Making China Modern

Making China Modern

FROM THE GREAT QING TO XI JINPING

Klaus Mühlhahn

The Belknap Press of Harvard University Press
CAMBRIDGE, MASSACHUSETTS
LONDON, ENGLAND

First Harvard University Press paperback edition, 2020
First printing

Book design by Dean Bornstein

Library of Congress Cataloging-in-Publication Data
Names: Mühlhahn, Klaus, author.
Title: Making China modern : from the Great Qing to Xi Jinping / Klaus Mühlhahn.
Description: Cambridge, Massachusetts : The Belknap Press of Harvard University
    Press, 2019. | Includes bibliographical references and index.
Identifiers: LCCN 2018008769 | ISBN 9780674737358 (cloth : alk. paper) |
    ISBN 9780674248311 (pbk.)
Subjects: LCSH: China—History—Qing dynasty, 1644–1912. | China—History—
    Republic, 1912–1949. | China—History—1949–
Classification: LCC DS754 .M84 2018 | DDC 951—dc23
LC record available at https://lccn.loc.gov/2018008769

For Sophia, Clara, and Julius

Our nation is new, but at the same time very ancient; it is modern and prosperous, but at the same time feudal and autocratic; it is westernized, but also intrinsically Asian. The world is transforming the nation, even as the nation is simultaneously transforming the world, and through this process the nation's innovation lies in its use of an unfathomable reality to challenge the limits of human imagination. As a result, the nation has come to acquire a sort of unrealistic reality, a nonexistent existence, an impossible possibility—in short, it has come to possess an invisible and intangible set of rules and regulations.

—Yan Lianke, *The Explosion Chronicles*

Contents

Timeline: China, 1644-2017

1644–1911	Qing dynasty
1683	Qing troops defeat Ming-loyalist Zheng Chenggong (Konxinga) in Taiwan
1689	Treaty of Nerchinsk between Qing China and Tsarist Russia
1712	Mission of Manchu official to Russia
1715	East India Company opens trading station in Guangzhou
c. 1700–1800	"High Qing," an age of prosperity and growth
1755–59	Conquest of central Asian lands (Xinjiang)
1757–1842	Foreign trade limited to the port of Guangzhou ("Canton system")
1780s	Literary inquisitions by the Qianlong emperor
1793	British Macartney mission to China fails to accelerate trade
1796–1804	White Lotus Rebellion
1799	Ban on import and cultivation of opium
1820–50	Economic depression under the Daoguang emperor
1840–42	First Opium War; Treaty of Nanjing opens Chinese ports to foreign trade; Hong Kong ceded to Great Britain; reparation payments; end of "Canton system"
1851–64	Taiping Rebellion
1856–60	Second Opium War; more ports opened; further rights granted to foreigners
1861	Founding of the *Zongli Yamen,* China's foreign office
1865–66	Opening of the first arsenals, producing battleships and armor
1873	Founding of China Merchant Steamship Company
1879	Japan seizes Ryukyu Islands, former tributary of the Qing
1883–85	Sino-French War
1890s	Beiyang Army formed by Li Hongzhang
1894	Hanyang Ironworks begin production
1894–95	Sino-Japanese War; Taiwan becomes Japanese colony
1895	"Self-Strengthening Army" created by Zhang Zhidong
1895–1911	Railway construction booms
1897	Qingdao occupied by Germany; Imperial Bank of China founded in Shanghai
1898	Hundred Days Reform, violently ended by empress dowager Cixi; Zhang Zhidong coins slogan "Chinese learning as substance, Western learning as function"

1899–1901	Boxer Rebellion and foreign intervention; 450 million tael indemnity forced upon the Qing
1901–11	New Policies (*Xinzheng*) reform program
1903	Commission on Military Reorganization
1905	Imperial Examination System abolished, to be replaced by universal school system; Sun Yat-sen founds Revolutionary Alliance (*Tongmenghui*) in Tokyo
1905–6	Study commissions investigate institutions and policies in foreign countries
1908–9	Representative assemblies established on local and provincial levels
1909–11	National census
Oct. 10, 1911	*Xinhai* Revolution begins with military uprising in Wuchang (today's Wuhan)
Jan. 1, 1912	Republic of China established, with Sun Yat-sen as provisional president
Aug. 1912	Founding of the Nationalist Party of China (*Guomindang*, GMD)
1912–16	Dictatorship of Yuan Shikai
1915–25	New Culture Movement
1915	Chen Duxiu founds journal *Xin Qingnian* (New Youth)
1916–28	Warlord era
Aug. 1917	Beijing government declares war on Germany
May 4, 1919	May Fourth Movement; students protest against Versailles peace treaty in Beijing
1921	Sun Yat-sen becomes head of the GMD government in Guangzhou; Communist Party of China (CCP) founded in Shanghai
1923–27	First United Front between CCP and GMD
May 30, 1925	Police of Shanghai's International Settlement opens fire on protesters
1926–27	Northern Expedition under Chiang Kai-shek reunites large parts of China, ends warlord era; persecution of Communists ends First United Front
1927–37	Nanjing decade
1930	Restoration of Chinese tariff autonomy
Sept. 18, 1931	Mukden Incident leads to occupation of Manchuria by Japan
1932	Japanese puppet state of Manchukuo set up in northeastern China; Shanghai War; Japanese attempt to take the city
1930–34	Jiangxi Soviet under CCP
1934	New Life Movement launched by GMD
1934–35	Long March of CCP from Jiangxi to Yan'an
Jan. 1935	Zunyi conference makes Mao Zedong leader of the CCP

1936	Three-Year Plan for industrial development by GMD government; Dec. Xi'an Incident
1937–45	Japan's War against China; Second United Front between GMD and CCP
1937	Marco Polo Bridge Incident starts the war; GMD government retreats from Nanjing to Wuhan, then to Chongqing; Nanjing Massacre
1940	Collaborationist "National Government" in Nanjing set up under Wang Jingwei
1941	US Lend-Lease Agreement extended to Chiang Kai-shek's government
Nov. 1943	Chiang Kai-shek attends Cairo Conference
Aug. 15, 1945	Capitulation of Japan
1945–49	Civil War between GMD and CCP
1945–47	Mission by General George C. Marshall to China to negotiate unity
Jan. 1949	CCP troops take Tianjin and Beijing
Oct. 1, 1949	Founding of the People's Republic of China
Dec. 1949	GMD forces retreat to Taiwan
1950–52	Land reform, Campaign to Suppress Counterrevolutionaries
1950	People's Liberation Army occupies Tibet
Feb. 14, 1950	China and the Soviet Union sign Treaty of Friendship, Alliance and Mutual Assistance
1950–53	Korean War
1953–57	First Five-Year Plan; nationalization of industry; collectivization of agriculture begins
1956–57	Hundred Flowers Movement followed by persecution of intellectuals in Anti-Rightist Campaign
1958–60	Great Leap Forward, resulting in a famine claiming around thirty million lives
1959	Uprising in Tibet quelled; Dalai Lama flees into exile in India
1960	Sino-Soviet Split
1962	Sino-Indian War
1964	Successful test of nuclear bomb; Zhou Enlai drafts Four Modernizations
1966	Beginning of Cultural Revolution
1968	Army restores order
1969–74	Deng Xiaoping is banned to the countryside
1971	Lin Biao attempts to flee and is killed in plane crash; Henry Kissinger secretly visits Beijing
1972	Richard Nixon meets Mao Zedong in Beijing

1976	Death of Zhou Enlai; death of Mao Zedong; Gang of Four arrested
Dec. 1977	National university entrance examination reintroduced
1978	Third plenum of the Central Committee decides on reform and opening policy; Four Modernizations taken up again; Democracy Wall in Beijing
1979	Establishment of diplomatic relations between US and PRC
1980	Establishment of four special economic zones; Zhao Ziyang becomes prime minister; introduction of one-child policy
1983	Campaign against spiritual pollution
1984	Acceleration of reform policy in both rural and urban areas; another fourteen coastal cities opened to foreign direct investment
1987	Campaign against bourgeois liberalization
1988	TV series *River Elegy* marks high tide of Cultural Fever movement
1989	Death of Hu Yaobang; violent suppression of demonstrations in Tian'anmen Square ends the democracy movement; Zhao Ziyang put under house arrest
1992	Deng Xiaoping's southern tour marks continuation of economic reform policy
1993	Jiang Zemin becomes president
1994	Tax reform
1995	Large-scale privatization of small state-owned enterprises
1997	Deng Xiaoping dies; Hong Kong is returned to China
1998	Zhu Rongji becomes prime minister
1999	Macau is returned to China; Falun Gong demonstrations
2001	China joins World Trade Organization (WTO); treaty of friendship with Russia
2002	Hu Jintao becomes leader of CCP
2003	Hu Jintao becomes president, Wen Jiabao becomes prime minister
2004	Thirteen amendments are made to constitution
2008	Olympic Games held in Beijing; large riots in Tibet; Charter 08 petition by intellectuals
2010	China becomes world's second largest economy after US
2012–13	Xi Jinping becomes leader of CCP and announces "China Dream"; beginning of anticorruption campaign; launch of first aircraft carrier
2013	Xi Jinping becomes president, Li Keqiang becomes prime minister
2015	Barack Obama and Xi Jinping sign Paris climate agreement; renminbi becomes official reserve currency
2016	For first time, China invests more money abroad than it receives

Maps

Making China Modern

Introduction

The rise of China in the late twentieth and early twenty-first century is undoubtedly one of the greatest developments remaking the world we live in. China's extraordinary and unprecedented economic growth in the recent past, its rapid catch-up in science and technology, and its increasingly robust projection of power on the geopolitical stage are shifting the global balance. In November 2012, at the opening of an exhibition in Beijing called the "Road to Renewal," China's president Xi Jinping spoke for the first time about the "China Dream" *(Zhongguo meng)*, which he described as "realizing the great renewal of the Chinese nation."[1] The exhibition told the story of China's twentieth-century recovery from the humiliations of the past that started with its defeats in the Opium Wars of the nineteenth century at the hands of Western imperialists.

If we are witnessing such a turning point, how should we understand it in historical terms? While many who study Chinese politics or economics today assume, per the government's official line, that China's rise is forty years old and began with the rule of Deng Xiaoping in 1978, historians should know that it has been much longer in the making. For over a century, China strove to overcome many past problems and its achievements are impressive. Yet how this drama will play out remains an unanswered question. History may be our only guide in gauging the possibilities of the future. To understand a rising China, we should be aware of the history behind it: the earlier periods of flourishing, the phases of decline and crisis in between, and the persistent efforts of recovery in the last century. Historical perspective will also reveal the reasons behind past triumphs and failures. For if China's age of prosperity and self-confidence is to define, to some measure, the twenty-first century, it is due to its historical legacy and experience, and its ability to overcome adversity.

What is suggested here is a reconsideration of China's modern history, which engages major dimensions of China's past for a more precise and nuanced understanding of its current dynamics. It is time to establish an up-to-date, profound, and comprehensive understanding of China's modern trajectory. The task is to explain just how today's China grew out of the past and what this might imply for the future. The country's past policies and actions can provide indicators and contexts for comprehending the present conundrums. Several questions are most relevant and pressing. What are the specific pathways that China has experienced, tested, and pursued? How do the problems that modern China is facing compare with the problems in the past? What can historical research contribute to understanding the current situation and the multiple and varying Chinese efforts to tackle the underlying challenges? What historical processes and events have affected the origins and transformations of institutions and structures that govern politics and economics in China today? In short, what can a historical perspective explain about the range of choices China confronts as it moves into the future?

A fundamental issue is the question of how far we have to go back to understand the making of modern China. Periodization is one of the most important and most significant tools of historical interpretation. Considerations tied to a period's movement from beginning to end are at the basis of historical explanations. There are many points in the impressively long history of China that can be seen to foreshadow the present. There are numerous writings, ideas, and decisions that can be related to contemporary China. What is sought here is a history that accounts for the making of modern China over the *longue durée*, recognizing the continuity of some of its most important institutions, the persistence of long-term problems and challenges, and its prominence on the international stage. We can find a valuable starting point for our narrative in a period called early modernity (roughly the mid-seventeenth through the eighteenth century).[2] In many ways, this period can be understood not only as a "late imperial" phase in the demise of traditional China, but also as an "early modern" forerunner of developments to come. By this time period, starting in 1644 with the reign of the Qing dynasty, many core institutions of late imperial China were developed and the empire reached its pinnacle. The basic institutions in society and culture that existed or were created in this period molded China's subsequent historical trajectory in the nineteenth and twentieth centuries and shaped its political choices.

It is important to point out that the term "modern China" in this book is used in a purely temporal sense, not as a normative framework. It refers to the timespan of almost three centuries across which any mature consideration of China's social, economic, cultural, and political development should look. Modern China in this book is also not understood as an absolute category, but rather as an evolving social construct involving the establishment of new institutions based on foreign or external blueprints and the mobilization of some specific indigenous institutional resources, political interests, and economic plans. It is not assumed that there is one universal or Western model for what it means to be modern. Such a conception would misread history, misjudge modern processes outside of Europe and the United States, and miss the many versions and variants of modernity. The persistent Chinese search for alternatives to and variants of Western modernity defies dominant and simple Western-centered concepts of modernity and modernization.

In this view, to be modern also does not assume a break with one's past. Although the idea of modernity is itself premised on the transformation of whatever is deemed premodern, historical roots and legacies continue to be relevant. Indeed, the coexistence of conditions traditional and modern, or indigenous and foreign, is part of contemporary life. There are many ways in which China's traditional social organizations continue not only to be politically and economically effective but also to play a significant role in issues of development. Modern in this book is understood to be relative in terms of both time and place, and a goal persistently and pervasively pursued by a variety of actors in China to make the country strong and wealthy. The making of modern China is, above all, driven by the frequently and clearly articulated Chinese desire to re-create a powerful, wealthy, and advanced nation.

This book aims to present the making of modern China by applying a historical approach that will bring to the fore China's experiences and own perspectives. Instead of stressing the role of frequently mentioned factors such as the weight of cultural traditions, the power of ideologies, and the struggles among China's old and new emperors, this book takes *institutions* as the starting point for understanding China in the modern period. This approach allows a wide-ranging, yet coherently organized, exploration of the history of modern China, covering all major events and important figures. Examining institutions and their roles in events, decisions, and processes yields a more precise and systematic understanding and a clearer explanation of historical developments. Institutions exert a profound impact on political decision-making, on social and cultural life, and on economic activities. Studying institutions therefore sheds light on why some countries prosper and others decline, why some develop faster and others slower, why some societies enjoy good governance and others do not.[3] Such an inquiry also has the advantage of being culturally and politically neutral. It does not apply external standards. And it opens up Chinese history for sustained comparisons. A brief consideration of what institutions are and why they matter, in China and elsewhere, will help make this clear.

The term "institution" is used vaguely in daily language. As defined in the social sciences, institutions are written or unwritten rules, or, to be more precise, social regularities arranged by human beings to achieve cooperation in a society.[4] They make it possible for members of a group to work together smoothly, based on the mutual trust that comes with sharing rules, common assumptions, expectations, and values.[5] In a functioning institutional framework, actors learn to rely on certain procedures with predictable outcomes, and therefore stick to them.

Progress in social and economic life depends on people working together and supporting each other. Cooperation is required at every level of society—from the small group of the family or clan to huge entities such as large firms or the state—for providing common goods and services, adjudicating disputes, maintaining order, and organizing education and welfare. It is a major challenge for people in any social group to keep cooperating over time, especially when the environment around them is changing. To sustain cooperation, they establish institutions assigning responsibilities and authority to selected members and also rewards or penalties to influence people's expectations, incentives, and calculations of returns or consequences from their actions. Rules become institutions when they are internalized by individual members and have become part of their worldview or conviction.[6] Hence, institutional rules are the fundaments of complex organizations such as government administrations, companies, and rural markets. Institutions manifest themselves in specific organizations, which follow certain scripts of tasks, functions, and divisions of labor, and embody mutual understanding, mutual trust, and common internal cultures. Institutions serve as the bases of all transactions and operate behind the scenes.

Institutions lay out a basic, intangible infrastructure that informs and coordinates the behavior of individuals in an organization. They are transmitted over generations from the past and go on to influence subsequent institutions. Institutional elements are moored in social memories and cognitive patterns. They shape preferences and choices. When a society faces a new situation or challenge, preexisting institutional elements condition the range of possible responses. Transmitted from the past, they provide a default mode for behavior in new situations.

While institutions provide a relatively predictable structure for everyday social, economic, and political life, they are not inflexible and uncontested. Institutions are dynamic and evolving scripts, in which patterns of behavior endure over time, but change can occur as a result of external pressure or internal challenges. Institutionalized behaviors can be hard to change, however. It is possible to generate new rules and mechanisms, but this requires conscious choices and actions. Scholars argue that institutions shape but do not necessarily determine behavior, as actors can choose whether to follow the rules or not. Newer institutional concepts emphasize that it is the interplay of organizations and their historical environments that defines and legitimizes organizational structures. Simply put, history matters for understanding institutional structures.[7]

As Douglass North maintains, "institutional change shapes the way societies evolve through time and hence is the key to understanding historical change."[8] Historical developments are shaped by the invisible changes within the institutions a society has established to organize cooperation and interaction among its members. Cultural and ideological elements also play their roles in maintaining continuity or driving change within institutions. We need contextual—in other words, cultural and historical information—to study institutions closely.

Institutions vary across societies. By enabling different kinds of relations and behaviors, they determine the effectiveness of organizations and policies, and produce varying economic and political outcomes regarding the enjoyment of rights and the allocation of resources in society.[9] Institutions can be inclusive, stable, efficient, and adaptive, but they can also be inefficient, contested, out of touch with changes in their environment, and extractive. Good, inclusive institutions promote cooperation and action benefiting a wide range of groups and individuals. Good institutions also facilitate development by promoting improvement and investment, and the dissemination of knowledge and skills through education. They maintain sustainable rates of population growth and foster stability and peace. They allow for the joint mobilization of resources and for beneficial policies such as the provision of public goods and services. More than anything, it is the quality of these institutional foundations that determines a society's welfare.

With the focus on institutions, the story of the making of modern China will take the reader beyond political history and integrate several subfields of history, in search of broader institutional structures and processes that can explain why certain developments occurred. Institutional history investigates how people cooperated and what arrangements they used to achieve common goals. Due attention is given to commerce, markets, and money. Institutional history refers to the study of how society was organized and how collaboration was achieved. It is concerned with the scripts behind organizations such as governments, villages and cities, economic entities, and the military. Taken together, these scripts interact in complex ways with religious and political views, indigenous cultural traditions, and transfers from the outside world. The perspective of institutional history is important in its own right, but also offers the basis for a more complete understanding of today's China.

Using this approach, this book aims to cover major aspects of Chinese history—not only rulers, ideology, and cultural practices, but also society, the economy, law, and justice—with a breadth that is missing in other histories for various reasons. It intends not only to relate the events involved in modern China's emergence chronologically, but to tell the story of how one development led to another over the sweep of more than three centuries. Focusing on institutional developments that were driven by Chinese plans and ambitions to become modern, it will offer a theoretically informed, balanced narrative that occasionally challenges conventional assumptions about Chinese history.

Approaches and Themes

The overall development of every society is shaped by institutions and their transformations—including by institutional failures and weaknesses that at certain times cause setbacks and social chaos. Studying how Chinese institutions worked and failed can contribute significantly to our understanding of China's letdowns and triumphs across the past centuries. Here, the focus is on the broad and complex transformation of Chinese society from 1644, by which point some of the most enduring institutions were in place, to the present day. This account will focus on institutions in the key areas of government, economy, sovereignty and secure borders, management of natural resources, and intellectual history.

Government must be seen as a meta-institution, since part of the function of a government is to organize and define the parameters for other social institutions, individually and collectively. Governments regulate and coordinate economic systems, educational institutions, and police and military organizations. Governments set the rules for other institutions through such means as enforceable legislation, decrees, and mobilizations of resources. But while government appears as a formal key actor and a basic unit of interest, it is by no means the sole actor establishing rules in Chinese society. Rather, it has to be seen as one agent among many. Across modern Chinese history, warlords, rebels, conquerors, clans, guilds, and local associations have also built or changed institutions. We will have to admit a wide range of relevant political actors and influences into Chinese history.

Another focus will be on the emergence and evolution of crucial *economic* institutions. Here, the question is how to think about the connections between government and economy throughout modern Chinese history.[10] The assumption is that rulers and their agents seek to maximize revenue, subject to certain constraints such as transaction costs, opportunistic behavior by state agents, and dependence on local elites or key constituents.[11] In this general institutional model, ruling authorities face a revenue imperative created by the need to finance political institutions and their functions. Rulers can meet their revenue goals by, for instance, specifying property rights that generate revenue as efficiently as possible. Although economic institutions powerfully shape economic outcomes, they are themselves determined by government institutions and governance systems and, more generally, the distribution of resources in society.

Another theme of the historical narrative involves institutions of national *sovereignty and territorial security*. China has frequently been forced to deal with challenges to its sovereignty and territory that threatened its existence. In fact, across its history, China has been ruled by non-Chinese peoples about half of the time. One result was the emergence of security institutions for effectively protecting borders and territory.[12] At the same time, however, an astonishing array of cross-border interactions allowed for the sharing of technological, institutional, and cultural achievements.[13] These transfers connected China to the outside world via its neighbors. The density and frequency of those connections and transfers posed the question of how to administer the openness to the world. The history of sovereignty and security therefore highlights not only the potential threats and rewards that in the eyes of governments can arise from border crossing, but also on the need to maintain institutions for managing territorial organization, at the center and periphery, and cross-border transactions.[14]

Much too often, the role of the *physical and natural environment* in shaping the conditions for human actions has been ignored in histories of China. In this account, the role of institutions for regulating the use of natural resources will be highlighted, giving the environment due attention. Environmental history has typically examined the influences of biology, climate, and geography, while casting man as "a prisoner of climate," as Fernand Braudel put it, and not a maker of it.[15] Recently, scholars have shifted the emphasis to human impacts on the planet. China is a case in point. It has a long and well-known history of natural calamities that inflicted loss and destruction and forced state and society to create tools for disaster prevention and crisis response. Yet by the twentieth century, China also inherited the dramatic environmental impacts of a millennium of refashioning nature for economic ends, resulting in ever-increasing costs and intensifying efforts to ensure access to fundamental resources such as air, soil, and water.[16]

Finally, any history of institutions also has to take note of the importance of *intellectual history*—the thought, ideas, symbols, and meanings that gain currency in a society. Institutions are embedded in cultural contexts and normative traditions. Social institutions and structures are based on processes of cultural symbolization and the social production of meaning.[17] What is meaningful and what constitute reasonable choices for social actors all depend on their perception and interpretation of social reality, which is filtered through symbolic systems. For the analysis of institutions, the cultural landscape of symbols, therefore, is as important as social and economic structures. In this thematic area, the focus will be on how groups within society made sense of their social, political, and global environments. This book will explore the values and symbols within Chinese society that informed the behavior of actors and institutions. It will reconstruct what it meant to be Chinese and how this definition changed over the course of time.[18]

The aim here is to explain, with reference to institutions, the choices Chinese society has made in the past and confronts today. This perspective will reveal how Chinese society continues to draw on historical symbolic and institutional resources for a whole range of contemporary purposes, from maintaining institutional practices to setting aspirational objectives. People in China still think within the historical Chinese idiom and frame the world in long-term perspectives. They construct a sense of China's rightful place in the world according to their historical experiences. China's past offers a broad and powerful repertoire of strategies and meaningful rules that continue to inform China's behavior in the present.

Outline and Chapters

This book proceeds in four parts, each containing three chapters, arranged in chronological order. The first part, "The Rise and Fall of Qing China," covers the period from 1644 to 1900. It starts off with an overview of the glorious era, a period in which China attained great size and power as the strongest, wealthiest, and most sophisticated Eurasian empire, despite the destructive, violent, and traumatic conquest by the Manchus in the mid-seventeenth century. In the early modern period, China had one of the world's largest and most efficient economies. The early Qing era demonstrated great military strength, material prosperity, and social stability, supporting an enormous expansion of territory and population in an increasingly commercialized but primarily agrarian economy. Global links fueled a commercial revolution that made China a center of the world economy. Some of its industries—for example, the textile, iron production, and ceramic industries— were also among the world's most advanced. A range of highly efficient and

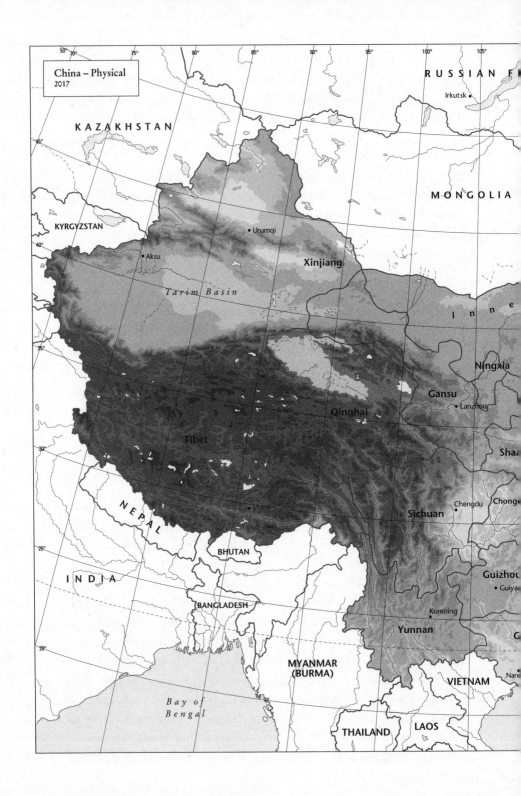

China – Physical
2017

sophisticated institutions such as the imperial government (a highly complex and effective administrative organization), the examination system, social welfare, and a free market system enabled Chinese society to thrive. Many institutions operated on the basis of informal rules rather than formal law. These developments not only shaped China, but helped to form the early modern world in which China was dominant.

After 1830, China slipped into a deep crisis. Caught up in widening economic crisis, institutional failure, and military disruption, it could no longer build on its historical heritage. On the contrary, China's position in the world suffered a steep drop. Demographic and economic trends, on top of severe degradation of the environment in the nineteenth century, increasingly eroded the Qing capacity to govern a rapidly changing society. Large rebellions, coupled with Western and Japanese imperialism, further weakened the government. China also fell behind the advanced technology of the West. These events and factors marked the era known in China as the "century of humiliation," a chapter in the country's history that featured an unrelenting series of wars, occupations, and revolutions. During its decline, China became so impoverished that most of its people, despite working long hours, earned small incomes, had insufficient diets, were not able to accumulate resources or capital, and had no access to welfare. As fiscal revenue fell dramatically, most government institutions became paralyzed. China's nineteenth-century descent to the point that it was unable to capitalize on its historical advantages or defend itself against social disorder and foreign imperialism was mainly caused by institutional and political failure.

China would display remarkable resilience, however, after 1870. It suffered the era of imperialism, but managed to survive it better than most parts of the world, in that it stayed largely intact and was able to lay the foundations for future development. Beginning in the late nineteenth century, Chinese leaders attempted to reform and rebuild existing institutions, initially relying on a state-directed industrialization program focusing on defense industries and infrastructure. The early efforts of institutional reform were too late and limited, however, and were largely unsuccessful in restoring the vigor of the dynastic system.

The second part, "Chinese Revolutions," tells the story of the emergence of a new Republican China, experiencing rejuvenation and national awakening in the time between 1900 and 1949. It was only after the defeat of the

Boxer Rebellion in 1900 that deeper institutional reforms in education, military, economy, and government were implemented. The New Policies by the empress dowager in response to the Boxer debacle shaped China's modern political agenda by introducing constitutional and legal reform, parliamentary government, local elections, court systems, higher education, economic and finance policy, upgraded transportation, management of foreign affairs, tax reform, and the creation of a new army. The rise of a professionally trained army was especially instrumental to the militarization of Chinese political culture in the twentieth century. Army officers and cadets also became forces of political change in China when they denounced the Qing throne and started to support the Republican movement. Under the leadership of Sun Yat-sen, China in 1912 became the first republic in Asia to begin literally "reconstructing" a modern nation-state and citizenry. New institutions were created to shape a new, strong nation. But what followed was an extended period of regional military leaders, who continued building military capabilities. Economically, China gained strength and became more robust in the early twentieth century, especially in the treaty ports, during a phase historians refer to as the "golden age" of Chinese capitalism. Shanghai became the hub of international trade and commerce in Asia and home to China's first middle class, embodying the promise of Chinese modernity. After the reestablishment of a central government in Nanjing in 1928, headed by Chiang Kai-shek, institutional reform and strengthening continued and expanded.

The focus increasingly shifted from reform to innovation. As part of this, the Chinese government sought to remove traditional institutions and replace them with new institutions to stem economic and political decline, to restart economic growth, and to facilitate social development. During this period, a host of new government institutions were built, a modern banking system was established, and a wide variety of new laws governing state and economy were passed. China opened its doors widely to new ideas, establishing a dynamic system of higher education that featured strong, state-run institutions and creative private institutions, aided in no small part by foreign-sponsored schools and institutions. As a result, Republican China did facilitate modest economic growth and social improvement, although these successes were limited to urban areas along the coast. While in the long term these efforts might have been successful in lifting China out of poverty, the Second World War and the ensuing Civil War brought this development to a grinding halt. The achievements and successes of this period were largely undone by the Japanese invasion and the protracted battle between the Communist Party and the Nationalist Party. War and civil strife continued to impede institutional reforms and thus led to a long delay in China's entry into the global scene of industrial development and technological innovation.

The third part, "Remaking China," explores the nature of the early People's Republic between 1949 and 1977, and the Chinese Communist Party's attempt to transform Chinese society. When national unity was eventually achieved in the 1950s, a variant of the socialist Soviet model was introduced, continuing the project to build a new and more powerful institutional structure in China. Under Mao Zedong, the ruthless pursuit of state prerogatives that had been underway in Republican China was continued and augmented. The massive infrastructure of the government apparatus of the People's Republic of China (PRC) was created, and shifted the balance of central versus local interests in favor of the central state. With the attempt to make China into a socialist country, central authority and state capacity were restored, as well. The PRC demonstrated capacity to formulate, implement, and monitor nationwide policy initiatives that, for the first time since the fall of the empire, resonated to the level of villages. Above all, the Chinese Communist Party (CCP) succeeded in planting itself and the state into society and developing deep roots. Rural collectivization allowed the state to reallocate resources from China's huge agricultural economy to develop heavy industry and defense, as well as infrastructure, education, and basic welfare. The socialist state was able to penetrate society down to the grassroots level and extract resources to an unprecedented extent, but its success was fractured and highly uneven. Mao's government still had to deal with relentless resistance to its initiatives and discontent. Heterogeneity and pluralism were limited, but prevailed. Conflicts between official and unofficial cultures persisted. The gap between urban and rural interests only widened and, to the extent that the old social inequalities were erased, they were replaced by new ones. This was a society whose capacity for inequality, contention, conflict, and violence was undiminished.

The downside of these developments revealed itself in the 1960s, when the overambitious initiatives of the Great Leap Forward and the Cultural Revolution inflicted massive destruction and loss of life, upending much of what had been achieved in the early 1950s. The PRC also failed in addressing long-term issues of poverty, environmental decline, and technological underdevelopment. An important observation is that, during its first three decades, the CCP was good at institutional destruction, but less successful at establishing new institutions. If anything, this suggests that Maoism intended a revolution of the state and of the political system that in the end it was unable to achieve. Still, the tumultuous destruction of the remnants of the bureaucratic state (and the rise of new intermediate command authorities) during the Cultural Revolution made possible the ascendance of a new administrative elite in the post-Mao era that has since become a key factor for stability.

The last part, "China Rising," tells the story of how the PRC, as it emerged from the ruinous policies of the first thirty years in 1978, managed to preside over an astonishing economic revival. The Cultural Revolution's disruptions, and the new pragmatic leadership of Deng Xiaoping, created conditions that, by 1978, made much more fundamental change possible. China's reform and opening strategy has been successful thanks to its economic orientation, but equally because of the gradual and experimental nature of the most important institutional changes. China has undergone a successful transition to a market economy, and seen impressively high growth rates in its gross domestic product (GDP). In the 1980s, reforms focused on the revival of the market economy and rural growth. The 1990s brought a push for privatization and transformation of state-owned enterprises (SOEs) into profit-oriented corporations. China's rise came about through fundamental changes of policy combined with gradual institutional adaptations. But it also depended on the deep historical roots of China's current institutions—such as China's legacy of administrative experience, sophisticated markets, and education.

A decentralized and inclusive economic institutional structure emerged that was oriented toward promoting rapid economic growth. Genuine improvements were achieved in the size of China's economy and the prosperity of its citizens. As average incomes have risen dramatically, hundreds of millions of Chinese people have been lifted out of poverty. The institutional reforms in the economy aiming at inclusiveness and openness have unleashed private enterprise, creating many new companies and markets, and a middle class of an estimated 300 million people with rising consumer appetites. This development reshaped China's economic structure, reducing reliance on agriculture and raising the share of industrial production—and, more recently, of services provision. Equally important is China's new position as a key player in the world economy and its ambition to project power on a global scale.

At the same time, profound challenges have emerged. China has not changed its political institutions; it remains an authoritarian, one-party state. Popular demands for political participation and democracy have been resolutely quelled, often by shows of force and violence. In 1989, the government even committed a massacre of unarmed protesters calling for more freedom of thought and speech. These actions, combined with a spread of high-level corruption, damaged the legitimacy of one-party rule. In response, heavy-handed nationalism and maintenance of rapid growth at all cost, as well as a strict anticorruption campaign, aimed to reinforce legitimacy.

The increased social inequality and environmental depredation associated with economic reforms in the PRC raise questions about their sustainability. Social tensions and conflicts are on the rise. Nervous debates often question the direction of Chinese society amid widespread and rapid change. Uneasy feelings of anxiety and uncertainty cloud the prospect of the future. Among the most crucial and most anxious questions being discussed are: What is the proper level of autonomy from the party state for institutions that are supposed to somehow serve a broader public purpose? Is China's political system adequate to handle its diverse society and vibrant economy? How much longer can the delicate balancing act be sustained?

Key Insights

Taking a historical perspective on the evolution of institutions yields a number of important insights. First, it emphasizes that China's move to a central place in the world is a change that has been in process for more than one hundred years, and is still ongoing. The decades since 1978 are merely the latest chapter. Since the middle of the nineteenth century, Chinese elites have brought about institutional innovation, destruction, and modification to make China prosperous and strong again. China's historical trajectory has been a long and steady, but also rocky and painful return to eminence and centrality.

In a nutshell, this book understands the making of modern China as a process of overcoming institutional weaknesses and dysfunctionalities that were standing in the way of prosperity and power.[19] China's ability to recover from the nineteenth-century crisis relied on important institutional changes that facilitated progress in terms of skill, expertise, and capital and thus allowed the realization of its historical potential. The difficult and slow emergence of a set of new formal and informal rules eventually established more inclusive economic conditions and unlocked economic opportunities. Through a long and complex process, the reforms of the institutional order created a more level playing field, removed entry barriers and discriminations, and encouraged initiative, leading to stability and growth. China was able to recover from the brink of near destruction in the nineteenth century and to reclaim its lost centrality in the world.

China's rise was not the outcome of adhering to one single institutional model; rather, it was based on many layers of institutional experiments and adaptations, drawing on China's own historical legacies and a wide range of foreign models. Among them were creations of military-industrial complexes under direction of the state in the late Qing and the warlord era, a national developmental state during the Nanjing decade, war-time economic mobilization during the Second World War, and a planned economic system during the era of Mao Zedong. Common to all these models were extractive institutions intended to siphon resources from the economy for the benefit of different ruling elites (whether they were imperial elites, warlords, military state officials, or party-state bureaucrats). These institutions achieved various degrees of political centralization and were able of generate some amount of growth. But it was not until the introduction of more inclusive economic institutions in 1978 that the Chinese economy really took off.

China's slow and unsteady rise over the course of the twentieth century was fueled not only by global opportunities, political ambitions, and sustained institutional innovation, but also by historical legacies. The historical legacy of its own social institutions and the creative adaptation of a broad spectrum of novel institutional forms eventually allowed China, in a gradual process full of setbacks and resistance, to arrive at adequate institutional solutions for some of the long-term problems facing the country (especially in the economy, but also other areas such as infrastructure, technology, and the military). Historical advantages upon which China could build included the comparative sophistication of the premodern Chinese institutions, an ingrained emphasis on meritocracy and education, and the long experience of having run such a complex administrative organization as the Chinese imperial bureaucracy.

China's rise is, however, partial and unfinished. Despite spectacular achievements and substantial progress, core issues remain unresolved. The biggest challenge facing China is the need for political reform. In the early twentieth century, China removed political institutions that had been key to the past stability of the empire—most notably, the emperor, the examination system, and the local gentry. To replace these, China cherry-picked from the global menu of political institutional models, subsequently opting for a constitutional monarchy, a constitutional republic, military dictatorship in the warlord period, a Chinese version of fascism in the 1930s, and several forms of state socialism—including Stalinism in the 1950s and its Chinese variant, Maoism, in the 1960s. Every institutional transfer left its mark on Chinese political institutions. All inserted fragments of rules and codes into the institutional mainframe. The result is an institutional bricolage whose internal contradictions yield frequent policy shifts and an inherent instability. The various institutional models had one main characteristic in common, however: they were all extractive political institutions that concentrated power in the hands of a narrow elite such as the dynastic clan, military officers, or party leaders. While China experimented with many institutional models for a political system in the modern period, its ruling authorities showed little interest in building institutions that would distribute power widely and support political pluralism. Even after 1978, no convincing, enduring, and efficient institutional equivalent to the country's economic liberalization has been established. On the contrary, economic modernization, based on inclusive economic institutions, was decoupled from political development, which continued to be driven by exclusive political institutions. Whether the country's economic rise can continue if China fails to pursue long-delayed political reforms is an open question.

There is also the problem of popular legitimacy. All Chinese governments in the modern period have brought about their revolutions on the battlefield. In each case, victory was achieved with violence, and then needed to be defended with further violence. This fundamentally compromised the ability to govern; governments faced more dissent, saw greater opposition to their policies, and resorted more to repression. Political institutions forged on the battlefield and through military campaigns lacked a legitimate basis. The lack of legitimacy also explains the constant efforts of indoctrination and propaganda, and the priority assigned to economic growth as means to deliver welfare.

The historical account suggests that China is and has always been a major and active player in the world. China was at the center of an interconnected and global network of engagement in the past and remains so in the present. Its domestic politics were therefore fundamentally linked to international dynamics. Various global powers tried to control it and take advantage of its huge market, but they ultimately failed to do so. China demonstrated remarkable resilience. It managed to remain independent and keep its territory intact, even in times when it was very weak and under intense foreign pressure. At the same time, it constantly sought to align itself with international partners and supporters, seeing foreign assistance as crucial to both economic development and national security. China tried to walk a delicately thin line, resisting external control and intervention, while building and strengthening foreign links to promote its social development and economic growth. The years since 1978 have seen the Chinese nation-state ascend into the ranks of global powers, yet it remains unclear what role it aspires to take beyond the pursuit of its own narrow interests and how it will enforce those.

For China, the twentieth century was an era of border insecurity and almost incessant war. This led to an increasing militarization of society, and to a deeply embedded sense of national vulnerability. Conflicts destroyed China's great cities, devastated its countryside, and ravaged the economy. Years of fighting, as well as frequent changes of the ruling powers and the administrative structure, contributed to the collapse of social and political order. China built vast military forces that were meant to make it more stable and secure, but analysis suggests they consumed tremendous amounts of energy and investment. As vulnerability, internally and externally, became China's great national theme, nationalism became another strong force, uniting state and society behind the goal of national rejuvenation. The surge of Chinese nationalism collided time and again with the fact that China is a country of immense size and enormous diversity. Issues of how to deal with a historical legacy of multiethnic and cultural pluralism in a post-imperial and nationalistic setting remain unresolved. With the status of so-called "national minorities" contested, and the potential for future violent conflicts, the fundamental question is how the Chinese nation-state will position itself vis-à-vis ethnic diversity at home.

China's historical experiences in the modern period also provide lessons in the causes and consequences of environmental crisis. Despite a high degree of specialized knowledge and a history of effective management in imperial China, China neglected environmental stewardship in the nineteenth and twentieth centuries, even as rapid industrialization and challenges such as climate change pushed the country into environmental crisis.[20] Millions of hectares of agricultural land were polluted, as were the air and water. Environmental degradation has been a consistent factor in the making of modern China, threatening to undermine the country's stability, growth, and security. The environmental crisis has had broad effects on quality of life throughout Chinese society. It has demanded and will continue to demand enormous efforts and investments by Chinese society to cope with its consequences.

In short, the enviable successes and indisputable achievements that have marked the emergence of modern China have also left a lot of unfinished business. Institutional reforms in key areas of politics, national security, foreign relations, and the management of natural resources have been partial and insufficient. All its attainment of wealth and power notwithstanding, China faces an increasingly uncertain future—and a future that all of humanity will confront together. Under today's globalized conditions, the making of modern China is not an exclusively Chinese story. Rather, it is a shared story of our time.

PART ONE

The Rise and Fall of Qing China

The Qing rulers were China's last imperial house. Established in 1644 by the non-Chinese people called Manchus, it was a dynasty that lasted until the founding of the Republic of China in 1912. Especially during the reigns of two exceptionally capable rulers—the Kangxi emperor, who ruled from 1661 to 1722, and the Qianlong emperor, who ruled from 1735 to 1795—remarkable political, economic, and cultural institutions were created that would be inherited by modern China. This unusual legacy is convincingly documented by the monumental set of scrolls produced to record the inspection tours these two conducted through their vast empire. One of the most beautiful and impressive scrolls portrays the Qianlong emperor's entry into Suzhou in 1751. The scroll shows in great detail the prosperity and sophistication of daily life in the cultural capital of China. The busy streets are lined by numerous shops and restaurants trading all sorts of goods, from fresh fish to silk. As the Qianlong emperor, accompanied by a large entourage, enters Suzhou on a white horse, the elegantly dressed people there bow in deference to him. The depiction of the event is testimony to the Qing emperors' political ambitions to preside over a prosperous, unified, and culturally refined empire.

By the time of the tour in 1751, the Great Qing had attained enormous size and was perhaps the most powerful Eurasian empire of its time. Demographic growth, expanded communication networks, rapid commercialization, and new forms of critical thinking had enriched social and intellectual life in the seventeenth century. The empire was also not closed to the outside world. On the contrary, it stood at the center of economic networks and flows that incorporated it into the larger South China Sea economy and, beyond that, into the global economy. Seen from a global perspective, the Qing age of glory and splendor contributed to the formation of the early modern world, in which it came to occupy a central place as the most advanced region. As the scrolls suggest, what was distinctive about Qing China was less its central state capacity than its flourishing local society. Even when the state was able to impose policy on local society, the central bureaucracy could sustain those initiatives only by enlisting the support of local elites and by adapting plans to existing social networks within local communities.

During the nineteenth century, however, powerful and unstoppable forces transformed the Chinese world and eroded the foundations of Qing prowess. After 1800, various factors combined to create an unstable and dangerous situation for the ruling dynasty. The empire lost its global economic leadership as it experienced economic fracturing, social turmoil, and the imposition of European imperialism. Economic decline and falling living standards prompted popular uprisings that claimed countless lives and disrupted everyday life in many parts of the country, while population pressures contributed to widespread social dislocation. At the same time, natural calamities deepened poverty and human misery, and foreign powers increased their demands for economic and political concessions. These forces resulted in the astonishing decline of imperial China, which went from being a leading and prosperous world power to being referred to as the "sick man" of Asia in less than a hundred years.

This first part of *Making China Modern* focuses on the grandeur of the Qing and on the reasons for the subsequent decline that turned the once leading empire into a laggard among the global powers of the nineteenth century. It highlights the emerging social, political, and economic constraints that left China unable to capitalize on its early economic and technological leadership. Institutions play a central role in this story. The principles of minimalist governance, including light taxes, little direct involvement in local society, and encouragement of local initiative for social and political initiatives, had enabled the Qing to consolidate control over China with relatively few resources. The downside of this approach came to light, however, in the nineteenth century, as the relationship between the central government and local society was revealed to be volatile and fragile. Demographic and economic trends, as well as a severe degradation of the environment in the nineteenth century, overwhelmed the small institutional apparatus, making it more difficult for the state to control local society. Political upheavals during the second half of the nineteenth century caused by economic crisis and the privations of foreign imperialism further eroded the capacity of Qing institutions to govern a society torn up by conflict. Qing governance ultimately led to periods of what Pamela Crossley calls "local hypertrophy"—the concentration of power in regional networks often operating against the interests of the central government.[1] Hence, the limited ability of the small Qing institutions to mobilize and support a growing population in turbulent times resulted in massive political and social disruptions. It is important to note that the turmoil brought about by contact with European nations and the United States—and later, Japan—is only one part of this narrative. More vital to highlight are the internal demographic, political, social, and economic developments that, by producing structural tensions inside Qing institutions, led to the downfall of imperial China.

The severe crisis of the nineteenth century came as a shock to the intellectual world of late imperial China. As it prompted a critical intellectual self-examination at the end of the Qing empire, new concepts concerning the state and the people found their way into Chinese political thinking. The center of the polity moved conceptually from the dynastic house and a Confucian bureaucracy to the nation and the military. Intense discussions of how to make China strong and wealthy again marked a pivotal moment in the creation of a distinctively modern Chinese national identity, defined above all in nationalistic and military terms. These ideas laid the foundations for the painful convulsions and political revolutions of the twentieth century.

ONE

Age of Glory

1644–1800

The Qianlong emperor's inspection tour of 1751 fell into a period representing the zenith of imperial splendor, a time of cultural efflorescence, economic power, and military expansion. Historians sometimes call this period the "High Qing," referring to its status as the peak, the last pinnacle of an imperial history lasting almost two millennia. The Qing dynasty ran an empire that in many respects was "modern" (although the term was not used in China before the end of the nineteenth century) even before China's encounter with the "modern" West. At its core was a set of efficient institutions that allowed the Qing to promote economy, engage in border-crossing interactions, cede space to local governance, and maintain an imperial bureaucracy of light societal penetration. The civil service examination systems enabled broad elite participation in governance on the basis of achieved merit rather than inherited birthright. The vibrant Qing market institutions were neither stagnant nor a closed system.[1] In fact, they were deeply integrated into the world's economy through trade, and allowed many foreign goods, techniques, and even decors to circulate among the imperial elites. Vibrant and open intellectual discussions were emerging that advocated evidence-based and precise scientific inquiry. The Chinese empire was also the dominant power in East Asia. It was at the center of a web of peaceful relations managed through the tribute system. Before the arrival of the West, China was deeply tangled up in links leading around the globe to Asia, Europe, and America, and it was watched from outside with a sense of admiration.

Nonetheless, in the course of the eighteenth century, challenges appeared on the horizon. The worsening of environmental conditions—a process that continues into the present—hampered productivity in agriculture and thus undermined the most important and dynamic sector of the imperial economy.

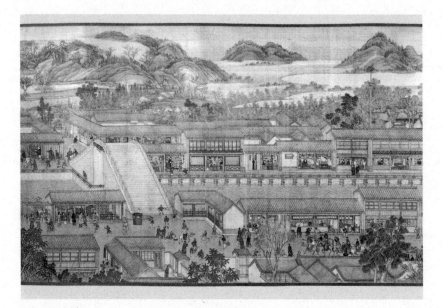

1.1. The Qianlong emperor entering the vibrant and wealthy city of Suzhou on his
Southern Inspection Tour in 1751. Silk handscroll by Xu Yang, 1770.
Purchase, The Dillon Fund Gift, 1988, The Metropolitan Museum of Art

Further growth of agricultural output became ever more difficult. Farmers
struggled to maintain the average volume of harvests. Existing technologies,
having more or less exhausted themselves, could not deliver further development or economic growth. A lack of sustained innovation failed to generate
necessary technological and scientific breakthroughs. The autocratic imperial system, captured by entrenched interests and prone to corruption, became
increasingly resistant to change.

The Physical Environment in Late Imperial China

Most historical accounts relegate the natural environment to a minor role
in the drama of Chinese history. In conventional histories, nature is backdrop; it becomes significant only with natural disasters such as earthquakes,
floods, and droughts. Today, given the heightened awareness of climate
change, environmental historians have begun to reexamine those older con-
ceptions. They have shown how the human relationship to nature is constantly

at work in history. Frontier lands are also being examined from new perspectives, revealing diverse and precarious areas of the environment and their fragile interconnections with the wider world.

The physical and natural environment in China has, across millennia, been constantly and heavily affected by human activity. By the Qing dynasty, China was experiencing enormous environmental problems and pressures, partly due to precarious natural conditions, but also as the result of centuries of conscious and industrious exploitation of nature for economic purposes. The interaction between human society and nature thus rendered China an ecologically vulnerable area long before its twentieth-century boom of industrialization.

The territory of the Chinese mainland proper measures some 5,000 kilometers from north to south, stretching from the center of the Heilong (Amur) River to the southernmost tip of Hainan Island. From west to east, the nation extends about 5,200 kilometers from the Pamir Mountains to the confluence of the Heilong (Amur) and Wusuli (Ussuri) rivers. In imperial times, China's territory was slightly larger, as it included what is today the independent country of Outer Mongolia, the small areas in Manchuria bordering Russia and in Central Asia.

China's geography is highly diverse, with hills, plains, and river deltas in the east, and deserts, high plateaus, and mountains in the west.[2] The topography of China is marked by a gradual descent from major mountain ranges and high plateaus in the west to low-lying plains and coastal areas in the east. In the south, the land is dominated by hills and low mountain ranges. The majority of the population resides in the extensive alluvial plains in the east, including the Northeast Plain, the North China Plain, the Middle to Lower Yangzi Plain, and the Pearl River Delta Plain, which are China's most important agricultural and economic bases. China has more than 1,500 major rivers, which total 420,000 kilometers in length. More than 2,700 billion cubic meters of water flow along these rivers, constituting 5.8 percent of the world's total. Most of China's rivers are situated in the east; the major ones include the Yangzi, Yellow, Heilong (Amur), and Pearl rivers. The largest Chinese river is the 6,300-kilometer Yangzi, the third-longest river in the world after the Nile in northeast Africa and the Amazon in South America. Northwestern China has a small number of rivers, with no connection to the sea and little runoff.

China's climate is equally varied, ranging from tropical in the south to subarctic in the northeast. China is subject to a strong monsoon climate, leading to a distinctive weather difference between the wet subtropical climatic zone in the southeast and the dry continental climatic zone in the northwest. The climatic transition zone between South and North China runs along 33–34°N, roughly following the Huai River. Continental climate patterns predominate in North China, where the winter tends to be cold and dry. Subtropical weather is found in the south, with ample rain and hot temperatures. During the summer, both south and north are subject to increased precipitation associated with the summer monsoon; however, average rainfall in the north is considerably less than in the south. On average, there is just enough rainfall on the North China Plain for agriculture. Long stretches of hot and windy conditions prevail during the spring and summer seasons and, compared to other regions of the world at similar latitudes, the North China Plain receives considerably less average precipitation. This makes irrigation ever more important. The vast majority of annual rainfall occurs in July and August, often in localized downpours. Periodically, a reduction of annual rainfall, particularly in the critical spring months, results in crop loss. Agricultural communities in the north perpetually face the risk of droughts. In the south, the main problem is not too little but too much precipitation. When dikes and other defense structures along the large rivers fail, floods wash over the landscape. High population density and the productivity of regional agriculture in the south thus depend upon continued commitments and capabilities to control the waters with engineering feats.

Historians have long recognized that booming demand for natural resources of all kinds is central to the environmental history of the late imperial period. The insatiable thirst for nature's riches deeply transformed the natural landscape of the Chinese empire. The story of agricultural expansion is crucial in this context, since agricultural needs provided a constant impulse to requisition and exploit nature's resources. Even though China is one of the largest countries in the world, its amount of arable land has been relatively small. Concentrated in the river basins of eastern and southern China, it is mainly to be found in the Northeast Plain, the North China Plain, the Middle-Lower Yangzi Plain, the Pearl River Delta Plain, and the Sichuan Basin. Out of 9.6 million square kilometers in total, only 1.3 million square kilometers are suitable for farming, representing some 14 percent of all land area. Of the remainder, 28 percent is pasture, 24 percent is forest, and the rest is used for human settlement or is otherwise uncultivable. Because China in the late

1.2. Workers in a paddy field, 1927.
Scherl / Bridgeman Images / SZT3023475

imperial period already had a large population, the area of cultivated land per capita was also small. In North China, conditions for agriculture were especially difficult because of soil salinization caused by the climate. Hot spring and summer temperatures dry out the soil and dissolve salts to the surface.

Northern China traditionally has been the center of wheat, millet, barley, and soy cultivation. In the early modern period, crops such as cotton and hemp were produced. In the southern part of China, rice farming became more and more common toward the end of the first millennium. Over the centuries, most of lowland central and southern China became a mosaic of leveled paddy fields surrounded by low mud walls that needed rebuilding to some extent each year. Walls and terraces were built on the slopes to allow rainwater to gather, stopping the earth from slipping downhill and preventing the loss of soil. A parallel development was the long-term drainage of the vast swamps of what is now the North China Plain and the central and lower Yangzi valley, and their conversion to farmland. If drainage work was neglected for long, however, the swamps tended to reappear.

Aside from agriculture, the booming late imperial economy also saw increasing demands for building materials and fuel. In the past, there were extensive forests sprawling across the plains, especially in the eastern part.[3] There is evidence that the wide-ranging Loess highlands in North China had significant forest cover at one time, but the expansion of human populations and their agricultural activities left the region largely stripped and barren. In the process, the larger part of China's original forest cover was gradually destroyed. With the removal of the forests, many wild animals lost their habitats. Thus, hunting gradually became a less significant part of the economy, except in some frontier zones. As the timber needed for houses, boats, and fuel slowly became scarce, there were substantial shortages of building materials and fuel in many areas. Along with the majority of forests and wild foods, the environmental buffer was lost, which had previously protected against the failure of harvests due to droughts or floods.

Demands for mineral resources also led to significant impact on the natural environment. China has a wealth of mineral deposits, and the nation ranks third in the world in total reserves. According to China's Ministry of Foreign Affairs, 153 different minerals have been confirmed, including fossil energy sources of coal, petroleum, natural gas, and oil shale. China has one of the largest coal reserves in the world, totaling 1,007.1 billion tons, mainly distributed in North China, Shanxi, and the Inner Mongolia Autonomous Region. These riches were exploited early on in Chinese history. Since antiquity, gold, tin, zinc, iron ore, copper, clay, coal, salt, and other minerals were excavated, mostly through open-pit mining, and traded throughout China. Some of these commodities entered global markets. During the Qing dynasty, coins in the empire were minted in Yunnanese copper, sold to shippers from Boston, and exchanged for sea otter pelts off the Alaskan coast.

In fact, the unprecedented rush for natural resources affected the forests, grasslands, and highlands not only of the empire, but of regions far away. By 1800, there was an amazing display of frontier and foreign products for sale in the urban markets of the Chinese empire. Records and sources prove the range of these materials: sandalwood from Hawaii, birds' nests from Borneo, pearls from the Philippines, silver from the Americas, copper from Yunnan, medicinal plants from the Himalayas, opium from upland Southeast Asia, jade from Xinjiang and Burma, sea turtles from Sulawesi, sea cucumbers from Fiji, mushrooms from Mongolia, ginseng and pearls from Jilin, sable from

Siberia, and sea otters from Hokkaido, Alaska, the Pacific Northwest, and the California coast. As demand for these resources grew, markets flourished. China's demand for fur from Siberia and the North Pacific in this period was so huge and hunting so intense that, by the early nineteenth century, sea otters, sables, and other species were on the brink of extinction across the world—from Alaska and Mongolia to the Pacific coast in California. Many resources showed signs of depletion: animal populations were significantly diminished, forests had been cleared, and coastal areas had been deprived of their diverse wildlife.[4]

The Chinese empire also worked to harness nature to eliminate or reduce risks to human lives, property, infrastructure, and agricultural production. The large rivers were flanked by levees to stop flooding. The problem was most acute along the Yellow River, also called "China's sorrow," but happened with other rivers, as well. After merging with the Wei River, the Yellow River enters the North China Plain, from where it flows to the river's mouth in the Bohai Sea, the small downstream gradient causing the flow to slow considerably. Due to the low velocity, about one third of the sediment picked up in the Loess highlands settles on the bed, one third is deposited in the estuary region, and the remaining sediment is flushed into the Bohai Sea. This silt deposit has been the determinative factor in shaping the North China Plain. Sedimentation raised the river until it regularly spread over its banks and across the landscape, eventually carving a new channel to the sea. To deal with water calamities, imperial China developed a sophisticated system of water management using dikes, dams, river diversions, and other measures.[5] During the imperial period, villages formed associations to build and maintain local flood control and irrigation systems. Imperial governments were focused primarily on large translocal and regional systems that stabilized drainage along large rivers such as the Yellow or Yangzi. Although officials put forward competing theories for flood control, a fundamental technological commitment to building dikes to restrict the river's flow to a defined bed remained a fundamental tenet of river control. In many ways, the history of water management in late imperial China is a story of unbroken confidence in human capacity to control immense natural forces.

These and other efforts aimed at staving off hunger and malnutrition, including the introduction of new crops, land reclamations, emergency prevention, and welfare policies, all affected the environment directly. But there

were also indirect effects which should not be underestimated. Exploiting and controlling nature enabled periods of relative safety, stability, and growing food security. With the development of efficient agricultural techniques, population growth accelerated. Especially after 1500, population growth was extraordinary. Over a period spanning half a millennium, China's population grew from approximately 70 million in 1400 to approximately 400 million in 1850 and 500 million around 1930, implying annual growth at an average of 0.4 percent.[6] The most rapid growth occurred between 1700 and 1850, when the population almost tripled.

Most regions in the eastern half of the country developed a distinctive pattern of urban settlements. Clusters of market towns formed along the dense regional networks of rivers, creeks, and manmade canals. Geographic specializations arose in the marketing and production of agricultural and handicraft products. The resulting economic geography had no clear boundaries between urban and rural districts or between farming and non-agricultural activity. High population density in the eastern coastal regions led many to migrate to less populated but also less developed regions. The area of land under cultivation increased significantly, as homesteaders departed for China's frontiers in search of arable land. Large numbers of settlers found opportunities to improve their livelihood by clearing and farming large tracts in regions along the borders, such as Sichuan, Yunnan, Guizhou, Taiwan, Manchuria, Mongolia, Tibet, and Central Asia. Slowly, the wildernesses along the frontiers and the remote regions began to disappear, as well. Thus the unprecedented population growth in the late imperial period led not only to high population density in the eastern part of the country, but also to internal migration and settlement in the open borderlands and highlands in the west.

Intensification of farming is, of course, one of the few options available to increase agricultural output once virtually all potential settlement areas have been claimed and all agricultural land has been developed—and this point was reached in the late imperial period.[7] More intensive use of human labor therefore became the most important characteristic of the imperial agricultural economy. Multi-cropping and inter-cropping expanded dramatically. These developments required shifts in institutional structures and farming practices, as animals could no longer be allowed to graze and fertilize fields following a harvest. With less grazing opportunities available, farm animals largely disappeared from the countryside. The intensification of farming also required an increase in the quantity of water needed each year, which forced communities to expand and manage their irrigation networks. The pressing need to find additional forms of fertilizer led to novel uses of organic sources, ranging from mud and human excreta to stalks and bean cake.

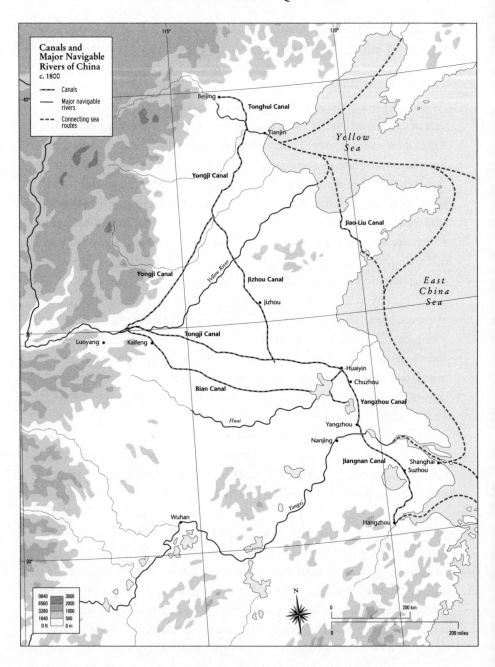

Through this long-term struggle with natural forces, human ambitions have deeply and literally molded the ecology of China and the history of its environment. By 1750, much of the original flora and fauna had all but vanished. The relationship between the manmade and the natural worlds made for a tenuous and delicate ecological balance. Soil and water supplies were considerably degraded by intensive human labor and ingenuity, including complex, engineered solutions that required increasingly costly and risky efforts to maintain. Rising population density, internal migration, land reclamations, and demand for food and fuels kept up the pressure. With further population growth in most of farmable China after 1750, the threat of diminishing returns loomed large. In the face of soil degradation, soil erosion, and desertification, late imperial China had no choice but to work ever harder to avert catastrophic system failure in the form of floods, droughts, and other calamities. The late imperial state employed an impressive array of technologies and practical strategies to deal with natural disasters. During droughts, for example, officials worked to quell social disorder by selling grain from massive state-run granaries at below-market prices, offering tax remissions or substantial reductions, personally investigating disaster areas, giving relief according to the degree of disaster, encouraging local elites to operate soup kitchens or charitable granaries, and setting up public shelters for famine refugees.[8] That China was able to maintain unity over such a large territory and in such unpredictable circumstances for such a long time is remarkable. It required that the state build and maintain sufficient administrative capacity for the upkeep of dams, irrigation systems, disaster prevention, and emergency relief.

Governing Late Imperial Society

Governing a country so huge and diverse represented an enormous challenge to every ruler of the Chinese empire. Governance—in the sense of enforcing order and exercising authority by way of setting up institutions, coordinating, and negotiating rules, norms, and services—was key to social stability and economic development. Western observers in the past have tended to depict governance in China in simple terms, describing it as a unitary empire ruled by an autocratic emperor who commanded a huge bureaucracy to enforce his absolute power on a lethargic populace. In more recent decades, historians have shown that the institutions in imperial China were more flexible, much more creative, and more efficient. Several core institutions and fundamental concepts were developed and highly refined over several dynasties and they formed the backbone of late imperial Chinese governance. Among them were institutions for ruling the empire and dealing with ethnic and cultural diversity, doctrines such as the Mandate of Heaven, the examination system, and the imperial bureaucracy.

Very early in its history, China became a unified empire (in 221 BCE); however, unity proved to be fragile and elusive for many centuries. Despite intensive efforts at unification, centralization, and standardization by many ruling houses, the empire remained stubbornly multiethnic, marked by ethnic diversity and a multitude of cultural traditions and religions. An astonishing ethnic and cultural complexity prevailed. Many dynasties came from outside of China and were of non-Chinese origins. Ethnic complexities and intermixings were not limited to the northern pastoral zone; in the rice-growing south, a majority of the population was made up of identifiably non-Chinese, aboriginal people. This cultural and ethnic ferment has caused historians to wonder whether the very concept of China simply "did not exist, except as an alien fiction."[9] Not only is the word "China" a foreign coinage, but even such roughly comparable Chinese terms as "Zhonghua" and "Zhongguo" have not achieved a stable, definitive meaning in traditional Chinese discourse.[10] Significant ethnic diversity was always present in the Chinese empire, although this pluralism often gets lost in most history texts' indiscriminate use of the word "China" or "Chinese culture."

Throughout its history, China was also remarkably open to external cultural influences. A silver ewer unearthed from the tomb of a man who died in northwestern China in 569 was decorated with scenes from the Trojan wars. Central Asians clearly influenced the plastic arts of sixth-century North China. The ruling elites were passionate collectors of foreign artifacts. An early sixth-century Northern Wei prince is said to have possessed dozens of crystal, agate, glass, and red jade drinking vessels that were "all from the western regions" as well as horses from as far west as Persia.[11] In the south, stone pillars at several sixth-century Chinese royal tombs closely resembled those of ancient Greece. A sixth-century bowl from Tashkent, together with some Persian coins, was discovered in far southeast China. After their introduction from India in the sixth century, Buddhist scriptures translated from Sanskrit attracted more readers among ordinary Chinese people than the supposedly native "Chinese" Confucian classics.

The empire turned to Confucian teachings only after the life of the historic Confucius (c. 551–479 BCE). The Han dynasty (202 BCE–220 CE) as well as the reunified empire after 589 CE, forged by the Sui and Tang dynasties at the end of the period of division, turned to Confucianism as official ideology. It was in many ways a substantially new empire, as shown, for example, in records of literary collections. Some 38 percent of the books in the Tang imperial library were newly created Tang-era works. Many of those publications promoted Confucianism as a unifying teaching. According to Samuel Adshead, before the sixth century, "continuity of political form was no more characteristic of China than it was of the West."[12] After that, however, the Sui and Tang dynasties so successfully imposed their unified, imperial model that, by the eighth century, "China had achieved a multiple preeminence" in East Asia and "at least the illusion of a succession of essentially similar dynasties governed by cyclical process." These dynasties also revived the notion of the so-called dynastic cycle based on earlier Han dynasty concepts dating back to the third century BCE.[13] Many internal ethnic distinctions were also beginning to disappear through cultural intermixing and education such as the examination system, although some peoples in more inaccessible parts of central China long maintained notable cultural differences. What we call "China" had by that time been more or less permanently established through a consistent vision and spreading of a reconstructed Confucian culture.[14]

This Confucian-cultural China soon came to be governed by vastly different ruling centers, some of them hailing from regions as far outside Chinese borders as Inner Asia, Mongolia, and Manchuria. The so-called conquest dynasties were established by non-Han peoples that ruled parts or all of China, but numerous other rules had their origins outside of China proper.[15] The conquest dynasties were not simply regular Chinese dynasties, but were steeped in the traditions of Inner Asia or the vast grasslands of the northeast—not only militarily, but culturally, politically, and ideologically. Han Chinese society interacted with non-Han peoples from the steppe region who often outdid them militarily. Central and North Asian ideas and practices had profound effects on the nature of governance in China. After the Yuan dynasty, Mongol practices and ideas found their way into Ming institutions. The first emperor of the Han-Chinese Ming dynasty drove the

Mongols from China, but he adopted their strict and more hierarchical system of political and military control over the Confucian bureaucracy.[16] Consequently, governance during the late imperial period was based on a blend of different Chinese and non-Chinese institutions, traditions, and practices.

Making this mixing possible was the fact that all models agreed on the monarchy as the best and only legitimate form of government. The Chinese notion of the emperor as the "Son of Heaven" and absolute ruler was also highly attractive to rulers from the steppe in the north. One of the Confucian classics, The Book of Odes *(Shijing),* stated clearly that "under the wide heaven, all is the king's land; within the sea boundaries of the land, all are the king's subjects." The emperor presided over "all under Heaven" *(tianxia)* on the basis of the Mandate of Heaven *(Tianming).*[17] This was another concept the conquerors found useful because, without that mandate, government would not be considered legitimate. It could consequently be argued that, if Chinese rulers had lost the mandate, the claim to power by the conquerors was legitimate and in accordance with Chinese ideas.

Over time, *Tianming* came to be seen in Confucian writings as concern for the welfare of human beings. This mandate was dependent on the ruler's ability to educate the people and to offer protection from human and natural harm. If a ruler ceased to rule justly or wisely in these terms and began to rule only with his self-interest in mind, then he could be seen as having lost the Mandate of Heaven. Heaven would punish the emperor for failing to fulfill his responsibilities by inflicting natural disasters and by encouraging the people to overthrow their ruler and government and replace them with a new regime based on a new mandate. In that case, an attempt at overthrowing the ruler might be justified. The Mandate of Heaven thus came to represent the moral order of the universe. In Chinese cosmology, the human and natural worlds were inextricably linked. When the proper order was respected, the physical world ran smoothly and the human world prospered. When that order was not respected, anomalous or destructive events, such as earthquakes, floods, eclipses, or even epidemics, would take place. In fact, many problems facing the government were understood in cultural-religious terms. Chinese rulers, officials, and commoners believed that natural disasters were brought about by human actions that violated heavenly principles and disrupted cosmic forces. Therefore, when drought struck, it was important for rulers and officials to make a "self-accounting" and show contrition for possible offenses.

Predicting natural phenomena that were particularly difficult to forecast, such as solar eclipses, was a way of assuring people that the central authority was indeed in touch with the powers of heaven, and thus worthy of their allegiance. Making accurate predictions became so important that emperors sought out the best astronomers and mathematicians they could find, even if they were European Jesuits or otherwise not Chinese. Aside from forecasts, rituals played an important role in demonstrating that rulers governed in accordance with heaven and had legitimacy. A number of rituals were regularly conducted by the emperor at the Temple of Heaven in the capital. During times of drought, for instance, rainmaking rituals to move the heart of heaven were as important as pragmatic measures in the repertoire of official responses. The sharp distinction some modern scholars make between ritual performances and "utilitarian" administrative behavior did not exist for most imperial officials.[18] benevolent father figure

Classic writings on governance conceptualized the proper relationship between an official and his people in familial terms, so officials were expected to behave as "fathers and mothers" who could not help but be moved to action by the people's suffering during a drought. Over the centuries, a wide range of texts associated certain rituals with ideals of benevolent rule and good governance. As a result, upright officials were expected to take the sufferings of their people seriously and do all they could to alleviate distress during times of disaster. Rituals *(li)* provided one of the most important venues in which behavior associated with the ideal of benevolence could be enacted and demonstrated. It was through these performances that the relationship between officials and local communities was constituted at the local level.

The rule of the emperor in everyday affairs rested on an ordered and ranked bureaucracy—another Chinese institution that the conquest dynasties found useful to maintain. The bureaucracy was based on clear rules and its personnel were selected based on meritocratic civil service examinations *(keju)*, not hereditary social claims or reliance on local military power. That good governance could be established through the "development of people" *(zuo ren)*—that is, by educating and training future officials rather than by taking them as they were—lay at the very basis of the Confucian administrative system. A comprehensive and public examination held at fixed, three-year intervals made success or failure in the competition for government positions dependent upon a candidate's knowledge and qualifications.[19] The civil service examination system was the main vehicle for selecting officials, and the late imperial state exerted great efforts to ensure its integrity and effectiveness. The system, which can be traced back to the seventh century CE, evolved over several dynasties into a complex and efficient institution that played a key role in Chinese society. The examinations fell mainly in the portfolio of the Ministry of Rites *(libu)* and, for the examinations in the capital, in that of the Hanlin Academy. The task of the Ministry of Rites was to train examiners and copiers at any level of the extensive system covering over 17 provinces, 140 prefectures, and around 1,350 counties. It also had to recruit security guards and other personnel. The wide-ranging organization for running the examination system involved the management of over a thousand examination places in total and perhaps hundreds of thousands of examiners, supervisors, and security personnel. The ministry was also responsible for publishing and periodically updating rules in the manuals on which the examination system was based.[20] Those rules were detailed and took up the space of twelve volumes.

The candidates were tested under strict surveillance. At the provincial level and above, candidates were hermetically sealed off into tiny examination cells *(kaoshe),* where they had to answer questions and write essays. The content of the examinations was dominated by the Confucian classics. Examinees had to know the Four Books *(sishu)* that are the authoritative works of Confucianism (Great Learning, Doctrine of the Mean, Analects, and Mencius) and the Five Classics *(wujing)* made up of the Classic of Poetry, Book of Documents, Book of Rites, Book of Changes, and Spring and Autumn Annals. They were required to cite important passages and discuss their content. Certain classical and modern rhyme schemes also had to be mastered, as demonstrated by the examinee's own composition of poetry in specified forms. In the Ming dynasty, for example, the so-called eight-legged essay *(baguwen)* became particularly popular, in which candidates had to craft concrete responses to questions under eight main headings and in 700 characters. From the seventeenth century, questions on practical aspects of statecraft, called *jingshi,* were also included, testing knowledge of history, geography, economy, justice, agriculture, nature studies, and certain emperors. These questions, however, were weighted less than other sections.

Who participated in the examination system? The so-called "ladder of success" was theoretically open to the entire male population (with the exception of criminals and Buddhist or Taoist monks) but, in fact, the examinations were not a mechanism for real social mobility. Taking part in the exams was not a ladder for the great majority of peasants and artisans to rise from the mass of ordinary people to the elite. Social mobility was not an officially declared aim, nor was the system specifically designed for it. Statistically, candidates from wealthy counties were more likely to pass the examination. Regions in the south of the country were therefore disproportionately represented by the successful candidates. As the archives also show, peasants, traders, and artisans did not make up a significant proportion of the candidates participating in examinations at a local level.[21] It was the intent of the institution, however, to rule out formal barriers and exclusionary criteria based on origin, region, or age. The main goal was not upward mobility but a limited circulation within the government of elites from gentry, military, and merchant backgrounds. The large pool of examinees also created a well-qualified, highly educated social class working in other occupations: fiction writers, dramatists, ritual specialists, genealogists, medical doctors, legal counselors, and teachers. The creation of an educated local elite, and its social circulation with government personnel, would prove to be key to the social and economic development of the late imperial society.

The system went to great lengths to ensure competitiveness and fairness. The examinations were to be as fair as possible for all, allowing talent and skill alone to determine success. After candidates had submitted their exams, the papers were anonymized, stamped, and taken to evaluators who could see only code numbers on them. Exams were first checked intently on the basis of formal criteria such as legibility and completeness, then handed to workers whose job it was to copy them in red ink and assign each paper a number. Proofers checked that copies corresponded with the original, and then the copies were sent to examiners for grading.

During the late imperial period, registrations for the examination increased due to both population growth and economic growth. The level of competition in the examinations was very high. A fixed number of titles could be bestowed and this quota could be changed only by imperial decree.[22] In

1400, there were about 30,000 candidates out of a total population of 65 million (1:2.200). Two hundred years later, half a million candidates participated in the examinations out of a total population of 150 million (1:300). By the end of the eighteenth century, the total number of candidates grew to nearly three million throughout the country.[23]

The increase of candidates was visible everywhere. Whereas about 8,000 candidates were tested at the provincial-level examinations lasting three days in Nanjing in the seventeenth century, the number of candidates increased to 18,000 in the eighteenth century. In 1766, when examinations in the capital lasted for 35 days, more than 2,000 candidates had to be examined. This kept 86 evaluators busy for 27 days, and 706 duplicators for 26 days. It took the examiners 20 days to produce their ranked list. The entire examination cost 4,089 silver taels. The intense competition also explains the high number of policemen and security guards at the places of examination, which were filled with thousands of candidates in a single examination period.

The examination system was not static. Long before the arrival of western culture and science in the nineteenth century, extensive discussions on whether the system was achieving its goals took place. Those discussions, above all concerned with the selection of the very best talent, focused on both examination content and organizational aspects of the system. Concerns about evaluation standards were expressed and efforts made to limit the observed "inflation" of grades. A growing use of technocratic language replaced the traditional political and moral focus.[24] Another discussion pertained to the goal of the institution. Again and again, debates considered whether, in light of the considerable effort made, the personal pressure applied, and the possible sources of error, the aim of recruiting the best candidates could be at all achieved. Radical changes were considered. In 1636, members of the local association of scholars of the so-called restoration society (fushe) even recommended that the whole system be abolished, to be replaced with a system of recommendation and commendation for testing purposes.[25]

Numerous reforms were undertaken to adjust the system and to make it more efficient in response to criticism and reservations. The curriculum was continuously adapted and reformed a number of times.[26] Emperors Yongzheng and Qianlong criticized, for example, the strong focus on philological and literary questions and lamented the neglect of practical aspects and matters of statecraft. Over and over, the right balance between general and specialized knowledge was discussed. Under Emperor Qianlong, the statecraft section within the exams *(jingshi shiwu)* was moved to the top of the examination catalogue. New western content, calendar calculation in particular, was also introduced.

The value of the imperial examination system as an institution of the imperial state would be hard to overestimate. It was a unique and remarkable institution, unmatched in early modern Europe. Millions of examination papers were produced, copied, graded, and ranked within the three-year examination cycle. This challenge was met relatively smoothly, both logistically and organizationally, for several centuries. As there were cases of abuse and fraud from the very beginning, the system developed detailed mechanisms to deal with such sources of error and weakness. The examination system is best described as a highly sophisticated, dynamic system of rules and processes, attuned to the possibility of abuse, errors, and inaccuracies at every level. It developed mechanisms capable of responding and fixing malfunctions. There was a critical awareness of the system's own shortcomings (concerning assessment, for example) and, accordingly, there was an elaborate system of testing, checks, and reviews to minimize dysfunction and ensure equity. It regulated, coordinated, and organized a central task: the recruitment of suitable personnel for state service. It did so by choosing a small group, albeit from a social elite, based on clear and transparent rules and norms to judge candidates' capabilities for civil service. Taking cultural symbols such as the study of the classics, painting, literature, and calligraphy as a point of reference also enabled the dynasty, together with its elites, to reproduce the institutional conditions necessary for its own survival. The examination hierarchy reproduced acceptable social hierarchies by redistributing wealth, power, and influence through education.

The existence of a central bureaucracy staffed by highly educated and competitively selected individuals allowed the empire to govern the huge country rather efficiently for many centuries. It permitted the drafting of a unified budget, the central management of transregional infrastructure and welfare, the establishment of a regulatory system, and a centrally controlled justice system and military. The military force was there for dealing with unrest and major security challenges, but unlike the practice in Europe and Japan, military commanders stood under central command and were not made governors of territories (that is, feudal lords). In the Ming and Qing dynasties, the civil and military chains of command were sharply differentiated, and even when civil officials had military responsibilities, they exercised them by giving orders to the military officers who actually led the troops. In the Ming dynasty, hereditary military personnel were assigned military colony lands to cultivate under the direction of hereditary military officers. This was called the *weisuo,* or hereditary military garrisons. Regular troops were recruited from among the soldier-farmers.

On behalf of the emperor, the bureaucracy pursued the maintenance of social order, the defense of the empire against foreign threats, and welfare goals such as the alleviation of poverty and greater equalization of landholding. The purpose of any Chinese government, therefore, was to provide peace and stability and to protect the people of China from the vagaries of nature, from external enemies, and from themselves.[27] The state apparatus itself was comparatively small. The two most important levels of local government were the province *(sheng)* and the county *(xian).* The lowest unit under control of the central government was the *xian.* The main task of the province was to broker between the *xian* and the central government. The number of *xian* scarcely changed in late imperial China. Despite its vastly larger population and territory, the empire had only 1,360 counties serving a population between 300 million and 400 million in 1750, compared to 1,173 counties for a population of 70 million in 1400. Limited revenues and the concern that adding officials could undermine administrative effectiveness in general made the court reluctant to expand the bureaucratic structure. As a result, however, the size of the bureaucracy lagged far behind the growth of population.[28]

Each county was ruled by a magistrate, who was always a native of another province according to what was called the rule of avoidance, designed to prevent the entrenchment of local power at the expense of the center. A magistrate could employ up to some hundreds of subordinate officials and clerks, depending on the size of the county, who were organized into roughly a dozen specialized bureaus for litigation, markets, and the like. An even larger number of messengers and runners supported the officials and clerks. Most regular officials were salaried, although their salaries were inadequate, forcing members of the local administration to rely on irregular fees, hidden payments, and kickbacks for large parts of their incomes. Limitations on the size of the bureaucracy help explain why the imperial administration never penetrated below the county level. Population growth meant that average county populations during the Qing dynasty reached a large multiple of comparable Song figures. This increased the burden on the near-static administrative structure. Insufficiently funded and poorly staffed, local magistrates depended on the cooperation of local gentry, which in turn reinforced pressures to keep taxes low, since any efforts to increase taxes placed local officials in direct conflict with the same elites whose support was essential to managing local affairs and preserving social order.

The administration of the empire was organized into a rather impressive and tightly run bureaucratic machine.[29] There was an elaborate system of checks and balances at every level designed to ensure effective central control over officials in the provinces and counties. Governors and governors-general of the provinces duplicated one another's efforts and monitored one another's adherence to central directives. A similar structure was found at lower levels of the bureaucracy, too.

The central state's commitment to a relatively small government forced the late imperial administration to rely on local, non-bureaucratic communities for the implementation of central initiatives and for support. This was accompanied by the formation of associations and groups within society itself such as kinship organizations, and merchant and artisan guilds. In addition to kinship groups and guilds, some of which controlled substantial wealth, village-level institutions included associations for crop-watching, defense, and maintenance of temples and irrigation works and water conservancy, along with revolving credit associations and associations to build bridges and schools, endow ferries, and repair roads. These associations worked in partnership with the state to achieve their goals of maintaining order and providing welfare services. The late imperial government was consistently compelled to rely on local elites to perform a wide range of quasi-governmental but nonetheless essential tasks. These included supervision of education; propagation of ideology through public lectures and recitations of the "Sacred Edict"; leadership of state-sponsored ceremonies of community bonding and political loyalism such as community rituals; mediation of conflicts to avoid lawsuits or armed feuds; and management of local-level public works projects. Local elites also served as tax-farmers and leaders of local militia. Local society was able to thrive in the late imperial period, and was marked by diversity, prosperity, and sophistication.

The practical business of village life fostered literacy and numeracy, both of which reached substantial levels in the late imperial period. Historical links between education and social mobility reinforced this tendency, as did popular appreciation of learning and culture. Strong household demand for education, coupled with low prices for teaching services and for books, produced levels of literacy in the late imperial period that outstripped much of preindustrial Europe. Work on age-heaping (the tendency of uneducated people to give their ages in rounded numbers) also suggests levels of numeracy in the Chinese population that were much higher than in countries with comparable or even slightly higher levels of development.[30] Widespread use of bookkeeping and accounting by households, business, lineage trusts, and guilds confirms the high level of commercial orientation and numeracy.[31]

Late imperial governments promoted the ancient *lijia* system of assigning responsibility to 110-household units for allocating tax and labor burdens across their members. Until the eighteenth century, each unit was supposed to be responsible for collecting the tax payments of its member households. Partly overlapping with the *lijia* was the *baojia* system consisting of hierarchically organized units of 10, 100, and 1,000 households. Each unit was led by one head of household who was theoretically held accountable for all the member households. To that end, he maintained population registers, kept the peace, resolved disputes, reported offenses to the magistrate, and gave expert testimony in criminal trials or civil litigation. This state-organized system of grassroots community administration extended uniformly across the empire. No household was officially permitted to evade the system.

Overall, the fact that the Confucian system of governance worked well explains the eminent longevity of the empire's institutions. For the most part, the late imperial period was marked by remarkable public welfare, security, and stability, especially when compared with the "dark" medieval and early modern ages in Europe, where countless wars were waged by noble courts and religious forces. The sources and self-descriptions from late imperial rulers, however, consistently display a bias toward harmony, peace, and decorum that does not fully reflect the more complicated reality. There is always a danger in taking accounts of Chinese history at face value, given their tendency to report more harmonious conditions than warranted. The entire official textual tradition offers a normative vision that is not simply a description of fact. There were in reality, of course, ups and downs in the late imperial governance.

The imperial system repeatedly faced severe problems such as poverty, destitution, insurgency, famines, and displacements resulting from natural calamities.

Despite the emphasis on rituals and benevolence, violence was a constant factor in the practice of imperial rule. Violence was in many ways systemically embedded in the local society and economy, as well as in the state's administrative apparatus. Local strongmen and militia leaders, insurgents (often called "bandits"), and other leaders of heterodox sects coexisted in local society and operated in a rough, fluid equilibrium. In its efforts to forestall or contain violent activity at the local level, the empire often collaborated uneasily with the former—and individual power holders (whether official or unofficial) routinely and clandestinely relied on the latter. And this was the case in the good times. In times when central authority collapsed—at the end of the Ming, for instance—the violence factor in local society could grow disastrously.

More routinely, concerns about maintaining stability triggered regular imperial campaigns over the centuries to educate *(jiaohua)* the lower classes, and to inculcate the Confucian four social bonds and the eight virtues *(siwei bade)* among the population at large. But for confronting popular disorder, incipient or actual, the imperial state also resorted to unrestricted and systematic use of violence—a practice symbolized in the word *jiao* (extermination). Aggressive, even preemptive violence was often inflicted without hesitation on enemies of the empire.[32] The late imperial system was so highly autocratic that there was no real limit on the emperor's power within the government or toward society. Rebels were eliminated, and officials were harshly punished if they dared to utter criticism of the emperor.

The empire also faced chronic and severe constraints on increasing the state's revenue because of the dependence on the static and stagnant arable land tax. Raising greater revenues meant increasing the tax burden and thus provoking resistance or outright rebellion. As a consequence, public spending was limited to programs that addressed fundamental issues of external and internal security. Expenditures on the military and border defenses were made to protect the population. The central government's spending on civilian public goods focused on measures intended to stabilize and increase agricultural productivity, such as investments in water control, irrigation, and the network of granaries designed to limit price fluctuations and stave off famine.

Over extended periods of time, the granary system worked well and helped avoid increases in grain prices following crop failures.[33] Such programs contributed to general welfare and thus added to the astounding stability of the imperial system. They also mobilized local contributions, highlighting the need for magistrates to maintain cooperation with local communities. Major construction and infrastructure projects could be accomplished with these arrangements between the central state and local communities, such as the construction and maintenance of the Grand Canal spanning a north-south route over a thousand kilometers in length, that delivered large-scale economic benefits for centuries.[34] At the same time, cozy relationships between central administration and local community leaders also raised the ever-present potential for corruption. Within the imperial bureaucracy, corruption was a huge concern, for if the court could not rely on officials to report impartially about conditions throughout the realm, imperial rule was at risk.

All of this, of course, meant that the theoretically unlimited power of the emperor was in reality considerably restricted by China's large size, limited revenues, long communication lines, small bureaucracy, and dependence on local associations and elites. The emperor, moreover, was supposed to observe ritual correctness, guarantee general welfare and social harmony, and follow precedents set by his predecessors and ancestors. Yet when foreign rulers, such as the Mongols or the Manchus, took power, they found it advantageous to maintain that restrictive system of governance. Its highly sophisticated structure allowed them to rule the huge lands of China by occupying the highest central positions in the government and thus having control over the crucial relays in the circuits of power. As one scholar puts it, the key goal of the imperial administration was "system maintenance rather than maximal efficiency."[35]

Manchu Conquest and the Great Qing Reconstruction

After 1600, the central power of the Chinese Ming dynasty (1368–1644) started to decay rapidly because of a combination of demographic pressure, corruption within the bureaucracy, mounting budget deficits, and the growing power of local tax collectors, landlords, and moneylenders. The rebellion that Li Zicheng led from 1630 to 1645 succeeded in occupying the capital for a short time, signaling the Ming dynasty's growing weakness. For the Manchus hailing from the northeastern provinces of Liaoning, Jilin, and Heilongjiang, and from Inner Mongolia, the Chinese empire's apparent inability to quash its social uprising and secure its borders was their long-awaited chance to extend their power beyond the Great Wall and gain access to the riches of China.[36]

The Manchus descended from peoples of northeastern Asia collectively called the "Tungus," a group that also included the Jurchen. Under their previous name of *Jin* (1125–1234) they once briefly ruled over China. Under the leadership of the charismatic Nurhachi (alternatively Nurhaci, 1559–1626), the horse-riding, animal-hunting Jurchen tribes that traversed the northeastern wilderness organized themselves into an ethnic confederation. Nurhachi also spurred the Jurchen expansion toward China, south of the Great Wall. In 1635, Nurhachi's successor, Abahai (1592–1643), renamed his people to the Manchus to remove the historical memory that, as Jurchen, they had been under Chinese rule.

In the early seventeenth century, Nurhachi and his successor organized the Manchu people into a military system called the Eight Banners *(Baqi)*. It was based on Inner Asian roots traceable to the Mongols and their predecessors, but was also influenced by Chinese imperial institutions of direct rule over Jurchen tributary people. This continued a tradition of hereditary enrollment in specific military units. Banners were separated from the rest of the population and mostly housed in garrisons, strategic areas, and larger cities. Overseeing the garrisons was a commander *(jiangjun)*. In theory, every adult male was supposed to become a soldier and the Banners were made up of companies, each of which was to furnish three hundred soldiers. Before the Manchus conquered China proper, they organized separate Manchu, Mongol, and Chinese Banners. Hence, the Manchu conquest of China was carried out by a diverse group of people, the majority of whom would by any definition qualify as Ming defectors, since they had served in the Ming armies or militia at one time or another. To speak of the Manchu conquest is therefore inaccurate, since it was a multiethnic alliance of Manchus, Mongols, Central Asians, Koreans, and anti-Ming Chinese rebels that invaded the Ming empire. The Banner forces combined Inner Asian cavalry skills with Chinese abilities in engineering and firearms to create a military power that was neither purely Inner Asian nor purely Chinese.

1.3. Manchu nobleman with servants and advisers, Beijing 1901–1902.
George Rinhart / Getty Images / 530729552

The Eight Banners continued to increase in military power in the border region northeast of the Great Wall. China north of the Yangzi came rather quickly under Manchu control, and with much less bloodshed than had been caused by the rebellion led by Li Zicheng. South of the Yangzi, however, it was a very different story. Urban resistance in the Yangzi delta, particularly in its wealthy and culturally developed cities, was intense. Extinguishing the disparate pockets of militant Ming resistance took thirty years and the conquest left urban elites profoundly mistrustful of the Manchus. In the infamous massacre of Yangzhou, the Banners engaged in a ten-day slaughter of the urban population, allegedly killing hundreds of thousands.[37] Taiwan, which was a base of the pirate world reaching from Japan to the Philippines, became a launching point for the combined resistance of Ming loyalists and those struggling to retain local independence under the leadership of Zheng Chenggong (1624–1662). They made dangerous forays into the mainland province of Fujian and threatened stable Qing control there. In 1645, the Qing court ordered that all adult males must adopt the Manchu practice of shaving their foreheads and braiding the rest of their hair in a queue, as well as wearing clothing in the Manchu style. This was met with great objection by many Chinese. Many Chinese officials and literati refused to serve the new dynasty and expressed their opposition to the new Manchu empire in art, literature, and private writings.

The Manchus eventually established control throughout the territory ruled by the Ming and established China's last imperial dynasty with the name the Great Qing. It ruled China from 1644 until 1911. When the Manchus swept into China, they followed their original method for controlling areas outside their homeland, here using Han Chinese administrative structures to rule over the Han Chinese areas.[38] Forming an effective government based largely on Chinese bureaucratic models, the court reasserted strong central control and extended Chinese territory to the north and west (Chinese Turkestan, Outer Mongolia, and Tibet).

The Qing imperial court understood that the environmental crises of the age posed a real threat to the imperial status and pristine purity of their homelands, acknowledging the challenges of disappearing wildernesses. The emperor responded with a mandate to protect the unspoiled natural areas of the Manchu and Mongolian homelands in the north. The Qing state also started a "purification" campaign to restore the land to its original form, by barring Chinese settlement in Manchuria, establishing controls on trade, and repatriating Chinese hunters and gatherers.

Hence, the Manchus formed a dynasty that was based on the Chinese imperial system whereby an emperor, in this case the great Qing emperor, would rule over all "Under Heaven" (*Tianxia*) based on the Mandate of

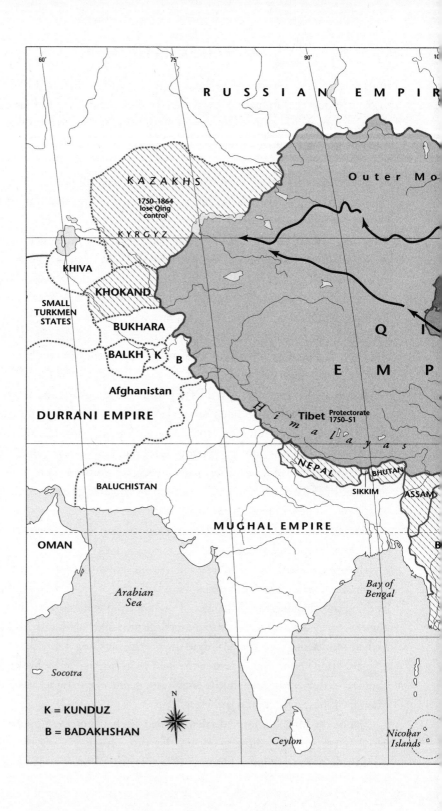

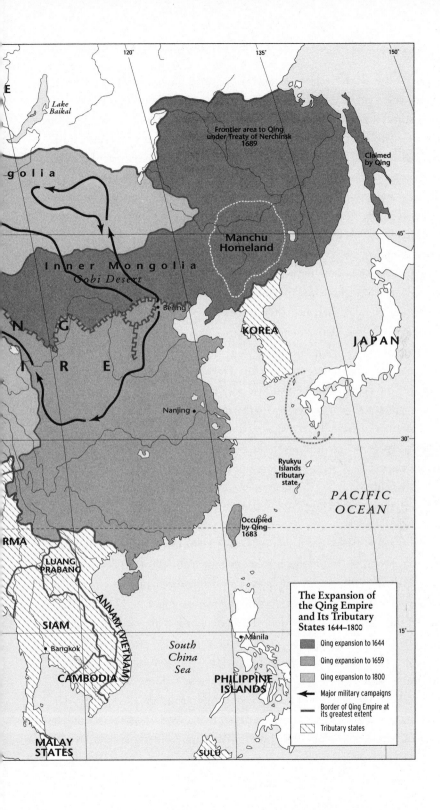

The Expansion of
the Qing Empire
and Its Tributary
States 1644–1800

■	Qing expansion to 1644
■	Qing expansion to 1659
■	Qing expansion to 1800
←	Major military campaigns
—	Border of Qing Empire at its greatest extent
▨	Tributary states

Frontier area to Qing
under Treaty of Nerchinsk
1689

Claimed
by Qing

Manchu
Homeland

Lake
Baikal

golia

Inner Mongolia
Gobi Desert

Beijing

KOREA

JAPAN

N G
I R E

Nanjing

Ryukyu
Islands
Tributary
state

PACIFIC
OCEAN

Occupied
by Qing
1683

RMA

LUANG
PRABANG

SIAM

Bangkok

ANNAM (VIETNAM)

CAMBODIA

South
China
Sea

Manila

PHILIPPINE
ISLANDS

MALAY
STATES

SULU

120°   135°   150°

45°

30°

15°

Heaven, and with the help of a highly developed bureaucracy. At the same time, the rulers of the Qing empire pressed for the unification of the Manchu, Mongol, and Tibetan regions. This was achieved by various long-term and flexible policies of connecting the great Manchu khans with the lamas' spiritual influence from Tibet; creating family ties with marital diplomacy between Manchus and Mongols; employing rituals preserved from the Mongol state audiences; and engaging in reciprocal tribute with frontier regions. These policies allowed the Qing to control about two-thirds of the steppes of the Great Khanate. This was a great achievement as, for the first time in Chinese history, the northern grasslands ceased to be the origin of security threats and challenges to the Chinese empire. Under the direct supervision of the Manchu Qing emperor, Manchu-Mongol-Tibetan affairs were administered by specific government agencies such as the Court of Colonial Affairs *(lifan yuan)*, the Imperial Household Department *(neiwu fu)*, and the military system of the Eight Banners.

A separate government system for Tibetans, Manchus, and Mongols emerged. This Great Khanate had not only its capital of Beijing, but also a summer capital at Chengde, along with the ancient royal palaces of the Mongols and a capital in Lhasa in Tibet. Manchu nobles held state audiences in all these locations, repeatedly confirming the imperial mandate of the Qing dynasty's Manchu emperors. These two systems, one for the Han Chinese areas and one for the Manchu-Mongol-Tibetan areas, were the core of the diarchic political and legal system of the Qing dynasty. This form of flexible and adaptive governance merged earlier systems: the vassal state system, the system of appointing national minority hereditary headmen, as well as the centralized system of prefectures and counties. It subsequently became the hallmark of the development of the Qing. The Qing empire employed a particular mechanism of governance over "a domain in parts."[39] Consequently, statements, edicts, and official documents of the Qing empire were deliberately designed as imperial communications in more than one language. Typically these were in Manchu and Chinese, and very commonly in Manchu, Chinese, and Mongolian. After the mid-eighteenth century, they were frequently in Manchu, Chinese, Mongolian, Tibetan, and the Arabic script of many Central Asian Muslims, often called "Uighur." The goal was the simultaneous expression of imperial policies in multiple languages, within multiple cultural frames, and to multiple ethnic audiences.[40]

The Qing rulers of the later part of the seventeenth and early eighteenth centuries were particularly capable of deploying this particular mode of multi-ethnic governance, which demanded cultural sensibility and constant mediation among different cultural spaces and ethnic constituencies, as well as the articulation of a unifying imperial vision of universal sovereignty and territorial expansion. Foremost among them was the energetic and hard-working Kangxi emperor (r. 1661–1722) who reorganized the court to adopt Chinese institutions, giving it stability and legitimacy that it could not gain by conquest alone. The other emperors governed under the titles of Yong-zheng (r. 1722–1735) and Qianlong. The early Qing period was also one of remarkable stability and continuity as Kangxi (1654–1722) and Qianlong (1711–1799) ruled for roughly sixty years each. During their time on the throne, the empire went through a period celebrated in Chinese historiography as the "prosperous age" *(shengshi).*[41] In 1736, the Qing undertook a major institutional innovation by creating the Grand Council. It was a small committee placed on top of the regular bureaucracy, featuring its own personnel, archives, research groups, rapid communications networks, and effective modes of command and control. The Grand Council was able to tap the grain and other resources of China proper to support commerce, colonization, and military provisioning deep into Inner Asia.

The Qing dynasty's standing military was made up of two separate forces: the multiethnic Banner armies, composed mostly of Manchus and Mongols, and the Green Standard armies, and staffed mainly by ethnically Chinese. (Ethnic separation was, however, not always strictly maintained.)[42] The Banners were the elite armies of the ruling dynasty. They had the task to secure the north, the homeland of Manchuria, and a handful of garrison cities at strategic locations scattered around the empire. They reached the peak of their might and numbers during the eighteenth-century frontier campaigns. In the nineteenth century, there were roughly 150,000 Banner troops based in the region around Beijing. The Green Standard armies stood below the Banner forces. They were responsible for maintaining control throughout the empire. Their numbers were proportionally greater: 550,000 soldiers were enlisted in the early nineteenth century.

The High Qing period was a time of peace and social order, material splendor, cultural refinement, technological progress, and continued territorial

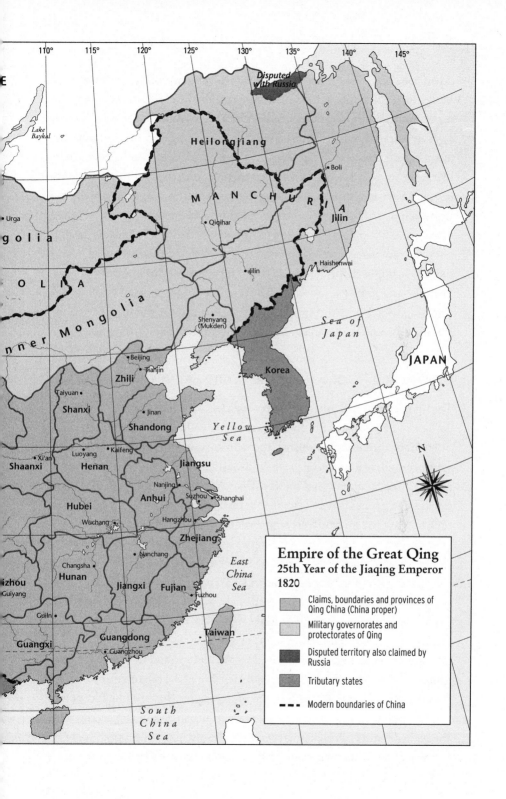

Empire of the Great Qing
25th Year of the Jiaqing Emperor
1820

expansion. The Qing empire reached its height of political control over Manchuria, Mongolia, Chinese Turkestan, Tibet, and China, as well as the states recognizing Qing superiority in the system of court visitation known as the tributary system (discussed later). It continued vigorously to push for territorial expansion with ongoing campaigns in Southeast and Central Asia. Until the mid-eighteenth century, the Qing could be compared with expanding Eurasian empires, including the Russian empire and potentially the British empire. The Qing had advanced gunpowder weaponry, and excelled in mapmaking, applied diplomatic techniques, and data collection. Qing military systems were so well developed that the empire could move men and supplies swiftly and efficiently to any front that needed reinforcements quickly. The Chinese empire boosted sophisticated central command and bureaucratic logistics. It was in this time that the Qing became the largest of all the land-based empires, as well as one of the most powerful in the world.

Growth and Prosperity in the "Long Eighteenth Century"

The Qing empire had inherited a very sophisticated and, by premodern standards, highly productive economic system. A wide range of advanced technologies in agriculture, industry, and transport were available and enabled solid economic growth. The previous dynasties had laid the basis for late imperial China's economy and society. This included the formation of institutions and structures that underpinned several centuries of steady development, such as a tax system based on registration and assessment of privately held land, accompanied by a shift to an agricultural regime based on smallholder ownership and tenancy, the expansion of markets for commodities and factors, the penetration of money in commercial exchange, and the extensive development of private commerce. The empire also was at the center of global trade, mainly with Europe in an unbalanced commercial relationship based on Qing exports of tea, porcelain, silk, and other goods.

After a brief interruption caused by the chaotic and destructive Ming-Qing transition, China's economy returned to a phase of growth and expansion. Three main factors contributed to the rapid growth of the Qing economic system: population growth; the increase in urbanization (especially since the higher density of urban markets made the distribution of goods more effective); and the pragmatic policy of the Qing court to develop the empire's commercial transport infrastructure. The Qing economy continued growing for over a hundred years, from the late seventeenth century until roughly 1800. Following the collapse of the Ming loyalist resistance in Taiwan in 1683, the Qing rulers overturned the maritime trading ban and also revoked the coastal evacuation policy. These policies allowed Chinese-European trade to start again. During the eighteenth century, the mounting demand for Chinese products in the European market and the subsequent influx of American silver into China revived the commercialization of the Chinese economy to a far greater degree than in the late Ming period. New markets were being explored, and merchants were extending their businesses across provincial lines and into the South China Sea. China's domestic economy was fully commercialized and, in some small ways, even industrializing.

In analyzing the various institutions that were in place in China at this time, it is important to keep in mind that the very economic structure of China's large continental empire was highly conducive to development and growth. Unlike Europe during this period, which was composed of many small states with their own political systems, currencies, national boundaries, and tax systems, Qing China was one vast continental market with few impediments to the movement of goods across provincial boundaries. Also contrary to widespread notions in the West, which imagined the imperial state in China to be consistently hostile to private commerce, the Qing state was active in facilitating economic growth. The Chinese state's pro-commercial attitude originated in the late Ming period, when the growth of the commercial economy began to be seen as an inevitable reality. Beginning in the late sixteenth century, many objections that had been raised—to silver's use as currency, to internal commerce, to foreign trade, and to merchants—lost ground to a school of thought emphasizing the "natural law" of the market economy. This thinking proposed that the market economy would flourish under appropriate nurturing, not government control. The pragmatic attitude toward commerce continued to grow in the Qing bureaucracy and became de facto government policy by the eighteenth century. Hence the Qing government actively "nurtured" business through various means. One, for example, was the expansion and interlinking of separate road and canal networks to increase the speed of commodity supplies. Another was the stimulation of new production and marketing sectors by offering incentives for entrepreneurs.[43]

The Qing economic basis was predominantly agricultural. Around 80 to 85 percent of the population lived in the countryside at the end of the Qing dynasty, and most people had some relationship to farming or to something that was a byproduct of farming. Agriculture practices showed an impressive level of sophistication. Improved yields, among the world's highest at that time, were achieved with an intensification of plowing enabled by an increased supply of labor and natural fertilizer per unit of land. Equally important for the agricultural growth in the late imperial period was the introduction of many new grain crops. The most important foods imported at this time were sweet potatoes (or yams), corn *(zea mays)*, and peanuts. These crops were introduced to Southeast Asia from America in the sixteenth century, and a few decades later they entered China, where they soon became widespread in both the north and the south. Their diffusion was amazingly rapid. Given their different suitable environments for cultivation, they enabled many areas that had never been suitable for growing food grains to produce rich harvests. Thus, the agricultural development improved thanks to the enlargement of areas under cultivation, but also thanks to the introduction of new crops from the new world and improved seeds (especially early ripening and high-yield Champa rice varieties from Vietnam). As farm equipment was advanced and specialized, efficiency also kept food prices low. Food production could therefore largely keep up with population growth as crop yields rose. Yet the high efficiency of Chinese agriculture could not easily be improved upon. Real and substantial improvement would have to wait until the advent of chemical fertilizers and modern machinery in the twentieth century.

Qing China had large transaction markets for land in which forms of ownership and user rights could be purchased, sold, rented, mortgaged, and divided. Under the *yitian liangzhu* (two lords to a field) or *yitian sanzhu* (three lords to a field) system, ownership of a single plot could be vested in parties endowed with separate rights over the surface and subsurface. Rights could then be sold, leased, or used as collateral. Tenants as well as owners could freely exchange their access rights. The multiplicity and divisibility of rights to land helped ordinary villagers to sustain their livelihoods in a dynamic environment.

While agriculture's role was central, industrial production was a significant part of overall economic activity. Industries included salt manufacture, sugar making, oil pressing, textile production, dye making, mining, smelting, metallurgy (casting), tool making, coal mining, papermaking, painting, ink making, armament manufacture, pottery and porcelain making, boat and cart crafting, pearl and jade polishing, and more. The textile industry was especially developed. Official textile workshops were located throughout the country, with the greatest concentration and the most important centers in Jiangnan, south of the Yangzi. Private textile workshops for silk and cotton were also centered in the Yangzi River delta, where competition spurred high-quality weaving. Porcelain production was another very important industry. Porcelain was made throughout the country in both the north and south. Jingdezhen in Jiangxi, with its fine, soft, white kaolin clay, became the center of the porcelain industry. The porcelains were thin and delicate—thanks first to the superior quality of the clay and second to the high temperatures at which they were fired. The enterprises involved the labor of hundreds of artisans, who produced a large variety of superior porcelain. Blue-and-white porcelains were not only popular in China, but also much in demand in distant markets in southern Asia, the Middle East, and Europe. In early modern Europe, Chinese porcelain was called "china" (hence today's name of the country in western languages), and it was very widely known and appreciated. For example, August the Strong (1670–1733), king of Saxony, was an enthusiastic collector of Chinese porcelain. He accumulated over twelve hundred "blanc de chine" wares. He later established the Meissen porcelain factory to re-create the exquisite quality of Chinese porcelain. By 1700, a ship arriving in England might carry more than 150,000 pieces of porcelain. In 1722, the British East India Company filled some 400,000 orders to satisfy the demand for "chinaware" among the well-to-dos. The Dutch East India Company shipped some six million blanc de chine pieces from Dehua, Fujian, in the seventeenth century, and this number represented only about 16 percent of ceramic exports at the time. It is estimated that by the close of the eighteenth century, at least seventy million pieces of porcelain had made their way from China into Europe via maritime routes.[44]

In industry, many technologies developed as early as the tenth century in areas like steelmaking. Through constant tinkering, they became far superior to the industrial technologies found in Europe before the eighteenth century. There were also important books that discussed industrial and craft technology: "Heavenly Crafts Revealing the Uses of Things" (Tiangong kaiwu), a

1637 work by Song Yingxing (1587–1666); "Comprehensive Treatise on Agricultural Administration" *(Nongzheng quanshu)*, published in 1639 by Xu Guangqi (1562–1633); and "Treatise on Armament Technology" *(Wubei zhi)*, published in 1621 by Mao Yuanyi (1594–1640?).[45] That a large number of books on production techniques appeared during the late Ming dynasty is a noteworthy phenomenon in itself. Some of these works, especially Xu Guangqi's, also reflected a great deal of European technological knowledge. This new knowledge had been brought from abroad by European missionaries. Innovations were developed through tinkering and experimentation, and produced different ways of increasing, for example, the efficiency of fuel used in making steel or the speed with which cotton could be spun into yarn or yarn woven into cloth. The kinds of science-based innovations that became central to Europe's technological advances in the latter half of the nineteenth century, with the development of electric power and the modern chemical industry, were largely missing.

Massive population growth, along with stable living standards, defined the late imperial economy. The Chinese economy boomed, driven by expanding markets. A pronounced proliferation of markets and commercialization penetrated rural society to an unprecedented degree. China's domestic trade developed quickly, too. A large percentage of China's farm households were able to offer a significant percentage of their produce for sale and began relying on markets for some goods instead of producing them themselves. Interregional trade included low-cost, bulk staples such as cotton, grain, beans, vegetable oils, forest products, animal products, and fertilizer. While most agricultural products were used and consumed by their producers, by the end of the eighteenth century, 10 percent of the grain harvest, 25 percent of raw cotton, 50 percent of cotton cloth production, 90 percent of raw silk, and almost the entire tea harvest were produced for sale in the marketplace.[46]

The Qing dynasty witnessed not only growth in the number of markets and market towns, but also the development of more efficient market structures. These structures emerged when central markets collected goods from lower markets. There were markets that served entire regions, markets that served sections of regions, and an increasing number of local markets that served the producers and consumers. China also had a long-distance trading system that brought grain from the interior to the coast, or from the lower Yangzi to

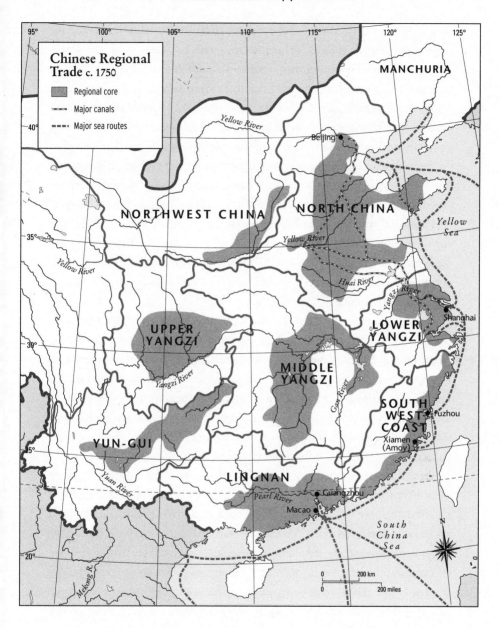

Chinese Regional
Trade c. 1750

Regional core

Major canals

Major sea routes

MANCHURIA

Yellow River

Beijing

NORTHWEST CHINA

NORTH CHINA

Yellow Sea

Yellow River

Yellow River

Huai River

Yangzi River

UPPER
YANGZI

LOWER
YANGZI

Shanghai

Yangzi River

MIDDLE
YANGZI

Gan River

YUN-GUI

SOUTH
WEST
COAST

Fuzhou

Xiamen
(Amoy)

Yuan River

LINGNAN

Pearl River

Guangzhou

Macao

South
China
Sea

Mekong R.

N

0   200 km

0   200 miles

Beijing in the north, and moved products from the coast back into the interior. Late imperial China had many cities with populations of over a million inhabitants. Supplying them required a sophisticated domestic market system making use of an extensive network of roads and canals. The Grand Canal, constructed under the Sui dynasty (581–618), shipped massive quantities of grain from the river valleys of central and southern China to provision government officials and troops in the less productive, more volatile north.

Simultaneously, markets serving the producers were evolving. These canals included periodic markets, which only met a few days a week, to which farmers could come and bring their produce. They changed into stationary markets that operated every day, with full-time merchants working in them. Rural and town markets operated periodically or continuously. Approximately 80 percent of the population lived within a day's journey of a market town and could take a portion of their produce to the market and become involved in market activities.

The Qing dynasty also saw the development of specialized groups of merchants. There were merchants who operated only within local marketing communities. But there were also long-distance merchants, whose economic activity demanded extensive traveling. Guild halls were established in distant parts to represent and serve the interests of merchants from other parts of China who conducted business there. As aliens in those distant communities, perhaps not even speaking the local dialects, the long-distance merchants relied on the guilds for their business.

In the financial sphere, too, the Qing empire developed institutions that were advanced by premodern standards. It is well known that China was the first country to use paper money on a nationwide scale. For most of its history, however, the Chinese economy operated under a bimetallic copper-silver monetary standard, meaning that both copper and silver were in circulation, with no regular issue of official paper currency. Officially minted copper coins with an opening in the middle (allowing coins to be tied together into "strings" of up to a thousand) were used for everyday transactions. Silver "shoes" (shoe-shaped ingots cast by private firms) were used for wholesale trade and larger transactions and for paying taxes to the government. As European trade expanded, an array of imported silver coins from Europe, the Americas, and Japan came into circulation. The exchange rate between copper and silver, theoretically constant at 1,000 standard cash per silver tael (a weight and traditional measure of money consisting of around 37.5 grams of pure silver), varied widely over time, across regions, and among different trades. During the Qing period, all Chinese people had to pay part of their taxes to the government in silver as opposed to goods-in-kind. This meant that the farmers, especially, had to sell what they produced on the market to acquire currency for their taxes. In fact, one could say that the Qing government's tax policy was one of the factors that pushed marketization, and thus economic growth, in China during this time.[47]

Equally important is that China developed a banking system to complement its domestic trading system. By the eighteenth century, money changers from Shanxi and pawn brokerages (*dangpu*) from Anhui made small loans as a means of putting their excess capital into play so it could earn interest. Over time, their expansion into providing credit within local market communities developed into the earliest native Chinese banks (*qianzhuang*). As we have seen, China had a vast market in which a large number of commodities moved both within local systems and over longer distances. Conducting this kind of business with heavy, metal money was difficult and inconvenient, however, especially if a merchant had to carry huge bags of silver over long distances. It would also make the merchant vulnerable to robbery along the road, increasing the risks for his business. To address this problem, remittance banks were established. The banks were often referred to as Shanxi banks because merchants from the province of Shanxi in northwestern China were the main investors and eventually became the bankers for all of China. Shanxi merchants established a network of private exchange shops, referred to as *piaohao*, which provided commercial remittances from one area to another, making profits on the exchange rates between silver and copper (mainly copper coins and silver coins or ingots). The Shanxi banks and others could transfer large sums of money over distances of thousands of kilometers without actually having to transfer the currency itself. The remittance bank would take cash deposits from a merchant in one place and issue him a remittance certificate, which the merchant could then take elsewhere to pay someone with whom he was doing business. That person could in turn go to a bank in his area and exchange the certificate for coins. This system required banks with the organizational capacity to keep books, perform well, and build up trust over generations. Local "money shops" specialized in money exchange between copper and silver, and verifying the genuineness of silver or strings of copper cash. They also issued loans against a variety of collateral. By the eighteenth century, there was a vast network of such banks and they were extremely important for the development of commercial activity in China.

Because its currency depended on silver and copper, China under the Ming and Qing dynasties had enormous unmet demand for precious metals. Through most of the sixteenth century, China's main source of silver was Japan. Both Chinese and European shippers worked the routes from Japanese docks to mainland China. As the economy grew, and with it, the number of transactions in the marketplace, the populace needed greater quantities of silver than Japan was able to produce. After the 1570s, silver was brought from a new location with huge deposits: Latin America. This was a new opportunity for the European shipping companies that operated across Asia, Europe, and the Americas, with the Philippines serving as gateway and Manila as the key port of transit. It marked the beginning of a truly global world economic system. The large-scale imports of silver from mines in the Americas to China beginning in the sixteenth century and lasting until the end of the eighteenth century linked the major world regions and transformed both intra-Asian trade and China's domestic economy. The end results were massive silver flows into China from other parts of Asia, Europe, and the Americas in exchange for export goods such as silk, tea, porcelain, and other manufactures. European nations during this time had very few commodities aside from silver to sell to China. Throughout this period, transactions were made using minted and raw silver. Even as early as the 1720s, Mexican silver dollars were used as the main means of payment in the commercial world in southern China. The use of Mexican silver dollars was convenient and reduced transaction costs, since they were already coined and their silver content was reliably accurate. Despite modest attempts to control trade, Qing China became the final repository for much of the world's silver. According to one estimate, almost 30 percent of the silver mined in North and South America made its way to China, but perhaps the proportion was still greater. Indeed, this inflow of silver from the European colonies is one reason for the phenomenal economic expansion of the eighteenth century. China's domestic economy was transformed as the availability of silver made it the medium for taxation, deeply affecting the agrarian economy as well as urban markets.[48]

Taxes were levied mainly on agricultural production, presumed to be the foundation of the empire's economy. China's fiscal system was centered on the taxation of privately owned land. In the mid-eighteenth century, official fiscal data show land taxes accounting for 73.5 percent of officially recorded revenue, with the balance coming from the salt tax (at 11.9 percent), native customs (that is, taxes on internal and foreign trade, at 7.3 percent), and miscellaneous taxes (at 7.3 percent).[49] The Qing dynasty's receipts from the salt tax were a significant item in the national revenue for two reasons. First, apart from the land tax, the government had very few other sources of tax revenue. Second, salt was a broadly used commodity. The state did not regulate how salt was manufactured; it only required a license for the transport of salt. The land tax was assessed by combining two factors: the number of adult males in the household and the units of land, evaluated according to the presumed yield of the household's cultivated fields. The tax burden thus fell onto property holders and was in proportion to their holdings. For most of the Qing era, the aggregate fiscal burden on the Chinese people was not excessive; the population was probably even "undertaxed."[50] There were also very few taxes on manufacturing, wholesale trade, and retail sales. The commercial sector as a whole was not seen as a potential source of state revenue. The domestic and maritime customs services collected modest tolls on the long-distance transport of commercial goods. The government also generated revenue from licensing some large wholesale traders in major port cities and transportation centers. Overall, the Qing state taxed the movement of only a relatively small number of goods that it recognized as essential for daily life and as good sources of revenue for state coffers.

Records from this period also show the emergence of large and sophisticated Chinese firms that were active in sectors ranging from mining and textile manufacturing to food production.[51] These enterprises were much more flexible, innovative, and effective than western views have tended to recognize. Various Chinese forms of partnership allowed entrepreneurs to assemble investment capital and reinvest profits for the long term in ways surprisingly similar to those made possible by western joint-stock companies. Merchant families successfully adapted traditional institutions, such as the lineage trusts more often associated with gentry families.[52] These allowed them to raise capital for the growth of their enterprises and to establish themselves as wealthy merchant families, rather than remove their money from commerce in a bid to enter officialdom. In some instances, families, including some very high officials, moved their capital in and out of commerce quite flexibly, minimizing conflicts between firm ownership stakes and official status.

Chinese law, which was one of the most advanced and sophisticated legal systems in the world during this time, left the regulation of private matters largely to the people directly engaged in them. While county magistrates also ruled on civil and commercial as well as criminal matters, broad swaths of economic and social life were governed by private custom, with disputes adjudicated and sanctions imposed by family, clan, and village elders, by local gentry, and by mercantile associations.[53] With certain exceptions, while the state set out specific parameters for economic activity, it was mainly within the local economic communities and social institutions that Chinese customary law for the handling of economic affairs emerged. The absence of commercial and civil codes introduced an element of uncertainty into private ownership. Private property rights in Qing China were genuine and substantive, but enforcement was less reliable. Legally enforceable claims remained somewhat secondary to the political standing of the property holders. Faced with the fundamental possibility of arbitrary government confiscation that could not be legally challenged, property holders tended to seek protection by wooing political power. Despite elaborate and generally reliable informal arrangements for recording, protecting, and transferring rights to land and other material assets, the foundation of property rights in imperial China depended on politics rather than law. This had implications for economic change during the nineteenth century and beyond, to which we will return later.

In practice, then, the Chinese state under the Qing took a laissez-faire approach to the economy, as the state did not regulate or tax commercial activity. In the traditional handicraft industries, the desire to produce more goods with less labor input certainly did exist, and it led to the constant refinement of production processes. But the minute division of labor in traditional industries led to fragmentation. Every stage in the work process was relatively independent and there was no overall coordination of the production process. The links in the chain of production were also mostly small units (family or small workshops) that did not command financial resources to systematically explore or invest in new technologies. While the late imperial state could have been expected to be able to requisition resources to push for innovation, it left economic affairs largely to themselves. Unlike in early modern Holland or England, there was also no formal market for public debt. The lack of proper financial instruments for government or private borrowing additionally restrained intuitional capacity and rendered the traditional state prone to fiscal predation or confiscation in times of budget shortfalls.

Governed by a rather small administration extracting small, and in fact declining, fiscal resources, the economy of Qing China nonetheless delivered food, clothing, and shelter to an immense and growing population despite mounting demographic pressure and without widespread technological advancement—surely an impressive achievement. In the absence of major disasters or challenges, the development proceeded smoothly. In the face of new threats or unanticipated needs, however, the imperial government would by and large lack the capability to mobilize new resources.

END 9/5/23

A Chinese Enlightenment? Intellectual Life during the High Qing

The dominant strand of philosophical thinking in the late imperial period is known as "neo-Confucianism." This is a general term referring to the renaissance of Confucianism during the Song dynasty and to the various subsequent philosophical schools of thought that developed from that renaissance. The revival of Confucianism followed a long period in which Buddhism and Daoism had dominated Chinese philosophy. It became a vital intellectual force that provided a platform for intellectual exchange and intense debate.

As the name indicates, neo-Confucianism is a reinterpretation of the philosophy dating back to the pre-Qin era based on the thinking of Confucius.[54] The tradition of China's culture, as well as its entire intellectual development during the existence of the Chinese empire, was shaped by the philosophy of Confucius, from the early phases of the Han dynasty in the second century to at least the beginnings of the Republican period in the early twentieth century. The following passage from the Analects describes some of its basic assumptions: "The Master said: Guide them with policies and align them with punishments and the people will evade them and have no shame. Guide them with virtue and align them with *li* (ritual) and the people will have a sense of shame and fulfill their roles."[55]

Confucius believed in the importance of moral education and personal cultivation. To Confucius, becoming a fully responsible and good human being was by necessity a cultural process. The method for pursuing education and cultivation was *li,* often translated as ritual practice or propriety. Specifically, Confucius referred to the rituals of the Zhou dynasty (1046–256 BCE), of which he was master. More generally, the term denoted a broad range of behavior from political protocol to court ceremony, religious rite to village festival, daily etiquette to disciplines of personal conduct. *Li* was the underlying cultural and moral syntax of community. The ultimate goal of education and self-cultivation lay in the dissemination of the comprehensive ethical virtue *ren,* translated as benevolence, humaneness, goodness. The term *ren* is so ambivalent that disciples in the Analects frequently question Confucius on its meaning. The Chinese character for *ren* consists of two elements, *person* and the numeral *two,* suggesting that benevolence is fundamentally part of social nature. Hence, the Confucian person is irreducibly social, fully cognizant of the specific complex of social roles and relationships that shape his being. This social definition of a human being makes social approval an important motivation for proper conduct. The threat of social disapproval or shame, on the other hand, works as an equal deterrent against unwanted conduct, more effective than the law or criminal punishments.

The excellence or virtue *(de)* achieved by members of the community empowers them as likely models of propriety for future generations. Because the authority of a community so constructed is internal to it, the community is self-regulating, and its effectiveness is dependent upon authoritative, exemplary leaders rather than on the application of some external institutional regulatory system. Propriety leads to proper conduct in one's relationships by reinforcing traditional social norms while at the same time demanding that they be whole-heartedly learned and "made one's own" *(yi).* The idea of "rightness" *(yi)* in a Confucian society, applied always within a social context, implies notions of "harmony." Proper actions are "right" if they are in complete harmony with the actions of others.[56]

It is worth repeating that what stands out in Confucian philosophy is its focus on moral conduct and education. Confucianism conveys the notion that self-cultivation and concrete actions are reciprocal conditions, the former concerned with the inner, moral world and the latter with the outer, communal world. Early Confucian scholarship involves critical introspection, but always combined with an interest in social practice and greater consequences for family, neighborhood, and the state.

Starting in the tenth century, neo-Confucianism was an intellectual reaction to the challenges of Buddhist and Daoist philosophy. It incorporated Buddhist and Daoist concepts to produce a new and more sophisticated Confucian metaphysics, in which the focus shifted almost exclusively to the inner, moral world of a person. The southern Song philosopher and official Zhu Xi (1130–1200) emphasized the "learning of Principle" and the "learning of the Mind and Heart." He asserted that the myriad things of the universe are all manifestations of a single "principle" (*li*, which is not to be confused with *li*, the ritual) and that this principle is the abstract essence of morality. By understanding the principle that underlies the universe (an idea similar to Buddhism's teaching that all things in the universe are manifestations of the single Buddha spirit), men may understand the moral principles that they must put into practice to achieve harmonious family life, good government, and peace under heaven. While there were different approaches to the way in which human beings are to understand Principle, neo-Confucianism agreed on the need to place emphasis on the inner self as the main arena of self-cultivation and self-improvement.

The thinking surrounding the "learning of the mind and heart" is also often identified with the Ming official and thinker Wang Yangming (1472–1529). Wang argued that, since every living thing is a manifestation of principle, one need not look outside oneself to understand principle (and therefore morality). One should consult one's own heart (or mind), wherein the principle surely lies. Since principle is considered to be the basis of human nature, it follows that anyone who realizes his or her inner world comprehends the Principle of the universe. Wang wrote: "There have never been people who know but do not act. Those who are supposed to know but do not act simply do not yet know. When sages and worthies taught people about knowing and acting, it was precisely because they wanted them to restore this original substance, and not just to have them behave like that and be satisfied."[57] This school of Heart-Mind (*xinxue*) rapidly gained influence during the Ming. Although Wang's philosophy tended to encourage greater freedom of thinking and intellectual exploration and thus provided an important impulse to philosophical thinking, it was limited by its focus on the inner world. Since Wang believed that action automatically flowed from the moral introspection, real-world problems of action and social issues receded into the background. At the same time, Zhu Xi's Neo-Confucian interpretations of the classics were adopted as orthodox. These teachings, especially by the Cheng-Zhu school—emphasizing loyalty to the ruler, moral cultivation, and the power of exemplary behavior—also achieved canonical status because they underpinned the examination system. They were the basis for the highly influential examination syllabus known as "Essential Ideas of the School of Nature and Principle" (Xingli Jingyi). As a result, the examination system gradually became a test in formalism and dogma; it was not interested in new interpretations of the meaning and implications of the classics. Imperial conservatism was meant to protect absolute imperial power, to the point that any ideas that questioned the intellectual or philosophical validity of the system were discouraged.

During the beginning of the Qing dynasty, many scholars became critical of the intellectual confines of neo-Confucianism metaphysics' speculation and the Heart-Mind school's idealism. The literati and scholars had experienced the shock of violent conquest as a very real trauma and they started to explore the specific reasons for the Ming collapse, a dynasty with which they had mostly identified. Several schools emerged that decidedly distanced themselves from neo-Confucian doctrines. The grand claims of the Heart-Mind school were now criticized as misguided and inflated concern with subjectivity, sensual indulgence, volatility of the self, and neglect of the social order. The so-called statecraft school (jingshi xue) shared an intellectual outlook that concerned itself with problems of order and practical administration. This concern with order was different from that of orthodox neo-Confucianists. The latter generally conceived of order in moral and spiritual terms, while among statecraft scholars the concern was mainly with the secular order of state and society. They tended to see statesmanship in institutional as well as moral terms. Statecraft Learning became influential in the eighteenth century. It gained prominence as China's growing problems underscored the need to deal with real-world issues.

Another school was the "School of Evidential Research" (kaozheng xue), which devoted itself mainly to textual criticism. Sometimes this school is called the New Text School (jinwen xue) or Han Learning, since some of its main protagonists, such as Gu Yanwu (1613–1682), preferred to use materials dating back to the Han dynasty instead of those from the Song-Ming period. Their work tended not only to question widely accepted orthodox interpretations of classical Confucian texts, but also to challenge the authenticity of standard versions of some of the Confucian classic texts, by throwing doubt on their provenance, date of writing, or authors. Some scholars' claims that some of the standard versions were the result of forgeries led to passionate debates.

A sense of the influence and role of those schools can be gained from the work of three remarkable scholars who lived and worked during the Ming-Qing transition.[58] Huang Zongxi (1610–1695), a native of Yuyao, Zhejiang, lived during the period of violent conquest. Actively resisting the Qing troops, Huang threw his support to the southern Ming rebels. When they failed, he devoted his life to teaching and writing. He became a leading authority in history, promoting precise historical studies on practical application of statecraft (*jingshi*). His main work was "Waiting for the Dawn: A Plan for the Prince" (*Mingyi daifang lu*). He pointed out the main flaws of the Chinese empire, which he saw as a monarchic autocracy that had emerged since the Yuan dynasty (1271–1368) and that was harmful to China's development. He felt the emperor had been "attributing all interests and benefits to himself while attributing problems to other people." He advocated "the rule of law" and was opposed to "the rule by the people."[59] He also spoke out against the practice of agriculture receiving special attention and the constraint of commerce, as he believed that industry and commerce were equally important. His views shocked the academic circles of the time, but exerted enormous influence on the rising democratic trends in the late Qing dynasty.

Gu Yanwu (1613–1682) from Kunshan, Jiangsu, was another famous thinker in this period. After his defeat in the anti-Qing struggle, he went to various provinces in the northern part of China, made many friends, and settled down in Huayang, Shaanxi, in his old age. He was conversant with the classics, history, astronomy, geography, phonology, epigraphy, military affairs, and farm matters. Gu Yanwu based his consideration of applied statecraft on his studies of history and historical geography. In his most important work, "Record of Knowledge Acquired Day by Day" (*Rizhilu*), he meticulously laid out his ideas on history and on human affairs, including systems of government offices, as well as the course of historical affairs, concentrating on practical matters. He was also interested in systems of taxation, the iron and salt monopolies, transportation of grain by waterways, and military affairs. To him, the neglect of these affairs during the Ming brought about their demise. Gu Yanwu took as the core of his philosophy the concept of "all under heaven" *(tianxia),* a term that covers all affairs from the welfare of common people to philosophy and thinking. His emphasis on the duality of practice and ideas was based on the theory that *qi* (tool) is a solid substance, while *li* (principle) is the objective law. He proposed that the objective law depends on solid substance, and that "the world is made up of substance." He looked at history from an evolutionary perspective, and called for advancements in politics to be made to keep up with the times. He stressed learning for practical purposes, striving to reverse the tide of impractical learning. He was against the politics of monarchical autocracy, proposing that "harmony and stability could be attained by empowering the people" and that "it is the responsibility of everyone to safeguard the country."[60]

Wang Fuzhi (1619–1692), a native of Hengyang, Hunan, also lived in the transition period between the Ming and Qing dynasties, and he participated in the resistance against the Manchus. After the defeat of the resistance, he wandered through southern China, finally finding refuge at the foot of Chuan Mountain in Qulan, Hengyang. His studies focused on the historical phonology of the Classical language, historiography, and geography. He believed the downfall of the Ming stemmed from the "empty talk" *(kong tan)* of neo-Confucianism and the ignorance of officials who focused on issues of statecraft. He was convinced that the scholasticism that had dominated Chinese thinking since the Song dynasty had distorted the original tradition of Mengzi and Confucius. He refuted Wang Yangming's theory of innate moral knowledge and looked for alternatives in Chinese thinking by returning to Confucian thinkers of the Han dynasty. Through his careful study of the original classics, he wanted to access and restore their original meaning *(puxue)* and complexity. He also wrote about the rise and fall of Chinese dynasties. Here, he especially pointed out the role of foreigners and non-Han people in this process. In general he described the influence of foreign ethnicities as harmful and dangerous to China. Wang adopted a strong anti-Manchu stance in his writings. He also insisted that the Chinese be distinguished from the non-Chinese, as each should stay in its own territory and respect the sovereignty of the other, to avoid the possibility of invasion or integration. He denied that foreign rulers could claim any legitimacy to rule over China.

He also sharply denounced Chinese who had helped or served the "barbarians" when they ruled over China. In Wang Fuzhi's work, we see the emergence of proto-nationalist positions that would gain great attraction and popularity at the end of the nineteenth century.

Confronted with the opposition and even outright hostility of a large number of literati, the Qing empire sought to incorporate them. The Qing continued public examinations to recruit for government service among the Han-Chinese population and to keep options for mobility open. They also started large official compilations and editions that employed many scholars.[61] This included the compilation of the official history of the Ming dynasty (Mingshi), the Kangxi dictionary, editions of text collections called congshu, and the largest encyclopedia in the world at that time—the "Complete Library of the Four Treasuries" (siku quanshu), which contained almost 3,500 of the most important texts of the Chinese tradition on over 2.3 million pages. These impressive projects were, however, also accompanied by a literary inquisition. Reaching its zenith in the 1780s, there were intensive efforts by the Qianlong emperor to purge China of "evil" books, poems, and plays. He sought to destroy works by Ming loyalists who he believed were writing subversive histories critical of the Manchu conquest. As many as three thousand works may have been destroyed by the inquisition in this period. Among the censored works were books considered disrespectful toward the Qing emperors or previous ethnic minority dynasties that could be viewed as analogous to the Qing. Writers who criticized the Qing dynasty could expect to have their entire output obliterated, regardless of the content of individual works.

Intellectual development in early Qing China resembled in some ways the intellectual tendencies in Europe during the same period. Many aspects point to the similarity between early Qing China and Enlightenment Europe, such as the availability of knowledge made possible through the production of comprehensive encyclopedias, the recovery of original texts, the desire to overcome scholasticism and metaphysical speculation, a growing interest in real-world problems, outspoken critiques of despotism, emphasis on rational argumentation and on the precise empirical gathering of facts and data, and the development of science. The Enlightenment is often seen as more or less a unique moment in European history—an exceptional turning point that affected only Europe. As recent scholarship has demonstrated, however, it was produced in a context of global synchronicity, in which China played a major role.[62] It was through European missionaries and translations of Chinese philosophical texts, published for the first time in 1687 as *Confucius Sinarum Philosophus*, that Europe would come to learn about and admire enlightened Chinese philosophical and political thinking. We can also, however, see differences. Unlike their European counterparts, who lived in different small states and countries and could easily escape government censorship by moving to neighboring states (where scholarship was also pursued in Latin), Chinese thinkers had no chance to remove themselves from the pervasive supervision and repression of the Qing empire. This limited their abilities to confront problems in government and society in a critical manner.

The Qing Empire and the East Asian World Order

China's relations with its neighbors were fraught. China was frequently confronted with security threats from adjacent neighbors that it could not easily overcome by military force. Given the long history of raiding and invasion by the peoples of the northern steppe, close attention was paid to the institutions of frontier defense. Emerging security issues were rooted in the geography of the North China Plain, where the first Chinese states emerged, and also stemmed from the difficulty of defending the extensive borders of China's huge territory. Flat and without natural defensive barriers such as mountain ranges or big lakes or rivers, the North China Plain rendered Chinese states defenseless to outside attack. This was especially problematic after the introduction of horses, which transformed steppe nomads into a formidable fighting force. Stretching east from the Mongolian plateau, north to densely forested taiga and south to the fertile Liao River Plain, the region consisted of three ecosystems that brought nomads, hunting and fishing peoples, and sedentary agriculturalists in contact with one another. The Khitan Liao (916–1125), Jurchen Jin (1115–1234), and, five hundred years later, Manchu Qing conquest dynasties indicate the dynamic political forces emanating from northeast Asia.[63]

Due to China's huge, continent-like size, the country had (and still has) more adjoining neighbors than any other country, except perhaps Russia. There were on average usually twenty or more immediately adjacent countries, from Japan in the east, to Vietnam in the south, to Himalayan kingdoms in the southwest, and to Russia and central Asian Khans in the north. Along its long border, China confronted very different terrains and faced different opponents, including tribes, nomads, and bureaucratized states. Under those circumstances, border defense was also logistically complex. Chinese dynasties used many strategies to deal with security issues along its extensive borders, including temporary accommodations, alliances made and abandoned, ambush and treachery, the careful cultivation of domestic resources and morale, psychological warfare, and raw military power. In other words, vulnerability to security threats has always been the main driver of empire's management of its foreign relations. Seen from the Chinese empire, the world was a chaotic and complex terrain of risks and uncertainties, stretching from the heartland to land borders and to the coasts.

Maintaining peaceful relations with foreign peoples along and beyond China's borders was a critical concern for any Chinese dynasty. It was also critical to the legitimacy of Chinese regimes. Again, imperial legitimacy derived from the Mandate of Heaven, which was conferred on a virtuous ruler. Not only domestic disasters but also foreign threats could undermine the basis of the mandate. Bringing northeast Asia, as well as the borders in Inner Asia and Tibet, under its firm control has to be seen as one of the great achievements of the Qing empire. At the same time, the Qing also established and maintained good relations with his neighbors in East and Southeast Asia. The Qing empire was the dominant economic and geopolitical center of an East Asian regional order that facilitated two centuries of stability and prosperity.[64]

The main institution established by the Chinese empire for managing good, peaceful relations with countries that did not belong to the empire, but surrounded it as its nearest neighbors, was the so-called tribute system.[65] The Qing dynasty requested periodic tribute missions from neighboring states at regular intervals and expected them to conform to the norms of Chinese ritual practice. These norms were detailed in the Collected Statutes of the Great Qing *(Qinding da Qing huidian)*, a legal code, and the Comprehensive Rituals of the Great Qing *(da Qing tongli)*. The rituals were designed to establish a clear hierarchical relationship between the Chinese emperor as Son of Heaven and the rulers of subordinate neighboring states. Unlike the European system where treaties and diplomatic conferences defined international relations, the world under the influence of Chinese civilization was ruled by a set of rites, which highlighted the symbolic sovereignty of the Chinese emperor. Foreign relations were no different than any other Chinese social relations, in which hierarchies of age, gender, social position, and official rank were understood as the natural order of things. Distant states that offered tribute to the Chinese emperor were seen as his vassals, even if they enjoyed autonomy. Greater proximity to the Chinese center meant enhanced bureaucratic control. People from beyond China's frontiers could come to be transformed, their ethnic differences erased as they adopted Chinese culture. Usually, however, relations with China did not involve loss of independence, as these states were largely free to run their domestic affairs as they saw fit and could also conduct foreign policy independently from China.

In this system, the center was the Chinese emperor, and the position of the other countries was reflected in the number of tributes they had to offer within a certain period of time. Foreign rulers were thus expected to honor and observe the Chinese ritual calendar, to accept nominal appointments as members of the Chinese court or military establishment, and, especially, to send periodic missions to the capital to demonstrate fealty and present tribute of local commodities. The tribute system was formalized in two key institutions: the recognition by the superior state known as "investiture," and the periodic sending of embassy envoys to the superior state. Investiture involved "the explicit acceptance of subordinate tributary status and was a diplomatic protocol by which a state recognized the legitimate sovereignty of another political unit and the status of the king in that tributary state as the legitimate ruler."[66] The tribute missions served a number of purposes: they formalized the political and diplomatic relationship between the two sides; exchanged information about important events and news; established rules for trade; and facilitated intellectual and cultural exchange. The missions themselves could consist of hundreds of people, including scholars, officials, interpreters, physicians, messengers, and assistants. Tributary envoys from continental neighbors were received and entertained by local and provincial governments in the frontier zones. Those from overseas were welcomed by special maritime trade supervisors at three key ports on the southeast and south coasts: Ningbo in Zhejiang for those from Japan; Quanzhou in Fujian for those from Taiwan and the Ryukyu Islands; and Canton in Guangdong for those from Southeast Asia. The frontier and coastal authorities forwarded foreign missions to the national capital, where the Ministry of Rites offered them hospitality and arranged audiences with the emperor. All envoys received valuable gifts in acknowledgment of the tribute they presented. They were also permitted to privately trade merchandise at designated, officially supervised markets, both in the capital and on the coasts and frontiers. Thus, copper coins and luxury goods, notably silks and porcelains, were exported, and pepper, other spices, and similar rarities were imported. On the western and northern frontiers, the main trade goods were Chinese tea and steppe horses. Far from balanced, the combined tribute and trade activities were highly profitable for foreigners, so much so that the Chinese established limits for the size and cargoes of foreign missions and prescribed long intervals that must elapse between missions early on.

Situated directly on China's border, Korea and Vietnam were most strongly committed to the tribute system. Both states sent prominent princes, statesmen, and scholars as regular tribute-bearing embassies to the Chinese court, to display their loyalty to the Chinese emperor. They also adopted the Chinese calendar and the Chinese writing system, incorporated classical Chinese learning into their cultural canon and accepted seals of authority and investiture of their rulers from the Son of Heaven in Beijing. As smaller states lying next to the Chinese empire, participation in the tribute system secured autonomy for them at the relatively small cost of offering ritual respect to the Chinese emperor. More distant states such as the Ryukyus, Siam, Champa, Khoqand, and Burma sent periodic tribute missions to China, too, though on a far less regular basis. Their tributary missions were allowed to trade at the borders following a prescribed route to the capital, and trade was also permitted at controlled markets in the capital after the emissaries had been received by the emperor. Doing business in China was clearly the main motivation behind their tributary visits, with some Central Asian merchants posing as representatives of rulers to gain access to the Chinese market.

While Korea, Vietnam, the Ryukyus, and a number of kingdoms of Central and Southeast Asia actively engaged in tributary trade with China, Japan sent no tributary missions during the Japanese Tokugawa period (1603–1808). While Japan had also adopted Chinese writing and held China's Confucian tradition in great respect, it did not accept tributary status by the Qing empire and was left outside the formal system. China-Japan direct trade nevertheless continued through Nagasaki, as well as indirectly through the Ryukyus and Hokkaido, and through the coastal trade that the Chinese state defined as piracy. Consider, for example, the fact that the Ryukyus took part in tributary relations with China to obtain access to the Chinese market, even when they were ruled by Japan, which itself had broken off those relations. Ryukyuan merchants traded far and wide throughout Southeast and Northeast Asia and the Pacific Islands from at least the fifteenth century. That gave rise to the "water frontier," linking southern coastal China and Indochina in the eighteenth century, and thereby contributing to the transformation of the domestic economies of the East Asian region.

Independent from, or at the margins of official tributary missions, were extensive trade networks, which developed among China, Vietnam, Korea, the Ryukyus, Inner Asia, and insular Southeast Asia, strengthening transregional economic linkages. Those trade linkages were largely autonomous from central state controls, which is why they, as mentioned above, were often associated with piracy by Chinese officials. They carried on an extremely lucrative and multisided trade, selling Chinese products (raw silk, silk textiles, and porcelain) to European merchants while transporting Southeast Asian commodities (deer skins and camphor from Taiwan, medicines and spices from Southeast Asia) to China and Japan. In all this trade, Mexican silver was the common currency of exchange. The preconditions for this roundabout trading were the Chinese and Japanese official sea trade bans. The incremental development of a network of international trade gave these adventurers a golden opportunity to operate outside the law, and, acting as part merchants and part pirates, they carved out an extremely profitable niche. In short, despite the imposition of interstate trade restrictions by both the Qing and Tokugawa governments, through both tributary and informal networks, dynamic East Asian trade continued, underlying the region's economic vigor.

In the eighteenth century, large regions of East Asia, with China at its center, experienced a long epoch of peace and prosperity, on the foundation of a tributary-trade order, at a time when Europe was more or less continuously engulfed by war and turmoil. If tributary and private trade were the basis of the regional order, so too were common elements of statecraft in the neo-Confucian orders in Japan, Korea, the Ryukyus, and Vietnam. In many ways, China subsidized peace and stability through maintaining the tributary-trade order. This meant sanctioning the regimes of favored local rulers, as well as ensuring a sustained transfer of resources to them via direct subsidies and guaranteed access to lucrative trade. At the same time, China abstained from intervening into other countries and respected their independence. Even Japan bought into the system through its behind-the-scenes domination of Ryukyu tribute missions. Through these, it secured lucrative trade with China while, in its own version of a tributary order, it subordinated the Ryukyu kingdom to Japan. Likewise, Vietnam implemented its own sub-tributary order with Laos.

China's leadership in Asia was by no means unchallenged, however, and China's foreign policy principles were more flexible and pragmatic than many western observers have assumed. The Qing court proved quite willing to adjust or completely forgo tributary norms to preserve peaceful relations with the peoples on its border. Perhaps the most notable example of this was the Treaty of Nerchinsk (1689) establishing the border with czarist Russia and the terms of trade. Until the arrival of the British and the French in the nineteenth century, Russia was China's only imperial neighbor. The Russian expansion to the east was initially motivated by commercial interests. The vast, dense forests of the Siberian Taiga were home to many fur-bearing animals, such as sable, fox, bear, and deer, whose pelts were highly valuable commodities in European markets. Groups of Russian traders and Cossacks began to enter the area, followed by the Russian army, undermining the Siberian Khanates in the sixteenth century. One of the major difficulties for Russian merchants and troops was the shortage of food as most areas in eastern and northern Siberia were unsuitable for agriculture. Though no diplomatic relations existed, illegal trade was beginning to flourish, with the Chinese exporting food, tea, and spices in addition to large amounts of silk and cotton in exchange for furs, silver, and gold from the Russians. The trade was hugely beneficial to Qing China because it ran a huge surplus. By the end of the Ming dynasty, the Russians' eastward expansion across Siberia had brought them finally to the shores of the Pacific, north of the Amur River.[67] They now had their eyes on the climatically milder and fertile regions along the Amur River that were conducive to the development of an agricultural economy and would allow a reduced dependence on the trade with China.

The Qing dynasty soon became alarmed by the growing Russian activities and influence in the northeast, especially the building of forts and small settlements. In 1685, the court sent troops to expel the Russians from their settlement, Albazin, on the Amur River. In this first military engagement between China and a European nation, the Chinese troops defeated the Russians and destroyed the town. Four years later, the czar sent a mission to China to negotiate the border in the Amur region. With the help of Jesuit translators, the text of a diplomatic treaty was negotiated on terms of equality, and established a compromise which gave equivalent status to the two great empires of the Eurasian continent. Under its terms, Russia was compelled to withdraw its forces from the region and destroy its fortifications, in return for obtaining trading rights with China. A border was drawn that went straight east from where the northern Mongolian frontier is today. It gave China the whole Amur basin and what is now the Russian maritime province, including the island of Sakhalin. The agreement helped to keep peace and allowed licensed trade along the borders. The 1689 treaty of Nerchinsk with Russia was China's first with a European power, and was for the Qing a first encounter with the practice of European diplomacy in its Westphalian form. In 1712, toward the end of the Kangxi reign, the Qing court sent a mission under the Manchu official Ayan Gioro Tulišen (1667–1741) into Russia to investigate conditions there. After his return, he published a travelogue on Russian geography, culture, and products that gained widespread attention.[68] In 1727, Qing China and Russia signed the Kiakhta Treaty, which reaffirmed the stipulations of the earlier agreement. Beijing would accept two hundred Russian merchants into the capital every third year, while also allowing for a flourishing border trade. The Qing court also permitted Russia to establish an embassy in Beijing. The economic importance of this ensuing trade was not negligible, especially for Russia. By the end of the eighteenth century, 10 percent of its foreign trade came and went across the border with China. The Russians continued to sell fur, sable, tiger, and wolf that were highly valued in China, and the Chinese side exported food, cotton, and increasingly also manufactured goods, including silk, porcelain, and furniture.

In another example of the diplomatic pragmatism of the Qing empire, a year after his decisive victory over the Zheng Chenggong (also known as Koxinga) resistance in Taiwan in 1683, the Kangxi emperor decided to relax his own sea ban and to permit coastal settlement. Invoking the interests of both state finance and popular livelihoods, he proclaimed the opening of all coastal ports to private licensed and regulated maritime trade and established a network of customs stations to collect taxes. The tribute system as an organizing device for intra-Asian diplomatic relations remained in place, but with

Kangxi's decision, its economic significance was diminished. The goods exchanged with the Qing through tribute missions decreased and the levels of trade outside the tribute system increased. After 1684, a larger and growing percentage of the empire's maritime trade was conducted with nations such as Portugal and eventually England, which never held or sought the status of tributaries. Private Chinese maritime trade not only flourished, but did so legally and openly.

Sometimes, the tributary model was challenged when China's neighbors questioned its claim to regional hegemony. Between 1637 and 1730, Korean officials and leaders contemplated a "northern expedition" against the Qing, erected altars to the Ming rulers, and reiterated their loyalty to the Ming by retaining the Ming calendar. In 1730, members of its embassy to Beijing were asked to explain why their identification plaques bore a Ming and not a Qing date. Japan not only refused to participate in the Chinese tributary system but constructed an alternate, Japan-centered world order. In 1715, the shogunate declared that only Chinese traders holding registrations would be permitted to dock in Nagasaki. Since domestic shortages of copper had driven the Kangxi court to purchase supplies in Japan, the Qing throne tacitly acquiesced to this direct refutation of its tributary model.

From the perspective of the tribute system, those episodes indicated recurring periods of disintegration, during which Chinese regimes had to negotiate and deal with their neighbors on equal terms. They point to the innovations and contributions made by the conquest dynasties. The Qing emperors mostly originated in the borderlands and used the Chinese tributary model in the conduct of interstate relations when it worked to their advantage. But they were also willing to alter the practice of the tribute system or to bypass it entirely if circumstances made it necessary or if it seemed more efficient. The Qing dynasty thus skillfully blended Chinese and Inner Asian practices to rule a diverse group of subjects within and beyond its borders.

This approach to handling relations with neighboring countries allowed the Qing empire to become one of the world's most influential empires by the eighteenth century. Its domain stretched from India to Russia and from Central Asia to Vietnam, and formed the geographic foundation for the modern Chinese state. It had reached the zenith of its position in Asia as it was secure against invaders and stood as the regional, if not global, hub for a wide and booming network of trade and business. Even though Qing rulers did not intervene directly in other countries, they often influenced them decisively through diplomacy, education, and culture. The Forbidden City in Beijing was recognized as the center of the eastern Asian region—the city to which outsiders were drawn and from which important impulses in terms of thinking, taste, and style originated. Even many contemporaries in Europe saw Qing China as a model for how an enlightened, cultivated yet powerful empire should be organized.

TWO

Reordering the Chinese World

1800–1870

A new external force loomed large beginning in the nineteenth century. Economic linkages to Europe and territorial expansion by European states intensified, producing political and economic instability in the Chinese empire. These processes date back to the early period of the European Renaissance in the 1400s, when European traders started to challenge Arab control over the lucrative trade in Asian spices and other luxury items and sought to reach Asia independently and by themselves. Transoceanic passages brought European trading houses into contact with the dynamic networks and vibrant centers in East Asia and above all in China. The Portuguese, and then the Spanish, were later followed by the Dutch and British and their East India companies through the 1600s and 1700s. Other European powers, as well as the United States, arrived in the 1800s. While the growing European presence was increasingly felt along the China coast, before 1800 its effects were limited and the empire seemed to have little to be concerned about.

But after 1800, growing global trade and political expansion produced disruptions that could not easily be contained and that resulted in a fundamental reordering of the balance of power in China. An economic downturn hit the Chinese empire, which was related to changes in global markets and in consequence led to rural impoverishment. The situation of rural populations was worsened by environmental problems and the inability of Chinese government institutions to provide efficient relief. The changes of the terms of trade, the influx of opium, and the spread of new ideas posed stiff new challenges that the empire's institutions found difficult to adapt to and to manage. At the same time, Europe pursued vigorous, strong-arm policies aimed at expanding its political and economic reach into China at a time when the West was entering a period of rapid scientific and technological development. It eventually worked to the disadvantage of China when the European nations—with their technological progress, first in ships and guns, and then in industrial power—moved to enforce their political and economic interests with military power.

Over the nineteenth century, imperial institutions were profoundly rattled by internal decline and external pressure, and increasingly unable to respond to the mounting challenges. The growing antagonism between local governments and grassroots communities was aggravated by rapidly worsening economic and environmental conditions, such as flooding and droughts. The ensuing crises hastened the erosion of government control in China and along the borders. In the hinterlands, disaster-stricken and land-hungry peasants joined rebels and openly challenged Qing authorities. Along the borders, the government had to relax its grip, and witnessed the rise of secessionist movements.

The Advent of Western Imperialism

The Portuguese had already established outposts on the African coast, in the Indian Ocean, and at Malacca in the fifteenth century, where they focused on extracting handsome profits by exploiting regional commercial networks and trading systems between the China coast and Southeast Asia.[1] In 1513, sea voyages eventually brought the first European explorer, Jorge Álvares (d. 1521), from Portugal to southern China. Becoming involved in what the Ming court considered smuggling and piracy, the Portuguese were not really welcomed, but they would not be forced out of China, either. By 1557, they had taken control of a settlement at the walled-off end of a coastal peninsula south of Guangzhou (Canton)—the area that is today Macau—and were trading periodically at Guangzhou. For many decades, European trade was mainly conducted in those two places. Macau especially served as a gateway for Europeans into China. Jesuit missionaries who came to China during the Ming dynasty generally did so through Macau.

Europeans tried to open alternative trading channels for their booming trade with the region, but with limited success. In 1575, Spanish ships from Manila visited Xiamen (Amoy) in a futile effort to obtain official trading privileges. Soon western trading houses were actively engaging in illegal trade activities on the Guangdong and Fujian coasts. The Dutch East India Company, after unsuccessfully trying to seize Macau from the Portuguese in 1622, took control of coastal Taiwan in 1624 and began to open trade links from its base in Taiwan into the nearby Fujian and Zhejiang provinces. In 1637, a squadron of six English vessels entered Guangzhou by force and sold its shipments there. Early British traders were associated with the (British) East India Company, a firm chartered by and partly invested in by the British Crown, but mostly held by private owners.[2] The company had earlier established trading centers in India, and its Asian trade gradually surpassed Holland's and Portugal's. From the East India Company's perspective, the China trade was highly profitable and had great potential, even more so than trade with British India. China offered products and goods such as porcelain, silk, and tea that had huge markets in Europe. The company was eventually allowed to open a trading station in Guangzhou in 1715.

The transactions between the Asian and Western European countries were complicated by the changes related to the Ming-Qing transition, as well as by the competing economic and colonial ambitions of the western nations. The Qing empire had initially started to relax its ban on foreign trade after the recapture of Taiwan in 1683. However, Chinese merchants, customs officials, and Qing officials protecting their profits and interests in Guangzhou were unwilling to allow the trade monopoly to be broken up or to have any part of their business in Guangzhou transferred to other ports in the north. In 1757, the Qianlong emperor responded to pressure from his local officials and implemented a new foreign trade policy whereby all ships from overseas were barred from every Chinese port, with the exception of Guangzhou. With the East India Company unwilling to accept this directive, in May 1759, the English merchant James Flint sailed straight into the northern port of Tianjin, close to the capital Beijing, to file a complaint with the Chinese emperor. No subject in the Chinese empire, however, was allowed to address the emperor directly. For this violation of protocol, in 1759, the Qianlong emperor severely punished his officials in Guangdong, condemned Flint to a three-year jail term in Macau, and then expelled him from China after his sentence had been served.

Still, the frequent observation in western books that the Chinese government rejected foreign traders and blocked trade with Europe on its shores is a major misinterpretation. Although foreign trade was not a dominant source of revenue for the imperial household, it was taxed at a number of ports along the Chinese coast and generated considerable and welcome income for the court. The court sought to permit trade, but in a controlled and managed fashion. Controlling foreign trade was necessary because of piracy or, to be more precise, smuggling. While taxes on merchandise and trade provided the Qing with critical revenues to meet a range of urgent domestic needs and foreign threats, they also created incentives for wide-ranging smuggling activities that would allow merchants to evade taxes and other fees. Smuggling was a very profitable enterprise. Japanese and Filipino pirates and smugglers, in league with Taiwanese and Chinese partners, transported silver, porcelain, tea, silk, and women up and down the Pacific coast without paying duties. To meet this challenge to its authority, the Chinese state fought back with an extensive campaign to stamp out smuggling and piracy, and asserted its prerogative to limit trade and to police trading posts. The Qing eventually outlawed all coastal trade except for the designated ports, admonishing local authorities to apprehend shippers and charge them with piracy and smuggling.[3]

The confluence of events in the mid-1700s prompted Qing China to develop a system, often later called the Canton system, that allowed the court to supervise and regulate trade with the West.[4] Starting in the 1760s, China began to strictly enforce this system. In this system, several locations were opened for foreign trade. In general, the point of trade was determined by the general geographic direction from which foreign merchants approached. Most traders from Europe approached China from the South China Sea, to which the largest port was Guangzhou. Guangzhou became the designated port for all European cargo ships. Europeans were consequently referred to as *yangren*, or "people from over the sea." Japan and Korea traded at the port of Zhapu, near the mouth of the Yangzi River; Russians were allowed to do business at Nerchinsk on the Mongolian border; and merchants from Central Asian states traded at Kashgar in Turkestan. No other ports or cities were allowed to receive foreign merchants.

This policy was not meant to be simply restrictive; rather, its motivations were related to concrete issues of security, practicality, and fiscal considerations. The decision was a response to information about the activities of the British East India Company in India in the 1750s, when Britain started to effectively annex India. Thereafter, the Qing court was worried about similar foreign infringement upon Qing territory. The creation of the single port of call for all European vessels in Guangzhou was also a practical decision, because, in reality, Guangzhou was the only port that provided the facilities that foreign traders needed. Guangzhou had enough merchants and sufficient capital to bring goods from the interior in the required volumes to make it worthwhile for foreign ships to make the long passage from Europe to China. Vessels came only once a year, given the length of the trip. Merchants bought everything they could to fully load their ships before embarking again. The Qing policy, however, was also integral to broader state efforts to extract fiscal resources and enforce central tax authority. Revenues from foreign trade went directly to the imperial court's own treasury. The Qing court looked with new intensity for money after the military expeditions into Inner Asia and the 1757–1758 conquest of Xinjiang had proved very costly. It wanted to secure a critical revenue stream, which was best accomplished if trade was concentrated on a few spots along the coast.

Before the arrival of the British, European merchants who did business at Guangzhou resided on the island of Macau. European traders were allowed to arrive only during the trading season from October to March. They had to obtain Chinese permits when passing through Portuguese-held Macau, and then anchor at Huangpu district just south of Guangzhou. There they were able to barter only with licensed Chinese merchants called *cohongs.* On the Chinese side, trade was supervised by a superintendent of maritime customs for Guangdong province, appointed directly by the emperor. He licensed local merchants and levied duties and fees from them before each foreign ship was allowed to embark. The Chinese merchants assumed fiscal responsibility for the conduct of each foreign vessel with which they were trading.

As the East India Company colonized India for Britain after the 1750s, British-sponsored Asian trade began to extend from India to the South China coast and thereby to integrate parts of South China into the world market. By the late eighteenth century, trade at Guangzhou began to grow significantly, fueled to great extent by the British demand for Chinese tea. Products from India, such as cotton, were imported through Guangzhou, while British ships in exchange transported tea, porcelain, and silk back to Europe. The Chinese merchants and middlemen involved in this trade made fine profits, and were able to set up their own, new trade links, which extended from the Pearl River delta upland, along the coast, and into the great rivers, as well as to parts of Southeast Asia where they already had a presence. The taxes and duties earned through the Canton system created highly attractive proceeds for the court, as well. The Qing empire was interested in continuing the economic exchange, at least as long as the empire's sovereignty was not seriously endangered. Hence, for many decades, this well-functioning system benefited both sides, the Chinese and the Europeans.

The growing trade volumes at Guangzhou soon ran up against the limits of too few piers, licensed merchants, and carriers. The trade also was under the clear control of Chinese authorities and Chinese merchants. In late 1792, the British East India Company made Sir George Macartney (1737–1806), an experienced diplomat and colonial administrator, head of a diplomatic mission to China to negotiate the opening of northern port cities to British traders and to allow British ships to be repaired on Chinese territory. Macartney arrived in North China in 1793 with three ships full of over a hundred staff, guards, and scientists, as well as a large number of presents including clocks, telescopes, weapons, textiles, and other products of technology. The presents were meant to display the advances of European civilization, and to gain the Chinese emperor's favor by impressing him. Macartney, however, taken on tour around the palace in the Chinese capital, noted the commanding splendor of the imperial pavilions and gardens. With humility, he wrote that the palaces were "furnished in the richest manner" and "that our presents must shrink from the comparison and hide their diminished heads."[5]

The Qing court treated the British party as a tribute mission and required Macartney to submit to the formal ceremony of kowtowing (touching his head to the ground) before the emperor. But Macartney refused unwaveringly, insisting he bowed only to his own king. Therefore, the emperor declined to give in to British demands. In a written reply to King George, the Chinese emperor Qianlong explained his decision at great length. He wrote:

> Surveying the wide world, I have but one aim in view, namely, to maintain a perfect governance and to fulfill the duties of the state; strange and costly objects do not interest me. If I have commanded the tribute offerings sent by you, O King, are to be accepted, this was solely in consideration for the spirit which prompted you to dispatch them from afar. Our dynasty's majestic virtue has penetrated unto every country under Heaven, and Kings of all nations have offered their costly tribute by land and sea. As your Ambassador can see for himself, we possess all things. I set no value on objects strange or ingenious, and have no use for your country's

manufactures. This then is my answer to your request to appoint a representative at my Court, a request contrary to our dynastic usage, which would only result in inconvenience to yourself.[6]

The British East India Company was not willing, however, to accept this verdict as the final say. If anything, it hardened the company's determination to break free of the trade limits and expand its lucrative business with China. The British had become a nation of tea drinkers, and the demand for Chinese tea continued to rise. It is estimated that the average London family at the time spent as much as 5 percent of its total household budget on tea. Meanwhile, however, northern Chinese merchants had begun to ship Chinese cotton from the interior to the south to compete with the Indian cotton that Britain had used to help pay for its tea purchases. The British tried to sell more of their own products to China to prevent a trade imbalance, but there was not much demand for heavy woolen textiles in a country that favored lighter cotton padding and silk. Needing to sell goods from the British Indian empire to pay for Chinese trade commodities, the British merchants found their solution. Increasingly in the eighteenth century, the commodity shipped to China was Bengal opium.

The use of opium was well known in China. It was traditionally used to cure diarrhea, induce sleep, and reduce the pain of diseases like dysentery and cholera. The opium poppy had been introduced between the fourth and seventh centuries by Arab traders, and it was cultivated widely for centuries long before the East India Company arrived in Asia. The British East India Company secured a monopoly on opium trading in Bengal in 1773 and in Bombay in 1830. From the 1770s, the company sought to expand trade in Guangzhou, often trading opium for tea, silk, and porcelain. Greater opium supplies spurred increases in demand and usage throughout China, in spite of repeated prohibitions by the Chinese government and officials. The British worked hard to expand the trade. They bribed officials, worked with smugglers to deliver the opium into China's interior, and distributed free samples of the drug. The cost to China soon became massive as the drug started to affect a growing percentage of the population. The economic consequences for China were negative, as well. Silver began to flow out of the country to pay for opium. Many of the economic problems China faced later were related, directly or indirectly, to the opium trade.

From then on and far into the twentieth century, opium assumed an out-sized role, ultimately epitomizing China's nineteenth-century crises and challenges.[7] It was the *casus belli* that opened imperial China's treaty ports, and became the metaphor for the falling dynasty's weakness and disgrace. It accelerated western penetration into China, especially for the British, significantly helping to pay for the upkeep and administration of the western mercantile presence. In the nineteenth century, opium was the main commodity linking China to global markets and an important part of China's modern commercial transformation. It was the cash crop that led some Chinese to new prosperity, and that also exposed them to heightened levels of scrutiny and harassment by the state. Purging China of opium became one of the great projects of the modernizing Chinese states of the twentieth century, and the "opium plague" came to be routinely invoked by foreigners to explain Chinese backwardness and by the Chinese to explain national humiliation. The drug became an indispensable revenue source for any number of secret societies, warlords, political movements, occupying armies, and "national" governments—and, as such, it was integral to the power struggles among them. By the early twentieth century, few significant aspects of Chinese life had been left untouched and undamaged by opium.

Already in 1729, rising opium use in China provoked an imperial edict that strictly forbade the sale of opium for personal consumption. Under pressure from the Chinese government, the East India Company stopped exporting opium directly to China in 1796 and began selling it in Calcutta to private (mostly Chinese and South Asian) merchants, who continued to deliver it to China. Able to deny responsibility for opium, the company retained other trading rights. As the Chinese government became increasingly wary of the opium trade and ever-expanding British influence, both the import and cultivation of opium were prohibited in China in 1799. The ban reflected the broad inroads that Indian opium had already made, and was ineffective. Weak state control in regions at the periphery, such as Xinjiang (Eastern Turkestan) and the provinces of Yunnan, Guizhou, and Sichuan, allowed foreign opium from central Asia and northern India to penetrate, and domestic cultivation to spread, despite official prohibition. In Xinjiang, traffickers and cultivators thrived under cover of the territory's uncontrollable expanse and fragmented authority, abetted by official lethargy. Indeed, drug-smuggling networks subverted and hence obstructed the efforts of officials to extend central governmental authority into the local arena. In China's southwest, Han and non-Han locals depended on the trade of opium for income. When local officials realized they would be unable to suppress cultivation, they taxed it for revenue instead.

Recognizing these problems, the Qing court enacted more stringent policies. The central government had promoted a program of crop substitution, but it was carried out half-heartedly and did not even begin to address opium's deeply embedded role in the aforementioned socioeconomic structures. Hence, the administrations enforced absolute prohibition and the emperor decreed even stricter laws against importation and sale of opium. Consumption and cultivation were criminalized in 1813 and 1831, respectively, and draconian new regulations on trade followed in 1839. In Eastern Guangdong, however, home to some of the most important drug-smuggling networks of the nineteenth century, the government's efforts to stamp out the illegal opium trade and arrest the smugglers faltered. Thus a culture of illegality became normalized as people were drawn in by their social networks to participate in a drug-running economy that became ever more lucrative. Qing authorities could not compete with the financially and militarily powerful secret societies and opium-distributing syndicates, not only in Eastern Guangdong itself, but in the regions to which members of these organizations traveled. As the opium prohibition failed, the lack of enforcement revealed deep-seated problems of the institutional structure of the empire such as overextension and crippling executive inefficiency.

Confronted with growing economic and social problems, the government debated the idea of legalizing the drug through a government monopoly similar to the one on salt. Legalization, as proposed by Xu Naiji in 1836, would also permit the import of foreign opium. But with the social and economic harms of addiction becoming ever more clear, the court voted in 1838 against legalization and in favor of sending one of its most capable officials, Lin Zexu, to Guangzhou. With orders to do whatever was necessary to shut down the opium trade for good, Lin went to work with vigor. Addicts were rounded up, forcibly treated, and taken off the habit, and domestic drug dealers were harshly punished. Lin's most important objective was to stop foreign supplies and force foreign merchants to sign pledges of good conduct, agreeing never to trade in opium and to be punished if found in violation. This self-confident and forceful policy, however, eventually led to war with Great Britain.[8]

As news of the events in Guangzhou reached England, public opinion there was divided. Some British citizens felt troubled by the drug trade with China. Their concerns were overruled, however, by those with business interests in increasing England's China trade, and those who favored teaching the "arrogant" Qing court a lesson. In June 1840, with the arrival of a British fleet at the mouth of the Guangzhou River, the first Opium War began. The war lasted almost two years and was a complete disaster for the Qing empire. By the summer of 1842, the British fleet celebrated victory as it reached the Yangzi, and prepared to shell the old capital, Nanjing, in central China. The Qing court capitulated shortly thereafter. Negotiations with the British were held onboard a British ship and in a small temple just outside of the city walls of Nanjing. The technological superiority of the British fleet was obvious, and it was a form of warfare the Chinese military had not seen before. The newly applied technology of the British armory included four steamships able to move upstream and support platforms for heavy guns, as well as modern rifles that fired more rapidly and with greater accuracy. Moreover, Britain could muster garrisons, warships, and provisions from its nearby colonies in Southeast Asia and India. The Chinese emperor therefore acted under the impression that he had no choice but to sign the peace agreement on British terms.

The Treaty of Nanjing (August 1842), the first of the so-called unequal treaties, opened China to the West and marked the beginning of a growing western dominance in the nation. According to its terms, the Qing had to open Guangzhou and four other ports for direct trade between foreigners and Chinese. The island of Hong Kong was ceded to Britain in perpetuity, and China agreed to pay twenty-one million silver dollars in reparations to the British merchants who had been driven out of Guangzhou. Twenty-one million silver dollars represented a considerable burden for the already strained Qing treasury. A supplementary treaty signed the following year gave Britain extraterritoriality—that is, full exemption from local laws for all its subjects in China. In 1843, France and the United States, and in 1858, Russia, negotiated treaties similar to England's Nanjing Treaty, including provisions for extraterritoriality.

Europeans fought a second opium war with China from 1856 to 1860, when the Qing were preoccupied with quelling a huge rebellion that operated under the name Taiping Heavenly Kingdom (*Taiping tianguo,* discussed below).[9] British merchants wanted greater access to the Chinese market than the provisions on the Nanjing Treaty had granted. They were waiting for any pretext that would afford an opportunity to revise the treaty system. Possible excuses were soon provided by local Chinese efforts to undermine the treaty provisions. China and Britain had initially disagreed on whether foreigners were allowed to enter the walled Chinese city of Guangzhou. Though Guangzhou was declared open in July 1843, the Europeans were confronted with growing opposition by the local population. After the first Opium War, the city of Guangzhou became a center of anti-European agitation. The literati of the city's great academies protested against "barbarians" entering the city. A movement emerged in Guangdong province, promoting the fortification and militarization of villages and small towns for self-defense. This movement also adopted an anti-Qing sentiment, since the court had signed the resented treaties. Local society rose up against the European presence, acting to protect their economic interests and their homeland increasingly without recourse to the Qing authorities in the capital. Finally, the British backed away from their demands and the anti-foreign movement in Guangzhou won a victory, despite the fact that the Beijing court conceded a "temporary entrance" into the city.

In the strained atmosphere in Guangzhou, where Governor-General Ye Mingchen (1807–1859) sided with local elites to resist the British, a momentous incident occurred in October 1856. Guangzhou police seized the *Arrow*, a Chinese-owned, British-registered smuggling ship flying a British flag, and charged its Chinese crew with piracy. British consul Harry Parkes (1828–1885) quickly dispatched a small fleet to fight its way up to Guangzhou to rescue the *Arrow*. French forces joined the venture on the grounds that a French missionary had been officially executed in Guangxi. Meanwhile, the British government sent Lord Elgin (James Bruce, 1811–1863) as emissary, charging him to gain reparations and a new treaty. The Russian and American governments declined to take part in military actions, but later sent their representatives to take part in diplomatic negotiations. At the end of 1857, an Anglo-French force bombed and occupied Guangzhou while waiting for reinforcements from Europe. After the spring thaw in March 1858, Lord Elgin set sail northward to the Dagu forts outside of Tianjin. He wanted to navigate upriver to Beijing to negotiate a revision of the treaty, but evasive Manchu officials refused to grant permission. In response, Lord Elgin decided to

2.1. Signing of the Treaty of Nanjing onboard HMS *Cornwallis*, 1842. Engraving by John Platt, 1846.
Brown University Library / Bridgeman Images / BMC474570

attack the Dagu forts. Against a lackluster Chinese defense, the battle-hardened Crimean war veterans from Europe quickly took possession of the forts. European forces had the advantage in technology and firepower, especially given the steam-powered and heavily weaponized ships in the fleet, but their victory owed also to superior training and morale.

When negotiations were held in Tianjin, the Qing representatives had no other option than to comply with the new demands of the British and French. The Russian and US diplomats also gained the same privileges. During June 1858, four Tianjin treaties were written to provide for, among other benefits, the opening of ten more ports for foreign trade, the permission for foreign ships to travel up the Yangzi, the residence of foreign diplomats in Beijing, and the freedom of Christian missionaries to move around as they

wished, spreading their gospel. Almost a year later, in mid-1859, Lord Elgin's younger brother, the designated British plenipotentiary Frederick Bruce (1814–1867), arrived at the Dagu forts on his way to consummate the ratifications of the treaties in Beijing. When a Qing emissary announced that his party had to take a special route over land, used for tribute missions, Bruce refused to do so. He stressed that his diplomatic mission was not to be confused with a tribute mission and ordered his small fleet to take up positions off the shoreline. This time, however, the Qing military was prepared. The Mongol general Senggelinqin (1811–1865), having anticipated the attack, had reinforced the forts and deployed capable troops. When the British and French troops eventually attacked, they were repelled by the gunfire from the forts and suffered heavy losses. This first defeat by an imperial army thought to be far inferior in almost every respect came as a shock to the British and other western nations. The sense of unassailable western superiority was shattered and replaced by a stinging desire for vengeance.

Once news of the rout reached England, the British government did not hesitate to start planning its reprisal. What happened next was unprecedented. France and Great Britain formed an armada the likes of which the world had not yet seen. The fleet that departed for North China in the summer of 1860 numbered 41 war vessels and 143 transporters, carrying 24,000 Indian, British, and French troops, artillery, and engineers; thousands of horses and mules; and thousands of support personnel.[10] The allied force under the military command of General James Hope Grant (1808–1875) and General Charles Montauban (1796–1878) conveyed Lord Elgin, the emissary, back to China, where they arrived at the end of June. Lord Elgin's orders were to procure the ratification of the treaty, and to extract an apology and war indemnities from the emperor for the attack on Frederick Bruce's detachments. On June 26, 1860, the allied countries officially declared war on China. The invasion began in August.

This time, however, the allied troops surprised the Qing military with an attack from the land. Expecting an attack from the sea, the defense of the Qing military stood no chance. They were surprised and, by August 21, 1860, the forts were in the hands of the European allies. Subsequently, Lord Elgin pressed ahead toward Beijing. Negotiations with Qing emissaries were revived, but went nowhere. Again, the thorny issue of kowtow arose, with Lord Elgin refusing to bow, and the Qing negotiators unable to concede. In mid-September at a place called Baliqiao (Eight Mile Bridge) at the western edges of Beijing, the Qing's Mongol Banner made its last stand. It launched a fierce attack against the allied forces, but was destroyed by artillery, which it confronted head-on. Almost all ensuing battles were also lost. The empire had to watch helplessly as even the capital Beijing was occupied in mid-October 1860, driving the Xianfeng emperor (r. 1850–61) out of the city to his summer palace at Chengde. The Qing army lost over five thousand men, and there were considerable losses on the western side, too.

After occupying Beijing, the troops set out for a palace complex on the outskirts of Beijing called Yuanmingyuan (the Garden of Perfect Brightness), built by the Qianlong emperor at the height of the Qing empire. In revenge for the Qing military's violence against the thirty-nine English and French prisoners it had captured, Lord Elgin ordered the British army to destroy and burn Yuanmingyuan to the ground. It took two full days of burning and demolition to destroy the hundreds of exquisite palaces and buildings in Yuanmingyuan. Ironically, this had been a palace complex, perhaps the only one in the Qing empire, that featured a section of European-style buildings, fountains, and formal gardens. Called "Western Mansions" *(Xiyang Lou)*, it was modeled on Italian baroque architecture, which the Chinese had become acquainted with from drawings and descriptions by Italian and French missionaries. At the center of Western Mansions was a Mediterranean-style landscape of fountains, basins, and waterworks surrounded by a palace, pavilions, aviaries, and a maze. This section of the palace reflected Qing China's curiosity about foreign objects and interest in foreign civilizations. The gardens also had hundreds of Chinese-style palace buildings—art pavilions, pagodas, temples, and libraries—as well as Tibetan and Mongolian-style buildings.

Before burning the rich and lavishly appointed palaces, British and French soldiers and officers carried away as much loot as they could.[11] A French soldier wrote: "I was dumbfounded, stunned, bewildered by what I had seen, and suddenly Thousand and One Nights seem perfectly believable to me. I have walked for more than two days over more than 30 million worth of silks, jewels, porcelain, bronzes, sculptures, [and] treasures! I do not think we have seen anything like it since the sack of Rome by the barbarians."[12]

Parallel to the British and French attacks on Beijing, activities of the Russian empire in the north increased, as well, where Imperial Russia was quick to take advantage of growing disorder in Manchuria.[13] The interests of the Russian government in the east had been revived through competition with British activities and interests in the Chinese empire. A Russian mission, directed to Kuldja (Yining) by way of the Irtysh River, succeeded in signing the Sino-Russian Treaty of Kuldja in 1851, which opened Kuldja and Chuguchak (Tacheng) in Central Asia to Russian trade. Another initiative was directed to the Amur watershed under the command of Count Mikhail Nikolajevitsch Muravyov (1845–1900), who had been appointed governor-general of eastern Siberia in 1847. The Russian governor-general of eastern Siberia pursued an aggressive strategy. In 1854 and 1855, he deliberately violated the 1689 Treaty of Nerchinsk, which delineated the boundary between Russia and China, by sending settlers down the Amur River to set up colonies along the river banks. By 1857, Muravyov had sponsored four expeditions down the Amur. During the third one, in 1856, the left bank and lower reaches of the river were occupied by the Russian forces. In May 1858, Muravyov forced the Qing general Yishan to sign a treaty at Aigun (Aihui), by which the territory on

2.2. British and French forces looting the Old Summer Palace in 1860. Godefroy Durand (1832–1896). *L'Illustration*, December 1860.
Wikimedia Commons

the northern bank of the Amur—an area of approximately 150,000 square miles—was transferred to Russia and the land between the Ussuri River and the sea was placed under joint administration of the two countries. Beijing, however, refused to ratify the treaty. After the Anglo-French allies attacked northern China in 1860, the Russian negotiator Nikolay Ignatyev (1832–1908) acted as mediator to negotiate the evacuation of the forces from Beijing. Soon after the allies left Beijing, Ignatyev secured, as a reward for his brokering, the Sino-Russian Treaty of Beijing 1860, which not only confirmed the Treaty of Aigun but added a further 100,000 square miles to the area granted to Russia in the earlier treaty, ceding to Russia the entire territory between the Ussuri River and the sea. Russia also received trade concessions in Manchuria.

A younger brother of the emperor, Yixin (1833–1898), better known under his title of Prince Gong, was appointed imperial commissioner in charge of negotiation with the Western European powers. Peace was restored by the 1858 Treaty of Tientsin (Tianjin) and the 1860 Convention of Peking (Beijing), the latter of which involved the Qing empire's three distinct treaties with the United Kingdom, France, and Russia. These weakened the Qing empire significantly. The 1858 and 1860 treaties extended the foreign privileges granted after the first Opium War and confirmed or legalized the developments in the treaty-port system. Great Britain, France, Russia, and the United States would have the right to establish embassies in Beijing, marking the first opening of the capital to foreign nationals. The Qing court was to pay indemnities to Britain and France of eight million taels of silver each, and compensation to British merchants of three million taels of silver. Eleven additional ports were opened to foreign residence and trade, including Niuzhuang, Tamsui (Taiwan), Hankou, Nanjing, and Tianjin. The lease of the New Territories was ceded to Great Britain. Foreigners, especially merchants and missionaries, were allowed free movement throughout the interior. Hardest to swallow for Qing authorities were not necessarily the economic rights given to western governments, such as trade and the opening of treaty ports, but the non-economic political privileges that affected the stability of social order. Chief among them was the legalization of opium, which would all but guarantee a deepening of the social and economic problems caused by opium addiction. Also highly disturbing was the right granted to missionaries to spread Christianity, sure to be resisted by the elites of Confucian society and local religious groups. It was foreseeable that this stipulation would cause numerous local incidents that would put the court in an uncomfortable position between local society and foreign missionaries. The same was true for another clause in the Convention of Peking that permitted British ships to carry indentured Chinese workers to the Americas. The demand for Chinese workers in plantation economies and for railway construction rose sharply with the limitation and ultimately abolition of the slave trade in the nineteenth century. To many contemporary observers, the ensuing "coolie trade" had many commonalities with the earlier slave trade—including brutal patterns of recruitment, frequent cases of kidnapping, inhuman conditions of transport, and high mortality rates of laborers performing the work. In fact, the two practices were at times hard to differentiate, especially in places like Cuba where Chinese and African slaves worked side by side on the same plantations. Qing authorities felt responsible for their subjects even when they lived abroad and were very much concerned about their treatment by western powers.[14]

During the turbulent years of 1858 to 1860, the Qing bureaucracy was divided between two parties, one inclined toward war and the other toward

Territorial Losses
1850–1900

Qing China c. 1900

BURMA   Previous Chinese vassals and
to Britain   territories with date of loss
1886

- - -   Modern boundaries of China

peace. It was the peace-favoring group's leaders—Prince Gong, Guiliang, and Wenxiang—who took charge of negotiating with the foreigners. They were driven by pragmatic considerations, believing that war could not be won and that settlements offered the only way out of crisis. In 1861, in response to the establishment of the foreign representatives in the capital, the Zongli Yamen (Office for General Management of the Affairs with Foreign Countries) was founded to deal with foreign affairs, with its main staff filled by members of the peace faction. A year later, in 1862, the Qing court set up the School of Combined Learning *(Tongwen Guan)* in Beijing to teach foreign languages and subjects.

The two opium wars brought an end to the tribute system and replaced it with the treaty system. The change was significant and the consequences were far-reaching. The tribute system's disappearance meant the loss of a significant institution based on a hierarchical model that had produced stability and prosperity in China and East Asia for several centuries. It was replaced by a new set of western-inspired, exogenous rules, enshrined in treaties, based on interstate competition among equal actors. The sudden demise of such a central institution by outside pressure severely affected the entire institutional order of Qing China. A pillar of Qing rule had collapsed, profoundly weakening the entire structure of the empire. Institutional change became inevitable.

The treaties of Nanjing (1842), Tianjin (1858), and Beijing (1860) were carefully written to convey formal equality between the Chinese and British empires. Concealed in the formal language, however, were a number of provisions that clearly disadvantaged Qing China.[15] It was the lack of reciprocity in some essential aspects that made the treaties essentially unequal. Both the opening of ports and the provisions for extraterritoriality were unilateral. In other words, China received no reciprocal privileges in Europe or European dependencies. Likewise, the low fixed tariffs required from China were not matched by any tariff concessions by the British or other European states. The most-favored-nation provisions were also nonreciprocal. As the Chinese began to study international law in the late nineteenth and early twentieth century, these undeniable inequalities became the focus of a protracted campaign for treaty revision. This campaign would eventually achieve some success, though not before World War II.

The problem was far greater, however, than specific treaty provisions. The treaties that effectively limited Chinese sovereignty became the foundation on which the larger system of western (and later, Japanese) imperialism was built. Two aspects were central in this respect: tariff autonomy and extraterritoriality. For the western powers, one of the reasons for going to war with China was the arbitrary way in which tariffs and fees were collected under the Guangzhou system of trade. In the treaties, the British determined low, fixed tariffs, usually of 5 percent *ad valorem*. In an age of rising global trade, fees taken from tariffs on imports were an important source of revenue for any state, allowing investments in infrastructure and the support of domestic industries. Slashing this income clearly made it difficult for China to make investments to facilitate the country's development and to catch up in industrialization. The inability to impose protective tariffs to nurture domestic industries would also be crippling. In the 1850s, western powers, led by the British, demanded the establishment of the foreign-administered Chinese Imperial Maritime Customs. The Imperial Maritime Customs gradually expanded its operations and eventually came to include port facilities and navigation at the treaty ports, handling China's first postal service, and ultimately managing tax collection for the Salt Administration.[16] All of these steps arguably improved the efficiency and enhanced the revenue streams of the imperial government, but at the cost of foreign control over key parts of China's fiscal apparatus.

"Extraterritoriality" was equally problematic for China.[17] Again, the term refers to an international norm allowing a power to exercise various judicial functions within a territory beyond its own borders. Extraterritorial courts place resident foreigners, with or without diplomatic or official status, under the jurisdiction of their own states, and thus exempt them from the jurisdiction of the host state. This, of course, runs counter to the usual practice of exclusive internal jurisdiction that has been a foundational element of state sovereignty in the modern international system. Exclusive internal jurisdiction holds that no state may exercise governmental authority—legislative, executive, or judicial, within the territory of another state. Western powers in China, however, have often found it more useful to resort to more flexible legal constructs and preferred personal extraterritorial jurisdictions over territorial jurisdictions in their dependencies. Constructing and upholding difference between the Westerners and the Chinese, or between the center and the periphery, has long been identified as a key tenet of colonial rule. Despite formal legal language stressing equality, Western imperialism in practice involved inequitable treatment, hierarchical relations, and unequal legal status. Western powers sought to produce and sustain differences among various populations, entailing spatial segregations and development of multiple jurisdictions. Extraterritoriality was the logical outcome of the need to operate and protect Western agents in ambiguous legal conditions by shielding them from Chinese authorities. It allowed foreign powers to engender different colonial formations through gradations of sovereignty, and to preserve differences in legal status.

Without extraterritoriality it would be impossible to sustain the legal complexities and ambiguities of the treaty system. The multitude of jurisdictions in China indicates the degree to which imperialism on the China coast was flexible and opaque. It was simultaneously diffuse and tangible, and oscillated between secretive and visible forms of control and sovereignty. Recent historical work concludes of imperial formations in general that they were mobile, flexible polities of imperial control dependent on shifting categories and moving parts.[18] Extraterritoriality allowed powers to operate securely and safely beyond the territorial boundaries of empire.

Western historians of colonialism have rarely discussed the historical specifics of imperialism in China and beyond.[19] But Chinese historians have long described a special manifestation of colonial rule called "semi-colonialism," by which they have meant a transitional state in which various forms of hegemony by a foreign power coexisted with remnants of the formal political sovereignty of the dominated country. China did not fall entirely under foreign rule, but neither was it fully independent or able to exercise full sovereignty. Global colonial practices collided with indigenous local practices, creating transitory institutional formations caught between different, conflicting forces in the global, national, and local realms. The outcome of these dynamics was uncertain and might tend toward either independence or full colonization.[20] Semi-colonization was a state of ambivalence which, in China, also opened up possibilities of resistance against more expansive and complete forms of outside imperialist rule.

Commercialization and Innovation in the World of the Treaty Ports

As a consequence of the treaty system, a growing number of Chinese cities along the coast and major inland waterways were opened to foreign trade and settlement. Most of those cities were so-called treaty ports, which quickly developed into booming and busy urban centers. Many of China's most celebrated cities today were once treaty ports that gradually came into prominence during the second half of the nineteenth century. There was, above all, the "pearl of the East," the metropolis of Shanghai. Short of its rank, there were the booming cities of Tianjin, Shenyang, Guangzhou, Hankou (Wuhan), Amoy (Xiamen), Qingdao, and more. Most of the major cities of the nineteenth century rose and grew prosperous through international trade (with the exception of the capital, Beijing). The rise of Shanghai and Tianjin, originally small towns, as important and prosperous big cities depended completely on their status as world trade ports. These Chinese cities not only expanded, but also underwent profound transformations, becoming centers of hybrid Chinese-European societies, conduits for the new and foreign, and drivers of fundamental change that radiated far beyond urban China.

The treaty ports were commercial centers where foreigners from the treaty powers had special permission to reside and conduct business, according to a series of agreements between China and eighteen other states. Between 1842 and 1914, ninety-two towns in all were formally designated as treaty ports. Foreigners representing official, business, and Christian interests established residences in about half these centers. Established through the "unequal treaties," the treaty ports were protected by legal arrangements and foreign gunboats. Although China ceded no territory in these places, recognition of extraterritorial status for foreign nationals amounted to a de facto relinquishment of Chinese authority over the foreign and Chinese inhabitants of the treaty ports. A rich variety of legal forms actually supported the various cities that are often, misleadingly, simply called treaty ports.[21] The classical colony—that is, the unlimited and unconditional cession of a relatively large territory—was an exception. Only Hong Kong in 1841 to 1997, Macau in 1887 to 1999, and Taiwan in 1895 to 1945 were colonies entirely ruled by foreign powers (Great Britain, Portugal, and Japan). Blurred genres of colonial rule,

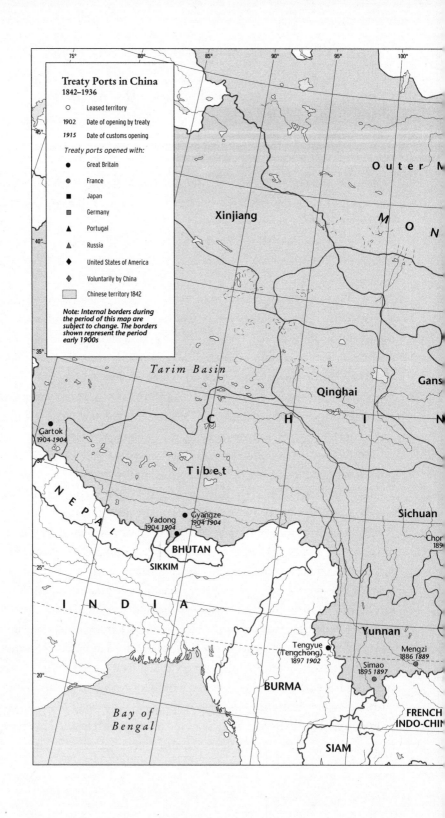

Treaty Ports in China
1842–1936

○	Leased territory
1902	Date of opening by treaty
1915	Date of customs opening

Treaty ports opened with:

●	Great Britain
◉	France
■	Japan
◼	Germany
▲	Portugal
△	Russia
◆	United States of America
◈	Voluntarily by China
▨	Chinese territory 1842

Note: Internal borders during the period of this map are subject to change. The borders shown represent the period early 1900s

Outer M

M O N

Xinjiang

Gans

Tarim Basin

Qinghai

C H I N

Gartok
1904 *1904*

Tibet

Sichuan

N E P A L

Yadong
1904 *1904*

Gyangze
1904 *1904*

Chor
189

BHUTAN

SIKKIM

I N D I A

Yunnan

Tengyue
(Tengchong)
1897 *1902*

Mengzi
1886 *1889*

Simao
1895 *1897*

BURMA

*Bay of
Bengal*

FRENCH
INDO-CHI

SIAM

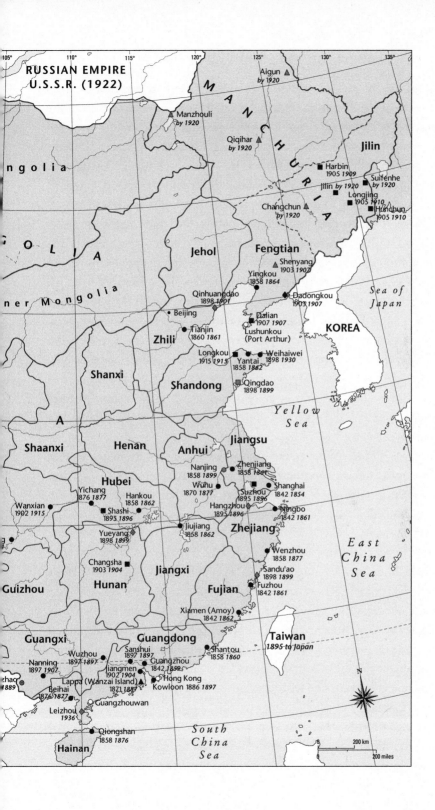

RUSSIAN EMPIRE
U.S.S.R. (1922)

MANCHURIA

Aigun
by 1920

Manzhouli
by 1920

Qiqihar
by 1920

Jilin

Harbin
1905 1909

Jilin by 1920

Suifenhe
by 1920

Longjing
1905 1910

Hunchun
1905 1910

Changchun
by 1920

Mongolia

GOLIA

ner Mongolia

A

Jehol

Fengtian

Shenyang
1903 1907

Yingkou
1858 1864

Qinhuangdao
1898 1901

Beijing

Dadongkou
1903 1907

Sea of
Japan

KOREA

Zhili

Tianjin
1860 1861

Dalian
1907 1907

Lushunkou
(Port Arthur)

Longkou
1915 1915

Weihaiwei
1898 1930

Yantai
1858 1862

Shanxi

Shandong

Qingdao
1898 1899

Yellow
Sea

Shaanxi

Henan

Anhui

Jiangsu

Nanjing
1858 1899

Zhenjiang
1858 1861

Hubei

Yichang
1876 1877

Hankou
1858 1862

Wuhu
1870 1877

Shanghai
1842 1854

Suzhou
1895 1896

Wanxian
1902 1915

Shashi
1895 1896

Hangzhou
1895 1896

Ningbo
1842 1861

Yueyang
1898 1899

Jiujiang
1858 1862

Zhejiang

Changsha
1903 1904

Jiangxi

Wenzhou
1858 1877

Guizhou

Hunan

Fujian

Sandu'ao
1898 1899

Fuzhou
1842 1861

East
China
Sea

Xiamen (Amoy)
1842 1862

Taiwan
1895 to Japan

Guangxi

Guangdong

Shantou
1858 1860

Wuzhou
1897 1897

Sanshui
1897 1897

Nanning
1897 1907

Guangzhou
1842 1859

Jiangmen
1902 1904

zhao
889

Lappa (Wanzai Island)
1871 1887

Hong Kong

Kowloon 1886 1897

Beihai
1876 1877

Guangzhouwan

Leizhou
1936

Qiongshan
1858 1876

Hainan

South
China
Sea

N

200 km
200 miles

such as leased territories, were more common. To maintain harbor facilities and naval bases, foreign powers leased small bordered territories from the Qing empire for limited times. In these, western powers exercised restricted sovereignty. Examples included Qingdao (German), Weihaiwei (British), Kowloon (British), and Port Arthur (Lüshunkou, Russian). Usually the leaseholds served as logistical bases for military and commercial interests. For this reason, they were often close to resources in the hinterland and offered access to important domestic and international trade routes. The leaseholds had small, local Chinese populations that could constitute ready workforces for foreign companies. In order to have a permanent presence in major Chinese cities and in treaty ports, foreign powers also established so-called urban settlements or foreign concessions. These were clearly defined residential areas under foreign administration that were leased to a foreign government for a limited time. Foreign powers operated around twenty settlements in China, the best known example being the International Settlement in Shanghai. Around the treaty ports, western imperial powers made use of "spheres of interest," or "spheres of influence," that gave them clearly defined economic, cultural, and often also military privileges in certain regions. In a "sphere of influence," the Chinese government typically retained full sovereignty over Chinese subjects, but otherwise obliged itself to give preferential treatment to a foreign government and its nationals.

Settlements, leaseholds, colonial bases, and spheres of interest had different jurisdictions and were based on different legal constructions. A unique hybrid formation emerged. Various institutional forms engendered complex, blurred jurisdictions that applied personal more often than territorial jurisdictions. In the various concessions and leaseholds, the Chinese population found itself completely or partly under foreign consular and colonial jurisdiction. Protected by extraterritoriality, which made them exempt from Chinese law, these foreign concessions were both international and Chinese at the same time. This hybrid, dual character gave them the basis to profit from development in China, but also provided a safe haven for Chinese businessmen and thinkers who wished to escape from the war chaos and restrictions in China.

Shanghai, by far the most important of the treaty ports and China's premier trade port thanks to its convenient location, was home to more than half the foreigners in China. Citizens of many countries and all continents came to Shanghai to live and work, and those who stayed for long periods, some for generations, called themselves "Shanghailanders." In many ways, Shanghai dominated the "treaty-port system" of Sino-foreign economic and political interaction.[22] As Shanghai developed into one of the world's most modern cities, comparable in every respect to Paris, Berlin, London, and Tokyo, it became an alluring model of modernity and daily elegance to foreigners in the other treaty ports and also to the Chinese population.

Originally separate, the British and American settlements were combined in 1863 into an International Settlement, which expanded to cover an area of 21.5 square kilometers by the 1930s. The French opted out of the International Settlement, and continued to maintain their own French Concession. In 1900, British owners held long-term leases on about 90 percent of the land within the International Settlement area; they still held 78 percent of its land in 1930. Residents of the International Settlement paid fees to support services such as running water, a police force, and the maintenance of a public garden, which became notorious for allegedly refusing admission to the Chinese inhabitants of Shanghai.[23] Meanwhile, the adjacent French settlement of Shanghai, popularly known as "Concession," grew to cover an area of 10 square kilometers. As formal privileges were extended through local practices, the major treaty ports became zones where foreigners enjoyed not only autonomy but also considerable authority over their Chinese neighbors. In Shanghai, the two foreign settlements each maintained autonomous courts, as well as police forces controlled by foreigners.

The Shanghai Municipal Council (SMC), created in 1854 to manage the International Settlement, was like the oligarchic leadership of a small state. Its nine members were elected by only thirty to forty foreign land owners or renters in the early years, and by about two thousand of those in the 1920s—still only a fraction of the settlement's foreign population. It was during those years that Chinese residents of the International Settlement protested against what they called "taxation without representation." Although well over 90 percent of the district's residents were Chinese, they were not represented in the SMC. Eventually, the SMC agreed to accept five Chinese representatives in an expanded council of fourteen members. Shanghai's French Settlement was run differently. It resembled a small monarchy, in which the French consul-general presided over a council of municipal affairs and was the chief judge in the district's court.

2.3. Nanjing Road in Shanghai, featuring a Sikh police officer in British service and a European family, c. 1900.
chinasmack.com

Tianjin was second only to Shanghai in importance. By 1914, Britain, France, Japan, Italy, Russia, Austria-Hungary, Germany, and Belgium had all leased residential areas in Tianjin. The British concession of 4 square kilometers was the most important of these, and British owners privately held a further 8 square kilometers of land in other parts of the city. Guangzhou and Hankou (Hankow) were also major treaty ports. Proximity to Hong Kong strongly affected the economy of Guangzhou. Westerners clustered in Shamian, a riverfront area separated from the city by a small canal. In the Yangzi River port of Hankou, a series of foreign concessions stretched for more than 5 kilometers along its riverfront, and behind these zones a district with European amenities such as a golf club and a race course was jointly managed by the foreign communities.

What clearly distinguished the treaty ports from other Chinese cities was their role as industrial centers. Until 1895, foreign companies were prohibited by treaties from setting up industrial enterprises on Chinese territory. More than half the foreign investments went into treaty port areas, which became hubs for the distribution of new commodities, new technologies, and new forms of production. The treaty system accelerated the arrival of new technologies and institutional forms initially only to the treaty ports themselves, but these soon became staging points for the diffusion of new technology and knowledge into the domestic economy and into China's governmental apparatus. Early examples include financial institutions such as banks, the Shanghai stock exchange, shareholding companies with limited liability, and new forms of local self-government.[24]

In the nineteenth century, most of the investment in the treaty ports was related to trade and transport, such as shipping and shipping yards. Many of China's railway companies took on foreign loans, and the steamships plying the inner waterways were all owned by foreign trading houses like the British firms Swire (established 1816) and Jardine (established 1832), and Japanese shipping companies.[25] Most of the nearly one hundred foreign companies in China up to 1894 were engaged in shipbuilding and ship repair in the treaty ports, processing of exports and imports, or other light manufacturing. There were also a few, largely unsuccessful attempts to establish textile or soybean processing plants. The first factories in these areas were built with foreign money, but the Chinese government and private capital soon developed their own industries. It was only in the early twentieth century that foreign investment also went into Chinese industry. The first Chinese industrial enterprises developed out of existing companies, mostly in handicrafts. Nearly all of modern China's industries were located in or on the periphery of the major treaty ports. Shanghai became an industrial center for Jiangnan, where flour milling, textiles, matches, porcelain, electricity, machine manufacture, and shipbuilding industries sprang up. Guangzhou was the center of tobacco and cigarettes, textiles, and agricultural products processing.[26]

In the treaty ports, "foreign firms" (*yanghang*) from all over the world established branch offices. Many foreign banks—City Bank of New York, Hong Kong and Shanghai Banking Corporation (HSBC), Yokohama Specie Bank, General Bank of the Netherlands, and others—maintained a presence there as well. Foreign financial institutions became an integral part of China's modern international market economy, as they infused cash into the Chinese economy. With the completion of the transcontinental railway constructions in North America and in Europe in the latter half of the nineteenth century, which had required substantial loans, China with its need for investments became a highly attractive financial market. Consequently, the interest in

China's capital markets was higher than in Europe or the United States. Loans and securities went from big western financial institutions to smaller banks, from there to new Chinese banks, and then to the old-style remittance banks and money-exchange shops. The number of Chinese seeking the new banks' financial services grew rapidly in the nineteenth century. The banks were also connected with the trading houses, which relied on bank loans to conduct their business. The biggest bank at that time, the Hong Kong and Shanghai Banking Corporation, offers an excellent example of the trans-regional circuits of the treaty port world. Founded in Hong Kong in 1865 with only five million Hong Kong dollars in capital, within twenty years it became the largest financial institution in China, with offices and representatives in most treaty ports and major cities. The bank also managed the Hong Kong government accounts in Southeast Asia and issued banknotes in Hong Kong and Thailand. Up until the 1920s it also handled many of the loans for the Chinese government, making substantial profits from this business.[27]

The treaty ports became connected not only to the West, but also to the maritime world in Southeast Asia. Merchants from Guangdong set up a far-flung trading network that connected the harbor cities in China with Taipei, Singapore, Hong Kong, and the Philippines. In Batavia (Jakarta) and Saigon (Ho Chi Minh City), Chinese merchants traded with Dutch and French residents, with foreign companies, and with companies operating out of China. Although Southeast Asian elites and Europeans were both wary of growing Chinese wealth and competition, they came to depend on the expanding markets that linked China with Southeast Asia. The transregional network for marketing medical and pharmaceutical products was highly developed. In British Malaya, for instance, Yu Ren Sheng, a company that began trading in Chinese medicine in the 1870s, came to link the Malayan peninsula to southern China's treaty ports, offering banking services alongside its medicines to contract laborers. In Rangoon, Burma, in 1909 an overseas Chinese entrepreneur by the name of Aw Boon-haw (1882–1954) invented a liniment that became a very popular cure-all. Trademarked as Tiger Balm, it was marketed not only in treaty-port China, but throughout maritime East Asia and allowed the inventor to build one of the most powerful commercial empires in twentieth-century China.[28]

Through the treaty ports, new knowledge and new institutions entered China. New information and new ideas on a broad range of subjects— including engineering, medicine, international law, jurisprudence, political representation, and democracy—reached urban Chinese society above all through the wide dissemination of printed materials. The tremendous influence of the printing industry, especially the periodical press in Shanghai and other treaty ports, propelled the intellectual transformation of urban China.[29] In Chinese newspapers, the first commercial advertisements appeared in 1858. Shanghai newspapers came to rely on them as their main source of revenue, and with this shift, the newspaper business was no longer dependent on government or missionary funding. The leading newspaper in Shanghai was *Shenbao,* founded in 1872. It was quickly joined by a great number and variety of other periodicals published in Shanghai. Among the most noteworthy of them was *Current Affairs* (also called *China's Progress, Shiwu bao*), founded in 1896.

Book publishers found growing markets in the treaty ports, as well, and developed new reading materials and genres. One of the largest publishing houses was Commercial Press, which printed translations of world classics. John Stuart Mill's *On Liberty* (1859) as translated by Yan Fu (1854–1921) and many translations of western literature by Lin Shu (1852–1924), for example, were very popular and had considerable influence throughout the country. China's urban network of treaty ports led and directed cultural change in the nineteenth and twentieth centuries. This vast network, with Shanghai as its center, spurred the transformation of the Chinese urban population. In their thoughts, tastes, and daily activities, the educated and affluent groups of the urban population began to abandon traditional ways of living and started to embrace what they saw as modern lifestyles.

Christian missions sprang up in the treaty ports and itinerant missionaries began traveling to most parts of the country.[30] At the same time, there were disagreements about the methods and goals of the Christian missionary groups who came from western imperialist states. China's exposure to Christianity from the sixteenth century on had primarily happened through European Catholics. In the sixteenth century, the Jesuits had arrived first with the Portuguese, followed shortly thereafter by the Dominicans and Franciscans who arrived with the Spanish, and later by the Protestant and Catholic churches under the British, Germans, and Americans in the nineteenth century. The theological disagreements among the European powers and missionary groups appeared to the central government in China, concerned with imposing political and economic order, as unsettling influences from which they had little to gain and much to lose. While the missionaries were often met with resentment by officials and the population, their cultural activities and educational initiatives became very significant—perhaps the most significant aspect of the missionary enterprise.

Most of the nineteenth-century missionaries were British or American Protestants—young men and women inspired by the Great Awakening in the United States and evangelical revivals in Britain. Some of the most influential of these missionaries were more interested in spreading western educational ideals than in saving souls. Robert Morrison (1782–1834), sent by the London Missionary Society, started publishing books in Chinese in the 1830s. Elijah Bridgeman (1801–1861), sent by the American Board of Commissioners for Foreign Missions, published magazines in English and Chinese in Guangzhou. Western churches also began to establish parochial schools in China, such as St. John's University in Shanghai. St. John's first set up faculties of western learning, national learning, and theology, but later it expanded into the four faculties of literature, science, medicine, and theology, with curricula including western languages, mathematics (algebra and calculus), western science, astronomy, chemistry, mechanics, geology, and navigation. Unlike most foreign military officers, diplomats, and traders, the missionaries were mostly well-versed in Chinese and could serve as mediators between China and the West. Some later went back to the West and took positions in western universities teaching Chinese.

The spread of western-sponsored activities, schools, and institutions of higher learning prompted Chinese efforts to create a new education system. In 1863, the government established the *Guang Fangyan Guan* (Foreign Language Institute) at Shanghai and another School of Combined Learning in Guangzhou one year later. In 1874, the comprador Tong King-sing (also called Tong Jingxing, 1832–1892), the reformer Xu Shou (1818–1884), and some supportive western diplomats and scholars established the School of Sciences *(Gezhi shuyuan)*, later often simply called Shanghai Polytechnic.[31] Launched to introduce western science to China, this institution sought to educate the Chinese about foreign countries and general scientific topics. It offered instruction in astronomy, mathematics, medicine, manufacturing, chemistry, weaponry, and geology. Tianjin's Beiyang Academy of Western Learning (now Tianjin University) began by teaching industrial engineering, western learning, mining, mechanical engineering, and law. In 1897, the mayor of Hangzhou, Lin Qi, established the "Qiushi Academy" based on the western higher education system. It would later develop into Zhejiang University. In less than a generation, higher education in China developed away from a narrow focus on technology and foreign affairs into a broad new educational system, similar to that of western universities. Universities, colleges, teacher training colleges, and various specialized schools for training in industry, commerce, law, government administration, and medicine sprang up, mostly in the treaty ports. By the early twentieth century, China already had more than 140 institutions of higher learning, with an enrollment of over 27,000 students.

The establishment of the treaty ports, the growth of foreign trade, and the influx of new educational institutions and opportunities tilted urban growth toward the expansion of large cities on the coast. A gap began to open up between the coastal cities and the interior heartland. Despite the often poor working conditions in the nascent industries—whether the employers were foreigners or Chinese—there was always a surplus of peasants in China's densely populated countryside seeking employment in the cities. Many Chinese cities along the coast doubled in size as Qing restrictions on travel to and residence in the cities were relaxed. Overall, around 85 percent of all Chinese continued to live in the countryside. But with over a tenth of the population living in urban areas, the big cities became a leading force in demanding political and social change.[32] They gave rise to the workers who organized themselves in associations, the students who protested against government abuse, and the shopkeepers who promoted nationalism.

Shanghai and other cities also became centers of nationalist and later revolutionary agitation. Toward the end of Qing rule, urban China (first in the treaty ports and then beyond) and China's urban diaspora collaborated in fostering an intense form of political nationalism, aided by the rapid development of communication of news and ideas by telegraph and train. Most of these large cities were linked by railroads, highways, and ocean or river communication routes. People and ideas traveled more quickly from place to place. In late imperial China, official correspondence took ten days within a province, and three months from Beijing to a more remote provincial capital. The new rail lines reduced the time needed to travel that distance from two days (by boat) to three-and-a-half hours (by express train). Once telegraph lines were in place, communication between the treaty ports, and also between other cities, was practically instantaneous.

The great population mobility associated with these large cities provided fertile breeding grounds for alternative sources of authority. These alternative social structures could build on traditions and organizations that had evolved long ago. There were, for instance, secret societies and criminal gangs. The traditional Green Gang (qingbang) and the Hong Gang (hongmen) groups, including the Heaven and Earth Society (tiandihui), operated from their bases in Shanghai. The Green Gang was originally formed by workers involved in the transport of grain along the Grand Canal. When those grain shipments declined and eventually ended, due to the change in the course of the Yellow River around 1855 and competition from ocean shipping, the boatmen and workers joined local rebellions or shifted to the coast to join the salt smuggling trade. They also spread to treaty ports—above all, Shanghai—forming a powerful underground force in Chinese society.[33]

Another type of organization that commanded authority in the treaty ports, and also other cities in China, was the huiguan or tongxianghui, the guilds or native place associations, which represented and assisted merchants and workers who came to the city from particular areas, provinces, and regions. The guilds advocated their shared interests vis-à-vis foreign or Chinese authorities, and assumed specific roles in the division of labor regarding trade. In places like Shanghai, Tianjin, and Hankou, they controlled areas of the Chinese city in which their members lived, where their dialect was spoken, and where their sort of food was served. Crucially, they also provided contacts with countrymen abroad. But, while powerful, the native place associations always competed for allegiance with the new trade and labor organizations and with secret societies of various kinds, from anti-Qing agitators to criminal gangs and everything in between.[34]

Overall, the new urban China in the treaty ports was full of opportunity but was also unruly territory, with complex links across time and geographical space. Its violent and rebellious underworld was hard to control. In the treaty ports, then, complex power systems came into being, which included the official government, western agents, business associations, labor organizations, and secret underground societies. With several layers of authority—Chinese, foreign, official, and popular—none of which was dominating, these treaty ports provided ample opportunities for pushing economic, social, and cultural boundaries. The resulting urban scene could support considerable experimentation through new and hybrid cultural forms.

In terms of urban design, new architectural forms emerged that mixed the Chinese national style with elements from New York, London, and Paris. In literature, the openness of Shanghai and the ability of writers to negotiate the terms of creativity with the outside world made the city a "cultural laboratory" for the invention and reinvention of Chinese culture, producing the "Shanghai modern."[35] In politics, similar effects were noticeable. Free from censorship and arrest in the foreign-administered districts of Shanghai, political dissidents could discuss and disseminate their ideas about equality, participation and, above all, nationalism.[36] Thus Shanghai became a center for the negotiation of diverse political and cultural projects.

To conclude, the treaty ports were an important aspect of a system of semi-colonial control imposed on China by the treaty powers. As Chinese nationalism developed, particularly after World War I, Chinese nationalists viewed the treaty ports with resentment as sites of foreign privilege vis-à-vis the Chinese population and as symbols of external constraints on China's sovereignty. Strong and ambivalent views about the nature of the treaty ports indicate how important they were and how much the nationalist critique continued to shape the ideology and institutions of the Chinese nation-state after 1911. But the treaty ports can also be viewed in more positive ways. Their business and consular communities promoted technological and economic innovation, along with institutional changes in areas such as education, finance, jurisprudence, publishing, and culture. Despite the confined social life typically experienced by the foreign residents of the treaty ports, the large and open urban centers offered wide intellectual horizons. Shanghai in particular has been described as a cradle of the development for the Chinese civil society. Despite the small size of China's nineteenth-century treaty ports and trade, they played a catalytic role in initiating processes of change that slowly but eventually resulted in a remarkable transformation of China's society. This pivotal role was explicitly recognized in official statements in 1984, when China's central government granted special privileges in foreign trade and investment to fourteen coastal cities as part of its program of economic reform and opening to the world. Almost all were former treaty ports.

Economic Downturn

Following the success of the Qing's 1755–1759 military campaign under the Qianlong emperor, which incorporated vast zones of Central Asia into the empire, the quest for military expansion waned and the need to continue institutional innovation and centralization abated. The budget available to the central government peaked in the late 1770s and diminished thereafter. By 1800, the budget was running about 15 percent lower. Growing fiscal problems had a debilitating effect on the capacity of the Qing administration at all levels. The Jiaqing emperor (r. 1796–1820) introduced a range of political reforms to reinvigorate the administration, uproot corruption, and deal with signs of widening political unrest, especially in the wake of a huge and costly uprising called the White Lotus rebellion (see below). The reforms intended a "sustainable political development" that toned down the ambitions of the Qing state and articulated a more conservative notion of "sustaining the prosperity and preserving the peace" *(chiying baotai)* as the empire's central goal.[37] These political reforms did little, however, to enhance the state's infrastructure and governing capacity. On the contrary, state capacity continued to decline significantly and visibly. The beginning deterioration in the ability of the Qing state to govern a growing, diverse society, let alone "nurture" a booming economy, was already being aggravated by the ever-expanding size and complexity of the population. In conjunction with the regime's growing conservatism and declining administrative rigor, an economic crisis occurred. While the cities along the coast and waterways found themselves at the center of a beginning economic revolution that would fundamentally reconfigure China's economic system, the extensive landlocked areas inland from the coast were put at a growing disadvantage. Poverty and misery began to spread in the vast hinterlands.

The economic problems emerging after a century of impressive growth were rooted in various issues.[38] Some were primarily domestic. Many scholars have pointed to population growth and the pressure it exerted on resources as one of the most pressing problems—perhaps *the* most pressing problem—confronting the Qing state in the late eighteenth and early nineteenth centuries. The increase of the population during the eighteenth century continued uninterrupted down to the mid-nineteenth century. Intensifying use of land, water, and fuels were exhausting forests, fresh water supplies, grasslands, and other natural resources. The degradation of the environment pushed China to the brink of ecological crisis. Overall agricultural productivity probably started to fall after 1800. In North China, production of cotton and other non-food crops deteriorated, reflecting a shift toward subsistence farming of vegetables and grains to meet the food consumption needs of the growing local population.

The domestic slump had consequences for financial and monetary conditions. Household incomes and purchasing power in the countryside suffered. The terms of trade also started to worsen for China in the nineteenth century largely due to the net outflow of silver on a massive scale after 1827, which reached its peak level during the 1840s. This constituted a reversal of the centuries-long pattern of silver flowing into China. As discussed already, the surging opium imports that came with western imperialism were certainly a major factor. But there were also other, more global economic forces behind the reversal of China's trade balance. In the first decades of the nineteenth century, global mine production of silver fell significantly when colonial governments in Latin America were overthrown. Data from the second decade of the nineteenth century show a decline of almost 40 percent, followed in the third decade by a further decline of 11 percent. The skyrocketing price of silver made it expensive for China to import. European markets for porcelain, one of China's principal export items, began to falter. By the 1780s, Europe was domestically producing high-quality porcelain which increasingly substituted for ceramic imports from China. Within a few decades, one of China's primary sources of wealth and prosperity was lost.

With the supply of silver falling, China paid out 34 million Mexican silver dollars to purchase goods—above all, opium—from abroad in the 1830s. The disruption of the currency system was one of the major causes of a protracted economic decline in the early part of the Daoguang reign. Known as the Daoguang Depression (1820–1850), it marked the end of the increases in commercial prosperity that had started in the Kangxi era in the 1680s.[39] The drain of silver inflated the value of silver still circulating in the domestic economy, deflating the value of the copper coinage used by ordinary people. As a result, real prices and wages came under additional pressure and stagnated or declined—a drop that was even steeper in silver terms. Adding to the misery, this in effect raised people's taxes, because taxes had to be paid in silver. The depression therefore hit peasant taxpayers hard, as they found it increasingly difficult to convert their copper cash, earned in daily sales of their goods, into silver taels for taxation. As the tax burden grew heavier, many small land-holders operating on small margins became insolvent and had to give up their farms, usually selling them to larger landlords. Meanwhile, the value of land and other property, usually also measured in silver, plummeted. The de-pression also resulted in a credit crunch that caused the collapse of many native banks. Capital markets dried up as increased transaction costs and falling prices put stress on manufacturers and they had difficulty paying back their loans. To lower their costs, businesses cut their workforces, leading to higher unemployment. The income gap between rich and poor widened, giving rise to a wave of tax- and rent-resistance movements and other forms of civil unrest.

The economic depression and its underlying factors also affected the Qing state. Tax revenues declined for the Qing state to the point that the annual silver outflow to address the imbalance of payments was equivalent to one quarter of each year's land-tax assessment. With the tax quota still frozen at its 1713 level, the government's surplus income steadily deteriorated. As gov-ernment spending on payroll and public projects shrank in real terms, corrup-tion and embezzlement spread, and the Qing government became increasingly hamstrung and inept. It was still expected to regulate the grain market via the granary system, maintain water works and flood control, and deliver famine relief, but its capacity to fulfill these responsibilities fell precipitously.[40] Officials neglected infrastructure as the cost of maintaining dams and irriga-tion systems increased in real terms. They allowed the emergency stores of grain held in granaries to decline, making it less likely that hard-hit commu-nities would see adequate relief efforts. Such actions and inactions resulted in more frequent disasters and exacerbated the suffering when they happened. The state was no longer capable of alleviating people's hardship. Victims of subsistence crises could no longer count on help from local governments. And as funding for defense evaporated, military efficacy plummeted—just at the moment when new domestic and foreign threats had to be countered.

It was not only the central government that grew administratively and fis-cally weaker. The collapse of businesses also aggravated the already grave fiscal problems of local governments, which responded by intensifying re-source extraction. On the brink of bankruptcy, they started levying unsanc-tioned surtaxes to make ends meet.[41] As local governments became financially unstable, they essentially competed with local communities for shrinking local resources, increasing tax fees and aggressively eliminating illicit activities such as salt smuggling and pirating that threatened state revenue. From 1857, when it was implemented across the empire, the likin *(lijin)* tax increased the cost of transport, which further depressed the entire rural economy. Local tax bullies reemerged, and the competition for resources between local governments and grassroots communities intensified. When the state became part of their problem, local communities struggled for survival by strengthening communal solidarity to fend off predatory agents from local governments. Tax riots, attacks on hated officials, and similar protests were essentially defenses against aggressive methods of resource extraction from local governments. The economic downturn also played a significant role in the outbreak of the Taiping Rebellion itself, a point to which we will return below.

For about twenty years, from 1840 to 1860, opium occupied the highest value in Sino-British trade. But after 1860, growing quantities of machine-made goods were imported into China and opium imports faded away. With the revival of silver production and the growth of tea and silk exports in the 1850s, silver once again began to flow into China, stabilizing the financial and monetary situation. New problems emerged, however, to prevent real economic improvement. The first wave of products from the European Industrial Revolution brought goods such as linen, woolens, umbrellas, petroleum lamps, matches, leather shoes, candles, and buttons, all of which competed with and eventually supplanted indigenous products. With the opening of the treaty ports, western trading houses could gain direct access to the markets and products of the Lower Yangzi region. This put pressure on rural handicraft production and caused rural unemployment. The widespread perception at the time, at home and abroad, seems to have been that economic crisis brought the Qing empire perilously close to collapse.[42]

Expansion of China's international trade was the most obvious effect of the treaty-port system. China's maritime customs data show the volume of exports doubling and imports rising by 77 percent between 1870 and 1895. Despite its modest scale, international trade had a significant effect on prices inside China. Major domestic commodity prices gradually aligned with international market prices throughout the Pacific Basin. Domestic prices for rice, wheat, and cotton moved in accordance with shifts in global markets.

This demonstrated a significant change. Several decades of unrestricted trade forged unprecedented global links affecting big and important sectors of China's economy. By the late 1880s, millions of villagers inhabiting the areas in the lower Yangzi area who grew, bought, or sold rice, or worked for or traded with partners who engaged in those activities, were affected by distant producers, consumers, and traders of rice. Toward the end of the nineteenth century, China's farmers had become unknowing participants in far-flung networks of international commerce, influencing and being influenced by the volatility of global markets. This also meant that they became much more vulnerable to changes in exchange rates, fluctuations in the value of the currency, and globally set energy and transaction costs such as shipping fees and customs fees.

The growth of treaty-port cities was matched by the decline of many inland cities thanks to changing patterns of trade and modes of transport. Steamer shipping along the coast and the Yangzi diverted trade from smaller inland waterways. The decline of the Grand Canal, China's main north-south waterway, spelled the decline of significant towns along its route, especially in northern Jiangsu and Shandong. At the same time, the haulers, boat people, horse and foot travelers, and the innkeepers serving them lost their livelihoods as China's interior transportation industries were not able to compete with the new, faster means of transportation. Rural migrants bypassed once-prosperous towns such as Jining and Yangzhou for Shanghai. However, treaty-port status alone did not determine a city's fortune. Ningbo, one of Qing China's great centers of commercial activity and among the first cities to be opened to foreign trade as a treaty port, was adversely affected by the rise of Shanghai. Merchants from Ningbo shifted their capital, and often their families as well, to the new center of action, joining their counterparts in Guangzhou to become Shanghai's new elite.

The development of manufacturing in the coastal areas fell far short of its potential. The expanding inflow of goods, new technology, and new knowledge during the latter half of the nineteenth century stimulated development in and around the treaty ports, but did not yet extend beyond the urban borders and affect larger swaths along the coast. On the contrary, conflicts often arose when new ventures clashed with the vested interests of the informal monopolies that still promised to deliver tax payments to official patrons. Prior to 1895, a fierce debate raged in Chinese intellectual and political circles about whether railways should be built at all. Railway advocates argued that only by adopting modern industrial technology, such as railways, steel mills, gunboats, and so on, could China hope to thwart the imperialist ambitions of foreigners and catch up with the West's technological development. This school of thought, which became known as the self-strengthening movement, attracted some of China's most powerful officials, including Li Hongzhang (1823–1901), Zhang Zhidong (1837–1909), and Liu Mingchuan (1836–1896). Opposition to railways, meanwhile, came from conservatives including the Mongol Grand Secretary Woren (1804–1871), Liu Xihong (1800–1899), and Yu Lianyuan. Among the worries they voiced were that railways might facilitate invasion by foreign armies, might cause massive unemployment among traditional transport workers, and might be unprofitable and therefore drain state finances.[43] Such arguments were also underpinned by a restrictive coalition between officials and traditional transport firms that opposed steamship shipping or railways because the competition threatened their incomes. Silk weavers, too, resisted the introduction of new manufacturing techniques. As landowners and merchants understood that the best way to secure their interests was to build good relationships with the official class, vested interests based on patronage networks between officials and traditional enterprises impeded economic innovation.

The imperialist states forced to grant railway concessions to Russia in northern Manchuria, to Japan in southern Manchuria, to Germany in Shandong, to Belgium in central China, to France in the southern provinces bordering Indochina, and to Great Britain in the Yengzi delta. After 1895, railway construction accelerated and by 1911, China had about 9,300 kilometers of railways, though this was anything but an integrated system. Inland China, however, was cut off from this infrastructure improvement. Thus, the rural villages in the interior could not participate in the development taking place along the coast.

Modern Chinese industrialization began with the late Qing national defense industry in Nanjing. Shipbuilding and weapons factories in Jiangnan, Fujian, and Hubei led the first phase of Chinese industrial production. As the internal exchange of regional goods and materials combined with international trade, the Chinese economy transformed into one with large urban centers serving as hubs for collection and distribution of industrial and consumer goods. The cities were connected by railroads under foreign control and management.

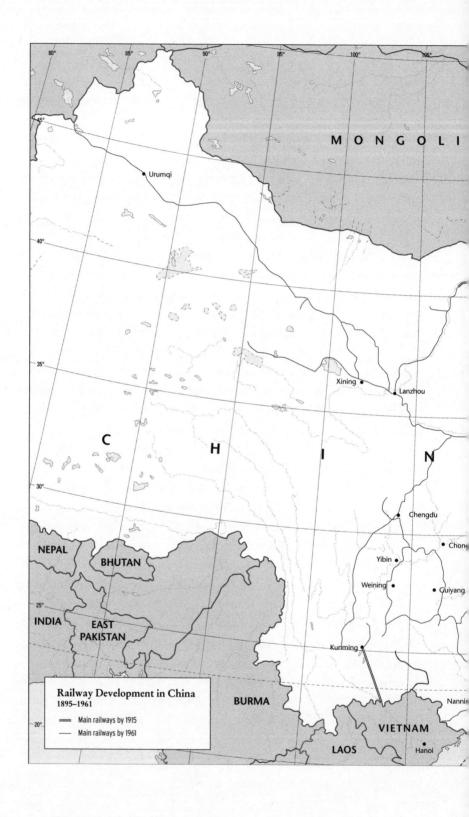

Railway Development in China
1895–1961

Main railways by 1915
Main railways by 1961

By the time China's own light industries developed, bringing factories for textile weaving, milling grain into flour, producing matches and soap, and small-scale machine-making, they were also located near the coastal treaty port cities rather than in the interior. Chinese businesses producing noodles, textiles, matches, electricity, machinery, chemicals, and processed agricultural commodities sprang up all over the Yangzi delta, from Beijing to Tianjin and in the Wuhan region. They operated first with foreign capital and later with Chinese government and private investments.

Most peasants, unable to earn income from home production, wholly reliant on harvests from tilling their small parcels of land, and faced with increasing tax burdens, were unable to maintain even modest standards of living. The disruption of China's traditional market network led to a longstanding situation in which the coastal areas became wealthier and the interior and isolated regions of the country grew more impoverished and underdeveloped. The gap between the urban and rural areas became ever more acute. China's traditional economic structure was gradually transformed as the internal economy, with its foundation in village agriculture and peasant handicraft industries, disintegrated.

This caused far-reaching social changes in the rural communities. Chinese rural society has long been characterized by the existence of voluntary associations. These mushroomed in the nineteenth century as people dealt with growing overpopulation, economic hardship, social dislocation, social unrest, and collective violence exacerbated by lineage feuding.[44] As support networks capable of responding in a variety of ways to social threats, voluntary associations mainly concerned themselves with issues of survival. They provided the solidarity that was the only hope of protection against extortion, exploitation, and predatory extraction by the local state. They took various forms, with some arising as religious sects (*jiao*) and others as popular, secular organizations and brotherhoods (all called *hui*). These vehicles for social cooperation were outside the state's control, and acquired important functions in the coordination of social and economic life in the villages. For example, water conservation and distribution collectives in Shanxi and Shaanxi and similar groups in southern Taiwan organized to share irrigation channels. Cooperatives in southern Fujian worked for the preservation of common markets for the distribution and sale of porcelains and other local products. Associations organized sacrifices to Guandi, the god of war, or the Dragon King in North China. Village alliances sprang up in the Hakka areas for martial arts and self-defense training.[45] These local groups and organizations had overlapping functions, and represented basic units of grassroots Chinese initiative in the countryside. Thus the differences between urban and rural regions also grew in terms of social structure and organization.

What caused the economic and social quandaries that bedeviled the once flourishing Qing empire? Should the West and its imperialist policies be faulted? Or were the causes homegrown, inherent in the unresolved problems of imperial institutions? No simple answer is possible. What is certain is that, in the nineteenth century, China slipped into a deep economic crisis that lasted for over a century and established the roots of an overall political and social decay that later Chinese governments found difficult to address. The economic quandary was the single most important factor, given that its effects crippled many other institutions in the Chinese empire. Questions about the economic impact of foreign imperialism on Qing China have been at the center of a heated debate since at least the 1960s.[46] Chinese nationalist and Marxist historians have long claimed that imperialism, the "unequal treaties," and the forced opening of China brought about China's subsequent economic troubles. Many Chinese intellectuals and historians have equated capitalism with foreign imperialism and exploitation, condemning both as external encroachment. On this basis, they have also argued that China's isolation from the rest of the world and from global capitalism after 1949 was a necessary period of unlocking indigenous sources for a twentieth-century regeneration. Providing a counterargument are western liberal historians who maintain that the overall western "impact" was an important impulse for modernization. They emphasize how western companies and institutions brought new technology, new knowledge, and new ideas.

The terms of this broad debate, however, have also changed in light of China's rapid development across the last four decades, which would not have been possible without its opening to the world and attracting foreign direct investment. Scholars have recently proposed a more nuanced interpretation. Kenneth Pomeranz, for example, argues that "while people so far apart as modernization and dependency theorists often argue that imperialism's worst political legacy was that it left twentieth-century China (or other Third World countries) with a state incapable of promoting development, it may be more accurate to acknowledge that much was done to develop certain modern sectors and regions and to look instead at how state strategies adopted under foreign pressure shortchanged other policy and geographic areas."[47] Robert Y. Eng suggests a similar approach: "If we are to understand the modernization process in China and Japan as a whole, we must go beyond citing various internal or external factors that might have facilitated or retarded modernization and even beyond weighing the relative importance of internal versus external factors. Rather, we must try to understand the organic links and dynamic interactions between domestic and foreign forces."[48] This is to say that the reality of economic imperialism was more complex than most accounts acknowledge. It caused economic disruptions in certain areas of the Chinese economy, but at the same time it provided important stimulus for innovation and growth in other areas. Studies of the history of foreign companies in China, for instance, have shifted to a narrative of multiplayer competition and economic interaction, rather than of simple western exploitation. Chinese businesses faced numerous hurdles, most of them domestic, but in general and especially in the treaty ports, they were much more able to compete with foreign firms than has been previously assumed.[49] Chinese businesses in the urban areas were agile and adaptable to the challenges presented by new foreign firms and new products. They also learned from their economic competitors and were quick to adopt new technologies and methods. Many merchants focused on new opportunities brought about by imperialism. They also went abroad to Southeast Asia, Australia, Hawaii, and the United States in pursuit of economic endeavors, even shopping for foreign citizenship and holding multiple passports. It is because of the resilience and adaptability of the Chinese economy in the coastal areas that rapid development in the treaty ports was possible in the first place. Several large urban areas became the foundation of Chinese industry and entrepreneurship and replaced the former base of cottage industries in rural villages.

Equally important, however, were the structural consequences. Seen as a whole, and despite new chances and positive developments in the treaty ports, China's economic system became fragmented. The scope and quality of this early Chinese industrialization was rather modest and remained small. The economies of the coastal industrial cities gradually extended into the surrounding areas, but the rate of expansion was quite slow. Traditional economic patterns continued to prevail in the regions between the interior heartland and the large urban areas. In general, the economy split into separate production and marketing systems: the interior versus the coastal regions, the villages versus the cities, and agriculture versus industry. Inevitably, this led to severe disruption and plunged rural China into a downward spiral of pauperization.

Environmental Disasters

Beyond the general economic slump, environmental degradation put pressure on life in the countryside. Indications of environmental fiasco became more conspicuous and frequent during the nineteenth century. The large-scale nineteenth-century environmental crisis manifested by these disasters could no longer be ignored.

Around that time, the population in China was estimated to have reached an unsustainable 400 million. Since the expansion of arable land had long since failed to keep pace with demographic growth, per-capita acreage dropped quickly in the latter half of the eighteenth century. It reached a precariously low point in the first half of the nineteenth century, clearly becoming a cause of peasants' misery and a driving factor of the nineteenth-century crisis. The growing desire for land and unprecedented demand for natural resources, including soil, energy, and water, accelerated ecological degradation. Population growth caused demand for timber to soar. Growing market demand, fueled by the development of domestic and international trading networks, further intensified the exploitation of frontier resources, which rendered this process unsustainable and environmentally damaging. By the 1850s, the new crops introduced earlier had exhausted the soil of the few nutrients left behind by traditional crops, and in the case of corn, depleted the soil to a far greater depth than rice, barley, or sorghum ever had. As fields failed and were abandoned, they aggravated the erosion problems that had been created by deforestation. The inevitable results were worse shortages of goods necessary for subsistence, more damaging floods and droughts, and an increasingly impoverished rural population.

Due to increased silt accumulation in the river bed, the Yellow River changed course in 1855, affecting three provinces and destroying huge agricultural areas. One of the country's most disastrous floods occurred in 1887 in the middle and lower reaches of the Yellow River, where the river spilled over its newly found bed. The fatalities numbered between nine hundred thousand and two million people. (The next major flood, in 1931, would be even more disastrous. And in 1938, the Yellow River would change course again after GMD troops blew up its dikes to prevent further Japanese invasion.) Management of the Yellow River had been a preoccupation of governments for thousands of years, since without periodic dredging, and occasionally embankment, it had the tendency to fill with silt, given the sandy, light soil of the northern Chinese plains. Emperors in the early nineteenth century were acutely aware of the need to maintain waterworks on the Yellow River and also for the Grand Canal. Nineteenth-century officials could draw on precise knowledge and long experience of river management, including the damming of tributaries and release of the water to clean silt from the Yellow River's bottom. The Qing court's declining finances and state capacity, however, kept it from immediately and effectively dealing with river issues.

The shift of the Yellow River was emblematic of the pressing environmental changes in North China, which also saw temperatures drop in the middle of the century and aridity rise. The most powerful El Niño conditions in five hundred years developed in the last quarter of the nineteenth century, killing tens of millions in drought-induced famines, and driving much of Asia, Africa, and Latin America further into the conditions that gave rise to the term "third world."[50] By the 1870s, drought and famine were acknowledged by regional governors in China to be major and persisting problems. One of the most disastrous famines in recent Chinese history took place between 1876 and 1879. The "Great Famine in the North," in the provinces of Shanxi, Henan, Shandong, Zhili, and Shaanxi, affected between 160 million and 200 million people and claimed at least 9.5 million lives. The immediate cause was the three-year drought that had withered crops from 1873 to 1876. Other disasters were less severe but occurred in China's economic and cultural heartland. The effects of droughts in Jiangsu province, in 1873, 1880, and 1892, rippled through some of the empire's wealthiest cities and provoked fears of failed harvests, rising prices, and divine judgment. Refugees from collapsed local ecologies joined refugees from the rebellions and wars, bloating the populations of coastal and riverine cities. The desertion of what had been some of China's most productive land only contributed to the social disorders of the nineteenth century.[51]

Large-scale migrations of excess populations, north to Manchuria and Mongolia and also south and southwest, further unsettled society in the nineteenth century. Twenty-five million people migrated from Shandong and Hebei to Manchuria, and more than nineteen million left China to settle in Southeast Asia and the lands around the Indian Ocean and South Pacific. The Straits Settlements, British crown colonies, provided a waypoint from which many traveled on to the Dutch Indies, Borneo, Burma, and places farther west. The emigration of Chinese from the heartland was one of the greatest movements of people in modern times.[52]

During emergencies such as famines or flooding, charitable donations from merchants and gentry to provide disaster relief were common and important. In the late nineteenth century, there were numerous charitable associations, large and small. Qing China maintained a complex system of social welfare that dwarfed its counterparts in western premodern states. Its task was to maintain subsistence levels for people in urban and rural areas in times of distress. This would also ensure social stability and prevent unrest. To provide these welfare services, the Qing state relied not only on public funds for granaries, but also on private contributions for charitable associations by local elites. Most of these charities were designed specifically for the care and shelter of the poor and relief of human suffering broadly understood. "Charity" as a concept referred quite specifically to the giving of money, goods, labor, or other forms of aid for the alleviation of human misery.[53] There were charitable halls *(shantang)*, which took a leading role in caring for people in distress; poorhouses *(pujitang)*; and orphanages *(yuyingtang)*, originally private ventures which were gradually mandated by the administration. Buddhists established soup kitchens *(zhouchang)* and provided lodging to the poor. Outdoor relief centers distributed food and clothing and helped keep the wandering poor from entering cities already saturated by the constant flow of people from the countryside. Refugee relief stations organized by the combined efforts of government and charitable societies made significant humanitarian contributions to caring for the poor and alleviating rural and suburban poverty. Soup kitchens and free clinics channeled the refugees and the disaster-stricken into certain areas and places, attempting to keep their suffering and infectious diseases from circulating broadly. Seen as potential troublemakers, they were not encouraged to find their own ways across the countryside.

Another important category was made up of associations that operated gruel kitchens or grain contributions to fight occasional food shortages. They performed functions similar to relief centers, but were more permanent. Often they were located just outside a city wall, and offered food to beggars and the poor. Other associations provided clothes, such as the societies established by some individual officials and members of the literati to help the poor through cold winters. Another area that became the focus of charitable activities was medicine. Some associations provided herbal medicine or vaccinations to those who could not afford medical treatments. Foreign missionaries were also a source of relief, and their generosity and sacrifice earned the respect of even initially hostile officials. Collectively, these measures had worked well in the past. In the nineteenth century, however, their piecemeal efforts were unequal to the needs of a vast population set adrift by environmental collapse and natural disasters on a huge and unprecedented scale.

The Chinese state found it ever more challenging to fight the deepening environmental crisis. More and more effort and resources were required to maintain dikes, manage granaries, and support settlements in precarious natural conditions. Augmented by global climate shifts, weather patterns became more unpredictable. Floods and famines occurred with growing and frightening frequency. This was not only an indication of worsening environmental problems, but also the result of a weakened state capacity during the final years of the imperial system. The environmental difficulties were thus an institutional and an environmental problem at the same time. Imperial institutions were overwhelmed and could no longer deal with an increasingly threatening situation. The environmental crisis acted as a threat multiplier, contributing to economic and political instability and also worsening the effects of both sudden-onset disasters like floods and storms and slow-onset disasters like drought and desertification. Those disasters contributed to failed crops, famines, and overcrowded urban centers—all of which in turn inflamed political unrest, intensified the impacts of war and civil strife, and led to even more displacement.

Rebellion and Unrest in Rural China

As traditional mechanisms and instruments of welfare provision and philanthropy were upended by sheer overload, many people in the nineteenth century had no choice but to resort to predatory survival strategies.[54] They armed themselves, rioted, attacked granaries, stole food, and robbed the rich—then often sought cover among the religious sects, bandits, triads, and rebel groups forming in remote hilly and mountainous regions. A series of ever-larger domestic rebellions reflected the misery in the countryside and further contributed to the erosion of rural society. These began with the White Lotus Rebellion (1796–1804), included the Nian and Miao uprisings and many smaller bandit uprisings and rice riots, and culminated with the vast Taiping Rebellion (1851–1864). Several prolonged conflicts also occurred between Muslims and Han Chinese in northwestern and southwestern China.

In 1796, the White Lotus Rebellion erupted in the economically marginal areas of Sichuan, Hubei, and Shaanxi. The White Lotus Society can be traced back to the salvationist teachings of Pure Land Buddhism during the Eastern Jin dynasty (317–420). It appeared first as an organization or society in the twelfth century and reemerged as a powerful force in the late eighteenth century.[55] Buddhism as practiced among the scholar-officials and at court must be contrasted with the lively sectarian movements among the broader population that were an integral part of popular culture. Some of these sects, such as the White Cloud sect and the White Lotus sect, belonged to a consistent undercurrent of messianic movements in China, which lasted into the nineteenth century. It has also been said that they were to some extent influenced by Manichaeism (in Chinese, *Monijiao* or *mingjiao*, translating to "bright teaching"), since the color white is frequently associated with the Manichaeans.[56] These sects were regarded as heterodox by Buddhist clergy and government authorities alike. Their beliefs centered on the arrival of the Maitreya, or Future Buddha, which would lead to the destruction of demons and other evildoers and would bring about prosperity and universal peace. As the leadership of the White Lotus Society turned more and more against the Qing dynasty, it attracted adherents who did not necessarily share its spiritual and particularly ascetic vision. Later, bandits, impoverished peasants, and bankrupt merchants and smugglers joined the sect. The Qing army could not suppress the White Lotus Society on its own and had to rely extensively upon the elites in local areas and their militias and mercenaries to crush the rebellion. It took about a decade to finally defeat the White Lotus Society uprising in 1805.

The White Lotus Rebellion dealt the Qing court a heavy blow, from which it never really fully recovered. The campaign to suppress the rebellion was expensive and nearly wiped out the entire budget reserves of the court.[57] While the sect itself eventually succumbed, it gave way to successors and splinter groups. One of the boldest was the "Eight Trigrams" *(bagua)* or Heavenly Principle *(tianli)*. They set up an elaborate organization of communications and military deployment, even infiltrating the population of eunuchs and officials inside the imperial city. In 1812, two leaders of the sect hatched a plan to gain control of Shandong and Zhili provinces and to stage a coup d'état in the Forbidden City by assassinating the Jiaqing emperor. When the plot was uncovered, eight Banner soldiers under the command of a prince, the later Daoguang emperor, arrested the rebels, who were later executed. Manchu Banners were dispatched to the neighborhood of Beijing to hunt down the last of the Eight Trigrams units and their supporters. In total about twenty thousand people were killed in the campaign. Defeat of the Eight Trigrams rebels and furious persecution of their sympathizers allowed the Qing dynasty to eventually quell the revolt.

The later, more violent, and longer upheaval called the Nian uprising (1851–1868) was staged by the *nian*—plundering gangs that ravaged northern Anhui, southern Shandong, and southern Henan.[58] By 1850, these gangs were relying on pillage, banditry, salt smuggling, gambling, and kidnapping to make a living in the impoverished, environmentally precarious, flood and drought-prone plain between the Huai and Yellow (Huang) Rivers. The very diverse membership base of the *nian* included White Lotus sectarians and Triad secret society members, demobilized government soldiers, and displaced peasants. Their activities spread as repeated floods of the Yellow River in the early 1850s worsened rural livelihoods and added many refugees to their ranks. From 1856 to 1859, *nian* leaders consolidated their bases north of the Huai River by winning over the leaders of walled communities, the consolidated villages that had long before been fortified with walls for self-defense. Clan and lineage heads from those villages were given important roles among the *nian* leaders. The *nian* strategy centered on guerrilla tactics as they effectively employed a powerful and fast cavalry to raid distant areas and carry loot back to their home bases. The real source of their strength, however, was popular support and widespread sympathy for their cause. Using slogans such as "rob from the rich and succor the poor," they sacked government food convoys and distributed the spoils of their raids evenly among their members. They also strictly prohibited unauthorized robbery and rape. The *nian* increasingly adopted an anti-Manchu language and, in defiance of Manchu rule, let their hair grow long. In response, the throne declared the *nian* a rebel movement that had to be quelled. The imperial suppression campaign was led by the experienced and well-respected Mongol general Senggelinqin (whom we encountered above as successful defender of the Dagu forts in 1859). He led a forceful cavalry of Manchu and Mongol Bannermen into the area in 1862. While his campaign scored some victories, he was unable to completely halt the rebellion. The general himself was killed in an ambush in Shandong in May 1865. The court then dispatched two of the most capable Chinese generals, Zeng Guofan (1811–1872) and Li Hongzhang, to succeed Senggelinqin. Their new tactic was to try to drive a wedge between the walled city leaders and their men, offering amnesty to defectors, registering loyalist peasants, and appointing pro-Qing village heads. Finally, Li Hongzhang set up encirclement lines along the Yellow River and the Grand Canal as part of the strategy that would destroy the revolt in 1868. The rebellion, which had started in a small area with a handful of robbers, had lasted eighteen years and affected a large stretch of the northern plains. The lasting damage of the Nian Rebellion, with its insistence on base areas, mobile guerrilla tactics, and popular approval, was to severely obstruct imperial control and further weaken government administration throughout North China. It laid bare the growing feebleness and fragility of the imperial institutions. The Nian's ultimate demise may be explained by its lack of a coherent ideology and governance system—and also by its inability or unwillingness to collaborate with the concurrent Taiping Rebellion, which could have created a formidable force.

Around the same time that the *nian* raged on the North China Plain, an even larger challenge arose in the south, this one also emerging from a small, rural locality and in the beginning involving just a few discontents. In the 1850s, two relatively obscure Christian sectarians in southern China, Hong Xiuquan (1814–1864) and Yang Xiuqing (1821–1856), attracted a small following which started to gain momentum. As the movement grew, the leaders daringly launched a separatist state called the Taiping Heavenly Kingdom (*Taiping tianguo*, 1851–1864) that challenged the Manchu empire and its claim of legitimacy. Their call for liberating the Han-Chinese by exterminating the Manchu rulers, which they characterized as the "Manchu demons" and

2.4. Secret societies or brotherhoods, which had their own rules and codes, were, in foreign eyes, often the initiators of revolts and rebellions. Engraving, 1884.

"mortal enemy of us Chinese," resonated with growing popular sentiment about the Manchu dynasty of the time. In the rebels' declarations and proclamations, the Manchu emperor was no longer referred to as the grand emperor of China, but as the "Tartar dog"—an immoral, alien ruler who hailed from a race "inferior" to the Chinese.[59] The initial emergence of the Taiping rebels was similar to the outbreak of the White Lotus Rebellion, during which sectarians persecuted by the authorities chose a path of open revolt and managed to attract a large following of non-sectarians, who also despised Manchu rule and came in conflict with the state on their own. What set Hong Xiuquan and his men apart, however, was not only their Christian beliefs, but also their boundless ambition to create a new rival rebel state (guo).

The Taiping movement originated in the Hakka migrant communities in the mountainous regions of northern Guangdong and Guangxi. Hong Xiuquan was born in 1814 in a village north of Guangzhou, into a rural family that centuries earlier had served the emperor at court. Close to both Guangzhou and Hong Kong, Hong's birthplace was in an area increasingly in contact with the outside world. It was a classical emigrant county, with a population divided between Cantonese speakers and Hakkas, and was already linked to international trade through the ports that bordered on the area. Having passed the local entry-level civil service examination in 1827, Hong was sent the following year to the city to take the exam for the prestigious shengyuan degree. Along with him came his family's hopes for social betterment. Hong failed his exam, however, and subsequently took a teaching position in a rural school. He went back to Guangzhou and failed again in 1836, and after a third failure in 1837, he returned to his village, became ill, and had fits of vivid dreams and hallucinations, the meaning of which eluded him. After one final, failed attempt at the exam a few years later, Hong read a Christian tractate that a foreign missionary in the port city of Guangzhou had happened to give to one of his cousins. In it, he encountered an abridged story of Christianity, emphasizing God's call to man and religion as a moral endeavor. The text seemed to explain his dream-visions from six years before. Hong reinvented himself as a religious visionary based on his reading of the Christian texts.[60] In 1843, with the local area in disarray after China's defeat in the Opium War, Hong Xiuquan announced to his astounded family that his dreams were revelations: he was the reincarnated son of Jehovah and younger brother of Jesus Christ. In his dream, Jehovah had given him a sacred sword and told him to purge the world of demons, corruption, and sufferings. The demons were none other than the idols worshipped by the Chinese in their Confucian and Buddhist temples. Hong Xiuquan baptized himself, then smashed the Confucian icons in his surroundings.

Despite Hong's use of Biblical language, his religious vision would seem to be very similar to the White Lotus legend in which the Venerable Mother sends the Maitreya Buddha to Earth through reincarnation and creates a new world free of corruption and suffering. Similarities were also to be found in the sectarian organization. On his way to Guangxi to recruit believers for his Heavenly Father, he founded the "Society of God Worshippers." Operating on the model of Buddhist religious sects, many local congregations sprang up in the wake of Hong Xiuquan's and his cousin's travels. Soon the widely autonomous local god-worshipping societies had hundreds of followers. They took Hong Xiuquan, whom many had never met, as their spiritual leader. By the mid-1840s, Hong Xiuquan shifted his rhetoric. He seemed no longer primarily concerned with demons, the wrong teachings of Confucianism, and the need to replace those with the worship of God. He started to belittle the Manchu rulers as the wrongful and inferior usurpers of China. His twin goals were to drive the Manchus from power and establish himself as emperor. This was an important and far-reaching change, by which a rather traditional religious movement slowly morphed into a political one that urged not only rebellion against religious ideas, but the establishment of an alternative state. Hong Xiuquan was adept in many ways at combining traditional institutional elements derived from popular religions and sects with new Christian teachings and political language. For contemporaries, the movement simultaneously spoke to familiar concerns and offered radically new perspectives. China had to reorganize society based on diverse institutions that merged its traditions with elements of the West's industrialized societies. The Taiping rebels also believed that a lasting international peace would be established when the Heavenly Kingdom joined forces with the foreign Christian states overseas to form a universal Christian state. This creative recombination of old and new elements provided the Taiping rebels with the powerful vision of a new Heavenly Kingdom that promised to be better governed and more just, and above all, to return China to the Han-Chinese. This was a message that won the Taiping many adherents in troubled times, not so much because of its religious content as because of its promise to set wrongs right and create a better, more efficient, and domestically and internationally more secure state. Like many previous founders of millenarian sects and anti-government movements, Hong Xiuquan remained an inventive but unpredictable man throughout his life, profoundly affected by the times of uncertainty and anxiety around him. He managed to attract the local poor, the displaced, and the disadvantaged. He pulled them into his society and, in time, melded them into a formidable army that the Qing court found tough to defeat.

The Qing government began cracking down on the god-worshipping societies aggressively, and tried to arrest Hong on several occasions. Meanwhile, however, the sectarians had armed themselves well, moved north, and entered the Guangdong-Hunan-Yangzi corridor—an area already in turmoil having experienced incidents of tax resistance and revolts in the 1840s. Along the way, the rebels expanded their ranks by recruiting desperate and resentful tax resisters and allying with preexisting secret societies in the region. By 1850, the rebel movement had gained strength and extended its activities. After winning a decisive battle against government forces in January 1851, Hong Xiuquan announced the formation of a Christian state he called Taiping Tianguo, the "Peaceful Heavenly Kingdom." He anointed himself ruler of the new state as Heavenly King *(tianwang)*. Having by now mobilized twenty thousand men and women as soldiers of God, Hong began to attack cities in south-central China. The Taiping army continued to grow rapidly and eventually captured most major cities in the Lower Yangzi area. The victory of the Taiping rebels from south to north was made possible not only by the successful recruitment of a following of aggrieved peasants, but also by the indirect support of protesters launching parallel resistances against local officials. Many distressed peasants welcomed the invading rebels by offering them food, drinks, and local intelligence.

After Hong's army conquered Nanjing in March 1853, the city became the capital of the Taiping Tianguo. This came as a huge blow to the Qing dynasty, revealing to the Manchu court how grave this crisis was. Shockingly, in the course of the takeover the Taiping soldiers had mercilessly slaughtered the local Manchu population, made up of a garrison of Banner troops but also their families, and numbering perhaps fifty thousand people.[61] The court was now at risk of losing control over large swaths of southern China, including important commercial centers, strategic infrastructure assets, and historic cities. The collapse of the dynasty appeared within reach. It seemed as though all of China was rising up against Qing rule.

Hong Xiuquan, however, promised his followers a brighter and more peaceful future: "When disorder reaches its extreme, then there is order, when darkness reaches its extreme, then there is light; this is the Way of Heaven. Now, night has fled and the sun has risen! We only wish that all our brothers and sisters on earth would rush from the demon's treacherous gate and follow God's true Way . . . they would one and all improve themselves and improve the world . . . enjoying universal tranquility *(taiping)*."[62] The new Taiping Kingdom adopted ambitious policies to reform Chinese society. After 1853, Taiping leaders initially tried to institute policies for widespread land redistribution, gender equality, and the enforcement of religious practices that might best be described as Christian egalitarian fundamentalism.[63] The 1853 "Land System of the Taiping Kingdom" described a future Taiping society in glowing colors: "There will be fields and all will cultivate them; there will be food and all shall eat; there will be clothes and all will be dressed; there will be money and all will use it; inequality will cease, all will be fed and warm."[64] Women were also allowed to own and inherit property, work in the fields, and serve in government.

Especially after Hong Rengan, a cousin of Hong Xiuquan educated in Hong Kong, arrived in Nanjing and took over the government as the so-called Shield King in spring 1859, the Taiping policies became more systematic and moderate. Hong Rengan envisioned the future China as "a country of wealth and civilization." This could be achieved by making it part of the global industrial economy. He promoted the establishment of hospitals, railways, schools, banks, newspapers, steamships, and arsenals, and a land system by which poorer regions would receive assistance from the surpluses of wealthier regions. In terms of government, many imperial institutions were copied, among them the Six Boards. Most remarkable, the Taiping also built a new examination system for selecting loyal officials, despite the close relationship of examinations with the empire and with Confucian teachings. Even in the Heavenly Capital, they believed, talent should be selected by examinations—with Confucian classics replaced by Christian classics. By early 1861, however, the Taiping examinations had begun to reincorporate the Chinese classics, as well.[65] Students sitting for the district exam in the spring of 1861 wrote examination essays not only on religious doctrine but also on the Analects. Even though this practice was short-lived, it did point toward institutional innovation. The Taiping approach of combining traditional rules with new ideals served as a pattern or blueprint for institutional adaptation.

The Taiping state was an amalgam of indigenous and exogenous institutions, combining repertoires of mid-Qing protest and revolt with ideologies of western provenance newly imported into the empire by way of translation and transfer. These hybrid, reformist programs gave the Taiping state the reputation, among twentieth-century revolutionaries and scholars alike, of being China's first modern revolutionary state.[66] It also paved the way for later governments which, in one way or another, all combined Chinese and foreign institutional components in similar hybrid formulas.

But these radical ideas encountered stubborn resistance by the old elites of the empire. The social and cultural plans of the Taiping alienated most local elites, who by the late 1850s began to join forces with the Qing court in the fight to defeat the Heavenly Kingdom. And despite its Christian persuasion, the Taiping Rebellion was seen as a menace for order as well as a blasphemy by most westerners in China. For the western powers, the Taiping Rebellion prevented the expansion of trade that was at the center of foreign interests in China. Most foreign countries and companies were therefore willing to help the imperial armies fight the Taiping. European governments, and Britain especially, believed the Qing empire should and could be compelled by force to accept western terms. Such a weak and submissive Qing empire tied into international trade through accepted treaties was much preferable to a fundamentalist, revolutionary state, even one carrying the Christian Bible. The Qing state, already weakened considerably by the opium wars, had no choice but to rely on limited western military aid, especially in supplying weapons. In eastern China, the Qing also received help by a mercenary army led first by the American Frederick Townsend Ward (1831–1862), then by the Englishman Charles Gordon (1833–1865). The Qing court also counted on Han provincial officials, who built regional armies autonomous from the central government, to put down the Taiping movement. In this context, Beijing suspended the time-honored "rule of avoidance," which barred imperial officials from holding positions in their native provinces. Scholar-officials were now fighting in and for their hometowns. Zeng Guofan and Li Hongzhang recruited local militias and drew on the newly imposed *lijin* transit tax in central Chinese provinces devastated by the war. These efforts

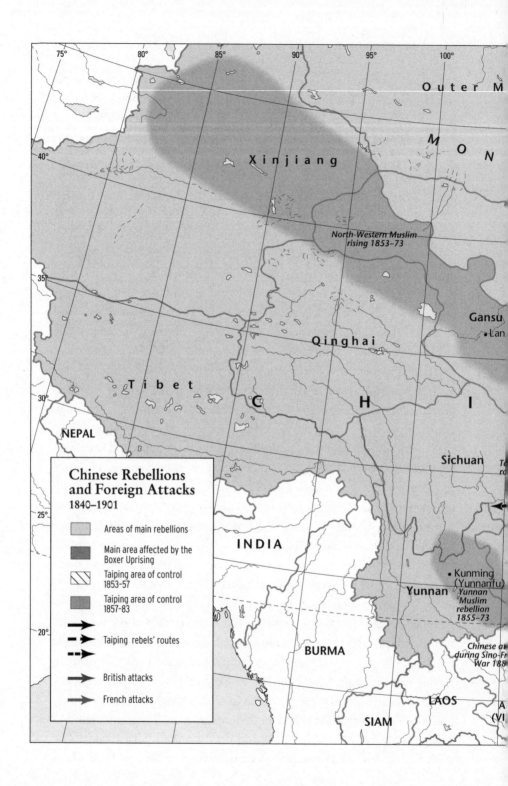

75° 80° 85° 90° 95° 100°

Outer M

M O N

X i n j i a n g

40°

North-Western Muslim
rising 1853–73

35°

Gansu
•Lan

Q i n g h a i

T i b e t   C   H   I

30°

NEPAL

Sichuan   To
ro

Chinese Rebellions and Foreign Attacks
1840–1901

25°

Areas of main rebellions

Main area affected by the
Boxer Uprising

INDIA

Taiping area of control
1853-57

Taiping area of control
1857-83

•Kunming
(Yunnanfu)
Yunnan *Yunnan*
Muslim
rebellion
1855–73

Yunnan

Taiping rebels' routes

20°

British attacks

Chinese a
during Sino-Fr
War 188

French attacks

BURMA

LAOS

A
(VI

SIAM

MANCHURIA

Jilin

Mongolia

OLIA

Inner Mongolia

KOREA

• Beijing
Main area of
Boxer uprising
1900–01
Zhili
• Tianjin

Area of
Boxer
uprising
1900–01

Shanxi

Shandong

Taiping
northern
expedition
1853–54

Nian
invasion
1868

ou

Kaifeng
Nian rebels
1853–68

Jiangsu

Yellow
Sea

JAPAN

Shaanxi

Henan

Main Nian
centre

Anglo-French
campaigns
1850–60

N

A

Yangzhou
Zhenjiang
Nanjing•
Taiping
capital
Songjiang
• Shanghai

Hubei

Xiantao

Anhui
Hangzhou

ing advance
e to Sichuan
1856–63

Ningbo
Zhejiang

East
China
Sea

Taiping
advance
1850–53

Jiangxi

Opium War
1839–42

Hunan

Guizhou

Fuzhou

Guizhou
Miao tribal
rising
1854–73

Fujian
Xiamen
(Amoy)

Tamsui
(Danshui)

Guangxi

Jintian
Outbreak of
Taiping rebellion
1850

Guangdong
Hakka-Cantonese
War 1855–57
Guangzhou•
Hong Kong

Taiwan

N

cks
ch
85

Hanoi

Sino-French war
1883–85

200 km

NAM
TNAM)

Hainan

South
China
Sea

200 miles

were aided by discord and disagreements about policies and strategies among the Taiping leaders. Since the Taiping membership was diverse, differences regarding policies and beliefs had surfaced early on. As Taiping leadership's infighting began to widen, the Qing empire's officials in central China were finally able to mobilize enough support to destroy the Taiping in 1864. Eventually the imperial army conquered Nanjing in a violent, bloody massacre.

The Taiping civil war had devastated China for about fourteen years. The part of the country south of the Yangzi or Jiangnan, China's economic center, was hit hardest. The damage to human lives and property was staggering. Total lives lost have been estimated from twenty or thirty million at the low end, to perhaps seventy million at the high end. Contemporary accounts by Chinese and westerners describe extraordinary destruction across a huge area, which left the remaining rural populations devastated by poverty and misery. Suspicions that people had already harbored about the Qing's capacity and strength were therefore reinforced. And the price paid for this victory by the court was heavy. The local militias that bore the brunt of the fighting, led by Chinese officers and assisted by the western powers, did not disband after defeating the Taiping. In fact, they subsequently assumed an even greater role in maintaining order. The government was even compelled to permit them to retain the tax on goods passing through their domains *(lijin)*. Hence, while the ruling dynasty eventually managed to suppress what had been, up to that point, the gravest challenge to its rule, and to restore basic order to the heartland, it had difficulty keeping rivals and new rebels in check along its far-flung borders. The uprisings roiling China proper not only inspired followers on the periphery, they also presented the diverse populations in the borderlands, who had long aspired to greater autonomy, with a unique opportunity to pursue their goals. For them, it was now or never.

The Erosion of Qing Control over the Borderlands

Various rebel forces emerged in China's distant and unruly border regions in the north, west, and southwest, all of which areas were at least partly, if not predominantly, inhabited by ethnically diverse groups and Muslims. The fact that China had direct control over these northwestern frontiers, versus mere political influence or a tributary relationship, dated back to the eighteenth century. The name Xinjiang (New Frontier) for the Central Asian province was probably used for the first time in 1768.[67] After the devastation caused by the eighteenth-century conquest of Xinjiang, the Qing's policy was to avoid interfering in the practices and religions of the indigenous population. Instead, the court tried to rule as far as possible through existing political and religious structures. A complex and hierarchical native, civil, and religious bureaucracy evolved in which the *begs* (rulers) and *akhunds* (spiritual leaders) controlled their villages or towns formally in the name of the Qing emperor but by means of Islamic law. Although the region was heavily garrisoned, Qing control of Xinjiang also depended on merchants from China to help supply the Qing military garrisons, and a complex relationship emerged between the Han Chinese, Hui Muslim (Chinese Muslims), and local Uyghur traders.

The Qing dynasty's military administration encountered constant political and religious resistance, however, to its control of Xinjiang. The revolts received support from Islamic groups in the Central Asian khanate of Khoqand, a Muslim Turkic state that existed from 1709 to 1876 within the territory of today's Kyrgyzstan, eastern Uzbekistan and Tajikistan, and southeastern Kazakhstan. Islamic religious leaders were increasingly drawn to so-called New Teaching, based on the Sufi order of Islam. The spread of Sufism, a mystical version of Islam inviting Muslims to find the truth of divine love and knowledge through direct personal experience of God, had the profound effect of galvanizing the Muslim population against Qing rule. Despite its long-standing policy of noninterference in religious issues, the Qing court clearly saw the political challenge to its rule presented by the dissemination of New Teaching. Labeling it a heterodox sect, the Qing court tried to subdue it. This resulted in a number of violent upheavals in 1781, 1815, 1820, and 1847, and in each case, regaining control over the region took the Qing several years. Aside from religious reasons, the neighboring khanate of Khoqand backed the rebels because its merchants, who profited from illegal northwestern border trading in Chinese tea and rhubarb, resented Qing restrictions and taxes on commerce.

Muslim rebellions also occurred in other parts of western and southwestern China—above all, in Yunnan, Shaanxi, and Gansu. They mostly originated from local conflicts between the Chinese and Chinese Muslims in those provinces. Yunnan had also been plagued by growing tensions between Muslims and Chinese since 1821. A dispute between Chinese and Muslim miners in central Yunnan triggered a larger confrontation in 1855, which provoked the persecution and slaughter of Muslims in and around the provincial capital, Kunming, in April 1856. This caused a widespread revolt of Muslims in Yunnan, which lasted until 1873. Lack of unified leadership weakened the Muslim rebellion, and the unrest was brought to an end, partly through the Qing policy of pitting the rebel leaders against one another. In Shaanxi, small disturbances had been seen as early as the Qianlong reign. When government officials sided with the Chinese, the Muslims started to rise up against both the Chinese and the authorities. The unrest quickly spread throughout the entire region, involving both Chinese Muslims and Turkic Muslims. The first full-scale military confrontation with Qing troops, often identified as the beginning of the northwest Muslim rebellion (1862), occurred when Muslim militias laid siege to the city of Xi'an. The siege continued for over a year. Zuo Zongtang (1812–1885), a former protégé of Zeng Guofan, was ordered to Shaanxi with a part of the Huai Army (the Qing dynasty military force that had defeated the Taiping Rebellion in 1864. His troops initiated irrigation projects, dug wells, planted trees, built roads and bridges, and promoted silk and cotton production.[68] In the late 1860s, after economic reconstruction had begun to revive the northwestern economies, he moved his troops forward and succeeded in restoring Qing rule there in 1873.

The revolts inspired other ethnic and language groups to follow suit. Beyond religion, the Chinese empire had a wide array of different languages and ethnic groups who often could not be clearly distinguished. Nonetheless, over the centuries, they had developed strong communal ties and their own identities. The Miao settling in West Hunan and spreading over the Guizhou and Sichuan borders were a population of several hundred thousand who practiced settled agriculture. They had established close family links by intermarrying, and shared a set of distinctive religious and social customs including worshipping the White Emperor Heavenly Kings *(baidi tianwang)* and using an informal oath-taking legal system. Han migration into the impoverished and neglected areas had long caused disputes about access to land, water, forests, and other resources. Those conflicts eventually led to a large anti-Qing uprising in Guizhou in 1854–1873, when the Miao rose up together with other disgruntled and disadvantaged groups. The revolt was eventually suppressed by military force.

These conflicts exposed late Qing vulnerabilities at the far-flung frontier areas of the empire, which not only domestic rebels but also foreign powers sought to exploit. In the north, Tsarist Russia's expansion into Central Asia further complicated the Qing campaigns against rebels in the northwest. In the eighteenth century, khanates in Central Asia had prevented Russia from annexing the traditional heartland of the old Silk Roads. Their merchants, particularly those from Bukhara (today's Uzbekistan), had controlled commerce and often excluded Russian traders. The Russian government, pressured to compete with British expansion and to act on behalf of its commercial interests, gradually turned its attention to the region starting in the 1830s.[69] Facing only fragmented opposition, Russia targeted one khanate after another. By 1873, Russia had brought the region under its control. In fact, by closing borders, severely restricting international trade, and eliminating all significant Central Asian polities, Russia and China destroyed the Silk Road economies in Central Asia. Both the domestic Chinese component of the Silk Road economy and its long-distance component were thus largely put out of business. The direct result was the severe decline of Central Asia, and its long-term slide into poverty, backwardness, and relative isolation.[70]

Russian merchants now had access, on equal footing, to Central Asian trade. The original economic objectives of expansion had been to increase commerce and incorporate additional territory, but a new motive developed due to the US Civil War. Russia had been buying most of its cotton from the United States, but the North's blockade of international trade with the South had temporarily shut off supplies. Russia's newly acquired lands in central Asia seemed ideal for growing cotton that could substitute for the United States' product. As Russia became increasingly drawn into central Asia, it also developed a greater interest in the adjacent region of Xinjiang. China's weakness, as demonstrated in the rebellions and lost opium wars, prompted Russia to capitalize on Muslim rebellions. The Qing permitted Russia to trade and station consuls in the town of Kashgar along the old Silk Road, yet denied those privileges to other foreign powers. Russian traders arrived in Xinjiang, as did geographers, adventurers, explorers, and natural scientists. Russia accumulated a wealth of information, including maps and descriptions of critical locations in Xinjiang. Asserting that the Muslim revolts in China's far west threatened to affect its central Asian possessions, in 1871 the tsarist government sent troops to occupy Ili, in northern Xinjiang, declaring that it would withdraw once the Qing restored order. Lacking any means to forestall the Russians, the Qing had no choice but to accept their takeover of Ili.

From 1874 to 1875, the Qing government discussed the status of Xinjiang.[71] The fate of Xinjiang was debated by Zuo Zongtang (1812–1885) and Li Hongzhang, governor-general of Zhili at the time. Zuo's Zongtang's success in the northwest had not only been hard won, but required a constant struggle for funds, men, and resources. At the same time, the Japanese invasion of Taiwan in 1874 had demonstrated to the court the ongoing weakness of Qing maritime defenses. Li Hongzhang argued against the recovery of Xinjiang on the grounds that the court needed to focus its limited resources on coastal defense. Retaking Xinjiang would not be worth the massive expense, as it would always be an unruly trouble spot with barren land that offered little economic perspective. Zuo countered that the security of the entire north of China, including Beijing, depended on the retention of Xinjiang. Xinjiang remained in his eyes a vital imperial possession, valued at first as a strategic buffer zone, but increasingly as an integral part of China, despite its remoteness and worsening poverty. He also believed that, with proper policies, Xinjiang could be developed. In the end, the campaign to regain Xinjiang was approved. Zuo continued his strategy to complement military action with efforts to revive local economies to win over the local population. After lengthy preparations, he marched into Xinjiang in 1876 and quickly captured the town of Urumchi, which had become the most important center in the region. By the following year, he restored Qing control over nearly all of Xinjiang. Within a year, much of the north had been retaken and Zuo's troops were heading south. With the fall of Kashgar and Khotan in early 1878, the Qing reconquest was complete, with the exception of the Ili region, which remained under Russian control. The Qing court started negotiations with Russia that were concluded with the Treaty of Petersburg in 1881. Thereafter, Ili was returned to the Qing empire. A war had been averted and Qing China had, for a time, secured its central Asian province. Even when weakened, the Qing empire had also demonstrated that it could still be a formidable opponent for any enemy, domestic or foreign.

Many western accounts, with their focus on the British treaty system, tend to underestimate the complexity and significance of Russia's land-based imperial presence along China's borders. Russia participated in the semi-colonial order along the coast, but parallel to that, it also expanded forcefully over land. Overall, the Tsarist empire after 1855 extended control over the immense stretches and swaths of Turkestan and Siberia. The Tsars also terminated the independent Central Asian Islamic emirates of Bukhara and Chiva. They successfully took control of the Silk Road economies. Toward the end of the nineteenth century, Russia came to share a huge transcontinental border with Qing China. Russia also started to build the ambitious Trans-Siberian Railway to connect the Far East to the imperial center and integrate the vast Siberian stretches.[72] Along the Russian-Chinese border, trade boomed, but imperial rivalries persisted. Overall, the Qing court had to witness the formation of a major threat from the west and the north as well as an erosion of its power—but at the same time, it responded with vigor and demonstrated resilience. Unlike the multiple setbacks on the coast, along the transcontinental border, the Qing court held its own. This in fact, gave the Qing dynasty a boost and allowed it to better manage the disadvantages of the semi-colonial situation.

Even though the Qing government had successfully and with great effort quelled the threatening rebellions in many parts of China in the second half of the nineteenth century, the long-term consequences were even more difficult to deal with. One of the most important consequences was what historians have called a "devolution" in power from the center to the regions.[73] In the post-Taiping era, the Qing granted provincial and local authorities unprecedented rights to collect taxes for their military campaigns, as well as the right to serve in their own districts. The introduction of the *lijin* tax, placed on goods passing through their domains, gave provincial governments access to a source of funding of their own to sponsor local militias. Even as the bureaucracy was restored to order, the central government was never able to fully recover those rights. Society was more militarized than before, and families with mixed commercial and land interests made sure they dominated local militias. Militarization was particularly evident in peripheral and frontier areas. Regional military regimes, which were crucial for defeating the Taiping, continued to thrive and proliferate, becoming the de facto rulers in many parts of China. The professionalization and accelerated growth of regional military regimes, however, did not deter the growth of sectarian activism, the politicization of brotherhood societies, and the explosive growth of violent state-resisting protests. Some brotherhood associations were long active in South China and overseas Chinese communities. Such communities included the Tiandihui, which ignited the Lin Shuangwen Rebellion in Taiwan of 1785–1788 and lent major support to Sun Yat-sen's Republican revolutionary movement in the late nineteenth and early twentieth centuries. These secret societies later provided the revolution with manpower as well as financial and organizational support.

Perhaps even more dangerous for the Qing throne was the growth of anti-Manchu sentiment. Gradually, popular perception, as well as the view of elites, was that the Manchu rulers had lost the Mandate of Heaven and that new Chinese rulers were about to emerge, as many of the rebels claimed. This perception emboldened many discontented groups to opt for open revolt—a path that had rarely been taken before the 1830s. The rebellions had therefore permanently weakened the Qing by throwing into question the legitimacy of Manchu rulers, by pushing militarization, by prompting local elites to adopt new strategies of survival, and by increasing the intervention of foreign powers. For all these reasons, the mid-century uprisings accelerated the erosion of Qing control and the growth of an anti-Manchu nationalism that would precipitate the dynasty's downfall in 1911.

THREE

Late Qing Predicaments

1870–1900

During the last quarter of the nineteenth century, the court faced seemingly intractable problems on many fronts. Uprisings, economic depression, environmental degradations, and foreign threats made reform of the empire's institutions imperative. Chinese attitudes toward the respected Confucian tradition were challenged. China's thinkers and officials had to respond to crises originating from the twin challenges of domestic disorder and foreign intrusion. They embarked on efforts at careful institutional reform that aimed at selective transfers and learning from the West. The adoption of military technology, and of applied sciences such as engineering, was seen as particularly important to strengthen the empire and restore its vitality.

After the second Opium War and the suppression of the Taiping Rebellion, a period of relative stability and peaceful foreign relations ensued. It was a period that favored policies focused on reform and self-strengthening of institutions. The Qing dynasty seriously attempted but was ultimately unsuccessful in remaking itself into a more effective state. Despite ambitious intellectual and political efforts, the empire's decline accelerated. Toward the end of the nineteenth century, a new series of military conflicts interrupted reform efforts and demanded full attention. To the court's disbelief and shock, the Qing military squarely lost every battle—despite its costly acquisition of new armaments and technologies. China reached its lowest point in modern history in 1900 when an international expedition force marched on Beijing on a punitive expedition to suppress the Boxer uprising and occupied the imperial palace, driving the court into exile at Xi'an.

Cherry-Picking and Self-Strengthening

With the rapid loss of social and political control, a sense of crisis began brewing in intellectual and political circles. The recognition that something was deeply wrong not only beset the court and officials, but gradually also spread throughout China's intellectual circles. Although there was initially little understanding of the specific economic, demographic, or structural problems responsible for China's crisis, the probing and wide-ranging search for answers led to remarkable changes in intellectuals' thinking and scholarship, and initial attempts to reform the empire's institutions. It was understood at the time that the causes were both external and internal. Partly to blame were homegrown problems—specifically, departures from the enlightened political norms and ideals of antiquity, including the practice of remonstrance. Another factor, however, was the challenge of western imperialism. Chinese thinkers were aware that they confronted a new world of social changes brought about by new technologies (such as steam engines in boats and trains, newspapers, and telegraphic communication) and new social and economic practices presented by Europeans in treaty-port society from Guangzhou to Tianjin. Nineteenth-century intellectual thinking did not merely or even primarily consist of reactions and defensive responses to the West. It engaged with much older questions of how to come to terms with and understand China's own rich cultural tradition in light of changed circumstances. Those debates informed and shaped how the late Qing intellectual and political scene grappled with the dawn of a new era. Specifically, the debates should be traced back to the eighteenth century, a time before the onslaught of the West. This earlier instance of Qing scholarship's going through a significant and irreversible transition in Chinese intellectual history provided the basis for later Chinese thinkers' efforts to understand and explain the nineteenth-century crisis.[1]

The social and intellectual community of Qing scholars was increasingly devoted to the exact study of textual problems, as epitomized in the work of Dai Zhen (1724–1777)—a polymath and philosopher who, however, never passed the highest level of civil service examinations in the capital. The revolution in scholarly discourse that took place during this time was based on the philological tradition of evidential research (*kaozheng xue*, or "investigations based on evidence") that could, as we have seen earlier, be dated back to the seventeenth century and had a lasting influence still in the nineteenth century. According to Benjamin Elman, it was "a mode of empirical scholarship that sanctioned new, precise methods by which to understand the past and conceptualize the present. As a style of scholarly method and representation, evidential studies marked the beginning of an unprecedented strategy for research."[2] Thinkers in the *kaozheng* tradition were more interested in verifiable facts than in the abstract speculations and discussions of philosophical concepts related to cosmological correspondence that abounded in the neo-Confucian idealist tradition of thinking. The emphasis on hands-on empirical study and meticulous philological investigation led to a new focus on textual authenticity—and, in turn, to a renewed interest in the tools of textual analysis. Scholars in the movement were deeply engaged in such concrete subjects as textual criticism, historical linguistics, classical studies, historical research, mathematical astronomy, and historical geography, and in refining tools of investigation and auxiliary disciplines such as epigraphy, bibliography, and collation of texts.

Kaozheng learning stressed not only the value of empirical evidence, but also the need to identify, extract, and validate that evidence through careful research. As scholars and critics began to apply textual analysis to the Confucian classics, it followed that they would seek the most ancient and most original sources in their desire to recover the undistorted meanings of the classical tradition. Commentary no longer focused mainly on the concepts and philosophical ideas in the texts, but instead took the form of detailed textual criticism and evidence-based arguments. The use of empirical criteria as an approach to discuss doctrine reveals the profound social and political implications inherent in this turn to philology. The empirical approach favored by Qing classicists, "to search truth from facts" (*shishi qiushi*—a slogan that would reappear and gain prominence in China in 1978), emphasized proof and verification as essential for the preservation and analysis of the classical tradition. Textual criticism, not philosophy, became the methodology to restore a more reliable image of the past and to access a more remote and original history of the creative possibilities of Confucian thinking than the orthodox and moralistic interpretations provided by neo-Confucianism.

Qing literati revolted against the abstract learning of the Song dynasty, choosing instead to go far back into history, to Han dynasty sources, to overcome the limitations or distortions they found in Song and Ming editions and commentaries. Because of this return to Han dynasty sources, this school was also called Han learning *(Hanxue)*. The return to antiquity *(fugu)* was part of an emerging secularism and a rise of critical consciousness that probed the neo-Confucian claims of unquestioned authority. Although the *kaozheng* movement itself weakened in the nineteenth century, it spawned a philosophic rebellion and prepared the ground for new social and political arguments.

Passionate debates erupted among the various schools, especially between the New Text and Old Text schools. The so-called New Text *(jinwen)* classics were versions recorded in clerical script *(lishu)* that had been in use during the early Han dynasty. During the middle of the second century BCE, however, pre-Han versions of the Confucian classics were discovered in buildings where Confucius had allegedly resided. These texts were written in the ancient script *(guwen)* of the Zhou dynasty. Following the discovery of the Old Texts, Chinese scholars debated the authenticity of, as well as the differences between, these texts and other versions, but after the Eastern Han dynasty, the New Texts more or less disappeared from the intellectual scene. Cast into long oblivion, New Text proponents did not reappear until the nineteenth century, when they focused mainly on the *Chunqiu*, or Spring and Autumn Annals—one of the Five Classics traditionally regarded as having been compiled by Confucius. This official chronicle of the State of Lu, covering the time from 722 to 481 BCE, is the earliest surviving Chinese historical text arranged in annalistic form. New Text scholars maintained that it was the key to exploring the Confucian teaching of the classics. And thus it followed for them that the Gongyang Commentary *(gongyang zhuan)*—rather than the Zuo Commentary *(zuo zhuan)* favored by the Old Text school *(guwen jingxue)* and most evidential scholars—offered the best and most reliable basis for understanding the original vision of history supposedly discernible in Confucius's editing of the Chunqiu.

These issues might sound purely academic, but New Text scholarship during the late Qing dynasty had a practical and political purpose. Above all, it tried to revive the political activism of the Western Han dynasty (206 BCE– 8 CE).[3] It offered a new view on the Confucian tradition as a useful resource for solving the pressing issues associated with the western intrusion. Moreover, New Text philology was highly critical of what were considered bookish textual studies and helped to revive an interest in statecraft *(jingshi)*. New Text scholars began to refute the orthodox doctrine set forth by scholars in the neo-Confucian tradition by arguing that the Old Text sources on which it was based had been forged by scholars during the reign of Wang Mang (45 BC–23 AD). Wang, one of the most controversial of China's emperors, had seized the throne for himself and his usurpation had marked the end of the former Han dynasty. Supplanting the Han, he had proclaimed the Xin "new" dynasty and instructed scholars to make changes to Confucian texts and sources. New Text scholars claimed to have unearthed hidden, original versions of sources which would bring new legitimacy to oppressed lines of thinking. New Text studies played an important role in the steady drift toward new forms of political discourse. The arguments these scholars called orthodox and corrupted, and worked to replace, had been used since the Yuan-Ming transition in the fourteenth century to justify a highly autocratic form of government. Insisting that new ideas were needed in a time of political, social, and economic turmoil, New Text scholars championed pragmatism and the value of political activism and reform. They promoted the traditional pattern of Confucian reform, but adopted increasingly radical positions and, as the nineteenth century approached its end, called for sweeping changes.

Many literati realized that the institutions of the imperial system were no longer adequate and efficient and that changing historical conditions required new institutional solutions. Even before the Opium Wars, some came to believe that if the Chinese empire hoped to cope with its problems, fundamental changes were unavoidable. To "accord with the times" became the slogan of a generation of statecraft (*jingshi*) scholars who during the early nineteenth century sought pragmatic solutions to China's growing crises. Wei Yuan (1794–1857) and Feng Guifen (1809–1874) were among the most influential thinkers of the statecraft school. Their point of reference was a golden age in pre-Qin antiquity, mediated through writings on political reform by Gu Yanwu (1613–1682). Like other scholars of the nineteenth century, they shared a great admiration for the seventeenth-century thinker. As a token of their recognition, a group of statecraft scholars, including Wei and Feng, erected a temple in Beijing in the 1830s to commemorate Gu. The members of the statecraft school shared an intellectual outlook that concerned itself with problems of social order and an institutional approach to order. This goal led statecraft scholars to secure social order through the reform of government institutions. Their concern with order was different from that of orthodox neo-Confucianists, who generally conceived of order in moral and spiritual terms. Although statecraft thinkers maintained that moral knowledge should and did remain at the core of civilization, such scholars were prepared to concede that new and other types of knowledge were worth studying, even when they were not based on moral principles. They took a piecemeal approach to the technocratic and institutional innovation needed to improve the workings of the bureaucratic apparatus. By using coercive and managerial institutions instead of exclusively relying on self-cultivation and moral exhortation, they tried to achieve a better and more efficient government of society and a more stable social order.

Wei Yuan, a scholar and official, played a prominent role in the critical review of Qing governing institutions and scholarship in the first half of the nineteenth century.[4] He worked with a prestigious circle of scholars, advisers, and officials serving the governor-general of Liangjiang provinces.[5] The group sought to adjust Qing governing institutions to cope with the new challenges. Wei Yuan and his collaborators compiled an important collection entitled "Essays on Qing Imperial Statecraft" (*Huangchao jingshi wenbian*, 1826), which offered information and practical perspectives on issues of government administration and innovation. In 1844, Wei published his best-known work, the "Illustrated Gazetteer of the Countries Overseas" *(Haiguo tuzhi),* on the geography and material conditions of foreign nations. This work was the first to make use of translations from western sources to warn about the growth of western commercial and naval power in maritime Asia and to argue for the reassertion of Chinese control over this region to counter increasing western influence. The work brought a wealth of new information about world geography and the global dimensions of western power to its readers. Most significant was its geopolitical analysis of China's historic ties with Southeast Asia, and its calls to reorient the Qing strategic vision to take account of global maritime trade and western power. Wei also concluded that it was the West's more advanced military technology that allowed it to overcome China. He therefore stressed the foreign-policy implication that China must bolster its military capabilities: "Before the peace settlement [of the first Opium War], it behooves us to use barbarians against barbarians. After the peace, it is proper for us to learn their superior techniques in order to control them."[6] Wei Yuan proposed that the Qing empire actively work to transfer elements of western technology and thereby become strong enough to deal actively with European states. He outlined a detailed plan for maritime defense which included "building ships, making weapons, and learning the superior techniques of the barbarians." The overarching goal of his reform agenda was to revive the greatness of the Chinese empire and to restore "wealth and power" *(fuqiang).*[7] Like many thinkers of his time, Wei Yuan was both a scholar and an influential official who served the dynasty and had the ear of its governors. His proposal would later become concrete policy.

In the decades that followed, other Chinese scholars went further than Wei, proposing not only the purchase and eventual production of western military technology, but also the establishment of translation offices and institutions where students could study western languages and subjects in addition to Chinese classics. Feng Guifen was one of the leaders of this effort.[8] Feng was a classically educated scholar who had a successful career as an official in his own right, and also served as an adviser to the leading Qing statesmen of the mid-nineteenth century. In the midst of the Taiping crisis and the second Opium War, when China again suffered defeat by European powers, Feng completed a collection of essays that gained the attention of his contemporaries and later generations. His forty "Essays of Protest from the Hut near Bin" *(Jiaobinlu kangyi),* with a preface dated November 1861, were sent to Zeng Guofan in 1862. But because of widespread hostility to his ideas, these writings were not published until much later. In his essays, Feng argued that the West's technological and military superiority came not only from steamships, firearms, and military training, but from more efficient institutions in four critical areas: education ("employing people's talents"), economy ("profiting from the land"), government ("keeping the rulers and people close"), and science ("calling things by their true names").[9] Feng concluded that China would have to implement ambitious reforms in all these areas to catch up with western countries. The way for China to strengthen itself *(ziqiang)* was to learn from the West, not only about technology and military strategy, but also about education, economy, government, and science. Beyond acquiring foreign weaponry, Feng insisted, the Chinese must manufacture, maintain, and employ new technology themselves.

In his essay "On the Adoption of Western Learning," Feng argued that China should learn from the West while retaining Chinese values. He wrote:

The principles of government are derived from learning. In discussing good government, the historian Sima Qian said, "Take the later kings as models," because they were closer to his own time, and customs, having changed, were more alike, so that their ideas were easy to implement because they were plain and simple. In my humble opinion, at the present time, it is also appropriate to say "Learn from the various nations," for they are similar to us and hence their ways are easy to implement. What could be better than to take Chinese ethical principles of human relations and Confucian teachings as the foundation *(ti)*, and supplement them with the techniques *(yong)* of wealth and power of the various nations?[10]

This approach came to be known as "self-strengthening" *(ziqiang)* and its primary goal was to maintain the essence or the core of Chinese civilization while adding superior knowledge and technology from abroad.

Western learning as a movement intended to facilitate selective borrowing from the West. It called for the introduction of western thought to strengthen Qing institutions. While the approach aimed to reform the overall institutional structure, it was also evident that it could lead to questioning single institutions. Interestingly, the one institution especially singled out for scathing criticism was the one that in many ways worked best. Many late Qing thinkers were convinced that the examination system was to blame for the troubles that befell the Qing empire. Feng wrote: "Our nation's emphasis on civil service examinations has sunk deep into people's minds. Intelligent and brilliant scholars have exhausted their time and energy in such useless things as the stereo-typed examination essays, examination papers, and formal calligraphy. . . . We should now order one-half of them to apply themselves to the manufacturing of instruments and weapons and to the promotion of physical studies."[11] Feng advocated abolishing the examinations and replacing them with elections, believing public opinion was a better gauge of civil servants' worthiness than any examination.

The Qing court was slow to pick up those proposals, and change came only gradually to some central institutions and policies. To the extent that the Qing court responded to crises confronting China, basically the same pragmatic approach and mode of thinking prevailed that the court had long applied to tackling domestic problems of statecraft. This changed around 1870. The long and bloody campaigns to subdue the mid-century rebellions convinced Zeng

Guofan, Li Hongzhang, Zuo Zongtang, and other leading officials in affected provinces that China needed to make bolder and more far-reaching steps. The fact that Qing China had lost the second of the Opium Wars (1856–1860) also deepened the sense of crisis in the country. The Qing thus needed to make more serious, ambitious efforts to acquire advanced western knowledge and technology to shore up the Confucian order. Witnessing the advanced military weaponry and technology during the westerners' cooperation in the battle against the Taiping further heightened officials' determination after 1870 to undertake broad and, if necessary, costly self-strengthening efforts.

The goal of self-strengthening was to restore the Qing dynasty to its original, robust stability and prosperity by adopting a broad range of western techniques and technologies, revitalizing orthodox Confucian ideology, reconstructing the traditional low-tax fiscal regime, and reforming regular civil-service examinations. Much later, in 1898, the intellectual premise behind self-strengthening was summarized by Zhang Zhidong's famous phrase, "Chinese learning as substance, western learning as function" *(zhongxue wei ti, xixue wei yong),* also known as the *ti-yong* formula. *Function* meant the functional applications and useful instruments that should be derived from western learning, while *substance* referred to ethical order and the central bonds between a ruler and his subjects, or between a father and his sons within Confucian teachings.

In the ensuing period of recovery and reconstruction known as the Qing Restoration, Zeng Guofan, governor-general of the Liangjiang provinces, played a leading role.[12] Early in his life he was greatly influenced by the Cheng-Zhu school of neo-Confucianism. He tried to give life to old ideas mainly by infusing them with moral idealism. Zeng firmly believed in the importance of moral leadership for the creation of an exemplary center. Moral idealism, however, was only a part of his formula. Zeng added the new dimension of interest in pragmatic statecraft to his philosophy. This is seen most clearly in his emphasis on *li* (propriety, rites) as the guiding precept in Confucian statesmanship. Zeng's concept of *li,* influenced by the School of Han Learning or the New Text movement, was very broad, referring in his thought not only to moral and ritual propriety, but also to devices of statecraft. Zeng was thus willing to use both moral and institutional power to achieve order. What is perhaps more important is that, as Zeng and other proponents felt compelled to use western technology to defend the values at China's core, they needed a clearer notion of what that core was—and a vigorous policy to popularize that core among the Chinese population. The unrest affecting many parts of the country had led Zeng to believe that the central values and practices (rites) of the Chinese civilization were no longer being observed. In response, traditional learning and values needed to be revived and promoted by, for example, having official printing offices publish the classics and histories. Those who lacked education, Zeng realized, could be instructed with songs. At one point during the Taiping war, he composed a song titled "Love the People" to teach his military men how to behave while on campaigns.[13]

Zeng was a famously strict father. His "Family Letters and Family Instructions" were first published in 1879. Filled with advice and moral exhortations, they reveal his sincere belief in Confucian ethics and moral self-cultivation. As head of the family, he urged his family members, especially his younger brothers and sons, to be obedient, selfless, loyal, dutiful, self-disciplined, and diligent. He appealed to his male family members to withstand the seductions of laziness and leisure and to stay focused on collective goals and values. Conservatism is perhaps a necessary part of any restoration, and Zeng's influence helped to bring Chinese conservatism into full swing during the Qing restoration—indeed, he became an icon of modern Chinese conservatism. Zeng Guofan's "Family Instructions" is one of the most printed books in modern China.[14]

The idea of self-strengthening provided the rationale for the broad reforms the Chinese state attempted in the 1870s, when its leaders intended to systematically introduce western devices and technology into China. Leaders sought to adopt the best of western technology, particularly armaments, to the service and preservation of the Qing dynasty. They drew from the practical "statecraft" (jingshi) traditions to adapt selected bits of western models and techniques to strengthen national defense, infrastructure, and industry, as well as to gradually reform state institutions. But the policy was not met by unanimous support. Some scholars were opposed to westernization and proposed a more fundamentalist approach refocusing on Confucian family values and a rejection of foreign innovations.

An important focus of institutional reform was the need to solve the government's chronic budget deficits. The likin (lijin) tax, originally levied on internal trade to help fund the anti-Taiping effort, became a regular and important component of China's fiscal system, which provided funding to some self-strengthening policies. There were also new taxes on seaborne international trade being collected by the foreign-administered Imperial Maritime Customs (although most of these revenues went to foreign nations as war reparations). The land tax was still the major tax, but it amounted to no more than 2 percent of China's gross domestic product (GDP) at the time. In the mid-nineteenth century, the land tax had contributed about 77 percent to the overall revenue, but by the end of the century it generated just 35–40 percent of officially recorded revenue.[15] Even under fiscal pressure, however, the Qing state refused to change its policy of light direct taxation on agricultural production. Since 1713, there had been a freeze of the land tax. It was the *lijin* system, then, that became more important in restructuring the Chinese fiscal regime. By the end of the century, *lijin* tax payments made up 15–19 percent of all revenues, and levies from maritime customs fluctuated between 11 and 17 percent; together, these taxes from domestic and international trade made up more than a third of revenues. The considerable increase in state revenue, however, did not necessarily improve the central government's fiscal situation. Commercial taxation and the *lijin* had essentially become local revenue after the 1860s, part of the ongoing process of fiscal as well as political decentralization.

Aided by newly acquired fiscal resources, regional leaders such as Li Hongzhang (1823–1901) and Zhang Zhidong (1837–1909) sponsored a small number of western-style, capital-intensive enterprises which were financed by the state and, under the direction of officials, managed by merchants. Those enterprises operated by and large under a scheme known as *guandu shangban* (official supervision and merchant management).[16] That specifically meant that management was shared between the government and merchants, and investment capital was raised through either selling shares to private investors or procuring government loans. Although these enterprises, which included shipping companies, arsenals, factories, and shipyards, were fraught with inefficiency and corruption, they did have their successes.[17] Attention was particularly directed to naval and military development. The Jiangnan Arsenal in Shanghai and the Jinling Arsenal in Nanjing were both established in 1865, followed by the Navy Yard at Mawei, near Fuzhou, in 1866. When Japanese visitors came in 1873, they were impressed by the Jiangnan Arsenal; this was during the time when Japanese reformers initially relied on Chinese translations of European scientific treatises.[18] Output was disappointing,

3.1. Harbor, shipyard, and factory buildings of the Fuzhou or Mawei Arsenal, c. 1867–1871.
Canadian Center for Architecture, distributed under a CC BY-SA 3.0 license

however. The shipyard at Fuzhou, for example, built only fifteen vessels before it was almost entirely destroyed by French forces in 1884, during the Sino-French War of 1883–1885. Other enterprises founded under *guandu shangban* arrangements included the China Merchant Steamship Company (1873), the Shanghai Cotton Cloth Mill (1878), and the Kaiping Mines (1877)—all of which deployed technology acquired from the West. China's Hanyang Ironworks in Hubei, on the Yangzi, began production in 1894, seven years ahead of Japan's Yawata complex. Initiatives like these gave rise to regional military-industrial complexes under provincial governors. Governor-General Li Hongzhang's purview, for example, included arsenals, a shipping company, the Kaiping and other mines, China's telegraph system, and a monopoly on cotton spinning. Another complex, built under the guidance of Governor-General Zhang Zhidong, consisted of the Daye Iron Mine, the Pingxiang Coal Mine, and the above-mentioned Hanyang Ironworks.

The impact of the new industrial policies came not only from their direct applications and military purposes, but also from the western knowledge and techniques introduced through the many educational facilities attached to the

arsenals.[19] In 1867, the Qing court established the Academy of Naval Administration *(chuanzheng xuetang)* in Mawei harbor in Fuzhou. In 1868, the
Jiangnan Arsenal added a school for translators to the training for modern
engineers it had established. In 1880, Zhili's Governor-General Li Hongzhang
established the Tianjin Naval Academy. Many military academies and specialized training schools were subsequently set up in other places around the
country, all in the interests of "employing the best technology of the barbarians to defeat the barbarians." Military academies, especially naval academies,
began to offer instruction in modern mathematics, mechanical engineering,
physics, geography, and so on, thus offering another powerful channel for
"new learning." All these count as side effects, but they gradually resulted in
significant institutional innovations.

Some of these new companies carried out quite amazing feats of reverse
engineering to understand and produce foreign machinery. Yet they found it
hard to compete against western-owned shipping concerns and imports.
Overall, the industrial sector of the Chinese economy was dominated not by
private entrepreneurs but rather by a system of bureaucratic capitalism.[20] In
this style of management, officials authorized, planned, and oversaw projects,
while day-to-day management was left in the hands of private merchants and
local elites, who also provided most of the financing. In most cases, investment

and risk were shared by the public and private sectors, with officials—or, more precisely, members of officials' staffs—setting policy. This tended to obscure the locus of decision-making and responsibility, allowing business to be burdened by political patronage, local loyalties, and corruption. Moreover, government-appointed sponsors tended to use the enterprises as bases for their regional power. The central government was not only unable to supply capital but, given its own budget problems, also looked for ways to extract resources from the enterprises, just as it had profited from the salt trade. Under such circumstances, the enterprises never fully developed, and often slid into decline after initial years of investment.

The China Merchants Steamship Company (CMSC) deserves a closer look as a well-researched example illustrating the financial and political challenges facing these early efforts—and also their significance.[21] With the opening of the Suez Canal in 1869, which halved the travel time between China and Europe, steamships revolutionized China's shipping business. Some leading western firms had begun to form joint-stock steamship companies, with much of their capital raised from Chinese investors, in the early 1860s. The CMSC was established to counter the dominance of foreign steamship lines in the highly lucrative coastal freight service and to make sure that investments and profits would benefit Chinese, not only foreigners. The CMSC was probably the first Chinese joint-stock company sponsored by the Chinese state. As with all firms operating under the *guandu shangban* scheme, management was shared between the Qing government and merchants. Even though the company was government-sponsored, it was owned and administered privately by risk-taking shareholders. Most of the capital was raised through sales of shares, although this was difficult in the beginning. While considerable Chinese investment went into western shipping companies, Chinese merchants initially hesitated to purchase shares of Chinese companies. This changed, in the case of CMSC, when the joint-stock enterprise was reorganized under the management of two merchants (compradors), Tang Jingxing (1832–1892) and Xu Run (1838–1911), who served as actual managers from 1873 to 1885. Tang and Xu were also the largest shareholders. During their time, share capital increased, reaching one million taels by 1880 and two million by 1882. Yet the CMSC had to rely on government loans to supplement merchant capital.

3.2. Compradors, likely Tang Jingxing and Xu Run, c. 1875–1880s.
Private collection, photo © Christie's Images / Bridgeman Images

CMSC acquired a fleet of thirty vessels and soon had the highest tonnage among steamship companies in China. It had the considerable advantage of being the only Chinese-owned shipping company permitted by the imperial government. Beyond giving it assured business through government contracts to transport tribute rice, this meant it had access to government loans and enjoyed preferential treatment in the acquisition of real estate and the payment of fees and transit dues. Between 1878 and 1883, the company purchased nine new ships and extended its operations beyond Chinese waters to the United States, Japan, and Southeast Asia. But the financial panic of

1883 in Shanghai drastically altered the company's fortunes by damaging its capital base. The government also compelled CMSC to divert valuable resources to prop up the navy for the imminent wars (as will be discussed below). At the same time, management was embattled for other reasons. The merchant directors, who suffered heavy losses in the financial crisis, were accused of misappropriating funds for their own benefit. In 1885 they were replaced by Sheng Xuanhuai (1844–1916), who had been buying CMSC's shares and become the largest shareholder. During his directorship between 1885 and 1902, which he maintained from a distance having other tasks in the government, capital investment stagnated and the tonnage of the fleet remained constant, while competition by foreign steamship companies in Chinese waters rapidly intensified. Several new shipping companies entered the market, too, including the Nippon Yusen Kaisha (Japan Mail Line). Chinese merchants began losing confidence and turning their backs to the company. Without adequate management and private capital, the company steadily lost business and market share.

Compounding the problems were the compradors, those Chinese agents that foreign firms employed in the treaty ports to act as their links to Chinese commerce. Compradors were able to accumulate vast wealth from the new enterprises, but while they were active in supplying capital and managerial personnel to the enterprises, most lacked technical training and knowledge themselves. Many engaged in risky speculation and misappropriation of company resources. Embedded in exclusive communities with strong family, regional, and political ties, their focus was on those communities' concerns rather than national economic interests. These shortcomings impeded efforts to construct and maintain the new enterprises. In all cases, vested interests and patronage networks between officials and enterprises hampered economic development. Inevitably, CMSC and other *guandu shangban* enterprises all faced similar problems. Their intimate bond with the government was an asset but also a burden. They were charged with political and commercial missions that were contradictory and hard to reconcile.

But the self-strengthening endeavors were significant in another respect, in that shareholding quickly became an integral part of the Chinese business tradition.[22] This was an important and far-reaching institutional innovation, blazing the way for efficiently raising capital for business enterprises and for the emergence of a capital market for the trading of shares. Both, in turn, were important steps toward further developments of the economy. At the same time, this innovation from the West was modified. In the emerging Chinese shareholding structure, major shareholders were directly involved in the management of the company, and the government played a major role as a lender. Early shareholding arrangements therefore did not engender a division of ownership (public-private) and control, nor did they weaken the impact of the family or the government on ownership.

The Chinese efforts were ambitious, but effectively limited by an unwillingness to fundamentally change political processes and institutions. There was no effort to overhaul the empire's political system. There was no initiative to draft a modern constitution or commercial law, and no reform of the currency system. Railroads were not built in earnest until the late 1890s and the development of steamships was restricted and slow. Preoccupation with military and naval developments meant that reforms during the self-strengthening period were only piecemeal. Most limiting was the Qing restoration's inability to raise sufficient funds for the defense industry and for other modernization programs such as the building of railroads. The private sector was reluctant to invest, and the government had limited tax revenues. China's lack of government revenue was one of the main reasons that the Qing government failed to develop a successful broad industrialization and economic modernization. It made for a striking contrast with the government of Japan, which was able to raise revenue in excess of 10 percent of GDP, particularly in the late Tokugawa period, when the percentage was even higher. Overall, it was this lack of political leadership to carry out institutional reforms that kept the self-strengthening policies from achieving more.

That said, the Qing restoration and its emphasis on self-strengthening did succeed in creating a few success stories in business, especially in shipping. A feeble start at industrialization was made in some localities with the late Qing national defense industry. Shipbuilding and weapons factories in Jiangnan, Fujian, and Hubei, as small and problematic as they were, led the first phase of Chinese industrial production. While falling short of its initial grand plans and high hopes of restoring the dynasty to prosperity and power, self-strengthening in the late Qing nonetheless created early experiences of industrialization and limited examples of gradual institutional innovation, above all in business, upon which later generations could build.

China's Lost Wars

Western imperialism represented a novel military threat, completely unlike the land-based invasions China had traditionally fought at its northern frontier. Europe's growing projection of military power in East Asia undermined the economic, political, institutional, and ideological position of the Qing empire. Conflicts in the last quarter of the nineteenth century wrung several humiliating concessions from China, the tributary order collapsed, and Qing capacity to defend the borders declined. From another perspective, however, the turbulent period that began in the mid-nineteenth century illuminates the dynamics of the late Qing system, revealing not only its institutional overload and obstacles to change, but also its resilience as China avoided a complete breakup of the country.[23]

Some military conflicts were triggered by anti-Christian incidents. The violent opening of China led to a growing anti-foreign and anti-Christian movement concerned with China's loss of territorial rights and self-determination. This movement first emerged in the treaty ports, then spread to other cities throughout China and into the countryside. The central demand was that the government take a tougher stand vis-à-vis foreign demands, foreign intrusion, and foreign religious influences. The nineteenth-century mission movement in China began with Protestants, driven by the dynamism of the evangelical revival in Great Britain and the United States. Although Catholic missionary orders came later to China, their congregations grew much faster. As the treaties had permitted missionary work in treaty ports since the 1840s, Christian missions sprang up there and itinerant missionaries began traveling to most parts of the country. The Beijing Convention (1860) extended this privilege throughout the empire, granting the right to acquire property to build and run schools, hospitals, orphanages, and churches and to use them for any purposes that would promote the missionaries' goals. In 1900, there were approximately 1,400 foreign Catholic priests, monks, and nuns in China serving close to one million Catholics. Meanwhile, China's Protestant population numbered perhaps 250,000 and was served by more than 3,000 Protestant missionaries. Like all foreigners, missionaries enjoyed extraterritorial rights.

Despite Chinese resentment, both official and popular, of the Christian missions, they enabled rich cultural and educational interactions. Education and science, rather than religion itself, were advanced most by the missionary enterprise. Missionary work contributed to and inspired various reform efforts in China, including the introduction of western medicine, schools for girls, higher education, the anti-footbinding movement, and more.[24] Missionary activities challenged traditional beliefs, social customs, and the leadership role of the gentry, not to mention the authority of Chinese officials. Still, Christianity came to have a deep bearing, as some religious elements and cultural translations found their way into Chinese social institutions. While the Chinese, especially peasants in impoverished regions, were often open to missionary work and many converted to Christianity, the elites tended to associate missionaries with the exploitation of China and with the promotion of new technologies and ideas that threatened their positions. Most resented were the special benefits that missionaries arranged for Chinese converts to Christianity, which included both legal and extralegal privileges. These resulted in hard feelings toward both the missionaries and the Chinese Christians. Anti-missionary riots flared up from time to time after 1860. In the late 1860s, Chinese sentiments against Christians were inflamed by rumors that Chinese children were being killed by Europeans to make medicine, and that Christian orphanages were buying and selling Chinese children or using them for sacrifices. Such demonizing stories fanned the hostility toward Christianity and, in 1868, incited uprisings in Yangzhou (a new treaty port), including an incident of an enraged mob of thousands surrounding the British missionary headquarters. Similar rumors led to the Tianjin Massacre of 1870. The entire city was engulfed in days of rioting, causing the deaths of more than thirty Chinese Christians and twenty-one foreigners. The conflict led to a general decline in relations between the Chinese government and Christian missionaries. Another series of anti-Christian riots broke out along the Yangzi in the 1890s. As missionaries responded to this hostility, they altered their missionary objectives and methods by, for example, promoting medicines and forms of secular education that accommodated Chinese values.[25] Missionaries expanded the church in China in the late nineteenth century and introduced new institutional foundations, especially in education.

Despite the buildup of popular anti-Christian hostility inside China, the 1860s and 1870s were relatively peaceful with regard to China's foreign relations. But changes already underway would soon result in a series of wars which, taken together, constituted another heavy blow to the Qing empire.

3.3. An advertisement card for a French chocolate company depicts Christians worshipping in the Episcopal Chapel of Beijing. French chromolithograph.
Private collection, photo © Look and Learn / Barbara Loe Collection / Bridgeman Images / LLL3105593

By the 1870s, a new international order was emerging. Having witnessed the changes within China and the growing weakness of the Qing empire, China's neighbors gradually adjusted to the new reality—a world in which western powers rather than China dominated East Asia. More distant neighbors, such as Burma and Thailand, were quick to end their tribute relationships with the Qing as the Qing-dominated world order was superseded. Thailand sent its last tributary mission in 1853, and in 1882, Bangkok formally declared the end of its tribute relationship with the Qing. In Burma, China had to give ground to the British who wished to supplant its influence. Starting in 1852, Burma gradually lost its independence to Britain. In 1885, the British established a protectorate over Burma, and in 1886, Burma came under the rule of British India.

But even the countries that were culturally and geographically closer to China—Vietnam, the Ryukyu Islands, and Korea—realized that a new era had come and that they needed to rethink their alliances with China. In Vietnam, a country that had followed the Chinese model for centuries, China confronted a European power similar to the situation in Burma.[26] France was laying claim to China's Indochinese tributaries, such as Annam and Cambodia, and expanding its influence into Guangxi province. During the late Qing, the Nguyen dynasty (1802–1945) governed the country. The fact that it was a fragmented dynasty, however, facilitated the efforts of France to gain control of the country. French merchants, advisers, and missionaries began to arrive in Vietnam in the early nineteenth century. By the mid-1870s, France had forced Vietnam to sign treaties that allowed it to become the dominant power in South Vietnam and in modern Cambodia. Nationalists in North Vietnam turned against France, which responded by occupying both Hanoi and Haiphong in 1882. The Nguyen court appealed to the Qing for assistance. Li Hongzhang intended to avoid a conflict and find a solution to put on the negotiating table, but the Qing court overruled him and chose to go to war, believing that self-strengthening efforts had already bolstered the navy's military capabilities and created a more forceful fleet. This led to the Sino-French War (1884–1885). The new Qing navy was no match, however, for the French battleships, which approached Fuzhou on China's southeast coast and sank nine out of eleven Chinese vessels without losing a single one of their own. A peace agreement was signed, under which the Qing gave up its claim over Vietnam, which became part of French Indochina. After driving the Chinese forces out of Vietnam, the French commander attempted to enter Guangxi province, but a Qing counterattack in 1885 sent the invaders fleeing back to Hanoi. French Indochina was established on October 17, 1887, merging Annam, Tonkin, and Cochinchina (which together form modern Vietnam) with the Kingdom of Cambodia. Laos was later incorporated after the Franco-Siamese War in 1893. A piece of Chinese territory was later also added to French Indochina, however, which was called Guangzhouwan. It was a small enclave on the southern Chinese coast ceded by Qing China to France as a leased territory. Qing China had prevailed and defended its borders, but also suffered a diminishment of its influence in the region.

The most shocking loss in the series of foreign wars that punctuated the last two decades of the nineteenth century came in 1894 and 1895, when China was defeated on land and sea in a war with Japan—a war that began with a conflict over control of Korea.[27] Like China, Togukawa Japan had been facing growing internal economic and social troubles since 1853, when US Commodore Matthew Perry sailed into Edo Bay and triggered a public debate with his demand that Japan open its ports to American vessels. Japan, however, took a markedly different path than China. Japan negotiated persistently and then agreed to Perry's demands, signing the Treaty of Kanagawa in 1854, which opened two ports for the provisioning of ships (although not for trade) and permitted an exchange of diplomats. The final stages of the demise of the Tokugawa period began with the Meiji Restoration in January 1868, when a group of well-educated, ambitious young men seized the palace grounds and proclaimed a new government in the name of the fifteen-year-old emperor, Mutsuhito, who now was called the emperor Meiji. They replaced the shogun with a temporary council of princes. Shogun Tokugawa Yoshinobu paused briefly, then decided to submit to the new regime rather than throw Japan into civil war, and the young Meiji emperor became the figurehead of the new government. Japan eventually was made into a constitutional monarchy as Emperor Meiji promulgated a constitution, Asia's first, on February 11, 1889. It created a sovereign emperor who appointed the cabinet members and held final legislative power over everything but the budget. At the same time, it created a popularly elected legislature, the Diet, along with an independent judiciary, and it gave the Diet the crucial right to veto budgets. The new Meiji government put great effort into long-term plans to develop a modern army to replace the samurai class, to reform its education system, to abolish the rigid four-class structure of samurai, peasants, artisans, and merchants, and to emphasize a new form of nationalistic Shinto religion to legitimize their reforms. The Japanese also started an ambitious naval program intended to surpass similar programs of the Qing empire.

The new Meiji government wanted to bolster Japan's international position and to project its influence onto adjacent territories like the Liuqiu (Ryukyu) Islands, today part of Okinawa prefecture, and Korea. For almost three hundred years, the Ryukyu kings had been both tributaries of the Qing and subject to the rulers of the southern Japanese domain of Satsuma. In 1871, China's position on the islands was weakening: sailors from Liuqiu were shipwrecked on Taiwan and then killed by local Taiwanese. Japan demanded reparations from the Qing, which would have meant that the Qing recognized Japan as having sovereign rights over the Liuqiu Islands. When the Qing failed to respond, Japan announced that it had annexed Liuqiu (henceforth Ryukyu) and several thousand Japanese marines landed on Taiwan. Japan declared its sovereignty over the islands in 1872, stationed troops there in 1875, and in 1879 seized all of Ryukyu, overthrew the local ruling house, and transformed it into the Japanese prefecture of Okinawa. China's attempts at appealing to US and British mediators failed.

Japanese businesses also began to look for a foothold on the East Asian mainland for the supply of coal, iron, wheat, and labor. The same expansionist groups who proposed that Japan take over the Liuqiu Islands also argued for an aggressive policy toward Korea. Following the model set by European powers in China, Japan forced Korea in 1876 to sign a commercial treaty, which required the Korean court to renounce its status as a Qing tributary state. Thereafter, China and Japan clashed repeatedly on the peninsula and came close to war in the mid-1880s. In 1882, anti-Japanese protests in Korea created a pretext for Japan to dispatch its naval forces for the first time. When, in 1884, riots in Korea threatened foreign missionaries, Japan responded by dispatching troops to restore order and putting a reformist group in power at the Korean court. Qing forces under the command of Yuan Shikai restored the Korean king to the throne. In 1885, Qing and Japan tried to solve their conflict in Korea with the Convention of Tianjin, in which both sides appeared to promise to pull back their troops from Korea.

In Beijing, advisers at the court were alarmed that the loss of Qing authority in Korea corresponded with the rise of Japan as an expansionist sea power that would sooner or later challenge Qing influence over Korea, Taiwan, and perhaps even areas along the Chinese coast. In 1894, supporters of the Donghak movement (literally, the Eastern Learning movement, which originally aspired to revive neo-Confucianism in Korea, and gradually evolved into the religion known today as Cheondoism) began to stage an uprising in Seoul, and King Gojong (1852–1919) of Korea petitioned Li Hongzhang to send troops to restore order. When China, in line with treaty stipulations, accepted Korea's request for military aid, the Japanese press declared that China must be challenged. As three thousand Qing troops arrived in Seoul, the Japanese, citing the Convention of Tianjin, shipped about eight thousand troops to Korea. In July 1894, they arrested King Gojong and installed a new government of young pro-Japanese modernizers. This group explicitly annulled all relations, formal and informal, between Korea and the Qing empire, and requested that the Japanese army drive away the Qing troops. Hostilities began in July, and the Sino-Japanese War was declared on August 1. While the war was fought first on the Korean and then the Liaodong Peninsula, the most important combats happened on the sea, since both belligerents relied on their navies to deliver their troops to strategic positions in Korea. A decisive naval battle occurred on September 17, 1894, when the Japanese Combined Fleet encountered the Chinese Beiyang Fleet off the mouth of the Yalu River. The fight at sea lasted from late morning to dusk and resulted in an overwhelming Japanese victory. The Beiyang fleet was almost completely wiped out, with most of the war ships having fled or being sunk. With this severe setback, China abandoned northern Korea. In October, the Japanese troops quickly pushed north and entered Manchuria and the Liaodong Peninsula. By late autumn Japan had won so many devastating victories on land as well as on sea that it left the Chinese court asking for peace negotiations. When a peace treaty, the Treaty of Shimonoseki, was signed the following April 17, the Qing court was forced to cede suzerainty over the province of Taiwan and southern Manchuria's Liaodong Peninsula. Japan also claimed a large indemnity and extensive commercial rights in China. The treaty granted Japanese ships the right to navigate the Yangzi River and Japanese enterprises the right to build and operate their own factories in China. China had to pay 200 million silver taels to Japan. As important as the victory, however, were two wartime developments that would reverberate later. The first occurred in Port Arthur, where Japanese troops massacred hundreds of civilians after defeating the Chinese in November 1894. While Tokyo launched an investigation and apologized, foreign reporters expressed shock and outrage. Equally significant was the outburst of nationalism and patriotic fervor in Japan during the war that signaled lasting popular support for the Japanese expansion in China.

Since Russia's position in the northeast was threatened by the handover of the Liaodong Peninsula to Japan stipulated by the Treaty of Shimonoseki, the tsarist government approached Germany and France (Germany, France, and Russia together were called the tripartite powers) with a plan to take joint military action against Japan unless it relinquished its claim for the Liaodong Peninsula. Facing the resistance of three European countries, Japan backed down and agreed to the tripartite powers' demand that it accept an additional indemnity of thirty million silver taels from the Qing in lieu of the Liaodong Peninsula. The money paid to Japan as part of the Shimonoseki and Tripartite agreements represented about a third of the Qing treasury at the time, and was more than six times the annual income of the Japanese government.

A peace treaty so costly and, to Chinese eyes, a defeat so humiliating had two consequences. In terms of the Chinese economy, the period after 1895 was ironically marked by a burst of economic activity and a spectacular phase of growth. The 1895 treaty provisions, which granted Japan and by way of most favored nations clauses also all other foreigners rights to establish factories, had a profound impact, leading to a rapid expansion of foreign investment in industrial and mining ventures and, at least as important, to the emergence of private Chinese enterprises in competition with them. The role of the Chinese compradors as partners of foreign merchants became obsolete, and China was made into a base for foreign manufacturing. The decade before 1904, the year China introduced its first-ever Company Law, saw a big wave of market entries by new firms. Among the eighty-three shareholding Chinese companies launched were nine spinning mills, twenty-eight steam filatures in the lower Yangzi area, eight flourmills, one match factory, three machine works, four oil presses, and one winery. The crisis also changed official attitudes toward business activities. The Qing court established quasi-public banks funded by the state. China's first modern bank, the Imperial Bank of China, was founded in Shanghai in 1897. The Qing empire now saw itself engaged in a "trade war" *(shangzhan)*, with a determination to do everything possible to recover the rights to exploit economic resources that had been lost to foreigners. Officials were actively engaged in promoting industry and merchants were more than willing to cooperate.

In terms of political development, the consequences of the peace treaty were less positive. Military defeat in the Sino-Japanese War of 1894–1895, by a nation long regarded as a little brother rather than an equal, inflicted a profound and unsettling political shock, especially as the Qing empire was now viewed as the "sick man of Asia." The lasting political reverberations of the Treaty of Shimonoseki were severe. The structure of commercial, diplomatic, and strategic relationships between the Qing empire and the western treaty powers dating back to 1842 collapsed. Japan gained significant ground. This was the first time that Japan had taken massive territorial concessions from China, a move that threatened the territorial integrity of China and harmed the interests of the European imperialist powers, particularly Russia. In the ensuing years, Japan was able to settle most of its debt, finance continued industrialization, expand its educational programs, and renegotiate its one unequal treaty with the United States in 1911, all thanks directly or indirectly to the massive infusion of cash from the Qing government after 1895.[28] Diplomatically, China responded by seeking new international allies. While in Moscow in the spring of 1896, Li Hongzhang signed a treaty awarding Russia rights to industrial development and military occupation in the northeast, expecting that this would create a block to further Japanese encroachment there. The framework for a wider and in some ways more decisive war had been established, and Japan's development as an imperialist power had been accelerated. That the Qing empire's recovery would be stalled became all but inevitable.

The Boxer Crisis

By the mid-1890s, China was under considerable pressure by foreign imperialism. The Japanese, British, French, and Russians had already staked their claims. Britain removed Bhutan, Sikkim, and Nepal from alleged Chinese jurisdiction and sought influence or domination in China proper; France successfully challenged Chinese claims to modern Vietnam, Laos, and Cambodia, as well as southwestern China; and Russia annexed lands all across China's northern frontiers. Japan had taken over Taiwan and controlled Korea. Other powers would soon join in the attempt to capitalize on China's weakness, among them the German Reich, which was looking for a harbor colony in northern China. In November 1897, two German missionaries were murdered in the prefecture of Caozhou, West Shandong, by members of the Big Sword Society (Dadaohui), one of the many self-defense associations that had turned anti-Christian. This gave Germany a long-awaited rationale for a military occupation of the Jiao'ao Bay, in the eastern part of Shandong province. In March 1898, a treaty with China was signed giving Germany a ninety-nine-year lease of a territory in Jiao'ao Bay. German interests in China were by no means limited to this small territory directly ruled by German colonial authorities. With this treaty, Germany also secured rights to build railways, start mining operations in a corridor along the railway lines, and deploy troops in Shandong.[29]

Shandong became Germany's primary entry point to the Chinese market. By declaring Kiaochow (in China the city is called Qingdao) an imperial "protectorate" (Kaiserliches Schutzgebiet) in April 1898, the German emperor

Wilhelm II barred the constitutional organs of the German Reich, such as the Reichstag (the parliament), from legislating for Kiaochow. Unlike the British crown colony Hong Kong, Kiaochow was under tight supervision by the authorities of the motherland, with little room left for self-government or self-administration. Germany developed Kiaochow into a colonial base for German expansion in China and East Asia. Kiaochow served as a repair dock and coal station for the German navy. The colonial government also established a large commercial harbor. German and Chinese businesses settled in Qingdao and it soon became the second largest trading port in North China. The government in Berlin and colonial authorities in Kiaochow formed two major syndicates, one for the railway and the other for mining operations, which were composed of large banks, heavy industrial enterprises, shipping companies, and trading houses. These syndicates raised capital for two companies established in 1899: the Shandong Railway Company built a railway to Jinan, the provincial capital of Shandong; and the Shandong Mining Company exploited mineral resources along the railway. The companies were obliged to use supplies from Germany, to apply German technologies and standards, to coordinate the price policy with colonial authorities, and to yield a portion of their profits to the German government.

Immediately thereafter, a large domestic uprising broke out in the vicinity of the German colony in Shandong. From 1899 to 1901, a series of violent, local conflicts—first between Germany and China, and later involving seven other countries, as well—escalated into a large international crisis, leading to the dispatch of the largest international expedition force the world had ever seen. The two sides saw themselves caught up in not just military and economic conflict but in a clash of civilizations. The conflicts occurred at sites within the German sphere of influence, at the outskirts of the German colony. This region, with its large coal seams in Boshan and Weixian, along the railway line from Qingdao to Jinan, was the focus of German economic interests. Beyond the expectation that the railway and mining operations would become profitable enterprises, their quick completion was also seen as a precondition for Kiaochow's overall development. Any delay would cause losses for the companies and hold back the colony's economic development.

As in many other localities, railway construction by western firms encountered numerous problems. Peasants were unwilling to sell their land because they were not satisfied with the compensation offered. Despite protests, the companies decided to continue construction even if some plots of land had not yet been purchased. With this policy antagonizing the rural population, it took only a minor incident, such as a dispute between a local peasant and German railway worker at a market in Dalü, in the German sphere of influence, to ignite violence. Angry peasants gathered to stop the railway workers from continuing track construction. When news of popular unrest reached Kiaochow, the German governor, Jaeschke, decided "to teach the peasants a lesson." He swiftly ordered about a hundred soldiers to the area to quell the unrest. The troops stormed three villages, killing twenty-five people.[30]

Following these events, German soldiers occupied the city of Gaomi for two weeks. Here, an incident occurred that drew the attention of officials all over China. Gaomi, the seat of the local magistrate, was a relatively wealthy city known for its literati.[31] Many houses displayed signs of academic honors or official appointments. The German troops took up residence in the academy (shuyuan) of Gaomi, which housed a famous library. On leaving Gaomi, German soldiers destroyed the academy and burned the library's books. This was not a random act of property destruction; it was an auto-da-fé of Confucian classics, in line with the widespread belief among westerners in China that more than the mere construction of a railway line was at stake. In these local conflicts, they saw themselves as engaged in a war against not only rebellious peasants, but Chinese civilization in general. The enlightened, progressive West, in their view, had to overcome the backward Confucian civilization—with arms, if necessary. In 1900, Jaeschke wrote to Berlin: "In China there is at the moment a fierce struggle between two different ideologies: the national Chinese Weltanschauung, which rests on centuries-old traditions, and the cosmopolitan occidental Weltanschauung."[32]

Chinese resistance continued as peasants repeatedly removed surveyors' rods. A new conflict arose in the spring of 1900. In the lowlands of the Haoli district north of Gaomi, the population feared that the railway would block the delicate drainage systems of the lowlands and cause floods. But the railway company portrayed these fears as mere pretext to block its progress.[33] Again, the company urged the governor of Kiaochow to resort to military measures to protect ongoing construction. In the meantime, the rural communities of Haoli district invited leaders of the spreading Boxer movement to teach them fighting techniques and magic. The Boxers United in Righteousness *(Yi-hetuan)*, known to westerners as the Boxer Rebellion (1899–1900) or simply the Boxers, was a spontaneous mass movement that aimed to drive out all things foreign and restore the Qing *(fu Qing mie yang)*. It was thought to be an offshoot of the Eight Trigrams Society *(Baguajiao)* which had historically fomented rebellions against the Qing dynasty in the late eighteenth and early nineteenth centuries. More recently, however, the Boxers had evolved out of the merger of two specific traditions: the notion of invulnerability from the Big Sword Society *(Dadaohui)*, which had been active in southwestern Shandong from the mid-1890s and had killed the two German missionaries in 1897; and the mass rituals of spirit possession practiced by the so-called Spirit Boxers *(Shenquan)* which emerged around the same time in the northwestern part of the province. The Boxers were mostly poor farmers, seasonal agricultural workers, and unemployed canal workers who had lost their jobs due to the rise of coastal shipping. They believed that, through magic spirit-possession rituals, they could become invulnerable and acquire superior fighting power. Only loosely organized, they met spontaneously at boxing grounds in rural areas and altars in cities (often, in both cases, attached to temples). After the Yellow River broke through its dikes in August 1898, leading to widespread flooding, the Boxers' promises of self-defense and healing gained them a large following in the disaster-stricken villages and communities. The Boxers, too, saw the evolving conflict in Shandong as a clash of civilizations. They saw the presence of foreigners, and especially the construction of the railway, as angering the ancestors and gods. The Boxers believed this was the real reason that natural calamities had descended on Shandong in recent years.[34] Facing the rapid spread of the Boxers throughout northern China, and growing attacks on foreigners, German colonial authorities decided to retreat for a time. Jaeschke ordered all German personnel back to Kiaochow and railway construction was stopped. The Boxers of Haoli celebrated their victory and enjoyed a broad and significant boost in appeal.

The seemingly powerful Boxer fighters were tacitly permitted, sometimes even encouraged, by Qing officials to attack foreign communities, especially missionaries and their installations, throughout Shandong and Zhili provinces.[35] Throughout the spring and early summer of 1900, the Boxers spread across North China destroying railway tracks and churches. Tens of thousands of them streamed into Tianjin and Beijing, combing the cities' quarters for western missionaries and Chinese Christians. Tensions and disputes between foreigners and Chinese escalated as Boxers started to burn and loot buildings occupied by western banks or firms. Foreigners, including diplomats, felt threatened and called for protection by foreign military. The immediate response of the western powers was to put a small relief force of two thousand marines, pulled together from various naval forces stationed in China, under the command of the British Admiral Sir Edward Hobart Seymour (1840–1929). The contingent was ordered to advance to Beijing, secure the foreign diplomatic compounds, and protect the foreign population. This small, lightly armed force was able to board a train on June 10, 1900, but never made it to Beijing. Finding themselves under relentless attack by Boxers as well as the Qing Army, the troops exited the train and turned around to make their way back on foot, exposing themselves to even heavier attacks. Soon they also ran out of food and ammunition. Exhausted, they finally reached Tianjin on June 26. Seymour's expedition, immediately recognized as a painful humiliation by the Boxers, resulted in 62 dead and 232 wounded. For the Boxers it was an important victory. Suddenly it seemed that, with the support of a mass uprising, the Qing dynasty had some chance of defeating the imperialists.

Meanwhile, the allied powers pulled together more substantial reinforcements, mainly from the western naval bases scattered across Asia. Their quick arrival in Bohai Bay took the local Chinese garrison by surprise, and they were able to occupy the Dagu forts on June 17. The Qing court called this attack an act of war and, emboldened by the defeat of the Seymour expedition, it assembled troops for the defense of Tianjin and Beijing. Events were happening fast. On June 19, notes were sent to foreign embassies ordering them to leave the capital. The next day, as the German minister Clemens von Ketteler made his way through the diplomatic quarter to the Zongli Yamen (a quasi-foreign office) to discuss the conditions of the evacuation, he was shot dead in the street. By June 20, Boxers started to attack the diplomatic community in Beijing and laid siege to the foreign legations in the Chinese capital, including the embassies of Russia, France, Japan, the United States, Great Britain, Germany, Italy, and Austria-Hungary. On June 21, 1900, the imperial court issued what amounted to a declaration of war against the allied powers. With this, full-scale warfare broke out in North China. In the ensuing chaos and violence, around 250 foreigners (primarily missionaries) were killed

3.4. American troops marching in the Forbidden City during the Boxer Rebellion, 1900.
Bettmann / Getty Images / 514877178

by the Boxers, and so were tens of thousands of Chinese (most of them Christians). The foreign legations remained under fire for almost the entire month of July, but were able to hold off the Chinese forces.

By early August, a multinational coalition of nineteen thousand soldiers, including British, French, Japanese, Russian, German, Austrian, Italian, and American troops, was mobilized from Tianjin, which had been occupied in late July. The force reached Beijing on August 12 and prepared immediately to attack the city gates. It entered the city on August 14, and by opening the way for British units to relieve the legation compound, quickly lifted the siege of the legation quarter and the Northern Cathedral. The next day, allied troops began the occupation of Beijing's center that would subdue the Chinese army and the Boxers, and force the Empress Dowager Cixi and the Guangxu emperor (1871–1908) to leave the Forbidden City and seek refuge in the old city of Xi'an.

Even greater reinforcements were on their way from Europe for what would turn out to be a naval operation of unprecedented scale. On seeing off the German battalion, Wilhelm II delivered his famous "Hun Speech" in Bremerhaven on July 27, 1900. He said: "Should you encounter the enemy, he will be defeated! No quarter will be given! Prisoners will not be taken! Whoever falls into your hands is forfeited. Just as a thousand years ago the Huns under their King Attila made a name for themselves, one that even today makes them seem mighty in history and legend, may the name German be affirmed by you in such a way in China that no Chinese will ever again dare to look cross-eyed at a German."[36] Vessels carrying roughly ninety thousand European soldiers, among them twenty-two thousand Germans, arrived in Tianjin's Bohai Bay in early August. The troops were placed under the command of the German field marshal Alfred Count von Waldersee (1832–1904), but they arrived too late to help with the defense of the embassies in Beijing. The Qing court was practically defeated by the time the large and impressive armada arrived. The allied army instead carried out at least seventy-five "punitive expeditions" around Beijing and Tianjin, as part of a strategy to inflict both physical and symbolic harm on China.[37] Thousands were killed for allegedly slaughtering Europeans. One example of such a "punitive" expedition was the violence planned on October 6 and 7 by Waldersee and Jaeschke when they met in Tianjin. They authorized German troops to carry out punitive actions in Shandong against not only the Boxers themselves but also the broader civilian population that had supposedly provided support to the insurgency. On October 23 and November 1, three villages came under heavy artillery fire without warning and were destroyed. The more than 450 people killed included many women and children.[38]

Almost immediately after their arrival in China, members of the eight armies turned to looting. It began with the occupation of Tianjin in late July and stretched well into October 1900 in Beijing. Later, diplomats and missionaries joined the soldiers in looting. The sack of Beijing was similar to what had occurred at the Summer Palace forty years earlier, as "loot fever" had taken hold among the foreigners. The ensuing phase of uncontrolled plunder affected not only Beijing and the new Summer Palace on its western outskirts, but many other cities and towns in the province of Zhili. The German commander Waldersee admitted quite frankly in a November 1900 diary entry the extent of damage and destruction inflicted by looters on Beijing and other wealthy, centuries-old cities.

> By the permitted plundering for three days after the occupation, which was followed by private plundering, the population [of Beijing] must have suffered great, not even quantifiable material damage. Each nationality assigns

to another the palm in the art of looting; but the fact remains that they have all plundered thoroughly. . . . There is now a rich trade going on with the objects acquired in the plundering. Already traders, namely from America, have arrived making fortunes. . . . If one is so naïve at home to believe that all this was done for Christian culture and propaganda, he will be disappointed. Since the Thirty Years' War and the raids of the French at the time of Louis XIV in Germany, similar devastation has not yet occurred.[39]

From 1900 to 1902, Beijing and Tianjin were placed under foreign occupation. Barracks were built in Tianjin to house thousands of foreign troops, and a provisional government was set up there by the allied forces. As it tried to transform and develop the city, the city walls that had encircled the city for centuries were removed for "military and hygienic purposes."[40] The provisional government also installed running water, street lamps, and telephone lines. Public toilets were introduced, as well as a system for garbage disposal. Another innovation brought western-style policing.

The Boxer Protocol, the concluding document of the war, was signed on September 7, 1901, roughly a year after the allied forces had entered Beijing.[41] The settlement had an undeniably draconian character: Prince Duan, the father of the heir apparent and a major supporter of the Boxers, was sentenced to death as the main culprit (although the throne was allowed to replace the death sentence with banishment to Xinjiang, a possibility generally offered by Chinese law). In all, six senior officials were given death sentences, and more were punished in other ways, such as by demotion in rank. The court also promised to send a member of the imperial family to Germany and Japan to express "regret" for the murder of their diplomats. The Dagu forts had to be dismantled and disarmed. The Chinese government also had to prohibit by law the founding of anti-foreign societies. The nations that had sent armed forces against the uprising gained the right to post permanent garrisons in North China. The most devastating clause, however, concerned the huge indemnity of 450 million tael, excluding interest, which far exceeded the Qing government's annual budget of 250 million tael. This sum represented the sum of all claims submitted by other countries for military expedition costs, damages to property, and lives lost. There was, however, no process by which the validity of the claims and their amounts was assessed. Each country made its claim based on its own calculations. Russia's accounted for 29 percent of the total indemnity, followed by Germany at 20 percent. China was obligated to pay some twenty million taels annually, meaning that it would take thirty-nine years to pay off the entire sum with interest. The requirement to make this large annual payment mortgaged the budgets of Chinese governments for decades to come, with significant consequences. This provision of the settlement placed a crippling burden on the finances of the Chinese state, and at the same time intensified the grip of foreign powers on Chinese revenues. Robert Hart (1835–1911), Inspector General of the Maritime Customs Service, and other foreign expatriates living in China argued that China was in no position to meet those financial demands without finding new sources of revenue. In the end, they persuaded the allied powers to raise custom tariffs on imports to 5 percent (from 3.17 percent) and to begin taxing some goods that had been exempt—in particular, goods for consumption by foreigners such as European wines, liquor, and cigarettes. These measures, by generating significant additional revenue estimated at eighteen million taels, made it possible for China to meet the payments demanded by the Boxer Indemnity.

The lost wars in the final years of the nineteenth century would later be recognized as an important turning point. People inside China and globally saw the many setbacks—the stiff diplomatic settlements; the poor performances of the Chinese military; the foreign occupations of major cities, including the capital; the untold numbers of people, many of them bystanders, who lost their lives; the destruction of cities and cultural treasures; the humiliating flight of the court—as ample proof of the Qing empire's profound weakness. The immediate effect was a further deterioration of the Chinese imperial government's control, not only at the borders, but also inland. The recognition spread that the Qing empire was no longer able to rule and defend the country. This crisis point was noted by none other than the Empress Dowager Cixi herself, who wrote: "The dynasty has been brought to the precipice."[42] And thus, forces of radical reform arose in a Chinese society that sought to remake China—forces that the dynasty, it soon became clear, would be unable to withstand.

The Rise of Chinese Nationalism and Militarism

China's lost wars had two immediate consequences. First, the demands and proposals for reform became more urgent and radical as China teetered on the brink. It was in this period that Chinese nationalism emerged and became a powerful political factor in Chinese politics. Second, the series of grave setbacks on the battlefield convinced governing elites that the self-strengthening movement had been a failed approach and that China needed to reset and rethink its efforts. Needed instead were much broader and deeper policies to stabilize social order and defend the empire against foreign and domestic threats.

As we have seen, Chinese thinkers throughout the nineteenth and twentieth centuries engaged in debates over how to update China's technology while retaining traditional values and culture. Only gradually did some thinkers accept that simply importing western guns and machines was not enough. The ineffectiveness of reform efforts increasingly convinced them that the traditional system itself was hindering both China's modernization and its ability to deal with outside challenges confronting the nation. The debate intensified during the last quarter of the nineteenth century as China was slowly partitioned into various spheres of influence. After 1900, with the disastrous defeat of China by the Japanese armed forces over dominance in Korea, and the occupation of Beijing and the Forbidden City by the allied troops, and the foreign powers' subsequent scramble for Chinese concessions and spheres of influence, the more conciliatory and pragmatic programs of the "self-strengtheners" were discredited. Fears for China's survival mounted.

Information about foreign realities and ideas, formerly confined to a narrow circle of reformers, now began drawing the attention of a concerned, nationwide audience. Chinese thinkers at the end of the Qing dynasty turned to new, western ideas including social Darwinism, parliamentarianism, constitutionalism, and nationalism to address ongoing Chinese concerns about state stability, personal self-cultivation, and economic performance.[43] Better knowledge of western countries and the international order was provided in no small part by the translations that had begun in 1860 but showed their full effect only around 1900. The American missionary W.A.P. Martin employed a team of Chinese assistants to carefully translate Henry Wheaton's *Elements of International Law* in 1864 to aid Chinese officials in understanding the meaning of western treaties and the norms on which they were based.[44] The writer and translator Wang Tao (1828–1897) rendered into Chinese a work on French history and a military history of the Franco-Prussian War which became a favorite of Li Hongzhang. He also founded the China General Publishing Company *(Zhonghua yinwu zongju)* and in 1874 began to publish a

Chinese newspaper. It featured his own editorials calling for China to take up the science, industrial transformation, and parliamentary system of Britain.[45] An account by Huang Zunxian (1848–1905) of his experience as counselor to the Qing embassy in Meiji Japan had received little attention when it first appeared in 1887, but found an avid readership ten years later, following Japan's naval victory over Chinese forces.[46] Huang's work joined a wave of translations—many by Yan Fu (also called Yen Fu, 1854–1921), China's foremost interpreter of western thought—that exposed Chinese audiences to theories like Thomas H. Huxley's social Darwinism and its insistence that nations had to evolve, adapt, and progress or face extinction. Yan's translation of Huxley's famous speech on social Darwinism went through more than thirty editions in the ten years following the initial 1898 Chinese translation. Yan's 1902 translation of Adam Smith's *The Wealth of Nations* also won a large audience.[47]

Unlike earlier writers on self-strengthening such as Wei Yuan and Feng Guifen, Yan Fu advised his readers that western technology could not be transferred without also borrowing the science and political and educational systems that fostered development and progress in the West. In an essay called "Learning from the West" he argued that efforts of reform in China should extend to the foundations of Chinese society:

> The foundation *(ti)* and the use *(yong)* mean the same thing. The body of an ox should have the use of carrying heavy things; the body of a horse should have the use of carrying something to a distance. I have never heard that the ox is the body or the foundation, while the horse is for use. The difference between Chinese and western knowledge is as great as that between the complexions and the eyes of the two races. We cannot force the two cultures to be the same or similar. Therefore, Chinese knowledge has its foundation and function; western knowledge has also its foundation and function. If the two are separated, each can be independent; if the two were combined, both would perish.[48]

With those words, Yan Fu criticized Zhang Zhidong and other contemporary thinkers who believed western techniques could be layered onto Chinese cultural foundations. Yan Fu's call was for new legal, political, and spiritual institutions to be introduced to China to "enrich the state and strengthen the army." He recognized that it was not the West's technology but its institutions that had given western countries such strong advantages. If these could be established in Chinese society, China would become powerful again, too. Yan Fu also was a proponent of Herbert Spencer's social Darwinism and, applying evolutionary biology theory to questions of society, he emphasized that individuals and nations were constantly competing, adapting, and progressing. It was necessary for China to modernize, he stressed, or it would fall prey to foreign countries. Pointing to the experience of Peter the Great's Russia, he warned that modernization had to be full-spectrum rather than limited to simple purchases of defense technology, which would only lead to ruin. Yan Fu's writings and translations helped to shape many contemporaneous debates in China. His commentaries on western social philosophers and attempts to reconcile their ideas with contemporary Chinese realities, and China's own intellectual traditions, were as influential as the actual translations he produced. His powerful statements prepared the way for institutional change.

Reform thinkers were also inspired by the New Text tradition as reshaped by Kang Youwei (1858–1927), who turned Confucius into a leader and prophet.[49] Kang honored Confucius not only as the New Text's "uncrowned king," but also as founder of China's unique religio-cultural order, similar to Jesus, Muhammad, and Gautama in other world religions. In his writing, beginning in the 1880s, Kang looked for Confucian precedents for radical change and sociopolitical reconstruction to save China. He described "Confucius as a reformer" (to quote the title of an 1897 essay) and attempted to reinvent Confucianism as a philosophy of social change, recasting Chinese history as a linear process leading toward a utopian end, rather than a series of repetitive, dynastic cycles. He wanted to demonstrate that far-reaching reform, including reorganization of institutional structures and introduction of new institutions, was fully in line with Confucian principles. To him, a failure to reinvent Confucianism would spell the future collapse of the entire imperial system. He also advocated constitutionalism as an urgent requirement for China's survival.

The reform program designed by Kang Youwei, together with his followers Liang Qichao (1873–1929) and Tan Sitong (1865–1898), had a brief trial in the so-called Hundred Days of Reform *(wuxu bianfa)* of 1898.[50] The initial reform effort was approved by the young Guangxu emperor and lasted for only slightly more than a hundred days, at which point it was abruptly terminated by the empress dowager and court conservatives in a coup d'état. Mainly, Cixi and her supporters worried about losing their own power. Six reformers were executed without trial, but Kang Youwei and Liang Qichao, among others, managed to escape with help from foreign legations. The Guangxu emperor was kept under house arrest for the rest of his life, living on a small island in the Forbidden City's lakes. Virtually all of the Guangxu emperor's far-sighted reforms were revoked. It was a missed final opportunity and fatal mistake for the dynasty.

Even if short-lived and only on paper, the decrees and edicts issued over the summer of 1898 by the young emperor were notable. He wanted to reform the examination system to emphasize knowledge of current affairs over the classics; to convert Buddhist monasteries to public schools; to abolish Manchu privileges and many government positions; and to establish new bureaus for commerce, industry, and agriculture. The army and navy were to be modernized. Low-level officials and even ordinary literati were encouraged to send memorials directly to the emperor. The reforms attempted to use the existing dynasty and its court as a basis for top-down social innovation and economic development. Pragmatically, the reformers saw how the court's support would help reshape and invigorate the bureaucracy. They were in no position to challenge the Qing dynasty by calling for its overthrow, nor did they intend to. On the contrary, inspired by the models of Peter the Great and the Meiji emperor, they favored using the emperor's autocratic powers to drive innovation.

When the official reform policies came to their sudden end in the fall of 1898, the voices demanding deep institutional reforms were not silenced. To the contrary, they became louder and more radical. Younger officials and literati were increasingly taken with the idea that political modernity lay in popular power *(minquan)* and a strong state. They stressed the need for more thoroughgoing adoption of western institutions to counter conservative resistance inside China, and also to counter western imperialism and Meiji Japan's emerging national power outside of China. A movement for broad and deep change emerged among younger elites who were attracted to the creative appropriation of various notions they saw as crucial to China's recovery: the nation-state; mass citizenship; the combination of constitutional monarchy and representative government (local self-government and national parliaments); and commercial development.

Among all those who called for institutional reform, Liang Qichao's thinking had the most lasting influence.[51] He was the leading publicist of reform and innovation in the decade preceding the Revolution of 1911. After 1898, he went into exile in Japan, where he became highly visible as a writer and publisher of journals; "Renewing the People" *(Xinmin congbao),* published between 1902 and 1907, was an especially popular periodical. He wrote extensively about topics in history and politics and his opinions, while often controversial, influenced a broad range of young scholars and officials. Among them were both reformers who believed the Qing could be renewed and revolutionaries who saw the end of the Qing empire as unavoidable.

Like Yan Fu, Liang came to see "wealth and power" as the only salvation for a China living under the threat of national demise at the hands of Japan and the technologically advanced, insatiable, imperialist powers. Liang and other reform-minded scholars wanted to explore the origins of China's dynastic weakness and to develop remedies. An erudite Confucian scholar, Liang came to believe that the source of the West's wealth and power lay in certain institutions, and above all, in its political systems. His writings consistently argue that weak nations are ruled by selfish monarchs, while strong nations come into being when the people are able to exercise rights and powers. When people have rights, they identify with their countries and develop a sense of ownership. Liang clearly believed that political institutions determine the relative wealth and power of nations. He deplored China's lack of any "national [or statist] consciousness" *(guojia sixiang),* perceiving no shared, civic concern for the state of the Chinese nation. To his mind, the nationalist energies generated by popular participation in the political process were the key force driving any dynamic society forward. After a trip to the United States and Canada, he wrote:

> The weaknesses of the Chinese people can be listed as follows: 1. Our character is that of clansmen rather than citizens. . . . 2. We have a village mentality and not a national mentality. . . . 3. We can only accept despotism and cannot enjoy freedom. . . . When I look at the societies of the world, none is so disorderly as the Chinese community in San Francisco. Why? The answer is freedom. The character of the Chinese in China is not superior to those of San Francisco, but at home they are governed by officials and restrained by fathers and elder brothers. . . . Now, freedom, constitutionalism, and republicanism mean government by the majority, but the overwhelming majority of the Chinese people are like [those of

San Francisco]. If we were to adopt a democratic system of government now, it would be nothing less than committing national suicide. . . . To put it in a word, the Chinese people of today can only be governed autocratically. . . . [52]

In other words, Liang Qichao saw the creation of a community of new citizens as the key to China's revival; out of them a new viable and constitutional system would grow, providing the foundation for an invigorated and strong nation. Insisting that the new citizens (xinmin) should have and exercise "rights" (quan), Liang offered ideas that were simultaneously nationalistic and politically liberal.

New thoughts spawned political and social change. Repeated military defeat encouraged negative evaluation of the self-strengthening effort and a recognition of China's overall backwardness.[53] The Qingyipai, a powerful alliance of prominent conservatives who had steadfastly opposed self-strengthening initiatives, suffered a rapid loss of influence amid an explosion of new civic and academic associations. With opposition removed, considerable resources and efforts went into building modern armies rather than new political systems, much to the exasperation of the intellectuals and reformers. Qing regional authorities presided over the reorganization of China's military forces to protect China from further imperialist aggression and to support the dynasty. A defining characteristic of the Qing empire had always been its focus on military affairs. Now, however, "militarism" emerged from the almost incessant internal and external conflicts. As used here, that term refers to the dominance of the military in politics—even to the extent of using policy to allow armed forces to achieve greater autonomy, extract more of a nation's economic resources, and dominate part or even all of its regional and national power structure—and the ascendancy of military values and symbols in social life. An increasing proportion of Chinese elites, wishing to shore up national defense and erase the humiliations suffered by imperialism, considered it necessary to instill greater martial spirit and military skill in the Chinese population.[54]

The building of new modern armies goes back to the waning years of the nineteenth century. Most modern armies were initially regional. Zeng Guofan, Zuo Zongtang, and other local Hunan literati were able to organize, despite no other backing, a powerful Hunan Army (Xiangjun) to contend with the

Taipings across hundreds of kilometers of territory. The Hunan Army was completely under the control of local leaders—official Qing armed forces were only auxiliary to it—and provided its own salaries and food rations. It employed two methods of raising money. First, it set up customs stations on the main communication arteries and exacted new *likin* transportation taxes from traveling merchants. Second, it took advantage of the Qing court's authorization of the sale of blank certificates of office and gave out various official ranks to obtain contributions. Another important regional army was the Anhui Army *(Huaijun)* raised by Li Hongzhang. Both armies made some use of western arms, but were trained in traditional fashion, and remained loyal to the Qing state. As their loyalty to the throne was rewarded with official ranks and titles, local elites were drawn into the Qing system and bureaucracy. While large numbers of their troops were demobilized after the crushing of the Taiping rebel state, many were also kept at imperial command to quell other rebellions and to defend China against the West and Japan. Yet in the long run, the legacy of those armies contributed to a militarization of regional authority which would create serious problems for the imperial state.

The crushing defeat of the Sino-Japanese War sped up changes in military policy.[55] In the aftermath of the war, with its best armed forces destroyed, the Qing government found itself in a position of profound weakness. Increasingly ambitious efforts were made to restore China's military strength, this time by building new regional armies. The first two of these new armies were sponsored by officials Yuan Shikai (1859–1916) in North China and Zhang Zhidong in Hubei. In 1895, Zhang Zhidong, then acting governor-general of Liangjiang, created the "Self-Strengthening Army" *(Ziqiangjun)* in Nanjing. It consisted of thirteen battalions of carefully selected men who were organized based on the German model and trained by a team of thirty-five German officers. This force included cavalry, infantry, artillery, and engineering units, and also had medical and support personnel. To provide trained officers for his new army with the right military values, Zhang also created a new military academy in Nanjing in 1896. When he was transferred back to his former position of governor-general of Hunan and Hubei, Zhang created another military academy in Wuchang and began to reform the troops in these two provinces. Zhang Zhidong trained his New Hubei Army, as it was later called, with a strength of seventy to eighty thousand troops. The combination of the Hanyang Ironworks, Hanyang Arsenal (in contemporary

Wuhan, the capital of Hubei), and many new schools also made the middle Yangzi a base for new political forces. In 1911, the New Hubei Army would launch the Republican Revolution and bring an end to two thousand years of Chinese imperial history.

Meanwhile, at the directive of Ronglu (1836–1903), the increasingly influential Manchu grand councilor and superintendent of the northern ports, Yuan Shikai began to build a new army in 1895 to shore up the weakened defenses of North China after the war with Japan. Before the century came to an end, the "Military Defense Army" *(Wuweijun)* was formed in Zhili, with Yuan as commander in chief. Yuan Shikai later renamed the army the "Newly Created Army" *(Xinjian lujun).* This new army was to total some seven thousand men, also trained by German instructors. Yuan's army rapidly expanded to form the Beiyang (Northern) Army, stationed near the capital area, which soon established itself as China's most modern fighting force. Yuan relied on various enterprises, as well as on local agriculture, to raise money for his army. The Beiyang Army had officer training schools, staff colleges, foreign instructors, and modern armaments. Most notable among these schools was the Beiyang Military Academy in Tianjin, which would produce the Beiyang clique of officers that dominated Chinese politics after 1911.

From the Taiping Rebellion on, China marched step by step toward militarization broadly conceived. As the number of armed soldiers gradually increased, those controlling these military forces were in position to obtain growing economic resources and to gain political power. New armed forces were created based on western military models of training, equipment, and organization. The concurrent rise of nationalism provided another impetus for capable and ambitious young men to pursue careers in the military. Studying in Chinese military academies took on new prestige. Others attended military academies abroad in Japan or Europe. With that, professional military men entered the national stage, seeking power and influence. The militarization of local elites during the great rebellions and wars was linked to their growing politicization, and ultimately gave them a significant role in overthrowing the dynasty.

Events in the final years of the nineteenth century proved pivotal in the creation of a distinctively modern Chinese identity shaped by nationalism and militarism. No longer aligned with the dynastic house and the elite bureaucracy, the polity conceptually centered on the nation and the military. The new military men in the empire drew their conclusion from the nineteenth-century crisis: the fate of China was irrevocably linked to national strength. The strength of the nation, moreover, required more than strong defense capabilities; it demanded that the masses be mobilized, drilled, and trained as militant members of the nation. What is often overlooked is that this was not the only possible conclusion. Another perspective, as promoted by Liang Qichao, was to note that mass citizenship and recruit armies also implied, however silently, at least the potential for full-fledged political rights and active membership in a national community united by ethnic, historical, and cultural ties.

❖ ❖ ❖

China's downfall in the nineteenth century was dramatic and astounding. The early Qing era demonstrated great strength, material efflorescence, and social stability, and saw enormous expansions of territory and population in an increasingly commercialized but primarily agrarian economy. Its industries—for example, of textile and porcelain producers—were among the world's most advanced. In the nineteenth century, however, China fell far behind many European countries. Within the relatively short period of a hundred years, a comparatively prosperous and well-administered country at the edge of modernity turned into a nation of chaos, corruption, backwardness, and poverty. Flourishing rural cities with academies and busy markets declined into neglect and destitution. What had been one of the most formidable militaries in the world had its self-confidence shattered as it proved unable to defend borders or win wars.

What were the reasons for China's free fall? Generations of scholars in the West and in China have sought explanations in China's traditional culture, variously blaming the Confucian rejection of commerce; the fundamental incompatibility of Chinese tradition with science or innovative thinking; a reliance on *guanxi* (favoring those in one's social network in business dealings) that invited corruption and mismanagement. None of these arguments is entirely convincing, however, since these same traditions had not proved to be hindrances before as the Chinese empire grew and developed for hundreds of years. On the contrary, they provided the stability and good governance that allowed the empire to flourish. Other scholars have blamed western imperialism, which exploited Chinese resources and forestalled indigenous development.[56] At the same time, doubts have appropriately been voiced that imperialism affected much of China beyond the treaty ports in the nineteenth century.

In recent years, scholars such as Kenneth Pomeranz and Jack Goldstone have argued that, toward the end of the eighteenth century, the dynamic economic expansions in China and Western Europe both hit ceilings due to mounting ecological constraints.[57] Such constraints caused widespread hardship, diminished state revenues, and proliferating unrest in both parts of the world—but Western Europe managed to transcend these difficulties through its easy access to energy resources and large-scale emigration to the Americas. These historical variables, according to both Pomeranz and Goldstone, allowed further political centralization and the Industrial Revolution to take hold in Europe, even as China and most other Asian states suffered prolonged economic crisis and political disintegration. Not all scholars are persuaded, however, that the variance in development outcomes can be fully accounted for by the differing availability of coal and colonies.

To understand the causes of China's downfall more comprehensively, it is useful—in fact, indispensable—to place China in a global framework. China's crisis in the late Qing period was not unique, but typical of how empires in the nineteenth century were challenged.[58] On a global scale, empires in the nineteenth century were entering a phase of upheaval and crisis in which many of them grappled with new and profound challenges related to the spread of nationalism, the advent of new military technologies, and changes in global climate. Nationalism threatened the cohesion of the multiethnic architecture of almost all the empires. The global market of new, efficient, and affordable weapons such as machine guns and explosives emboldened rebels and facilitated uprisings against imperial control. Changes in global climate patterns put pressure on the imperial economies in the northern hemisphere that relied on agriculture. These challenges placed growing stress on existing imperial structures and institutions, forcing them to adjust or fail.

China's nineteenth-century decline can only be understood as a confluence of several specific historical factors, some of them global and outside of the Qing's direct control. A focus on institutional development offers the best and most accurate explanation for understanding late Qing challenges and obstacles to modern development. First, ecological constraints certainly played a significant role. Environmental degradation and a change in global climate patterns exacerbated an already precarious situation and resulted in wide swings of rainfall amounts in North China and increased flooding in the south. As China's premodern agriculture struggled from diminishing yields in a time of demographic growth, spreading rural poverty put pressure on Qing institutions. Second, the effects of imperialism deepened China's economic woes. Outflows of silver and, later, competition from western textiles and other products pushed the domestic economy into a depression, so that prices fell and rural incomes dwindled. Third, the influx of foreign capital, technologies, knowledge, and institutions into the treaty-port world increased the divide between coastal areas and hinterlands, eroding social stability. Fourth, political institutions in the empire clearly failed to address the pressing problems and to find effective solutions for dealing with the economic downturn, regional imbalances, rural poverty, and social unrest. In this reading, it was a combination of these several factors, rather than any overarching single factor such as general resource limitations or cultural orientation, that constrained China's development both shortly before and after the start of the treaty-port system.

In a rapidly changing world, China lacked the leadership to respond to new challenges and adjust to new realities. Internally, it faced increasing population, social complexity, and geographic mobility; externally, it faced imperialism. It became painfully apparent that China needed institutions capable of mobilizing its economic and human resources to a much greater degree than ever before. The Qing institutions failed in this respect because court could not agree on the need to act, much less on a specific plan to modify the institutional order and set China on a new path. Political power continued to be narrowly concentrated in the hands of the weakened Manchu court, and the court was above all concerned with protecting vested interests and maintaining power. With this priority overruling all other considerations, institutional changes were avoided for fear of undermining the rule of the Manchu dynasty. The essential problem for Qing's economic, social, and fiscal policies was the political center's hesitation in adapting to the changing environment for fear of losing power.

In a context of rising populations, stagnant and declining per-capita revenues, and global competition, China was crippled by institutional exhaustion. Its lack of institutional modification or innovation restricted the center's capacity to mobilize resources to implement new administrative initiatives or to address national emergencies. Limited revenues and no fiscal provisions for local governance forced emperors to deal with substantial financial irregularities. Thus the empire was left to depend on severe punishments and cultural symbols and practices to fight against graft and defend the imperial institutions. As the imperial system lost internal cohesion and began to fall apart, its function and reproduction became increasingly reliant on local power brokers' willingness to spend their own scarce resources, like material and political incentives, to redress complaints and create consent. Fundamentally, China was misgoverned because the state remained too small, too cheap, and too weak for too long.[59] Its fiscal and administrative decay started in the Daoguang depression and worsened throughout the nineteenth century. As compared to the peak years of the mid-eighteenth century, the Qing state became much more insolvent, corrupt, and inefficient. The fact that a mere thirty thousand officials and officers ran the single largest empire in Asia had benefited the population in the past, but now meant that China's administrative, financial, and military abilities fell woefully short. Confronted with western imperialism on its coast, China had to pay a heavy price for its lack of governance.

Why did political institutions that had been effective and innovative in the seventeenth century become so dysfunctional in the late Qing? The reason can be found in the closely aligned incentives of the imperial household and the bureaucratic, scholarly, commercial, and landowning elites. These created a tight web of vested interests and rent-seeking behavior which, once established, impeded institutional change and proved extremely difficult to remove. Late imperial Chinese society displayed strikingly interdependent sources of formal and informal influence and power. Public office offered the surest path to prestige and wealth. At the same time, money was essential to finance the long preparation needed to pass the civil service examinations. As part of late Qing self-strengthening programs, the merchants setting up Chinese enterprises were officeholders in the bureaucracy or had intimate links to the bureaucracy. The state at various levels relied on extracting resources from society, and cooperated with individuals and businesses to take advantage of rent-seeking opportunities in profitable sectors. This tight integration of economic resources, status, and political power provided a pillar of stability but also presented daunting hurdles for institutional reform and innovation. The fact that property rights were limited and incomplete may have played a role, as well, as this facilitated what might reasonably be termed a *patronage economy*. The absence of secure property rights and of institutional restraints on imperial power produced a domestic economy in which only land was suitable for long-term, passive wealth holding. There were no impersonal financial arrangements or transactions.[60] Overall, an extractive institutional system emerged that benefited the merchant-official at the expense of the population.

Global trade and the importation of foreign commodities into the Chinese market began the gradual evolution of the Chinese economy into a modern one based on urban areas. Other factors fueling the transformation of the Chinese economy were finance, modern industrial production, and the construction of a modern transportation system. The influx of foreign capital investment gave rise to a system that was then expanded and developed by Chinese entrepreneurs themselves. China's growing if still feeble efforts to modernize society and industrialize the economy did bear some fruit. But the development was too slow and too confined to the coast, so that few ripples reached the rural hinterlands. From the end of the nineteenth century onward, degrees of distance from commercial hubs took on ever greater economic significance.

Social disruption, economic fragmentation, and institutional weakness resulted in a substantial loss of control both internally and externally. Among the large, modern countries, China became one of the most penetrated as an unparalleled number of foreign actors tried to influence its political, economic, and cultural evolution. China saw its southwest occupied by the French, its northeast by the Germans, its south and center along the Yangzi by the British, its northwest by the Russians, and its north by the Japanese. The devastating loss of Taiwan to Japan in 1895 and failure of the comprehensive Hundred Days of Reform in 1898 came to be seen as evidence of the overall failure of Qing reforms. After that, even more foreign powers demanded spheres of influence, especially for constructing railroads and mines. In 1900, an international army suppressed the anti-foreign Boxer Rebellion in northern China, destroying much of Beijing in the process. Each of these defeats brought more foreign demands, greater indemnities that China had to repay, more foreign presence along the coast, and more foreign participation in China's political and economic life. Little wonder that many in China were worried by the century's end that the country, to quote the favored metaphor of the time, was being sliced up "like a melon." An enduring legacy of nineteenth-century decline was border insecurity and Chinese fears about losing control over parts of the Chinese territory—fears that would continue to loom large in the twentieth century.

The Qing crisis prompted intense discussions among thinkers and literati of the reasons for China's downward spiral and the best way to reverse it. New Text notions emphasized historical change and advocated practical adjustments of institutions to changing times. These notions combined with empirical research prepared the ground for later reforms, and were important "early modern" stepping stones to a modernist vision of political and cultural transformation. Initially, discussions focused on the use of western arms and other technologies to defend Chinese *substance*, as defined by the *ti-yong* formula. The vague *ti-yong* formula was a kind of umbrella concept, however, covering many different ideas. Reformism as found in the treaty ports was distinctly different from the reformism of the self-strengtheners. Certainly, the treaty-port reformers played a role in self-strengthening; many of them even served on the staffs of Li Hongzhang and other self-strengthening leaders. But before 1890 there was little communication between the worlds of the treaty ports and the literati-gentry in the hinterlands. In Ming-Qing society, gentry elites moved frequently between the countryside and administrative centers. Academies were mostly placed away from urban commercial centers. This ended, however, when most colleges and universities were located in coastal cities. This parallels the socioeconomic effect of the treaty ports, since analysis indicates that, prior to the late nineteenth century, the ports had no significant transformational impact on the hinterlands. A great cultural gap thus opened up between the intellectual worlds of the treaty ports and of the gentry-literati. The situation began to change in the 1890s, when western learning for the first time spilled out of the treaty ports into the inland cities on a large scale. This was made possible mainly by the emergence of new social institutions. Traditional academies were renovated or gave way to new schools. Curriculum reform gave a prominent place to western learning. Educational changes were especially noticeable after the Sino-Japanese War of 1894–1895. Many voluntary associations called *study societies* appeared among scholar-officials, their number reaching over sixty between 1895 and 1898. Another important institutional innovation at the time was elite journalism. Newspapers and magazines were founded by literati themselves.

Most were politically oriented and ideologically charged. They spread beyond the treaty ports into the inland cities and had circulation agencies in almost every major city in China proper. Elite journalism helped bridge the gap between the scholar-gentry and the treaty ports and aroused nationwide interest in western learning.

The intellectual ferment that ensued had a number of dimensions. Focusing on the new sociopolitical thought, the spectrum of ideas included Zhang Zhidong and his followers advocating a self-strengthening position on one side, and Kang Youwei and his sympathizers promoting constitutional reform on the other. There was also a liberal group forming around Tan Sitong and Liang Qichao. Several ideas seem to have been important for late Qing liberal intellectuals, including social contract theory, the organic state, sovereignty, and the territorialization of the state. These ideas emerged in the context of social Darwinism and nationalism, and the interpretation of historical development as a struggle of nations and nation-states.[61] The liberal group represented a new departure, elements of which began to challenge the foundations of the traditional social and political order—the Confucian cosmological myth. The myth had been made up of a fusion of family and political ethics and based on the cosmological belief that sociopolitical ethics were embedded in the cosmic order. By contrast, the reform-oriented intellectuals emphasized the importance of Chinese citizens, as the basis of national destiny, to the nation's defense and well-being. Militarization and mobilization of citizens, they believed, would empower China to stand up for its rights in the world. Together, these notions represented a new conception of the state, but also a new conception of what it meant to be Chinese. In the 1890s, the radical reformers shook the Confucian foundations of the Qing empire and spearheaded an intellectual nationalist movement that was to culminate in the May Fourth movement in 1919. This new focus on the nation and Chinese citizens, together with the disintegration of the old cosmological and political vision, affected Chinese intellectuals across all political camps. Time was running out for imperial rule by a Manchu dynasty. Its existence was no longer assumed; on the contrary, it was increasingly seen as a fundamental impediment to the power and wealth of the Chinese nation. A new age of ideologies and political mobilization of the masses was about to begin.

What also stands out in this period of modern China is its resilience in the face of crisis. Humiliation was transmuted into a uniting force, transformed from shame into a stimulant to the construction of a new and modern national identity. It was also a turning point in shaping China's modern political and military culture.[62] The abashed sense of living in a paradise lost, of having fallen so far behind other countries, would become a curious badge of resolution. It would compel the country to strengthen and develop, to finally catch up with the West, to regain its ability to defend itself, and to restore China's honor. Even the weakened dynastic empire demonstrated a capacity not only to withstand shock, but also to restore stability in the wake of potentially destabilizing disasters. The devastating Taiping Rebellion (1850–1864), which exposed the weakness of Qing rulers, was suppressed by regional leaders who possessed the highest level of civil service examination degrees. These men mobilized troops and funds in their home provinces and defeated the rebel armies. The victorious generals, all of them Han Chinese, then restored control to the throne, even though it was occupied by the non-Chinese descendants of Manchu invaders. As other early-modern land empires dissolved within the nineteenth century, it seems that only the Qing empire persisted as a national entity. The Ottoman empire was eventually broken up into numerous countries. Russia was divided into national provinces united under a federation structure. China is unique in that it went into the era of revolutions as a unified entity, based upon the territory of the previous empire.

Ironically, the same resilient forces that provided coherence also worked against institutional reforms whenever those reforms threatened the standing, incomes, or future prospects of the political and economic leadership groups that dominated the imperial polity. In the short term, resilience kept the territory of the Qing empire intact during the time of crisis. The long-term cost, however, was that it postponed necessary change, adding to the radicalization and conflict of the tumultuous twentieth century. For a long time after 1900, and in many ways even today, China continues to struggle with the late Qing institutional conundrum of needing to replace the empire's long-lasting institutions with a viable order capable of fostering economic reconstruction, spurring technological progress, confronting foreign military encroachment, and building a legitimate political system. China's problems since, and many of the conflicted solutions to address them, have been rooted in its late nineteenth-century crisis.

PART TWO

Chinese Revolutions

Two years after the Boxer catastrophe, in May 1903, a young teacher and writer, Chen Duxiu (1879–1942), who in 1921 would become the Chinese Communist Party's first general secretary, helped establish a political association called the Anhui Patriotic Society. Its constitution, which Chen helped to draft, declared: "Because the foreign calamity is daily growing worse, the society seeks to unite the masses into an organization that will develop patriotic thought and stir up a martial spirit, so people will grab their weapons to protect their country and restore our basic national sovereignty."[1] Among the new political elites that emerged after 1911, there continued to be a widespread consciousness of a glorious past that had been lost during the country's catastrophic decline at the hands of western imperialism in the nineteenth century. The nineteenth century increasingly came to be identified with national humiliation *(guochi),* to which the young, new elites reacted by calling for revolution and "national salvation" *(jiuguo).* The combination of recollections of ancient grandeur and outrage at China's decline provided the starting point for Chinese revolutionary nationalism. Beginning around 1900, this development would not only bring a quick end to the Qing dynasty, but would fundamentally shape the formation of a new republic.

Revolutionary nationalists saw revolution as essential to national strengthening and modernization—to making China a "rich country, strong state," to restoring its greatness, and to creating an age of national flourishing. As Benedict Anderson and Etienne Balibar have shown, nationalism is rooted in an understanding of a nation as a political community, or "imagined community." The elements of this imaginary consist of a common history, rights to a territory (that needs to be defended), ethnicity, and a common historical *telos* (that must be fought for). Revolutionary nationalism was restrictive and exclusive, as it emphasized the unique and binding aspects of a common legacy.[2] Based on this concept of what a real nation should be, Chinese nationalists envisioned the Chinese nation-state as a sovereign, revolutionary, political organization grafted onto the Chinese people as an imagined community.[3] Yet, while they pursued similar goals, Chinese nationalist intellectuals and officials were deeply divided on how to revive China and restore its greatness. Chinese political leaders and thinkers since have often disagreed fiercely, resulting in wide shifts in the selection of political strategies, foreign models, and methods. The first half of the twentieth century was therefore dominated, shaped, and irrevocably characterized in China by the problem and practice of revolution. Given this multitude of political lines and ideas, it is fair to say there was not one Chinese revolution. There were many.

The revolutions in China stemmed not only from internal and regional causes, but also from the influences of global discourses and events. They can be understood as parts of "global moments" and sometimes even "global movements." China's many revolutions should therefore be viewed and explored as global events, linked to local and national developments simultaneously playing out elsewhere. A look around the world at the beginning of the twentieth century would have revealed a global political landscape in the process of being reshaped by national revolutions.[4] The prior century was ushered in by dramatic transformations along the "revolutionary Atlantic"—that is, the French and American revolutions—and in the mid-nineteenth century they were followed by the Great Rebellion in India (1857–58) and the American Civil War (1861–65). The turn of the twentieth century brought a cluster of revolutions, in Russia in 1905, Iran in 1905, and Turkey in 1908. All these combined to make a case for revolution as the way to bring about effective and fast historical change. They also seemed to demonstrate that Chinese problems could be solved by revolution alone.

The original meaning of the word revolution, or *geming*—the righteous, Heaven-mandated removal of a previous regime—accurately described, in most Han people's eyes, the fall of the Manchu Qing dynasty. But thereafter, the word took on a new meaning. It was now also used, first by the Japanese, in a sense more aligned with the western concept of revolution. For the rest of the century, this broader and eventually more radical concept spread quickly among thinkers and political elites. The term came to be associated with the violent overthrow of a monarchical system (as in the French and Russian revolutions), and with that, the total transformation of the socioeconomic and even intellectual conditions of a people and nation. The modern period saw a rapid multiplication of terms related to revolution. To be sure, in China and in all of its governments, it was assumed above all that revolution meant prevailing in battle, whether against warlords, rival political parties, competing ideas, or different forms of ideology (or *weltanschauung*). But other adjectives soon added new dimensions to the concept, extending it to economic, social, and cultural revolutions with potential to transform life in China more profoundly than the military or violent dimensions of making revolutions.

The immense impact of this was that, in the course of the twentieth century, more and more Chinese came to accept the revolutionary praxis as the norm for building a new nation. Some of these proposed revolutions challenged ancient ideas and practices, while others focused on imposing new values, yet all transformed Chinese people's lives. The notion of revolution was centrifugal and pervasive, as new fields of knowledge and social practice were permanently integrated: psychology, behavior, law, the practices of producers, consumers, buyers, and importers, and more. Revolution, then, involved cross-fertilization, by which a broad range of areas and activities were organized or reorganized.

To be a revolutionary state meant to implement a new political order, with new sources of legitimacy. Any return to the world of empire as it had existed before became unthinkable, even dangerous. Defenders of the existing order were portrayed as old and obsolete, reactionary and counter-revolutionary, or at the very least "conservative." A revolutionary nation-state was a lofty, ambitious attempt to respond to a whole range of deep problems the old order had been incapable of solving, from governance to security to economy. Revolutionaries expected that radical change or overthrow of the political system would solve their economic problems, guarantee their civil rights, and allow their participation in political life. They also hoped that a strong nation-state would be more assertive in standing up to the interests of the world's great powers and foreign capitalists. For an awakening China just emerging from the Qing dynasty, this dominant theme of making a national revolution therefore gathered into itself a whole set of crucial issues including foreign encroachment, national self-determination, the production of "Chineseness" and other forms of national belonging, public participation in political discussion, public education, social equality, prosperity, and economic growth. China needed to be not only imagined but constructed in all these areas. The vision had to be made into lived reality.

The 1911 Revolution achieved its goal of ending the dynastic system, but it led to dictatorship, warlordism and, above all, further revolutions. Perhaps most importantly, it mobilized the new social groups—students and intellectuals, workers, women, the emerging urban bourgeoisie, and certainly the military—that would shape the first half of China's twentieth century. Following the overthrow of the dynastic system, revolutionary efforts were extended to the building of a new state and the formation of a new nation. The Nationalist Party of China (Guomindang GMD)—led by Sun Yat-sen and, later, Chiang Kai-shek—promised a republican era that would literally "reconstruct" China into a modern nation-state and citizenry. To build this new, strong nation-state, ambitious initiatives were undertaken and investments made to develop industry, education, the military, and the government. In the 1920s, however, an alternative, oppositional effort to form a powerful, wealthy nation-state out of the remains of the Qing empire was launched by the Chinese Communist Party. The communist movement that, after initial setbacks, was able to gather momentum in the rural areas by mobilizing and arming peasants also had the goal of creating a new China. Its vision for the nation was to develop it, once it was liberated from the yoke of the past, into a modern society that was also an egalitarian, communist one.

Overlapping and competing with the particular issues of revolution was the broad allure of modernity. Revolution was, in the minds of many intellectuals, needed to make China modern, but modernity was also seen as something independent, a day-to-day culture and lifestyle that could be achieved and practiced outside and almost independent of political revolution. Shanghai and other treaty ports, in particular, came to embody the promise of modernity in the early twentieth century. The general attractiveness of an urban and secular modernity broke through at different points and in different ways in the republican era, but never simply on western terms. During the republican period, diverse architectural elements, forms of urban organization, material objects, and cultural activities were combined, mingled, and juxtaposed in slender urban spaces in China, often in sharply contradictory ways. Hence, the chapters in this part also explore the cultural forms and social practices current in urban China in the first half of the twentieth century, and what these reveal, suggest, or obscure. All of these—architecture and urban spaces; economic underpinnings of foreign trade, commerce, labor, and leisure; words and images consumed by the populace; new roles for women, youth, the family, and citizens—contributed to create the ideal and the complex reality of a China in revolution.

When war broke out in 1937, there were many internal struggles and daring experiments underway by governments, intellectuals, and the business world to create a new China. These were abruptly cut short. Japan's attack, the culmination of decades of expansion and pressure, led to the outbreak of nationwide hostilities that started the war in Asia, earlier than the Second World War in Europe. A united China rallied passionate resistance against the overwhelming Japanese war machinery and fought a bitter war, but the costs were tremendous. In 1945, when Japan capitulated, China was exhausted, its cities destroyed. Rather than cooperate to rebuild, China's two remaining major political camps, the Nationalist Party and the Communist Party, staged a final, brutal battle for control of a devastated nation.

FOUR

Upending the Empire

1900–1919

Political change had been expected but, coming at the end of a decade of an incremental institution-building process known as the "New Policies" (*xinzheng*), by which the Qing court had already largely transformed the organization of the Chinese state, the Revolution of 1911 itself came as something of a surprise. The abolition of the centuries-old system of civil service examinations, the election of various province-level assemblies (albeit by a very small and elite group of voters), the establishment of modern schools and universities, and the influx of western commodities and techniques all took place during the last years of Qing rule. The reforms were ambitious, but came too late to avert the erosion of legitimacy that had set in during the nineteenth-century crisis. It is an irony that the belated but farsighted reforms became a trigger for revolution.

China's 1911 revolution ushered in a period of political disorder that lasted until 1928. The "first republic in Asia," with Sun Yat-sen as its short-lived first president, was quickly followed by a constitutional monarchy under Yuan Shikai, equally short-lived. With the Qing dynasty and Manchu rulers removed, it soon turned out that neither the republican movement nor any other social group was able to fill the political vacuum. The imperial system was wrecked, but no other institution arose to replace it. The outbreak of the Great War in 1914 made the situation even more confusing and unpredictable. As the European powers focused their resources and energies on Europe and withdrew from Asia, Japan saw an irresistible opportunity. Immediately after the Great War, the global protest wave that emboldened students and intellectuals to demand emancipation, awakening, and political participation set the stage for the May Fourth movement in 1919. With Chinese generals, the Japanese military, republicans, and passionate students hungry for change

(209)

all laying claims on the coveted legacy and remnants of the Qing empire, intense jockeying for power ensued.

The New Policies

In many ways, the political experiments to remake the Qing empire into a modern nation-state started after 1900, in the last decade of Manchu rule. Responding to the severe crisis of the empire exposed by the Boxer episode, the court embarked on a program of reform that went far beyond anything previously tried. The New Policies aimed at broad-ranging reforms meant to make the imperial government more efficient and more involved in many areas of society and economy. Recent research has shown that the New Policies were not simply a superficial effort by a collapsing dynasty clinging to power and doomed to fail, but truly a "new beginning" that ultimately led to China's turn to "big government" to seek national rejuvenation and awakening throughout the twentieth century. While the goal of the imperial system's reform was not achieved—the dynasty's fall from power could not be avoided—the policies had far-reaching impact and considerable long-term significance. They represented a reversal of the long decline of the government's size and capabilities, and a clear move toward the construction of a more intrusive, expansive, and powerful state. This development would continue far into the late twentieth century.

On January 29, 1901, a decree issued by the Empress Dowager Cixi, still in exile in Xi'an, started a new phase of ambitious reforms, based to an unprecedented degree on learning from the West. The edict said: "Now that the peace negotiations have commenced, all affairs of government must be thoroughly overhauled, in hopes of gradually achieving real wealth and power." The new course called for adopting "all the fundamentals that have made the foreign countries rich and strong," including "governing methods, people's livelihood, educational systems, the military, and financial affairs." The text added: "Making these changes is a matter of life and death for our country. . . . There is no other way."[1] Reorganizing the Chinese polity to survive in a world of imperialism had become a matter of great urgency.

In April 1901, a political affairs office was formed to sort through reform proposals systematically and manage the implementation of various new policies.[2] One goal of the reform was to make the bureaucracy more efficient by improving administrative organization and coordination among agencies. New institutions would be created based on formalized rule systems that would be capable of providing more inclusive and efficient forms of governance. For instance, the venerable six boards were abolished and replaced by cabinet ministries. A new Ministry of Justice took over from the Board of Punishments. The Board of Revenue was reorganized into the Ministry of Finance and the Zongli Yamen was replaced by a Foreign Ministry. Several ministries were established that had no predecessors. The Ministry of Trade was China's first-ever government agency focused on regulation and support of commerce. Other new ministries included the Ministry of Education, a Ministry of Police (later Ministry of the Interior), and a Ministry of Posts and Communications. Other developments included the establishment of the state bank in 1905, followed by the birth of a national currency, with the yuan as the new monetary unit.

Constitutional and legal issues were at the center of the reforms as the search for a new constitutional order to replace the traditional imperial political system started for the first time in earnest. This would prove to be one of the most important turning points in modern Chinese history.[3] The reforms were also driven by modern China's overwhelming impulse to join the world on equal terms and to end the practice of extraterritoriality. Although debates about constitutional monarchy date back at least to the 1880s, attempts at constitution-making were not made before 1905. In 1905 and 1906 two study commissions were sent abroad. They were charged with the task to study constitutional systems around the world and to prepare a comprehensive report. The Imperial Constitutional Commission visited Europe, Japan, and the United States in 1905. A second commission called the Constitutional Government Commission was sent to Japan, Germany, and Great Britain in 1906. In one report by those delegations, officials concluded that the "real reason why other countries have become wealthy and powerful lies in the fact that they have a constitution and decide important affairs through public discussion. Their monarch and people form one indivisible unity."[4] Many officials and intellectuals saw the origins of China's weakness in the distance between the ruler and the ruled—in itself a rather Confucian concern. Through constitutional reform, a closer and more organic relationship between state and society could be formed. It is important to note that those efforts of constitution making were informed by intentions not so much to empower the people as to bring together monarchy and people in a tighter bond.

The work of the commission resulted in the 1908 document "Principles of the Constitution" (xianfa dagang). It envisioned a type of government with a monarch (usually a hereditary position) as head of state and regulated by a written constitution. The authority of the monarch would not be derived simply from religious concepts, or the Mandate of Heaven, or the inheritance of the throne, but from a constitution that spelled out basic rules. The emperor retained the power to make and promulgate law. Under the principles, the emperor could issue imperial decrees, but he was not permitted to use them to change or abrogate laws. The parliament had only consultative functions and was subordinate to the emperor. Although the people were granted certain fundamental rights, the principles did not grant a general and equal right to vote. This version of constitutional monarchy took the Meiji constitution of 1889 as its model. It was decided in the end, however, that a "preparatory period" of ten to fifteen years should precede the implementation of constitutional government. The Qing constitution therefore never went into effect, due to the Xinhai revolution in 1911, but the "Principles" led to the establishment of representative bodies, called assemblies, on the local level (in 1908) and provincial level (in 1909) that soon became important political platforms. In 1910, even a national assembly began to meet. Members of the assemblies were elected by male citizens who fulfilled voter registration requirements regarding property and education. Most assembly members came from the provincial elites, including officials and merchants. The assemblies had no legislative functions, but were platforms for debates on policy-related issues.[5]

In 1902 an Office for Legal Reform was established.[6] It was headed by two officials regarded as specialists in legal matters, Shen Jiaben (1840–1913) and Wu Tingfang (1842–1922). The office had three main tasks: to study and translate important western texts on legal thinking and legislation; to evaluate the Chinese legal tradition in light of these; and to draft new laws based on a synthesis of western law and Chinese tradition. A few years later, the Qing government started to overhaul the institutional structure. With the same edict that created a Ministry of Justice, an Imperial Supreme Court was established. The court quickly moved forward with an ambitious reform program. In all, twenty-six translations from foreign countries were published, including one text on penology. An examination of foreign law was conducted by sending study delegations to various countries. Members of these missions not only collected written law and sought discussions with leading legal scholars but also made visits to police offices, procurators, courts, and prisons.

The reformers introduced the separation of civil and criminal law. The office drafted separate criminal and civil codes and also rules of criminal and civil procedure. After lengthy discussions, the reforms finally went into effect in 1910. The execution of sentences and legal punishments was another main area of the reforms. In 1905 physical penalties ranging from tattooing to torture, slow slicing, and the beheading of corpses and public exhibition of heads were abolished. Some other physical punishments, like flogging, were replaced in the same year with fines. The concept of collective responsibility was also abolished. The newly drafted criminal code limited punishments to three basic forms: fines, imprisonments, and death sentences. Imprisonment became the main form of punishment for most offenses. Within a very short time, public displays of painful punishments disappeared. The death penalty, too, was no longer to be carried out publicly but only behind the walls of a prison.

In 1909 China adopted its first law of nationality, defining as "Chinese" all children of Chinese fathers regardless of their place of residence.[7] This principle of *jus sanguinis* (determining nationality status by bloodlines) was based on new, nineteenth-century ideas about ethnicity, and directly conflicted with the notion of citizenship as a territorial concept. China had decided to treat other countries' ethnically Chinese citizens as Chinese subjects—despite its inability to offer protections to them.

Economic development through trade and industrialization was another major point on the reform agenda of this period's government. China's first Company Law was published in 1904.[8] Even as it asserted government control over companies by requiring registration, it aimed to make it easier for entrepreneurs to establish them. It introduced the protection of limited liability, required the publication of annual reports, and put in force clear accounting regulations. Merchants were offered assistance to attend meetings and expositions abroad and to develop products for export. The Ministry of Commerce actively supported the establishment of Chambers of Commerce in the most important cities and in the provinces.[9] By 1909, approximately 180 such chambers were bringing together local merchants, entrepreneurs, and brokers. The chambers soon turned into important channels of communication between the government and the world of business. They also provided forums for the establishment of professional associations. As these new forms of legal organization appeared, they inspired the creation of still others. Groups advocating social reform quickly took their place alongside trade associations.

The New Policies also marked an important turning point in the development of the military.[10] On August 29, 1901, an edict suspended the traditional military exam, clearing the way for modern military education. A decree issued on September 11 of the same year, recognizing the value of trained officers and soldiers, directed all provinces to establish new armies based on western models and to set up military schools. Another decree, issued the next day, ordered the division of army units into separate standing armies, first-class reserves, and gendarmerie divisions. The court also discussed reforming the traditional Green Standard and Banner armies, but no solution was agreed upon. Instead, these were often made reserve units. Implementation of reforms varied from province to province. Progress was greatest where powerful and capable governors-general were in office, as, for example, Yuan Shikai in Zhili or Zhang Zhidong in Hunan and Hubei. Elsewhere the process was less successful. Existing troop units were simply renamed or reorganized and officers were deputized to train in the new military academies. Foreign, often Japanese, instructors were hired to qualify Chinese officers, and occasionally to drill Chinese troops.

In 1903 a Commission on Military Reorganization was set up. It developed a plan to create a national military force, called the New Army, composed of thirty-six divisions of approximately 12,500 men each, totaling some 450,000 men. Individual provinces took responsibility for organizing, training, and financing one or more divisions of the New Army. Two divisions from North China, known as the Beiyang Army and under the command of Yuan Shikai, provided the first units of this national army and constituted China's strongest military force for the next decade. As military service acquired new prestige among the educated strata of society, it became an important channel of social mobility.

The government also pursued far-reaching reforms in the area of education. The most dramatic move was the abolition of the civil service examination system that had existed for more than a millennium. It was replaced by a new educational system based on western models, which introduced a whole range of new subjects while retaining Chinese classics in the curriculum. Prefecture-level academies were converted into public high schools, province-level academies were transformed into universities, and primary schools were newly created. By 1909, 52,000 new schools had already been created, in which nearly 1.6 million students were enrolled.

In time, unintended consequences of the reforms would come to upend the empire, as illustrated by the abolition of the exam system. As early as the seventeenth century, the Qing court had controversially begun the sale of examination degrees, in hopes of financing the massive costs of the examination system and raising funds for the cash-strapped empire. The proportion of titles sold increased rapidly: 30 percent of academic titles were purchased before 1850, and after that, the rate increased to 51 percent. In the years that followed, the court tried, with only partial success, to restrict the number of sales.[11] The unforeseen and far-reaching consequence of title sales was that they undermined the normative framework of an institution that had promoted the principle of meritocracy. Increasingly, it instead reinforced the symbiosis of power and money among political administration and economic players. The institutional legitimacy of the once inclusive exam system suffered mightily as it contributed to spreading clientelism and patronage of economic and political special interests. Calls increased for a system considered "unnatural" as well as "outdated" to be discarded. Meanwhile, new forms of education spread in the treaty ports and beyond, so that the imperial examination system was not only delegitimized but consciously decanonized. Literary and cultural forms enshrined by the system became, as western perspectives spread, symbols of backwardness, particularly in the minds of reformist Chinese intellectuals. Traditional forms of knowledge were discounted as superstition as the new intellectuals propagated the "modern sciences" of European and US origin as the only valid path to knowledge, enlightenment, and national power.[12] Thus, in a rather short period of time—just a few decades—the imperial examination system was so thoroughly delegitimized and decanonized that, after 1900, its abolition seemed inevitable.

When the court did abolish the examinations in 1905, it destroyed what had been one of its most powerful means of sociocultural control. For centuries, as one of imperial China's most sophisticated and functional institutions, the examination system had unquestionably contributed to popular acceptance of the entire imperial system. The reasons for its abolishment are not simple ones having to do with the institution's backwardness, the traditionalism of its contents, bureaucratic ignorance, or the superiority of western modernity. In a much larger sense, at a crucial point in history, this was a failure to adapt and keep an institution's foundations from eroding. It should not be presumed that the classical civil examination inherently presented obstacles to the development of a modern Chinese state or to the process of modernization. Certainly, it would have remained possible to choose an elite cadre to serve the imperial state at the highest levels based on a classic education centered on moral and political, rather than technical, instruction; indeed, the selection and training of elites in the rising nation-states of Europe during the early modern eras emphasized the value of classic humanistic education. Nor should it be presumed that the classical exams could be abolished without ramifications beyond their own removal. They were part of a highly integrated field of cultural, social, political, and educational institutions that had, in combination, effectively met the needs of the dynastic bureaucracy and supported the late imperial social structure. By axing one of the most essential pillars of the state, the court destroyed the many connections that had tied classic virtues to dynastic power and elite status.

The New Policies also tried to solve the problem of budget deficits, which had been long in the making but brought to a crisis point by the increased spending associated with reform projects. The basic problem was China's dwindling revenue stream. The capacity of the central administration to collect taxes had been severely diminished during the course of the nineteenth century. Taxes were underreported and remittances to the central government often withheld by the provinces and local governments. On top of the Boxer indemnity, the need to finance ambitious reforms such as the creation of new schools, a legal system, and the military made the budget problem even worse. Falling revenues together with increased financial obligations created large deficits. To close the gap, the government took out massive loans from banks and foreign governments, and also sought to extract more resources through fiscal reform. To increase tax collection, the government demanded annual contributions from the provinces based on thorough audits of province-level finances. It also nationalized profitable industries, mines, and shipping lines. As a result of those policies, China's revenues leapt by over 70 percent in a five-year period, from just over 70 million taels in 1903 to 120 million taels in 1908.[13] The New Policies, it seemed, had at least stopped the long-term trend of fiscal decentralization.

Finally, the New Policies saw the emergence of a more activist state interested in transforming cultural and social practices by introducing new forms and technologies of governing. A growing use of social surveys, for instance, reflected China's transformation from a dynastic empire to a sovereign state in which the people—not tradition, classics, or Heaven—stood as the source of political authority and legitimacy. A national census was conducted between 1909 and 1911, beginning a movement toward producing more data and knowledge about Chinese society to be used in governing.[14] Equally important was that this new census deployed a single template to count the entire population. The message was that this nation-state's political community was founded on the principle of abstract equality among its citizens, not a hierarchy of social or ethnic groups. The survey gathered empirical information including population statistics, sociological and ethnographic facts, economic data, cultural artifacts, and archaeological evidence. Information gained by surveys and other means was used to support increasingly interventionist policies. For instance, an ongoing campaign was waged in the countryside against superstition, which was blamed in part for the spread of the Boxer movement.[15] New to the Chinese vocabulary, "superstition" *(mixin)* was a term introduced by Jesuits in the seventeenth century. Land attached to temples was confiscated and nationalized, so that revenue from those plots could be used to fund new public schools. Thus a movement originally launched in the name of the Confucian state against religious sectarianism came to be associated with the pursuit of progress, science, and national defense.

The reformers identified numerous social problems that held China back and impeded development. Measures were taken to remedy these ills. Among the first decrees was one proclaimed on February 1, 1902, lifting the ban on Han-Manchu intermarriage. The ban had been upheld since the beginning of the Qing dynasty, although there were exceptions for certain groups. The new goal was to relax ethnic segregation in the interest of shaping a common and equal people. The same decree called upon Han Chinese to abandon their tradition of foot-binding, stressing that the practice "harms creatures and violates Nature's intentions."[16] Many initiatives, both state-sponsored and advanced by civil society, aimed at improving the social position of women. In spring 1907, a Regulation for Women's Education was decreed which made it official that women could receive education. Another area that attracted the attention of reformers was drug abuse. Opium smoking was now recognized as a habit that harmed not only the addict, but society as a whole. An edict announced the plan to eradicate opium production and consumption in China within ten years.[17] Opium houses were closed as part of the prohibition movement that was in full swing by 1906.

In broad historical perspective, the New Policies were a significant chapter in modern Chinese institutional history. Designed to create a range of new institutions, the reform policies of the twentieth century's first decade attempted to usher in what could best be described as a modern, activist, and fiscally efficient state. The vision was of a state that could mobilize sufficient financial resources, by collecting taxes centrally and making wise use of borrowing and other financial policies, to render China strong and wealthy. The restructuring of the bureaucracy undertaken for this purpose established institutional patterns that would shape the republican and communist governments that came later. Campaigns and movements seeking social transformation laid down new forms of governance to which later regimes would also resort. The reach of government extended deeper into society than ever before. Yet, some governmental functions could not be brought or kept under the control of the central state. In areas including the military, education, and finances, the New Policies' boost to political power accrued to local and provincial elites more than it did to the imperial state.

As top-down reforms were launched by the court throughout the 1900s, they were also often simply outpaced by developments in Chinese society. The elites who dominated local and provincial assemblies increasingly distanced themselves from the Qing court. These local leaders, who drew their power from a combination of commercial wealth, landholding, military power, patronage, and education, constituted a new kind of elite that had emerged toward the end of the nineteenth century. Considerably more urbanized than the traditional gentry, they not only assembled to discuss local and provincial affairs, but also in many cases ran newspapers and hosted lecture series that were increasingly critical of Qing rule. The provincial assemblies established by the New Politics were among many new venues from which opposition could emerge.

The influx of new ideas contributed to a growing radicalization and rapid politicization of China's intellectuals, many of whom spent this decade in Japan. Studying there, they heard lectures by exiled political figures, saw foreign newspaper reports, and read Japanese translations of western social and political thought. New political concepts gained popularity, such as *minzu* (nation or race), *minquan* (people's rights), *minzhu zhuyi* (democracy), *shehui zhuyi* (socialism), *gongheguo* (republic), and, not least, *geming* (revolution). Thus, while Kang Youwei's idea of a constitutional, Confucian monarchy had appeared revolutionary in 1898, Kang was considered by the first decade of the twentieth century, by most progressive thinkers and activists, to be hopeless and backward. Even Liang Qichao, one of the most prominent and widely read advocates of constitutionalism and an admirer of liberalism, was outdone by a cultural and political vanguard made up of activists like Zhang Binglin (Zhang Taiyan, 1868–1936), the editor of the influential *Minbao (People's Journal)* published in Tokyo. Zhang and many of his followers disapproved of what they saw as a pro-western bias in the institution-building process and advocated an alternative form of democracy, rooted in social equality and Chinese utopian traditions. Zhang Binglin and Zou Rong, author of the devastating essay "The Revolutionary Army," published in Shanghai in 1903, were the first Chinese to articulate a full-scale anti-Manchu ideology.[18] Zou Rong vehemently advocated the overthrow of the Manchu government. "Expel all Manchus who live in China, or kill them for revenge," he demanded, and "Slay the Manchu emperor!" Zhang Binglin had been one of the first in China to publicly cut off his queue—a specifically revolutionary gesture. Zhang and Zou opposed alien Manchu rule over native Han Chinese. To them, the Manchus were supplanting a vibrant, native Chinese culture with a primitive and barbarian tribal culture.

Perhaps the most severe challenge to Qing rule stemmed from the rise of such racialized, nationalist rhetoric. Collectively, the institutions put in place by the New Policies altered the way in which China was imagined, at least by those members of the elite who participated in them. This newly emerging class believed deeply in modern nationalism and reform, promoted the creation of modern institutions, and questioned the basis of Manchu rule over China. The reforms thus initiated a process by which China was separated from the Qing empire.[19] To be sure, the terms for China in Chinese—such as *Zhongguo, huaren*, and *Han*—date to much earlier times, but the emerging understanding of China and the identity of the "Chinese" or "Chinese citizens," even as it incorporated older notions and terms, was a very new and modern invention. At this important juncture, conceptually, the new China was born. Moreover, it reordered the ethnic landscape by introducing demographic concepts like overseas Chinese and national minorities. The overseas Chinese were identified as a group that could help China solve its problems, overcome its dependence on the West, and regain the respect of the rest of the world. Meanwhile, numerous ethnic populations were defined as minorities and like the Manchus they were perceived as inferior and alien to China. Defining their various statuses and relationships to and within China was part of the process of negotiating what constituted China and who were the Chinese people. Overall, the nationalism promoted by the reforms rapidly moved beyond the control of the Qing state and fused with racist, nationalist ideologies in the newspapers and revolutionary groups. The radicalization of this entire generation might be seen as another unintended consequence of the New Policies reforms. Bold institutional innovation failed to save the empire, because it came too late, but it did shape the new China.

The Republican Movement and the 1911 Revolution

In the first decade of the twentieth century, the Qing dynasty faced pressure from a political movement seeking to abolish the monarchy and establish a republican system.[20] Mostly, this movement, like its leader Sun Yat-sen himself, was thriving less in China than in overseas Chinese communities and foreign-controlled parts of China, such as Hong Kong and the treaty ports concessions. Sun was born in 1866 in Cuiheng, in the county of Xianshang—today, the city of Zhongshan in Guangdong province, not far from Macau. His family could not afford the classical education that would prepare him for civil service examinations. Instead, in 1878, Sun was sent to join his older brother in Honolulu, where he attended a missionary school. After that, he went to Hong Kong and graduated in 1892 from the Hong Kong College of Medicine as one of its first Chinese students. Sun's upbringing was markedly different from other leading figures of the time. He felt more at home abroad than in China, and spoke and wrote English more comfortably than classical

Chinese. By training, he was a western-style professional with little schooling in the Chinese classics. At the same time, Sun identified himself as a southerner, stressing his links to overseas communities in maritime China and to the southern anti-Manchuism of the Taipings and the Triads. What also set him apart was his outspoken, unremitting activism for the overthrow of the Qing dynasty.

The year 1894 marked Sun Yat-sen's entry into politics. Motivated by an incipient nationalism and spirit of revolution, he returned to Hawaii to set up indisputably the first organization dedicated to anti-Qing revolution, the Revive China Society *(Xingzhonghui)*. Because of his revolutionary activities, he was soon banished not only from China but from Hong Kong, as well. In 1905, with the financial support of Japanese sponsors, he founded the Revolutionary Alliance *(Tongmenghui)* in Tokyo, which ultimately evolved into the Nationalist Party *Guomindang* (GMD, or KMT in the older literature), at which point the flag of the Revive China Society became the flag of the GMD. He also founded the above-mentioned *People's Journal (Minbao)* as the political organ of the Revolutionary Alliance in Tokyo in 1905. For the next few years this organization took the lead in promoting a republican revolution for China. The movement was of a nature more ideological and rhetorical than practical. Despite many efforts and ambitious plans, the Alliance did not succeed in orchestrating local uprisings in China, let alone a national revolution.

The fact that Sun had so many foreign contacts and was so much a child of foreign-occupied treaty ports and the overseas Chinese diaspora alienated him from revolutionaries and reformers in China proper. He was often faulted for insufficient familiarity with China's realities and social practices. Two factors, however, contributed to his preeminent role. First, like nobody else, Sun was able to obtain support and raise money from overseas Chinese merchant communities. He connected especially with entrepreneurs hailing from Guangdong and Fujian who had gone abroad to run businesses all around Southeast Asia and, to a lesser extent, the Americas and Europe. Giving speeches to overseas Chinese communities and exile groups and engaging in other fundraising activities, Sun honed his political skills. His pioneering use of oratory in gatherings created a model for modern Chinese leadership which later politicians would follow. Second, only Sun Yat-sen had something of a revolutionary vision to offer. Beginning with a 1905 speech in Tokyo at the founding of the Revolutionary Alliance, he worked on a compendium of ideas regarding China's political and social future. Eventually his speeches were combined in the published work for which he is best known, "Three Principles of the People" *(sanmin zhuyi)*. Sometimes criticized as vague or eclectic, his three principles of nationalism, democracy, and livelihood nevertheless outlined an appealing political program for a new future of China. In his own words: "The San Min Principles are the principles for our nation's salvation."[21]

The principle of nationalism *(minzu zhuyi)* placed emphasis on racial cohesion based on the concept of *minzu* (race) instead of *guojia* (state). This principle assumed that a Han race existed which formed the ethnic basis for the single grand nation of China. Sun explained that "the Chinese people are of the Han or Chinese race with common blood, common language, common religion, and common customs—a single, pure race."[22] The Chinese nation should be united to withstand imperialist domination. Sun decried that the people of China had no national consciousness: "The Chinese people have shown the greatest loyalty to family and clan with the result that in China there have been family-ism and clannism but no real nationalism. Foreign observers say that the Chinese are like a sheet of loose sand."[23] This choice of terminology suggests that Sun Yat-sen's vision of China had as much to do with protecting the Chinese people as a race as it did with preserving the sovereign territory of the country. Sun alludes several times to fears of "racial extinction."

The principle of democracy *(minquan zhuyi)* stressed that China must be a republic since a monarchical system generates factionalism and bureaucratic in-fighting. While Sun aimed to empower China's citizens with political representation via a national assembly, and with political participation via the rights to elections, initiative, referendum, and recall, he repeatedly highlighted China's need to restrict freedoms and its need for strong government. Sun believed that the Chinese at the beginning of the twentieth century had excessive personal liberty, and that some of it should be relinquished for the sake of national strength and independence. China, he thought, needed more social discipline and durable order, and less emphasis on individualism and the rights of the people. Insisting that a new and powerful form of governance alone would allow China to become prosperous, strong, and respected, Sun created a powerful argument that would be invoked time and again in China.

Of the three principles, the third, supporting people's livelihood *(minsheng zhuyi),* was the least carefully defined and most vulnerable to conflicting interpretations. In his words, *minsheng* refers to "the existence of society, the welfare of the nation, the life of the masses." By invoking this principle, Sun sought to respond to the social problems, especially inequality, unemployment, and poverty, in western capitalist societies at that time. But he went to great lengths to distinguish his response from socialism, which he viewed as mired in constant in-fighting over the correct interpretations of Karl Marx's writings. To him, "the problem of livelihood is the problem of subsistence (and not of ownership)."[24] The republic he envisioned would care for the subsistence of the population. This principle thus highlighted the need to create a viable socioeconomic system via industrialization, equalized land ownership, and a just tax system, although the means to these ends remained somewhat unclear.

On the eve of the 1911 revolution, Qing rule faced challenges on many fronts. Social and institutional changes, while meant to strengthen Qing rule, in reality frayed the fabric of the dynastic system. The merger of nationalist political action in China with patriotic activism among Chinese workers and students abroad created a new political dynamic that simultaneously challenged the Qing government and foreign firms and governments (particularly American and Japanese). It manifested itself in 1905 boycotts and demonstrations against America's immigration laws, and in 1908 protests against Japan's objection to a Japanese ship's being investigated by Chinese port authorities. These public political actions demonstrated the growing influence of urban population groups such as merchants, shopkeepers, office workers, and students. Revolutionary cells were founded in many places and students also reached out to local secret societies. The Qing New Army, mainly under provincial control and therefore under Han Chinese command, also became a fertile breeding ground for Han-Chinese nationalism. As the army's loyalty to the reigning dynasty became questionable, control gradually slipped away from the ruling house.

Foreign encroachments into Chinese territory, in the form of money-lending for the construction of railways and the development of mines, gave rise to rights recovery movements during the mid-1900s. The movement to recover Chinese railways, in particular, was a direct precursor to the 1911 revolution.[25] Railway policies had fluctuated as the Qing court searched for efficient ways to finance the heavily burdened projects; they ranged from encouraging private management to favoring joint official and private ventures to arranging official companies, before eventually shifting toward centralizing railway construction and putting management in the hands of the newly established Ministry of Post and Communication *(youchuan bu)*. When the ministry decided to take over construction projects from the provincial governments of Hubei and Sichuan and complete them using foreign loans, that move triggered strong anti-foreign and nationalistic reactions from local elites and railway company shareholders. Protests against railway nationalization later spread into wide-ranging popular struggles against encroachments by foreign powers and against a Qing court seemingly incapable or unwilling to protect China. The movement reflected the complexity of the "multiple nationalisms" circulating at the time, which simultaneously promoted many different groups' diverse agendas: expressing patriotic sentiment against foreign encroachment, calling for constitutionalism, demanding provincial self-governance, condemning the Manchu court for mishandling the railways, and railing against the economic burdens of reform policies.

Tensions erupted in the city of Chengdu as protesters took to the streets in the summer of 1911. They were demonstrating against the nationalization of the Chengdu-Hankou railway line ordered by the central government. Construction of the railway had originally started in 1904 relying only on Sichuanese funds and no foreign loans. On May 18, 1911, the Qing court appointed a Bannerman (1861–1911), Duan Fang, to take over railway management as director-general of the Canton-Hankou-Chengdu railway *(duban yuehan chuanhan tielu dachen)*. Two days later, Sheng Xuanhuai, the minister of posts and communication, signed a loan from Britain, Germany, France, and America for the extension of the line to Guangzhou (Canton). The public was informed that all Chinese capital raised for the construction of the first stretch of the railway would be returned to investors. But because the reimbursement would come in the form of government bonds, not cash, the announcement aroused dissatisfaction on the part of the Sichuanese. They argued that the government's decision to nationalize the railway amounted to stealing not only the railway but also the property of Sichuan. A Railway Protection League *(Baolu tongzhi hui)* was set up on June 17, which organized protests in the city. As the antagonism of shareholders and local

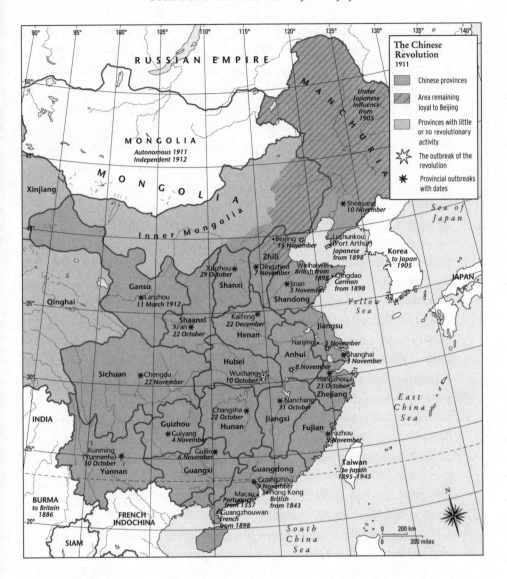

officials deepened, the court decided to send a loyal official, Zhao Erfeng (1845–1911), known as "the butcher" because of his harsh policies as frontier commissioner in Tibet and Kham (in the border region between Tibet and Sichuan). This provoked the eruption of a popular uprising. Meanwhile, members of the Revolutionary Alliance *(Tongmenghui)* infiltrated Chengdu urban society and started organizing revolutionary forces, participating in the protest movement through shareholders' meetings and the Railway Protection League. Their demands now widened and included self-governance and local autonomy. In September 1911, on orders by the court, Zhao ordered that his men open fire on a crowd of protesters who, demanding the release of nine leaders of the Railway Protection League, had surrounded and set fire to government buildings in Chengdu. The situation quickly escalated into a major armed conflict between Zhao's army and the militias—organized by the revolutionaries—flowing into Chengdu. As the city was besieged from four directions and under attack from thousands of local militias and bandits, the government called in reinforcements from Wuhan to quell the uprising with military violence.

At this fraught moment, made more precarious by local tax revolts, food riots, and other small protests elsewhere, it took only a small incident to push the Qing empire over the edge. After a bomb went off accidentally on October 9, Qing authorities discovered a wider plot in Wuhan among the local military.[26] The authorities also obtained lists of alleged members of a revolutionary organization. When local units learned of the imminent arrests of some of their members in the local military garrison, they decided to rebel. A coup attempt was planned for the next day: October 10, 1911. Within days, the revolt spread to other cities and provinces. To avoid further arrests, revolutionaries still at large seized the main arsenal in Wuhan. When, after two days of intense negotiations, the commanding colonel, Li Yuanhong (1864–1928), joined the revolutionaries, the Manchu governor-general of the area decided to flee. This set off a chain reaction. By the end of November, fourteen provinces had established revolutionary (often military) governments and seceded from the Qing empire. On January, 1, 1912, the Republic of China was established, led for a brief period of forty-five days by Sun Yat-sen, who had been in the United States during the events in Wuhan.

With the court putting up almost no resistance, the emperor abdicated in February of that year. And thus the collapse of the Qing empire was like a silent implosion: quick and relatively bloodless, belying the profound historical significance of the moment. With these events, not only was the Qing dynasty overthrown after nearly 270 years of continuous rule; the entire imperial-dynastic system that had endured for over two thousand years came to its end. Quite suddenly, China found itself entering a new century promising radical change and the chance of renewal. It became Asia's first republic and, in so doing, became one of the first continental empires to reinvent itself by adopting the nation-state form.

It is important to note that Sun Yat-sen did not play an active role in sparking the revolution. Only after its outbreak did he become recognized as its leader. He gained his legitimacy to perform that role because he alone could credibly claim that he had fought decades for the revolution, laid out a vision of the future, and, not least, attracted substantial financial support from overseas. Only after the fact did he fashion himself into the "revolution's iconic leader." With Sun Yat-sen on the sidelines, what then caused the revolution? The principal agents, ironically, were not members of Sun's alliance, but all the new institutions created by New Policies reforms. The New Armies, the chambers of commerce, the provincial assemblies—all of these institutions were dominated by local Han-Chinese elites who wanted a greater say in shaping their own future. In the final analysis, the Qing dynasty was upended because its own army commanders refused to defend it and because local Chinese elites withdrew their support for it.

The 1911 revolution, whether because of the initial weakness of its protagonists or through a series of unfortunate historical coincidences, rapidly led to the restoration of Yuan Shikai to the vacant imperial throne. In the negotiations between Yuan Shikai (acting as the premier of the National Assembly) and the revolutionaries in January 1912 to avoid civil war, Yuan held the advantage of controlling the most powerful army in China. Sun realized quickly that Yuan Shikai had a strong power base in North China, and that his own support from the south was much weaker. At heart, Sun was a pragmatic realist who was well aware of his vulnerability and lack of experience in government. As a result, Sun decided to give up the presidency in favor of Yuan in return for promises that Yuan would move the capital to Nanjing and commit himself to a democratic republican political system. Yuan Shikai did neither. However, Sun's withdrawal from the presidency in 1912, while often portrayed as a fatal miscalculation, may have spared him a failure in government, and a potentially devastating blow to his authority. It also gave him a chance to organize the *Guomindang*, or Nationalist Party (GMD), which was officially established on August 25, 1912, and would serve as the main vehicle for his political career until his death.

Yuan Shikai ruled China for four years, from 1912 to his death in 1916, essentially as a military dictator. His main support came from leading army officers, and he was the first Chinese leader who generally appeared in public wearing a uniform.[27] The first years of the republic featured continuing struggles between Yuan Shikai and the former revolutionaries over whether ultimate power should reside in the parliament or the presidency. Yuan Shikai—in a rather traditional manner—favored a centralized state with a strong and powerful ruler, based on the assumption that only such a hierarchical and centralized system could hold the country together. The conflict fully erupted after the elections for the National Assembly in late 1912.[28] The electorate was limited by gender, wealth, and education, but forty million men, representing about a tenth of the population, voted on the national level for the first time in Chinese history. Several parties were on the ballot, with the GMD emerging with a large majority of seats. When Song Jiaoren (1882–1913), the main organizer of the GMD's electoral victory and most likely candidate for premier, was assassinated in March 1913—some say on orders from Yuan himself—revolutionary leaders in the south (with Sun Yat-sen's support) broke with Yuan's government and revolted. Yuan Shikai quickly suppressed this revolt, later known as the Second Revolution. After he had eliminated the opposition and bribed or threatened members of parliament, Yuan Shikai was elected to the presidency and then had the GMD banned. Sun Yat-sen took refuge in Japan. Yuan went on to arrest Sun's supporters and closed down China's first parliament on January 10, 1914. The presidency had become a military dictatorship.

The final act in this drama was yet to come. In 1915, Yuan Shikai made the fateful decision to revive the monarchy, with some new features, and to place himself on the throne as emperor. He believed that China's political turmoil might be resolved by a constitutional monarchy. The nation was renamed from Republic of China (*Zhonghua minguo*) to Empire of China (*Zhonghua diguo*), indicating a modern national Han Chinese monarchy as opposed to Manchu Qing dynasty. Vehement opposition came from the leaders of the Nationalist and Progressive parties, the local elites, and Japan. By the start of 1916, it was clear that the provinces, under new military rulers, had also turned against Yuan Shikai. Another source of opposition came from Yuan's direct subordinates, General Duan Qirui (1865–1936) and General Feng Guozhang (1859–1919), whose powers Yuan had attempted to curtail. When he called on them for help, they both withheld support. After only eighty-three days, on March 22, 1916, Yuan announced the abolition of the new empire. The revolt, however, continued to spread, with more military leaders declaring the independence of their provinces. Meanwhile, Yuan Shikai became gravely ill and died on June 6 of the same year.

During his time as president and briefly emperor, Yuan Shikai continued making institutional reforms, despite the fragility and unpredictability of the political situation. These efforts are highly remarkable, as the example of the reintroduction of the examination system shows. In 1916, Yuan Shikai made an ambitious attempt to reinstall the examination system to build good and modern institutions on historical foundations. His goal was to establish a standardized, normative, and rule-based state apparatus. He defined new procedures for personnel advancement and promotion as well as a new ranking system.[29] Regulations for nationwide civil service entrance examinations were also developed, intended to test a combination of literacy and technical knowledge. After the exams, a two-year probationary period was meant to follow, after which a candidate could be assigned to a ministry based on recommendations. The new examination system should become the primary channel to gain access to civil service positions. The examinations were held only once after Yuan's death, even though recruits were later at the core of the Beiyang government's administration. Even though this attempt was short-lived, it did point the way for institutional innovation. The approach of combining traditional rules with new content served as a blueprint for other institutional innovations.

After Yuan's failed emperorship, Duan Qirui and other Beiyang generals assumed control of the government. They appointed Li Yuanhong president, assuming that his connections to the revolution in the south would neutralize southern resistance to a resurgence of Beiyang control. Li was able to make gestures toward reviving the republic, but soon disappeared from the political stage. Real power came to reside in Duan Qirui, who held the position of premier beginning in June 1916. When the National Assembly reconvened on August 1, its delegates confirmed Duan as premier and elected Feng Guozhang (1859–1919), the leader of another emerging faction of the Beiyang Army, as vice president. The entire central government quickly became mired in factional power struggles.

The course of events from the revolution of 1911 to the chaos of 1916 had grave consequences. This was a revolution, China's first to be labeled as such, that faltered quickly after its initial success. Great expectations were raised only to be dashed against the hard realities of Chinese politics. Yuan's defiance of constitutional procedures and his dissolution of parliament set precedents that were later repeated, just as borrowing from foreign entities for political purposes would appear again. China was a republic in name, but the reality was arbitrary political rule based on military power and behind-the-door brokering. Many were disillusioned with the republican experiment; the long-anticipated parliamentary system and the greater social and civic equality that new social groups such as students, officers, businesspeople, and intellectuals had hoped for remained elusive, prompting a decade of soul-searching by China's intellectuals. The most famous product of these reflections was Lu Xun's (1881–1936) novella *Ah Q*, the fictional account of a revolutionary who is as unable to become a real citizen as he is uninterested.[30] How were China's Ah Qs to be made into citizens? As the nation rapidly descended into warlordism and factional strife during the 1910s and 1920s, instead of uniting into a strong, healthy, and organic society as the revolution had promised, the need for a new approach based on scientific reason and objective truth—in short, a new culture—was seen as the only solution. This search for new impulses and models was to be undertaken, however, in a fundamentally changed global environment.

China and the First World War

The heavy internal crisis in the newly founded Chinese republic erupted at a time when profound changes were under way in the international order. An unsettling international breaking point, the July Crisis, began with the assassination of Archduke Franz Ferdinand in Sarajevo on June 28, 1914, and culminated in the British declaration of war on Germany on August 4, leading to the outbreak of war across Europe, which soon escalated into war of unprecedented scale: a world war. In global history, the First World War marked an important turning point, as it ushered in the slow but unstoppable disintegration of global empires and the parallel rise of anticolonial independence movements worldwide. Both developments were to have an enormous impact on China's search for a new beginning. China's internal development and changes in global society became interlocked. Although no country was able to shield itself from external influences—via trade, migration, smuggling, and disease—China was one of the most open and accessible countries. A large number of foreign actors from Europe, America, and neighboring countries such as Japan yielded influence on its political, economic, and cultural development, sometimes without approval or even against the articulated will of the Chinese government. During the First World War, a disintegrating China became ever more tied up in global developments.[31]

Japan pursued far-reaching strategies in the Great War precisely because the war presented unique military opportunities to bring new initiatives into play and to change the regional balance of power in East Asia. For China, by contrast, as a semi-colonized country where hostile imperial powers including Germany, Britain, Japan, and others had carved out spheres of interest, the war was another threat in a long series of risks to its territorial integrity. It was, however, also an opportunity to enhance its standing on the global stage.

The perils that the Great War represented for China had mostly to do with Japan. The war theater in China, where the military confrontation between Japan and Germany eventually unfolded, was the German colony Kiaochow in Shandong province. On August 7, 1914, the British government asked its Japanese ally to confront the German navy in East Asian waters, based on a provision in the 1902 treaty between Japan and Britain. Japan dispatched a note to Berlin on August 15, 1914, demanding that Germany withdraw its fleet from East Asia and transfer the administration of the German colony Kiaochow to Japan. With this move, Japan pursued a number of objectives. Japan was eager to enter the war and be a full member of the Triple Entente (consisting of France, Russia, and Britain) that fought against Germany, Italy, and Austria-Hungary. It also viewed the German colony as an important naval base and strategic location that would facilitate the Japanese military expansion on the mainland. Finally, by establishing control over the harbor of Kiaochow, Japan hoped to promote trade between China and Japan, thus benefiting Japanese businesses. When Germany refused to hand over the colony, Japan responded with a declaration of war on August 23, 1914. With this, World War I had reached Asia. At the same time, the Imperial Japanese Navy attacked other German possessions in the Pacific: Japan seized coaling stations on the German Mariana Islands abandoned by the German Pacific Fleet in its rush back to Europe.

The German Reich immediately issued a call to arms for all adult male Germans in China. The ensuing battle of Kiaochow received wide news coverage in Germany as well as in China, where it was perceived as the first major military confrontation of the war. Five days after the Japanese declaration of war, over thirty thousand Japanese troops arrived in the outlying coastal waters before Qingdao. The Japanese troops first began a siege of the city and blocked all ship traffic. On September 2, 1914, troops landed on the coast and started to cut off land links. The fighting started two weeks later, when German troops tried to break through the siege. Japan responded with heavy artillery fire on the fortification in and around Qingdao on October 31, 1914. The German troops fought back until Japan launched a final attack on the city. Outgunned, exhausted, and with no hope of reinforcements, the remaining four thousand German troops surrendered on November 7, 1914. More than two hundred German soldiers were killed in battle. Japanese losses were higher, with as many as 422 casualties.[32]

China protested several times against the unjustified Japanese occupation of the territory of a neutral state. It was in this context that Japan, in January 1915, presented its infamous "twenty-one demands" for securing its gains in China. Japan's leaders were worried that after the war they would lose out to western powers. Japan therefore asked for endorsement of its railway and mining claims in Shandong province; the yielding of special concessions in Manchuria; control of the Hanyeping mines; access to harbors, bays, and islands along China's coast; and the dispatch of Japanese advisers to control Chinese financial, political, and security institutions. When Yuan Shikai, still president, refused to sign, Japan threatened military intervention. In the end, Yuan Shikai signed a series of Sino-Japanese agreements on May 25. Yuan's acceptance of all but the last point (the dispatch of advisers) was a watershed event. It greatly increased anti-Japanese sentiment in China: Japan now became the main threat to China's independence.

China's hope of receiving support and gaining a greater say in international politics was behind its decision in the middle of 1916 to send workers to Europe. Its intention was to strengthen the Allied countries' workforces to establish political links with them, even though China was still in theory a neutral country. The British and French governments, to make up for labor

4.1. Workers of the Chinese Labor Corps washing a British army tank, spring 1918. Photographer David McLellan, IWM / Q9899

shortages in France, as well as to release British dockworkers in French ports for military duty, employed over 140,000 Chinese contract workers between 1916 and 1918.[33] During their sojourn in France, these Chinese workers were employed in a wide variety of war-related jobs, both behind the lines (in transportation, armaments and munitions production, machinery maintenance, and aerodrome construction) and at the front (making road repairs, digging trenches, and burying war dead). In evening schools set up by Chinese students in France, the workers were taught to read and write. When they returned to China after the war, they became an important driving force for social and political change. In the French factories in particular they had also become committed labor activists and acquired the skills and techniques of political mobilization.

After the German declaration of the unrestricted submarine war in early 1917, the US government severed diplomatic relations with Germany and called upon other neutral powers, including China, to do the same. An intense public discussion in China ensued.[34] This alone is noteworthy: never before had important foreign policy decisions been publicly discussed to such an extent. It reflects how in the span of just a few years the existence of the republic had led to a political way of life, in which citizens confronted political leaders over issues of public interest. The government and the public were bitterly divided on the question of China's entry into the war. Li Yuanhong, as president, opposed the step, but Duan Qirui, the premier, favored moving toward entry into the war. Sun Yat-sen, now in Shanghai, argued that entering the war could not benefit China since it was a colonized country. Rather, it would create additional threats from Japan. But respected intellectuals including Liang Qichao and Zhang Junmai (1886–1969) argued that the war provided China with a chance to enhance its international status and, during peace negotiations after the war, to regain some sovereign rights it had lost to imperialist powers in the nineteenth century. Under heavy pressure by Duan Qirui, the parliament in the end voted to sever diplomatic relations with Germany, and Li Yuanhong was compelled by his premier to give in.

The debate, however, erupted again when the United States formally declared war in April. Duan Qirui wanted China to do the same, but was again opposed by Li.[35] On May 23, Li dismissed Duan and called on Zhang Xun (1854–1923), another of the Beiyang generals and also a monarchist, to mediate. As a price for mediation, Zhang demanded that Li dissolve the parliament, which he did, reluctantly, on June 13. The next day, Zhang entered Beijing with an army and set about to restore the Qing dynasty. Telegrams immediately poured in from military governors and generals denouncing Zhang and the coup. Duan recaptured Beijing a month later, on July 14. This ended the second attempt to restore the imperial system. With Duan Qirui in power again, the Beiyang government declared war on Germany on August 14, 1917. The rationale behind this step was that only by formally becoming a member of the Allies could China secure a seat at the post-war peace conference, where the Chinese diplomats could leverage world opinion and diplomatic channels to regain Qingdao, and push for negotiations regarding the unequal treaties. Japan strengthened its position in China by providing Duan Qirui with loans of some 145 million yen in 1917 and 1918. These "Nishihara loans," like the Reorganization Loan of 1913, were meant to support pro-Japanese camps in China. In return, the Beiyang government secretly acceded to the stationing of Japanese troops in Manchuria and Mongolia and to Japan's presence in Shandong, undermining its official intentions.

The shift in the balance of world politics caused by the war coincided with China's yearning for change in both the domestic and international systems and afforded China a chance to launch its own initiatives in world affairs by actively joining the Triple Entente. The war signaled the collapse of the existing international system dominated by empires and the coming of a new world order. Although China was fragmented and torn, it nonetheless thought of itself as a global player, despite its domestic weakness. In consequence, the First World War as a global event shaped the evolution of Chinese diplomacy and foreign relations, and popular perceptions about China's role in the world.

These connections among developments globally and in China came into even fuller view after the war. Independence movements worldwide demanded the recognition of the colonies as sovereign actors, and envisioned the creation of a new, non-colonial world order based on the principle of self-determination. Many factors contributed to this moment: the weakening of the European colonial powers due to losses suffered in World War I; the rise of new powers such as Japan; the opening of political space for colonized peoples as a result of the war; and the shifts in the global economy, which gave new economic impetus to the colonies. There were also new and daring ideas in play, such as Woodrow Wilson's January 8, 1918 "Address on the Fourteen Points for Peace."[36] The American president proclaimed:

An evident principle runs through the whole programme I have outlined. It is the principle of justice to all peoples and nationalities, and their right to live on equal terms of liberty and safety with one another, whether they be strong or weak. Unless this principle be made its foundation no part of the structure of international justice can stand. The people of the United States could act upon no other principle; and to the vindication of this principle they are ready to devote their lives, their honor, and everything that they possess. The moral climax of this the culminating and final war for human liberty has come, and they are ready to put their own strength, their own highest purpose, their own integrity and devotion to the test.[37]

Wilson's Fourteen Points were met with much praise and acclaim, especially in the colonies. They were understood as a signal for the dawn of a new, post-colonial world order.

Wilson's powerful words were not the only source of inspiration. As he stated himself, his speech to Congress was merely a reaction to the much more explicit and far-reaching assurances given in the "Decree on Peace" issued by the Bolsheviks a few months earlier, in October 1917. Therein Lenin emphasized in strongest terms the right of self-determination, in the sense of an undisputable worldwide secession right, explicitly also for colonized peoples in overseas territories. The decree adopted by the Second Congress of the Soviets stated:

> If any nation whatsoever is detained by force within the boundaries of a certain state, and if [that nation], contrary to its expressed desire whether such desire is made manifest in the press, national assemblies, party relations, or in protests and uprisings against national oppression, is not given the right to determine the form of its state life by free voting and completely free from the presence of the troops of the annexing or stronger state and without the least desire, then the dominance of that nation by the stronger state is annexation, i.e., seizure by force and violence.[38]

The founding of the Communist International, or Comintern, in Moscow in March 1919—which proclaimed as its concrete goal the global liberation of workers and peasants, including those in the colonies, and aimed for world revolution—also played a role in this context. All of these factors indicated that the imperialist world order was facing major challenges and upheavals at the end of the First World War. The justification for colonial rule was challenged by new visions and values, which suggested that colonized peoples could no longer be denied an equal position on the international stage. A vision emerged of a new world and world order that would not be based on the survival of the fittest or victor's justice anymore, but on principles of self-determination, equality, and freedom.

The articulation of this vision, however, was no longer exclusive to European or American politicians and intellectuals; thinkers and activists from colonial areas also played a decisive part. This globally forged vision was immediately noticed by a global audience and embraced enthusiastically in China and other countries. A 1919 English language pamphlet of the Shanghai Student Union read: "Throughout the world, like the voice of a prophet, has gone the word of Woodrow Wilson strengthening the weak and giving courage to the struggling. . . . And the Chinese have listened and they too have heard."[39]

Protests demanding independence and self-government broke out in many parts of the colonial world. The "1919 Revolution" in Egypt was unable to present its calls for independence at Versailles, but it led to a protest movement that eventually achieved Egyptian independence in February 1922. The largely peaceful rebellion in Egypt was watched closely in the colonial world and was the beginning of a global protest wave. Following the events in Egypt, Mohandas Gandhi became inspired by the power of protest and civil disobedience. Almost parallel to the events in Egypt, the Indian National Congress passed a resolution for the "self-determination of India" in December 1918. By March 1919, however, it became clear that Great Britain would block any discussion on the status of the Indian colony at Versailles. When Gandhi, who appeared at that point for the first time as a national leader of the independence movement, called for civil disobedience and a nationwide strike, Britain answered with violence. This bloody episode provoked collective outrage against the colonial occupation in India, and was widely reported by the international press. Like Egyptian and Indian nationalists, Koreans were also trying to gain a hearing for their independence at Versailles. Korea had been annexed by Japan in 1910. On March 1, 1919, demonstrators organized nationwide public readings of a declaration emphasizing the Koreans' right to their own nation. In total, more than a million Koreans probably took part in the protests that went on until early summer. Japanese authorities responded with violence and repression: around 50,000 protesters were arrested, 15,000 injured, and 7,500 executed. Similar demonstrations and street protests also took place in Latin America and North Africa.[40]

The events in those countries were closely reported back in the Chinese media. During the 1920s, one of the most influential journalists and commentators, Zou Taofen (1895–1944), wrote several articles about Mohandas Gandhi, whom he celebrated as the leader of the Indian independence movement. These appeared in *Life Weekly* (*Shenghuo zhoukan*), one of the most widely distributed magazines of the republican period, which in 1933 regularly reached perhaps 1.5 million readers.[41] One of the articles was titled "Gandhi's Strategy for National Salvation" (*Gandi de jiuguo fang'an*). Zou wrote that Gandhi's central accomplishment was his nationalist program of civil disobedience against the colonialists' overwhelming power. The article ended by stating: "It is crucial for China to learn from Gandhi." Zou also wrote several articles about Kemal Atatürk and his successful struggle to end allied occupation after the end of World War I and to achieve Turkish independence. "Turkey in the Near East and China in the Far East have a lot in common," Zou observed. "Seeing how Turkey was able to pull itself out of a dangerous crisis, we have to do whatever it takes to enable China to also win its future back."

The view that China was closely connected to other regions of the world struggling for independence was widespread and extended into the rural interior. Twenty-seven-year-old Mao Zedong (1893–1976) was in Changsha when 1919 protests shook the world. In his *Xiangtan Newspaper*, he published several reports about the events in India, Egypt, Turkey, Afghanistan, Poland, and Hungary. On July 14, 1919, Mao reported that Afghanistan was following the Indian example and protesting against its British colonial masters. He wrote: "When the fox dies, the hare grieves, so how could [Afghanistan] fail to pick up the sword?"[42] Two years later, when Mao ran the "Self-Study University of Hunan" in Changsha, he considered knowledge about the anti-imperialist struggle in the world to be essential for the development of political consciousness. For example, he proposed that his school send correspondents to New York, Moscow, Tokyo, Cairo, and Calcutta to provide the students with regular reports on world events.

Anticolonial activists from different countries did not just inspire each other from afar but sometimes met in person. The Versailles Peace Conference provided a reason for numerous activists from colonial areas to hold lengthy rallies in Paris. Other, very different places also saw gatherings with discussions: At a New York farewell meeting for the Indian activist Lajpat Rai in 1919, which was organized by an American supporter of the Irish independence movement, a Chinese delegate delivered a speech on Sun Yat-sen's political ideas.[43] In addition to New York and Paris, the International Concession in Shanghai became an important place for anticolonial activists to gather and exchange ideas. Important leaders of the Korean and Vietnamese independence movements (among them, Syngman Rhee and Ho Chi Minh) often stayed in Shanghai, where they were in close contact with Chinese intellectuals.

The unprecedented protest wave that spread across the globe in 1919 was based on global transfers and cross-border processes made possible by new forms of communication, mobility, and exchange. During the twentieth century, regions far apart from each other were brought into contact and developed what could be called a conceptual political proximity, despite their geographical and cultural distances. The creation of these transnational connections was possible only because ideas and people started to circulate globally in the twentieth century. They did so because of the spread of new technologies.

The "second media revolution" during the second half of the nineteenth century (the first one having been the invention of the printing press) was crucially dependent on the intercontinental "wiring of the world" by electric telegraphy. Starting in London at the end of the nineteenth century, the British colonies in India, Southeast Asia, Australia, South America, and South Africa could be reached safely and cost-effectively through a network of submarine cables.[44] The Danish Great Northern Telegraph Company had been active in East Asia since 1871: the Siberian line was finalized in 1900. A second cable was run from the United States to East Asia. The Pacific Cable Board (1879–1902) operated by Canada, Great Britain, and the United States was in charge of coordinating the construction of the trans-Pacific cable connection, which was made available to the public in 1902. With China's connection to the worldwide telegraph network around 1900, the region was integrated into the global relay of messages in real time and almost without delay. As a result, demonstrations and marches were from then on held according to a global political calendar and employed a global protest repertoire.

New forms of mobility supplemented this new system of communication. Thanks to new technologies such as steamships, and construction feats such as the finalizing of the Suez and Panama canals, travel multiplied and accelerated. Intercontinental travel changed fundamentally over the course of the nineteenth century. Small communities of traders, who transported goods on their own backs or in small boats, gave way to large corporations like major trading houses. Instead of lone pilgrims or priests, widely networked religious organizations (for example, Christian missions) spread not only their beliefs but also their languages, writings, and building styles. The few, fearless adventurers, military commanders, and travelers of past centuries who brought distant societies together were replaced by thousands or even millions of refugees and immigrants who fled across borders, and later by tourists, who traveled across the world. All of these travels deepened and extended the connections between distant parts of the world and eased the transfer of goods, ideas, and cultures. The mobility of large groups of people, including not merely tourists, diplomats, and aristocrats, but also masses of students and unskilled workers, was a stand-out characteristic of globalization around 1919.[45]

These travels enabled students and activists, among others, to move from country to country and, in East Asia, from city to city. In the early twentieth century, staying abroad or studying abroad became an integral, almost indispensable part of any academic education. Chinese, Korean, and Japanese student clubs were established at all major universities in Europe and the United States. For example, a large group of Chinese students attended Columbia University Teachers College, several of whom went on to become important spokesmen for the May Fourth movement. Particularly noteworthy were Hu Shi (1891–1962), Sun Ke (1891–1973), and Tao Xingzhi (1891–1946). This international exchange of students and intellectuals led to the development of transnational circuits of agitation and emancipation. Labor mobility played a role, too. During the nineteenth and twentieth centuries, perhaps over nineteen million Chinese workers resettled in Southeast Asia and areas around the Indian Ocean and the southern Pacific Ocean.[46] The demand for Asian workers rose rapidly after 1900, when the slave trade was first restricted and then completely abandoned.

Non-state actors gradually appeared on the scene and sought to shape and develop transfers of people and goods. They established independent, non-governmental organizations (NGOs) with far-reaching consequences. In 1912, Li Shizeng (1881–1973), Wu Zhihui (1865–1953), and their friends organized the "Society for Frugal Study" (*Jianxuehui*) in Beijing. Li Shizeng and Wu Zhihui were anarchists who followed the French theorist Élisée Reclus, who saw a dialectical connection between education and revolution. In general, they believed the success of social revolution was dependent on the development of science and education—and therefore that society should encourage students to sacrifice their comfort, live frugally, and study abroad in France. The students should work part-time to earn a living while attending French universities to study modern science and technology. France, renowned in China at the time for its scientific achievements, was the favorite destination of Chinese students going overseas. Over the course of two years (1912–1913), the society sent a hundred students to France. In 1916, a successor was set up in the form of the Sino-French Education Association *(Hua Fa jiaoyuhui)*, which was founded by Li Shizeng, Cai Yuanpei (1868–1940), Wu Zhihui, and others in Paris.[47] Some 1,600 Chinese student workers arrived in France between 1919 and 1921 through joint arrangements made by Chinese leaders of the association and their French counterparts. The organization had branches in Beijing, Canton, and Shanghai. Year-long preparatory schools for those intending to go were established in Beijing, Chengdu, Chongqing, and Baoding in 1918 and 1919. The first group of students sent to France arrived in March 1919. The program ended in late 1921 for financial reasons. Among the students were several later leaders of the Chinese Communist Party—including Zhou Enlai and Deng Xiaoping, who would go on to greatly influence the fortunes of the country for more than half a century. Many of the students who worked in France benefited from higher education, and some were also employed as general workers, teachers, technicians, and journalists. In the factories they also learned the techniques of political mass protests, such as demonstrations, strikes, and boycotts. Long before the first translations of texts by Marx, Engels, or Lenin into Chinese, Chinese students in factories came into contact with the world of the European labor movement.

Reports about the global wave of anticolonial protests, as well as intensive contacts and exchanges with different parts of the world, suggested two things to the contemporary Chinese public: that China should participate in this international trend for a new post-imperial era to avoid remaining hopelessly backward and be left behind; and that the great powers were not about to grant independence and self-determination without pressure from the colonialized and the oppressed. Both played a major role in the outbreak of protests on May 4, 1919, in Beijing and other cities.

Awakening China: The May Fourth Movement

Following the model set by protesters throughout the colonial world, Chinese students and intellectuals also took to the streets. The immediate cause was the intention of western leaders, who were assembled at Versailles to define the shape of the postwar world, to confirm and accept the occupation of the eastern portion of Shandong province (formerly the German Kiaochow) by Japan rather than return it to China.[48] The movement began when students at

Beijing schools and universities learned about the negotiations at Versailles. They were so outraged that on May 4, 1919, they demonstrated in Beijing—not only against the western powers for disregarding China's territorial rights but also against the Chinese government for being too weak to stand up for China's interests. Within days, demonstrations spread across all of urban China. Chinese workers and students in France also actively started their own action and wanted to inject themselves into international politics. News was exchanged between China and France and petitions were written. Among other actions, sit-in blockades were staged by students and workers in Paris that prevented Chinese delegates from going to the conference and participating in the negotiations.

Specifically, the demonstrators demanded the reestablishment of territorial sovereignty; the complete recognition of China's right to self-determination through nullification of the so-called unequal treaties that had been in place since the Opium Wars; and an end to extraterritoriality. Ignoring the protests, the great powers at the negotiating table in Versailles adhered to their plan. But the Chinese delegates refused to sign the peace treaty because of the protests in China.

Compared to Egypt, India, or Korea, China's May Fourth movement was not only very late but also relatively small. China had around 130,000 new-style schools with more than four million students, but only a small fraction went to the streets to demonstrate. After all, China was in a very different and much better situation: the country's independence was an accomplished feat that was not up for discussion. In fact, China belonged to the allied powers of Versailles. China's biggest problems in 1919 were domestic, given its disunity and internal fighting. There was something brewing that was more important than the political protests and public demonstrations in Beijing and other Chinese cities in the spring of 1919. This was the social and cultural upheaval that took place between 1915 and 1925 and culminated in 1919, which is commonly referred to as the New Culture movement. It started in September 1915, when Chen Duxiu (1879–1942), a Francophile who would later be dean of Peking University, changed the name of his journal *Qingnian zazhi* (*Youth Magazine*) to *Xin qingnian* (*New Youth*), with the subhead "La Jeunesse" as of the second issue. The journal gained its well-known importance after its move from Shanghai to Beijing in 1917. The incident in Shanghai of May 30, 1925, where the police of the International Settlement opened fire

4.2. Jiang Menglin, Cai Yuanpei, Hu Shi, and Li Dazhao (left to right) belonged to the most important intellectuals of the May Fourth movement. The photograph was taken in Beijing, 1920.
Collection of Institute of Modern History, Chinese Academy of Social Sciences, Chinese Modern History Archives

on protesters and sparked mass demonstrations all over China, marked the end of the May Fourth movement, which originally tended toward non-violent protests rather than armed revolution.

The New Culture movement has been interpreted in different ways. Some scholars see it as the start of a "Chinese enlightenment" and a slow turn toward embracing western modernity. Others, however, read it as the first phase of a radical and blind anti-traditionalism in which the seeds would be sown for the Cultural Revolution.[49] The May Fourth movement certainly displayed a profound shift of paradigms, which should be interpreted as a clear break, as opposed to the prevalent thesis of continuities in China's transition from tradition to modernity. But with this it followed a more general trend in the colonial world. With great determination, a revolution in the form of a completely new beginning was to be brought about in China and elsewhere. But it also meant that, first, there was much that needed to be demolished. Thus, the vogue word of the turn of the century was *po* (break) or *pohuai* (destroy), a concept with problematic consequences that became a mantra for Chen Duxiu and would also become that later for Mao. In his 1918 essay "On

Iconoclasm," Chen Duxiu writes, "Destroy! Destroy the idols! Destroy the idols of hypocrisy!" The object of destruction was to be everything traditionally Chinese. In this context, Hu Shi formed the 1921 catchphrase "down with Confucianism" (dadao Kongjiadian). The first issue of the journal *New Youth* included the publisher's important "Appeal to the Youth" (jinggao qingnian). Unlike the reformers before him, Chen Duxiu contended in this text that what China needed was not merely a technological strengthening, but a spiritual awakening. Chen advocated new ideas like cosmopolitanism, self-determination, science, and freedom as central elements of his remedy. This appeal to the youth had slightly Darwinist underpinnings. At stake was the political survival of China as an independent nation. The catchphrase "survival of the fittest" led to a two-pronged strategy. The objective was to save China (jiuguo), and to achieve this goal, the people, especially the youth, had to be spiritually awakened. Literature and art should induce in a whole new generation of educated activist youth a commitment to creating a "new China." Many Chinese writers asserted in books, as well as in other media such as newspapers and journals, that China lacked a real society. They critiqued the Chinese by portraying them as unenlightened, parochial, and foolish people (yumin) who were neither nationalistic nor capable of participating in politics. Such anxiety about the absence of functioning social institutions reflected earlier contentions of Liang Qichao's call for New Citizens or Sun Yat-sen's characterization of China as "a sheet of loose sand" (yipan sansha) made up of four hundred million individuals. Nation building, for both Liang and Sun, was to fix the incomplete and fragmentary social institutions so that Chinese society could turn into a cohesive "national social body" (minzu tuanti). The chaos and fighting after the 1911 revolution seemed to confirm the intellectuals' alarm and demonstrate the pressing need to create enlightened citizens for a new society. During the height of the May Fourth movement, leading social scientists such as Fu Sinian and Tao Menghe echoed the same sentiment about the requirement to create a new organic society made up of real political citizens. Indeed, the numerous social engineering projects and political campaigns of twentieth-century China, such as national reconstruction, the New Life movement, rural reconstruction, and land reform, to name just a few, could all be seen as attempts by different political camps to create their corresponding ideal society or "new society" (xin shehui). In this discourse, the May Fourth leaders obviously refused to see the nation-state and the individual as two separate entities. In their view, both needed to form an organic bond. In their writings, they imagined individuals first and foremost as citizens of the state and members of a new society.

This endeavor's strict division of old and new had far-reaching consequences. For Chen Duxiu, the old was backward, and therefore equaled the enemy that had to be eliminated. China's problems lay within the traditional cultural essence itself. Here, the iconoclasm reached a radicalism that lasted for the entire twentieth century in China. Of course, the place of the old had to be taken by something new, and this new element was the imaginary realm called the West. Accordingly, the term "new" won unforeseen importance and was used to an almost inflationary degree in contemporary writings. Chen Duxiu was among the first to declare his belief in a new age and a new civilization based on progress and modernity. In the article "The Year 1916," he wrote:

> The epoch in which you are living—what epoch is this? It is the beginning of the 16th year of the twentieth century. The changes of the world are evolutionary, different from month to month, year to year. The shining history is unfolding faster and faster. . . . To live in the present world, you must raise your head and proudly call yourself a person of the twentieth century, you must create a new civilization of the twentieth century and not confine yourself to following that of the nineteenth. For the evolution of human civilization is replacing the old with the new, like a river flowing on, an arrow flying away, constantly continuing and constantly changing.[50]

Of course, what Chen Duxiu emphasized here was not just the necessity to create a new civilization of the twentieth century, but also the desire for a new consciousness about time and history. The term for civilization *(wenming)*, a neologism taken over from the Japanese *(bunmei)*, soon caught on and was used together with terms such as *Dongfang* (East Asia) and *Xifang* (Western Europe) to define "eastern" and "western" civilizations as dichotomous and contrasting categories within the common vocabulary of the May Fourth movement. This was based on the assumption that western civilization was characterized by dynamic progress, which had led to wealth and power. Chen idealized many of those aspects of western civilization that he found lacking in China's own culture.

Naturally, the students and professors began by trying to imagine what this new civilization would actually be like. Chen Duxiu emphasized France's role in this, because it was there that the most important modern doctrines had been invented: the theory of human rights (Lafayette), the theory of evolution (Lamarck), and socialism (St. Simon and Fourier, who were later followed by the Germans Lassalle and Marx). This is just another example of the enormous role that international connections played in the protests, demonstrations, and debates of the May Fourth movement. But other intellectuals looked to Gandhi or Atatürk as inspiration for activism. While studies of the May Fourth movement have so far been mainly concentrated on the West's role in motivating its members, the movement's outlook extended much further and was of a truly global nature. The new age was always thought of as a new era in a global sense. This was connected to the fact that 1919 saw, perhaps for the first time, the manifestation of a global public sphere, through which actors on different continents started to communicate and exchange ideas.

The new culture movement, however, also promoted cultural change. Hu Shi, a former student of the American philosopher John Dewey, promoted the use of vernacular language *(baihua)* in literature rather than the classical style. By 1918, most of the contributors to *New Youth* were writing in *baihua,* and other journals and newspapers soon followed suit. Students at Peking University began their own literary journal, *New Tide (Xinchao).* It became the main venue for new experimental literature inspired by western forms. Many new literary journals were founded in its wake. New fiction was published that used new literary styles and techniques to explore China's ambiguous cultural and political situation. Spoken drama also emerged. This was the beginning of a period of immense artistic creativity.

All activists of the May Fourth movement shared a desire to replace the principles of Confucianism with new political and social institutions to bring China in line with the modern world. The movement had demonstrated that it was possible to mobilize a whole new generation of students, workers, and even merchants across the country, who showed their will through strikes and work stoppages in factories. A political force, in the form of mass mobilization and public protest, had demonstrated its power. From then on, the May Fourth movement stood as a turning point in modern Chinese history, a moment of popular public mass mobilization from which future Chinese political movements would derive their inspiration. But at the same time, quickly after 1919, disputes among the activists surfaced. The crux of the difference between the liberals and the group that later became the Marxists was the question of political power. Responses to the 1917 October Revolution drove a deeper wedge between them. Hu Shi and the liberals rejected its value for China, but Chen Duxiu and his supporters were sympathetic and wished to learn from it. The fundamental difference centered on whether China's problems should be resolved by armed revolution or by slow, evolutionary change.

FIVE

Rebuilding during the Republican Era

1920–1937

GMD=nationalist party

With the demise of Yuan Shikai in 1916, the republic encountered difficult, perplexing conditions. The central government existed on paper only, while real power was exercised by numerous local warlords. Frequent battles for power among them caused loss and destruction for Chinese society, and also encouraged Japan and a new foreign actor, the Soviet Union, to expand their presences. Japan used military threat to widen its influence. The Soviet Union worked with both revolutionary parties, the GMD and the Chinese Communist Party (CCP), and forged an alliance between them with the goal to rebuild a central government that would be amicable and open to Soviet influence. With the support of the Soviet Union, the Northern Expedition was carried out in 1926–1927 to unite China and rebuild a central government. Contrary to Soviet expectations, as soon as the new party leader of the GMD, Chiang Kai-shek, defeated and coopted the most important warlords, he broke the alliance and banned the CCP.

One conclusion the May Fourth movement intellectuals drew from the lamentable state of affairs in China after the Qing was that the newly established institutions, such as the new government and parliament, were not efficient enough. They needed to be complemented by a new collective called the Chinese nation instilled into all citizens. This was in line with the dominant thinking of the new central government headed by Chiang and the ruling party, GMD. When China was reunited in 1928 and a new government came into power in the capital Nanjing, nation building became an overwhelming priority. Many efforts were started to get the long-postponed project of transforming China into a modern republican nation underway. The term "nation building" refers to centrally initiated and coordinated efforts or programs to modernize an economy and society, homogenize a population, elevate ideals of popular sovereignty, produce a progressive conception of history, create an unmediated and interiorized relationship between citizens and nation-state, and force congruence between a territorial state and culture. Parallel to nation building, however, the adoption of new institutional models for the nation-state and its organizations was also on the agenda and was continued. Specifically, this meant building a range of new institutions to bolster the new revolutionary republican system and keep it in operation. The open questions had to do with how open and inclusive this system should be and which groups should be allowed to participate in decision making. The two projects of nation building and institution building were not congruent, and were seen by most political camps as separate enterprises—which, however, ideally should complement each other. Much was achieved in China in terms of nation building and institutional reform, but these achievements were largely confined to the urban areas.

The reunification of China in 1928 was more a wish than a reality. Large areas were only loosely integrated (such as warlord-controlled spots in the border regions) or not directly controlled by the GMD (such as treaty ports or the insurgent areas to which the CCP had fled and built caches of resistance against the central government). Significant yet divergent developments took place in the treaty ports and CCP areas. In the treaty ports that were still administered by foreigners, urban, cosmopolitan cultures and modern industries continued their dynamic expansions. The rise of a relatively unrestricted and free public sphere allowed lively political debates and passionate discussions about culture and society in China. Shanghai and other coastal cities went through a "golden age" marked by prosperity, creativity, and diversity. By contrast, the CCP territories were located in unruly, unstable, and impoverished regions of the countryside far from the coastal cities. They became the stage for a reboot of the revolution. Fleeing from its former main base in Shanghai, the communist movement had to reinvent itself as a peasant revolution. Instead of strikes, it engaged in armed uprising. Land distribution displaced worker control over factories as the top priority. Not unlike the GMD, however, the CCP was deeply divided about the fundamental policies. Bloody party purges followed. Disunity also made the territories vulnerable to GMD attacks. Toward the end of 1934, the CCP was on the run again, and began its Long March to Yan'an in Shaanxi.

China under Warlord Rule

There was a widespread belief among Chinese and foreign observers that the cause of China's continued plight after 1911 was twofold. Apart from the external pressure of imperialism, the internal crisis of warlordism was robbing China of its future. Warlords were autonomous militarists who gained power through the devolution of military authority from the central state to the provinces or regional leaders. The diffusion of central power that had begun gradually in the late Qing had given way to the undoing of civil order and to the militarization of local society. This had important social consequences in the republican period, as a wider culture of militarism and violence took hold that shaped society and shook up the country. This process also finally caused the massive breakdown of central control after 1916, with the failure of Yuan Shikai's imperial ambitions and his subsequent death.[1] Thereafter, a power struggle arose among Yuan Shikai's former generals of the Beiyang Army. These generals, called Beiyang warlords, commanded personal military forces and acted independently of central authority. As the Beiyang Warlords jockeyed for power among themselves, regional warlords assumed power in other parts of China, as well.

The period between 1916 and 1928, when a new national government was eventually reestablished by the GMD in Nanjing, saw the rise of numerous regional rulers, almost all of them with military backgrounds. These men called themselves military governors *(dujun)*, but were referred to as warlords *(junfa)*. The duration of an individual warlord's rule could be very brief. Few of them enjoyed continuous periods of rule. Fighting among warlords was almost constant. After Yuan Shikai's death, Duan Qirui, the commander of the Beiyang army, assumed control of the remnants of central government and became the last Beiyang intendant. His power rested on a loose alliance of warlords in the north and northeast. The central government, which in official communication was referred to as the Beiyang government, was obviously weakened by these developments, but it never completely collapsed. It continued to function until 1920, when the "Zhili clique," based around Beijing and led by warlords Cao Kun (1862–1938) and Wu Peifu (1872–1939), forced Duan to flee and seek Japanese protection in Tianjin.

While it gradually lost its power over much of the country, the Beiyang government maintained control over the capital, Beijing. Sometimes, through

5.1. Muslim warlord and governor of Ningxia province Ma Hongkui receiving ice cream from his wife, 1948.
Pictures from History / Bridgeman Images / PFH1165917

coalitions with other warlords, it also controlled parts of North China. The Ministry of Foreign Affairs continued to represent China in international politics. The Beiyang government was also the recipient of customs revenues, though these were mostly used to pay debts from China's lost wars in the nineteenth century. The Beiyang government even continued institutional reform, especially in the education sector and the legal system. It defended Chinese interests in foreign policy and negotiated a raise of the customs tariffs with the great powers. All these were achievements that future governments were able to build on.

Given the many warlords and the considerable diversity of their policies, it is difficult to characterize the era as a whole.[2] Some warlords committed atrocities, allowing their troops to pillage and murder local communities. With these men in command, the period tended strongly toward violence and heavy extraction of resources from society. Some warlords exhibited particularly colorful characteristics: Zhang Zongchang (1881–1932), who was referred to as the "dog-meat general" (because his favorite game was called Eating Dog Meat), had a reputation for violence and womanizing. He ruled over Shandong in the 1920s, but also made several advances into the south. He briefly held Shanghai and Nanjing in 1925. Zhang's mercenary army numbered around fifty thousand, and included White Russians who had fought for the tsar against the Bolsheviks, and fled to China after the Bolsheviks. He was assassinated on a visit back to Shandong in 1932, having fled to Japan following his defeat in 1928 by GMD troops. Feng Yuxiang (1882–1948) had the nickname "Christian general" since he was known for his missionary zeal after converting to Christianity. He rose to power as a warlord in China's tumultuous north, with a main base in Shaanxi. He is reported to have, on occasion, baptized an entire army unit with a fire hose, ordering its soldiers to march to the tune of "Hark, the Herald Angels Sing." In areas under his rule, he implemented policies inspired by Christian Socialism, a movement of mid-nineteenth century Europe.[3] He pursued a program of social and economic improvement for all members of society, impoverished or wealthy. He vigorously suppressed prostitution, gambling, and the sale of opium. Some other warlords, such as Yan Xishan (1883–1960), the "model governor" from Shanxi province, also pursued long-term stability and economic development in the areas under their control, and cared for the welfare of the population.

Rents, tributes from landlords, taxes, money from criminal gangs, and revenues from the opium trade combined to deliver considerable wealth to the warlords. These resources extracted from society could have been used to provide public goods and services to the population; more often, however, they went toward weapons purchases. The warlords wielded effective military power but gained little popular support. Thus, for most of the warlord era,

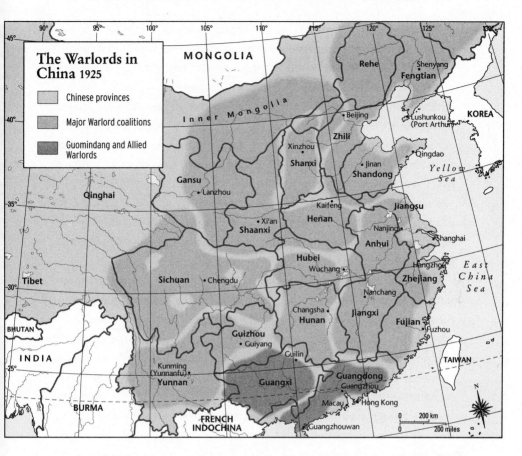

The Warlords in China 1925

Chinese provinces

Major Warlord coalitions

Guomindang and Allied Warlords

there was no clear basis for political legitimacy and despite their coercive power, the warlords oversaw inherently unstable regimes. Because most of them were strongly committed to the region they ruled, but harbored little concern for China as a nation, they also undermined the central institutions that had been in place. The single exceptions were the post office and the maritime customs service, both of which, amazingly, continued to work throughout this era. Without a single currency, a unified national administrative system, or a unitary system of national defense, China became increasingly fragmented socially, politically, and economically.

The absence of central control also, however, had some positive effects. Intellectual and artistic production was free from government intervention and entered a period of experimentation, innovation, and creativity. During the social and political upheaval of the 1910s and early 1920s, the film industry in Shanghai, for instance, produced rich and engaging popular entertainment including musicals, light comedies, episodes from traditional fiction and opera, martial arts adventures, detective stories, and morality tales.[4] The publishing business expanded, and journals and newspapers achieved circulations greater than ever before. Exciting new literature appeared, with authors experimenting with innovative forms and fresh topics. Many works now considered classics of modern Chinese literature were written and published during this time. In the treaty ports, schools and universities expanded and operated with little restriction. The foreign-dominated cities along the coast offered protection not only from predatory warlords, but also from Japanese expansion, giving rise to diverse, creative, bourgeois, and cosmopolitan cultures.

Amid the disruptions caused by warlordism and civil war, important economic changes occurred during the war years. Commercial development mainly centered on the treaty ports, but recent research shows the extent to which commercialization, and the development of foreign and domestic trade, also penetrated rural economies, especially in coastal locales. As expanding commercial networks presented new employment opportunities, families saw pathways to economic gain beyond simple landholding. After World War I, levels of foreign economic competition abated, and this period saw light industries increasingly filled with Chinese-owned businesses. In fact, in the postwar period, Chinese companies and trading houses made enormous profits serving western demand for raw materials and agricultural produce. With the revival of trade in the 1920s, exports to an exhausted Europe rose even higher and China's trade deficit shrank. China also experienced growth in the small, modern sectors of the economy along its coast.[5] As evidence of this period's rapid pace of industrialization, modern factory production grew 8–9 percent annually in the 1920s. The industrial labor force numbered some two million people, a quarter of them in Shanghai. Chinese banks increased in number and expanded their capital. Many new laws were passed to govern the economy in various ways. It is remarkable that the buildup of a new economic institutional order in the coastal areas proceeded strongly despite political turmoil.

The overwhelming social consequence of warlordism was the continued rise of the military in society. The warlord era fundamentally undermined the concept of civilian rule in China. The military became a leading institution, and it preferred military solutions to problems of control and governance. Meanwhile, having such a fragmented and locally militarized society turned China as a whole into a more vulnerable target. The political situation created serious potential for outside intervention.

United Front Revolution

Inspired by the global flows of ideas facilitated by the May Fourth movement, China's students and activists began to study western political ideas seriously. Several developments had contributed to the appeal of leftist ideas in China, beginning with the success of the 1917 October Revolution in Russia and the renunciation of the unequal treaties by the Soviet Union in the Karakhan Manifesto of July 1919.[6] Adding to these were the Great War among the world's leading nations and the rise of anticolonial liberation movements worldwide. Above all, the split of the New Culture movement into liberal pragmatism and left-leaning revolutionaries, and the deepening crisis in China, propelled Chinese intellectuals to search for an international alternative and more potent solution—this time, via Russia.

Young intellectuals were at first attracted to the ideas and activities of the Russian nihilists and terrorists who were mostly informed by the political philosophy of anarchism—the most radical and widespread philosophy of social transformation then available.[7] The Chinese writer Ding Ling (1904–1986), for instance, named the lead character of her most famous story "The Diary of Miss Sophia" (*Shafei nüshi de riji,* 1928) after Sofiya Perovskaya—the Russian revolutionary executed in 1881 for her involvement in the assassination of Tsar Alexander II.[8] The calculated use of violence for political ends advocated by the anarchists seemed necessary to many young Chinese at the time. In a nutshell, anarchism favored the autonomy of local communities and opposed monarchy, imperialism, and any kind of nationalism that envisaged a large, centralized state enforcing its authority. The idea of local communities as the source of social order and economic well-being resonated with many Chinese thinkers, and many in this period echoed elements of anarchistic thinking. The problem with anarchy was that, by definition, it lacked organization and discipline. Already concerned with China's fragmented situation, more and more intellectuals came to view the Russian Bolshevik solution—in which a centralized party of committed activists steps up to lead society toward commonly held goals—as more appealing and better suited to the problems of Chinese society.

In contrast to anarchism, Marxism was considerably less known to the Chinese. In early 1903, a brief excerpt from the *Communist Manifesto* was published in China. Five years later, in 1908, Chinese anarchists published a translation of Friedrich Engels's preface to the 1888 English edition of the *Communist Manifesto*. This was the first Marxist text to appear in complete form. Inspired by the Bolshevik Revolution of 1917, Li Dazhao (1889–1927), known as the "father of Marxism in China," was the first in China to draw attention to Marxism. In his essay "The Victory of Bolshevism," published in the October 1918 issue of *New Youth*, Li welcomed the revolutionary new order of the Soviet Union and briefly discussed the Marxist social and economic theories on which it was based.[9] Like Li Hanjun (1890–1927), probably the leading specialist in socialist theory of the time, Li Dazhao came into contact with Marxism through Japanese-language writings. The "Research Society for the Study of Marxism" he founded met regularly to discuss revolutionary theory. Only after the May Fourth movement, and in the midst of general disappointment regarding Wilson's allegedly empty promises of self-determination, did many more Chinese students and intellectuals begin to study Marxism. In 1919 and 1920, the Beijing daily paper *Chenbao* and its supplement, *Chenbao fukan*, published translations of writings about Marxist theory, mostly from Japanese publications. In the beginning, Marxism appeared to be a very broad ideology of emancipation, and attracted much interest from young students who wanted to be free of the yoke of the past and foreign domination. Interest in Marxism was strengthened by admiration for the Bolshevik revolution in Russia. What inspired the first Chinese communists was Leninism rather than Marxism.[10] Another important point is that most of these early communists were primarily nationalists. As ironic as this might seem, in light of the internationalist credo of Marxism and its subsequent Leninist variant, they were interested above all in China's national salvation. Recognizing this helps to clarify subsequent developments and the ultimate form that Marxism-Leninism took in China; specifically, it explains why the practical principles and organization of the Soviet revolution, more than Marx's original philosophical ideas, attracted the interest of Chinese communists. Leninism seemed to show a way toward building an organization and a new nation-state using the same tools that Lenin and later Stalin had used to create the Soviet Union.

At this point, the Comintern, the Russian organization founded in 1919 to spread communism across the globe, decided to facilitate the establishment of a Communist Party in China. It was an obvious move to gain influence in a country sharing a long transcontinental border with Russia.[11] Surveying the scene from Moscow, Comintern agents determined that the group around Li Dazhao at Peking University was most likely to participate in such an undertaking. They also identified a group of intellectuals associated with *New Youth* in Shanghai, including Chen Duxiu, Li Hanjun, and others, who could possibly form the nucleus of a new Communist Party. The timing of the Comintern search was fortuitous given the social-intellectual context. There had been many protests, demonstrations, and petitions demanding political change, but China remained stuck in conditions of backwardness and warlordism. The search for a new approach had taken on real urgency. In August 1920, a communist group was set up in Shanghai, consisting of students, teachers, and journalists. From the autumn of 1920 to the first half of 1921, similar communist groups were established one after another in Beijing, Wuhan, Changsha, Jinan, Guangzhou, and other cities, as well as in Japan and France. Names and organizations varied from place to place. Small, covert communist cells operated illegally, forming the backbone of the communist movement. The Socialist Youth Corps, able to operate somewhat more publicly, took on the task of recruiting new members for the party through its connections to urban youth. Finally, Marxist study societies, operating in public, worked to reach audiences as widely as possible.[12]

In November 1920, the communist group in Shanghai drafted the "Manifesto of the Communist Party of China."[13] This first public text issued under the aegis of the Chinese Communist Party (CCP) consisted of three sections: "Communists' Ideals," "Communists' Objectives," and "Recent Conditions in the Class Struggle." It articulated the communists' aspirations to create a new society that would abolish private ownership, practice public ownership of the means of production, destroy the old state apparatus, and eliminate social classes. "The goal of Communists is to create a new society in accordance with communist ideals," it proclaimed. "In order to make the realization of our ideal society feasible, the first step is the elimination of the present capitalist system. The elimination of the capitalist system requires strong power to defeat the capitalist countries. The power of the laboring masses—the proletariat—is growing stronger and is becoming more concentrated. This is precisely the result of class conflicts within capitalist countries. The form that this power takes is class struggle." The manifesto explained that the Chinese proletariat would have to engage in class struggle to destroy the capitalist system by force, and therefore that it must "organize a revolutionary political party of the proletariat—the Communist Party" to lead it in the seizure of political power and in the establishment of the dictatorship of the proletariat.

The CCP was officially established in July 1921, when the first congress of the CCP was convened in the French Concession in Shanghai. Attending the congress were twelve delegates representing fifty-three party members from seven localities; among these twelve were Mao Zedong (1893–1976) and Dong Biwu (1886–1975). The party's cofounders, Chen Duxiu (1879–1942) and Li Dazhao (1888–1927), were unable to attend. Two representatives of the Comintern, G. Maring (a pseudonym of Hendricus Sneevliet, 1883–1942) and Nicolsky, attended the congress as observers. The CCP believed that earlier Chinese revolutions (in 1911 and 1919) had not mobilized the people on a broad scale—indeed, that they had neglected workers and peasants. The CCP's deep admiration for the October Revolution also caused it to reject the social-democratic line of thinking backed by the Second International, an international socialist organization. From the outset, the CCP defined itself as a Marxist-Leninist party, a revolutionary party of the working class. Committed to socialism and communism, it was determined to ignite a revolution in China. The congress decided that the basic task of the party at this stage would be to establish trade unions of industrial workers and to "imbue the trade unions with the spirit of class struggle."[14] Hence, the First Party Congress adopted a sectarian, strict proletarian line and refused any notion of cooperation with other social groups such as urban shopkeepers, merchants, or intellectuals. The program passed by the congress called for the "revolutionary army of the proletariat to overthrow the capitalistic classes."[15] It demanded a dictatorship of the proletariat. Two documents were drawn up—the program and the party's "First Decision" to form industrial unions— both uncompromising in their opposition to collaborating with other parties or groups, or the intellectuals. The congress elected Chen Duxiu as general secretary; Chen Lida (1890–1966), and Zhang Guotao (1897–1979) would together form the party's Central Bureau.

This exclusive focus on the working class and hostility toward the bourgeoisie contradicted the policy favored by the Comintern. The subsequent period was dominated by Soviet attempts to compel the CCP to pursue a policy of cooperation with other groups, and in particular with the nationalists around Sun Yat-sen. The reasons for the Comintern line were both ideological and practical: Lenin and his successors believed that China was an undeveloped, agrarian, and poor country that was not yet ready for a proletarian revolution. Therefore it needed a nationalist, bourgeois revolution before socialism could be put on the agenda. The representative sent by the Comintern, Maring, was tasked with influencing the CCP to come into line with the Comintern plan. He suggested an alliance to the CCP by which it would cooperate with Sun Yat-sen's GMD. The CCP and the GMD indeed had some common goals and shared a basic worldview as revolutionary parties both dreaming of an independent and strong China without foreign imperialism.

North and central China, however, were still firmly under the control of Beiyang-connected armies. With few exceptions, the warlords viewed the GMD and the CCP with suspicion, if not hostility. By 1921, one of the few sympathetic warlords, Chen Jiongming (1878–1933), assisted Sun Yat-sen's efforts to head the GMD government in Guangzhou (Canton), reorganize the Nationalist Party, and build a revolutionary alternative to the Beiyang government in the north. Sun knew, however, that without outside support his government in exile would be unable to regain power over China. While the western powers, hesitant to get involved, refused to support him, the Soviet Union eagerly worked through the Comintern to back Sun's GMD. Subsequently, the Comintern sent an agent, Adolf Joffe (1883–1927), to Guangzhou to make clear that the Comintern would offer advice, money, and weapons—but only on the condition that a broad national alliance be established, including the small CCP. In 1923, Sun Yat-sen forged a coalition of nationalists, the CCP, and the Soviet Union. Sun Yat-sen was critical of communism, but found enough common ground between his own goals and the Soviet intentions to make the alliance work temporarily.

Between 1923 and 1927, the GMD (and CCP) worked closely with the Soviet Union.[16] A large contingent of advisers from the Comintern also advised on political matters, and assisted the GMD's efforts to build a modern and strong army at the newly founded military institute, the Whampoa

Military Academy *(Huangpu junguan xuexiao),* modeled on Moscow's Red Army Academy. Revolutionary ideology played a prominent role in the academy's teaching program, as political commissars lectured troops on the history of foreign imperialism in China and emphasized the importance of political awareness.[17] Chiang Kai-shek (1887–1975) served as the first commander of the school, and established a basis there for the almost exclusive control of the army. Chiang was born in 1887 to a salt merchant family from the town of Xikou, in Zhejiang province. Schooled in the classics, he was endowed with a deep sense of responsibility to engage in self-cultivation, maintain self-discipline, and observe traditional social rituals. Like many in his generation, he was driven by China's lost wars and the abolition of the examination system to join the military. Inclined to study military strategy, tactics, and technology, he enrolled in the Japanese military academies that he felt could give him the knowledge and skills to pull his nation back from the brink of disaster. In 1913, he met Sun Yat-sen in Japan and started to work with him. In August 1923, Sun sent Chiang to Moscow to study military and party organization, so that when the Whampoa Military Academy opened, Chiang was the obvious first choice for the position of commander. (Zhou Enlai, later second in command at the CCP, served as its political commissar.)

While the CCP hesitated to implement a Comintern policy it had viewed with reservations from the very beginning, the new Comintern representative, Mikhail Borodin (1884–1951), forcefully pushed the expansion of cooperation between the CCP and the GMD. The process was accelerated by promises of greater Soviet financial support and by the reorganization of the GMD that finally took place in January 1924. By 1925, Soviet support had made the Guomindang into a very different and much stronger party, organized along Leninist principles—that is, as a tightly organized and highly centralized political party. According to Comintern instructions, the main targets of the revolution were foreign imperialists and their Chinese collaborators. While fighting these opponents in cooperation with the GMD, the CCP was to strengthen its position within the GMD and more broadly within the nationalist movement by taking control of the peasant and labor movements. Stalin, who after Lenin's death in January 1924, took over the leadership of the Soviet Union, played an important role in implementing a "united front" policy. He first wanted Chinese communists to ally themselves with the left factions within the GMD to increase their influence within the movement. Even when the non-communists in the GMD lashed out at CCP members for what they considered an undermining of the GMD, the Soviet leader still insisted that the only political path for communists in China lay in the alliance with the GMD. Stalin's policy provided vital assistance to the un-usual and uneasy cooperation.

The alliance was formally called the United Front (1923–1927). It helped the CCP to increase its membership, and enabled communists to develop personal relations with GMD soldiers and officials in organizations such as the Whampoa Military Academy that would prove invaluable in later years. Wang Jingwei (1883–1944), who in the 1920s ascended into Sun Yat-sen's inner circle, worked with Zhou Enlai in the political department of the academy, where they devised propaganda campaigns. Between January 1924 and May 1926, communist influence in the GMD grew steadily and the CCP grew from just under a thousand members in January 1925 to almost fifty-eight thousand by April 1927. The communists' influence in the urban areas was especially boosted by the demonstrations of the May Thirtieth move-ment (1925). With the protection of the nationalist armies in the south, the CCP was also able to work in the countryside and to develop its influence among the peasants.

Those successes and experiences in inciting revolution were valuable, but also came at a cost. The CCP could neither develop a basis of its own in urban China nor build up solid support in the southern countryside. Because it was allied with the GMD, the CCP could not develop a coherent policy for rural areas. From an attitude of indifference, it veered to a radical plan of land confiscation—from which it later had to retreat when that plan was opposed by the right wing of the GMD. As a partner in the United Front, the CCP was compelled to compromise and maneuver. In the end, by exposing its small group of members to the jealousy and distrust of their allies, it alienated its own base of supporters.

When, on March 12, 1925, Sun Yat-sen died of cancer, the almost imme-diate result was a power struggle between the left and right wings of the GMD. Sun's two most likely successors were the right-leaning Chiang Kai-shek and the left-leaning nationalist Wang Jingwei. The two differed, as well, in their political instincts. Chiang had started to doubt the usefulness of the alliance with the Soviet Union, and grew convinced that the Soviet Union used the United Front to undermine the nationalist leadership. Wang Jingwei insisted on sticking to the alliance and the United Front policy. Chiang Kai-shek moved quickly to secure his role as successor, pushing aside his rival. After officially becoming the leader of the National Revolutionary Army on June 5, 1926, Chiang Kai-shek went on to carry out the Northern Expedition first conceived by Sun Yat-sen as a core mission of the United Front aimed at reunifying the country.[18]

With the Northern Expedition, Chiang Kai-shek pursued two goals, hoping both to secure his leadership of the party and government and to eliminate the remnants of the Beiyang warlord network that still controlled large swaths of North China. In July 1926, the Soviet-supplied National Revolutionary Army, one hundred thousand men strong, left its stronghold in Guangzhou, Guangdong province, to overpower the warlords. Soviet military advisers were attached to every unit of Chiang's expeditionary force, and Soviet aircraft and pilots flew reconnaissance missions over enemy positions. At the same time, communist agitators and propagandists spread out, persuading warlord subordinates to defect to the nationalist side while encouraging strikes and peasant revolts. But the warlords did not give in easily; they defended every inch of territory. The Northern Expedition was a bitterly fought civil war that took the lives of perhaps three hundred thousand people. By March 1927, the National Revolutionary Army had overrun Hunan, Hubei, Jiangxi, Guizhou, and Fujian provinces and captured many important cities, including Shanghai, Nanjing, and Wuhan in southern China.

Once victory seemed within reach, Chiang broke with those forces that had provided crucial support. Conflicts between him and his supporters on the one hand, and the CCP, Soviet advisers, and the GMD left wing on the other had become worse during the Northern Expedition. The rift widened as Soviet advisers suspected Chiang of wanting to establish a military dictatorship. Chiang ended the cooperation with the Comintern at the end of 1926 and shortly thereafter banned CCP members from serving on GMD committees. On April 12, 1927, he decided to finally purge the party, government, and army of all communists through brutal campaigns of extermination and bloody massacres. Not all groups and leaders within the GMD

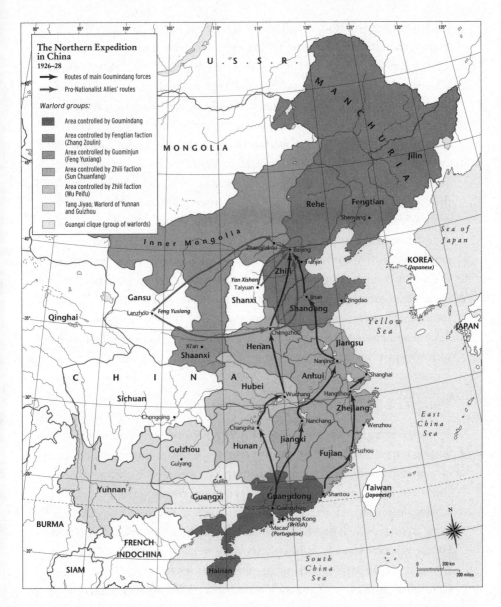

The Northern Expedition in China
1926–28

Routes of main Goumindang forces

Pro-Nationalist Allies' routes

Warlord groups:

Area controlled by Goumindang

Area controlled by Fengtian faction (Zhang Zoulin)

Area controlled by Guominjun (Feng Yuxiang)

Area controlled by Zhili faction (Sun Chuanfang)

Area controlled by Zhili faction (Wu Peifu)

Tang Jiyao, Warlord of Yunnan and Guizhou

Guangxi clique (group of warlords)

were willing to go along. Wang Jingwei, holding the industrial center at Wuhan, opposed the "White Terror" against the CCP and its sympathizers. In January 1928, however, Chiang's troops occupied Wuhan and brought unified military governance to the whole territory along the Yangzi. At this point, northern China was still in the hands of powerful warlords. On April 7, 1928,

Chiang resumed his northern offensive against the remaining warlord forces. Many generals shifted their position either toward neutrality or toward Chiang Kai-shek. By the end of 1928, most of China had been brought under Chiang's control, even though a few northern warlords continued to reject his authority until the Japanese launched full-scale war against China in 1937.

This effort of national unification was the continuation, and in a sense the culmination, of the prolonged warfare in China that had begun with the collapse of the Qing empire. It was fought to achieve unified control over the entire territory of China. The Northern Expedition was not the last war over the control of China. For several decades more, China would be continuously at war in one form or another, at enormous cost.[19] Yet the successful completion of the military campaign was an impressive victory and important boost for Chiang Kai-shek. When he went on to eliminate known and suspected communists from within his party and from the cities under nationalist control, he pushed the Communist Party to the brink of destruction. The final consequence, therefore, was that the United Front policy, devised and pushed through by the Comintern since 1920 and imbued with such hope, was an utter disaster for the CCP.

Nation Building during the Nanjing Decade

By 1928, Chiang Kai-shek had done away with his main contenders inside and outside the Nationalist Party. He had reunited China and enforced the idea of a united republic. The city of Beijing was renamed Beiping—that is, "northern pacification" (with the capital element removed from the name). Chiang decided to place his government at Nanjing, the former capital of the Ming dynasty, which had been the last dynasty by a Chinese ruling house. For the first time since 1911, the country was governed again by a single center. It was a single-party government under the leadership of one man— Generalissimo Chiang Kai-shek (da yuanshuai). While this achievement was widely admired and cherished, in many cases entrenched regional or provincial powers were merely superficially coopted but not removed. There were provinces that refused to pay taxes to the central government. The reach of the state remained limited, and the government had only a shaky grip on large swaths of the country. Chiang's leadership, too, was far from secure and continued to face serious challenges. The basic causes of opposition against him were wariness of Chiang Kai-shek's growing personal power and fear of Nanjing's centralizing pretensions. What followed as a consequence, especially in the period from 1928 up until the early 1930s, was a prolonged and complex drama involving political maneuvering and occasionally large military battles between Chiang and the various opponents looking to expand their sway or conspire against him. Chiang's challengers included the Guangxi warlords in 1929, the warlords Feng Yuxiang and Yan Xishan in 1930, the communist insurgency in Jiangxi in the early 1930s, Guangzhou followers of the conservative GMD leader Hu Hanmin in 1931, Fujian dissidents in 1933, and Guangdong and Guangxi militias again in 1936.[20] All openly revolted and tried to topple Chiang's government. Hundreds of thousands of troops were involved—and tens of thousands died. Chiang's responses were equally violent and dubious. Espionage, covert activity, and assassinations, as well as large bribes to various warlords, contributed to Chiang's success in clinging to power. The price was high. In the areas affected by fighting, the conflicts led to a deterioration of already desperate living conditions, alienating and often displacing the population. Refugees, deserters, migrants, and paupers were later easily recruited into the CCP.

After 1927, most GMD leaders agreed on some broad political goals, including an anti-communist stance and a strong belief in a one-party system, the need for political centralization, and a high degree of control over society and the economy.[21] In theory, the GMD controlled the state and would rule through a system of so-called political tutelage until Chinese society was mature enough to be entrusted with the practice of democracy. Recall that democracy, nationalism, and livelihood (social welfare) made up the "three principles of the people" devised by Sun Yat-sen as official ideology. The regime that took shape after 1927 was neither totalitarian nor democratic, but oscillated indecisively between those ends of the political spectrum. For a one-party dictatorship, the Nationalist Party was strikingly diverse, composed of several factions. While these groups all considered themselves to be part of a nationalist revolution and thus agreed on broad goals, they had diverging political persuasions and interests. Political orientations within the GMD member base ranged from leftist to traditional to conservative. Competitors from within the GMD persistently challenged Chiang's authority on theoretical grounds and on practical issues of governing. Chiang found the bureaucracies of the party and the government difficult to run. In general, his authority

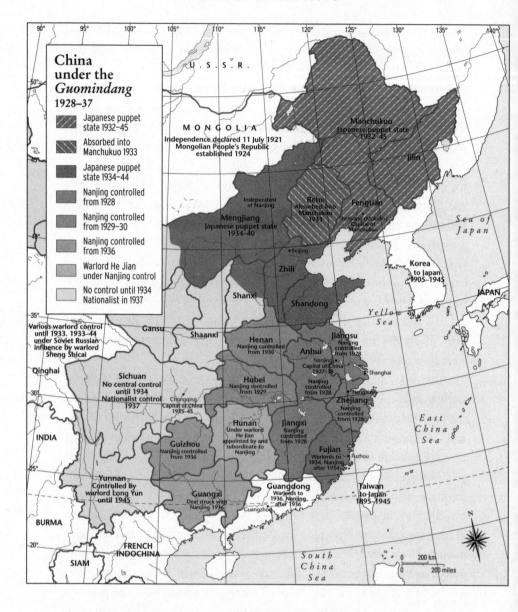

China under the *Guomindang* 1928–37

Japanese puppet state 1932–45

Absorbed into Manchukuo 1933

Japanese puppet state 1934–44

Nanjing controlled from 1928

Nanjing controlled from 1929–30

Nanjing controlled from 1936

Warlord He Jian under Nanjing control

No control until 1934 Nationalist in 1937

U.S.S.R.

MONGOLIA
Independence declared 11 July 1921
Mongolian People's Republic established 1924

Manchukuo
Japanese puppet state
1932–45

Jilin

Independent of Nanjing

Rehe
Absorbed into Manchukuo
1933

Fengtian
Shenyang (Mukden)
Capital of Manchukuo

Mengjiang
Japanese puppet state
1934–40

Beijing

Zhili

Korea
to Japan
1905–1945

Sea of Japan

JAPAN

Shanxi

Shandong

Yellow Sea

Various warlord control until 1933. 1933–44 under Soviet Russian influence by warlord Sheng Shicai

Gansu

Shaanxi

Henan
Nanjing controlled from 1930

Jiangsu
Nanjing controlled from 1928

Anhui
Nanjing Capital of China 1927–38

Shanghai

Qinghai

Sichuan
No central control until 1934
Nationalist control 1937

Chongqing
Capital of China 1935–45

Hubei
Nanjing controlled from 1929

Nanjing controlled from 1928

Zhejiang
Nanjing controlled from 1928

Hangzhou

INDIA

Hunan
Under warlord He Jian appointed by and subordinate to Nanjing

Jiangxi
Nanjing controlled from 1928

East China Sea

Guizhou
Nanjing controlled from 1936

Fujian
Warlords to 1934. Nanjing after 1934

Fuzhou

Yunnan
Controlled by warlord Long Yun until 1945

Guangxi
Deal struck with Nanjing 1936

Guangzhou

Guangdong
Warlords to 1936. Nanjing after 1936

Taiwan
to Japan
1895–1945

BURMA

FRENCH INDOCHINA

SIAM

South China Sea

0   200 km
0   200 miles

N

rested on unstable coalitions of GMD supporters and regional allies (warlords and local elites). What these supporters had in common was little more than a fragile allegiance to Chiang Kai-shek as leader, or to the party itself.

Uneasy coalitions could be found in the highest echelons. From 1928 to 1947, Chiang Kai-shek served four times (usually briefly) as president of the cabinet, the Executive Yuan. During other periods, the cabinet was presided over by H. H. Kung (1881–1967), T. V. Soong (1894–1971), or one of their political allies. T. V. Soong (Song Ziwen), the brother of Madame Chiang Kai-shek (Song Meiling [1897–2003]), was a leading figure in the government. He had obtained a bachelor's degree in economics from Harvard University in 1915 and undertook graduate studies at Columbia University from 1915 to 1917. In 1928, Soong joined the nationalist government, serving as minister of finance (1928–1933), governor of the Central Bank of China (1928–1934), minister of foreign affairs (1942–1945) and acting president of the Executive Yuan (for two months in 1930 and again in 1932–1933, after which he served as formal president from 1945 to 1947). However, he often disagreed with Chiang on government spending levels and on policy toward Japan.[22] H. H. Kung also played an important role, serving as governor of the Bank of China and as finance minister for most of the same period, taking over from T. V. Soong. He had the reputation of being the richest as well as perhaps the most corrupt political figure in China. Kung and Soong formed the core of a faction called the Political Study Group, which in general advocated policies for economic development. The Sun, Kung, Soong, and Chiang families would remain at the center of a financial and political complex through the entire period of the nationalist republic in China.

Chiang's rule also relied on the Chen brothers (Chen Lifu [1900–2001] and Chen Guofu [1892–1951]), who headed the so-called CC-Clique.[23] This group derived its power from within the party and, specifically, from the Nationalist Party's Organization Department, which ran the party from the national level all the way down to the grassroots and was modeled after the Bolshevik Party structure. The CC-Clique asserted power by influencing appointments in the party and in national and provincial administration, and monitoring the press and other educational and cultural institutions. The group as a whole had a nationalist and traditionalist intellectual outlook. The group opposed radical reforms, was strongly anti-communist, and worked to revive traditional moral values. On Chiang's instructions, one of the Chen brothers, Chen Lifu, was also appointed to head an intelligence service called the Investigation Section of the Organization Department (of the GMD). Later, in line with his governing style of creating networks of rival organizations loyal only to him, Chiang asked Dai Li (1897–1946), a former and trusted Whampoa student, to head a new Bureau of Investigation and Statistics in the Military Council. The two intelligence agencies

5.2. Chiang Kai-shek and his wife, Song Meiling, with US General Joseph Stilwell, c. 1930.
FPG / Getty Images / 104527648

both engaged in covert operations against proclaimed and assumed op-ponents. They bought off enemies, carried out assassinations, produced anti-communist propaganda, and engaged in clandestine collection of data through infiltration, torture, threats, and bribery.[24]

Another faction was the Whampoa or Huangpu group. Its members were mostly former military staff and students who had studied under Chiang at the military academy. They dominated the Military Affairs Commission in command of the nationalist armed forces and were fiercely loyal to Chiang Kai-shek. They also organized a group called the "Blue Shirts" to combat the ills of liberalism, corruption, communism, and the Japanese threat. The Blue Shirts were modeled on similar fascist groups in Europe, although Chiang's interest in fascism seems to have been superficial, mostly focusing on its ten-dency toward cults of personality and emphasis on discipline.[25] The secret core of the association was the *Lixingshe* (Act Vigorously Society). Ultimately reaching half a million members, it used security training, political indoctrination, mass recruitment, clandestine operations, the infiltration of regional warlord armies, and propaganda efforts to fight against communism. It dominated army training and influenced the police, universities, high-school summer camps, the Boy Scouts, and the New Life movement. Although the CC, Political Study, and Whampoa groups shared strong loyalties to Chiang Kai-shek, they pursued slightly competing political priorities.

Chiang Kai-shek had two important inner-party rivals: the left-leaning Wang Jingwei and the conservative Hu Hanmin. During the first years of the Nanjing decade, both tried to undermine him. While in the end they remained on the sidelines, they continued to contest Chiang Kai-shek's hold on power. Only the growing threat by Japan compelled the two competitors to cooperate. After a short resignation in December 1931, meant to demonstrate that no other leader could replace him, Chiang Kai-shek returned to power in January 1932, heading a new government in which Wang Jingwei, after uneasy negotiations, served as president of the Executive Yuan. With this, Wang and his group, the "Reorganization Faction," were brought back into the fold of the new government, but with no real power.

The structure of the government, adopted in 1928, was in accordance with Sun Yat-sen's schema of five branches as outlined in his *Lectures on Democracy (minquan zhuyi)*. Three of the five were inspired by western liberal political institutions: an Executive Yuan (or cabinet *xingzheng yuan*) to run daily operations through various ministries and committees; a Legislative Yuan *(lifa yuan)* to pass laws; and a Judicial Yuan *(sifa yuan)* for adjudication. The remaining two stemmed from the traditional Confucian bureaucracy: the Supervisory Yuan *(jiancha yuan)* oversaw government offices with the powers of consent, impeachment, censure, and audit; and the Examination Yuan *(kaoshi yuan)* focused on qualifying individuals for civil service.

The Examination Yuan deserves a closer look, as it provides an example of the strengths and weaknesses of GMD institutions. It had two departments: the examination commission *(dianshi weiyuanhui)* and the ministry for personnel *(quanxu bu)*. The first department was responsible for the exams, and the second was responsible for commendation, promotion, and office ranks. These added up to only a small organization; during the republican era, the Examination Yuan had no more than two hundred employees.[26] The first minister of the Examination Yuan was Dai Jitao (1891–1949), a leading and influential party theoretician who had led the political department of the Whampao Academy in the 1920s and, in 1924, directed the GMD propaganda department. In his writings, he tried to combine and reconcile Sun Yat-sen's theories with the Confucian tradition.

The Examination Yuan held its first examinations to fill higher positions in civil service in 1931 in Nanjing. These examinations were called Gaokao (not to be confused with the university entrance examinations of the same name in today's People's Republic of China). In 1933, more examinations were conducted in Nanjing, this time for entry positions and general civil service aspirants. The content of the exams largely followed the structure of the examinations during the Beiyang period. They contained three sections. The most extensive section focused on general knowledge and linguistic skills. Many questions concerned traditional philosophy, literature, and history and required very good command of classical Chinese. This was complemented by a second section testing expert knowledge of finance, administration, and other professional content. The third section contained questions on the GMD's party doctrine *(dangyi)*, testing familiarity with party congress documents. In this third part of the exam, Sun Yat-sen's writings took center stage. Thematically, the section on party doctrine placed most emphasis on nationalism, modernization, and anti-communism. Designed to be selective, the examinations were pitched at a very high level of difficulty. The Examination Yuan organized the exams regularly and with much effort. As in imperial times, grading was anonymized. Examiners were isolated for several days in specific examination buildings. When they finished, the Yuan's chairperson, Dai Jintao, would announce and publicly display the results.

Unlike its imperial predecessor, the republican Examination Yuan had only limited impact. Most civil service positions were filled without the examinations. During the Nanjing decade, only about 1 percent of all civil servants were recruited through examinations. Almost all positions were assigned based on personal recommendation. In 1936, the institution stabilized and examination candidates regularly took administrative positions. Still, however, only a small percentage of civil servants gained their positions by exams.

The nationalist government also undertook a number of significant initiatives and reforms to follow up on its agenda of reconstruction and national development. The republican era was a time of change and innovation, especially in the urban areas. Some of those reforms were very successful, managing for example to slowly improve China's international standing. China became an important member in international organizations such as the League of Nations. The republic also moved to steadily reduce foreign privileges in China and make China a more equal trading partner through treaty revision and tariff reform. In 1930, the government succeeded in restoring tariff autonomy. It gained the right to decide the percentage of import taxes on goods coming into China. Also, during this time, the Maritime Customs Service that handled these tariffs started to replace foreign employees with Chinese.[27] A number of foreign concessions were returned to Chinese control—for instance, the British leasehold in Shandong, Weihaiwei. The regime thus achieved some of the major goals that Chinese nationalists had set long before. As a result, customs revenue increased enough to cover about half the government's expenses, leaving the rest to come from industry and agriculture.

The period of political tutelage, during which no elections were supposed to be held, was based on a special provisional constitution, also called the Tutelage Constitution (1931). It was designed to cover the period of transition from party tutelage to constitutional, democratic rule. In an important innovation, gender was added to race, religion, and class as a basis that could not be used to discriminate against citizens. The issue of writing and instituting a permanent national constitution and multi-party national assembly was a major cause for debate within the party and in society. After a lengthy process of discussion and political maneuvering in the early 1930s, the draft text of a new national constitution was published in May 1936. The constitution was explicitly based on the three people's principles. In fact, it declared China to be a "Three People's Principles Republic." While granting political participation to the people, the constitution clearly limited the fundamental civic rights of the citizens. Individual rights could be abolished by a simple parliamentary majority if circumstances were thought to call for that.[28]

Law and criminal justice were high on the agenda of the government in Nanjing.[29] In general, the nationalists adopted all major legislation from their predecessors in the Beiyang government, but tried to modify and revise the laws to bring them in line with the new political and constitutional order. A modified version of the criminal code was made public in 1928, too, passed by the Legislative Yuan, together with new laws for criminal procedures. A revision of the prison law was adopted in 1928 and remained in effect, with only a few modifications, until 1949. Intense public and legislative discussion accompanied further work on these codes in the 1930s. After four years, a new criminal law code was promulgated on January 1, 1935; revised criminal procedures followed one year later. Between 1929 and 1931, a modern civil code was adopted that explicitly strengthened women's rights in matters of marriage, divorce, and inheritance. Those changes, however, affected in reality only the urban areas.

After 1928, the Nanjing government also strove to implement a new legal system and to increase the number of new legal institutions. In 1930, the government laid down a comprehensive plan aimed at replacing all traditional *yamen* courts within ten years. The new courts were divided into civil and criminal benches, and there were three levels of courts: the Supreme Court, the provincial high courts, and the district courts. Each court had a procurator, who was given a monopoly on prosecution in all criminal matters. The criminal trial was to be conducted as an oral accusatory process in which, during a hearing, the procurator brought the charges and the defendant was allowed to defend himself by pointing out exonerating or mitigating circumstances. The draft criminal law introduced legal representation by lawyers on behalf of both the defendant and the plaintiff.[30] In major Chinese cities, bar associations sprang up quickly.

The government also intended to reform the education sector fundamentally and, above all, to expand China's system of higher education to meet the needs of national development.[31] An organizational law for Chinese higher education was approved in 1928. It required that each university should have a school of science, engineering, medicine, or agriculture. Reforms began in earnest in 1932 under the leadership of Zhu Jiahua (1893–1963), who was named minister of education. A German-trained geologist long active in nationalist developmental policy, Zhu brought to his job strong academic and political credentials. Rapid development followed. By 1936, the number of universities and colleges had increased to 108 with 41,922 in-school students and 11,850 faculty and staff. Those institutions were mostly located in the big cities in the eastern part of China. This dynamic and evolving system of higher education included public institutions (Peking University, Jiaotong University, National Central University) and a pure research institution, the Academia Sinica, complemented by a range of private colleges and universities (Tsinghua University, St. John's University, Peking Union Medical

College, and Yenching University). China's public universities were designed largely according to the German Humboldtian model of a research university, while many of the leading private colleges were supported, advised, or even run by American institutions. The Ministry of Education also began to move higher education away from the focus on humanities and social sciences in favor of science, engineering, and, at the secondary level, vocational training. Government financial support for the applied sciences increased markedly. From 1931 to 1936, the percentage of students in the fields of science and engineering doubled in public institutions. Parallel to the expansion, the government tightened its grip. In the 1930s, institutions of higher education were required by the Nationalist Party to politicize education. The Ministry of Education ordered all schools to add military training and courses on the Nationalist Party's ideology to their curricula as a means of building discipline and loyalty to the party.[32] The GMD government worked hard to increase the number of six-year compulsory primary schools and secondary schools, as well. At the same time, authorities made sure to centrally regulate and supervise the schools, as education was enlisted to serve the practical needs of the state. They were key to cultivating loyalty to the nation, to the party, and to its ideology based on the three people's principles.

Reformers also targeted urban poverty and other "social problems" such as drug abuse, prostitution, and gambling.[33] They followed an urban social reform program based on progressivist ideas that were also popular in the West. In the republican period, social problems came to be seen as major obstacles to the modernization of China. Social relief and intervention came in the form of workhouses and poorhouses, as well as other state-run institutions such as orphanages, where the poor engaged in compulsory labor and were trained to be productive. Incarceration of varying degrees of stringency and harshness became the prime method of dealing with those sections of the urban population that the state was otherwise unable to assimilate into its vision. This was part of a wider trend by which not only criminals but also lepers, madmen, ethnic and religious aliens, and the poor were confined to special spaces which they often experienced as somewhat disciplinary and punitive, if not predominantly so. While inroads were made against prostitution, gambling, and drugs, all remained fairly common.

In its efforts to build a modern nation, the government also confronted religious institutions. Confucian, Daoist, and Buddhist traditions were deeply embedded in the fabric of rural life, and brought deeper meaning and community to the lives of most rural folk. China never had a national, hierarchically organized established church. The term "religion" *(zongjiao),* with its Christian-derived connotation of personal faith practiced within a congregation, entered the Chinese vocabulary only in the late nineteenth century, borrowed from the German term for religion and translated via Japanese texts. In the early twentieth century, reformers tried to transform and modernize Chinese traditions by reorganizing them into hierarchically structured congregations subordinate to the state, essentially remaking them in the image of western churches. For instance, the state legally recognized the Chinese Buddhist Association as the official representative of the entire national community of Buddhists. Similar organizations were formed for other religions. These were not, however, seen as religious organizations per se, but rather treated as a type of "cultural organization" *(wenhua tuanti).* The government thus saw religions as various strands of China's cultural tradition. Religious associations were also required to register with the Social Affairs Bureau and the local branch of the Nationalist Party. This meant that, like all cultural associations, they fell under the control of party and state. Demanded of them were loyalty to the party, state, and official ideology, and also active contributions to the public good in the forms of charity, welfare, and activities to promote ethics and education. As for the ritual, often syncretistic, practices of ordinary Chinese people involving ancestor and local deity worship, the GMD government labeled these as superstitious and tried to eradicate them.[34]

The army became an increasingly powerful component of Chiang's government given its military orientation, which external circumstances naturally reinforced. Chiang Kai-shek was convinced that China needed foreign support for its military modernization. There was, however, only one country willing to offer sustained military assistance: Germany. Forced by the Versailles Treaty of 1919 to downscale its military forces, Germany had left many high-ranking officers seeking employment. Some of them ended up in the service of Chiang Kai-shek. For ten years, Max Bauer (a one-time chief of operations for Field Marshal Erich Ludendorff) and forty-six other highly decorated German officers would develop ambitious plans for the modernization of China's Central Army. They drew up a thirty-year program and were charged with beginning to implement it.[35] One of the leading military strategists of the time, General Alexander von Falkenhausen (1878–1966), headed these military advisers from 1934 to 1938. They were a large, tight-knit group of German former colonial officers experienced in "small wars"—often, colonial counterinsurgent campaigns—who had previously been deployed in areas of unrest from Africa and the Middle East to China. As well as developing policies of military modernization, these German advisers aided China's nationalist government in devising tactical measures and strategies to crush the communist revolution. Von Falkenhausen, for instance, recommended the blockhouse strategy the British had used in the Transvaal in colonial Africa—and that strategy proved very effective in Chiang Kai-shek's fifth encirclement campaign against the communists' base areas, carried out from autumn 1933 to autumn 1934. More generally, the advisers crafted a plan to develop a relatively small but well-trained and well-equipped army. Under von Falkenhausen's leadership, the German advisers also trained military staff that reported to Chiang Kai-shek for military operations and policy decisions.

As Chiang Kai-shek found himself surrounded by political rivals within the party, challenged by a swelling communist uprising, fighting unyielding warlords, and responding to a Japanese invasion in the early 1930s, he recognized the need to go on the offensive. It was imperative that he offer a compelling, guiding political idea. Only a powerful vision could effectively counter the appeal of communism. In Jiangxi province (where the communist Soviet base area was located), the New Life movement *(xinshenghuo yundong)* was launched in 1934 and spread via posters, pamphlets, public lectures, and the organization of mass demonstrations.[36] The New Life movement aimed to reinvigorate the spirit of Chinese society through a series of campaigns designed to transform social practices. The movement used an eclectic mix of traditional and Christian ethics to facilitate a social and cultural transformation. Changes in everyday life, it was believed, would lead to China's cultural and social regeneration and thus the strengthening of the nation-state. A leaflet authored by Chiang explained that the New Life movement promoted a "regular life" guided by four virtues: *li* (behavior), *yi* (justice), *lian* (integrity), and *chi* (honor). "These virtues must be applied to ordinary matters such as food, clothing, shelter and action," it explained. "The four virtues are the essential principles for the promotion of morality. From these rules, one learns how to deal with men and matters, how to cultivate oneself and how to adjust oneself to surroundings. Whoever violates these rules is bound to fail and a nation which neglects them will not survive."[37] The day-to-day activities of a movement promoting courtesy, cleanliness, and social order were left to a large extent to the police, the military, and even the scouting movement. New Life instructional committees were set up throughout the country and, by 1935, more than 1,100 counties had such committees. Gradually the New Life movement became more militaristic as it mimicked the style and trappings of the European right-wing youth movements also springing up in fascist Europe in the 1930s. Officially, the movement intended to "thoroughly militarize the lives of the citizens of the entire nation." The purpose of this complete militarization was spiritual rather than martial, however, as the aim was to cultivate "courage and swiftness, the endurance of suffering, a tolerance of hard work, especially the habit and ability of unified action." The New Life movement, however, had only a slight impact on the population and never was able to catch on with the public. It slowly faded from sight after 1937, although officially it did not end until 1949. While it failed to entice the masses, it stands as first of the many large, government-led mass movements that would become a hallmark of China's twentieth-century history. The New Life movement coined slogans that remained obscure, but set a pattern for policies to reeducate and mobilize the masses for political ends. It has often been compared to fascist movements in Europe, but a more interesting and illuminating comparison is with the post-1949 mass campaigns of China itself. Especially after that year, mass campaigns became an important tool for the communist government to rally the population behind its goals and to enforce policies. The organizational prototype provided by the New Life movement turned out to have more impact than any message it tried to deliver. The idea of a countrywide political campaign that bypassed the regular institutional order to quickly and flexibly realize political goals was a significant and far-reaching innovation that would play out after 1949 on a far bigger scale.

Through initiatives like the New Life movement, the Nanjing government also tried to control the public sphere. Sun Yat-sen had already envisioned the establishment of a propaganda state in the 1920s.[38] The nationalist government under Chiang Kai-shek started in 1928 to pursue this notion, although it was never able to enforce complete control of public intellectual life. In a propaganda state, all forms of public communication are influenced and regulated by the state. The goal is to bring public life in line with the norms of state ideology. Officially, this was justified in China by a need to "educate" the people until they were fully ready for basic freedoms such as freedom of expression and the press. Accordingly, the Nanjing government censored the press. It also arrested or otherwise intimidated intellectuals who publicly voiced criticisms of the government.

The Nanjing government made tremendous progress in building a set of national state institutions that featured a rational division of responsibilities, a high degree of technical professionalism, and a basis in legal routines. Those institutions were able to assert the authority of the center even as they delegated powers to provincial and local levels. In many ways, this continued the policies started in the late Qing period, beginning in 1900, to achieve greater centralization and modernization. But the strategy suffered from several shortcomings. Recruiting enough trained and competent civil servants was a constant challenge, especially in the countryside. The bureaucracy was probably weakest at the level of local government of rural areas. Corruption and rent-seeking networks ran rampant. Without more resources, the Nanjing government was simply unable to build a strong, efficient administration. But lacking a strong civil administration, it was unable to extract the resources it needed from Chinese society. Tax officials at local levels used tax collection as a means of extorting all kinds of unauthorized extra fees from farmers, simply continuing similar practices during the late Qing and the warlord period. A large share of the fees and taxes never made it to the treasuries' coffers. During the entire span of the Nanjing decade, the government had to struggle with insufficient government revenue and inefficiency in taxation. Making things worse, most of the revenue (for instance, from maritime customs) went to defense spending. The republican government was therefore constantly forced to look for alternative sources of income. It found them by taxing the growth and consumption of opium. Although such taxation was officially part of a control system intended to reduce the use of the drug, taxes on its growth, distribution, and consumption continued to be an important source of income for the central regime.[39]

By the mid-1930s, then, the nationalist government had achieved a relative degree of consolidation, although it remained fiscally weak, politically vulnerable, and timid in face of criticisms. But it could claim a fair degree of control over most of China proper: the economic heartland of the rice-producing center and the industrialized eastern cities. It also had built new institutions that were striving to develop and transform China into an industrialized modern country. Western historians have long held a rather negative view of the achievements of the republican era and its main leaders, Sun Yat-sen and Chiang Kai-shek. Authoritarianism, corruption, "hypertrophic military establishment"—such labels paint a picture of a downtrodden government and era "doomed to fail."[40] Recent research has developed a more positive and revisionist interpretation and provided a more sympathetic portrait of Chiang Kai-shek as a patriotic defender of China. Revisionist histories have also debunked the prevalent interpretation that the Nanjing decade was a politically monolithic time, firmly under the leadership of Chiang Kai-shek. Instead, the image emerges of a nationalist government deeply divided and contested. Severe divisions about openness and inclusiveness as well as shortcomings of the institutional environment remained. A balanced judgment must recognize that much was achieved of lasting significance for China's development, especially regarding institutions. Precedents and patterns were established or continued that the communists could build on in the 1950s. Without doubt, despite all its failings, the Nanjing government was the most effective administration China had seen since the mid-nineteenth century.

The Rise of the Chinese Developmental State

If the GMD government's first priority was building a strong, defensible, and authoritarian state, economic development and industrialization were second on its agenda. There was broad consensus within GMD circles that economic modernity was key to national recovery and China's national assertion. A policy for industry was drafted which ranged from improvement of the infrastructure to electrification and reform of the silk industry. This was accompanied by the reorganization and growth of economic bureaucracy in China in the mid-1930s with the intention of developing plans and tools to stimulate, regulate, and control the economy. The Chinese national development state came into being.[41]

There were two diverging and competing concepts in play. The first was Wang Jingwei's and T. V. Soong's economic policy, which envisioned the development of a national *(minzu)* economy, combining state control with support for China's private sector. The plan was to develop a domestic market for industrial goods by improving income in the rural sector. This was based on a vision of economic development that entailed control and planning by the state but gave private enterprises space to grow. By promoting the growth of private enterprises, economic growth would be initiated, but state control would make sure that China did not become decentralized, but rather transformed into a unified and centralized unit, achieving autarky sufficient to resist foreign economic control. By contrast, Chiang Kai-shek favored the development of military-oriented heavy industry. This priority, which can be traced back to late Qing reforms, not only emphasized state control but saw the state as owner and manager of industrial enterprises. Consequently, private enterprises and domestic consumption would be given only a peripheral role. At the center would be heavy industrial development oriented toward the defense industry. During the first half of the Nanjing decade, Wang Jingwei's concept dominated. In the mid-thirties, with the growing Japanese threat, Chiang Kai-shek's ideas gained the upper hand.[42] Also notable is that both concepts continued to have impact beyond the republican era: Mao's emphasis on heavy industry in the 1950s was similar to Chiang's industrial policy in the 1930s, while the Deng Xiaoping policy after 1978 resembled the early plans of a national or *minzu* economy.

Global economic conditions complicated the ambitious plans of the republican government. In the 1920s, the Chinese economy had improved markedly and Chinese businesses, from textiles to tobacco, were thriving. But when the Great Depression took hold in the West between 1929 and 1933 and international trade collapsed, China's exports in silk, tobacco, cotton, and soybeans suddenly nosedived. Exports of Chinese silk, for instance, fell by two-thirds. Rural incomes broke away and in some areas, tens of thousands died of malnutrition. The hard times made it more difficult for the government in Nanjing—already an unstable, fragmented political coalition—to institute financial and rural reforms.

After the depression, the growing urban population (5–6 percent of a total population of five hundred million in 1938) in northeastern China (Manchuria), the lower Yangzi provinces, and China's eastern and southeastern coastal regions was again experiencing significant economic growth thanks to an increase of commercialized urban markets and a recovery of import-export activity. In large part, this was the result of economic policies that clearly tilted in favor of urban centers. The new capital of Nanjing, for instance, received huge investments meant to transform the ancient city into a modern metropolis.[43] A massive upgrading project started in 1928 to remake the old city into a modern capital, complete with government ministries, universities and colleges, and residential districts of western-style houses. The old inner city was torn down to make space for the new buildings and for the broad new boulevards, which crisscrossed the city and met at a huge circle, the focal point of the new capital. The new Nanjing would function as a "source of energy for the whole nation," and "a role model for the whole world." It would "glorify the nation's culture."[44] Similar projects of redesigning urban spaces and improving infrastructure were also carried out in other cities, such as Tianjin, Canton, and Chengdu.

Perhaps the most impressive, and certainly the most extensive, achievement was the construction of national infrastructure. Investments were made in much-needed ports, waterways, highways, railroads, and airports. Projects in this sector were often made in cooperation with international agencies or foundations, including the League of Nations and the Rockefeller Foundation. In the decade leading up to 1937, China's paved roads doubled to a total of 115,000 kilometers. The railway system also improved as the GMD nearly doubled the lines to total some 25,000 kilometers by 1945. Great strides were made in flood control and water conservation. Civil aviation was promoted, and by the end of the Nanjing decade, through official joint ventures with Pan American and Lufthansa, China's major cities were connected by flights on regular schedules. Yet, overall, the construction of infrastructure was unsystematic and limited for the most part to certain areas in Manchuria, the east coast, and the lower Yangzi region. The new developments did little for landlocked counties in the interior.

In the face of more aggressive Japanese policies toward China, the nationalists also made concrete plans to develop the national economy by increasing military expenditures. In this respect, they followed the models of Italy and Germany, which had both used similar policies to end periods of economic stagnation. This had important consequences for the political economy in China. Crucial parts of the economy came under the control of the state, although private firms still made up an important part of the economy. Two bodies were charged with the task of developing the economy and the defense-related industry: a National Economic Council established in 1931, and a secret National Defense Planning Council formed one year later. The latter was charged with producing a national development strategy to link reconstruction with national security, strengthening the security of state and nation while broadly promoting the development of economic infrastructure. To this end, the National Defense Planning Council carried out over fifty research projects and produced numerous reports, from economic development to infrastructure to demography. The end result of economic planning was the Three-Year Plan for Industrial Development compiled in 1936. This plan designated the provinces of Jiangxi, Hunan, and Hubei as areas where both heavy industry and the arms industry should be concentrated in the future. The supplies of natural resources from neighboring provinces were also to be delivered through railways that had yet to be constructed. The plan proposed to build iron and steel works at Xiangtan in Hunan, establish iron and copper mines in Sichuan, open coal mines in central and southwest China, and start machine and electronic industries, also at Xiangtan.[45] Most of those companies were state-owned enterprises (SOE). The plan envisioned a development to make China militarily and industrially self-sufficient through the domestic production of steel, machinery, arms, trucks, aircraft, and electrical equipment in the interior. This also included efforts to build self-contained enterprises made up of work units. Beginning in the early 1940s, government and state-owned enterprises routinely used the term *danwei* (work unit) to identify organizations, as well as subordinate entities within those organizations. In the Dadukou Iron and Steel Works, the largest state-owned enterprise, staff and management were all organized in different administrative *danwei*. The *danwei* also provided social services and welfare. Employees lived in factory apartments and dormitories, bought their daily necessities at factory cooperatives, purchased vegetables grown at factory farms, and went to factory clinics and hospitals for medical treatment. Almost a decade before the *danwei* became ubiquitous in Chinese society under CCP rule, the nationalists started to experiment with this form of social organization.

In the late 1930s, feeling increasingly threatened by Japan's advance, the state in China planned for a larger role and more direct, interventionist involvement in the economy. In these moves can be discerned the beginning of "the planned economy that would mark Mao's China."[46] In this phase, capitalists were given no role in society or government, and the party under Chiang became anti-capitalist. Throughout his career, Chiang Kai-shek would tightly control the various organizations of bankers and merchants in urban China.[47] He would turn to them to raise funds—sometimes with the help of

Du Yuesheng's Green Gang, who employed such means as threats, property destruction, and even kidnapping.

The military budget of the Nanjing government was relatively large in terms of overall government spending, with 40–48 percent of annual expenditures devoted to military purposes.[48] (Military spending in the 1930s, however, probably never exceeded 2 percent of China's gross domestic product.) Only 8–13 percent of the total budget during the 1930s, for example, was allocated to the operations and maintenance of civil bureaucracy. Those military expenditures may have also had substantial economic side effects: roads being built, peasant soldiers learning how to operate and repair machines, and some industrial development occurring (for example, of chemicals for munitions, steel, and infrastructure). For the most part, however, the plans were never realized. As a result, Nanjing's large military spending extracted resources from the economy which, while they did succeed in shoring up China's defense capabilities, could have been used instead for investment or consumption in the private sector.

Despite positive trends in population growth, and economic development of an estimated 5.5 percent annual growth rate in the industrial sector and 1–2 percent in agriculture, the overall development of the Nanjing decade was highly uneven.[49] Although, from 1931 to 1936, industry grew at a healthy annual rate of 6.7 percent, this was from a very small base. The contribution to the overall economy was small. The entire economic development of the 1930s benefited urban China along the east coast, in the northeast, and in the upper Yangzi provinces, but little was done to modernize agriculture in the hinterlands. The government noticed the rampant and growing problem of rural poverty, but rural reform remained outside Nanjing's purview. The power of the government rested in large part on its ties to wealthier elites, who had vested interests in maintaining existing economic relationships.

Urbanism and the Chinese Modern

For the nationalist government and its elites, modernity above all meant bureaucratic rationalization and industrial technology, municipal planning, urbanization, professionalization, the rise of the nation-state, the disciplining of a new citizenry, and the emergence of a nationalist discourse. Those were projects targeting the nation collectively as an object of development. But there was another side of everyday modernity in urban spaces which was more subjective, unyielding, and individualistic. In Shanghai and other cities such as Tianjin, Wuhan, and Canton, driven by the border-crossing trade of goods and ideas, global enterprises, and transnational capitalism, the social fabric and the material foundations of everyday life were remade. Cosmopolitan connections and entrepreneurial ambitions shaped a new era of public culture and social activism. They also introduced a material transformation of everyday life that undergirded this vibrant public culture. Cities were sites of production, zones of contact between cultures, and places where experiments in making money, making revolution, and constructing a new nation could be conducted. These changes took place against a backdrop of economic prosperity that many cities along the coast and the upper Yangzi had been experiencing. Apart from the nation, the cosmopolitan city was the main locus for the construction of a Chinese modernity in the republican era.[50]

In recent years, a growing literature on urban culture and commerce in Shanghai and other urban centers has laid a new foundation for scholarly understanding of Chinese modernity.[51] This scholarship has made clear that Chinese modernity cannot be understood as merely adopting external elements. Rather, Chinese appropriation of foreign elements occurred in specific localities where both ordinary Chinese consumers and the cultural elite blended foreign and traditional influences as they constructed urban modernity. The experience of modernity in China should therefore be seen as a complex process. There was no single notion of Chinese modernity. Instead, different views contested, interacted with, and influenced one another. Chinese material culture in the twentieth century was increasingly eclectic. Global elements fused with the domestic to such an extent that it became impossible to say which was foreign and which was Chinese. These new urban centers were the bases for transurban, translocal, and transnational connections across which people, goods, and ideas traveled. The resulting urban scene facilitated considerable experimentation through the creative appropriation of cultural forms, such as the modification of traditional Chinese opera. In literature, the openness of the city and the ability of writers to creatively experiment with new forms and themes, partly deriving from other parts of the globe, made the city a "cultural laboratory" for the invention and reinvention of Chinese culture. This produced the "Shanghai modern" effect—that is, a Shanghai version of modern life and culture. The cultural matrix that came into being in Shanghai and other cities connected print culture, cinema, bookstores, opera, spoken theater, and other forms of artistic expression. Rather than thinking about the creation of a new China and Chinese people from a theoretical perspective (as intellectuals such as Liang Qichao and Chen Duxiu had since the turn of the century), young activist publishers, editors, and authors worked to spread "new" knowledge, "new" practices, "new" styles, and values tied to being modern among the public.[52]

In terms of urban design, the result was an architectural pluralism that mixed different national styles with abandon. Neoclassical forms and axial planning derived from western architecture were integrated with elements from the increasingly popular Chinese-revival style. The sociocultural influence of global transactions was not confined to urban architecture or literature. During this period, western-style schools, hospitals, multistory buildings, automobiles, telephone services, and tap water appeared, together with modern infrastructural projects and factories. Western movies, dancing, billiards, and western-style fashion were also popular among urban residents whose lifestyles resembled those of their counterparts in the great cities of western Europe and the United States. The Chinese city turned into a cosmopolitan center with a culture and everyday life that followed closely behind global currents of the day. Change and the ability to adapt to it were commonly hailed as essentials to live in the modern world.[53]

Much of this was made possible by the spread of new institutions. At the center was the lively and competitive market for print media, especially in treaty ports, most of them still under foreign control in the 1930s. In this market, the provision of information or opinion was used to attract a broad readership willing to pay for the service. One scholar calls this "print capitalism."[54] The term refers to media enterprises run as for-profit businesses and funded by commercial advertising revenues as well as subscriptions and sales of individual copies of printed matter. Publishers operating on this model can be traced back to the nineteenth century, but they flourished in the early twentieth century. This market for information and entertainment became the institutional foundation for the spread of words, ideas, and thought as China's intellectuals learned to maneuver and use the evolving public sphere.

These changes in the realm of culture and everyday life had profound political and social implications. Modernity is not just an experience and a lived reality; in intellectual terms, it is a critical engagement with the past and the present, reflecting on historical circumstances as well as possibilities for the future. In the course of the 1930s, urban China evolved toward a more open society. Individuals and groups could make their own choices regarding trade, travel, and social relations, and increasingly they also took an interest in social affairs. The politics in those discussions could be liberal, conservative, reformist, or revolutionary. As an example, consider the intense discussions of democracy. Many liberal intellectuals stressed the importance of liberal democracy featuring secret-ballot elections, an independent judiciary, freedom of association, and a free press. They pointed to Europe and America as models—and also, to a degree, Japan. But political instability, assassinations, and autocratic political tutelage convinced other intellectuals that democracy was not going to work in China quickly or easily. It prompted some Chinese thinkers and writers to question the applicability of western-style liberal democracy to China and to search for alternative versions of "people's rule" *(minzhu)*. Anarchists sought to empower ordinary people in a different way through their places of work, be they farms, workshops, or factories. They wanted to sweep away repressive state structures and the formalities of liberal democracy. Marxists declared that democracy was class-based, for the benefit of a specific economic class—the workers or proletariat, in Karl Marx's model of political economy. They argued for a democracy for the proletariat, but not for capitalists or militarists (though some more pragmatic communists conceded that "bourgeois democracy" could be a temporary historical stage on the way to socialism and communism). The public intellectual field during the republic was lively and a mixture of competing thoughts that provided the intellectual and philosophical underpinnings for Chinese modernity.[55]

Educators, journalists, writers, students, and common readers engaged in lively debates, whether they revolved around a well-publicized matrimonial affair, a love-induced murder, a court sentence, a case of police brutality, an act of local vengeance, or a provocative opinion piece. Media sensations or scandals frequently sent ripples through urban communities, which bristled with rumors and incited public sympathy. Teahouses, street corners, and back alleys functioned as forums for sharing news and gossip. It was there that speech flourished, actions and motivations were mulled over, and possible motivations and causes were explored. These spaces functioned as hubs of neighborhood and local community dissemination of local and national news.

Journalists and commentators expressed deep sympathies with victims of injustice and went on the offensive attacking culprits, the corrupt, or the powerful. These debates easily spilled over to bigger social issues. Some sought to reevaluate the nature and rules of romantic love in an increasingly politicized climate. Others delved into issues of justice, the proper role of women, the question of equality, the role of sexuality, the evil of warlord rule, or the moral character of modern politicians and even the central regime. These informal forums became arenas of contestation between state and society and between elites and lay persons. Sensationalism in the mass media helped to mobilize a modern public, which might then engage in powerful critique of an actively intervening central government or of administrators pursuing projects of social engineering. The streets of Chinese cities periodically filled with protesting citizens. Temples, teahouses, and provincial hostels hosted politically minded literary societies, political party conventions, and labor union meetings.

These overlapping debates in the media and in public were waged among conservatives, liberals, and socialists. The left, for example, was diverse and included several groups. There were, for instance, the Shanghai workers and their union representatives, whose insurrections of 1926 and 1927 were portrayed by Communist Party organizers as efforts to create a "Shanghai Paris Commune" that represented the principles of the 1871 Parisian revolution.[56] There were also intellectuals who adopted Marxism and historical materialism as their guiding principles. Next to those more radical and violent groups were moderate socialists. In many quarters of the cities, their ideas had larger appeal than more strict Marxist or Leninist variants. Many intellectuals and students in this period favored a variant of democratic socialism that, as a political idea and a political movement, was closer to social democracy than to Marxism-Leninism. Activists in the first Chinese human rights movement in the 1930s were mostly liberal intellectuals critical of the government.[57] They founded the China League for the Protection of Civil Rights, which was especially concerned with the rights of persons held in custody and political prisoners (many of whom were leftists). Considering the political repressions carried out by Chiang Kai-shek and the nationalist government, the League demanded the recognition of fundamental political rights such as freedom of opinion, freedom of the press, and freedom of assembly. They defended their advocacy of fundamental rights against Marxist critics, as well as against the criticisms of the government's conservative supporters.

Another force to be reckoned with was Chinese conservatism, which must be seen as a reaction against the radical anti-traditionalism of the May Fourth movement. While there were different forms of conservatism in China, all of them found common ground in their desire to preserve China's cultural-moral heritage. Based on nineteenth century forerunners like Zeng Guofan, conservatism arose as a reaction to the horrors of World War I and to Enlightenment modernism. Conservative Chinese thought echoed the philosophies of Friedrich Nietzsche, Henri Bergson, Rudolph Eucken, Hans Driesch, and Bertrand Russell, as well as neo-Confucianism.[58] In the 1920s, Liang Qichao, for instance, thought that China's traditional emphasis on humanism, compassion, and self-cultivation should complement the technological dimension of modernity. Zhang Binglin, the classically trained scholar from the city of Hangzhou, went back to the sources of Chinese tradition in his search for a "national essence" (guocui), a Japanese neologism. And while, for Zhang and other revolutionaries, the Han ethnicity was an important aspect of this essence, it was more cultural than racial. Conservative thinkers approached Chinese traditional culture as a complex blend that offered meaningful values still relevant to their world. Liang Shuming (1893–1988) called for his generation to critically rediscover the values of Chinese traditional thought. He wrote: "We must renew our Chinese attitude and bring it to the fore, but do so critically."[59] National essence scholars came to be associated with those searching for historically rooted alternatives to the crumbling Confucian orthodoxy. They were also interested in Buddhist and Daoist spirituality. As it evolved, cultural conservatism became engaged in political dynamics linked to nationalism and modernity. A main concern was related to the questions of how to revive Chinese self-confidence in their civilization in the modern age, and how to save China. The cultural conservatives were nationalistic, but they also had an ambiguous relationship with a GMD political order that, in their opinion, lacked a true commitment to Chinese core values and national "essence." In their quest to recover and conserve the sources of tradition and to articulate traditional culture in a context of global modernity, they left a body of scholarship that remains a core resource for Chinese nativist thinking today.

The third force was modern China's liberal intellectuals and their liberal visions. Hu Shi, for instance, a leading voice of liberalism, called for pragmatism or what he preferred to call "experimentalism." Instead of adhering to abstract principles or "-isms" *(zhuyi),* he advised his contemporaries to search for specific solutions to concrete problems. He wrote: "We do not study the livelihood of rickshaw drivers, but we make an abstract talk about socialism. We do not study how to liberate women or improve family system, but we make an abstract talk about the *isms* of sharing wives and free love."[60] Criticizing Marxist arguments, he called for factory conditions and the status of women, for example, to be understood as separate problems and not treated as symptoms of an overarching system. Wanting to carry out specific and gradual reforms to China's problems, Hu rejected revolution as overall system change. While emphasizing liberties and pragmatism, republican-era liberals also advocated efficient governance, a "government with a plan," and political elitism. They often found themselves outside of the existing political institutions and therefore inevitably came into conflict with the ruling elite—especially with the nationalists after 1928, who followed a different state-building project that entailed political tutelage and one-party rule. The liberal vision of modernity was at odds with the visions of both the Marxists and the nationalist party-state.

The growth of public debates, of nongovernmental and even anti-governmental associations and organizations, of political movements, and of autonomy in cultural affairs in many places elicited heavy-handed responses from the nationalist government. Political repression became a primary instrument of nationalist rule. As early as 1930, the regime feared that it was no longer sustained by popular support. Determined to quash the rising tide of discontent and pluralism, it tightened controls over its critics. Political opponents were assassinated, critical reporters were arrested, and newspapers and journals were censored. The government had little respect for human rights. Because the territorial control of the government was still limited, critics could often find a safe haven in the foreign-administered treaty-port concessions or in the provinces controlled by Chiang Kai-shek's opponents. Chiang was also criticized for his continued struggle against the CCP in the face of Japan's increasingly aggressive policies. Yet, from Chiang's point of view, opposition to the GMD made China vulnerable to foreign attack, particularly from Japan. To him, resistance—especially in the form of the communist movement that, after 1927, had shifted its focus to the rural areas—represented a more urgent and immediate threat.

Restarting Revolution in Rural Base Areas

Since the middle of the 1920s, while still based in Canton, Mao Zedong had been looking for an alternative revolutionary strategy. Mao was born into a relatively wealthy peasant family in Shaoshan, Hunan province. After training as a teacher, he moved to Beijing where he worked in the library of Peking University. It was during this time that he began to read Marxist literature. In 1921, he was one of the founding members of the CCP and set up a party cell in Hunan. After Chiang Kai-shek launched his anti-communist purge, Mao Zedong retreated to rural Hunan, where he became convinced of the power of the peasantry. In his passionate, forty-page "Report on the Hunan Peasant Movement," which he submitted to the Communist Party in March 1927 (that is, shortly before the breakup of the United Front in April of that year), Mao described the seizures of power in Hunan by the poorest of the peasants and the landlords humiliated by the peasant associations. He praised how the village order was turned upside down, with women emancipating themselves from their husbands, and members of militias, secret societies, and even criminal gangs revolting and defying authorities and local elites. He also described, with sympathy, the peasants' feelings of vengeance when they punished local "tyrants and bullies" for earlier misdeeds. Mao provided an implicit critique of the revolutionary strategy pursued by the Comintern and the urban intelligentsia. He did not explicitly renounce proletarian leadership, but his report concentrated on the role and the strength of the poor peasantry. He was convinced that rural mobilization was the only way for the revolution to succeed in China. He wrote: "the present upsurge of the peasant movement is a colossal event. In a very short time, several hundred million peasants . . . will rise like a fierce wind or tempest, a force so swift and violent that no power, however great, will be able to suppress it."[61] Mao also made clear that violent excesses in the peasant movement were unavoidable and necessary to overcome the counter-revolutionaries and the power of the local gentry. Activist Communist Party cells, based on existing historic communities like villages, should inject themselves into the fabric of work, defense, education, and social life, creating caches of the revolution that could be gradually expanded to the entire country. Mao started to favor a strategy that combined agrarian socialism, anarchism, and Marxist-Leninist theory in pursuit of rural transformation. With most of the urban party cells being wiped out by the GMD in 1927, many CCP members became more or less convinced that Mao's strategy, if not his ideology, of rural mobilization was the only remaining possibility, and pointed to a viable path to restart the revolution.

Mao gained his impressions and insights about the revolutionary power of the peasants from Peng Pai's Peasant Training Institute in Guangzhou, where he was a student in the mid-twenties. Born to a wealthy landlord family in the southernmost province of Guangdong, Peng Pai (1896–1929) was educated in China's new schools and abroad at Waseda University in Tokyo from 1918 to 1921. After returning to China from Japan, Peng joined the newly established CCP, returned to his home area in Guangdong, and set about organizing peasant associations to resist local abuses like extra rents, local bullies, and pettifoggery by local elites. In late 1927, Peng Pai established Hailufeng Soviet (a revolutionary government council) on the southern coast. The Soviet lasted only four months until late February 1928. "Little Moscow," as the area was called—there was even a "Red Square" with an entryway copied from the Kremlin—was ruled by a coalition of peasants, bandits, and communists.[62] Its base of support was made up mostly of landless seasonal workers, vagabonds, bandits, deserters, smugglers, and prostitutes. The peasant alliance sought to side with the masses of poor, landless peasants against the group of landlords who were branded as evildoers for having exploited the masses for centuries. The whole process was intended as a form of "democratic terror" according to Mao Zedong. It was a form of terror that was exercised in the name of class justice, legitimized by the masses, and therefore regarded as democratic. The treatment of the opponents was indeed violent and cruel. During the mass trials—as these spectacles later came to be called—the accused were humiliated, beaten, and forced to wear dunce hats. Many accused landlords received death sentences, which were carried out by beheading. Their heads were placed on poles and displayed in the marketplace, a supplementary punishment that had been practiced in imperial China. There were also reports of ritual cannibalism. In traditional China, to eat the organs of one's enemy was to have complete revenge for his misdeeds. Bloody spectacles of revenge were an efficient way to assemble peasants, brand political targets, and transmit a clear political message. During the course of such campaigns, entire villages were razed. While Mao Zedong approved of terror as a weapon of the revolution, he rejected the scale of violence that was carried out in Hailufeng. Moscow also strongly disapproved of the "aimless and disorderly pogroms and killings."[63]

After the party's near destruction in 1927, a debate ensued about the reasons for the disaster. In this discussion, Zhu De (1886–1976), a brilliant military general who became one of Mao's closest associates, played an important role. Hailing from a poor peasant family, Zhu De attended the new schools, too. He went to Yunnan Military Academy in 1909 and studied military science in Germany and in the Soviet Union in the 1920s. His Soviet experience gave him authority. He agreed with Mao on two major points: that the CCP needed its own army, and that the party should refocus its efforts on rural areas. In this context, Mao Zedong told an emergency party meeting on August 7, 1927: "Power comes out of the barrel of the gun."[64] As a result, the ragtag Revolutionary Army was renamed the Red Army in May 1928. Out of these insights also emerged the strategy to mobilize the countryside to "surround the cities." Basically, Mao and Zhu laid out a plan that advocated enlisting the lowest strata of rural society, including seasonal workers, bandits, and vagabonds. With their support, the land of not only wealthy landlords, of which there were few in those areas, but also small landlords and rich peasants, should be confiscated and redistributed to poor peasants and landless workers according to their needs.

When the "White Terror" extermination campaign of the GMD against the communists was unleashed in 1927, the remnants of the Communist Party had to flee from Wuhan and Shanghai. These communists sought refuge in the countryside of Jiangxi province, where hills and mountains in the Jinggang area offered natural protection against nationalist pursuers. The Jinggang mountain range was classic outlaw country, controlled by organized bandit groups. Upon his arrival, Mao had to cultivate ties with local brigands and outlaws who were wary of the communists. Jinggang became the site of the first practical experiments that led to a specifically Chinese path of rural revolution. The party began to develop and test social, cultural, military, and economic policies that later became the hallmarks of "Maoism."[65] But those beginnings were rather messy, due to the poverty of the region and the diversity of party members. The fact that some policies were virtually indistinguishable from traditional bandit behavior remained a source of dispute for years.

For nearly a year and a half, under the protection of the Red Army, popularly known as the Zhu-Mao army, Jinggang's social, cultural, and economic life was shattered. By June 1928, most land in the area had been confiscated by the new power and redistributed to poor and landless peasants. The new owners of the land then had to pay levies to the new authorities. Not surprisingly, these radical social policies were met with virulent opposition not only by the landlords, but also by many peasants—including even those who had received plots through redistribution. The area had only a few big landlords, and the majority of peasants were poor and owned only small amounts of land. Few saw any benefits in land redistribution. They were, however, in favor of rent and tax reduction. This poor, mountainous area simply did not produce enough for the peasants to pay taxes and sustain the presence of a relatively large army. On the other hand, the Red Army needed resources to continue the revolution. Increasingly, the Red Army went on to make requisitions that further worsened the relationship between the local community and the communists.

After the Red Army's arrival, Jinggang soon became the target of concerted suppression campaigns by militias and armies of the nationalist government. Chiang Kai-shek was intent on wiping out the communist threat. These campaigns came at a time when several factors began to weaken the cohesion of the CCP. Internal discord erupted. In 1929, on instruction from the Comintern, the current leader of the CCP, Li Lisan, was replaced by Wang Ming and a new group of Comintern-trained revolutionaries sent from the Soviet Union to Shanghai. The arrival of Wang and his "Twenty-Eight Bolsheviks," whom Moscow had sent to take over the party leadership, led to conflicts within the CCP. Also at stake was the strategy for the future: Should the party focus on mobilizing rural areas, or instead try to instigate unrest and revolts in urban areas? Loyalists to Li Lisan, veterans who disliked being on remote control by the Comintern, and party members displeased by Wang's personality and style, began to reject his leadership. While the CCP was leery of the Comintern's efforts to rein in its internal affairs and to enforce compliance with the political course devised in Moscow, it was unable to rid itself of Moscow's oversight. Given the difficulties it experienced finding resources in the poor areas it ruled, the CCP depended heavily on support from the Soviet Union in the form of weapons, logistics, and money. In January 1929, it became clear that Jinggang could no longer be defended. It had to be evacuated. In early 1930, after more than a year of wandering, Mao and his followers were battle-hardened and thoroughly exhausted. They settled on the southern plains of Jiangxi province, in a small city named Ruijin.

Upon arrival, a violent internal party conflict erupted that would change how the party managed internal discipline and security. In Jiangxi, Mao and his followers encountered a preexisting local peasant movement unwilling to give up its autonomy and to subordinate itself to the newly arrived leaders and troops. In addition, Mao's evolving emphasis on peasant-based revolution presented the Central Committee in Shanghai with an explicit challenge to its focus on urban areas. The tensions that erupted in the so-called Futian incident had two immediate causes.[66] One was land reform. Mao advocated a land redistribution policy based simply on family size. He proposed that the more members a family had, the larger the plot it would receive through land distribution. Local Jiangxi leaders, more open to local interests, favored a less radical policy of land redistribution based on a family's labor power (family members that actually worked on the fields). A second controversy revolved around the military tactics that were to be employed to defend the communist base in Jiangxi against the anticipated attacks by Chiang Kai-shek's nationalist army. Mao advocated the tactic of "luring the enemy deep." The enemy forces should be enticed to move into the local area, before they were attacked. This tactic had enabled the Red Army to survive in the Jinggang mountains against superior enemy forces. The local Jiangxi communist leaders, however, feared that this policy would wreak havoc in their home districts, even if the tactic turned out to be successful in the long run. These conflicts were complicated by the real or alleged existence of a secret anti-communist group called AB Corps (with AB standing for anti-Bolshevik), which had been formed by the local GMD to undermine CCP policies by infiltration and covert intelligence work. Mao claimed that the cells of the local Jiangxi communists were made up of "AB members and rich peasants" and labeled his adversaries as "objectively counter-revolutionary." Both sides started to distrust each other. Under the pretense of weeding out the AB Corps, open fighting broke out between the newcomers and the local communists. In December 1930, the conflict led to a massacre of the local communists in Futian. Widespread, bloody purges followed and, in the end, Mao and his supporters prevailed. By the end of 1931, thousands of local Jiangxi communists had been arrested and killed. To be sure, Mao was not the only one behind the purges. The entire leadership supported them, albeit in pursuit of varying objectives. The purges spun out of control and soon became so widespread, decentralized, and spontaneous that for a time they could not be reined in by any of the top leaders. Yet it is also beyond doubt that the outcome of the events clearly favored Mao Zedong, as inner-party opposition to his policies was effectively quelled.

The Futian incident was the first large-scale, bloody, intraparty purge that occurred at a time of distress and fear. But it also reveals what was to become a pattern: violent purges to deal with inner-party dissent and to enforce discipline and obedience. The issue of party discipline and security was one that received great attention by the leadership. Until the Futian incident, party discipline was handled by the Committee for Eliminating Counter-Revolutionaries (CEC), established at the CCP provincial level in 1929. As a result of the Futian incident, the CEC was abolished in March 1931 and a new agency was created in its place. This agency was called the Political Security Department and it was designed to function as a branch of the communist government in the base areas. In the following years, the Political Security Department built a large network of agents who penetrated all levels of the party organization, the Red Army, and government agencies. The department was charged to train agents to uncover GMD enemy intelligence, to investigate counter-revolutionary activities, espionage, and counter-intelligence matters, and to solve cases related to espionage, imprisonment, and the execution of anyone considered an enemy or to be training enemies of the Soviet Republic and the Red Army. This was a far-reaching institutional innovation. On its basis, a shadowy, clandestine, and powerful security apparatus emerged to deal with suspected enemies within party ranks.[67]

In 1931, as the party prepared for a national congress in Ruijin, Wang Ming was called back to Moscow, where he stayed until 1937. Having repulsed the third campaign of the GMD military in September, the CCP leadership felt strong enough to use the party plenum in November 1931 to proclaim itself the government of the newly constituted Chinese Soviet Republic. Mao Zedong was named the governmental leader, both as "national chairman" (*guojia zhuxi*) and as prime minister. The CCP, which moved its central organization here, remained a separate organization from the government under General Secretary Bo Gu (1907–1946). The new rebel state had a population of about three million people. It was based on an entirely new set of institutions. Befitting its new government status, the leadership announced a wide range of new laws on land and labor, and adopted a basic constitutional program. The land reform program stipulated that anyone who was landless, or owned relatively small amounts of land (small and middle peasants) would receive plots sufficient to maintain them, taken from large landholders (rich peasants and landlords). The policy in Jiangxi was therefore relatively moderate. Families were given as much land as they could till, and the rest was redistributed to landless peasants and seasonal workers. But here, too, land reform was often met with resistance. Conflicts arose because of suspicion of the criteria used for classification of land ownership or those used for distribution. The government resorted to a flat tax on land that was marginally less (at about 38 percent of the realized harvest) than the tax imposed by the nationalist government. Shopkeepers were also taxed to provide the area with amenities, including repaired roads to take goods safely to market.

The city of Ruijin and a few outlying towns were equipped with electricity, cable communications, and telephones—things little known in China outside the largest cities. The CCP set up a radio broadcast enterprise in addition to its printing operations. In 1931, a constitution was promulgated. In addition to protecting the property of the residents, it explicitly recognized the property rights, cultural independence, and political participation of the Miao, Yi, Li, and Zhuang nationalities living in the region. The right of cultural minority areas to secede was explicitly guaranteed. A marriage law forbade arranged marriages, outlawed dowries, and made divorce possible at the request of either party. Public schools were opened to both male and female children.

There were public hygiene campaigns and the establishment of a rudimentary health system. The central authorities abolished all corporal punishments, which seem to have still been in wide use in rural areas. Inhumane treatment of prisoners was forbidden. This was proclaimed by Mao Zedong to be a "great historical reform."[68] To this end, two new ministries were established, offering the promise of a more formal approach to policing and justice after years of ad hoc populism. These were the Ministry of Judgments and the Ministry of Internal Affairs. These institutions would be in charge of all the base camp's courts, prisons, civil police, and legal matters. Generally speaking, it was the Ministry of Judgments that would run the prison sector. It effectively replaced the Committee for Eliminating Counter-Revolutionaries that had been running detention prior to this.

After Mao had risen to the pinnacle of power in the Jiangxi, he quickly found himself under criticism and pressure from the leadership. He effectively fell from power in early 1932. He was opposed by the "returned student faction," whose members dominated the Central Committee and had Moscow's support. The young, Moscow-trained Chinese communists were critical of Mao, who, unlike them, had no experience abroad and little in the way of credentials as a Marxist theorist. They also resisted his brutal policies of guerilla warfare and radical agrarian revolution. Mao's positions were reduced to ceremonial status. By the time Chiang Kai-shek took command of the "anti-bandit" campaign, in late May 1933, the communists in Jiangxi had abandoned Mao's tactics of mobile warfare in favor of a more conventional defense, on the advice of the German communist Otto Braun (1900–1974). Having learned from the failure of previous campaigns, and based on recommendations by his German advisers, Chiang Kai-shek began to concentrate on the construction of a network of slowly advancing blockhouses. An army of 800,000 men built an encirclement of mud and brick outposts protected by machine gun fire. In the battles, both sides suffered thousands of casualties, but by 1934, a total of 14,000 blockhouses and 2,500 kilometers of new roads had been constructed in the combat zone, providing an effective blockade of the communist areas. In early summer of 1934, the CCP leadership recognized that the situation had become hopeless. Losses had been mounting steadily, desertion was growing, and supplies dwindled due to the blockade. Eventually, it was decided to evacuate the main forces. On October 25, 1934, the Red Army broke through the first ring of encirclement and moved into southern Hunan. Thus, it commenced its famous Long March to the northwest. Few of the approximately ninety thousand people who joined the march were to survive.[69]

As it proceeded on its winding journey westward, the Long March halted at the town of Zunyi in Guizhou province in early January 1935. A five-day battle with GMD forces over a crossing at the Xiang River destroyed half the army. Against this backdrop of losses and defeats, a session of the CCP Politburo decided to put Mao back into power. Although the internal struggle was to continue until the early 1940s, forty-one-year-old Mao became the party's dominant leader. He regained control of the army and was able to pursue the policies he favored. At the same time, the immediate grip of the Comintern had finally been loosened. The Long March continued until October 1935, when the remaining troops reached an existing local Soviet area in northern Shaanxi under the command of a communist, Liu Zhidan (1903–1936). The Red Army set up their headquarters at Bao'an (today's Zhidan, named after Liu Zhidan). The march had lasted one year, during which the Red Army traversed eleven provinces, walked more than 10,000 kilometers, crossed five major mountain ridges, and forded numerous rivers. The losses were enormous. Only eight thousand soldiers survived the ordeal. The Long March was a daring but desperate maneuver. Its eventual significance, however, lay in mythology and legitimation. What it showed about the communists' will for survival and perseverance in the face of adverse conditions was taken as proof of not only the validity of the revolutionary cause but ultimately the correctness of its leader and his policies.

SIX

China at War

1937–1948

The GMD government had been making considerable progress in rebuilding China and was also close to destroying its main internal challenger—the communist movement—when the outbreak of hostilities with Japan reshuffled political priorities. From inside and outside the government, calls grew louder for a broad, national coalition to resist Japan. But it was only after Chiang Kai-shek had been abducted in Xi'an and held for two weeks, in December 1936, that he agreed to stop the fight against the CCP and to enter the Second United Front. This alliance was even more fraught than the first one. But on paper, at least, a unified and determined China entered the war to defend its territory.

The result was a long, bitter war of resistance that required enormous sacrifices, devastated China, and changed its history. Mounting losses and widespread destruction undid much of the progress that had been made. For the first years, China had little outside assistance. The help it obtained came mostly from the Soviet Union in the form of advisers, money, equipment, and ammunition. In 1937, the central government had to flee to Chongqing and in 1938 almost the entire eastern seaboard was lost to Japan. In 1939, when support from the Soviet Union slowed—and, in 1941, when it eventually stopped following the Molotov–Ribbentrop Pact—the outlook was bleak, and total defeat seemed near. Yet, much to the vexation of Japan, persistent Chinese resistance was able to thwart further Japanese progress.

For the remainder of the war, China was for all practical purposes divided into different areas. Chiang Kai-shek and the GMD controlled much of inland China, under difficult circumstances since Chongqing, the wartime capital, was remote and frequently attacked by air raids. The CCP built and expanded control over the rural areas in North China. The coastal areas from Manchuria to Guangzhou were ruled by collaborationist governments that were steered by Japan.

Following the Japanese attack on Pearl Harbor in 1941, China's lone fight ended, since it joined the Allies in a formal declaration of war against Japan, Germany, and Italy. With this, the war of resistance became part of the global war theater of World War II. China was able to obtain support from the West, mostly the United States. Equally important, entering the global war also provided an opportunity for the Chinese government to reclaim rights it had lost in the nineteenth century. Above all, the foreign administration of the treaty ports and extraterritoriality were abolished. With that important achievement, China finally left behind the humiliating legacy of imperialism.

Following the end of the global war, the two leading superpowers, the United States and the Soviet Union, despite their growing rivalry, agreed to strive for the establishment of a broad coalition government in China. Given the destruction and losses, this seemed the most reasonable way forward. During a few weeks of talks between Chiang Kai-shek and Mao Zedong in the summer of 1945, a postwar compromise in the form of a democratic and united China seemed a real possibility. Growing hostility, however, and a race to move into strategic positions vacated by Japan, made this vision a fleeting moment of hope with no real outcome. A mistreated and exhausted China had to endure yet another war, which ended in 1949 with an improbable outcome: China, the most populous country on earth, became communist.

Rising Tensions in Xi'an

The conflict between China and Japan had been long in the making. Japan had not always been a rival, however. In the beginning of the twentieth century, Japan served, as we have seen, as an important model for reform-oriented intellectuals and students. Japan became a competitor, however, as it remodeled itself as an expanding empire with continental ambitions. With limited resources and territory on the Japanese islands, Japan sought to secure access to resources such as foodstuffs, metals, and minerals in northern China—a region that was increasingly portrayed as its lifeline.[1] The Great Depression added fuel to Japan's continental ambitions. Protectionism in the United States and in Europe caused the Japanese export economy to shrink, forcing Japan to look for its own zone of economic autarky. Moreover, in

Japanese eyes, Chiang Kai-shek and his government resembled a predatory warlord regime that lacked real legitimacy to represent China. Japan saw itself as the true heir of East Asian empires, including the Qing. It promoted the ideology of pan-Asianism, arguing that the nations of the East should unite under Japan's leadership to resist western materialism and imperialism. Among its military leadership and in economic circles there was a widespread belief that Japan had a special mission and exclusive rights in China.

Just as the decline of centralized authority permitted the rise of warlords, it also provided room for the Japanese military empire to grow on Chinese soil. In 1928, when the Chinese warlord Zhang Zuolin (1875–1928) in Manchuria threatened to impede Japanese encroachment, Japan had him assassinated. The murder of Zhang Zuolin unmistakably indicated Japan's determination to gain control over Manchuria. The Japanese officers who carried out these and other acts on Chinese territory did not always have official orders; rather, they "were part of an empire-wide network of clandestine study groups and associations linking military officers and civilian ideologues" in Japan.[2] By pushing vehemently for Japanese expansion on the Chinese mainland, they intended to strengthen the imperial system in Japan. The leaders of the Kwantung Army, as the Japanese army in China was called, were strongly driven by such thinking. For instance, Colonel Ishiwara Kanji (1889–1949), the Kwantung Army's operations officer from 1929 to 1932, had a dark, pessimistic understanding of international developments. He believed that a great war between Japan and the United States was inevitable. In that scenario, the possession of Manchuria was an essential precondition for Japanese survival. Hence he approved of bold, clandestine action in Manchuria. On September 18, 1931, Ishiwara's forces blew up a section of the southern Manchurian railway tracks at a major crossroads in Mukden (now named Shenyang), and blamed Chinese military forces for the action. The matter of whether Tokyo military leadership knew that such action was planned and, if so, whether it was approved, remains controversial to this day.

With this step, the nationalistic officers of the Kwantung Army achieved in 1931 what their assassination of Zhang Zuolin had failed to gain in 1928. The Japanese army went on to seize Manchuria, arguing that its Kwantung Army had intervened to support a local revolt against the allegedly corrupt warlord government of Zhang Xueliang (1901–2001), the son and successor of Zhang Zuolin. The Kwantung Army also carried out attacks on Chinese regional armies in the area. By December the Japanese forces controlled most of Manchuria. Soon, the independent state of Manchukuo *(Manzhouguo)* was established. The Japanese authorities managed to convince the last Qing emperor, Puyi (1906–1967), to become the official ruler.

In China, a passionate public debate ensued over how to deal with Japan. The Nine Eighteen (or *jiuyiba*) incident, as the Mukden incident is called in Chinese, became a major turning point. The loss of Manchuria mobilized the Chinese public more than any prior instance of territorial loss. A huge patriotic response followed, as evidenced by the song "Along the Sungari River" *(Songhua jiang shang)*, composed by Zhang Hanhui (1902–1946) in 1935. Its lyrics became hugely popular:

> My home is in the Northeast, on the banks of Sungari River. A land of dense forests and deep coal mines, of high mountains and endless bean and sorghum fields. . . . My fellow countrymen live there, my old and feeble parents live there. On the tragic day of September 18, I left my native place, gave up the boundless hidden treasures. To rove, to rove, all day long to rove south of the Pass [of the Great Wall]. When, oh when, can I return to my beloved native land? When, oh when, can I recover the boundless hidden treasures? Oh my compatriots, my compatriots, when, oh when, can we recover our native land?[3]

Life Weekly, edited by Zou Taofen, also devoted many articles to reporting on the Japanese expansion and China's salvation movement, and this coverage helped to make it the most popular journal in the country, including in the large southern cities such as Shanghai (where it was printed). Activists such as Chinese refugees from Manchuria, through a lobbying group called Northeast National Salvation Society, and patriotic students demanded that the government put up determined resistance. Chiang Kai-shek, however, steadfastly refused.[4] He believed China lacked the military capabilities to challenge the Japanese army. While he pledged to resist Japanese aggression and saw it as the biggest threat facing China, in his diary he warned that rushing into a war could "cause our nation to perish instead of helping it."[5]

After the occupation of Manchuria, Japan eyed Shanghai as the next step in its invasion. On January 18, 1932, a Japanese agent allegedly organized the beating of five Japanese men, monks among them, and blamed it on a Chinese mob. As retaliation, Japanese expats in Shanghai began rioting in the city, burning houses, killing one Chinese policeman, and injuring more. This in turn prompted Chinese protests against the Japanese violence. Boycotts against Japanese goods and companies, as well as strikes, led to citywide student demonstrations, the reappearance of communist groups, and even anti-GMD protests. By January 27, the Japanese military delivered an ultimatum to the Shanghai municipal government, demanding a public denunciation and payments for damages to Japanese property, as well as the suppression of all anti-Japanese protests in the city. Although the Shanghai municipal government accepted the demands, three thousand Japanese troops entered the city. In response, Chiang Kai-shek ordered the Chinese Nineteenth Route Army to move in and put up a vigorous defense of Shanghai. For several months, Japan and China engaged in the battle that came to be known as the Shanghai War of 1932. Despite inferior military equipment and heavy casualties, the Chinese army kept the Japanese from taking the city. The Japanese even increased their troop numbers to nearly ninety thousand, supported by eighty warships and three hundred airplanes. The Japanese navy bombed and assaulted Chinese-controlled portions of Shanghai. Air bombing completely destroyed Zhabei, a district north of the International Settlement that was populated mostly by workers and migrants, sending 230,000 refugees fleeing to that settlement or elsewhere. On March 2, the Nineteenth Route Army pulled out of Shanghai due to dwindling supplies and manpower. Through the mediation of the League of Nations on May 5, China and Japan signed the Shanghai Ceasefire Agreement, which made Shanghai a demilitarized zone. China agreed to refrain from stationing troops in areas surrounding Shanghai, Suzhou, and Kunshan, and had to accept the presence of a few Japanese military personnel in the city. The agreement was widely regarded by the Chinese public as a humiliation. The bombing of residential areas in Shanghai caught the attention of the entire world, as it showed the horrors of aerial bombing of the civilian population. Four thousand Chinese soldiers were killed, as were probably a few thousand Japanese; Chinese civilian deaths stood at around ten thousand.[6]

Shortly thereafter, in 1933, the Japanese army continued its invasion of North China and took over the Manchurian province of Rehe (Jehol), which had been controlled by Zhang Xueliang. Given the unrelenting expansion of Japanese troops, Chiang Kai-shek sought to sign an agreement with Japan. His hope was to gain more time and breathing space for his government to prepare for the ultimate conflict that Chiang and most Chinese were certain was on the horizon. On May 31, 1933, the countries signed the Tanggu truce. A demilitarized zone south of Jehol province was created, which became the border between Manchukuo and China. With this, the Japanese advanced to what had been the line of the Great Wall and consolidated their territorial gains. From that point, they would become a constant military threat to Beijing and the whole of China. While this agreement benefited Japan and, again, seemed to confirm that the nationalist government followed an appeasement policy, it effectively avoided full-scale fighting between Japan and China in the following years, up to the eventual outbreak of the war against Japan in 1937.

Two years later, Japanese troops were mobilized again and reached the Chinese heartland. Here, in November 1935, Japan established a Chinese government, a "self-governing" *(zizhi)* regime in Hebei with the local Chinese official Yin Rugeng (1885–1947) as governor.[7] It was called the "The East Hebei Anti-Communist Autonomous Council," and had a population of six million people under the control of Japanese military advisers. A pattern was thus set for later collaborationist regimes in China proper. The imperial army was within striking distance of Beijing and Tianjin. As Japan relentlessly increased its pressure, the Chinese public, as well as several GMD generals, demanded that the Nanjing government redouble its efforts to fend off the Japanese army.

The continuous advance of Japan alarmed Stalin and the Soviet Union. Moscow informed the Chinese communists of its pessimistic assessment of the current situation in East Asia. Soviet leadership expected that a full assault on China was imminent and that, sooner or later, Japan would also attack the Soviet Far East. In July 1935, the Seventh World Congress of the Comintern called for the creation of worldwide "popular fronts" against fascism. Hence, the CCP was instructed to find ways to end the fight against the nationalist government and to direct its struggle against Japanese imperialism instead. On August 1, 1935, the CCP issued a statement underscoring those instructions. Under the Heading "To Inform Comrades in China of Anti-Japanese Resistance for National Salvation," it called for the GMD to suspend the civil war and to form a united front against Japanese aggression. This statement, referred to as the "August 1 Declaration," marked a turn in the CCP policy from "anti-Chiang, anti-Japan" toward a renewed cooperation between the two hostile parties to resist Japan.

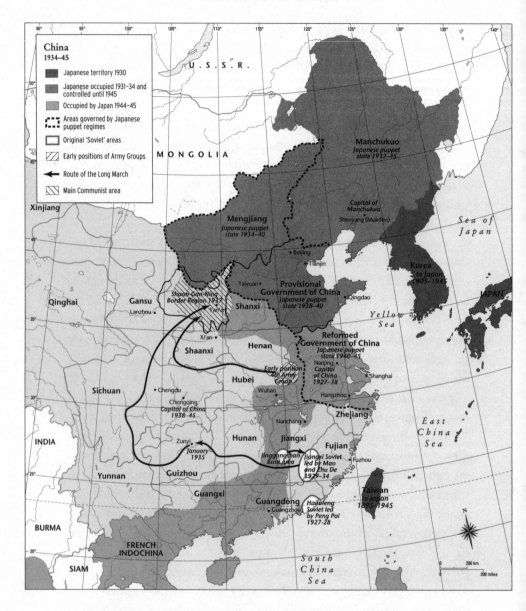

The CCP approached the GMD general Zhang Xueliang, who had over-seen the northeastern and northwestern armies in Shaanxi and Gansu in the campaign to suppress the CCP.[8] After initial contacts, a series of secret meetings were held between Zhou Enlai, second in command in the CCP, and Zhang Xueliang between April and June or July 1936. The purpose was to negotiate an end of military actions against the communists, the opening of trade with the areas under CCP control, a renewed cooperation between the two parties against Japan, and to that end, the formation of a united army. The talks were difficult but, by early December, the two sides had reached a tentative agreement. Zhang also provided money to Zhou Enlai for the purchase of food, fuel, and clothes—goods the CCP urgently needed, since the Long March had weakened its forces and depleted its resources. When Zhang, however, later tried to persuade Chiang Kai-shek to halt his campaign against the CCP, Chiang refused. Chiang Kai-shek's real intent was to mobilize enforcements for what might prove a decisive, final assault on the CCP. He believed his anti-communist campaign was on the brink of success.

The local troops under Zhang Xueliang were, however, resisting marching orders and delaying the "bandit suppression" campaign against the CCP. Frustrated with their slow progress in launching an all-out attack on the CCP headquarters, Chiang Kai-shek flew to Xi'an on December 4, accompanied by about fifty high-ranking GMD officials, including his senior military staff. He wanted to inspect the situation and prod the troops at Zhang's headquarters in Xi'an to begin the big final attack.[9] Rather than cooperating, however, Zhang decided to take Chiang prisoner. This detention, which lasted for almost two weeks, became known as the "Xi'an Incident" of 1936. Zhang's former aide Lu Guangji recalled the scene in the middle of the night of December 12 when Zhang revealed to his officers his plan to capture Generalissimo Chiang: "Zhang Xueliang with a grave countenance told us, 'Being driven into a corner, I came up with *bingjian*. I have tried by various means to persuade Chiang Kai-shek but he rejected all. There is no other way left. . . . I have asked you to come here today because I do not know if I will be alive tomorrow.'"[10] *Bingjian* is an ancient Chinese term referring to the rightful capture of an emperor by a minister to force him to mend his harmful policies. Clearly, Zhang felt that circumstances of national emergency forced his hand and legitimized just such a mutiny. In the early morning of December 12, Zhang made his move, arrested Chiang Kai-shek, and, by telegram, informed the CCP of his action. Mao Zedong and Zhou Enlai were taken completely by surprise, yet rejoiced to hear the news. While an exuberant Mao and CCP wanted to try Chiang for treason in a people's court of law—and would probably have sought his execution, too—Stalin intervened from Moscow. The Russian leader argued that a trial and execution of Chiang

Kai-shek would deepen internal strife in Chinese society, weaken its defensive capabilities, and therefore only benefit Japan's aggressive policies. Stalin was convinced that only Chiang Kai-shek had the ability to lead China into war against Japan. Therefore, he instructed the communists not to seek a public trial, let alone execution, of Chiang Kai-shek. Instead, they were ordered to seek a peaceful solution. On behalf of the CCP, Zhou Enlai was dispatched to Xi'an to take part in the negotiations. Chiang's wife Song Meiling and her brother, Prime Minister T. V. Soong, also came to Xi'an.

Meanwhile, Zhang started negotiating. He demanded that Chiang Kai-shek stop the campaign against the communist forces and instead lead a united front against Japan. An informal understanding was reached by which Chiang would lead a national alliance to resist Japan, but Chiang then refused to sign a written statement to that effect. After lengthy talks, it was agreed that his wife and brother-in-law, the Song siblings, would sign on his behalf. This, however, was unacceptable to many local officers in Zhang Xueliang's army and the CCP; they demanded a written statement by Chiang Kai-shek declaring the end of the fight between the CCP and the GMD, and the start of war against Japan. The situation became tense as talks came to a stalemate. Meanwhile, the Nanjing government mobilized the army and set troops in motion toward Xi'an. Zhang Xueliang feared that a new civil war could break out should Chiang be killed or detained much longer. He concluded that he needed to act quickly to release Chiang, and then fly back with him to Nanjing. Without informing the CCP or his own troops, Zhang put Chiang Kai-shek and Song Meiling on a plane to Nanjing. Chiang returned on December 26, after fourteen days of captivity, to an outpouring of public sympathy.

Eight months of negotiations ensued before the CCP and the GMD arrived at a plan for the Second United Front. Unlike the First United Front, this second effort at unity ensured the independence of both the GMD and the CCP. The GMD agreed to release all political prisoners and to stop its military campaigns against the communist areas. The CCP promised to terminate its pursuit of armed uprisings and radical land policies. The Second United Front planned for the eventuality of war against Japan, but both the CCP and the GMD assumed that essential support would come from the Soviet Union. Zhang Xueliang, however, was immediately arrested by Chiang Kai-shek. He would spend the next fifty years, until 1991, under house arrest.

The events in Xi'an had intriguing, unforeseeable, and far-reaching consequences. During those tense two weeks of negotiations and amid the uncertain back-and-forth engagement in the old imperial town of Xi'an, no one could have predicted the outcome. It was contingent on how a series of decisions played out. But the Xi'an incident ended up having an impact on China and the world that would be hard to overstate. Few events in modern history have been such complete game-changers or had such enormous consequences. As a result of the Xi'an incident, China was able to fully mobilize all of its military forces to repel Japan's further advance. In the following years, Japan's attempts to overcome persistent Chinese resistance consumed considerable resources. Ultimately, it was unable to defeat China on the battlefield and occupy the entire country. Moreover, had Japan not been bogged down in China, it would surely have deployed more troops and materiel to its other military campaigns against the United States in the Pacific theater and against the Soviet Union in the northeast. Without the Xi'an incident, World War II would likely have taken a very different course, both in Europe and in the Pacific. The event also marked the beginning of Russia's rising military power and political clout in China. The Soviet Union demonstrated that it was by far the most important and influential foreign country active in China and it continued to have great sway over Chinese politics. In August 1937, the Soviet Union and China signed a nonaggression pact, and the former quickly began sending funds, munitions, and military advisers, as well as more than three hundred aircraft with Soviet pilots.[11] For the first years of the war, the Soviet Union was virtually the only country providing support to China.

The Xi'an incident also proved decisive for the domestic situation in China because it demonstrated the influence of Chinese nationalism as a potent political movement that could transcend party politics to mobilize a large public, including students and the military. Nationalist passions were shown to be a dominant force in Chinese politics, even while Chiang Kai-shek had admirably stood by anti-communist principles and refused to yield to extortion. After 1936, he became the undisputed national leader accepted by all camps in the fight against Japan. Mao and the CCP, however, benefited more in the long run from their official recognition as a national force. No longer rebels or bandits (*tufei* as Chiang had called them), they were regarded as a legitimate part of a nationalist coalition.[12] The entire political field was reconfigured and structures emerged that would profoundly influence the

6.1. Japanese soldiers during the seizing of Shanghai, September 1937.
Keystone-France / Getty Images / 105212226

postwar development in China. The Xi'an incident activated powerful resistance against Japan, but also planted the seeds of the nationalists' undoing.

The Battle Begins

Rather than deterring Japan, the establishment of the Second United Front and the support of the Soviet Union convinced Japanese leaders that a full-scale war was inevitable and should begin sooner rather than later. On July 7, 1937, a minor dispute between Japanese and Chinese troops at the Marco Polo Bridge near Beijing finally led to open hostility between the two countries, escalating into the undeclared beginning of war in Asia. The Japanese government tried for several weeks to settle the incident locally. But in China, public opinion demanded decisive resistance to further aggression. The public expected Chinese troops no longer to recede. On July 17, Chiang Kai-shek declared, "If we allow one more inch of our territory to be lost, then we would be committing an unpardonable offense against our race."[13] When fighting broke out in late July, the battle for North China began. The Japanese quickly took Beijing and proceeded to capture Tianjin. Fighting continued into August, but it was soon evident that the region could not be held by Chinese troops.

On August 13, 1937, Japanese and Chinese troops clashed further in the south, this time for China's most important city, Shanghai.[14] It is not clear what precise events precipitated the first local skirmishes, but once they erupted they quickly got out of hand. Three months of bitterly fought and extremely destructive combat followed, in which Chiang Kai-shek deployed more than half a million men for the defense of Shanghai. Seeking an early standoff to gain the upper hand and engage the enemy in a decisive battle, he led his best-equipped, German-trained troops into the urban battlefield. Most were sent into the abyss. According to Chinese data, around 190,000 Chinese soldiers were killed or maimed in just those three months. Other estimates by the Japanese military and foreign observers push that number as high as 300,000. Whatever the final count, there can be no question that the Chinese military, though it fought bravely, suffered a devastating blow. It lost large portions of its best troops and most valuable equipment in the battle for Shanghai.

Civilian losses were horrible, as well. On the second day of battle, August 14—later to be known as "Black Saturday"—hundreds of civilians were killed. Several foreigners were among the many more who were injured. Chinese pilots accidently dropped their deadly payloads on Nanjing Road and the Great World Amusement Center in the International Settlement. Two weeks later, on another "Bloody Saturday" in Shanghai, Japanese air raids on Zhabei to the north killed hundreds of civilians who were crowded into a Shanghai railway station trying to flee the burning, shattered city by train. Shortly after 4 PM on August 28, 1937, the Chinese photographer H. S. Wong rushed to the station to document the carnage. He later described the scene: "It was a horrible sight. Dead and injured lay strewn across the tracks and platform. Limbs lay all over the place. I stopped to reload my camera. I noticed that my shoes were soaked with blood."[15] He then captured one of the most famous and influential war images of the twentieth century. It showed a lone baby sitting in the ruins of the wrecked Shanghai railway station, crying in agony. Taken a few months after the German bombing of Guernica during the Spanish Civil War, an incident famously portrayed in a painting by

6.2. Baby crying in the ruins of Shanghai train station, which was bombed by Japanese troops, August 1937.

Keystone-France / Getty Images / 104402087

Picasso, the photo showed the world that the horror of modern aerial warfare had simultaneously arrived in Asia, where it inflicted even heavier losses on a much larger, entirely unprotected civilian population.

The devastating battle for Shanghai revealed that the nationalist resolve to defend China was very real. Vast sacrifices were made. The determination of the Chinese also surprised Japan, as its army suffered more casualties than expected and it had to mobilize more materiel and men than originally planned. In the end, however, Japan had more men on the ground, and also far superior weaponry. Its advantages on the sea and in the air were decisive. Continuous shelling by the Japanese navy and relentless air raids pummeled Chinese defenses and extracted heavy tolls. During the first year of the war, Japan won victory after victory despite dogged Chinese resistance. In October 1937, the Chinese government started to move its administration first to Wuhan and then on to Chongqing in Sichuan, farther up the Yangzi and behind protective mountains.[16]

By late December, Shanghai and Nanjing had fallen, the latter city providing the site of the infamous Nanjing Massacre perpetrated by Japanese troops in December 1937 to January 1938.[17] In an attempt to destroy the morale of the population and to force the GMD government to sue for peace, long-range bombers mercilessly hammered Nanjing for three months. When the Chinese troops finally surrendered, the Japanese army entered the city. For six weeks, Japanese troops went on a spree of murder, rape, looting, and torture, seemingly throwing aside all restraint. Instead of enforcing a new order, the Japanese allowed Nanjing to descend into complete chaos. Atrocities imaginable and unimaginable were reported by Chinese witnesses and by the few foreigners, such as John Rabe (1882–1950), in the city trying to protect its population. Rabe was a German who worked for the German company Siemens. He also chaired a group of about two dozen missionaries, doctors, and professors, most of them Germans and Americans, who had established a neutral zone in Nanjing as a haven for Chinese refugees. In his diary, Rabe wrote of people being shot, doused with gasoline, and burned alive. He saw bodies of women lanced with beer bottles and bamboo sticks. In his entry for one day alone, January 3, 1938, Rabe reported several horrifying events:

> Early yesterday morning, the Japanese soldier had tried to rape Mr. Liu's wife. The husband came in and with some slaps in the face forced the Japanese to leave. That afternoon the soldier, who had been unarmed in the morning, returned with a gun, looked for and found Liu in the kitchen, and shot him, even though all Liu's neighbors pled for the man's life and one even knelt down before the Japanese soldier. . . . The Hanchung Men, the gate that was opened yesterday, has been closed again. Kröger saw about 300 corpses in a dry ditch near the gate: civilians who had been machine-gunned there. They don't want to let Europeans outside the gates. They probably fear that something about conditions here might get published too soon.[18]

The total number of people killed in Nanjing during the weeks of the Japanese rampage is unknown and estimates vary widely. Chinese historians put the number in the range of three hundred thousand.

Meanwhile, in North China, the Japanese met increasing resistance and suffered heavy losses in the Battle of Taiyuan's nearly two months of combat before eventually taking the city in November 1937. From there, Japanese troops moved quickly down the east coast of China making use of China's rail system. In April 1938, Chiang Kai-shek's troops managed to score a rare victory in Jiangsu province, boosting the morale of the troops and the public. In the hard-fought Battle of Taierzhuang, they beat back the enemy, temporarily halting the Japanese onslaught. But briefly thereafter, Xuzhou, a critical railway junction, was lost, which allowed the Japanese army to continue its advance westward and southward.

From June through October 1938, Japanese troops advanced toward Chongqing, fighting numerous battles north and south of the Yangzi River. In its desperate fight against Japan, Chiang Kai-shek's government committed a major act of violence against its own people.[19] In a reckless effort to halt the progress of the Japanese army, Chiang Kai-shek gave orders to open the dikes of the Yellow River. This June decision resulted in colossal flooding across the plains of central China, causing the deaths of perhaps close to a million people and the displacement of another three to five million. It slowed the Japanese advance by only a few weeks. Similarly, retreating Chinese troops chose to burn Changsha rather than leave anything of value behind for the Japanese. That action meant that an estimated twenty thousand people lost their lives before the Japanese fired their first shot. Changsha would later be successfully defended three times before the Japanese finally occupied the city in 1944. While this "scorched earth" strategy slowed the Japanese troops down, it ultimately could not stop them, and it did terrible damage to the Chinese population.

Meanwhile, Japan continued its advance with a vengeance. Japanese navy planes raided Guangzhou for fourteen months before the Japanese army took the city on October 21 and disrupted the railway supply line to Wuhan, where the temporary Chinese military command was located. It also captured the triple city of Hankou, Hanyang, and Wuchang—which together form Wuhan—over the course of October 25–26. Soon, the Japanese gained control over all the major railway lines and cities of China.

Incessant fighting and bombing during the first year of the war wrecked countless Chinese cities, crushed infrastructure, took millions of lives, and set even more millions of refugees in motion. The refugees moved from northern and eastern China into the unoccupied western parts of China. No reliable statistics exist on the refugees produced by the war, but analysis suggests that between eighty million and one hundred million were on the move during one phase of the war or another. Such numbers, representing 15 or 20 percent of China's total population at the time, add up to one of the greatest migrations in Chinese history. The displacements destabilized Chinese society and unraveled the fabric of social and political order; this was a gigantic upheaval that would reverberate throughout the war and beyond.

Already at the end of the opening phase of the war, the nationalist government had lost the best of its modern troops, air force, and arsenals, and a large chunk of the eastern seaboard where most of China's modern industry and railways—its major tax resources—were located. By the end of 1940, the Chinese efforts were successful only in the sense that they exhausted the Japanese attackers. The incursion of the Japanese army into China stalled. During the second stage of the war, lasting roughly three years until the end of 1943, the battle lines changed only slightly, although there were many skirmishes of limited, regional scale. In this period of relative stalemate, the Japanese army sought to consolidate and exploit its gains. Military actions by both the nationalists and communists primarily took the form of guerrilla warfare behind enemy lines. China was for practical purposes divided into at least several different regions, and most Chinese found themselves governed by either the Japanese or a collaborationist regime. The different institutions that were built in these various regions would shape diverging experiences and practices.

The Nationalist Government in Chongqing

Chongqing, located in Sichuan province, was designated the new provisional capital—a status the city retained until the end of the war in 1945. Apart from Sichuan, the nationalist government could also claim to control Yunnan, Hunan, southern Jiangxi, western Hubei and Henan, southern Shaanxi, and pockets of Guangxi and Guangdong. Large parts of those regions, especially Sichuan and Yunnan, had been in the hands of various warlords since 1911 and had suffered from the protracted wars among them. Because that made it hard for the nationalist government to establish control, it gained a footing in Sichuan only in 1935, later than in other areas. Even after 1935, the government's hold was tenuous. Militarists, as well as associations like the Green Gang and Red Gang, continued to wield great power in this unruly area. By moving their center of government so far to the west, the nationalists had entered a region with which they were not familiar and which they found hard to control. Chiang Kai-shek found himself trying to reorganize an army and rebuild a government in conditions that were beyond difficult. Chongqing was an important commercial hub for the economy of southwest China, but the landlocked region was isolated from the coast and relatively backward. Its industrial development lagged behind that of the coastal areas. Sichuan had few railways and highways, and only a small base of modern industries such as steel production. It offered, however, natural protection in the form of mountains and hills that would turn any Japanese assault by land into an arduous undertaking. The region also had rich natural resources and highly productive agriculture.

With the relocation of the nationalist government to Chongqing, development of the city and the area accelerated markedly.[20] The government committed funding for investment in infrastructure and housing. The Dianqian (or Burma) road connecting Yunnan and Burma was extended and improved. It quickly became a lifeline connecting nationalist China—or "Free China," as it called itself—to the world. Chongqing also became an aviation center. After 1941 (when stretches of the Burma Road had fallen into Japanese hands), US supplies would arrive here via airlift. Some two hundred factories and enterprises were also relocated and settled in the area—and that number grew by 1940 to more than four hundred. They formed a large industrial complex, and indeed the only such complex in the western part of China at the time. Chongqing became a center for the steel, machinery, and weapons industries.

The government relocated not only industries and defense equipment, but also libraries, museums, and radio stations. As a wartime capital, Chongqing became the new cultural center of a nation that had lost most of its cultural heartland to Japan. China's leading newspapers and publishers followed suit. Many institutions of higher education moved, as well.[21] Of a total of 108 institutions of higher education existing at the time in China, 57 were relocated to the southwest, almost half of these to Chongqing. A lively and diverse cultural scene developed.

These efforts of building a new capital by the nationalist government took place in the difficult and frustrating circumstances of warfare. Frequent air raids by the Japanese struck indiscriminately at military and civilian targets. The capital Chongqing and virtually all cities in the nationalist area, including Guilin, Kunming, and Xi'an, were systematically bombed. From May 1938 to April 1941, Japan's air forces launched 268 separate raids against Chongqing. A single raid could involve up to a hundred planes dropping incendiary and explosive bombs. The purpose was less to destroy military installations and factories than to break civilian morale and terrorize the population. The almost daily activity of running for air shelters profoundly shaped the lives of urban inhabitants. Many thousands of citizens were killed in just the first two days of heavy raids in May 1939. "When the Japanese bombers came to Chongqing," recalled Zeng Yongqing, a woman living in Chongqing, "in addition to dropping bombs, they also used machine guns to shoot people on the ground. The bullets came down like torrential rain, and the bombs came down like a thunderstorm."[22] In total, more than fifteen thousand residents were killed as a result of aerial bombing, and much of the city was destroyed.

The civilian population endured hardships beyond bombing, as well. Chongqing was under an economic blockade most of the time, since Japan had cut off most traffic links to eastern China. Manufactured goods were scarce and hoarding drove up prices. The government did not have the means to carry out rationing and price control, though it did supply government employees and the population with rice rations. Many people in the city had to spend their entire savings and sell their possessions for ever more expensive foodstuffs and basic necessities. A mother of three from Chongqing remembered that "to feed my children and myself, I sold everything I could put my hands on in our house."[23]

The area was therefore also ill prepared for the masses of refugees from the east that flooded Chongqing and its neighborhoods. After the fall of central and eastern China, by the end of 1937, millions of Chinese packed up all they could carry and left their homes in search of safety. As refugees later also poured into Chongqing, the population soared quickly. During the seven years of the war, the number of people living in Chongqing more than doubled to over one million residents, from roughly half a million in 1937. The arrival of so many refugees hailing from different parts of China caused profound social dynamics, but also tensions and challenges in Chongqing society. Given the mounting social problems, the government for the first time established a system of welfare provision. It also issued identification cards to refugees, which were used to allocate work, housing, and food. In the interest of food security, agricultural reforms were carried out. Peasants were supplied with pesticides as well as loans.

In general, the government tried to maintain control over political and social life. Because of the agreement with the CCP that led to the establishment of the Second United Front, the nationalist government was compelled to permit communists and other political parties to participate in Chongqing's political life. In 1938 (still in Wuhan), it conceded to the establishment of the People's Political Council (PPC). The PPC was a parliament-like forum, designed to provide a platform for broad popular participation in the political affairs of the nationalist government. It initially had about two hundred members. Together, the communists and the so-called third political parties claimed about fifty of these seats. Several of these smaller "third" parties had positioned themselves along the political spectrum between the CCP and GMD. Most influential among them was the Democratic League, founded in 1941 as a merger of six minority parties and groups that had emerged during the 1920s and 1930s. Independents without party affiliation were given seventy seats and the GMD held about eighty seats. The new council was thus a remarkable institution that reflected the search for a national unity transcending party affiliations and ideological conflicts during the first years of the war. In Chongqing, the CCP was even able to sell its party publications, as were other political parties. All this reinforced the emergence of a broad movement aspiring to realize a constitutional and democratic form of government. After 1940, however, many council members criticized the government's growing neglect of the principles of the United Front and the increase of censorship and repression. The critics were typically intellectuals, often foreign-educated, who resented political dictatorship. Despite growing government harassment, the war years in Chongqing were thus marked by a remarkably open and public debate on the values of a multiparty system and on the possibilities for democracy and freedom in China. Rarely before and after in Chinese history could the political opposition in China voice its concerns so freely, and publicly and forcefully demand participation in political affairs.[24]

The nationalist government also strengthened its control over the wartime economy. Economic planning became one of Chongqing's largest bureaucracies, expanding as the war continued.[25] The plans included blueprints for the development of military-related industries and for new infrastructural elements such as roads, railroads, and airfields. Crucial industries were nationalized. The government initially ran over sixty state enterprises, and that number grew to 103 by 1944.[26] State monopolies were established in tobacco, sugar, salt, and matches. In April 1941, the government regained the land tax in the areas under its control, taking over tax collection from the provinces. Since 1928, the agricultural land tax had been collected in money by the provincial governments or lower-level governments. The central government therefore had to purchase rice for its vast army on the open market. But with rice prices spiraling out of control (the average price in June 1941 was over twenty times higher than on the eve of the war) the cost of maintaining the army had become prohibitive. After taking over land-tax collection, the government started to assess the tax not in money but in kind—that is, mostly in the form of rice and other grains. This practice, which would be continued under the CCP after 1949, had the dual advantage of providing the government with food for its soldiers and lessening its need to print money. But it also kept grain out of the markets, which further contributed to spiraling prices and popular anger. The fact that taxes were rather high also led to popular discontent. With the loss of large chunks of territory in eastern China, the government had also lost essential revenue streams from agriculture and trade in China's most prosperous regions. Smaller harvests in 1941 and 1942, moreover, caused famine in Henan and Shandong, only made worse by government requisitions of grain. The government's revenue sources remained too limited, given the large bureaucracy it had to support, on top of an army that at times exceeded three million men. Between 1937 and 1939, total revenue fell by 63 percent while total spending increased by 33 percent.[27]

Facing growing deficits, the government resorted to printing currency inadequately backed by reserves. As a result, a galloping inflation shook the economy. Running at 230 percent a year from 1942 to 1945, it was nearly uncontrollable in nationalist territories. Declining government wages in real terms led to widespread corruption. Groups that were particularly hurt—including intellectuals, public servants, and students—became increasingly critical of the government's policies.

Critics of the regime, however, faced very real threats of arrest and even assassination. Factional politics and infighting paralyzed the government. The protracted war progressively weakened the nationalist government, which obviously provided a rare window of opportunity to the CCP—one that Mao was determined to use.

The Communist Areas

Exhausted, decimated, and constantly harassed by the nationalist troops on its Long March, the CCP sought refuge in north Shaanxi in the walled town of Bao'an in autumn 1935. Later, in December 1935, it relocated to Wayabao. During those years, the leaders holed up in caves dug into the soft loess soil of Shaanxi; pictures of these caves taken by American journalist Edgar Snow were seen around the world. Although territory held by the communists had shrunk in 1936 due to GMD extermination campaigns, the Xi'an incident (December 1936) and then the outbreak of war with Japan provided much-needed relief. In January 1937, the leadership was able to move into the largest city in the region, Yan'an. There, CCP leaders enjoyed a break from permanent battles and attacks. They used the time to rethink and readjust the course the revolution had taken.

Initially there were two base areas *(genjudi)* developed by the CCP in the desolate borderlands of Shaanxi, Gansu, and Ningxia provinces. On September, 6, 1937, the formal announcement came that these had been merged to establish the Shaan-Gan-Ning Border Region (the name was derived from the provinces of Shaanxi, Gansu, and Ningxia, where the area was located). Yan'an would be the capital.[28] This border region *(bianqu)*, with its population of about 1.5 million, was poor, entirely agricultural, and prone to disasters. For the most part, it lay in ruins. Years of warlord fighting, banditry, droughts, and epidemics had undermined the local economy and social order. Despite these adverse circumstances, the communist movement gained significant momentum here during the war against the Japanese. It remained the only base that was behind enemy lines and separated from both the coastline controlled by Japan and the area controlled by the nationalist government.

Shaan-Gan-Ning was the secure and relatively stable border region where the party leadership, including Mao Zedong, resided. Aside from it, there were also three other, larger border regions, all located in North China. Very soon after the outbreak of war, the Eighth Route Army crossed the Yellow River into Shanxi province and started to build a border area there. The establishment of the Jin-Cha-Ji (Shanxi-Mongolia-Hebei) Border Region was formally announced in January 1938, and it soon became the most important and successful of the border areas. The CCP also established two bases in western Shanxi and one in central Suiyuan (now part of Inner Mongolia) in early 1937; the three were merged in 1942 to form the Jin-Sui Border Region. Finally, there was the Jin-Ji-Lu-Yu (Shanxi-Hebei-Shandong-Henan) Border Region. Its origins began in October 1937 as the Taihang guerilla zone on the Hebei-Henan-Shanxi border. Expansion into southern Hebei and eastward into Shandong eventually resulted in its formal establishment as a border region in July 1941. The more important central and eastern China smaller base areas were Su-Wan (Jiangsu-Anhui), Subei (north Jiangsu), E-Yu-Wan (Hubei-Henan-Anhui), Xiang-E-Gan (Hunan-Hubei-Jiangxi), and Huaibei (Anhui, Henan, Jiangsu).

In the fight against Japan, the CCP infiltrated rural areas behind enemy lines in northern and central China to establish base areas or guerilla zones (youjiqu). Operating within the general framework of the United Front against Japan, the leaders of the Eighth Route Army adopted a strategy based on their experience in guerrilla warfare. They sent small columns into areas of northern China that the Japanese army had overrun but lacked the manpower to control. There, they incorporated remnant troops and organized the population to supply food, recruits, and sanctuaries for guerrilla units attacking small Japanese garrisons. From those base areas, the CCP tried to extend political control and wage guerrilla warfare against the Japanese army and Chinese collaborators. By mid-1940, it had established control over several areas, with a combined estimated population of more than fifty million people.

The CCP fought one major battle with Japanese troops during the entire war, called the Hundred Regiments Campaign. It extended from August 20 to December 5, 1940. In a surprise, CCP regiments attacked the transportation network in North China, singling out railway lines, motorways, bridges, and infrastructure installations. Facilities at important coal mines were also destroyed, halting production for nearly a year. The enemy response was ferocious: the Japanese waged a relentless attack on the communist troops, which included the use of poison gas, in a brutal attempt at complete annihilation. They also blocked all trade with communist-controlled regions, depleting the countryside of food and causing indescribable civilian misery. The CCP army reportedly sustained one hundred thousand casualties during the Hundred

Regiments Campaign. Mao Zedong was said to be especially upset as he had warned against this campaign, which was led by Peng Dehuai, believing it would put at serious risk the CCP's ability to consolidate its rule in areas under its control. Continuous attacks by Japanese forces and the collaborationist governments indeed decimated the communist-led forces and the areas the CCP ruled. In the years leading up to 1942, the communist areas were reduced by almost half. Neither the campaign nor guerilla warfare tactics could repulse or seriously threaten Japan. The most they could do was to continue tying down and wearing out the substantial Japanese forces.

Until the end of the war, the communists managed to recover from the setback. They greatly expanded the area under their control, extending it over four border regions and more than twenty base areas in North China. In the 1940s, the CCP made important changes to its policy. Mao Zedong, having spent much time studying the classics of Marxism-Leninism, began writing programmatic texts with the help of Russian-trained secretaries, in the interest of devising his own unique system of thought, later called "Mao Zedong Thought" *(Mao Zedong sixiang)*. Essentially, he sought to indigenize Marxist theory by insisting that local practice should influence and shape the further development of theory. He was outspoken in his criticism of those who would follow the classical Marxist texts blindly: "Many comrades seem to study Marxism-Leninism not to meet the needs of revolutionary practice, but purely for the sake of study. Consequently, though they read, they cannot digest. They can only cite odd quotations from Marx, Engels, Lenin, and Stalin in a one-sided manner, but are unable to apply the stand, viewpoint and method of Marx, Engels, Lenin, and Stalin to the concrete study of China's present conditions and her history or to the concrete analysis and solution of the problems of the Chinese revolution."[29] By contrast, the thinking of Mao Zedong intended to unite "the universal truths of Marxism-Leninism with the practice of revolution and construction in China."[30] This was a bold proposition.

Some of the most important changes resulting from this revisionist approach were related to the strategy for revolutionizing Chinese society. In many ways, the party altered its fundamental policies. On July 16, 1936, Mao had told Edgar Snow: "The fundamental issue today is the struggle against Japanese imperialism."[31] The increasingly ominous Japanese threat fused Chinese nationalism with communist political interests, and led the party to approach social groups it had fought against before. Urban members of the middle classes, rich peasants, and small landlords were wooed as allies in the national resistance against Japan. The great majority of the Chinese people, not only the peasants, were potentially part of the "patriotic" and "revolutionary" United Front. In other words, Mao Zedong deemphasized class struggle and instead reassured the "patriotic" members of the "bourgeoisie" that they would be welcome and that their property and status would be respected. This had clear practical consequences. The CCP's earlier radical policy of confiscatory land distribution was replaced by a much more moderate and popular policy of reduction of rural rents, interests, and taxes. Rent and interest reduction *(jianzu jianxi),* and particularly tax reform, demonstrated a new approach to equalizing rural income and land ownership through an incremental process that gradually shifted the burden of taxation from poorer peasants toward the more wealthy, while maintaining the level of state revenue. Flexible economic policies allowed Yan'an to achieve greater economic autarky and to deal better with the economic blockade, as well as the 1942 famine in North China. In Yan'an, the CCP pursued gradual transformation with flexible adaptation to local conditions, instead of uniform, radical, revolutionary change.

The moderation of class struggle rhetoric led to a revision of the CCP's views on working with other social classes and groups in Chinese society. As part of the United Front, the party explicitly welcomed urban professionals and intellectuals, seeing their knowledge, skills, and participation as helpful for revolutionary success. By adopting moderate policies and promoting nationalism, Yan'an acquired a positive reputation for social reform. The CCP touted the egalitarian, participatory, and cooperative achievements of its wartime resistance. This attracted many sympathizers from urban China. Most of the new arrivals were highly educated writers, teachers, intellectuals, and journalists. They came in search of a safe haven, but even more, they sought a new and brighter future in a liberated area of free and open discussion. By late 1943, the party reported that roughly forty thousand intellectuals had come to Yan'an since the beginning of the war. Their knowledge and skills were in high demand for building a central administration, mustering resources, producing supplies, and rallying support. The CCP needed large numbers of commanders, instructors, and general staff as well as engineers, technicians, and doctors for the growing army. This was required for expanding industry, finance, commerce, and agriculture in the border region as well as building up the performing arts, journalism, and education in military science and other disciplines. The CCP had been overwhelmingly made up of poor peasants, bandits, and soldiers, but after this point, membership became more diverse.

Another effect of the United Front policy was a wave of elections of political personnel to base area assemblies and offices. In the more secure and consolidated base areas, grassroots democracy could spread. Election movements took the form of mass mobilizations that reached deeply into rural areas, serving to educate the villagers and broadening political participation. Even as elections were held on the village level, however, the CCP made sure that its hegemony was not challenged.

Within a few years after settling in Yan'an, the success of this policy became evident. The change in Yan'an was spectacular. Across the border region, hundreds of machinery, chemical, paper, textile, and other kinds of factories and multiple levels of official administration had begun to operate. The CCP had established and taken over banks, trading firms, and clinics. Art and education absorbed large numbers of the newcomers. Theater troupes, writer groups, and cultural associations were founded. The number of schools increased many times over. The party operated over twenty establishments that it deemed to be college-level training centers or research institutes, and over thirty newspapers and journals. Although most of the facilities were poorly equipped and relied on a lot of improvising, their presence and operations transformed the region.

Mao also worked hard to provide the CCP with a more unified common language, justification, and purpose. Given the intense debates in the past, he felt it was time to strengthen and unify the party's political mindset. Once a new program, along with a consistent rhetoric, was agreed upon, Mao used his 1942 "rectification campaign" (Zhengfeng yundong) to enforce the "correct thinking" and to consolidate his political power. For Mao, the rectification campaign was a way to legitimize his leadership by sanctifying his understanding of the revolution, including his own Marxist interpretation of the role of armed peasant uprising. Previous political strategies used by the party, and alternative ideas of what it must do to defeat Japanese aggrandizement, were strongly repudiated. Above all, the campaign allowed Mao to criticize and attack internal rivals like Wang Ming, Zhang Wentian, and Bo Gu, who had spent time in Russia and enjoyed Moscow's backing. This was also the beginning of the canonization of Mao's writings. The rectification campaign was crucial to the creation of a cult of Mao and to crushing independent thought or dissent among intellectuals and party activists. In his speeches over the course of the movement, Mao stressed the importance of uniformity and orthodoxy, which were to be reinforced through "thought reform" *(sixiang gaizao)*.[32] A "coherent discourse community" was to be created that would be strongly rooted in a clearly defined system of ideas and language. What was once a loose gathering of activists would be transformed into a rigorous community of like-minded party members who had internalized the CCP's norms and values and would follow the same code of behavior. For this purpose, party cadres were called on to form study groups in which carefully selected texts were read and discussed collectively. (Eighteen mandatory texts altogether were collected in a small volume called "Rectification Documents.") This form of study had less to do with memorizing certain doctrines than with engaging in an open-ended process of self-examination. For example, participants were asked to write "thought examinations." Study, self-examination, and thought examination were expected to lead to a revelation of wrong thoughts, evil ambitions, and bad desires. Particularly through confession, cadres were supposed to rectify and reform their thinking.

The party counted on voluntary embrace of the ideas, but also deployed a set of coercive measures to keep the campaign going. Interrogations and mass rallies were among these measures, and terrified party members. At public meetings in front of large crowds, young volunteers were forced to confess to being spies and to name others.[33] Violence and torture were often used to extract these confessions. This coercion was accompanied by the expansion and strengthening of the CCP's security apparatus.[34] Intelligence work and an internal surveillance network were used to monitor party members who were in the process of rectification. Interrogations and arrests were made by CCP detectives and security agents with the goal of uncovering hostile agents, traitors, and Trotskyites. Some alleged enemies were executed after mass trials without any actual court hearings.

The campaign was in part a reaction to the need to consolidate the leadership, but also to the change of party membership that occurred in Yan'an. As we have seen, the educated groups which had come to Yan'an formed a diverse population. Many joined the party not long after their arrival.

Numerous new peasants and soldiers from the local areas also entered the party during this period. By the early 1940s, the number of party members across the country had reached eight hundred thousand—as compared to the forty thousand who were members when the war first broke out. Party membership of the CCP further increased to approximately 1.2 million in 1945. Rectification was an important vehicle to improve ideological and organizational discipline within a growing communist movement.

In Yan'an, the party also continued to receive considerable aid from the Soviet Union. Moscow sent money, fuel, military supplies, and other strategic goods.[35] Communist military power expanded dramatically. In 1937, the Red Army had seventy thousand poorly trained and primitively armed soldiers. By the time of the Japanese surrender, those forces had grown substantially into an army of one million regular soldiers, uniformly well trained and well equipped. Beyond these, there were also several million peasants organized in local militias.

At the end of the war, the CCP held its Seventh National Congress, from April 23 to June 11, 1945. The CCP constitution was amended and adopted Mao Zedong's thought as the party's guiding ideology. This new party constitution stipulated that "the Communist Party of China takes the Mao Zedong Thought that integrated Marxist-Leninist theory with the practice of the Chinese revolution as the guideline for all its work." During the congress, the CCP stressed its commitment to the United Front and a postwar coalition government. This is evident from the speeches delivered by its leaders: Mao Zedong gave the political report "On the Coalition Government." Zhou Enlai laid out the party's views "On the United Front." The congress worked out the party's political line, which was to "boldly mobilize the masses and expand the people's forces so that, under the leadership of our Party, they will defeat the Japanese aggressors, liberate the whole people and build a new-democratic China." In the mid-forties, the CCP thus clearly indicated its readiness to be a major political force in the postwar period, and also to enter a multiparty coalition with other political parties in China.

The Yan'an period turned out to be very significant for the CCP. The contrast of the situation between the early 1930s and the early 1940s could not be greater. In the beginning of the 1930s, the party had teetered on the brink of destruction, was mired in internal strife, and had little backing in rural society. It was forced to evacuate the Soviet region in Jiangxi and to flee pursuing GMD troops by marching thousands of kilometers across China. By the 1940s, the CCP controlled a large part of northern China, had built solid local governments, had learned to carry out social reforms, and was successfully managing local economies. While it is true that the United Front afforded the party a respite from the GMD assaults—and for that matter, that the CCP-ruled base and border areas suffered less damage from Japanese attacks than the bombed-out GMD areas—CCP rule had to deal with numerous other problems. They included the 1942 famine, an economic blockade, and the general poverty of the region. There is no denying that the CCP used the period in Yan'an well. It invested in local development and reform, while at the same time pushing through the consolidation and unification of the party by enforcing discipline and centralization. It continuously improved inner-party organization, extended its geographical reach, and found ways to enhance its public appeal. In the early 1930s, the CCP was little more than a ragtag army and political nuisance; a decade later, it was on its way to becoming a serious competitor for national power.

The Occupied Territories

Before 1945, Japan maintained a wartime empire on Chinese territory that included much of eastern and northern China. This empire was made up of several separate, independently administered regions. Since 1895, Taiwan had been under a colonial Japanese administration. Manchuria and the rest of the mainland were ruled indirectly through "military advisers" from Japan in collaboration with local Chinese officials. Several such short-lived governments were established before and during the war, in Manchuria, Inner Mongolia, and parts of northern and central China.

Manchuria became home to the most important of those "puppet" regimes. Only Korea and Taiwan were under Japanese control longer than Manchuria. Since the end of the Qing empire, Manchuria had been transformed quickly. Increased migration from northern China led to population growth and settlement of the vast plains. Around 1930, the population was estimated to be thirty million, of which twenty-eight million were ethnically Chinese or Manchus.[36] The remainder were Mongols, Koreans, and Japanese. The construction of the railroad lines connecting the southern port of Newchwang (Yingkou) with regions in the north, such as Harbin, and the opening of several ports in the first decade of the twentieth century, including Dairen (Dalian), stimulated rapid economic development centered mainly on the export of agricultural products. The main commodity of the region was soya. The soya bean and its byproducts made up some 80 percent of Manchurian exports. It was the most important export item of the region until the late 1920s, representing 59 percent of total world soya production. Consumed largely by the Japanese, soya would also, later, be shipped to Europe as cattle feed. Cities like Harbin and Dairen, bolstered by agricultural growth, trade, and foreign investments, began to compete with Shanghai in terms of services, prosperity, and urban life. The region was long governed by changing coalitions of Russians, Japanese, and Chinese warlords and only loosely integrated in the Chinese republic. Due to its economic interests in Manchuria, Japan intended to bring the area under its control.

After the Japanese occupation of Manchuria in late 1931, little resistance from the local population against the new rulers occurred.[37] Few might have welcomed the Japanese, but there also was little enthusiasm for the previous warlord regimes of Zhang Zuolin and Zhang Xueliang. Nor was the nationalist government in faraway Nanjing seen as a real and viable alternative. After the occupation, nationalist China appealed to the Council of the League of Nations, seeking a peaceful return of the region to China. A British diplomat, the Earl of Lytton, was charged to lead an inquiry into the status of Manchuria. Based on a visit to Manchuria by the Lytton Commission in April 1932, a report was issued in October of the same year. While the report refused to recognize Manchukuo as a legitimate state, and suggested measures to return it to China, it did highlight that the integration of Manchuria into the Republic of China had been more "nominal than real" and that "the relationship with the Central Government depended in all affairs—military, civil, financial, and foreign—on voluntary co-optation."[38] Japan did not, however, accept the recommendations of the report. In 1935, it withdrew in protest from the League.

In defiance of the League of Nations, the founding of the independent Republic of Manchukuo ("Land of the Manchus") was declared in March 1932. Its government was headed by the last Qing emperor, Henry Puyi, as head of state, and had its seat in the "New Capital" (Xinjing, today the city of Changchun in Jilin province). Manchukuo was envisioned as a multicultural polity to be made up of various ethnic groups, such as Japanese, Chinese, Koreans, Manchus, and Mongols, all living together peacefully. In reality, however, there was no real independence, as the Japanese army exercised supervision and tight control over all branches of the government and over Manchukuo's decision-making process. While "puppet state" is a vague term, it was often invoked to describe the situation. Moreover, Japanese officials were appointed to important positions in national defense, overseeing railroads, managing harbors, and so on. In 1934, Manchukuo was reconceived as an empire, and Puyi became an emperor again, this time of the Manchukuo empire.

Manchukuo was supposed to be a showcase for a new form of Japanese imperialism, centered on economic development of territories and public service provision. For reformist Japanese officials, Manchukuo became a convenient testing ground for new techniques of political administration, industrial management, and planning. In 1936, the government announced a first five-year plan for the development of industry. State companies, in which the government was a principal or important shareholder, were set up in selected sectors of the economy such as mining. The government intended to promote heavy industrialization and make Manchukuo a showcase of Japanese industrial might. The new empire's economic development was indeed stunning. In the 1940s, Manchukuo could point to a ready-made industrial base, ample production of wheat and timber, and extensive exploitation of its rich reserves of coal and iron. Over time, Manchukuo developed into a large, relatively industrialized country, with vast coal and iron resources, a vibrant market for consumer goods, and significant Japanese investments in education, infrastructure, and public health. It also ran an efficient public relations operation. Japanese businesses and organizations for publishing, radio broadcasting, film, and newsreel production were quickly established.

From the beginning, Chinese collaborators helped the new regime create its governmental structure and carry out its policies. Nationalist Chinese historiography tended to see this behavior as treasonous, but those cooperating with Japan saw little choice; it seemed a practical necessity. Moreover, motivations to work with Japan were diverse. The co-optation of landholding elites was a top priority for the Manchukuo government. Those elites had never supported the revolutionary rhetoric of the nationalist government. They were, above all, interested in maintaining stability and safeguarding the existing order, which Japan seemed to promise. Then there were also ardent Manchu supporters of Manchurian regional autonomy and self-governance, who hoped to pursue their dreams of independence from China with the help of Japan. Finally, religious salvationists reveling in eastern spirituality saw an opportunity to contribute to the establishment of a new East Asian religio-political order conducive to their beliefs. All these groups could be persuaded or coerced to join the "peace maintenance committees" that served as administration under the recently created Self-Government Guidance Department.

Although cooperation with the Japanese became the norm, there were also notable acts of resistance. Those were met with intensely brutal methods by the Japanese army. One of the most notorious incidents was the massacre on September 16, 1932, at Pingdingshan, near the industrial city of Fushun in Fengtian. Because that village had resisted Japanese troops it was entirely raided as an act of reprisal, and nearly three thousand civilians were killed. Chinese residents of Manchukuo, who were accused of transgressions, were also forced into labor service in concentration camps. Puyi reported in his memoirs that "corrective labor camps" were established throughout Manchukuo in the thirties.[39] Prisoners in the camps were forced into physical labor, mostly in mines or war-related industries. The Japanese military also established facilities in which prisoners were subjected to medical experimentation. In 1932, the small and remote village of Beiyinhe, about 100 kilometers south of Harbin, was picked as the site for the Zhong Ma Prison Camp. Surrounded by a high brick wall with barbed wire and high-voltage lines strung along the top, the compound itself covered a wide area with many buildings. The camp was divided into two wings. One contained the prison, laboratories, and a crematorium. The other had offices, barracks, warehouses, and a canteen. The camp was designed to hold a thousand people, but there were on average not more than five hundred prisoners. These included "bandits" (generally, Chinese and Koreans), suspicious persons, and criminal offenders. The purpose of internment, however, was to use the prisoners as human guinea pigs in a series of experiments to develop weapons for germ warfare. The mortality rate was very high. Normally a prisoner was kept no longer than a month for experiments before being killed. There was a ready supply of replacement "bandits" for the scientists. The experiments, all of them gruesome, focused on three main diseases: anthrax, glanders, and plague.

Beiyinhe was abandoned in late 1937, but only to give way to a much larger internment complex in the Pingfang area, closer to Harbin. Experiments were carried out on prisoners between 1937 and 1945 by a division called Special

Unit 731. Shiro Ishii (1892–1959), a physician and army officer, was in charge of this unit. Here, too, human guinea pigs were used to test diseases ranging from anthrax to yellow fever. Besides testing pathogens on humans, other secret research focused on the cultivation and dissemination of biological warfare agents. Thousands were killed. The internment center was destroyed by retreating Japanese troops in 1945 as the Soviet Red Army approached.

The Kwangtung Army played a central role in developing and governing Manchukuo. A new set of institutions was created under its direction with the goal to build a "model society." Those institutions can be best described as a combination of "military fascist" elements and Confucian norms of hierarchy, obedience, and respect. Initiatives were implemented through a state-sponsored mass organization called the Concordia Association (xiehehui, kyowakat). As a mediator between local communities and the government, the Concordia Association enrolled all officials, teachers, and important members of society in the task of implementing initiatives of the new state in their respective institutions. The Manchukuo state wanted to create a corporatist system in which each group had a set place and clearly defined function within the state. At the same time, individual rights were neglected, and resistance was subdued with dictatorial and often brutal actions.

Manchukuo played an important role in the making of Japan's colonial ideology. Manchuria was not only a strategic buffer zone between that empire and the Soviet Union but also a colonial frontier, even a potential utopia, awaiting the future arrival of intrepid Japanese settlers who would develop the region's vast potential. The Japanese government tried to use migrants to consolidate its hold on Manchukuo, sending large groups of settlers to Manchuria. Many returned home, however, when they realized how harsh the region's conditions were, especially in winter. Radical officers wanted Manchuria to benefit Japan not only materially but also spiritually. Their specific plans and initiatives were underpinned by a more cultural vision of the inevitable confrontation between East and West. Under Japanese leadership, Manchuria and China would be led into a holy war for the liberation of East Asia from western control, and then guided by Japan to succeed with modernization and development. The vision grew by the mid-1930s into the East Asian League (Toa Renmei) and the East Asian Community (Toa Kyodotai), and still later into the idea of the Greater East Asian Co-prosperity Sphere (Dai Toa Kyoeiken).

Collaborationist regimes also sprang up in the rest of China.[40] Initially there were numerous small, local governments, which were created in an ad hoc manner by Japanese Special Service agents co-opting local elites in occupied areas to set up so-called peace maintenance committees. As part of Japan's determination to obstruct the Chiang Kai-shek government, a decision was made to set up larger, economically more viable governments. Three such governments were established (apart from Manchukuo): a provisional republic in North China, the Mengjiang (Mongol United Autonomous) government, and a renewed Republican government in the Lower Yangzi.

In December 1937, "The Provisional Government of the Republic of China" was established with the help of the Japanese Imperial General Headquarters, as part of the latter's strategy to establish an autonomous buffer zone between China and Japanese-controlled Manchukuo. The "East Hebei Anti-Communist Autonomous Council," earlier established in 1935, was absorbed into the new government. Thus, the provisional government nominally controlled a large swath of territory in northern China including the provinces of Hebei, Shandong, Shanxi, Henan, and Jiangsu.[41] The former minister of finance in the Beiyang government, Wang Kemin (1879–1945), who had also studied in Japan, served as chairman in the capital at Beijing. The provisional government was a republic with legislative, executive, and judiciary branches. It issued its own currency and also formed its own army, called the North China Autonomous Army. It chose as its national flag the same five-colored flag that had been used by the Beiyang government in 1912. In general, many of the Chinese officials who worked with Japan had served in the Beiyang government. They had always resented the nationalist government, and saw a window of opportunity to resurrect, with the help of the Japanese empire, the Beiyang government—which in their eyes had always been the true successor to the Qing dynasty.

The Mengjiang government in Inner Mongolia was created in September 1939 with support from the Kwangtung Army. It also issued its own currency. In the Lower Yangzi region, a third government was set up called the "Renewed Government of the Republic of China," which was also dominated by former members of the Beiyang government.[42] The name of the government—the Renewed Government—reflected the rhetoric of the Meiji Restoration, which also claimed to renew good governance and restore the nation. The Renewed Government also used the Beiyang flag and controlled the provinces of Jiangsu, Zhejiang, and Anhui, as well as the two municipalities of Nanjing and Shanghai. It was headed by Liang Hongzhi (1882–1946), who had worked for the warlord Duan Qirui and earlier also served in the Beiyang government. Its structure was a constitutional republic, and its capital was Nanjing, although it had its offices in Shanghai. A ten-point "Political Program" *(Zhenggang)* also promised three branches of government (legislative, executive, and judicative), and a multiparty system. As its goals, the government emphasized anti-communism, economic reconstruction, and the replacement of modern "shallow doctrines" with "China's traditional moral culture."[43] The Renewed Government existed from March 1938 to March 1940, when all the provisional governments were subordinated, at least nominally, to a new national government in Nanjing, headed by Wang Jingwei.

In these areas collaboration rather than resistance characterized much of China's experience with the occupation. Inspired by European historical revisionism that subverted the French myth of national resistance, scholars also came to reexamine Chinese politics of heroic patriotism.[44] Local elites in the Lower Yangzi region entered into relationships of collaboration practically as soon as Japanese forces drove out the nationalist defense. There were incentives on both sides that made collaborative arrangements appealing. For the Japanese, the decision to found occupation regimes was intended to build more stable relations with the Chinese population. Functioning state institutions would sustain Japan's war effort by facilitating the restoration of order and productivity in occupied China. The local villagers were urged to return to a normal life of "peaceful living and blissful working" in the destroyed hometowns. As Japan saw its military costs escalate in China, it also considered it imperative that the occupation begin to pay for itself. To the Chinese population, the resumption of normalcy and stability was simply critical to survival. The war had produced terrible devastation and suffering, which came from actions by Chinese troops as well as Japanese ones. It was therefore far from unnatural for the two sides to collaborate. On the ground, pragmatic considerations prevailed during the Japanese occupation.

Throughout the war years, the Japanese government repeatedly approached the GMD government and proposed to find a diplomatic settlement. Japan made, on average, four diplomatic forays per year, and in one year, 1938, that number rose to eleven.[45] Chiang Kai-shek steadfastly rejected Japan's offers because he would not accede to any loss of sovereignty and territory. Others in the government, however, had different priorities. To them, the continued war and systematic destruction by aerial bombing was exacting too high a price from China. They pointed to the mounting burdens that an exhausted and profoundly shaken country could no longer shoulder. They were also highly critical of the United Front with the Communist Party, and the government's dependence on the Soviet Union. Wang Jingwei in particular sought to resolutely distance himself from leftists, socialists, and labor activists. While he had initially supported the nationalist policy of resistance against Japan, after compromising with Chiang Kai-shek in 1932, he advocated starting negotiations with that country. Japan, he thought, was preferable to Great Britain or the United States, to say nothing of the Soviet Union. It also seems that he believed in a pan-Asianist future. As Japan pursued an ever more aggressive policy, however, the "pro-Japan" group that included Wang Jingwei became marginalized and isolated within the GMD. Finally, when an attempt was made on his life, Wang Jingwei shifted toward the "peace movement" and the decision to collaborate with Japan. Wang Jingwei defected with a group of "peace advocates" *(heping pai)* to Hanoi to pursue a peaceful resolution to the military conflict with Japan on his own. He negotiated with Japan for over a year. Eventually, in 1940, a new "Reorganized Government of the Republic of China" was established in Nanjing under Japan's sponsorship, and he was appointed to chair it. To Chiang Kai-shek and the communists alike, he was a traitor *(hanjian)*, but he and his supporters had a different understanding of their role and goals.

Established with the slogan of "national reconstruction with peace and anti-communism," Wang's collaborationist government controlled most of the occupied areas (with the exception of Shanghai) from March 1940 to August 1945.[46] He set up a reorganized, formally autonomous nationalist government. Japanese authorities, however, observed Wang's government closely, and the Japanese army had the final say in all decisions. Nevertheless, his emphasis on the state's wartime role as protector of the people, on rebuilding the national economy, and on developing a close Sino-Japanese relationship suggests that he was motivated by more than just the quest for power. To create his vision of a new world order, he merged his versions of nationalism, pan-Asianism, and the three principles of the people into a new "Wang Jingwei doctrine" *(Wang Jingwei zhuyi)*. He also launched a campaign called the New Citizen movement, which incorporated civic elements of Sun Yat-sen's three principles. For Wang, Sun had already shown that it was possible to combine pan-Asianism and Chinese nationalism. Collaboration with Japan was therefore compatible with Sun's nationalist project. Wang believed that the nationalist state under Chiang Kai-shek had been either unwilling or unable to protect the people during the war, which was a point of departure he used to argue against the charge of treason and for the usefulness of collaboration with Japan, "a natural friend."

In the areas ruled by Wang Jingwei, local Chinese self-administration continued. Local communities also policed themselves and enjoyed the benefits of a temporary respite from the horrors of war. The vast majority of businesses in Shanghai and in the Lower Yangzi area did not relocate inland with the nationalists. Rather, they tried to keep their factories operating under Japanese rule. In these areas, a modest economic recovery was underway, supported in part by the objectives of the Greater East Asian Co-Prosperity Sphere—the Japanese program for coordination between the economies of Korea, Manchukuo, the Mongol Military Government, Taiwan, the occupied areas on the Chinese mainland, and the other countries occupied or dominated by Japan, from the Philippines to Thailand. Trade between the occupied areas and the rest of China, both licit and illicit, was also flourishing by this point in the war.

Global War

Since spring 1937, China had fought a bitter and desperate struggle against Japan. When Europe went into battle, as well, and consequently the Second World War erupted in the hot late summer of 1939, China had already been living with the horrific losses and far-reaching consequences of more than two years of brutal warfare on its territory. The outbreak of the Second World War had effects on the war theater in China, but in the long term it mainly changed China's international position. The start of global war offered both complex risks and multifaceted opportunities for new initiatives. Even if the concrete consequences were difficult to foresee, all parties and political camps in China knew that profound change was coming.

At the end of August 1939, the Soviet Union and Germany signed a non-aggression pact.[47] The countries, which had been ideological archenemies, pledged to cooperate in Europe. A few days later, World War II began with

Hitler's invasion of Poland. For China, and especially the GMD, this meant not only that Soviet support for its war effort would dry up, but that Japan would be able to free up forces along the Russian border and redeploy them in China. In late 1939, Japan indeed renewed its efforts and started several new initiatives to expand its occupied territories and defeat Chiang Kai-shek's government. Even worse, in July 1940, the British government temporarily conceded to Japan's demand that it close the Burma Road linking the British colony with China. The British military was already stretched thin in Europe; for the time being, it did not have the military capacity to open another front in southern Asia. The British decision essentially cut off the delivery of much needed war equipment and materiel via the Burma Road into nationalist China. In late September 1940, another blow came: Japan, Italy, and Germany joined in a military alliance, the Axis, and all remaining German military advisers were withdrawn from China. The country was left completely to its own devices in its fight against Japan. Isolated and without reliable international support, the GMD, and the CCP as well, were anxious as to what the future would bring. It was in this period that the United Front worked best and both parties cooperated in military and political matters.

Meanwhile, Chiang Kai-shek was looking for new allies. Since all the European states were consumed by the battle raging in Europe, the only realistic potential ally was the United States. By the end of 1940, when the United States was reconsidering its position of neutrality, it started to respond to Chinese requests for help. When the Wang Jingwei government was officially recognized by Tokyo in late November, the US government announced a loan to Chongqing, as well as the delivery of fifty military aircraft. In the spring of 1941, the administration of Franklin D. Roosevelt (1882–1945) also extended the Lend-Lease Agreement to China. The Lend-Lease Act of January 1941 was primarily a means for the United States to provide military aid to foreign countries. It authorized the president to transfer arms or any other defense materials for which Congress appropriated money to "the government of any country whose defense the president deems vital to the defense of the United States."[48]

The end of 1941 brought an important and sudden turning point. Japan's unexpected and devastating attack on Pearl Harbor on December 7 led to America's entry into the war and consequently also ended China's relative international isolation. The war went truly global. For the first time in years,

China could form new alliances. Within weeks, the China-Burma-India theater of war was established, with Chiang Kai-shek as supreme commander. From that moment on, China fought alongside the allies in an all-out war against the Axis powers. American assistance began to flow and was particularly important for sustaining China's war efforts. The United States sent supplies, military equipment, and advisers via a costly, difficult, and dangerous airlift over the Himalayan mountains, called "the Hump." The Flying Tigers, a volunteer corps of US fliers, also began to attack Japanese forces there.

The Americans equipped Chiang's best troops and trained his administrators. They also sent specialists to coach his intelligence services. For example, US officers worked, in the vicinity of Chongqing, in one of the most infamous prison camps run by the republican government. The camp system consisted of several different internment sites in Bai Gongguan and Zhazidong. The Sino-American Cooperation Organization (SACO) was set up not far from the prison camp under a secret agreement signed in 1942. From 1943 to 1945, American police officers and intelligence personnel were stationed there. They trained Chinese secret agents and spies and instructed nationalist secret services in interrogation techniques.[49]

In February 1942, the United States also sent a chief adviser, the highly decorated and respected General Joseph Stilwell (1883–1946), to Chongqing. As one of the few US officers fluent in Chinese, Stilwell often found himself in direct conflict with Chiang Kai-shek, whom he condescendingly referred to as "the peanut." Personal resentments aside, the two sides' priorities could not have been more divergent and conflicting. Stilwell's job was to convince Chiang Kai-shek to deploy his troops for bold attacks on Japanese positions, while Chiang Kai-shek hoped for large campaigns by the British and the Americans in Burma to relieve Chinese forces fighting in China. Chiang complained that Stilwell and the United States were not doing enough, and demanded more US operations. Stilwell accused his Chinese counterparts of unwillingness to send Chinese ground troops into battle and of cowardice, corruption, and incompetence.

Nonetheless, by joining the anti-Hitler coalition, China gained international recognition and stature, which offered a chance to finally move beyond its humiliating legacy of nineteenth-century imperialism. In January 1943, new treaties were signed between China, Great Britain, and the United States to revoke the last surviving remnants of western imperialism, reverse the system of legal extraterritoriality, and return all concessions, including the International Settlement and French Concession in Shanghai, to Chinese rule after the war. The treaties also canceled all Chinese debt assigned by the 1901 Boxer Protocol.[50]

In November 1943, Chiang Kai-shek attended the Cairo Conference, the only one of the international war conferences where China was formally represented. Given the great importance of the conference for Chiang, he prepared himself intensely, and went to Cairo with ambitious plans. As with the Beiyang government during the Great War thirty years earlier, Chiang Kai-shek saw China's role in the global conflict as an opportunity to gain some say in the shaping of the postwar world order. Chiang was convinced that China, as the only nonwestern country, would have a special role to play. His primary goal was clear: he wanted to secure critical military support. But beyond that, he would also demand the recovery of all lost territories—not only the territories occupied by Japan, but also territories in Tibet (where the British exercised influence), Outer Mongolia, Xinjiang (a region that, under warlord Sheng Shicai, had essentially become a satellite of the Soviet Union), Manchuria, and even Hong Kong and the treaty ports. As still another objective, he aimed to establish China as an equal power among the Allies, which could advocate in the interests of the nonwestern, colonial world.

In private conversations with Roosevelt leading up to the meeting, Chiang expressed the hope that the "policy toward British imperialism can also be successful, to liberate those in the world who are oppressed."[51] This ran up against strong British objections. Prime Minister Winston Churchill (1874–1965) stressed that while Great Britain would not seek territorial gains, it "intended to 'hold on to what they had,' including Singapore and Hong Kong, and would not give up their colonies without a war."[52] By contrast, a few days later during the follow up conference in Teheran (where China was not represented), Stalin made clear that he would fully respect China's claims in Manchuria and accept the prewar Manchurian borderline.[53] Churchill was also speaking out against Operation Buccaneer, a plan for an amphibious landing of Allied troops in the Gulf of Bengal, in which Chiang placed high hopes. In the end, the Allies agreed to open a second front in Europe and a land campaign in Burma in 1944. They also published a joint declaration requiring Japan to return all occupied areas in Manchuria, Taiwan, and the Pescadores to China. This was a considerable success for Chiang Kai-shek.

The Cairo Conference certainly displayed to the world how far China had politically recovered from the devastating setbacks of the nineteenth century. Through its official inclusion among the "Big Four," China was being treated, for the first time in modern history, as a great power.[54] It also claimed for the first time the role of advocate for the colonial world on the international stage. But the disputes and tensions revealed that China still had a long way to go to be viewed as an equal by the other great powers. Despite Chiang's urgent pleas for more help, Britain and the United States were quite content with the status quo, regardless of the burden it placed on China. They would continue to send just enough supplies and support to allow China to make life hard for Japanese forces. Actually helping China defeat Japan was clearly not a priority for the West.

After his departure from Cairo, Chiang Kai-shek stressed China's support for the establishment of an international organization, later called the United Nations (UN), to maintain peace in the postwar period. Shortly after Cairo, he telegraphed President Roosevelt in 1944: "Without the participation of the Asians, the conference [in preparation of the foundation of the UN in Dumbarton Oaks] will be of no relevance to half of mankind."[55] In Dumbarton Oaks, near Washington, DC, in 1944, the Chinese delegate, Wellington Koo (1888–1985), argued vehemently for the inclusion of passages in the UN Charter expressing the principles of universality, equality, and justice. Again, the western states repeatedly rejected such language, preferring to emphasize the absolute nature of state sovereignty. Resistance to Chinese objectives came mainly from Great Britain, but also, to a lesser degree, from the United States. Great Britain feared the boost that the human rights provisions would give to British crown colonies in their struggles for independence. One member of the American delegation even expressed concern about "the consequences such provisions would have for our Negro problem in the South."[56]

As agreed in Cairo, a North Burma campaign was carried out in 1944. The Anglo-American forces set out to retake Burma, which had been occupied by Japan in 1942, with the assistance of some of Chiang Kai-shek's best remaining forces. The campaign on the ground led by Stilwell failed to achieve its objectives, in part due to disagreements between Stilwell and Chiang Kai-shek—although the beginning of 1944 saw some hard-won success against Japan in the Battle of Myitkyina. Chinese resistance gradually increased, with mounting support from the American air force, as the Japanese army suffered attrition thanks to steadily lengthening supply lines and its own decreasing air cover.

It was during this same time that Japan started the final and the largest campaign ever conducted by the Imperial Japanese Army. The Ichigō campaign ran from April 17, 1944, to early February 1945. It attempted to secure a passage through the Chinese heartland to create a continuous land route extending from Pusan, Korea, to Indochina. It also aimed to eliminate airfields in Sichuan and Guangxi that were used by the United States to conduct air raids over Japanese cities. Half a million Japanese soldiers were mobilized, and they fought against seven hundred thousand nationalist soldiers. From April to December 1944, China suffered a string of grave defeats, and the nationalists lost more territory in several provinces, as well as many valuable troops. Increased American bombing of the Japanese home islands caused the Ichigō campaign to be drastically deprioritized; it was halted at the end of 1944 so that as many troops as possible could be redeployed to defend Japan. But by severely weakening the nationalist military and government, the Ichigō campaign had its impact on the ensuing civil war.

The end of the global war in Asia came swiftly and unexpectedly. A single US aircraft dropped an atomic bomb on the Japanese city of Hiroshima on August 6, 1945, the impact of which was equal to approximately twenty thousand metric tons of conventional explosives. Hiroshima was chosen because it was an industrial target that had not been damaged by earlier attacks, which would allow for accurate assessment of the bomb's effectiveness and shatter Japanese morale. Three days later, a similar bomb was dropped on Nagasaki. Nearly two hundred thousand people died in these cities within four days. With the tragedy of Hiroshima and Nagasaki, the final chapter of a cataclysmic war at long last came to its end. On August 15, 1945, Japan capitulated.

Civil War

In the final years of the war, the Second United Front between the CCP and the GMD had existed only on paper. In January 1941, GMD troops attacked and decimated a communist army attempting to establish itself in central China. They also imposed an economic blockade and impeded trade between the border areas and the GMD-controlled regions. From that time on, there was little pretense of unity. Chongqing deployed half a million men to prevent the communists from expanding their border areas in the northwest. Neither the CCP nor the GMD had doubted that civil war would erupt in China after the defeat of the Japanese. Yet when the US attacks of Hiroshima and Nagasaki forced the sudden Japanese surrender in August 1945, both the communists and the nationalist government seemed unprepared to act. Japanese troops were withdrawn from China, Taiwan, and Manchukuo, leaving most military equipment behind.[57]

The Soviet Union concluded a Treaty of Friendship and Alliance with the nationalist government on August 14, 1945. With that treaty, Chiang Kai-shek conceded to virtually all of Stalin's demands regarding Mongolia and the Sino-Soviet border in Manchuria. The secession of Outer Mongolia was China's most substantial territorial loss in the entire twentieth century. The Soviets also systematically shipped industrial equipment from Manchuria to Russia and reasserted their old rights to the Chinese Eastern Railway (a shortcut to the Trans-Siberian Railway connecting the Siberian city of Chita, to the Russian port of Vladivostok that was built between 1897 and 1903). Although the western powers directed Japanese troops in China to surrender to nationalist forces—and Japanese troops tried to comply—the CCP insisted on its right to liberate Japan-held territory. Rejecting Chiang's order to remain in place, they raced eastward and, in Manchuria in particular, were able to arrive in advance of nationalist troops. In those areas where the Soviet Red Army had disarmed the Japanese, Chinese communist forces obtained large amounts of arms and ammunition. It was only a matter of time before the nationalist government and communist troops would clash, as both sides attempted to extend the areas under their control.

Given the crucial role that foreign powers and international assistance had already played in defeating Japan, we should not be surprised that the influence of foreign states continued to be of utmost importance. The Chinese civil war was never purely domestic but had a significant international dimension from the beginning.[58] While the Soviet Union and the United States watched the situation in China carefully, both were ambivalent toward their respective Chinese allies. Neither Moscow nor Washington had a clear plan for coping with the situation in China.

Chiang Kai-shek's relations with the United States had soured during the war and, while he was optimistic, he was also uncertain as to what direction might be taken by the post-Roosevelt leadership in Washington. American attitudes were muddled, partly because China was not a high-priority concern in comparison to Europe, and partly because American officials were sharply divided in their evaluation of the situation in China. Some American leaders were convinced that the Chinese communists were obedient to Moscow, so that their victory would tip the balance in Asia in Stalin's favor. Rather than allow the Soviets to seize control of China, they argued, the United States should continue providing support to Chiang. Others pointed to the evidence of nationalism in the Chinese communist movement and contended that a Maoist China would not necessarily be hostile to the United States—and that Chiang was doomed in any event. They urged the administration not to take sides, to prevent a civil war if possible, and if civil war could not be avoided, to keep the United States out of it.

The Soviet Union, while in principle pledging support to the CCP, was equally conflicted. Stalin was not willing to make sacrifices for the benefit of Mao, whom he referred to as a "cave communist." Like President Harry S. Truman (1884–1972) in the United States, he did not want events in China to undermine his far more pressing national security agenda in Europe. Stalin's uncertainty was reflected in Soviet actions in the months following Japan's surrender. Soviet troops in Manchuria vacillated between arming the Chinese communists and pushing them aside, between being responsive to Chiang's requests and ignoring them. Very early, Mao confessed to party confidants that "Soviet policy cannot be understood."[59]

In summer 1945, Soviet and US policy both aimed at the creation of a coalition government. Deeply suspicious of the United States but also uncertain of Soviet support, Mao welcomed American mediation. The communists were not ready for another war. Even before Japan surrendered, United States officials, with Soviet consent, tried to mediate between the competing parties, hoping to prevent civil war. Once Japan capitulated, the eccentric American ambassador in China, Patrick J. Hurley (1883–1963), was charged to broker a lasting coalition government.[60] The first postwar American effort led to direct talks between Chiang and Mao. Mao Zedong traveled to Chongqing, where he landed on August 27, 1945, and had dinner with Chiang Kai-shek the same evening. It was the first time the two archrivals had met in twenty years. Across a period of six weeks, the two men held many private meetings, often walking in Chiang's garden. Aides ambitiously drafted documents that envisioned a new, democratic China, starting with a national consultative conference to devise the rules for elections to a national assembly. They also proposed that all Chinese armed forces be unified under Chiang's command. On the surface, the meetings had the appearance of going well. The two leaders issued a hopeful joint declaration on October 10, 1945—the national holiday of the Chinese republic—promising "peace, democracy, solidarity and unity." Their troops on the ground, however, pushed on. In November 1945, Chiang launched a major offensive against the communists and all negotiations ended. In late November 1945, Hurley abruptly resigned in frustration.

The GMD government returned to Nanjing in 1946. In the same year, the United States made another attempt to find a peaceful solution. President Truman reaffirmed America's commitment to a "strong, united, and democratic China" and dispatched General George C. Marshall (1880–1959), the well-respected American statesman and principal architect of the American victory in the war against Germany and Japan, to the country. Marshall's mission, which he pursued for virtually all of 1946, was to persuade Chiang and Mao that they should cease hostilities and form a coalition government. Yet midway through the year, his mission's failure became apparent, as Chiang and Mao were both clearly unwilling to set aside their resentments and hostility.[61] Fighting resumed in October 1946. Mao became convinced that the United States was committed to the GMD. An anti-American propaganda campaign was launched that accused the United States of trying to dominate China, and portrayed Chiang Kai-shek as the "running dog" of American imperialism. In response, the United States imposed an arms embargo and sent aid to Chiang after May 1947. Chiang decided to begin an all-out war, and his armies went on the offensive.

A full-scale civil war raged in China from mid-1947 through mid-1949. The Americans and Soviets kept a close eye on each other but neither side intervened militarily. In effect, the two emerging superpowers deterred each other and neither intended to put boots on the ground—as long as the other side remained on the sidelines, as well. The Americans were reassured to see Soviet troops brought home from China. The Soviets would do little to actively support a communist victory in China, and remained apprehensive almost to the end about possible military intervention by the United States. In the context of the emerging Cold War, we can see a characteristic pattern

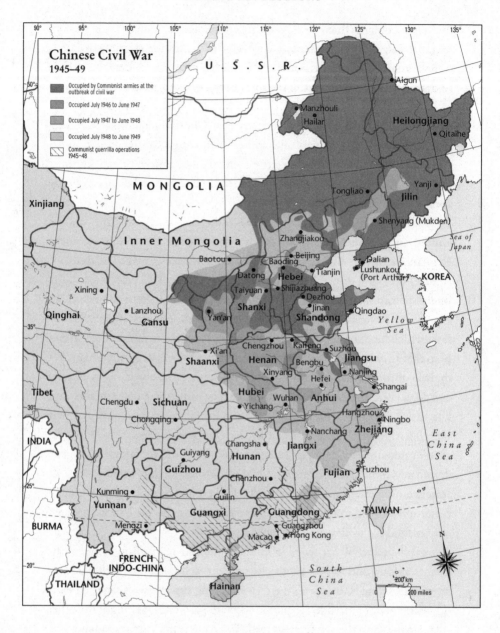

Chinese Civil War
1945–49

- Occupied by Communist armies at the outbreak of civil war
- Occupied July 1946 to June 1947
- Occupied July 1947 to June 1948
- Occupied July 1948 to June 1949
- Communist guerrilla operations 1945–48

for the first time: the United States and the Soviet Union avoiding direct military intervention. Instead, both superpowers armed their trusted agents, satellite countries, and allies to shape the outcome of conflicts in their favor. *proxy war*

Chiang's forces advanced on all fronts until they captured Yan'an itself in March 1947, but the rapid occupation of North China and Manchuria—with American aid, but against American advice—overextended the nationalist army and tied it to cities and railroad lines. Chiang Kai-shek's impatient insistence on ending the conflict with the CCP with a quick military offensive was a costly mistake. Combined with the tactical mistakes made in the decisive Huaihai battles in late 1948, these strategic errors lost the war for the GMD. *too quick + overly ambitious* When the communists counterattacked at the end of 1947, nationalist units were left isolated in the cities. Defections were high. The communists took Tianjin and Beijing in January 1949 and opened a southward offensive in April. Nanjing was taken on April 23, Shanghai on May 27, and Qingdao on June 2. By June the communist army had grown to 1.5 million men while Chiang's shrank to 2.1 million. The Guomindang government fled to Canton, then to Chongqing, then to Chengdu, and finally, in early December 1949, to Taiwan—to which Chiang Kai-shek had already dispatched three hundred thousand troops, much of the military equipment provided by the Americans, the government's entire gold supply, and many of China's greatest art treasures from the forbidden city in Beijing.

In 1949, the US government discussed the possibility of military intervention to come to the rescue of Chiang Kai-shek at the last minute. Foreign secretary Dean Acheson (1893–1971) steadfastly refused. In Europe, the United States worked resolutely for the containment of the Soviet Union. But in Asia, Acheson was convinced that the situation was not comparable. As he wrote in one report:

> It is even questionable whether we have anything to gain from political support of any of the remaining anti-communist public figures in China. They are likely to prove only slightly less impotent than Yugoslav royalists. The only vital political resistance to the Chinese Communists is something that is not yet evident. That force will take time to appear and develop; but inevitably it will, simply because a China under the Communists will breed it just as surely as Chiang's Kuomintang was the forcing ground of the Communists.[62]

But with China falling under communist rule, the United States began covert operations against Mao. The United States soon found itself pursuing a hedging strategy that committed neither to embracing nor to confronting the CCP.

The communist victory in the Chinese civil war was by no means to be expected. At the outset, government troops outnumbered the communists by a ratio of three to one, held a monopoly on airpower, and possessed vastly superior quantities of tanks and heavy artillery. Mao and the CCP leaders proved able military strategists, but they benefited enormously from the severe tactical and strategic mistakes made by Chiang Kai-shek and his generals. They were also aided by the decline in support for the Guomindang regime among the elites and Chinese people. When they reclaimed power over the coastal areas, GMD leaders had pushed aside the businessmen, intellectuals, and civic spokesmen who had stayed on under Japanese rule, accusing them of collaboration. The GMD also antagonized local elites in regions on the periphery, such as Manchuria, southwest China, and Xinjiang, by placing officials from the central government above local administrators. By doing so, the GMD lost the sympathies of those local elites who had supported the nationalist government before the war. Mismanagement, corruption in the army and the government, and record-high inflation chipped away any remaining popular support. When Chiang's troops and officials returned to regions that had been vacated by the Japanese, their arrival was often accompanied by looting and corruption. China's runaway inflation was due principally to the continued fiscal deficit, which the GMD government chose to deal with simply by printing money. That this was originally caused by the Japanese seizure of China's richest provinces in the first year of the war, and exacerbated by eight years of war and three years of civil war, is undeniable. But it is equally true that, in the face of peril, the GMD government did little to stem the inflation. Areas liberated by the communists were better governed, communist troops were better disciplined, and the communists' moderate land-reform programs won broad support in rural areas.

Right up to the very end of GMD rule, there were also other groups with alternative visions of China's future. These included liberal groups, factions of the student movement, regional organizations, secret societies, religious sects, and even factions in the ruling Nationalist Party itself. In particular, it was the Democratic League *(Zhongguo minzhu tongmeng),* reorganized as a party in 1944, which promoted a democratic alternative. It developed a pro-

middle ground b/t CCP + GMO

gram for a third way between capitalism and nationalist government on the one side and the Communist Party on the other. The party platform of the Democratic League formulated the following statement: "We want to unite Soviet economic democracy with Anglo-American political democracy in order to establish a Chinese form of democracy."[63] The Chinese human rights discussion after 1945 also emphasized the close relationship between economic, social, and political rights, as well as collective and individual rights. Zhou Jingwen (1908–1985) advanced the critique that, while political rights were constitutionally anchored in the West, many people were not able to avail themselves of these rights due to economic or social inequalities. From 1944 to 1948, Zhang Junmai (also known as Carsun Chang, 1886–1969) published several essays on the subject of human rights. The Chinese constitution from 1946, which foresaw considerable protection of the basic rights, was drafted by Zhang Junmai.[64] In his writings, he argued with conviction that the idea of human rights was the result of a historical interaction, an intercultural exchange between China and Europe. For this reason, he argued, the political philosophy of Confucianism was not only compatible with the idea of human rights in every regard, but had historically enriched it. Zhang Junmai perceived human rights to be the result of a complex transfer between western and eastern ways of thinking, whereby the cultural transfer did not harm the idea, but rather led to its improvement and maturation. While they lacked foreign support and any real political influence, the groups invested in democracy and human rights offered an eloquent alternative during the civil war.

❖ ❖ ❖

Born out of a deep sense of crisis, collapse, and scorn, China's first half of the twentieth century was marked by a profound and desperate longing for a clean slate, a new beginning, and a collective rejuvenation. All of its governments, even its warlords, aspired to revolutionary change of some kind. Numerous texts explored possible paths to revolution and branded those who rejected revolution as "counterrevolutionaries." Art and literature intended to transmit revolution. Businesses were selling national products for the sake of national revolution. To be sure, "revolution," an ambivalent and vague term, can mean different things to different people. The longing for revolution therefore inevitably led to tensions between different revolutionary approaches. Debates within Chinese society about the correct revolutionary path deepened political divisions and tore the social body apart, even in the face of outside threat. The revolutions in this period have often been described as failed or aborted. Certainly, the revolutionary drives fell short of their goals; they did not even come close to their lofty aspirations. The nationalist republic remained a fleeting vision while the first cultural revolution promoted by the May Fourth intellectuals never connected with a broader audience. The communist revolution was closer to the brink of destruction than to victory most of the time. China's revolutions generally seem to have been better at destroying the old than creating the new. Confucian academies disappeared, temples were closed, customs were abolished, elites were attacked, and centuries-old ideas were disparaged. Yet, those revolutionary projects, even when they failed to achieve their goals, often initiated profound transformations of Chinese society. A host of new institutions were introduced and tested, new social practices took hold in society, new technologies were embraced, working conditions changed, new patterns of mobility and everyday living were set. Changes were most pronounced in urban areas, but they also extended deep into the rural hinterlands. Steamships, highways, and railways crisscrossing the country brought new techniques and opportunities but also new challenges and risks. Dependency on markets increased, and global currency fluctuations came to influence rural living standards. Never before had Chinese society undergone such a flurry of different changes in such a short time—and often, those changes went in detrimental and very different directions.

Apart from revolution, war was another significant current in this period. In the first half of the twentieth century, China was almost continuously at war against internal or external enemies. The consequences were grave. Up to twenty million deaths were caused by the fighting between Japanese and Chinese troops, the mistreatment of prisoners of war, and the casualties suffered by civilian populations. Millions also died due to failures to maintain infrastructure and negligence in preventing and responding to floods and other disasters. Famines and natural disasters were widespread and frequent from the late 1920s to the late 1940s. For almost three decades of continuous and brutal warfare, total casualties of the Chinese population may have been as high as forty million. Equally devastating was the destruction of infrastructure, industries, and buildings, and the debilitating effects on the Chinese body politic. These wars, however, also showed how far China had come by mid-century. Decades of military buildup, military recruitment and training, and the spread of martial values and attitudes had made China significantly stronger in military terms and more capable of defending itself. In 1900, the country's debilitated military lost nearly every battle, but forty-five years later, it had managed to tie down one of the most formidable and efficient military machines in the world in a grinding, protracted war of resistance. In 1949, China was a scarred, but battle-hardened country.

The third overarching trajectory was the growth and spread of nationalism. In his study of how republican China developed into an independent sovereign state, John Fitzgerald characterizes the immediate period after 1911 as a time when China was at once "stateless" and "nationless," in the sense that, although the nation-state concept certainly existed in the minds of the Chinese elites, the form of neither the state nor the nation had been determined or fixed.[65] In this respect, the republican period saw profound changes. It created a clearer sense of national identity. The nation was formed in the context of national defense and state-building. It took shape as a consistent effort of the state mobilizing against foreign incursion. This process of representation or nation-defining, embedded in state-building, made "China" as a concept meaningful, tangible, and personal. Territorial division and occupation by foreign powers also invigorated a territorial notion of China that spanned the whole of the country's landmass. China, perhaps for the first time in its history, mobilized for international war as a country united behind the notion of nationalism. Most importantly, this was a main factor in avoiding military collapse—which, especially at the beginning of the war, had looked like a real possibility. The idea of China itself, however, did not cease to be contested, as the various state-making projects defined and represented the nation differently. The Chinese nation was created and re-created in the struggle between two highly competitive state-building parties over the content of the nation and the form of the state that would represent it.

The period saw a tremendous amount of institutional rebuilding and experimentation, although most governments were short-lived and their institutional reforms were fragmented and incomplete. The Beiyang and warlord governments established military dictatorships mostly built on existing traditional institutions, with some limited innovations in education or the military. The warlord regimes were as a rule exclusive and extractive, monopolizing power and wealth in their own hands. The GMD built an authoritarian one-party state in Nanjing and Chongqing. Its institutions were designed to control society and economy through an efficient bureaucracy reporting to the party leadership. It was a top-down system that extracted resources for state-building. It was less exclusive than the warlord regimes, but still prioritized state and party interests over private interests, and hence over disadvantaged groups and forces not connected to the party-state. The CCP in Yan'an established a different version of a one-party state: one that built on carefully managed and cultivated grassroots mobilizations. Discipline was achieved through control of public discourse and punitive campaigns. Moderate social reform benefiting the rural society in some ways made Yan'an more economically inclusive. Still, requisition of resources was a main goal. Finally, the regimes of collaboration in Manchukuo and other parts of China presented yet another institutional order. These satellite or puppet states were driven by external interests. Development and industrialization were pushed forward, but with the purposes of supplying Japan's war needs. The institutions were highly extractive and exclusive. Although the period left behind a bewildering institutional puzzle, in which the various pieces did not really fit together, all areas and regions had in common that they were ruled by narrow elites that organized society for their own goals and at the expense of most Chinese people. Political power was narrowly concentrated, and mainly used to create wealth and military strength for those who possessed it. Economic institutions were extractive because they were designed to be; they were mainly built to extract incomes and wealth from the majority of the population to benefit those in power.

In this fractured environment shaped by revolution making, war, and nationalism, the purpose and makeup of China's government institutions underwent an important, general change that characterized all regions and orders. In this period, a rather clear-cut development toward a strengthening of the state can be seen. For different administrations, starting with the warlords and ending with the GMD, increasing control over society and economy became a prerequisite for maintaining independence and pursuing economic development. This trend started long before the war but gained significant momentum across years of resisting Japan. This period also saw repeated efforts of mass mobilization in different regions by various governments. The horrors of war and displacement reinforced, in the minds of government officials, a deep fear of disorder, which caused them to build and expand impressive agencies for enforcing internal security. One can detect, above all, the steady and unrelenting rise of the power of the security state and its ever expanding capacity to intervene in the formation of the modern Chinese society. The expanding state was able to muster the service of whole generations of intelligence and law enforcement agents while also claiming their allegiance. The wartime regimes were keen to create powerful government agencies that extended a pervasive capillary network of control throughout society. Fully empowered clusters of secret police, law enforcement, and intelligence agencies emerged, with the capacity to deal with a large number of deviants and opponents. This concentration of power was interconnected with the other key activities the state took up as areas of concern, including the central registration of citizens, the extraction of resources through central taxation systems, patriotic education, social memory construction through school curricula and sponsored public memorials, and national identity propagation.

National economic development became a main priority of the government, one it would ultimately take seriously enough to regulate, control, and even nationalize (during the war) almost all industry. The plan for economic development was simple: develop industry by government and obtain the necessary resources for this by taxing agriculture at high rates. The private sphere of economic life was correspondingly restricted.[66] Of course, in this period the governments had only very partial success in implementing their economic controls and development plans. In the end, these may have remained, as Julia Strauss has argued, "strong institutions in a weak polity."[67] Neither the nationalists nor the communists were in a position to impose their vision of economic or political life on the wider population until after the war. Only then were they able to do so in the parts of the country they firmly controlled. As they demanded a greater degree of control and called for ever greater sacrifices from citizens for the collective good, the wartime regimes also had to demonstrate that they would provide aid when citizens suffered poverty and misfortune. A new compact between state and society was forged in which new ideas of social provision of goods and services played an important role. Despite some successful efforts in this direction, however, the Chinese governments mostly failed to honor their end of the pact. They ended up demanding much but providing little. During the entire republican period, nongovernment institutions and international relief organizations such as the United Nations Relief and Rehabilitation Administration, the Red Cross, and the Buddhist-inspired Red Swastika provided the main support for a population stricken by war and disaster.

Despite all the violence and destruction, the period also saw tremendous social and cultural changes. Chinese society became more diverse, more complex, more mobile, and more global. New social groups such as urban middle classes and professionals emerged, demanding participation and recognition. Between the May Fourth movement and other visions and historical currents, there were many hot debates in this period over what was or could be *modern* in China—debates which themselves demonstrated the plurality of Chinese modernity. The May Fourth movement (or New Culture movement), with its emphasis on education and individual autonomy, was followed by other cultural agendas that became increasingly utopian and radical, as politics became more cynical and polarized. Modernity is a complex and multivocal process. There were many visions of the modern—some iconoclastic and political, some secular and profane, some driven by intellectuals, some driven by consumers. The emphasis on agency and diversity is essential to understand the Chinese reinvention of tradition in a context of global modernity. It shifts the perspective away from evaluating the accuracy of China's borrowing from the West, which is the conventional approach (even when it includes a recognition of a unique Chinese perspective on western ideas), to instead exploring how traditional and new ideas were reinvented and redeployed in the Chinese quest to be part of the modern world.

The wars and revolutions also marginalized those who were hoping for a more tolerant and inclusive style of government. Any form of democracy was seen as possible only outside the corrupt institutions of party politics. The history of this period has often been portrayed as a struggle between autocratic state institutions on the one hand and popular movements demanding democracy on the other. As David Strand argues, such a dichotomy fails to capture the significance of civic life in republican China, where the meanings of citizenship, patriotism, rights, and justice were debated and negotiated, even amid institutional failure and Leninist party regimes.[68] Growing governance problems related to weakness, corruption, and repression constantly led to greater calls for active leadership and citizenship. The calls for political participation never resulted in institutional change, however. The biggest predicament of the republican period concerned political institutions, which remained exclusive and monopolized by those in power. The utopian vision of "new citizens" or a "new culture" never affected reality in the political system. The republican period was a time of great intellectual liberty and artistic creativity, but centered on a republic nobody believed in, a political system whose republican institutions no one was able or willing to invest in.[69] Critical Chinese intellectuals developed a deep mistrust of political institutions. The Chinese republic failed in ways that permitted some of its core values and practices to survive only as lofty intentions and future ambitions. Moreover, the desperate desire to shake off the historic yoke of feudalism and imperialism necessarily highlighted the view of "national salvation" (*jiuguo*) at the expense of political reform and left it to state agencies to shape political norms and processes. On the whole, reform of political institutions was often seen as both hopeless and useless.

In 1911, China had been at the forefront of a century of global change, renewal, and revolution. It not only became Asia's first national republic but in fact was one of the first continental empires to reinvent itself as a republic and to adopt the political form of a nation-state. Subsequently, while European empires destroyed each other during the First World War, China witnessed the first golden age of Chinese capitalism and made Shanghai the cosmopolitan center of Asia and the world. China also set out to create a dynamic system of higher education—one that would train the scientists and technocrats of later generations. It strengthened its army, rebuilt institutions, mobilized and disciplined its citizens, and successfully defended the country. At the same time, there was a striking absence of even minimal consensus on the nature of the Chinese constitutional political order. The divide between an institutional apparatus that seemed less and less amenable to popular participation and political movements gathering momentum outside the institutions impeded the establishment of a legitimate constitutional system that could claim popular support. That divide would yield the unresolved legacy of the Chinese revolutions of the first half of the twentieth century.

PART THREE

Remaking China

October 1, 1949, was a mild, sunny autumn day in Beijing. For days, the inner city had been cordoned off, busy preparing the large public ceremony for the proclamation of a new Chinese state, the People's Republic of China (PRC). Since 5:00 AM, a large crowd had been steadily gathering, and at 10:00 AM sharp, party leaders appeared on a podium overlooking Tiananmen Square. The physician Li Zhisui (1919–1995) stood next to Mao Zedong, who addressed the large audience. Later, in his memoirs, Li would recall:

> Mao's voice was soft, almost lilting, and the effect of his speech was riveting. "The Chinese people have stood up," he proclaimed, and the crowd went wild, thundering in applause, shouting over and over, "Long Live the People's Republic of China!" "Long Live the Chinese Communist Party!" I was so full of joy my heart nearly burst out of my throat, and tears welled up in my eyes. I was so proud of China, so full of hope, so happy that the exploitation and suffering, the aggression from foreigners, would be gone forever. I had no doubt that Mao was the great leader of the revolution, the maker of a new Chinese history.[1]

Like Li Zhisui, many contemporaries believed a new era was dawning that would be defined, simply, by all things being made new. A "New China" *(Xin Zhongguo)* was about to be born, thoroughly remade by the elimination of exploitation, inequality, war, and other ills of the past. It would feature a new society without classes, a new culture for the common people, and a new wave of development that would benefit all sections of Chinese society. As new practices were promoted, an enthusiasm for everything "new" would be carefully cultivated. A new calendar would be introduced and new international alliances would be shaped. Ambitious state initiatives would reconfigure business ownership, landholding, marriage, the organization of work and daily life, and the very under-standing of one's self, one's community, and one's past. This yearning for renewal was perhaps not in itself new; it could be traced to the beginning of the twentieth century, and above all to the May Fourth movement. But never before in China had there been initiatives so vigorously and deci-sively backed by the state and by popular support. A population worn out by war and destruction longed for a reset.

By the time of Mao's death, three decades later, hopes for renewal would be deeply shattered. The Cultural Revolution was the story of ef-forts to create a new China ending dramatically in chaos, internal strife, confusion, isolation, and destruction. The history of the first three decades of the PRC is, then, a history of aspirations and betrayals, of new begin-nings and hard landings, of experimentation and failure. Periods of construction were followed by phases of destruction. Ambitions and confidence, tempered by deep-seated anxieties, led to frequent policy changes, often involving violent and painful leadership struggles, policy reconfigurations, and system crises.

Like other communist parties, the CCP chose not to call its system and society *communist* but rather to use the word *socialist*. For the party, communism was to be a later stage in the development of Chinese so-ciety—the ultimate stage, when the institutions of the state would have "withered away." Communism was an ideal condition in which the Chi-nese people would not only enjoy material abundance, but also live in a perfect society that was democratic, harmonious, self-administering, and free of social classes, exploitation, and war. It was also a rational system, which would come about through the laws of historical development. Socialism was a transitionary phase on the way to that utopia. In this phase, the Communist Party as a vanguard held a monopoly on power over society and governed through a new institutional order described as democratic centralism. This meant that the central apparatus of the Com-munist Party and the state made the final decisions after consulting with various groups in society. Through that new institutional system, the party was able to exercise firm and at times harsh discipline over party members—especially leaders, called "cadres"—and over the cultural and intellectual activities of society at large. It also established state ownership of the economy and subordinated all economic organizations to the control and planning of the party-state.

By adopting a socialist system, China also became part of the international network of socialist states in Eastern Europe. Intensive cooperation emerged. Global connections and contexts reached deeper into Chinese society than ever before. Apart from the sharing of knowledge and technology, there was the particularly important need to comprehensively transmit a whole set of new institutional blueprints. Remaking China specifically implied an ambitious and broad program of transferal and establishment of new rules and organizations. After 1949, this was occurring in almost all social sectors, from the government to the social order, economy, and public culture.

Decisions and policies in the Mao era were broadly informed by the goals of communism and shaped by transfers from the Soviet Union, but building socialism did not take place in a historical vacuum. Although the revolution aimed for wholesale reconfiguration of the political and social landscape and full attainment of communism, the CCP knew from its experiences in the border areas that to reach this goal it would have to engage society and the Chinese people. While generally following the model and leadership of the Russian Revolution, the leaders of the CCP were nonetheless convinced that Soviet models had to be adapted and altered to fit the specific conditions in China, to garner widespread popular support.

Building on pre-1949 practices, society and economy in the PRC were reorganized in a unique way. Directives from the top echelons of the party reverberated through the large circuits of the bureaucratic state and into a dense network of social organizations at the grassroots level. The need for such a system was recognized in the 1950s and resulted in the creation of a whole range of new institutions, introducing the party-state, economic planning, state and party control over the cultural sector, social classification, and much grassroots organization of society. The history of the Mao era cannot be told without reference to these distinctive institutions.

The chapters in this part of *Making China Modern* explore the nature of the early People's Republic and the CCP's attempt to "remake" China's society into a socialist one on a path to communism. Under Mao Zedong, the ruthless pursuit of state prerogatives already underway in republican China was continued and augmented. The massive infrastructure that became the PRC's government apparatus was created, shifting the balance of center versus local interests firmly toward the central state. As it reconfigured physical space, staged public celebrations, and redesigned literature and arts, all came to be fundamentally transformed by CCP initiatives.

There was considerable achievement at the beginning of the 1950s. The new state invested in infrastructure, education, and health care. A vast government apparatus was created. But the outcomes of transformative policies such as land reforms and nationalization of industries were often far less clear. The hierarchical and centralized system of the party-state and the fluid grassroots campaigns were sources of strength, but at the same time rife with ambiguities and vulnerabilities. Implementing policies based on the new institutions proved to be much more challenging and difficult than the planners had expected. Many policies were sidetracked, compromised, or distorted, and some backfired. The problems, however, only spurred the party to renew and increase its efforts.

The escalating efforts to remake China led to two radically ambitious, nationwide campaigns of rapid transformation: the Great Leap Forward and the Cultural Revolution. Both claimed to reinvigorate the push to remake China and propel it into a new era, but in reality, both inflicted massive destruction and loss, upending many of the achievements of the early 1950s. The Great Leap Forward (1958–1960) was a policy to accelerate the transition to communism, formulated by Mao as he watched protests against communist rule erupt in Eastern Europe, conflicts with the Soviet Union increase, and an economic crisis reach a simmering point in China. He pressured the government to orchestrate a mass mobilization of workers and peasants with the goal of making a great leap in production and output. The Great Leap was not able to achieve its goals; to the contrary, it worsened the crises and was at least partially responsible for the 1959–1961 famine in which millions of people in the countryside perished. The Great Leap also caused the Sino-Soviet split of 1960, resulting in international isolation, so that China could no longer rely on outside help. A readjustment at the beginning of the 1960s rolled back many of the policies and sidelined Mao, who was blamed for the economic disaster.

economic disaster

Pushing back, Mao turned directly to the urban youth in 1966. Bypassing the party, he called upon the Red Guards to rise up against the party-state and eliminate the revisionism that he claimed had spread through the party and society. This call to arms jolted all major institutions in Chinese society, many of which ceased to operate after they were attacked by the Red Guards. What has become known as the Cultural Revolution decade (1966–1976) saw intense political struggles throughout society. Many were injured or killed by its violence. Top leaders, consumed by rivalries, constantly jockeyed for power. When Mao Zedong died in 1976, the utopia of communism seemed as distant as in 1949. The country's energies were sapped by decades of campaigns and struggles, and its hopes deeply disappointed by promises unkept and visions unrealized.

failure of CCP + Mao

SEVEN

Socialist Transformation

1949–1955

After the party achieved military control over mainland China in 1949 and 1950, it gradually moved toward civilian rule. During the early 1950s, the new power was, above all, busy establishing new institutions to transform China into a socialist country. This happened through several initiatives carried out in parallel. China entered an alliance with the Soviet Union in 1950 and, only a year after the end of the civil war, mobilized troops again for military intervention in the Korean War (1950–1953) in support of its new North Korean allies. This costly and brutal war, about which leaders were initially very ambivalent, forced the government to speed up the consolidation of its rule over China. At the end of 1950, nationwide mass campaigns were initiated to target domestic opposition and leftovers from the previous government. At the same time, a new administration was built and, in the rural areas, land reform was carried out. The media and publishing sector was brought under party control. Taken together, these processes succeeded in establishing new socialist institutions that intended to remake economic relations, daily life, and social practices throughout the country in the first years of the PRC.

Regime Change

The CCP was not carried to victory by a popular mass movement. Its triumph was realized on the battlefield, as the result of more than two decades of military perseverance against various enemies—and its victory could be achieved only by abandoning some of the original aims and core values of the communist revolution. During the 1940s, Mao and his party had scaled back policies aiming at radical transformation. Instead of striving for private property abolition, collectivization, dictatorship of the Communist

Party, and strict centralized planning, the CCP in Yan'an had called for a New Democracy, in which the CCP would cooperate with other political forces and refrain from instituting radical change. The party had also started to embrace nationalism, and advocated a united front to defend China against Japanese aggression. All of this meant that the goal of radical social transformation receded into the background, and national unification and resistance rose to the top of the CCP's agenda. Therefore, the party that came to power in 1949 was rather pragmatic and had not, in the preceding years, displayed much interest in seriously transformative policies.

We should not wonder, then, that the Soviet Union's leadership started to doubt the CCP's commitment to the cause of communism. In December 1949, Stalin called Chinese communism "nationalistic" and accused Mao of being "inclined toward nationalism."[1] Stalin recognized the new government only hesitatingly. As early as 1948, he made a prediction: "After victory, the Chinese government will be a national revolutionary and democratic government rather than a communist one."[2]

Doubts about popular acceptance also drove Stalin's and the Soviet advisers' constant urgings that the CCP should enter a coalition government with the smaller democratic parties in China, and work within existing political structures and institutions. The CCP's victory had been gained through the rapid disintegration of the GMD forces, as well as by assistance from the Soviet Union. By the time the PRC was established in October 1949, there were 4.5 million party members, the core of a new regime that was to rule a nation of 541 million citizens.[3] Whatever sympathies it might have enjoyed among certain groups in the population, on the eve of the victory the CCP did not have widespread support or acceptance.[4] A fundamental lack of legitimacy marked the rule of the CCP from the very beginning. To work smoothly and in a stable and confident way, a government needs popular consensus, generalized social acceptability, and credibility. Based on reports from that time, the majority of the population seems to have viewed the CCP with little more than curiosity.[5] Perhaps among urban workers, college students, and liberal intellectuals there was support of the CCP, but those groups made up only a very small portion of the population. Forcing the Chiang Kai-shek government into exile in Taiwan did not make China communist. In the mid-twentieth century, China faced tremendous problems as a country that was not only huge but also very diverse. The prospects for a smooth tran-

sition to communism were slim. By defeating the GMD government on th
battlefield, the CCP only brought upon itself a much bigger challenge: the
need to govern China and its border territories. There were still an estimated
two million armed men (and possibly women) throughout the country not
connected to either the CCP or the Red Army. The rural economy had been
ruined by war and the destruction of infrastructure. The urban economy suffered from rampant inflation and from insufficient supplies of food and
building materials. Large segments of the population were displaced. And a
new administration had to be created.

From 1949 to 1951, the mainland was effectively under martial law. During
the first two years, Military Control Commissions (*Junguan hui*) governed
China. Military officers and military political commissars were in charge of
pacification in most provinces, which was seen as temporary from the beginning. China was divided into six large regions, excluding Inner Mongolia and
Tibet, which were administered separately. Four of these regions—the central south, eastern China, the northwest, and the southwest—were run by
military-administrative committees, whereas northern China and the northeast were already given civilian people's governments in light of their successful conclusion of military consolidation.

Top priority was assigned to taking over the cities, given their economic
and political significance. The CCP followed a three-part strategy to accomplish this. First, organs of GMD political power—government departments
and offices, the police, the military, taxation bureaus, and the like—were to be
stripped of power, disbanded, and replaced by new CCP-led organs. Second,
economic units such as factories, shops, electricity plants, transport companies,
and so forth were to be maintained in their existing form, so that production
could be restored as rapidly as possible. Third, a new social order had to be
established and strengthened.[6]

There was no avoiding the fact that transition to full CCP control would
involve much conflict; many negotiations and numerous compromises had
to happen among the various political, market, and intellectual actors. Prior
to the takeover, political cadres were schooled by the CCP for that purpose.
When they arrived in any given city, they were well informed and knew what
to do. Their general goals were to achieve pacification, disarmament, and de-
mobilization, and in their immediate measures, the objective was to rapidly
target the most obvious holdover problems from the chaos that had preceded

the regime change, such as scattered soldiers, refugees, displaced persons, and homeless beggars. Right from the start, these efforts encountered a problem the CCP had not foreseen. Taming the urban chaos required not only repairing the devastating damage of the civil war, but also managing the expectations of poor and disadvantaged social groups for revolutionary justice and social compensation. The poor among the urban population had readily embraced the CCP's call to *fanshen* (to turn around, or to revolt), interpreting this slogan to mean that they were just as entitled to food and money as richer urban residents. Sometimes, zealous street-level cadres actively encouraged the penniless to demand immediate social justice, and allied with the poor against their more well-to-do neighbors.[7] Emboldened by revolutionary rhetoric and a change in power, the urban poor, beggars, and displaced people from the countryside began to use increasingly aggressive tactics to exact food or money from the wealthy, ranging from standing in front of stores and businesses, playing loud instruments, and preventing customers from entering, to smearing feces on storefronts, smashing windows, and even pulling knives on shopkeepers who did not offer handouts. Such actions disrupted businesses and forced many store owners to close down, hampering the recovery of the urban economy. The new municipal leaders often could only watch helplessly as their efforts to achieve stability and promote economic development were repeatedly undone. Tensions intensified as urban economies continued to deteriorate.

Ensuring a smooth takeover meant confronting these incipient problems in Tianjin and other North China cities already under CCP control. To that end, Liu Shaoqi (1898–1969) was dispatched to Tianjin in late April 1949 to investigate the situation and devise a strategy.[8] Liu Shaoqi had been in Moscow as a student in 1921 and a supporter of the rectification movement in Yan'an. Since then, he had served as the CCP's second in command. Perceiving that, at least for the time being, it would be impossible to pursue social revolution while also maintaining production, his conclusion was that the party had to greatly narrow the scope of revolution. He also suggested that the communists cooperate with former government clerks, local businesspeople, and technical specialists to ensure the uninterrupted provision of public services. His approach undercut the more radical ideas advocated by local cadres, who often came from poorer areas in the countryside. Liu Shaoqi also argued for strengthening the role of state organs, such as the Public Security Bureau. To prevent a political mobilization that could not be controlled from above, Liu wanted to postpone the goal of social transformation. Subsequently, the CCP started to steer a rather pragmatic course in implementing its new policies.

To deal with the challenges of the takeover, the CCP had to develop a specific approach to governance in the first years of its rule, up until 1953. The communists' adjusted strategy was to cooperate with existing structures and institutions and, at the same time, to organize and control at the grassroots level, calling on the "masses" to participate actively. This policy allowed the party to develop a specific form of governance. It conceived of governing the cities as a process of change, conflict management, continual experimentation, and ad hoc adjustment. The party encouraged local grassroots initiatives within a framework of centralized bureaucratic authority. At the same time, centralization was relentlessly pursued at the expense of local powerholders.

Experimentation had been a core feature of the Maoist approach to policy making since the revolution in the 1930s and 1940s.[9] Having learned from its experiences, the party gradually inserted itself into the traditional social and economic structures, and transformed those only progressively, at opportune moments, for specific reasons, and at an uneven pace in different parts of China. The party relied on experimentation, first testing policies in a few selected counties before implementing them nationwide. Even the land reform programs were carried out on this basis, since they were designed to identify and act on the needs of the majority of distressed farmers. Rural communist cells built on existing village communities, their work and debt cooperatives, and even the cults attached to religious shrines. In commercialized urban environments, communist organizers worked with market and transport organizations, first promoting the profitability of products, then attempting to shift the attention of merchants toward improving relations between producers and consumers.

With its greater flexibility and pragmatism, the new strategy worked well. In the cities, the new authorities were quickly able to restore order. There were many urgent tasks. Cadres were charged to enforce traffic regulations, control street vendors, and deal with petty crimes. To accomplish these goals, the CCP maintained a dual emphasis on propaganda work and the voluntary organization of supportive individuals at a grassroots level. To control street vendors, for example, the party encouraged peddlers, shop owners, and pedicab drivers to join local street associations. All peddlers were required to register for permits. Local vendors were also persuaded to meet and review their local situation periodically. The total number of peddlers was reduced and plans were initiated and implemented to regulate and lower the number of illegal kiosks on city sidewalks.

There were two substantially larger groups that the party had to deal with when taking over city governments: Refugees and beggars represented a more complicated problem. Keen to deal with the beggars first, the CCP called upon public security forces in each district to enforce the ban on begging by detaining any beggars they found. Since some cadres were initially hesitant to detain destitute parts of the population who had long been portrayed as natural allies of the party, an internal effort of "ideological mobilization" (si-xiang dongyuan) was first carried out, consisting of an extensive program of meetings involving all cadres. The first real roundups of beggars took place as part of the "winter relief program," designed for repatriation of refugees. Beggars were first taken to temporary "beggars' detention centers" spread out across the cities. There, they would be registered and investigated, and decisions would be made as to whether individuals should be transferred to custody centers in nursery schools, training units, relief homes run by private charity organizations, or elsewhere.

The official ban and roundups made begging in the cities suddenly risky and difficult. People who had relied on begging now readily went to the beggars' centers because they could get food and rest there. Others came in reluctantly, under coercion and fearful of being sent either to fight in Taiwan or to perform reclamation work in the northeast. Within a few weeks, most beggars had been cleared off the streets. In the centers, the detainees received education in the following topics: "1) to labor is honorable, to be a parasite is shameful; 2) in order to *fanshen,* beggars must labor; 3) the origins of begging; 4) the difference between the CCP and GMD on attitudes toward beggars."[10] Detainees who were able to work were sent off to join work teams assigned to cultivate barren land and clear debris from streets, canals, and riverbeds. Many city dwellers praised these and similar campaigns. When reformed beggars performed songs in the streets, local residents were reportedly astonished at the success of CCP policies. Shopkeepers greeted the beggars with cigarettes and candy. Some business owners noted a contrast with the GMD's prior ineffectiveness and commented that "the old society turned people into beggars, while the new society is turning beggars into productive people."[11]

The refugee problem was even thornier. For the party, the key to handling the refugee crisis was to raise awareness and persuade urban populations to share the burden. Those living in cities had to recognize that they were not economically separated from the surrounding hinterlands and that they should help pay for the cost of transporting refugees to the countryside, where they could engage in productive activities. They also had to accept some measure of responsibility for financing public works projects in the cities and the suburbs for refugees who could not be assured of productive labor back in their own hometowns.

Despite the delivery of help and relief, refugees continued to pour into the cities. The summer rains in 1949 caused widespread flooding and destroyed crops in northern Jiangsu, northern Anhui, and central Shandong, disrupting village communities and sending crowds into the cities. Refugees who had been repatriated previously often returned to cities in desperation. In response, the authorities called for the forced repatriation of all the "landlords and rich peasants," drifting "parasitic disaster victims," and "suspected enemy agents" entering the city.

Once the CCP had restored basic order, it started surveying the existing landscape of organizations and social groups. For instance, a "Comprehensive Report on the Investigation of Charity Organizations in Tianjin" categorized each of the city's relief organizations according to their role and social backing and divided them into four categories: institutions conducive to people's welfare, relief institutions with feudal characteristics, purely reactionary feudal and superstitious institutions, and charities that promoted religious propaganda. The report concluded: "Relief organizations of the ruling class are inherently reactionary and hypocritical, but some elements of their work and departments, if taken over and transformed by us, can be used for the people's welfare, while the reactionary, backward, superstitious and socially detrimental elements must be abolished completely. Our policy neither means total abolishment nor unprincipled preservation without differentiation. We follow a case-by-case principle."[12] The reform and dismantling of organizations followed a differentiated and gradual approach. Associations or organizations that were deemed to benefit the people, such as schools, orphanages, and homes for the elderly and disabled, were to be retained. The government would guide such organizations and gradually transform them. By contrast, *huidaomen* (superstitious sects) and secret societies in the business of "disseminating feudal, superstitious ideas" and "persistently carrying out counterrevolutionary activities" were to be dissolved without exception. The CCP was determined to suppress urban secret societies, which "thrived on the needs of people living beyond the reach of the government in the lowest strata of society." Together with various "quasi-religious societies," these secret societies had come to encompass around 40 percent of Tianjin's adult population.[13] Similar conditions existed in other Chinese cities, as well.

Most foreign organizations likewise had to cease operations and leave the country. Any organization or business under partial foreign ownership was hit with a large fine, and continued to be fined until its ties to foreign owners were terminated. Some foreign-owned charities and enterprises were confiscated outright, or accused of wartime collaboration with the Japanese and seized on that basis. The vast majority of foreigners left China voluntarily, and the rest were deported in 1950–1951.[14]

In the sensitive area of publishing, a similar policy was followed. CCP policies distinguished between those periodicals and enterprises that had been GMD-controlled and those that had not.[15] Formerly GMD-controlled tabloids faced takeover or termination. Regarding non-GMD-controlled periodicals, the policy was to investigate and deal with them on a case-by-case basis. Within a short period of time, many periodicals shut down—but a few remained and were allowed to stay in operation. The CCP needed to keep some papers in business, given its goals for outreach to urban populations. Information and new content could be delivered through them to groups that were otherwise difficult to reach. At the same time, new papers were founded under CCP control.

Similar approaches were also taken toward the numerous occupational and professional associations that combined to exercise considerable influence in urban society. Workers were heralded in official pronouncements as "masters of the country" (*guojia de zhuren*) and the "leading class" (*lingdao jieji*) that should rightfully "take charge" (*dangjia zuozhu*).[16] Trade union organizations were established in urban factories immediately following their takeover by CCP authorities. Under the provisions of New Democracy, the trade unions enjoyed considerable prestige and influence (for a time) as official representatives of the working class. They were even permitted to set up their own armed patrols to guard factory grounds and carry out inspections. In June 1950, the All-China Federation of Trade Unions subsumed the many independent trade unions. But there were also many workers not affiliated with unions, including rickshaw pullers, drivers of tricycles (used for transport of heavy items), night soil collectors, and practitioners of more respectable trades such as doctors, merchants, and lawyers. These groups, too, needed to be reeducated, organized, and categorized. This also raised questions of how to deal with existing trades and occupations when they escaped clear social categorizations based on Marxist theory. Few occupations in urban China could clearly be categorized as *proletarian*. Nonetheless, drivers of tricycles, the most important means of transportation in the cities, were categorized as workers and organized accordingly.

The new authorities found new ways to curb traditional vices by forcibly reeducating prostitutes, gamblers, and drug addicts to become productive members of society.[17] As a top concern, the CCP was committed to fighting that social scourge and long symbol of Chinese colonial humiliation, opium smoking. Here, too, the first step was to sort the people involved into categories—wholesale opium dealers, street-level dealers, owners of opium dens, and addicts—so they could be dealt with differently. Big opium dealers were summarily executed; smaller dealers were arrested and reeducated. Addicts, like prostitutes, were delivered to custody centers where they could be treated for medical problems and reeducated through work to become productive members of the new society. Within two years, opium had been stamped out, and prostitution had been drastically curbed.

Heavy-handed tactics were used to address urban criminality. After 1949, police had unfettered power to detain and convict criminals. They rounded up petty thieves, pimps, opium dealers, and vagrants, many of whom were subjected to "noncriminal" reform measures. The new government was also keen to tackle the problem of speculation and market manipulation by financial capitalists and fraudsters. It worked vigorously to stamp out currency fraud, especially in the form of counterfeiting.

In short, the new government's takeover in 1949 and 1950, especially of the cities, displayed a relatively high degree of planning, intensive preparation, and systematic execution. In general, the party favored gradual changes and nuanced responses over drastic and sudden interventions, but it was able to act decisively when its hold on power was at stake. It surveyed existing institutions, organizations, and associations in urban China, and used its categorizations of them to decide which it would work with to provide essential services to the population, and which were hostile and had to be closed. Its policies aimed at popular mobilization, but also emphasized popular participation and voluntary involvement. Extensive investments in education and propaganda accompanied the takeover. These policies, all in all, were effective and successful. Order in most cities was restored quickly, and open resistance against the new regime was minimal and short-lived. Still, there were risks in leaving many earlier structures and organizations intact. Soon enough, some of them came to be seen as potential challenges to the new government.

Governing China

In a country where the central government had been disintegrating since the late nineteenth century, political centralization and national independence were general hopes of the population. Building on developments of the republican era, the new state was designed as a modern nation-state. It penetrated society far more deeply, however, as its bureaucratic apparatus reached into even the most remote villages. This new state was thus able to wield far greater power than its republican predecessor or its late imperial counterpart in the nineteenth century.

The principles used to govern China in the first few years after the takeover, up until 1953, had been laid out by Mao Zedong in his 1940 speech "The Politics and Culture of New Democracy" *(Xin minzhu zhuyi de zhengzhi yu Xin minzhu zhuyi de wenhua).*[18] Mao argued that the Chinese revolution historically fell into two stages: democracy and socialism. The former was a special Chinese type of democracy to be called New Democracy. In this period preceding the establishment of socialism, the new government would be required to manage a coalition of four progressive (or "democratic") social forces. These were the same that constituted the United Front of the Yan'an era—the proletariat, the peasantry, the petty bourgeoisie, and the national bourgeoisie—but now, this coalition of social classes would be under the leadership of the Communist Party. The calculation behind the policy was that the alliance of the CCP with local or national capitalists (excluding counterrevolutionaries and traitors) would avoid economic collapse, and allow the CCP to draw on urban support.

Following its accession to power, taking into account the practical need to maintain political stability, the CCP at first assembled centrist political forces into what was formally a coalition government led by the CCP. Called the People's Democratic Dictatorship, it was explained and advocated as a unified dictatorship of the revolutionary classes under CCP leadership. In one of Mao Zedong's most influential and important speeches, "On the People's Democratic Dictatorship," given in commemoration of the twenty-eighth anniversary of the CCP on June 30, 1949, Mao Zedong talked at length about the emerging political and social order in the new China.[19] In China's new order, the people would exercise a dictatorship over the enemies of the people:

> Who are the people? At the present stage, they are the working class, the peasantry, the urban petty bourgeoisie and the national bourgeoisie. These classes, led by the working class and the Communist Party, unite to form their own state and elect their own government; they enforce their dictatorship over the running dogs of imperialism—the landlord class and bureaucratic bourgeoisie, as well as the representatives of those classes, the Kuomintang reactionaries and their accomplices—suppress them, allow them only to behave themselves and not to be unruly in word or deed. If they speak or act in an unruly way, they will be promptly stopped and punished. Democracy is practiced within the ranks of the people, who enjoy the rights of freedom of speech, assembly, association and so on. The right to vote belongs only to the people, not to the reactionaries. The combination of these two aspects, democracy for the people and dictatorship over the reactionaries, is the people's dictatorship. . . .[20]

The speech introduced several crucial and far-reaching concepts. Law as a tool, the systematic distinction between the people and the enemies of the people, the need of the people to reform themselves, the justification of violence against enemies, the use of mitigation and persuasion for members of the people (although individual cases might demand severe punishments or even the death penalty)—all these were fundamental concepts that would shape the political institutions in socialist China. While the dictatorial functions of the new state were made abundantly clear, Mao failed to mention any institutions through which "the people" might exercise their democratic rights.

Lacking a formal document to serve as the legal basis of the new state, the CCP organized the Chinese People's Political Consultative Conference (CPPCC), which convened in Beijing during September 1949. The 662 delegates to the conference reflected the CCP's intention to be inclusive, and therefore included representatives of not only the CCP, which dominated proceedings, but also a few left-wing members of the GMD and some representatives of the People's Salvation Association and of the smaller democratic "third parties." In September 1949, on the eve of the founding of the PRC, the Chinese Political Consultative Conference adopted three documents: the Common Program of the Chinese People's Political Consultative Conference; the Organic Law of the Chinese People's Political Consultative Conference; and the Organic Law of the Central People's Government of the People's Republic of China. During the period between 1949 and 1953, the Common Program provided the fundamental framework for the legal developments in the PRC while the two Organic Law documents outlined the formal structure of the future Chinese government. In general, the Common Program enacted a plan for gradual change while protecting China from "imperialism, feudalism, and bureaucratic capitalism." Article 7 stressed the necessity to suppress opponents and punish counterrevolutionaries. The conference named Mao as the new head of state and determined the membership of the Government Council, which operated as the central authority in China until the constitution took effect. Mao Zedong in fact now dominated all three institutions—party, army, and government. He also enjoyed enormous popular standing enhanced by his still growing cult of personality.

The party first turned its attention to building a viable state apparatus and to training cadres and staff to carry out important policies. The PRC set up a Soviet-style governing structure that provided for overall control by the CCP.[21] The party organization was at the core of the new state. It was the party that created and controlled the new civilian administrative apparatus, much as it had controlled the army during the revolution. At every level of government, decision-making power was in the hands of the CCP. At the top was the CCP Politburo, composed of roughly twenty full members and several alternates (the number varied slightly over time). The Politburo had a Standing Committee that usually had between five and nine members. This was the most important decision-making body, and presumably met one week. The Politburo was part of the larger Central Committee, which grew from seventy-seven to roughly three hundred full and alternate members from the Seventh Central Committee (1945–1956) to the Tenth Central Committee (1973–1977). While it was formally required to convene at least once per year, this rule was not always observed: in the years 1951–1953, 1960, 1963–1965, and 1967 no meetings took place). The Central Committee meetings were used to discuss policy, but usually decisions were not made in them, and thus they had little direct impact on day-to-day policy making. Members of the Central Committee were elected by the National Party Congress, theoretically the body with the highest authority. Yet its size and infrequent conventions made it more of a platform for announcing policies and top appointments. The National Party Congress met only rarely. The only three meetings to take place in the Maoist era were in 1956 / 1958 (two sessions), 1969, and 1973. During the meetings, the members of the Central Committee were elected for terms that eventually lasted up to ten years.

Reporting to the central party in Beijing were party committees on the provincial level. Party secretaries, the top officials in each province, headed these provincial committees and met regularly with the smaller, standing committees on the provincial level. The same structure was replicated at each lower level of government all the way down to the grassroots, where municipal and prefectural party committees and below-county and city district party committees were established. Party committees also existed in every rural commune, every university, every factory, and every residential neighborhood. This nationwide network of party committees exercised supervision and control over administrative processes at each level and, in short, extended across all social institutions and economic enterprises.

By 1954, when it was clear that its hold on power in China was secure, the People's Congress passed a constitution that affirmed the political primacy of the CCP, and, in effect, legitimized the PRC as a one-party dictatorship. The constitution was patterned on the 1936 Soviet constitution adopted under Stalin. The structure of the state was formally separated from the CCP. On the party side, there was the National Party Congress and the Central Committee; and on the government side, the National People's Congress and the State Council. The National People's Congress was similar to a legislature and the equivalent on the government side to the National

7.1. Mao Zedong, Liu Shaoqi, and Zhou Enlai, probably in the Eighth National Congress of the Communist Party of China, in Beijing, September 1956. hrchina.org

Party Congress. Initially it had 1,226 members, and that number was increased to perhaps three thousand by 1964. The National Party Congress was elected every four years. It also chose the State Council, the highest governing body. Headed by a premier, the State Council served as an executive governing body, like a cabinet, with several ministries and commissions reporting to it. The prime minister, the commission heads, and the ministers made up the State Council. The head of state was the president, whose largely ceremonial duties included signing laws into effect, making formal appointments for government leadership positions, and receiving foreign state visits. In the 1950s, Mao Zedong was chairman of the CCP and president of the PRC; Liu Shaoqi was chairman of the Standing Committee of the National People's Congress; and Zhou Enlai served as premier of the State Council. These three were the highest leaders.

In practice, however, the distinction between state and party was relatively meaningless, because government leaders almost always held simultaneous appointments in both the party and the state.[22] Since their party institutions and governmental structures are closely intertwined, communist regimes are often described as party-states. China's was based on a single, hierarchical in-

stitutional structure, subordinate to the top leadership in Beijing and faı
fully carrying out directives from the top echelon.

Official communist doctrine, however, was generally ambiguous about this. On the one hand, the party was granted a monopoly over political power as the "dictatorship of the proletariat" or, as it was later more modestly described, the entity playing the "leading role" in the system. On the other hand, in official theory it was a social organization rather than an organ of state power. As such, it was supposed to represent and defend the interests of social groups such as workers or peasants vis-à-vis the government. Government and party were intrinsically linked, yet remained distinctive. The party injected itself into local society and interacted deeply with it.[23] It also successfully gained compliance from a large part of the population by offering a Maoist political vision and a redemptive project for the damaged nation. The promise was that, based on scientific socialism and party guidance, China could be empowered to address its centuries-old problems of poverty and weakness. This was a party that not only established an authoritarian government, but also produced a community of unprecedented social unity and stability. Had the CCP not been able to elicit compliance and stability through its institutions, it could not have built the powerful developmental state it needed. With those, it could mobilize vast resources, both human and material, to transform the country and pursue industrial modernity.

On the local level, the CCP had little choice but to retain most government personnel from the previous regime. Already stretched too thin, it could not bring in enough new people to replace existing staff throughout the structure of Chinese government. These holdover staff, however, had to undergo political reeducation and lessons in the New Democracy program—a process that was also called thought reform *(sixiang gaizao)* or educational reconstruction. During its first years, the CCP was unable to staff the recently established political institutions with a new elite. Instead it had to rely on existing elites.

Establishing new, effective forms of governing was of central concern to the party and, in general, it followed Soviet models. Those formal bureaucratic processes competed, however, with informal means of governing through mass campaigns and bottom-up initiatives, which, as we have seen, were deployed widely before the takeover. While leaders carefully guarded their power to make decisions about strategic policies and the overall direction of the state and economy, they constantly relied on local involvement at a grassroots level. We see two things at work here: local actors trying new things out and being observed or finally noticed by the center; and central control through top-down bureaucratic processes being brought to bear, including or adapting some of the bottom-up ideas and actions.

China and the Cold War

Ever since the European expansion in the early modern period, China had occupied an important strategic position in the world. Global powers had tried but ultimately failed to influence and control it.[24] China managed to defend its independence even when under attack in World War II. At the same time, China could not isolate itself; foreign assistance was seen as crucial for both economic development and security, so it needed constantly to align itself with international partners and supporters. During the Cold War this task was greatly compounded. It became apparent that rivalry between the world's big powers, especially the Soviet-American confrontation, had a profound effect not only on China's international standing, but also on its internal development.[25] As a result, developments far outside of China's borders became vital for China and had an immediate effect on Chinese domestic politics. Foreign and domestic policy were inseparably intertwined.

Mao Zedong expressed his view in June 1949, shortly before the establishment of the PRC, that "China must lean either to the side of imperialism or to the side of socialism. Sitting on the fence will not do, nor is there a third road."[26] A clear and immediate reason for that statement was the need to counter the American strategy of containing and isolating the communist government that had begun to emerge before the end of the Chinese civil war. The United States had adopted an increasingly hostile attitude toward the CCP and started to actively support the GMD. Thus, the CCP had sought to break with the West and enter into an official alliance with the Soviet Union, although the relationship between the CCP and Moscow in the 1930s and 1940s had never been easy. Both parties decided to leave this legacy of distrust behind when they placed Sino-Soviet relations on a new footing in 1949–1950. On February 14, 1950, China and the Soviet Union signed a Treaty of Friendship, Alliance, and Mutual Assistance, in which the Soviets pledged to defend China from attacks by "Japan and her allies" (meaning the United States) and provide military and civilian assistance. They also agreed to transfer the Russian concessions in Manchuria obtained in 1945 back to China. In return, the Chinese side accepted the independence of Outer Mongolia and promised that no other country but the Soviet Union would be allowed to operate in Manchuria and Xinjiang. The two sides also decided to establish a number of joint stock companies in sectors from food canning to aviation. During Mao's visit to Moscow to negotiate the contract, Stalin also agreed to China's wish for a five-year $300 million loan. This was used to fund fifty key industrial and infrastructural projects intended to speed up the development of Chinese heavy industry, defense industry, and energy production.

The consequences of "leaning to one side" were far-reaching and can hardly be exaggerated. China became part of a larger web of cooperative relationships with all the "brother countries" of the socialist bloc. In numerous respects—including city planning, agricultural reform, higher education, labor camps, nationalist policies, economic models, propaganda, and intelligence work—the new state in China was closely modeled on Eastern European and, above all, Soviet experiences. For it, the Soviet Union and the world of state socialism represented an appealing alternative form of modernity. The socialist model aspired to achieve an industrial progress free of the darker aspects of exploitation, inequality, and imperialism that marred western modernity. It was the most obvious choice as the model that offered effective solutions to a wide range of pressing domestic political, economic, and social challenges. This is not to say that the Soviet model was without nuances. The Soviet Union and other socialist states offered several models, ranging from Lenin's pragmatic and moderate New Economic Policy (1921–1927), to the revolutionary or high Stalinist models featuring all-out campaigns to collectivize agriculture and forcefully speed up industrialization and urbanization (1929–1934), to the bureaucratic Stalinism that emphasized central planning and centralized management of the economy and the state.[27] For that matter, the fact that the Soviet model was readily available at a general level during the first half of the 1950s did not mean that Chinese leaders had to follow it. China's leaders were keenly aware that conditions in their country differed in key respects from the Soviet Union, and made their own judgments about which models should be applied and whether they should be modified in practice.

Still, there can be no doubt that China's links to Eastern Bloc countries and to the Soviet Union led to the most systematic transfer of knowledge and technology in its modern history—and that this "alliance was to have a deeper impact on China than any other alliance."[28] Following the signing of the treaty, roughly ten thousand Russians arrived in China to serve as expert advisers, mainly from 1953 to 1957, and quite a few remained until Nikita Khrushchev (1894–1971) abruptly pulled them out in 1960. Soviet advisers were attached to all Chinese ministries, regional and provincial governments, and major industrial enterprises.[29] China learned from the Soviet Union in many areas, including how to set up a central party apparatus to run a government rather than a war; how to manage government ministries; how to create a system of courts, procurators, police, and jails; how to embed political security functions into factories, universities, offices, and other work units; and how to set up Soviet-style mass organizations. The organization of the new People's Liberation Army (PLA) was consciously and directly fashioned on that of the Soviet army. Soviet educators also devised the Chinese system of higher education. Along with land reform and education, the new regime enacted truly transformative policy in urban planning. By rebuilding Chinese cities inspired by Soviet achievements, New China constructed urban centers that embodied modern forms. The new cities were planned to be functional, productive centers rather than the traditional, unregulated capitalist domains of consumption and exploitation that cities of Old China were said to be.[30]

In foreign policy, too, China sought close alignment with Eastern Bloc policies. The CCP was convinced that it was locked in pitched battle against imperialism and capitalism, and that its security depended on a close political and military alliance with the communist camp led by the Soviet Union. They were eager to close ranks with their socialist brothers-in-arms. A striking example is China's involvement on the Korean peninsula, which led to an immediate and bloody confrontation with the United States and a subsequent enmity between the two nations that lasted more than twenty years.[31]

The PRC was hardly well equipped to get involved in this confrontation between the world's superpowers, but given the proximity of the conflict, it saw no way to steer clear of it. As early as January 1950, when Mao Zedong met Stalin in Moscow, the two emphasized their mutual determination to provide assistance to the North Korean communist regime.[32] In mid-May 1950, the North Korean leader Kim Il Sung met with Mao Zedong in Beijing, where Kim told the CCP's leadership that Soviet leader Joseph Stalin had approved a military plan for a southern advance to reunify Korea. Although Mao urged caution and expressed hope that the United States could be kept out of the military clash, he promised undivided support to North Korea and declared that China would provide troops should the United States intervene.

On June 25, 1950, troops from communist North Korea (with Stalin's approval, if not his encouragement) crossed the thirty-eighth parallel, which had been established as the border between North and South Korea, and invaded South Korea, which was backed by the United States. North Korean forces moved south in a swift push that forced the South Korean forces into the southeast area around Pusan. Two days later, on June 27, the United Nations agreed to provide assistance to the retreating South Korean forces, resulting in orders issued to the US Seventh Fleet to patrol the Taiwan Straits. Through the summer of 1950, North Korean forces advanced and occupied almost the entire peninsula. As UN troops landed in South Korea (about half of them American), China requested that the United States not intervene. This request was not heeded. Successive military victories brought the UN troops up the thirty-eighth parallel and, following this, the decision was made by the American military leader, five-star general Douglas MacArthur (1880–1964), to cross it and approach the Chinese-Korean border along the Yalu River. MacArthur had his own broad and ambitious agenda. He wanted to expand the Korean War to the point of moving against China. He felt that the momentum of the recent victories and the progress of American troops on the Korean peninsula provided a unique chance to undo communism in China by increasing pressure on the Chinese leadership.

This step provided both a trigger and a justification for Beijing's entrance into the Korean War. China responded by again issuing a warning and beginning to mobilize troops. But Mao and the other Chinese leaders hesitated, and weeks of internal debate among the CCP leadership followed before troops were sent into battle. Many in the leadership thought the ongoing military campaign against Taiwan should take priority over Chinese involvement in Korea. On October 2, in a reversal, Mao informed Stalin that China was not able to send sufficient troops to Korea. In his stern reply, Stalin warned of the severe consequences of Chinese inaction. In the future, he cautioned, China would have to deal with two American bases in Korea and Taiwan

7.2. Troops of the Chinese People's Volunteer Army in North Korea, c. 1951.
Pictures from History / Bridgeman Images / PFH1187488

along its borders and would find itself under constant threat. He also insinu-
ated that China could no longer count on Soviet help. In another surprising
change of position, the Chinese Politburo decided three days later, on
October 5, in principle, to follow Stalin's policy and to send divisions of so-
called volunteers to North Korea's rescue. But by mid-October the leadership had still not set the troops in motion. After weeks of faltering, the Chinese
People's Volunteer Army (CPVA), commanded by the remarkable military
strategist Peng Dehuai, initiated its first campaign in Korea on October 25,
1950. In a surprise for US military leaders, it attacked South Korean troops in
the Unsan area.

For six days the Chinese volunteers fought alone. The Russian air force
flew its first mission in support of the CPVA only on November 1, much to
the frustration of Chinese leaders, who had been promised vigorous Russian
air support for the Chinese combatants on the ground. By the twelfth day,
however, South Korean troops had been forced to retreat from areas close to
the Yalu to the Chongchun River. According to Chinese statistics, about fifteen thousand South Korean soldiers were killed in this campaign. Conse-

quently, the North Koreans, aided by thousands of Chinese troops, drove the UN forces all the way back to Seoul. UN forces began a counteroffensive in mid-January, now taking the CPVA leadership by surprise. Mao ordered Peng to launch a vigorous counterattack; this strategic gamble led to the first major CPVA defeat on the peninsula. Both armies dug in and the battles that followed alternately brought victories and defeats for the CPVA. In April 1951, at the height of the Korean War, American president Harry Truman shocked American politics and surprised the world with his decision to remove Douglas MacArthur, whom he accused of unilaterally escalating the conflict. A ceasefire was signed in summer 1951 but sporadic fighting continued until June 1953. Stalin's death in 1953 led to an almost immediate change in Soviet policy. Less intransigent than Stalin, the new Soviet leadership pushed China to formally end the Korean War. An armistice agreement was signed on July 23 between the United States, China, and North Korea, dividing the two Koreas at the same border as before.

The outcome of the Korean War was naturally presented to the Chinese people as a victory, but it came at tremendous cost. Some 600,000 Chinese were killed and perhaps another 400,000 wounded. Scarce resources needed for China's reconstruction had been diverted to the war effort, away from other programs that urgently needed government investment. In 1951, military expenditures took up 55 percent of overall government spending.[33] From late 1950, resources for local relief efforts in the still ailing Chinese cities, and for social welfare, were significantly constrained by the heavy demands imposed by the Korean War. Grain, meat, and cotton were needed to supply the army of volunteers fighting in Korea. The war also brought personal loss to Mao, whose oldest son, Mao Anying, was killed in the conflict. Casualties for all sides were high. Over 36,000 Americans, 520,000 North Koreans, and 400,000 South Koreans are estimated to have been killed on the battlefield. In terms of human lives, then, this conflict was the third-costliest war of the twentieth century, outdone only by the world wars.

Mao and the other Chinese leaders had not rushed into the conflict. In fact, China's initial commitment floundered. It was Stalin who pressured China into entering the war. Anxious not to lose Soviet support that was seen as indispensable, the Chinese leadership gave in to his demands.[34] Once China had intervened, however, its war effort had three important and partly unforeseen consequences. First, China established itself as a rising international

中國人民志願軍出國作戰二週年紀念

1950-1952

紀19 4-3

(92)1952

800 圓

中國人民郵政

7.3. Stamp honoring the second anniversary of the Chinese People's Volunteer Army's dispatch to Korea, 1952.
Reproduced from Scott Catalogue, #173

power that was able to hold its own against far superior American forces. Because it showed determination in defending its territorial safety and safeguarding a neighboring, allied communist country, its prestige and its influence in the Eastern Bloc were greatly increased. Soviet leadership, perhaps for the first time, saw China as something more than a dependent satellite. Second, China reinforced its role as a protector and defender of nonwestern countries—a role that could be traced back to the First and Second World Wars. It would go on to support the Viet Minh in its war against the French, and later help the North Korean and North Vietnamese communist governments. It worked, too, with insurgents in Africa and Latin America. Third, waging war also allowed the CCP to consolidate the rule it needed to mobilize the Chinese population for a total transformation of Chinese society.

The Korean War also affected the situation across the Taiwan Strait. By the end of 1949, Chiang Kai-shek and the GMD government had fled to Taiwan and successfully rebuffed an attack of the PLA on the offshore islands in September 1949. It had also established a new administration and instituted a set of reform policies that were winning local support. Chiang Kai-shek spoke of a new beginning, "creating a new history" for Taiwan.[35] Yet

Chiang Kai-shek had little international support, since the US government was still highly critical of him. With the PRC repeatedly making clear that it wanted to reunite Taiwan with China and was not willing to accept the permanent separation of the island, Taiwan was deeply vulnerable to PLA attacks. Chiang and his intelligence services assumed that a massive PLA attack on Taiwan, supported by Soviet-supplied aircraft or even Soviet-piloted bombers, was only months away. Tensions were rising. The outbreak of the Korean War, however, unexpectedly changed the situation. Mao had to concentrate China's resources in Korea, postponing any attack on Taiwan. Moreover, war on the Korean peninsula prompted the United States to quickly resume its relationship with Chiang Kai-shek and the GMD government. That relationship grew closer in the 1950s and led to the 1954 signing of the Mutual Defense Treaty, not only securing the military survival of the GMD in Taiwan, but also creating the foundation for the US economic assistance that would play an outsized role in the reconstruction and development of Taiwan. Victory in North Korea came at a hefty price for the PRC: it deepened the fissure across the Taiwan Strait and, given the determined US involvement, made unification almost impossible.

Along with China's entry into the Korean War, a campaign of radicalization began in late 1950 that lasted until 1952. Two days after Mao decided to send Chinese volunteers to intervene in the Korean War, the CCP Central Committee issued the "Directive Concerning the Suppression of Counterrevolutionary Activities." This marked the beginning of a series of urban campaigns designed to bring potential opponents under full control and reeducate those people, especially intellectuals, who still held pro-US or pro-nationalist views. It was no coincidence that the decision to battle America on the Korean peninsula and the declaration of internal class struggle were made almost simultaneously.

The war also created much more pressure to speed up land reform and extract more resources from the rural economy. China's entry into the Korean War therefore led to alterations in economic policy. At the Second National Meeting of Finance in November 1950, Chen Yun pointed out that "the work of finance policy on the basis of the Korean War will be completely different from the finance policy on the basis of the recovery of the economy in peace time [in 1950]. Financially, an increase in military spending and military related expenditures is needed. . . . One of the questions to consider is whether we can fetch several billion kilograms of grain more from the farmers and whether farmers can afford this?"[36] The need to increase the state's extraction of resources from the countryside was a major reason for the start of land reform in late 1950. On November 22, 1950, Mao sent a telegram to regional CCP branches saying: "In the tense situation of the War, we need to annihilate bandits, intensify land reform, develop local militias, and severely suppress counterrevolutionary activities. Our party and our military need to be active to avoid the danger of passivity."[37] As these statements demonstrate, the three different concerns—the socialist transformation of society and economy in China, the fight against internal enemies, and international conflict during the global Cold War—were interlocked. This meant that the Korean War helped radicalization penetrate much further into Chinese society.

Cleaning Up

In the city, as in the countryside, the CCP wanted to create a "new society." Core to the CCP's general policy was to "increase production and achieve economic prosperity." For example, whereas Shanghai had long been a "bridgehead of imperialism" and a symbol for the "degenerated lifestyle of the bourgeoisie"—as evidenced by its brothels, gambling dens, and more sordid entertainment establishments—the plan was for it to become the "People's Great Shanghai" *(renmin de da Shanghai)*. To achieve such transformation, the CCP began its task of "purifying society" to "reduce the city's parasitic population" and transform cities of consumption *(xiaofei chengshi)* into cities of production *(shengchan chengshi)*.[38] To extend control over the population, it devised methods to supervise or remove parts of the population deemed unreliable or hostile to the new authorities.

After the takeover, the party continued to fear nationalist counterrevolutionary activities and foreign intervention. There was some basis for this fear. Having just overthrown the nationalist regime by means of war, the CCP believed it was still at risk when both the remnant forces of the GMD and hostile groups in local society put up resistance throughout China. Even after the establishment of the PRC in October 1949, at least 600,000 of the GMD rearguard remained on the mainland and numerous special-service agents, left behind by secret police units of the nationalist government, hid throughout China. In fact, it took until the end of 1950 for the CCP to establish full control over the mainland. The new authorities warned sternly that these nationalist remnants might collaborate with gangsters and criminals to undermine the new order. In part, the decision to send troops to the Korean peninsula in October 1950 compelled the government to tighten internal security, as it was feared that the United States might, in conjunction with the GMD in Taiwan, use the war to fuel unrest on the mainland.

As soon as the new Public Security Bureaus were constituted under communist leadership, the announcements were made at the command of the Military Control Committee: reactionary organizations were against the law; all special-service units were to be dissolved; their members would be registered; and their illegal weapons and radio transmitters would be seized.[39] The crime of "counterrevolution" was defined in the "Statutes of [the] State Administrative Council and the People's Supreme Court Concerning the Suppression of Counterrevolutionary Activities," dated July 1950, and the twenty-one articles of the "Statute on Punishment for Counterrevolutionary Activity," dated February 1951.[40] The purpose of the latter statute was "the suppression of counterrevolutionary activities and the strengthening of the democratic dictatorship of the people" (Article 1). Many Chinese citizens were sentenced based on these 1951 statutes. The term "counterrevolutionary activity" was only vaguely defined as "any activity that aims at overthrowing or undermining the democratic dictatorship of the people and the socialist system and therefore puts the PRC in harm's way." The 1951 statutes included a comprehensive list of concrete offenses, all related to security issues. For nearly all (95 percent) of the crimes listed in the statute, the applicable punishment was at least determinate imprisonment—and for many it was life imprisonment or even the death penalty. Further, the adjudicating institution had tremendous latitude to punish offenses through the principle of analogy (that is, specifying punishments for actions that had never specifically been declared against the law by referring to crimes believed to have similar impact) and retroactivity that allowed counterrevolutionary acts committed even before 1949 to be punished.

It was in this vague climate of war, fear, and suspicion, and with the specific intention to purge society of unreliable or hostile or "counterrevolutionary elements," that the CCP launched its nationwide Campaign to Suppress Counterrevolutionaries (*zhenya fan geming* or *zhenfan*). Lasting from 1950 to 1953, its main intention was to strengthen and defend the CCP's grip on power. The campaign ordered suspected former members of the GMD or its organizations, alleged nationalist spies, and former members of the nationalist military or secret police to register with the police at their place of residency. The campaign also attacked gang leaders, drug smugglers, and religious sect leaders. Most suspected "counterrevolutionaries" were given a chance to repent and reform, by which they could remold themselves through hard physical labor into "new persons" *(xin ren)*. Mao also described this process as "turning rubbish into something useful." But in some cases, counterrevolutionaries simply needed to be killed, because in Mao's words they "were deeply hated by the masses and owed the masses heavy blood-debts." The use of violence was thus justified by "great public anger" *(min fen ji da zhe)* and "blood-debts" *(xie zhai)*. The latter expression frequently occurred in Mao's speeches and writing. The concept of "blood-debts" was used to argue that earlier crimes committed by the enemies of communism compelled the party to seek retribution and retaliation. Mao also made it clear that counterrevolutionaries would still exist in China, so that campaigns would be necessary in the future. The socialist state had to be vigilant and could not afford to renounce the use of violence: "We cannot promulgate [a policy of] no executions at all; we still cannot abolish the death penalty. Suppose there is a counterrevolutionary who has killed people or blown up a factory, what would you say, should that person be executed or not? Certainly such a person must be executed."[41] Therefore it is not surprising that the campaign was violent: in less than one year, the counterrevolutionary campaign led to the deaths of 712,000 people, the convictions of 1.3 million people, the sentencing of 1.2 million to forced labor, and the arrest and subsequent reeducation of another 380,000.[42]

One account of an accusation meeting held on May 20, 1951, gives a sense of the fervor stirred up by the Campaign to Suppress Counterrevolutionaries. On that day, the Beijing Municipal People's Government summoned a huge public gathering to witness the accusation of some five hundred counterrevolutionaries. Luo Ruiqing (1906–1978), minister of public security, addressed the agitated crowd first, describing the crimes involved and suggesting that perhaps 220 of the accused should be sentenced to death. He was followed by Mayor Peng Zhen (1902–1997), who added his own impassioned voice to describe what must come next:

> "People's Representatives! Comrades! We have all heard the report given by Minister Luo and the accusations of the aggrieved parties. What shall

we do to these vicious and truculent despots, bandits, traitors, and special service agents? What shall we do to this pack of wild animals? ("Shoot them to death!" the people at the meeting shouted.) Right, they should be shot. If they were not to be shot, there would be no justice. . . . We shall exterminate all these despots, bandits, traitors, and special service agents. We shall shoot as many of them as can be found. (Loud applause and loud shouts of slogans: "We support the people's government! We support Mayor Peng.") . . . Tomorrow, conviction; day after tomorrow, execution. (Loud applause and loud shouts.)"[43]

Similar mass trials and accusation meetings were held in every urban area and in many villages. Organizing such events was a way to rally popular support behind the regime, extend the formal and informal coercive instruments of the revolutionary state, and establish a vertically constructed bureaucracy capable of maintaining control at all levels.[44] Significant personnel and financial resources were set aside for the campaigns, indicating the high priority the government assigned to them.

After the initial phase, the campaign extended its scope: government and party officials, who used to deem themselves safe, were suddenly also targeted. Among the government officials were many GMD holdovers that the new government suspected of trying to undermine it. Some had even managed to cling to party membership. They too were arrested and had to reform themselves through labor—or worse, were executed. The wave of suppression surged ahead until 1953, when the campaign finally ebbed.

Endowed with broad legal powers to take action against suspected enemies, the Campaign to Suppress Counterrevolutionaries relied heavily on people's tribunals *(renmin fating)* or military courts for its implementation. People's tribunals can be traced back to the period of the revolution before 1949, when they were instrumental to the fight against the CCP's enemies. People's tribunals, first introduced in 1950, existed alongside the people's courts, but they were ad hoc in nature and lasted only for the duration of a given campaign.[45] In the early years of the PRC, they were one of the most important levers by which the new government wielded state power.[46] Operating under the "organic regulations of people's tribunals"—a set of rules made public on July 20, 1950—they were formed by people's governments at the provincial level or above and were dissolved upon completion of their tasks. Their main task was "the employment of judicial procedure for the punishment of local despots, bandits, special agents, counterrevolutionaries, and criminals who violate the laws and orders pertaining to agrarian reform."[47] The tribunals were allowed to make arrests, detain suspects, and pass sentences ranging from imprisonment all the way to the death penalty.[48] The people selected to serve on tribunals came mostly from local party organizations, and many would go on to be appointed to positions in the regular courts, having received judicial training through their work in the tribunals. Bypassing the formal court system, people's tribunals, in cooperation with public security and party organizations, often carried out massive purges.

People's tribunals deployed devices such as mass trials and accusation meetings. Three specific formats were widely used in the process: the accusation meeting *(kongsu hui)*, the "big meeting to announce the sentence" *(xuanpan dahui)*, and the mass trial *(gongshen)*. Each form could involve up to tens of thousands of people. They were organized in a way that sought to best mobilize the populace, educate through negative example, and deter through public punishment. The accusation meetings, mass trials, and mass campaigns were meant to engage the populace. The people were to be "stirred up" *(fadong qunzhong)* and invited to participate in the action of the state, thus collectively reaffirming its popular legitimacy. The close and direct involvement of the masses in this process was carefully stage-directed. Those who served as material witnesses were not only thoroughly rehearsed in what they were to say and when, but carefully chosen in the first place for the degree to which they would excite the sympathies of the crowd. Organizers particularly favored very old, very young, and female witnesses, whose testimonies and grievances were more likely to arouse strong emotions.

As well as counterrevolutionaries, several other social groups were targeted by nationwide campaigns and movements in the early 1950s. For example, many party or government officials who came from the countryside into the cities found themselves in influential positions that gave them access to scarce resources. Soon after the takeover, corruption and waste spread among government officials, siphoning off important resources. As the central government began to recognize this as a severe problem it would have to deal with, Mao became convinced that these were the acts of GMD holdovers and the results of foreign influences. Soon the counterrevolutionary suppression campaign was interrupted and the "Three-Anti Campaign" *(sanfan)* was

7.4. "People's tribunal" convened to consider a "despotic landlord" in Guangdong province, 1953.
Bettmann / Getty Images / 514970462

launched instead—as an anti-corruption, anti-waste, and anti-bureaucracy effort. Each organization and department was required to search for "capitalist elements" within its ranks. Officials were ordered to list their social contacts and those of their family members, with a special emphasis on any family or friends who lived in capitalist countries or had worked for the GMD. This information was handed over to public security agents, to be used in the struggle against the counterrevolution.

In 1952, when the state purchase and contracting system had created many opportunities for bribery, fraud, and other undesirable behaviors, the party attempted to discipline China's capitalists and private entrepreneurs by launching the "Five-Anti Campaign" *(wufan),* this time outlining an anti-bribery, anti-tax evasion, anti-fraud, anti-theft of state property, and anti-leakage of state economic secrets agenda. These two "Anti" campaigns, designed to discipline the party state and to consolidate unified central leadership over the urban economic sector, proved hugely popular and drew general praise. They were also very effective. It was reported that the *sanfan* campaign brought to light some 1.2 million cases of government corruption.[49] The fact that just two hundred thousand of those cases involved party members shows that the campaigns targeted many more holdovers from the GMD than CCP members. While the campaigns differed in scope and intensity, all involved tribunals being used as a major vehicle to deal with target groups. Campaigns were also carried out in the second half of the 1950s.

To the great surprise of those who knew him, Pan Hannian (1906–1977), vice mayor of Shanghai and former chief of CCP intelligence, was accused in the spring of 1955 of historical crimes in public. It was claimed that he had, in the 1940s, sought cooperation with the Japanese secret service organs and had been "colluding with the major traitor Wang Jingwei." Together with the writer Hu Feng (1902–1985), and others he was indicted for organizing a counterrevolutionary clique. These revelations triggered another, even broader campaign against counterrevolutionaries. This campaign, known as the Campaign for Elimination of Counterrevolutionaries *(sufan yundong)* lasted five years and involved the exposure and criticism of roughly twenty million people in factories, residential units, and government agencies. In the first two years alone, 1.8 million people were investigated for past transgressions, and 20 percent of those were found to have committed crimes. Half of them were declared to be counterrevolutionaries or "bad elements."[50]

Millions of arrests were made by the police, the army, or people acting on behalf of the party without any involvement of the regular courts. Hundreds of thousands of "class enemies" or "enemies of the people" were sentenced to death in these campaigns, and executed. Mao himself set a quota for executions to be carried out, believing that counterrevolutionaries deserving death made up 0.1 to 0.2 percent of the population (between half a million and one million people).[51] According to reports by the Public Security Bureau, in the twelve years between 1950 and 1962, almost ten million people were arrested by central authorities for being counterrevolutionaries or bad elements, and roughly 1.6 million of these were executed. Many more were sent to labor camps by local authorities, factories, counties, and communes, which had the power to enforce law and impose sentences. By 1962, at least four million counterrevolutionaries or bad elements had been sentenced to labor reform, or *laogai*, meaning that they were sent to labor camps, reeducation centers, or work sites kept under surveillance. The number who died from starvation and disease exceeded half a million—and these were only the people punished for political offenses. Many others were sent to labor camps for crimes involving gambling, prostitution, drugs, theft, or illegal migration.[52]

With the campaigns generating so many arrests, the government had an urgent need to build a more extensive labor camp system.[53] Around the start of the *zhenfan* campaign, in May 1951, the PRC's labor camp system was founded. It was only in the Third National Conference on Public Security that the treatment of prisoners was finally discussed in a systematic way, and solutions were proposed regarding the management and placement of the arrested. As a sign of how central an issue this had become, the most important of the PRC leaders all attended the meeting. By 1952 there were 640 *laogai* farms, 56 of which were camps large enough to hold more than a thousand prisoners. Another 217 *laogai* units were involved in the industrial sector, with 29 of them having more than five hundred prisoners. Beyond these, the government operated at least 857 smaller, stationary *laogai* camps, plus mobile camps for the construction of railways and canals. In all, by 1954, China had over 4,600 camps, including the many relatively small units run by county and city governments. More than 83 percent of all labor camp inmates were now engaged in forced labor, mostly on agricultural farms, in mines, steel production, and on the construction of canals and railways. Three years later, in 1957, the Eleventh Bureau of the Public Security Ministry announced a consolidation effort by which the total was brought down to just over two thousand units, tending to be much larger. Of these, 1,323 were industrial enterprises, 619 were agricultural farms, and 71 were engaged in infrastructure projects. The economic focus had obviously shifted from agriculture to industry. *Laogai* slowly and inexorably assumed a prominent economic role, to the benefit of the socialist state. By assigning prisoners to dangerous, difficult, and exhausting work projects, the state offered some relief to the peasants and workers whose support it needed. Having created a sizable group of counterrevolutionaries and other enemies of the people to mark a contrast with the newly privileged group of workers and peasants, it further cemented their support. The full exploitation of prison labor cut the state's expenses, and the threat of being sent to the camps helped discipline the civilian workforce. Loafing was an offense that could result in a prison term, just as sabotage was. Just how many people were serving sentences at the end of the 1950s is unknown, but the number of arrests suggests the number was likely around twenty million.[54]

The death penalty was often carried out immediately or the next day.[55] Most executions were public. These public displays of excessive violence had a profound impact on society. They showed unequivocally what the "class struggle" ultimately entailed. In its campaigns against opponents, real or suspected, the CCP proved itself ready to employ violence and terror against its own nationals, and, if necessary, to substantially alter or ignore key provisions of its own fragile, socialist law. The intent was clearly to use calculated violence to liquidate opposition and caches of potential dissent. Still, the scope of arrests and executions and the willingness of local cadres to participate in the movement seemed to catch party leadership by surprise. Reckless arrests and executions, carried out regardless of whether there was clear evidence of wrongdoing, were common. The longer the campaigns lasted and the more blood was spilled on the execution grounds, the more the central party appealed to local units to exercise restraint.[56] It became apparent that campaigns were being used by many local individuals and groups (such as cadres and militias) to settle old scores with neighbors and to decide long-term local conflicts in their favor.

The numerous trials and campaigns drew in people from all sectors of society, mobilizing the rank-and-file cadres and rallying them behind government-sponsored objectives.[57] It was incumbent upon the central state to win over the leading local and municipal cadres it needed to implement its directives. The campaigns and tribunals thus played a very important role in imposing and enforcing norms; they provided a forceful set of ideological and moral incentives to ensure the compliance and responsiveness of low-level cadres and officials, as well as the broader population. While the judicial system continued to serve as the organizational core of the sanctioning process, mass trials and campaigns functioned as flexible and informal mechanisms for the effective, direct, and rapid transmission of sociopolitical norms and the mustering of broad popular support for enforcing them.

A prime vehicle for carrying out mass campaigns in the 1950s was a new institution: the Residents' Committee (*jumin weiyuanhui*) of each neighborhood, colloquially also called the neighborhood or street committee (*lilong weiyuanhui*). In December 1949, the city of Hangzhou created the first residents' committees as a "new mode of democratic organization" to replace the *baojia* system.[58] Such committees were subsequently established in all neighborhoods nationwide through a "neighborhood democratization movement" *(qujie minzhu jianzheng yundong)*, and by the mid-1950s, their efficient grassroots work and neighborhood activism accomplished a thorough reordering of political and social life.

Resident committees' officers were elected by residents and worked under the guidance of local government.[59] In their respective neighborhoods, the committees ran their own affairs, and offered important services to their members. They categorized people as either "good" (if they were revolutionary activists, for example, or workers) or "bad" (if they were criminals, GMD members, religious activists, or otherwise threatening). Families in the "bad" category were put under "special control" and surveillance by local public security agents.[60] As a mass effort of self-governance, not an organ of government, these committees also took care of people's welfare by monitoring crime and aiding citizens through conflict resolution or health care. They publicized new laws and party policies, mobilized residents to support government initiatives, and communicated the opinions of residents to the base-level government. Neighborhood committees organized newspaper reading groups, explained foreign affairs, and broadened residents' knowledge and political consciousness. Responsibility for social relief work was also transferred from local police stations to the residents' committees. Within them were welfare committees that took over the implementation of programs to offer shelter or give out food to people in need. During the Korean War, for example, as part of the "Resist America Aid Korea Campaign," residents were asked to donate money for airplanes and artillery. In the Campaign to Suppress Counterrevolutionaries, and the "Three-Anti" and "Five-Anti" campaigns, members of residents' committees were called on to inform on any neighbors, friends, and relatives suspected of waste, embezzlement, or corruption. Other campaigns involving residents' committees were aimed not at people but at vermin. The "Four Pests Campaign" (1958–1962), for example, called upon people to kill the four most common pests: flies, mosquitoes, sparrows, and rats. The populace embraced this campaign with enthusiasm but, like some other early policies, it was not well thought out. As their vigorous pursuit decimated the sparrow population, they removed a natural predator of insects, which multiplied enormously at the expense of crops.

By the time the Campaign to Suppress Counterrevolutionaries ended in 1953, the government had created 170,000 resident or work-unit security committees with an activist base numbering more than two million people.[61] These activists constituted a support force for the numerically weak public security units, solving a problem that had plagued the government since 1949. Operating under the leadership of the local public security agencies, work units, villages, and towns, the activists had a combined strength that allowed them to stretch across all facets of life and to protect the social order right down to the street and work-unit level. Their reach also enabled them to help the police, efficiently monitoring any suspected or minor counterrevolutionaries within their own work and living spaces. The residents' committees had two seemingly contradictory roles: promoting grassroots democracy and serving as a tool for "stability maintenance" and mass mobilization. Their close cooperation with local public security bureaus and local party organizations meant that the committees' neighborhood activists were able to translate government policy into pervasive and powerful public pressure.

In the cities there was a second organizational network called work units (*danwei*), which existed alongside the residents' committees and which managed to organize those parts of the population employed by the state and thus not included in the residents' committee system. Residents' committees principally included only family members of people who worked in a larger *danwei*, employees in small enterprises, retirees, housewives, and the unemployed. Members of a *danwei* did not usually participate in the activities of residents' committees. It was expected that, with industrialization, economic growth, and the completion of socialist transformation, the work unit system would eventually cover every single individual in the cities, and the residents' committees would eventually cease to exist. For the time being, the latter were still needed to carry out a total and thorough organization of the entire population.

Therefore, the residents' committees corresponded with the work unit or *danwei* system that was built up and expanded through the campaigns as well. Government and party organizations, state-owned enterprises, financial institutions, and educational establishments were all termed *danwei* or included different *danwei*. Typically, a *danwei* supervised almost all aspects of life for its employees. Housing, health care, recreational activities, rationed goods, and pensions were all organized through the *danwei*. The *danwei*-based welfare system was codified in February 1951 with the passage of the national "Labor Insurance Regulations."[62] The regulations set out both the tasks and responsibilities to be covered by the *danwei* system and the methods for financing it. According to the regulations, the workers were entitled to make use of various collective welfare services offered by the *danwei* such as sanatoriums, kindergartens, homes for the aged, orphanages, institutions for the disabled, and holiday facilities. *Danwei* employees were entitled to lifetime employment, but were not allowed to change *danwei* through their own initiative. Each *danwei* had several administrative departments or divisions, including a financial department, a security department, a party committee or commission, and so on. The *danwei* also served as the keeper of the personal files *(renshi dang'an)* that followed individuals from primary school throughout their lives. The files came to include school records, party membership, promotions and performance evaluations, and family history, as well as detrimental information such as any negative evaluations by superiors, written criticisms, and warnings.[63] They also contained a class label *(jieji chengfen)*, signifying family background and individual status. Security departments within *danwei* maintained separate files *(dang'an)* that were used to record criminal and disciplinary activities. These types of *dang'an* included criminal dossiers, labor reeducation dossiers *(laojiao dang'an* or *laogai dang'an)*, and public security dossiers *(gong'an dang'an)*. The contents of these *dang'an* were often lurid and contained information in writing that did not appear anywhere in public. The *danwei* also engaged in a variety of political activities under party leadership and supervision. Most importantly, the *danwei* had to implement the political campaigns devised by the central authorities by organizing meetings, discussing policies, and mobilizing members. Through the *danwei,* the CCP had the ability to carry out its policies down to the local level—a reach that had evaded its predecessors.

The CCP also created numerous mass organizations that helped implement central policies. The state-sponsored Women's Federation, for example, helped implement the campaign against prostitution and its assistance was a major factor in that effort's success. Various youth organizations made similar contributions. Mass organizations were important vehicles for boosting economic productivity and mitigating social problems, coming to the aid of refugees and war-torn families, and fighting poverty, prostitution, drug use, and child-selling.

The violence and pervasiveness of the political mass campaign succeeded in destroying most underground remnants of GMD forces. Whatever armed insurgencies, attacks, or acts of sabotage might have been attempted by the opponents of New China were almost completely forestalled. Thus, the CCP's campaigns achieved their primary goal, even as they also created a system for effective grassroots mobilization and established a host of new institutions to reorder social and political life. The CCP government managed to significantly consolidate its authority, and to establish key institutions of the Maoist era, including the work units *(danwei)* that set apart the industrial labor force, and the personnel dossiers *(dang'an)* that marked citizens with "good" or "bad" political records. The class labels *(jieji chengfen)* were also established that later, in the 1960s, would be further refined to sort good people into "five kinds of red" *(hong wulei),* and bad people into the "five kinds of black" *(hei wulei)* abbreviated as *di-fu-fan-huai-you* (shorthand for landlords, rich peasants, counterrevolutionaries, bad elements, and rightists).[64] Once resistance was quelled, these new institutions served to compartmentalize society by dividing citizens into separate state-created categories, with different entitlements. creating societal division

A Culture Made New

The Chinese communist effort to establish a new society after 1949 aimed for an extensive transformation of China's cultural landscape. Having won power on the battlefield, Mao and the party leaders needed to secure and sustain the majority of the people's support. The military conquest and consolidation of power had to be followed up by nationwide cultural renewal.[65]

The party's view of the cultural and intellectual life that had flourished in China before 1949 was that it was part of an obsolete and vanishing world; the work, beliefs, habits, and lifestyles of intellectuals, writers, artists, and professors were profoundly contaminated by their privileged upbringing, sophisticated education, and lavish ways of life, which had imbued them with disdain for workers and peasants, bourgeois political ideas such as liberalism, deeply pro-American values, and hostility toward the Soviet Union. Given their political predilections, some even secretly supported the Nationalist

Party or other political parties and undermined CCP rule. Even those who were indifferent to politics and refused to participate in political movements were nonetheless, for the party, roadblocks to the building of socialism. After 1949, the new authorities were eager to attack the institutions and people perpetuating this old, "backward" culture and to transform them. To create a new, communist culture, the entire cultural sector had to be reorganized to facilitate an intense politicization of the arts. New cultural institutions would mobilize the arts and literature for the political goals of the CCP and create and spread popular support for the government. After 1949, it became increasingly difficult for intellectuals, artists, and cultural institutions not to participate in the party's cultural policies.

After 1949, the Military Control Commissions gradually established Culture and Education Management Committees *(wenhua jiaoyu guanli weiyuanhui)* consisting of various bureaus. Together, these bureaus were to organize the takeover of the cultural and education sectors, including theaters, film companies, the broadcasting industry, media, print publishing, schools, and universities. Take, for instance, the Press and Publication Bureau *(xinwen chuban chu)* that exercised responsibility in that realm. Its first step was to quickly wrest from the GMD the entire state-owned publishing and distribution industry. The takeover of related private businesses, however, took longer to accomplish. In general, all private enterprises were required to register with the Press and Publication Bureau at the Military Commission to continue their operations. They had to provide information on their histories, finances, and operational management, on owners' and chief editors' past and current political positions and experiences, and on their relationships with other parties and organizations. The main criterion for approval and registration was political orientation. Pro-CCP institutions were always approved, while those with "neutral" or unclear political backgrounds had to stay out of business at least temporarily. Those institutions deemed reactionary were prohibited or not permitted to register.

Although the process of nationalizing the press, publishing, and distribution industry unfolded in different ways and to varying extents in Chinese cities, conformity with national guidelines was always emphasized and remained more important than regional differences. Overall, the private publishing industry continued to operate and even grow from 1950 to 1952. The idea of New Democracy allowed for the coexistence of multiple types of publishing and distribution enterprises. These included state-owned companies, book and periodical cooperative associations, individual bookstalls and retailers, private publishing, printing, and distribution enterprises, and joint state-private enterprises. But from 1953 onward, private publishing houses faced tightening restrictions. The PRC General Administration of Press and Publication (*Zhonghua renmin gongheguo xinwen chuban zongshu*) and Cultural and Educational Committee of the State Council of the PRC (*Zhengwuyuan wenhua jiaoyu weiyuanhui*) in the central government took over control of the press and publishing industry and stipulated that, after January 1953, newspapers, periodicals, and publishing houses had to apply for licenses to stay in business.[66] During this process, the methods used for regulation and restriction included forcing private publishers to terminate or change their business, incorporating private publishers into joint state-private entities, issuing or withholding the approval of applicants' business licenses, and suspending approval for some publishers until they implemented mandated changes. While some private publishers continued to operate after 1953, no private newspaper remained in business.

After 1953, nationalization of the entire publishing and print industry was gradually realized. Officials were assigned to lead joint private-public publishing houses and help them absorb other private publishers. When a private publishing house was absorbed, the majority of its employees were transferred to a state-owned entity and its private shares were transferred to a different joint private-public publishing house.[67] Some other private publishers were transformed into state-capitalist (*guojia zibenzhuyi*) publishing houses. By 1956, the nationalization and regimentation of private publishers in the PRC had been completed nationwide. Shanghai, a center of China's private publishing and distribution industry in the republican era, was left with few publishers, and those few were under state control.

A top-down hierarchical structure was built to connect the central state with local state press and publishing systems, to ensure control at the local level. First, the China Federation of Literary and Art Circles (*Zhongguo wenxue yishujie lianhehui*) ranked the existing literature and art periodicals, both national and local (that is, provincial and municipal). Local periodicals would focus on mass literature and the arts, and publish pieces that the masses could use for their cultural activities. The goal for national publications was that they be more comprehensive, publish higher-quality pieces, and provide direction for the local promotion of mass culture. National literary and arts periodicals would constitute the core of the nation's creation and criticism of literature and arts, organizing and supervising writers, and guiding the readership of the masses. These periodicals included *Literature and Arts Periodical (Wenyi bao), The People's Literature (Renmin wenxue)*, and *Talking and Singing (Shuoshuo changchang)*.

Second, the Ministry of Culture *(wenhuabu)* and the Central Propaganda Department *(Zhonggong zhongyang xuanchuanbu)* of the party's Central Committee, headed by Lu Dingyi (1906–1996), produced and disseminated new cultural forms. While ultimate power in shaping cultural policies was wielded by the Ministry of Culture, the Central Propaganda Department played a crucial role. Together, their purpose was to paint a sanguine picture of the future, inspiring the masses to hold steadfast in their faith in the party's vision. They monitored the national publishing houses that were meant in turn to provide leadership to local publishers. This nationwide regimentation meant that Shanghai was replaced by Beijing as the center of the press and publishing industry after 1955.

At the same time, state-owned distributors of print materials established monopolies. Foremost among these was the New China *(Xinhua)* Bookstore chain, which served as a clearinghouse throughout the country. Only books approved by the government were distributed in the Xinhua stores. From 1955 to mid-1956, the Ministry of Culture pursued an extensive and harsh program to take "reactionary, pornographic and ridiculous old books" off the market. These were eliminated in the process of compelling all existing booksellers and private book rental stalls to register as businesses. In 1955 the Ministry of Culture claimed that 80 percent of the novels found in old rental stalls in Shanghai were pornographic romances, fantastical martial arts adventures, and reactionary tales of spies and gangsters. Because they propagated "corrupt and reactionary thoughts and shameless lifestyles," these books had to be removed or replaced. Publishers had to cut many titles from their back catalogues and take them out of circulation. The ministry also compiled lists to inform local agencies of particular books that should be replaced or banned. Any newly purchased books had to come from government-run Xinhua Bookstore outlets. New popular art and literary forms were used for two purposes: to demonize enemies of the party and to acclaim the new socialist regime. Whereas communist artists largely employed cartoons and serial picture stories *(lianhuanhua)* to denounce their foes—Chiang Kai-shek and US imperialists—they used a traditional format, new year prints *(nianhua)*, to pay tribute to government policies and celebrate the achievements of the PRC.

Private ownership of press, publishing, and media was thus converted into government ownership, and state control was established over the entire sector—but more importantly, the content of what was published and reported was changed. In literary and arts publications, there was a push to create and publish new literature geared toward workers, peasants, and soldiers. A large majority of the publications were political in nature and guided by the editorial principle of promoting communist ideals. Even poems could not escape party politics; nearly half of those published in 1955 glorified soldiers and workers. Adhering to the CCP's cultural policies, the literary supplement of the Shanghai newspaper *Liberation Daily (Jiefang ribao)* mainly published short writings by workers, soldiers, and peasants, usually dealing with political movements. Newspapers, in their literary supplements, started publishing serialized works only by well-known CCP leaders or writers and artists close to the CCP.

Authors of the new literature adopted a style best described as a "combination of revolutionary romanticism with revolutionary realism."[68] It was intended to portray reality in a passionate and imaginative way, instilled with a utopian vision. Revolutionary romanticism meant that, through literary imagination, a vision of the world would be projected to which the audience could relate and toward which it would be inspired to strive. The task of this literature was to situate the present on a trajectory extending from the dark past to the bright future. While many leftist authors clearly and willingly took on the task of presenting the Communist Party's vision of the future, they also embraced, as a topic in its own right, the sympathetic and detailed portrayal of the lives of farmers, workers, and soldiers. Many of the texts described everyday work in the countryside or in the factories not only in terms of abstract state goals, but in terms of dignity and fulfillment. The authors saw themselves in conceptual proximity to the workers and peasants, and often, the proximity was physical. One of the most popular writers, Hao Ran (Liang Jinguang [1932–2008]), described how some of his stories came to be written: "It was harvest time and we cadres took turns watching over the threshing ground at night with the commune members. In the deep of night, I paced round the quiet square covered with grain and bathed in moonlight. As the cool breeze wafted over the fragrance of new rice, countless stirring events sprang to my mind all crying out for utterance. I turned a manure crate upside-down and spread a sack over it. Then by the light of my storm lantern I started scribbling on this makeshift 'desk.'"[69]

Meanwhile, those writers who refused to adapt to the new policies and guidelines saw their submissions rejected—even some who had been well-known critics of the GMD government. If in the eyes of the new government they had problems reforming their thoughts and renewing themselves, they could not get published. For instance, the essays of the respected May Fourth writer Zhou Zuoren were refused publication in 1952 owing to "thought problems."[70] That rejection signaled the fate of the leftist and progressive May Fourth tradition, which soon disappeared, replaced by the literary style of socialist realism mandated by the new authorities. Writers and journalists were often attacked and publicly criticized for deviating from the party line, for ignoring the viewpoint of the working class, or for failing to promote the progressive values of the CCP. As a result, many writers and journalists became timid or stopped writing altogether. Faced with a shortage of articles, newspapers resorted to cutting and pasting from government publications and rewriting pieces from other newspapers. Earlier, the papers had printed reports on movies and local operas, but after 1952 those sections now featured pieces of self-criticism by artists. By 1953, most papers were dominated by government propaganda.

Also unspared were those in education and academia. The system of higher education was reorganized, meaning that various universities were reshuffled and merged. The sector as a whole was expanded. From 1949 to 1960 total enrollment in the universities and colleges in China's mainland rose from 117,000 to 961,623. Here again, the process also facilitated the extension of central government control throughout the system at the expense of local governments and private institutions. The new government spurred the transformation of cultural or educational institutions, but it also demanded the allegiance of students, teachers, scientists, and writers, who had to demonstrate their loyalty. In general, CCP cadres believed that intellectuals lacked solidarity and worked only for their own benefit, scheming for power, status, and wealth. At the highest level, they perceived professors, scientists, and engineers to be transferring theories, methods, and equipment uncritically from capitalist societies and regarding knowledge as above class and politics. Nevertheless, the party also stressed that, no matter how elitist, opportunist, or wrong these people had been, they could change and be remade into new people through thought reform.

The start of a nationwide thought reform campaign can be dated to the summer of 1951, when Peking University organized political study classes for the faculty and staff and received Mao Zedong's enthusiastic support.[71] The Ministry of Education then proposed similar activities for universities and postsecondary schools nationwide. By September, over six thousand college faculty and staff in Beijing and Tianjin had been put through month-long study programs. In October 1951, Mao Zedong called for "a campaign of self-education and self-reform" on "the educational and cultural fronts and among various types of intellectuals." The "thought reform" of intellectuals *(zhishi fenzi)*, he stated, was "one of the important requirements" for China to "achieve democratic reform thoroughly and industrialization step by step."[72] The campaign was also launched to find intellectuals whose "thought problems" caused them to spread bourgeois or liberal ideas. In Shanghai, as in Beijing and Tianjin, the campaign began in colleges and universities. During a twelve-month period, it spread to secondary schools and research institutes and encompassed writers and newspaper employees, targeting ideological deficiencies or false political ideas of professors, writers, and other intellectuals. In the course of the campaign, intellectuals were forced to reveal their social backgrounds, which included education, previous jobs, political association, class background, and the background of family, friends, and relatives. They were asked to examine their political convictions and to identify those mistaken or false elements in their own beliefs, political activities, job performances, and lifestyles that did not correspond with the standards and models promoted by the party. They were urged to confess acts of corruption, waste, and other improper or unlawful conduct such as theft, prostitution, and gambling. Their ideas, attitudes, and behavior were then subjected to intense criticism by others and, if necessary, official investigation. It became compulsory to study speeches and articles by Lenin, Mao, and other communist leaders, as well as political documents related to recent campaigns. Intellectuals with "severe" political problems had to demonstrate their commitment by going to the countryside and toiling in work teams or assisting in land reform.

Young CCP activists, often students, were in charge of setting up meetings and procedures. They evaluated individuals' performance, investigated suspects, coordinated with the police, and prepared reports for higher party echelons. They received assistance from a larger group of activists, some of whom had received special training for the campaign. Mostly in their twenties and drawn from the establishments where they studied or worked, these activists helped set individual standards of performance, lead political study, keep records of small-group activities, and nudge and assist peers to heed requirements on confession and criticism.[73] Already regarded by the authorities as politically superior to their fellow intellectuals, these CCP members and activists were able to rise to positions of power in their organizations because of the roles and functions they assumed during the campaign. They were on the front lines of the thought reform of intellectuals.

For the CCP, the reeducation of intellectuals through political study, confession, and criticism was not the only objective of thought reform. The party was also keenly interested in gathering and storing data on individual backgrounds so that it could gain control over the cultural sector. Through monitored confessions and selected investigations, the local authorities collected a huge volume of data and valuable intelligence on the lives of intellectuals, artists, and specialists. This information enabled the authorities to distinguish, compare, and judge intellectuals in both political and moral terms and identify potential sources of support or resistance within universities, publishing houses, and so on. As the educated elite was regimented and absorbed into the state bureaucracy, it lost creative and intellectual freedom.

A cluster of powerful propaganda agencies oversaw the establishment of a whole new set of institutions to spread a new culture in the 1950s. A new cultural landscape came into being, engineered by the authoritative state, but also actively aided by idealistic artists and writers. This new culture was used not only to coerce, but also to persuade by delivering the socialist message to the masses and mobilize them for political gains. The new cultural institutions shaped social opinions, rewrote the past, changed attitudes, and helped to create a milieu within which government policies could succeed in building a better future. They created and maintained popular support, and compensated for the government's lack of legitimacy. Thus, the new culture was critical in helping to cement CCP rule. It shifted public perception in the urban areas to a more positive view of the new order. At the same time, the richness and diversity of the existing cultural fabric vanished.

Land Reform

China's revolution had its own pattern of development. It featured some similarity to the Russian Revolution but it also deviated from the Russian experience in significant and important ways.[74] These differences led to different debates and contentions surrounding the revolution, to different issues in building a socialist society, and ultimately to different experiences of communism in China. Unlike in Tsarist Russia, the peasants in imperial China were never strongly bound to the landlord's estates. As we have seen, most peasants were either tenants or owners of the plots they cultivated. They sold their crops at village markets in exchange for silver that was used to pay the landlords and the state taxes. Peasants were therefore part of local market networks. Those networks were dominated and often controlled by a local elite made up of landowners, wealthy merchants, and retired officials and their families. This powerful elite situated between the state and the peasantry was often able to resist the central government's power. Such an element was perhaps missing in Russia. In other words, in a Chinese rural society dominated by village-based networks, it was difficult to wield central power. Furthermore, in the nineteenth and early twentieth centuries, as internal uprisings and foreign imperialism repeatedly challenged Chinese central governments, local societies became ever more independent. As regional warlords rose to power, central power quickly crumbled.

Land reform was perhaps the most important sociopolitical goal of the CCP. Through a redistribution of the land, a more egalitarian society could be created that would eliminate rural poverty and economic inequality. The CCP also pursued other goals, however, such as establishing central control over the countryside and increasing tax revenues from China's huge agricultural production. In Yan'an, the party had softened its stance on land reform, but after the outbreak of civil war, it once again adopted a more radical approach. In May 1946, Mao issued a directive that called for heightening class struggle in the countryside. The areas the CCP controlled at that time were mostly located in North China. Land in those regions, he said, should be confiscated from "large landlords," "evil gentry," and "tyrants," and be given to poor peasants and landless rural workers. Special work teams were sent to the villages to start the process by dividing the local population into different categories: landlords, rich peasants, middle peasants, poor peasants, and laborers. A problem was that, given how enormously conditions varied throughout China, many villages in North China had no significant landholding class. In the next step, those in the poor peasant and laborer categories were mobilized against the so-called landlords, an ambiguous and relative category. Having identified the biggest landholders or landlords in the village, the work teams organized meetings of the villagers to discuss the bitterness of the past and denounce the landlords as symbols of past oppression. Only after such "speak bitterness" (suku) meetings ended with verdicts for the landlords were actual land reforms carried out. Free rein was given to young peasant activists who had scores to settle with landlords and "local bullies." This often resulted in the deaths of some people designated as landlords and rich peasants. This violence was soon deemed excessive by the party, not least because it disrupted agricultural production. Many of the young party activists were accused of "indiscriminate killings" and their methods were denounced as "leftist deviations." Land reform in North China was largely halted after a year and more moderate guidelines were drawn up.

The second phase of the land reform campaign was launched in June 1950, on the eve of the Korean War, with the passage of the Land Reform Law.[75] It ended around the same time the truce was declared on the Korean peninsula. In this second phase, land reform was carried out nationwide and extended to southern regions, where there had been no previous experience of social reform in the countryside and where communist power was almost non-existent. Its main aim was still to confiscate the landholdings of the landlords and to distribute them among the poorer peasants, but the new directives urged the work teams to safeguard the economically important farms of small and mid-sized land owners and to avoid disrupting the viability of the rural economy. Furthermore, rural enterprises enjoyed protection, even if owned by landlords. During the Korean War, fiscal concerns were a top priority.

When the work teams arrived in an area, ready to categorize rural communities into different classes, they were guided by directives from the Central Committee specifying that landlords usually made up about 4 percent of the rural population, and owned 40 percent of the land. They confiscated the land, houses, equipment, and property owned by those they deemed to be landlords, and by religious bodies, schools, and clans. In the subsequent redistribution of these assets, however, landlords were in principle entitled to shares of land equal to those of poor peasants. The 1950 Land Reform Law protected most of the lands of rich peasants who, according to the Central Committee, constituted about 6 percent of the rural population and controlled about 20 percent of the farmland. Rich peasants were also permitted to continue to rent land to others and to hire labor. Only leased land in excess of what the rich peasants and their hired laborers worked themselves was redistributed.

Land reform measures were inherently violent, and this violence was exacerbated by fears of counterrevolution generated by the Korean War. Work teams fanned resentment and turned local conflicts into class struggle. Some landlords and rich peasants were executed and others charged with criminal offenses. Most were assigned, along with their families, to undergo reform through labor in the poor peasants' associations or made to labor under surveillance by the village government—indeed, more than thirty million people were forced to work under such surveillance. In many cases, violence was carefully orchestrated to follow clear, prearranged patterns. Dramatic devices such as staging, props, working scripts, agitators, and climactic moments were efficiently used to engage the emotions of the crowd, stir up resentment against targeted groups, and mobilize villagers to enact the reform. The meticulous organization of such events allowed the regime to rally popular support and extend the coercive (formal and informal) instruments of the revolutionary state.[76]

On the whole, land reform was completed by the beginning of 1953 without major disruptions to China's vast and precariously balanced agricultural economy. Agricultural production even increased substantially in the early 1950s—although the gains probably had less to do with agrarian social reform than with the restoration of political order and revival of trade and transport after a decade of foreign invasion and civil war. At the same time, people in villages were encouraged to establish small mutual-aid teams which, although based on private property, led to sharing of draft animals and large tools. While land reform led to more equal distribution of land, however, it did not lead to more equally distributed rural incomes.[77] After land reform, the poorer peasants who made up more than 57 percent of the rural population owned almost half of China's land, but rich peasants' plots were often

twice the average size of those owned by poor peasants. Landlords, constituting 2.5 percent of the population, were left with little more than 2 percent
of China's farm land. As these numbers show, they were the main target of
land reform and they were practically eliminated as a social group in many
areas. Furthermore, poor peasants did not have enough capital and labor at
their disposal to make efficient use of the newly allotted land. Land that was
redistributed often produced less than it had before. Many areas were also
too impoverished to engage in land reform, as there were no landlords,
and existing plots could not be made productive due to the lack of tools and
fertilizers. In the end, while land reform generated significant changes in the
structure of land ownership, it failed to realize its goal of a more egalitarian
society in the countryside. Rural inequalities persisted, with peasants of the
middle and upper strata emerging as the winners in land reform. Poor peasants, including a growing number of new rural cadres, became disillusioned
and discontented, and complained that the promises of revolution had not
been kept. This failure was a major reason that the new government soon
started to push through its agenda of collectivization.

Land reform, beyond being an agrarian social reform to achieve more equitable land distribution, achieved other political goals. Most importantly, it
changed the relationship between the state and rural society. Because of land
reform, many landholdings that previously had not been reported to tax collectors were measured and assessed. Once it was determined how much each
plot was able to produce, it was possible to specify the amount of grain that
had to be given to the state as tax. Land reform thus helped the government
increase the area of taxable land and bring in new revenues. Grain and other
foodstuffs requisitioned from the countryside were valuable to supply the
cities or to trade with the Soviet Union for industrial equipment. Overall, the
state was able to considerably increase its rural tax base.

Land reform also had significant social consequences. Members of work
teams later became cadres in local villages, holding significant positions of
power. They became the new elites in rural society. These cadres did not
hail from local society but were brought in from the outside. Often, they
came from the regions in northern China that had been "liberated" first.
With their arrival, the land reform movement also disrupted the local networks of merchants, literates, and intermediaries who had long dominated
rural society and acted as brokers between the state and the peasants. A

major aim of land reform appears to have been this final destruction of the traditional rural social structure. Traditional institutions relying on estates, such as lineage halls and temples, were annihilated. The new state had a much more direct entry point into rural society and increased leverage for the extraction of resources.

The implementation of land reform was all but smooth.[78] Many peasants welcomed a fairer distribution of the land, but resented higher tax payments and party control. As recent Chinese research has shown, it became very violent over time due to increasing resistance in the countryside.[79] In many places, peasants refused to fully cooperate. Authorities also had trouble enlisting peasants to achieve their purposes. It was difficult to penetrate local society in the countryside. The party was unfamiliar with rural conditions in southern China, cadres did not speak the local dialects, and they had no social connections to the villages. When peasants started to criticize the government or refused to deliver their full grain quotas, cadres were helpless and saw no option but to resort to violence or coercion to carry out land reform. Problems also arose from the fact that the government pursued a single strict policy that was applied throughout the whole country, yet conditions in China were very diverse. Northern villages had economic and social structures that were very different from villages in the south. Some mountainous areas or poor regions could barely support a few rich peasants, let alone sustain a landlord class. Villages near market towns in South China tended to be prosperous due to sophisticated handicraft industries, but here, landlords were few and far outnumbered by rich peasants. In general, the boundaries between the categories introduced by the CCP to classify rural society into landlords, rich peasants, middle peasants, and so on tended to be blurred. There were areas where the vast bulk of the land was in the hands of small owners, and next came tenants who had contractually leased the land. But tenants were not necessarily much poorer than landowners and there was little hostility between them. Villagers therefore failed to participate fully in the campaigns. Peasants were also hesitant to carry out class struggle. The biggest problem in the countryside was perhaps not even inequality, but the small size of the farms. Most rural households supplemented their incomes with handicraft or other nonagricultural businesses.

The government and the party soon came to the conclusion that the peasants were not as revolutionary as they had assumed. They would have to be brought along by thought reform and education movements aimed at thorough changes of everyday culture. Culture, production, everyday life, division of labor, and social hierarchy would all have to become more conducive to revolution. The people needed to be turned into "state's peasants" *(guojia de nongmin)*. The countryside had to be entirely remade by eradicating "feudalist exploitation" and replacing it with egalitarian peasant communities. With this recognition, the government increased the pressure for transformation and strengthened its reeducation efforts, resorting to violent methods as it deemed necessary. Plans were made to bring greater changes to rural society and ready the nation for a great leap forward.

EIGHT

Leaping Ahead

1955–1960

In the mid-1950s, a part of the Chinese leadership around Mao Zedong came to the conclusion that the country needed to hasten its pace on the path to communism and to intensify social transformation. A number of domestic and international factors seemed to suggest that an acceleration of the socialist transformation could provide much needed relief and offer a solution for China's mounting problems. Domestically, the decision in the mid-fifties to implement a planned economy ran into steep hurdles and necessitated a significant revenue increase that was very difficult to achieve. Rural collectivization was enforced to increase revenue from the countryside, but output stagnated. Internationally, the death of Stalin in 1953 and the critical reckoning of Khrushchev with Stalin's rule sent ripples throughout the socialist world. Rising discontent in socialist countries alarmed the leadership in Beijing and prompted the search for a forward escape. The Great Leap Forward, started in 1958, was the answer. It was an attempt to deal with the accumulating challenges by mobilizing China's population to make major and sudden progress in industrialization and modernization. This daring gamble, however, ended in one of the worst calamities in modern Chinese history. Economic mismanagement and natural disaster led to a famine that killed over twenty million people.

Reorganizing Society

Many authors and studies refer to society under Mao Zedong or under CCP rule, but to imply that Chinese society remained separate and distinct from the government is misleading, and neglects to recognize an important aspect of PRC history. The reality is that the CCP government's persistent and

forceful efforts to transform Chinese society left deep and lasting imprints
on the social construction of China and the construction of the individual.
By pursuing an increasingly ambitious reform agenda, the state transformed
social practices and reached deep into society. The leadership and the party
did not only sit above society; they integrated themselves into social life, transforming society and becoming part and parcel of China's new social fabric.[1]

To manage "targeted" people (zhongdian renkou)—that is, selected segments of the population in each community to be specially monitored and
controlled because of their political, social, and economic backgrounds—the
new power took over the system of household registration from the nationalist government, but made it more systematic, extensive, and effective.[2] Using
records from the republican census as a foundation, the communist authorities reinstituted the household registers, which ordinarily had one page for
each member of a household (which could be extended to include a collective unit like a company dormitory, an apartment house, a boat, or a
temple). That page included entries for name, birth date, occupation, place of
work, family background, individual status, education level, marital status,
religion, and ancestral place of origin to be entered. Any time one of these
changed, the head of household was supposed to change the entry in the
register and report it to the local Public Security Bureau. The head of household
was held responsible for reporting all changes in the constitution of the
household. Individuals were registered as members of households. In general, the household registry was deposited in the "household registration section" (hujike) of each local police station. Food-ration cards were also given
to the head of the household, who in turn distributed them to other family
members. This grassroots institution was called hukou. It became the main
basis for resource allocation and subsidization for selected groups of the population. Based on hukou files, the police also kept a confidential list of
people to be specially supervised.

Hukou registration began as a tool to protect the revolution by identifying
and managing suspected enemies of the government. By the end of the 1950s,
however, everyone in Chinese society had been assigned an urban or rural
identity through the system.[3] Further, someone who was not registered to the
hukou of an area was not permitted to reside there. The hukou system thus
allowed the government to regulate and control internal migration—which
it did not only to stem the migration from rural to urban areas and from small

cities to large cities, but in fact to encourage migration in the reverse direction. To prevent rural residents from entering a city and benefiting from the valuable subsidies intended for urban residents, their right to enter had to be restricted. At the same time, the large groups of refugees and migrants already in the city had to be removed—a task that had to be approached with urgency given the national priority placed on rapid industrialization. Achieving this required that limited urban food subsidies be reserved for urban workers, not wasted on nonproductive refugees (who were needed in the countryside to produce more food).

In 1955, the government began to launch campaigns to relocate those members of urban society who were labeled as "parasitic" and did not have an urban *hukou*. Hundreds of thousands were persuaded or forced to relocate to rural villages. Relocation of migrants and refugees was usually accompanied by extensive propaganda efforts. The party's policy was to "heighten the general consciousness of the masses, obtain the sympathy and support of society, and create a formidable force of public opinion."[4] Through such means, a majority of a city's population could be swayed to personally participate in the various types of meetings and farewell gatherings organized to disseminate information about this campaign. The propaganda emphasized the long-term goals of socialist construction and "the bright prospects of rural socialist transformation." It aimed at creating "a new atmosphere" in which "mothers mobilized sons, wives mobilized husbands, elder brothers mobilized younger brothers, mothers-in-law mobilized sons-in-law, and targets mobilized other targets." Cadres reported with pride that "masses of urban citizens voluntarily organized themselves to help their rural brothers and sisters return to the village." This new atmosphere of popular, personalized social pressure was identified as "the driving force behind the upsurge in the mobilization work." Through these efforts, the campaign was reportedly transformed into a "movement initiated by the masses themselves." Mobilizing the urban population and getting urbanites involved was ostensibly a key factor for success of the campaigns that ultimately relocated hundreds of thousands.

In May 1955, Zhou Enlai signed a directive to take the household registration system that had been in place in the cities since 1951 and expand it to the countryside. With the promulgation of "Statutes of the PRC on Household Registration" *(Zhonghua renmin gongheguo hukou dengji tiaoli)* on January 9, 1958, this omnipresent and powerful institution was eventually given a legal basis.[5] The statutes stipulated that every citizen had to be registered at their place of residence by the Ministry of State Security. Overall, the *hukou* was one of the most central institutions the new government established. As well as a powerful tool for demographic intervention, it was the linchpin in the administration of urban neighborhoods during the 1950s, regulating access to scarce resources and entitlements based on residency.

An important goal of the CCP was to address the long-standing inequality between men and women by toppling an old patriarchal order based on male dominance over women's lives. Specifically, the reformers wanted to rid Chinese society of child marriage, concubinage, and the prohibition against widows remarrying. The official discourse portrayed marriage reform as an integral part of a larger socialist project of building a productive, liberated nation.[6] The New Marriage Law of 1950 was supposed to tackle those issues. The overarching goal as described in Article 1 of the law was the abolition of "feudal" marriage practices and the establishment of a new family order based on free spousal choice, monogamy, and equality between men and women. The law also proclaimed the right of a woman to seek a divorce from her husband. Overall, the law aimed not only to alter how Chinese couples married, but also to change the roles women and men played within families and communities. Consequently, marriage, family, and gender roles became key elements in China's revolutionary project to build a new society. The party wanted to cultivate the married couple as a new unit of political action that was emancipated, modern, patriotic, productive, and socialist.

The implementation of the 1950 Marriage Law ran into considerable resistance, however.[7] Across China, the campaign's mixed results suggested there were limits to the new state's reach. Husbands, mothers-in-law, and cadres resented the implications and consequences. Many husbands and their families had paid money to their brides' families at the time of their nuptials, and that considerable financial investment was made with expectations regarding the women's work in households and fields. The possibility of divorce threatened those agreements; under the new law a poor man might suffer a loss from which he could never recover. The law also threatened to upset the long-standing position of mothers-in-law who held power over daughters-in-law. Meanwhile, cadres in the countryside were hesitant to implement regulations they feared would alienate the male population. The communist government

婚姻自己作主張 登記回來喜洋洋

8.1. Propaganda poster concerning the Marriage Law of 1950. The slogan reads: "In marriage, keep an eye on your own interests, and return radiant after registration." Wu Dezu, & Landsberger, S. R. Print no. 0576. International Institute of Social History

thus devoted considerable efforts at a grassroots level to educating people about the law. It encouraged women to take advantage of their new rights as socialist citizens and, as women learned about those rights, divorce rates in some areas jumped higher. Yet the local officials often would not grant divorces, especially if family hardship could be proven. Criticisms about the lack of implementation led the party to renew efforts to enforce the law in 1953. As the hold of the new government strengthened, local cadres were instructed to strictly follow the text of the law. Still, it often remained very difficult for a woman to obtain a divorce.

Another area in which the state intervened to eradicate practices it viewed as backward and feudal was religion.[8] The consequences of land reform had already shattered the social and economic foundations of religious practices. The plots that local temples had relied on to finance their activities were confiscated and redistributed. The cadres also attacked the landlords and other local elites who would have been active in the temple associations. After 1950, no space was left for carrying out religious community festivals. But worship of ancestors and local gods continued to be carried out privately. Like the GMD, the Communist Party made a distinction between religion and superstition. Following the example set by the GMD, the new communist government recognized five religions—Daoism, Buddhism, Islam, Catholicism, and Protestantism. The CCP's policy toward religion was based on Stalin's policy. State agencies regulated religious affairs and restricted the educational and welfare activities of the religious organizations, and clergy were organized into "patriotic associations" such as the Chinese Buddhist Association, founded in 1953, which cooperated with the government. The new patriotic associations participated in political campaigns of the party and urged their members to refrain from burning paper money in sacrifices to spirits or participating in religious activities carried out in public. Religious leaders who refused to cooperate were imprisoned, allegedly not for their religious beliefs (since these were officially protected by the constitution), but for their counterrevolutionary activities.

The most systematic suppression was directed against the millenarian sects and redemptive societies. Those groups, many of which had emerged in the nineteenth century and grown rapidly in the first half of the twentieth century, were very diverse in terms of ritual and belief, yet shared certain general features: they were all committed to an ideal of universal salvation, regardless of family, lineage, or place of residence; they were generally based on doctrinal scriptures called "precious volumes" (baojuan); and they were relatively open to new members. Many believed in a creator deity and in three cycles (kalpas) of creation, destruction, and the arrival of a holy savior who would relieve the faithful from worldly misery. The party perceived those groups without exception as a counterrevolutionary threat to their rule. Their leaders were ruthlessly punished, often sentenced to death, and their members were forced to withdraw and cut all connection to the groups. This was accompanied by a large-scale propaganda campaign to educate the masses about the threat represented by these societies. There were exhibitions exposing the "crimes" of the sects, as well as public confessions of leaders describing their misdeeds. But despite unrelenting pressure by the state, the groups survived. Many members went underground and dropped visible signs of their membership. The religious practices persisted, as evidenced by numerous reports of stories continuing to circulate about holy water, secret stones, and mysterious, powerful places.[9]

Another key moment in the transformation of Chinese society came when the system of classifying ethnic populations was adopted and implemented. In the interests of social transformation and building a new socialist nation, it was an important project to construct the People's Republic of China as a unified, multinational state made up of different peoples. The centrality of *minzu* or "nationalities" as a concept can be traced back to the republican era. In 1953, the government issued a nationwide call for every ethnic group to declare its nationality. The multitude of *minzu* named as a result of this call made for a very long, confusing, and ultimately unmanageable list. In some areas, even single clans identified themselves as *minzu*. Facing such diversity in local Chinese society, the government hired social scientists and started an Ethnic Classification Project *(minzu shibie)*, the outcome of which was to consolidate the more than four hundred ethnic identities discovered by the 1953–1954 census into a more manageable number. The project was launched in Yunnan province in 1954.[10] Yunnan, located in southwestern China, is the province where almost half the classified minority groups reside. The communist ethnologists dispatched by Beijing to Yunnan to scientifically classify the various ethnicities used a linguistics-based system that had been designed in the early twentieth century by an officer in the imperialist British army, Henry Rudolph Davies, who had undertaken an expedition to Yunnan in 1894. Rather than strictly follow the Stalinist criteria for categorization (based on a combination of ethnicity, language, and history), the Chinese scholars modified the approach to fit the complexity of Chinese social conditions in the Yunnan countryside. One historian has described their classification as identifying "plausible communities" or groups with "ethnic potential"—meaning that they projected that certain communities could form *minzu* in the future. Needless to say, a classification informed by such an approach was full of artificial divisions.[11] In the government's census, more than two hundred groups in Yunnan had claimed *minzu* status, but a mere twenty-five of them were recognized by the new categories. After the research team had established its classification scheme in Yunnan, however, the central authorities employed extensive political propaganda to implement it nationwide. The classification work did not, however, end in 1954; at that point, only thirty-nine *minzu* had been recognized by the state. By 1964, this figure stood at fifty-three, and the last groups to be officially recognized were the Lhoba in Tibet and the Jinuo in Yunnan, in 1965 and 1979, respectively. In the years following the project, cultural and scientific works incorporated a rewritten history of China and its diversity that promoted a so-called "historic" and "ancestral" model of today's fifty-five *minzu* plus the Han Chinese *minzu*. Most surprising, the ethnic classification project managed to create some groups that had never actually existed. In the decades since, as the state has taught minority groups to accept these official categories, they have become social reality. It was only in 1987 that the central authorities announced the end of the national Ethnic Classification Project, thereby indicating that the fifty-six *minzu* figure was henceforth definitive. According to the constitution, the minorities were also granted self-determination rights in so-called autonomous areas, where they could maintain their languages, customs, and cultures.

As well as ethnic classification, there was also great interest in social classification: labeling and producing new classes in society. Since the revolution, people had been categorized as members of the "red types" (workers, poor and lower-middle-class peasants, revolutionary cadres, revolutionary soldiers, and dependents of revolutionary martyrs), or of the "black elements" (landlords, rich peasants, counterrevolutionaries, bad elements, rightists, and, implicitly, intellectuals). Personal files recorded every individual's details, including those essential pieces of information—class and political background. These categories began to matter a great deal as they became the basis for class discrimination. One's chances of a university education, a good industrial job, or being "sent down" from town to countryside to work as a peasant depended on how one was categorized. The Chinese leadership was inadvertently creating a new, communist *ancien régime* where everybody was allocated a relatively unchangeable status, with the "proletariat" at the top and the "black elements" at the bottom.

As we have seen, the CCP intended to create a new, collective subject: a modern, liberated, and self-fashioned type, the "new men and women" of China. Ascribing new definitions of gender roles, class, and nation was a significant part of the transformation of Chinese society. Problems of scarcity, rationing, and hardship made the process very consequential, since these categories became the basis for varying degrees of subsistence and entitlements. It was one of the important ways in which the concepts and ideas of a new socialist identity became literally embodied in the lives of people. Ascribing class, creating new bonds of belonging, and transforming the self all involved the enforcement of social discipline, which was a central aspect of this project. While the state was able to exert huge influence, its experience with marriage law and religion also demonstrate the limits of its power. Some existing social practices were difficult to change and stubbornly weathered even sustained and forceful campaigns.

Planning the Economy

After the communist takeover, China fell into a difficult economic situation. Production in the cities declined continuously during the first two years of communist rule owing to the lingering effects of the civil war and also the embargo imposed by the United States in 1950 that hampered China's foreign trade. The problems were compounded by the new government. The newly installed city administrations urgently needed funds, which they tried to raise by increasing taxes and other fees on businesses. Immediately following the takeover in 1949, many enterprises had been instructed to pay higher wages, which increased their costs of production. Business owners were also forced to purchase Victory Bonds to fund government operations, and this diverted money that would otherwise have been invested in production. The result was a marked rise in urban unemployment.

The CCP's economic policy, fundamentally inspired by Marxist theory, was that all means of production, including all enterprises and factories, should eventually be nationalized and operate under full state ownership. Leadership saw this as a precondition for creating a truly new and better society. Facing deepening economic troubles in the two years after 1949, however, the party adopted a moderate course and refrained from wholesale nationalization. Overall, economic policy in the first years of the PRC was pragmatic and flexible, and oriented toward growth. In an approach that corresponded with the New Democracy policy, Mao declared in June 1949 that "China must utilize all the factors of urban and rural capitalism that are beneficial and not harmful to the national economy and the people's livelihood, and we must unite with the national bourgeoisie in common struggle. Our present policy is to regulate capitalism, not to destroy it."[12] Chinese leaders looked favorably upon Lenin's New Economic Policy after the October revolution, which in key respects provided an economic model for China's moderate policy in the period of New Democracy. In the initial phase, the new government bought a number of enterprises, and some previous owners remained at their firms as managers or supervisors. In manufacturing plants and other industrial concerns taken over from the GMD, many managerial staff were also retained. Only a small number of key companies in the financial and defense sectors were outright nationalized.

The Bank of China, for instance, was taken over by the government and became the only bank authorized to provide credit for foreign trade. The history of the Bank of China began during the Qing dynasty. In 1905, the Qing established the Daqing Hubu Bank, which was renamed Daqing Bank in 1908. In 1912, Sun Yat-sen renamed it again as the Bank of China and made it the central bank of the new republic. After 1949, the Bank of China nominally remained independent but was effectively incorporated into the People's Bank of China as its foreign-exchange trading arm. The People's Bank of China, established in 1948 through the amalgamation of several regional banks, became the new central bank. In 1953, the government also extended its control over the economy by replacing previously independent chambers of commerce with the All-China Federation of Industry and Commerce.

By implementing these policies, the government was able to stabilize the economy relatively quickly. Well-calibrated measures such as control of the budgets, indexing of wages, and the issuing of a new currency—the Renminbi—brought inflation under control by the end of 1950. The successful stabilization of the financial sector led to an overall economic upturn. Private production expanded quickly in relative and absolute terms during the period from 1950 to 1953. Industry and agriculture recovered and grew to the extent that, by the end of 1952, output already surpassed the highest prerevolutionary levels. Thus, within the first few years, a mixed economy emerged, in which major industries that were already state-owned coexisted with a sizable sector of private manufacturing and trading enterprises, and a private handicrafts industry.[13] In agriculture, too, landlords had been disowned by the land reform movement, and the peasantry, now made up of individual private-property owners, dominated.

CCP leaders agreed that the mixed economy should endure only temporarily. In due course and once conditions permitted, all private ownership of means of production should be abolished. The crucial question, of course, was how long the stage of New Democracy could be allowed to last. At a June 1950 meeting of the Chinese People's Political Consultative Conference, Mao told anxious businesspeople, entrepreneurs, and traders that the mixed economy during the period of New Democracy would last twenty to thirty years. During this time, conditions conducive to a socialist transition would gradually develop. In reality, however, intraparty discussions had already modified the plan and debated the possibility of ten, fifteen, or twenty years.[14] Yet, other leaders, such as Liu Shaoqi, continued to adhere to Lenin's New Economic Policy and to Stalin's moderate advice. Stalin believed China was too backward for a transition to a planned economy, and that the government should continue to cooperate with private business to promote economic development. Liu Shaoqi and many others agreed. They also thought that the development of agriculture should be the first priority, with light and heavy industry coming second and third. This order of priorities was exactly in line with Lenin's and Stalin's recommendations. Liu also believed that the manufacturing industry needed to be modernized first so that it was able to supply machinery and goods for China's huge countryside. Only then could agriculture be collectivized. Instead of fast collectivization, he advocated the promotion of cooperatives that could jointly organize supply and marketing for rural producers, again conforming to Lenin's policy. This approach was also backed by another important leader, Zhang Wentian ([1900–1976] one of the twenty-eight Bolsheviks who had studied in Moscow and a Politburo member, Heilongjiang party secretary, and Berkeley graduate). Zhang and Liu wanted to protect the incentives necessary for agricultural growth, which meant sustaining the existing economy and its rich peasants until the conditions for a future transition to socialism and a collective economy had been created.

But after the consolidation of the CCP's rule, Mao Zedong started to short-circuit this long-term perspective and encouraged efforts to move forward with nationalization and economic planning.[15] Mao began to repudiate the moderate New Economic Policy model, which he thought had run its course. In February 1953, Mao stressed to provincial officials, as he had done many times, that Soviet methods should not be blindly imitated. He started to advocate a program of economic change that was more ambitious than anything that had been discussed in party circles so far. Many CCP members and government officials were bewildered and reacted to this shift with disbelief. The business community was shocked and felt deeply betrayed. To this day, there has been no entirely convincing explanation for the change in Mao's thinking, although several reasons have been suggested. According to one, after the Korean War, Mao felt that China should take advantage of the momentum it had established to press forward in its transition to a socialist economic system. Another theory says that Mao wanted to outdo Stalin and claim a leadership role for himself by transforming China successfully on a schedule he set. The most convincing explanation, however, relates to likely anxieties and insecurities within the leadership. Mao felt that as long as there were capitalists and market structures in China, the socialist project was at great risk of being toppled. In his speeches and commentaries, he frequently pointed out that communism would be secure only when all remnants of capitalism had been completely removed, just as the big estates and landholdings had to be liquidated in the countryside. The international situation, especially the threats of the Cold War and the ongoing conflict in North Korea, also kindled these worries. On numerous occasions, he mentioned the need to continue the revolutionary struggle. During a Politburo meeting on June 15, 1953, Mao stated: "The transition period is full of contradictions and struggles, and our present revolutionary struggle is more profound than armed revolutions. This is a revolution that will completely bury the capitalist system as well as all exploitative systems. The idea of consolidating a 'New Democratic order' is not in accordance with the real conditions of the struggle and hinders the advancement of the socialist cause."[16]

There were, however, also very pragmatic considerations. The mixed economy, while growing quickly, had inherent problems. As the institutions of China's socialist planned economy developed in the mid-1950s, it became obvious to both party leaders and owners of private enterprise that it was difficult to maintain private production in an increasingly socialist economy. The dual economy offered many opportunities for fraud, embezzlement, theft of government-supplied materials, and other violations of the law that became common problems. Because the Five-Anti campaign could only temporarily fix these problems, the PRC's leaders were inclined to attempt to implement socialist planning and state administration more quickly than anticipated. Meanwhile, many owners of private firms were critical of the mixed economy and were calling for solutions.[17] Their status as private enterprises operating in a state-dominated economy was confusing and uncertain, and they hoped that their evolution into joint state-private enterprises, operating under the management of the state, would mean better and more reliable organizational structures. Overall, the policies relating to private industry should be seen as ad hoc responses to new crises and distortions in the Chinese economy in the 1950s, the consequences of which drove both party and business toward socialization faster than anyone had initially anticipated.

Despite ongoing debate within the party, Mao Zedong announced a "general line for socialist transition" in October 1953. Following the path of development laid out by Stalin in the late 1920s and 1930s, this new policy declared a new phase in the transformation of the capitalist economy into socialist industrialization and collectivization. The existing economic structure based on private ownership would be replaced by a system operating exclusively on the basis of state and collective ownership. In that year, nationwide economic planning set out to develop a massive socialist industrial complex through direct government control.[18] The plan called for a development strategy based on maximum extraction of surplus from the rural areas to fund heavy industrialization located in the cities. With rapid industrialization given highest priority, the rural was subordinated to the urban and the centralized state focused on allocating resources based on China's economic, not social, needs.

The preamble of the 1954 Constitution of the People's Republic of China captures the sense that the time had come for an accelerated transition. It reads:

> From the founding of the People's Republic of China to the attainment of a socialist society is a period of transition. During the transition, the fundamental task of the state is, step by step, to bring about the socialist industrialization of the country and, step by step, to accomplish the socialist transformation of agriculture, handicrafts, and capitalist industry and commerce. In the last few years, our people have successfully carried out a series of large-scale struggles: the reform of the agrarian system, resistance to American aggression, aid to Korea, the suppression of counterrevolutionaries, and the rehabilitation of the national economy. As a result, the necessary conditions have been created for planned economic construction and gradual transition to socialism.[19]

Thus, in 1954, China described itself as a nation developing a new economic system based on public ownership and economic planning—the type of system the West calls a command economy, since in that system an economic plan made by a government centrally determines investments, prices, incomes, quotas, and production goals, and communicates these to all units as central commands. Implementation began in 1954 and continued vigorously through the "high tide" *(gao chao)* of 1956. The goal to nationalize all privately held businesses and industries was already achieved by 1956. In mid-1955, China's first Five-Year Plan, for the 1953–1957 period, was approved.

As Chinese communists went about developing state industrialization plans and programs, they could build not only on the model of the Soviet Union, but also on the nationalist government's experiences during the war. Several vice chairmen of the GMD National Resources Commission, a planning agency, later served in the State Council planning apparatus. The Soviet model of industrialization was extremely important, however, as was Soviet assistance, since so much had to be learned about centralized economic planning, management of large-scale enterprises, and the acquisition of technical knowledge and skills. The system was heavily dependent on technology and knowledge transfers from the Soviet Union.

The CCP thus set up Soviet-style economic planning agencies and industrial ministries to administer the investment of anticipated surpluses from agriculture into new industries. Entire new industries were created from scratch. At the core of this effort was the establishment, aided by Soviet experts, of 156 enterprises under central control. Most of those investments went to the northeast, which was already, due to Japan's earlier efforts, more oriented toward heavy industry than Shanghai, Wuhan, and other major industrial centers. New factories opened by the government produced electricity-generating equipment, chemical fertilizers, steel, ships, and motor vehicles. These projects were concentrated mostly in upstream industries—that is, in businesses that processed raw resources into intermediary commodities that could then be used by downstream industries to make finished products. These industries were considered strategic in the sense that they had the most linkages with other industries. For example, a petroleum processing facility that refined crude oil into chemicals, which were used by manufacturers to produce plastics, had important linkages downstream. China pursued a strategy that gave priority to heavy industry and therefore focused on industries in the upper and middle stages of the industrial economy.

Introducing a Soviet-style command economy presented a formidable challenge. The process of socialist transformation from the publication of the "general line" to the "socialist high tide" in January 1956 turned out to be rocky. China's economy was huge, complex, and very diverse. In the years before 1949, war and civil war had left the economy highly decentralized and regionalized, and different economic areas emerged that were almost autarkic. Central planning depended on precise data collection and elaborate plans being drawn up for industrial and commercial sectors specifying just how much of every product was needed and what inputs were required to produce that output. These plan targets then had to be broken down into individual production goals for each enterprise. Even in 1950s-era China, there were thousands of industrial and commercial enterprises. Backing up the plan was a system run by a government bureaucracy to contract for inputs and manage their distribution. In some industries, this system could base its allocations on precedents established in the republican era.

The hefty investment in strategic sectors led to substantial economic growth after the announcement of the general line. In 1956, as much as 48 percent of the public budget was funneled into industrial projects. The resulting increase in industrial production drove momentous gross domestic product (GDP) growth: from 1952 to 1957 it averaged 9.2 percent annually. Total industrial output nearly doubled over the course of the five years, from only 17.6 percent of GDP to 33.2 percent. Heavy industrial sectors were developed that supplied each other's demands, based on the government's investment decisions. By the late 1950s, heavy industry contributed 55 percent of total industrial output, up from 35.5 percent in 1952. As a result, the industrial working class grew from six to ten million, and with it, the urban population.

There were downsides to the system, however. The development had very limited spillover effects to benefit larger sectors of the population and larger areas. The growth achieved was resource- and energy-intensive, requiring substantial financial outlays. In particular, as huge investments in heavy industry caused budgetary deficits in the 1950s, pressures rose to export more grain. It was up to the agricultural sector to generate the enormous funds needed for these investments. Growing imbalances developed between industrial and agricultural regions in terms of their salaries, living standards, and welfare provision. The increasing inequalities spurred mobility in labor markets that could be regulated only by setting up tighter controls on rural-urban migration—contributing to a comprehensive effort of social engineering. Scholars have used the term "dual society" to describe the contrasting existence of urban areas subsidized by the state and rural areas reliant on their own resources and production.[20]

From 1953 to 1956, new economic institutions were established by the party that replaced existing structures. These institutional innovations established some degree of state centralization and enabled growth. The planning agency made forceful efforts to shift resources into industry, where they could be employed more productively, even if an industry itself was inefficiently organized.[21] This rechanneling of resources led to quick economic growth, but that effect was created not so much by technological innovation as by reallocation of labor and the redeployment of capital extracted from agricultural production. In other words, the economic institutions created in this period were extractive ones that requisitioned resources from agriculture and turned them into heavy industry investments. These extractive institutions, however, were not able to generate sustained technological change, both because economic incentives were lacking and because the planning bureaucracy resisted change. Once all the resources that could be reallocated to industry had been reallocated, few economic gains were left to be made. At that point, the growth of the Chinese command economy stalled, with lack of innovation and poor economic incentives preventing any further progress. Once CCP leaders recognized these constraints and limits, toward the end of the 1950s, the idea of a big leap held more appeal.

Collectivization in Rural China, 1953–1957

The year 1953 brought the decision to push forward with the next steps in China's transition to socialism, to abandon the economic policy of New Democracy by nationalizing all remaining urban private property and industry, and to swiftly introduce a planned economic system. This development had dramatic consequences for agriculture. The need to increase investment in industry made it imperative to find ways to raise agricultural output. In 1953, agricultural production did not grow fast enough to generate the huge amount of capital required to accelerate China's industrial output. Contrary to Stalin's advice to retain the rich peasant economy lest production be harmed, Mao Zedong and his supporters decided that the answer was to transform Chinese agriculture by pushing through, first, a program to establish cooperatives (in which tools and workloads would be voluntarily shared, even though land was still owned by individual households, and income would be generated by selling products on the market); and, second, a collectivization program (so that all land would be owned collectively by peasants who would be paid salaries for their work). Collectivizing would combine China's small farmers, their small plots of land, and their limited draft animals, tools, and machinery together into larger and presumably more efficient structures.

The idea was to achieve greater agricultural productivity by promoting cooperation in the countryside. As Mao noted in an October 15, 1953, speech:

> The rural work departments at all levels should look upon mutual aid and cooperation as a matter of vital importance. Peasants working on their own cannot raise production to any great extent, therefore we must promote mutual aid and cooperation. If socialism does not occupy the rural positions, capitalism inevitably will. Is it possible to take any road other than the capitalist or the socialist road? The capitalist road can also lead to increased production, but the time required would be longer and the course painful. We will not practice capitalism, that's settled. Yet capitalism is bound to spread unchecked unless we go in for socialism.[22]

Making frequent statements along these lines, Mao Zedong deliberately challenged the party bureaucracy's vested interests in the new democratic model and promoted a shift from gradual transformation to a more rigid model of social and economic development favoring rapid collectivization. Mao's push for profound and quick change in the countryside was met with resistance and contested within the party. The CCP had so far been relatively unified, but now arrived at a crossroads where important decisions affecting future developments had to be made. The first serious fissures of intraparty disagreement appeared.

This became evident in the Gao Gang affair.[23] In 1954, Mao's accusation of two high-ranking colleagues, Gao Gang (1905–1954) and his supporter Rao Shushi (1903–1975), of being traitors led to their purging. Initially trusted by Mao Zedong, Gao had been promoted in the final years of the civil war to become the party, state, and military head of northeastern China (Manchuria). In 1952, he was transferred to Beijing and appointed to head of the State Planning Commission of China (SPC) and member of the Politburo. In 1954, Gao tried to oust Liu Shaoqi and Zhou Enlai. He had his own reasons for doing so, and also represented a larger set of disgruntled party cadres. After 1949, this group of base-area veterans and military leaders shared a belief that they had received fewer high positions than their struggles during the revolution warranted. Of peasant background and little educated, they were often bypassed in promotions and saw many top positions go to more credentialed civilian leaders, who often supported the moderate group of leaders around Liu Shaoqi. Believing he had Mao's backing, Gao began to move against Liu and Zhou—but he was either misled by Mao or had misread his intentions. Mao instead attacked Gao Gang and Rao Shushi for undermining party unity.

It is important to understand that the kind of deep cracks the Gao Gang affair revealed were not restricted to top-level leadership; rather, they divided the entire party and even caused rifts in society. They appeared at all levels. Party cadres confronted public officials working in the new government; local cadres struggled against cadres sent to their villages from other counties; and cadres in urban areas were pitched against rural cadres. Cadres with ties to local communities tended to resist further changes, while younger cadres showed great eagerness to dash forward. The first years of socialism had not created an egalitarian society, but rather reconfigured existing tensions and created new hierarchies.

Within weeks after the National Party Conference, which occurred in March 1955 and proclaimed the defeat of the Gao clique, the CCP adopted active programs for agricultural collectivization and the socialization of industry and commerce. Mao Zedong had come to believe in the potential of small rural collectives to serve as catalysts in bringing about a fully socialist agricultural system. He also claimed that an organizational change in agriculture would lead to increases in output and that, therefore, China could move toward collectivization before the mechanization of agriculture. Given his belief that human incentives were more decisive than technology and resources, changes to "production relations" took precedence over changes to the "mode of production." With the rural situation still in flux following the disruptions of land reform, Mao judged it to be a moment "to strike while the iron is hot."

His opinions were explicitly at odds with recent Central Committee decisions. The Central Committee had opted to delay collectivization until China had the capacity to modernize agriculture. The Central Committee also argued that the rich peasant economy was most productive, and that this

economic form should be consolidated and maintained. Mao started to criticize Liu Shaoqi, Bo Yibo (1908–2007), the minister of finance, and others
for these policies, asserting instead that middle and poor peasants should be
encouraged to oppose rich peasants and ex-landlords, who were attempting
to reestablish their dominance over rural society. In Mao's view, only collectivization could prevent a restoration of the old order. From that point onward,
Mao pressed vigorously for the expansion of mutual-aid and cooperation
teams in agriculture.

As a first step in 1953–1954, farmers were encouraged to form mutual-aid
teams which would work together in farming. Mutual aid, in many forms, had
been familiar for centuries in rural China, as peasants pooled together to harvest each other's crops, or lend each other tools, plows, or animals. But this
had always been voluntary. The new state's policy was to register the existing
mutual-aid teams in the villages, determine their size and membership, and
also organize mutual-aid teams in areas where they had not previously
existed.

The second phase was to turn mutual-aid teams into "agricultural producers' cooperatives," in which the shared items used on a loan basis by the
mutual-aid teams became the permanent property of the cooperative as a
whole. At the same time, "advanced producers' cooperatives" were established
in which peasants pooled not only tools but their entire harvests, which were
split up among all work units that had participated in planting, weeding, and
harvesting. The size of the cooperatives still corresponded more or less to the
size of a traditional village. Such arrangements came about mostly through a
grassroots movement. In the summer of 1955, Mao gave a speech on "The
Question of Agricultural Cooperation," in which he described this grassroots
trend as a "socialist tidal wave" overtaking the countryside.[24] He called for a
campaign to accelerate the transition to socialism, wanting to launch China
on an even faster developmental path. He declared confidently that the peasants would be enthusiastic about collectivization, describing "an active desire among most peasants to take the socialist road." By the end of 1955, almost
all mutual-aid teams had been transformed into agricultural cooperatives. The
majority of poor and middle peasants had been cooperativized.

Seizing the moment, Mao began a campaign for collectivization in 1955–
1956. The reorganization and coordination of peasant labor was again stressed

by Mao as sufficient to bolster development. He also saw it as the only way to make progress, since rural China did not have and could not afford machinery and advanced equipment. The cooperatives were now reorganized into collectives or "state farms," in which peasants worked the land without owning it and received disbursements of grain or cash on the basis of the local cadres' calculations.[25] These state farms consisted of two hundred to three hundred households that were paid not according to the amount of land and other assets they had contributed but according to their labor in the fields. Collectivization required the incorporation of all peasants, as well as the end of most private ownership of land, the end of family farms, and the pooling of resources. While the richer and middle peasants resented collectivization, poorer farmers were often more inclined to welcome it. The land, livestock, and tools of rich peasants were merged into producer collectives. With these momentous developments, the family farming tradition disappeared from rural China.

At the same time, around the end of 1955, the harvest yields that had risen for five years flattened out, and economic problems appeared on the horizon. Agricultural output could not keep up with the demand created by fast industrial expansion or even with the increase in population. The stagnation was related partly to the disadvantage of the rural areas (lower wages, lower food supply, insufficient infrastructure) in relation to the urban areas, and partly to the mixed results of land reform and collectivization. China was hit by an agricultural supply crisis and found it increasingly difficult to provide its own people with enough grain. In 1953, urban rationing had already been introduced, so that the legal urban population received grain distributions from the state. From August 1955 onward, rationing was extended to the countryside and ration cards were distributed through the household system. The rations for the countryside were generally much lower than for the urban areas. While urban areas were subsidized by the state, rural society had to rely on its own resources and labor.

This unfolding crisis did not prompt a reconsideration or pause. Instead, it became a major argument for the quick introduction of the third stage of collectivization: the "unified purchase and sale system" of grain (tonggou tongxiao). The goal of the system was to improve food supply by controlling prices. Even before agricultural collectives were formed, the Chinese government had established compulsory procurement of grain from peasants, creating a government monopoly over key agricultural goods. After 1957, this would include almost all agricultural products; it was not until the mid-1980s that the system was abandoned. Peasants were forced to meet production targets established by the state grain monopoly and to sell what they grew at low, fixed prices. The quota was often higher than the yields of the past. With cheap farm products, such as cotton cloth, the markup on manufactured consumer goods by the state-owned enterprises was high, while wages were kept low and stable. Given these systematic biases in price setting, agriculture became an activity with low returns, while state-owned manufacturing became much more profitable. As a result, there was a steady incentive for people to leave the rural areas. Not wanting too many peasants to leave the farms, however, the government imposed restrictions on mobility by expanding the *hukou* system.

In the countryside, a dual economy emerged. After paying some of their grain in taxes and providing the quota the government demanded at low price for its stores, peasants were able to keep what remained for their own needs.[26] To convince the peasants to deliver their "surplus grain" *(yuliang)*, the state made patriotic appeals arguing that it was needed for the economic construction of the country and the supply of the army, whose members were almost exclusively peasants. The authorities also pointed to the system's advantages for the peasants, stressing that it stabilized prices, avoided exploitation by private traders, and promised relief in case of famine.

Many peasants, however, complained about the low purchase prices and resisted handing grain over to the state. The earlier policies of land reform and the introduction of cooperatives had also been resisted by many peasants, but at least there had been some winners to welcome them. But collectivization, and especially the unified purchase system *tonggou tongxiao*, increased the burden on every household. There were numerous cases of protest against the procurement of state-mandated amounts of grain and sometimes open rebellion in the countryside.[27] In response, the government reduced the quantity that peasants were allowed to keep for their own consumption.

By unleashing a broad campaign in the "high tide" of socialist transformation in 1955–1956, China completed collectivization rapidly, together with the equally and unexpectedly fast socialization of private business and handicrafts. By 1957, the majority of the rural population was organized into collectives. Mao certainly was the moving force behind the push toward collectivization. He prevailed over his colleagues who held different views by removing and deterring opponents, as in the Gao Gang affair. But he also used the ensuing sense of economic crisis as well as the tensions and fissures throughout society.

Surprise and euphoria among the leadership over the implementation of collectivization in such a short period of time allowed Mao to assert that collectivization would successfully address two crucial issues. First, it would effectively forestall the restoration of the prerevolutionary power structure that he and other leaders constantly feared. Second, it would solve China's food supply problem by remedying the shortfalls of land reform. He maintained that reports about resistance in the countryside and criticisms about agricultural social reform were actually instigated by landlords and counterrevolutionaries to attack the CCP and topple socialism.

By the end of 1957, however, it had become evident that collectivization was failing to fulfill its promises. The actual operation of the collectives encountered many difficulties. They were beset by complex accounting procedures, inefficiencies in work allocations, complications in planning the larger units, and inequities among members. Agricultural productivity stagnated, and not enough was produced to fund investments in the industrial development, to feed a growing urban population (nearly a hundred million people in 1957, up from sixty million in 1949), to supply the raw materials (for example, cotton and oil seeds) demanded by industrial manufacturers, and to engage in the foreign exchange needed to import industrial goods.[28] Disillusionment took hold within the party and society. Doubts spread as to whether the system of economic planning and collectivization could work properly in China. Migration from the countryside swelled as farmers, ignoring *hukou* restrictions, sought jobs and food in the cities. These negative developments also deepened disagreements between Mao and, on one side, some of the younger members of the leadership and, on the other side, veteran leaders such as Liu Shaoqi and Zhou Enlai. The former insisted on flexibility, mass mobilization, and fast transformation of the economy, while the latter stressed the necessity of a slow transition to socialism, the advantages of a centrally coordinated plan, and the need to learn from both the successes and failures of the Soviet experience. In the midst of this tense situation, unsettling news reports started coming in from Moscow that only increased anxieties.

Crisis in the Socialist World

In February 1956, Soviet leader Nikita Khrushchev stunned the socialist world with unprecedented and unexpected revelations. In a speech to the Twentieth Congress of the Soviet Communist Party, he disclosed at great length the extent of Stalin's brutality, terror, cult of personality, and deviation from Marxist and Leninist principles. By exposing some of Stalin's crimes—mostly, the unwarranted arrests of party members on trumped-up charges—Khrushchev dismantled the image of infallibility with which the communist system had surrounded itself. That the party had strayed from the correct path for decades, and that the Great Leader, admired by communists everywhere, could have been personally responsible for the deaths of so many innocent people, came as a profound shock to communists and their sympathizers throughout the world. The very basis of the communist system's legitimacy was shaken. Stalin's death, then, brought a thaw that exposed tensions within the socialist world and fragmented his vast empire. The fifteen years that followed were some of the most turbulent in the global history of communism and constituted the Cold War's most dangerous period. The world teetered on the brink of nuclear conflict.

Present in Moscow on that day was none other than Deng Xiaoping, head of the Chinese delegation to Moscow for the Twentieth Soviet Party Congress.[29] Like other foreign leaders attending the congress, Deng was not allowed to attend the private session in which Khrushchev made his speech, but he was allowed to read its text the next day. Deng immediately recognized the significant domestic but also international implications of that speech. Deng was aware that the massive criticism of Stalin would spill over to those who worked with Stalin and, as a consequence, weaken the authority of not only the Soviet Communist Party but other communist parties, too. He assigned two interpreters to work all night to translate the speech. He also carefully avoided addressing its content until Mao had a chance to decide how to respond. Therefore, when Deng returned to Beijing and reported on the speech to Mao (who was vulnerable to many of the same criticisms made of Stalin), Mao was immediately upset.

Khrushchev's revelations deeply unsettled Mao and the CCP leadership, who realized that global conditions had changed and that, as a result, China faced profound challenges. Khrushchev did not stop at criticizing Stalin's rule but also pushed for a "New Course" of reforms, which were soon implemented in the Soviet Union and Eastern Europe. These involved the relaxation of collective agriculture, permission for smaller private enterprises to exist, and in some countries, collective leadership of the Communist Party as a replacement for the so-called "little Stalins"—including Walter Ulbricht of East Germany, Boleslaw Bierut of Poland, and Mátyás Rákosi of Hungary, who had all been Stalin's trusted allies. Khrushchev also wanted to end violent class struggle, and, regarding international affairs, believed that a peaceful coexistence with the West was possible. He hoped that by limiting the arms race and abandoning violence, the socialist world would be able to resolve its internal differences, consolidate its regimes, secure its borders, and develop its economies.

At first, the greatest impact of the new Soviet policies occurred in Eastern Europe, the region where communism's hold was weakest. The sense of general relaxation ushered in by the post-Stalin era encouraged public articulations of grievances and discontent. As early as 1953, shortly after the death of Stalin, workers protested against low wages, lack of freedom, and Soviet rule in Czechoslovakia. This was soon followed by more serious and broader unrest in East Germany. The demonstrations and strikes were swiftly and violently repressed, but the workers succeeded in receiving higher wages. A larger crisis developed in Poland in June 1956. As in East Berlin and Plzeň, it was workers who started the protests. Low standards of living were the roots of popular discontent. In Poland, Soviet intervention was narrowly avoided, but when similar protests erupted in Hungary in the fall of 1956, the Soviet military moved in to quell them. Initially, the protests did not call for the end of one-party rule but only for modifications. Soon enough, however, protesters were demanding Hungary's withdrawal from the Warsaw Pact and the creation of a multi-party Popular Front government.

The resulting crackdown was harsh. On November 4, as Warsaw Pact forces entered Hungary and encountered heavy resistance, thousands were killed and many more arrested. It was an episode of violence that served to consolidate the communist regimes of Eastern Europe; the region was the first to stabilize after the restive period following Stalin's death. But unable to simply go back to earlier forms of governance, these governments spent the next decade looking for a more viable *modus vivendi* between communist regimes and society. Most East European governments settled on a more liberal, less austere form of communism from the late 1950s onward. Hungary, for instance, emerged after a period of repression as one of the most moderate countries in the bloc. Yet, it would be some time before the turbulence in the socialist world truly subsided. The forces Khrushchev had unleashed were powerful and not easily contained to Europe.

Watching workers in Poland and Hungary attempt to overthrow their communist regimes, using the revelations of the Twentieth Congress as evidence that communism could not work, the leaders in China became ever more alarmed.[30] On the one hand, Mao Zedong, who had always had an uneasy relationship with Stalin, welcomed critical discussion of Stalin's mistakes, particularly as they related to his misguided policies toward China. On the other hand, Mao believed that the Soviet Union's New Course, which de-Stalinization had made possible, was mistaken. His opinion was not shared, however, by those Chinese Communist Party leaders who dreaded Mao Zedong's monopolization of power. They seized on Khrushchev's speech to welcome the new policies, particularly insisting on the principle of collective leadership. Supporting the moderation of the New Course and thaw policy, they argued that China, too, should revise or slow down its own policies of rapid collectivization. Mao Zedong disagreed and was later to complain about how his views had been met with indifference by many party leaders in 1956.

Moreover, to Mao, who was always concerned about party power, popular unrest in Eastern Europe was evidence of the grave risks that lay ahead. The impact of a changing global situation could already be felt as, in the autumn and winter of 1956, discontent caused by collectivization and the implementation of the planned economy was on the rise in China. Grievances over inadequate food supplies were widespread in the countryside. Public demonstrations for better conditions for workers, more democracy, and freedom of speech were observed and reported on by the secret police in China. The situation was made worse by droughts in Hebei, Henan, and Shandong. Climbing average air temperatures constituted a warming trend that increasingly affected mostly western and northern China, with the most important temperature increases occurring in winter. Beginning in the 1950s, annual rainfall decreased in northern China, resulting in a higher frequency of spring and summer droughts.[31] Between these shocks to the agricultural system and ongoing peasant resistance, the state found it increasingly hard to enforce its grain quotas. More peasants streamed into the cities in 1957 to escape hardships in the new cooperatives and to seek employment in the rapidly expanding state-run factories where government policy kept wages rising rapidly. All over China, tensions flared. Thus, between the pressure of changes across the Eastern Bloc and the mutually reinforcing challenges of China's domestic economy and mounting environmental damage, the party was confronted with the greatest crisis since the 1949 takeover.

Mao Zedong was convinced that China needed to regain momentum both domestically and internationally. In a number of important speeches and articles in 1956 and 1957, it is clear how intensively he was searching for a way out of the crisis. His focus on the language and framing of Chinese politics enabled Mao to have powerful effects, and to bend the party's politics in a leftist direction. His speech "On Ten Major Relationships" (April 25, 1956) was an eloquent, systematic, and critical reexamination of the Soviet model.[32] He emphasized that China should not blindly follow foreign models but should develop its own path with confidence. Mao also described the relationship between the revolution and the counterrevolution, beginning with the observation that revolution and counterrevolution are antipodes. He predicted the continued existence of the revolution–counterrevolution contradiction in socialist society. Though this kind of contradiction was labeled antagonistic, it was changeable. In other words, the negative side (counterrevolution) could be converted to the positive side (revolution) if the social conditions and the policy were right. Mao said: "Thanks to the great strength of the people and to the correct policy we have adopted toward counterrevolutionaries, which allows them to transform themselves into new people through labor, quite a few of them have switched to no longer opposing the revolution. They take part in agricultural labor and industrial work, and some of them are quite enthusiastic and have done beneficial work."

Almost a year later, on February 27, 1957, Mao Zedong gave a talk entitled "On Correctly Handling Contradictions among the People."[33] In it, arguments made previously were taken up again and refined. Mao's central

(433)

argument was again that contradictions continued to exist under socialism. At the outset he drew a distinction between "contradictions between the enemy and us" and "contradictions among the people." Mao's "enemy" category was vague and flexible because the boundary between the people and their enemies was not absolute. He went to great lengths not to set up clear-cut rules and strict laws because he knew that, under certain circumstances, friends could turn into foes (as happened later, when even party members were accused of being rightists) and vice versa (although this happened far less frequently). In some ways, however, "enemies of the people" endured: especially from the late 1950s onward, class status was principally hereditary, so that the children of a landlord, for instance, were considered part of the landlord class.

These speeches, made within the time span of a year, incorporated features that had long characterized Mao's thinking, such as the emphasis on the role of ideas, the tendency to link class status to political thinking, and a belief in the necessity of struggle. But what set them apart was a pervading sense of uncertainty: Mao warned that the question of "whether socialism or capitalism will win is still not really settled." Class struggle, he concluded, would have to continue for a long time, even under socialism, and revolution would need to be reinvigorated and strengthened. He made very clear that he advocated not a thaw or peaceful coexistence, but a deepening and intensification of revolutionary struggle:

> It has been our long-standing policy to bring into play all positive factors and mobilize all forces that can be utilized. We implemented this policy in the past to achieve victory in the people's democratic revolution and to put an end to the rule of imperialism, feudalism, and bureaucratic-capitalism. Now [we are implementing this policy] to carry out a new revolution—that is, a socialist revolution—and to build a socialist country. Regardless of whether it is in the course of revolution or in the course of construction, we must always implement this policy.[34]

This also applied to international affairs, where he also advocated new and more aggressive policy aims. Deepening revolution in domestic and international policies was an integral part of Mao's strategy that would allow socialism in China to weather the crisis. At the same time, this strategy put China at odds with Khrushchev's New Course and with the emergence of a liberal and more humane socialism in Eastern Europe.

In 1957, after the Soviets launched the Sputnik 1 satellite into orbit, putting its space program ahead of the United States' efforts, Mao famously claimed that the "east wind prevails over the west wind." He advocated that the socialist world was not inferior to the nations of the West and should mobilize to contain US imperialism. China also urged Khrushchev's Soviet Union to regain the upper hand in the fight with capitalism. When Khrushchev declined, China unilaterally provoked a limited passage at arms in the Taiwan Strait in 1958. Mao calculated that his People's Liberation Army attack on the islands of Jinmen and Mazu would not result in an international and possibly nuclear war; he reasoned that the US government would shrink from any involvement. To the contrary, President Eisenhower threatened that if China went forward with an invasion of Jinmen, the US was prepared to deploy the atomic bomb against it. Under pressure from both the Americans and Soviets, the Chinese government ended its offensive in the Taiwan Strait. This episode further strained Sino-Soviet relations.

Domestically, the CCP decided at Mao's suggestion to launch a campaign for greater openness: the Hundred Flowers Campaign.[35] On February 27, 1957, Mao delivered a speech in which he encouraged open criticism, using the phrase "let a hundred flowers bloom and a hundred schools of thought contend." The Hundred Flowers Campaign was Mao's response to Khrushchev's thaw and to the reality of bureaucratic oppression and stagnation under state socialism in China and across the socialist world. Mao was convinced that the situation in China differed from the situation in the Soviet Union and in Eastern Europe, because the CCP had reeducated China's intellectuals. Having severed their bourgeois and colonial roots and reoriented themselves to a socialist view of the world, they could be trusted to usefully criticize the CCP in public, he believed. By suggesting ways to correct the faults of bureaucratic rule, they could bring the party to a new and higher level of "revolutionary success" in "serving the people." Not everyone shared that optimism; other leaders believed China's intellectuals were still bourgeois and should not be encouraged to comment on, much less publicly criticize, the CCP. Mao insisted, however—and the movement reached its climax in May 1957, in a thrilling and surprising month of public debate that fully confirmed the skeptics' fears.

Intellectuals were at first reluctant to speak out, but as the months passed, many began to voice their concerns. Many of the intellectuals and minority party leaders, finally emboldened to speak out, surprised Mao with the depth of their criticisms. Some said the party had taken a too dominant, too powerful role and that its thirst for power was not matched by competence in governing. This was the view of, for instance, the editor in chief of the *Guangming Daily*:

> In the past few years the relations between the party and the masses have not been good and have become a problem of our political life that urgently needs readjustment. Where is the key to the problem? In my opinion, the key lies in the idea that "the world belongs to the party." I think a party leading a nation is not the same as a party owning a nation; the public supports the party, but members of the public have not forgotten that they are masters of the nation. . . . Isn't it too much that within the scope of the nation, there must be a party man as leader in every unit, big or small, whether section or subsection? . . . For many years, the talents or capabilities of many party men have not matched their duties. They have bungled their jobs, to the detriment of the state, and have not been able to command the respect of the masses, with the result that the relations between the party and the masses have been tense.[36]

A student frankly criticized the lack of democracy in China: "True socialism is highly democratic, but the socialism we have here is not democratic. I call this society a socialism sprung from a basis of feudalism. We should not be satisfied with the party's rectification and reformist methods and the slight concessions made to the people."[37] Many writers and artists complained of having to obey narrow aesthetic rules and being constantly harassed by censorship. Jurists attacked the legal system as feeble and demanded judicial independence from the party and a strengthening of the court system. The cult that had formed around Mao was criticized, as well. In short, the intellectuals did not make the hoped-for suggestions of gradual improvements to party rule. Rather, just as in Eastern Europe, they voiced demands for more far-reaching political change, even to the extent of calling for a multi-party political system and democratic elections.

Mao and others in the party were shaken and responded by quickly putting an end to the criticism. Mao lashed back at those bourgeois intellectuals who obviously had not been able to efface their class origins despite the elimination of capitalism. He launched a punitive campaign to eradicate the rightists among the intellectuals and cadres (since a number of loyal CCP members had also offered some pointed suggestions for improvement). The Anti-Rightist Campaign took off in June and ran well into 1959. All those who had voiced criticism, regardless of their motives, as well as many who had made no criticism at all, were denounced and punished, and thousands were sent to labor camps. China's intellectuals and professionals inside and outside the party were threatened and intimidated. After Mao shared his estimate that up to 10 percent of all intellectuals were right-leaning and secretly opposed to socialism, many schools, universities, and newspapers took this as a cue that they should report 10 percent of their staffs as rightists. In all, this campaign, which Mao enlisted Deng Xiaoping to manage, branded some 550,000 intellectuals as rightists. During the Hundred Flowers period, Deng had urged local party officials to listen to criticism and not to fight back, but he was disturbed by how "arrogantly and unfairly" some intellectuals had criticized officials who were trying to cope with their complex and difficult assignments. During the Anti-Rightist Campaign, Deng strongly supported Mao in defending the authority of the party and in attacking the outspoken intellectuals.

As Mao's initiatives to deepen the revolution domestically and internationally strained China's relationship with the Soviet Union, increasingly bitter disputes and mutual accusations culminated in the Sino-Soviet split of 1960.[38] Khrushchev withdrew Soviet advisers from China. Chinese media published denunciations of Soviet "revisionists," clearly referring to Khrushchev. Beginning in 1963, Mao started to accuse Moscow publicly of betraying socialism while portraying China as its safe haven and himself as the true defender of Marxism–Leninism. China characterized the Soviet Union's attempt to dominate other socialist countries as "hegemonism" and described Moscow's efforts to gain influence in the developing world as "social imperialism." The split made China the adversary of both superpowers in the world at once. China increasingly stood alone and found itself in an unstable situation.

Red Banners

In 1958, China dramatically inaugurated the "three red banners" *(sanmian hongqi)* movement, consisting of the general line for socialist construction (which Mao had launched in 1953), the Great Leap Forward (1958–1960), and the rural people's communes. The general line for socialist construction referred to the directive to "go all out, aim high, and build socialism with greater, faster, better, and more economical results." With news media spreading the message that "speed is the soul of the general line," the Great Leap Forward became the embodiment of that ideal. The general line served as the guiding ideology while the Great Leap Forward was the specific policy and the people's communes were the main tool of its implementation.[39]

Undoubtedly, a complex mixture of forces and intentions, not all of them ideological, led to the articulation of the three red banners as China's way out of crisis in the late 1950s. It is clear that Mao was at odds with the Soviet Union and with the social and political ramifications of the Soviet model of development. He now openly rejected the Soviet system of long-term planning, substantial social stratification, and centralized control by large government ministries. The Soviet model assumed that agricultural surplus needed to be extracted by the government and made to serve urban development. Perhaps this had been possible in the Soviet Union in the late 1920s, when the model was invented, but the situation in China was very different. Chinese policy had to devise a way first to produce the agricultural surplus and then to siphon off a large part of it to invest in urban growth. The Soviet model also rested on assumptions about the energy and transportation sectors that were wholly incompatible with the Chinese realities of the 1950s. China faced bottlenecks in transport, energy, and construction materials that emerged as a consequence of rapid industrialization. By the mid-fifties, many in the bureaucracy started to realize that implementation of the general line threatened to overwhelm the economic system. They surmised from their daily work that it would take China a long time to acquire the necessary technical expertise for a planned economy. In Russia there were many more engineers and trained technicians per capita than the PRC education system could produce—it would take decades to close the knowledge gap—yet, without those engineers, mathematicians, technicians, and planners, the planned economy could simply not operate. The idea that China could quickly develop a Soviet-style system had never been realistic given its size, complexity, and uneven development. The Soviet-style planning apparatus in China was unable to overcome these challenges. The attempt to duplicate the Soviet strategies of development in China ran up against significant structural hurdles and created general economic instability.

Mao Zedong decided to resolve these difficulties in a single stroke by launching the three red banners movement to spur a decisive leap into communism. Although domestic and international political considerations were at the heart of the policy, the socioeconomic context mattered. Mao Zedong was not satisfied with the model of a centrally planned command economic system in terms of its economic performance, the restrictions imposed by it, or the rigid and technocratic decision-making it encouraged. Mao argued that such a system was too restrictive to allow for the dynamic development of industry and agriculture. He believed China would be much smarter to base its development on the mobilization of the population, rather than put its faith in top-down planning. The result of this thinking was the Great Leap Forward, designed to blaze an alternative trail and deliver China to a state of development surpassing industrial economies such as Great Britain.

Despite the often-stressed utopianism, the Great Leap Forward pursued two specific goals that were hardly in themselves utopian: finding a new institutional solution for China's food problem and accelerating industrialization. Leadership had repeatedly declared that increasing the food supply was problematic, as it would only lead peasants to keep and consume more, not sell more to the state. Meanwhile, the population was growing, from 550 million in 1950 to 670 million in 1960, creating an additional 120 million people to feed, stocks of grain dwindled perilously in the mid-fifties. The natural disasters that occurred in the second half of the 1950s only made things worse. The Great Leap Forward program embraced in the autumn of 1958 must be seen as both an attempt to escape crisis and a new push toward a vision of improved livelihoods in rural society.

Strong party propaganda accompanied the Great Leap Forward. Official reports focused on the promises of new rural life under the people's communes (renming gongshe) system. By pooling and precisely organizing labor and income, these new institutions were expected to achieve gains that were out of reach before the Great Leap.[40] People's communes would unify industry, agriculture, trade, study, and the military, thereby bringing development to landlocked and neglected areas. Cooperation through the commune organization was seen as key to tackling the problems that had burdened rural China in the past. Hence, the communes were instructed to start large water conservation projects, establish small factories, and manufacture goods that could increase rural revenue. They also promised to bring social welfare to the villages by running hospitals and schools and caring for the elderly and disabled within communities. Households were organized into teams, which in turn formed brigades. The brigades then made up communes. Each level of organization was responsible for certain tasks. The team took over specific jobs in agricultural work. The brigade was responsible for small workshops and elementary schools. The commune shouldered large-scale land reclamation projects, and the establishment and management of hospitals, high schools, small factories, and other sideline industries.

Public mess halls took over the management of food and in some places, at the beginning of the Great Leap Forward, provided free or heavily subsidized meals. Despite the resistance to collectives, the party relentlessly pushed for huge, militarized communes and collective dining halls—not simply because they were more productive but because they realized the promise of communism. The far-reaching social goal of the Great Leap was to reduce, through the communes, the differences between cities and countryside, between manual and intellectual workers, and between workers and peasants. By 1959, twenty-four thousand communes had been established consisting of between two thousand and twenty thousand households. Soon the party came to the conclusion that those communes were too big and ineffective, and split them into smaller ones. By 1963 there were seventy-four thousand communes. After the Cultural Revolution, the average size of communes was enlarged again so that their total number came down to some fifty-three thousand by 1978.

The method of mobilization was to induce enterprises and local cadres to apply resourcefulness and motivate their workers to expand production to unprecedented levels. Immense public works projects were an integral part of the Great Leap Forward. Huge irrigation systems were constructed. Villages and small towns were advised to build their own small industrial furnaces to boost iron and steel output. Larger enterprises were encouraged to throw out their existing plans and replace them with far more ambitious ones. The goal was to use manpower instead of machines or capital (neither of which China had) to rapidly set up a modern, more productive infrastructure. Though many of the projects were poorly devised and environmentally harmful, they mobilized millions of people for months at a time at massive steel mills and other work sites far from home. In a bid to catch up with the West, the goal was to double steel output from 5.3 million to 10.7 million tons in a single year. As villages experienced shortages of building materials and wood for fuel, houses and shops were pulled down. Mao Zedong applauded these efforts and suggested disassembling the old railways, as well:

> [We] must work hard, with all our might. In Shanghai over 100,000 tons of scrap steel were resmelted. [We] should retrieve scrap steel in a big way. Those railways that are temporarily of no economic value, such as the Ningbo and the Jiaodong lines, can be dismantled or moved to [economically] important places. First of all, [we must] guarantee [production of] metallurgical equipment, blast furnaces, open-hearth rolling mills, electrical machinery, major railways, priority engineering [projects], lathes, and cranes. [We] must make it clear to the cadres and the people that only by first guaranteeing a number of important tasks can [we] obtain ten thousand years of happiness.[41]

Higher production targets in industry were set independently, at the local level, and therefore no longer coordinated by the central planning agency with the rest of the economy.[42] With no mechanisms for coordinating these economic decisions on various levels, problems along the entire chain of production built up quickly. During 1958–1960, neither economic planning nor markets were used to coordinate the Chinese economy. The result was a collapse of industrial production and an enormous destruction of resources. Useful iron and steel products were melted in backyard furnaces to produce large amounts of unusable, low-quality iron. Local people encouraged to build such furnaces deforested their own natural areas to find firewood and exhausted themselves in producing substandard metal. Large, new construction sites also depleted supplies of cement, leaving little for better-planned projects. Economic output in the industrial sector plummeted: GDP per capita shrank by 17 percent in 1961.[43] The economic tragedy that befell China in 1960–1961 was entirely self-inflicted, undoing the achievements of the 1950s.

In the agricultural sector, too, a similar effort to increase production resulted in three years of harvest failures (1959–1961). The Great Leap Forward intended to make the family obsolete as a unit of production, as a home, and as a ceremonial unit, and to replace it with large, modern, militarized, and disciplined formations of labor. But new problems emerged, perhaps most evidently, the destruction of incentives to work productively. After peasants had become organized in huge communes with mess halls (so that more of

8.2. Men working on a backyard furnace during the Great Leap Forward.
Pictures from History / Bridgeman Images / PFH1178813

them could work on large, poorly planned construction projects or in the fields), they could see that those who performed no work were fed just as well as those who worked hardest. With few inspired to labor mightily for the general welfare, agricultural production plunged steeply; many mess halls ran out of food. Local party secretaries, pressured to make unrealistic promises for grain production, were forced to make good on those projections by emptying local storehouses, leaving local people to starve from lack of grain. When the environmental crisis deepened, especially as irregular precipitation in 1959 to 1961 worsened the spreading food shortages, catastrophe struck and the situation in the countryside spiraled out of control.

8.3. Starving peasant family during the Great Leap Forward.
Pictures from History / Bridgeman Images / PFH3431952

By early 1959, famine was widespread in several provinces, mostly in North China, and by the following year, it became a national crisis.[44] Henan, Gansu, Anhui, Guizhou, Qinghai, and Sichuan provinces were the worst hit. The famine took the most lives between January and April 1960, when all grain stores were exhausted and new crops had yet to come up. As the famished rural population seized on green crops in the fields (called *chi qing*), there was scarcely enough left to fulfill harvest quotas. After the crops were gone, rural people resorted to eating bark off trees, cornstalks, roots, bran, and wild plants, as well as insects, snakes, and toads. Others raided public granaries and store-rooms, attacked government agencies, and rioted. Once the villages in regions hit by famine were stripped of everything that could be eaten, people tried to flee to the cities where the food supply was better. For the most part, police and military stopped these refugees on the roads and at transportation hubs and turned them back. To stop news of the famine from spreading, information about the condition in the countryside and the refugees was blocked.

In 1959, Mao often seemed willing to believe the most improbable re-ports of success, but on other occasions seemed to suspect that claims were overblown as officials were afraid to disagree with him or bring him bad news. Again and again, Mao urged cadres to speak honestly and when they occasionally did, so long as his leadership was not at stake, he praised them for their openness. While there certainly were many reports of massive food problems, Mao and other leaders were probably not aware of the full extent of the famine. In October 1960, at last, Mao Zedong was handed a frank report on mass starvation in Xinyang. Within a month, investigative teams came down to the provinces to document the death toll. It is impossible to know the number of fatalities over the three worst years of famine, from 1959 to 1961. Statistics compiled by mainland officials estimate that between sixteen million and seventeen million people died from unusual causes; estimates by foreign analysts run as high as forty-five million. The estimates considered most reliable say that twenty-seven million to thirty million people perished as a result of the Great Leap Forward.[45]

Scholars have pointed to a multitude of factors contributing to this colossal disaster. First, all-pervasive politicization led to misconceptions, errors, and distortions. Local party officials, intimidated by the experience of the Hundred Flowers campaign, held back the truth of the death tolls. The extent of the catastrophe was hidden from view until early 1960—and by that time, the situation had spun out of control. Cadres also reported highly exaggerated production results during the fall of 1959 that in turn served as the basis for a new round of unrealistic assumptions and planning. In one report dated November 2, 1959, for example, the Ministry of Agriculture promised a "superb" harvest for the year, despite the fact that the yield was actually 15 percent lower than the year before. Reading this exuberant report, Mao saw fit to push for much larger grain requisitions, demanding 55 billion kilos from the countryside to speed up industrialization, even if it meant reducing rations in the countryside. With food procurement rates for 1959 set so high, little food supply was left to those in the countryside. China even continued to sell grain to the Soviet Union in exchange for foreign currency and industrial equipment.

Second, inner-party strife and dispute made course corrections of Great Leap Forward policies impossible. In the summer of 1959, the government recognized that this radical agenda was creating problems and tried to enforce a more moderate version, with Mao Zedong personally directing a readjustment (zhengdun) campaign. Faced with widespread opposition to the communes and rumors about serious food shortages, many delegates at the Lushan Conference in July and early August 1959 favored extending and broadening that readjustment. But when Peng Dehuai pointed to massive problems and the spread of famine conditions, Mao took it as a direct challenge to his leadership and launched an attack on Peng and his allies, labeling them a "right-deviating, opportunist, anti-party clique." Seeing Mao's accusation of Peng as a party traitor, no one else dared challenge the wisdom of the Great Leap Forward. The newly appointed minister of defense, Lin Biao, praised Mao's leadership and the infallibility of his thought at the Lushan Conference, even as he described the Great Leap privately as "based on fantasy; and a total mess."[46] By this point, intraparty negotiation and pluralism had all but collapsed. Any leaders voicing critical views were purged.

Third, there was simply a widespread, naive belief that a rapid state-socialist revolution was possible and would be successful in modernizing China. Behind this optimism was a high-modernist blind faith in the inevitability of progress: heavy industry, inventions, and massive public works would materialize, along with ambitious engineering projects, high productivity, and an abundance of resources. In the Chinese socialist context, this took the form of an irresistible vision of grassroots mobilization of the masses combined with the efficiencies of collectivization and the strategic clarity of five-year plans.

Finally, massive transfers of manpower from agriculture to industry created imbalances that were impossible to cope with, especially as they were exacerbated by population growth, ecological crisis, grain exports, and the waste of food supplies by public dining halls in the fall and winter of 1958 and 1959. Rapid urbanization during the period of the Great Leap Forward increased by millions the number of people entitled to urban rations and created immense pressure on supply systems. Between 1957 and 1960, the agricultural workforce dropped by about thirty-three million, while the rural non-agricultural workforce—most of it deployed to massive earth-moving projects—increased by more than fifty million, and the urban population by nearly twenty million. These seventy million new, non-agricultural workers had to be fed. The solution to this problem lay in the household registration system, extended to the countryside in 1958, which pinned peasants to their place of residence. From this point on, population policy became an important tool to relieve the cities of surplus workers and to settle those internal migrants in rural, underdeveloped areas. This policy was designed to help address economic problems such as urban unemployment and low work productivity. As in the Soviet Union, the rural population was denied the modest provisions of housing, food rations, and access to health care guaranteed to the urban workforce, and no effort was spared to prevent them from escaping their sorry situation. It is testimony to the rural population's desperation that, in spite of the *hukou,* the increase of the Chinese urban population between 1958 and 1960 was historically unprecedented.

Until recently, scholars have assumed that popular resistance to the Great Leap Forward was almost nonexistent, either because of the might of the state or because of the widespread support the CCP allegedly had. Partial access to archives now suggests that rapid collectivization, the Great Leap Forward, and the famine provoked a range of oppositional activities—even as fundamental support for the regime continued—including some activism from the redemptive societies. To be sure, a great deal of the everyday resistance to state disentitlement in the Great Leap Forward took the form of foot-dragging. People concealed harvested grain, did business on the black market, and engaged in clandestine migration. Whether they resorted to outright opposition or were simply motivated by sheer need or despair, many were forced to circumvent, undermine, manipulate, or ignore state policies. Theft, cheating, smuggling, and walking away were all strategies for resisting the collectivization enforced by the state.[47] The famine caused by the Great Leap Forward also led to an upsurge of popular religion, including greater activity on the part of the redemptive societies. More crucially, at this juncture, the apocalyptic messages of the sects reached wider audiences.

The Great Leap Forward's immediate consequences were its terrible waste of assets and horrifying destruction of life, but it also had long-term effects of great significance. At the grassroots level, villagers were left to their own devices to survive famine and fight for survival. The Communist Party had failed on a mammoth scale to keep the socialist state's promise to abolish poverty and prevent starvation. The already ambiguous legitimacy of the party was weakened dramatically by the Great Leap Forward debacle. Even after the famine ended, the party found it impossible to climb back from a legitimacy crisis rooted in the state's decision to take grain from a hungry peasantry. Anguished tillers rejected the communes and collectivization, convinced that they were predatory and inadequate to protect them or avert future famine.

What they wished for was a state guarantee against future starvation, but the party-state hierarchy was unwilling or unable to provide it. Socialist China's problems had only become worse.

In recent literature it has become commonplace to compare the Great Leap Forward to other forms of mass murder in the twentieth century—above all, with the Holocaust or the liquidation of the kulaks in the Soviet Union. During the Holocaust, European Jews were mass-murdered in a systematic process informed by a racist ideology. A similarly systematic campaign of violence was undertaken against the kulaks, whom Stalin wanted to extinguish as a class. In the case of the Holocaust and the liquidation of the kulaks, then, there was a clear intention to kill certain groups for political or racist reasons. In contrast, Mao did not launch the Great Leap Forward with any intent to kill off a portion of the population. The famine was the result of blind aspirations and an irrational optimism that led to dramatic economic misjudgments. In the case of the Great Leap Forward, the death of millions was the outcome but not the objective. There is a critical moral distinction between unintended consequences and planned mass murder. At the same time, in terms of responsibility for the staggering catastrophe, neither Mao nor the party can be exonerated. Mao did not precisely intend to starve the peasantry, but whenever it came to deciding on whether to support the countryside or the cities, the farmers or the workers, party and state clearly set their priorities on urban areas, accepting however implicitly that many, many millions of people must suffer.

NINE

Overthrowing Everything

1961–1976

After a brief respite and recovery from the failure of the Great Leap Forward, China was plunged into more mayhem in the form of the Great Proletarian Cultural Revolution *(wuchanjieji wenhua dageming)*. The Cultural Revolution itself was declared by the party to be a victory after just three years, at the 1969 Ninth Party Congress, but it actually dominated an entire decade and thus can be divided into three phases. The first phase lasted two years, from 1966 to 1968 (although the first signs actually appeared as early as 1962) and was shaped by mass movements, public rebellion, Red Guard rallies, and street battles. The second phase extended from the latter half of 1968 through 1971. This period was dominated by the rustication of the Red Guards, the rise to power of the People's Liberation Army (PLA), and the violent mass purges during the "cleanse the class ranks" campaign. The third phase, from 1971 to 1976, was a period when, after Lin Biao's defection, normalization and consolidation set in. Together, these three stages form the Cultural Revolution decade.

The Cultural Revolution was, despite its name, not at all limited to the sphere of culture. Rather, it was a violent, revolutionary mass movement intending "to sweep away all Monsters and Demons" and to "carry the Great Proletarian Cultural Revolution through to the end." Its stated goals were "to overthrow everything" *(dadao yiqie)* and to engage in a "full-scale domestic struggle" *(quanmian neizhan)*.[1] The leaders in support of more pragmatic and moderate readjustment—above all, Liu Shaoqi and Deng Xiaoping—were to be toppled. The mastermind behind the pandemonium was Mao Zedong, but he did not accomplish it alone. Not only did he have substantial support in the party, but amazingly and to his own surprise, when he publicly called upon the people to "rebel," and to "destroy the four olds," and to "bombard the headquarters," millions followed, carrying out a sustained revolution against the institutions of New China. These actions vividly demonstrated the tensions that had built up during the 1950s and that now spilled into the open. While the Great Proletarian Cultural Revolution did not create a major disaster or famine in the way the Great Leap Forward did, its overall impact on Chinese politics and society was pervasive, violent, and destructive, and it lasted for the decade of the Cultural Revolution itself and for many years thereafter.

Recovery from Disaster

By the beginning of 1961, it was imperative that the policies of the Great Leap Forward be rolled back. The Ninth Plenum of the Eighth CCP Central Committee in January 1961 formally approved a policy of "adjustment, consolidation, replenishment, and enhancement" of the national economy without, however, officially discrediting the entire Great Leap Forward. While mistakes were admitted, the Great Leap Forward policy was never officially refuted. Liu Shaoqi, who assumed the state presidency in 1959, and Deng Xiaoping were put in charge of the economy. The new leadership set out to stabilize the Chinese economy step by step under what the premier, Zhou Enlai, suggested in 1963 would be "the four modernizations" *(sige xiandaihua)*.[2] Zhou Enlai promoted the view that China should concentrate on developing "modern agriculture, industry, national defense, and science and technology." The four modernizations policy was a response to the problems created by the Great Leap Forward. After the three red banners, it sought to revive science and technology, and to renew bureaucratic management under a rectified Communist Party. The huge work projects that were characteristic of the Great Leap Forward were scaled back, agricultural output was revived, and efforts were undertaken to bring inflation under control. Engineers, scientists, and other educated Chinese who were attacked during the anti-rightist campaign were brought back and reinstated in their old functions to fix the economy. Reliance on the "Chinese only" technology of the Great Leap, which had made a virtue of China's international isolation and increasing tensions with the USSR, was reversed as China again sought international cooperation. Diplomatic recognition by France in 1964 was one result of this outward turn in the 1960s. In fact, the fundamental policies of reform that would work for China in the 1980s were already on the table and underway by 1964, but were terminated by the beginning of the Cultural Revolution.

The specific formula of economic policy during readjustment consisted of the following elements: balanced budgets, management of the economy based on financial indicators, elimination of extra budgetary funds, slower and sustainable growth, control over inflation, and acceptance of local markets as a supplement to the planned economy. Central planning was restored with one important change. Much of the planning and control of the economy was now done through monetary policy and at the provincial level and below, rather than being centrally managed in Beijing. One of the consequences of the Great Leap disaster was that provincial and local levels vetoed centralization and demanded greater influence on the shape of national policies.

In agriculture, readjustment policies aimed to revive production by lowering grain requisitions in the countryside, establishing local markets, and reducing exports of agricultural produce and imports of grain from the West. Local governments were allowed to implement their own agricultural policies and even to experiment with a return to household farming in some areas under their jurisdictions. The readjustment policy generally brought a retreat from collectivization. Mostly this happened within the framework of the household responsibility system, by which individual households in rural China took responsibility for agricultural production in the plots assigned to them while formally working under the system of collective ownership of land and of equipment. While the collectivized communes were maintained in name, control of farming was in many places more or less returned to individual households. The huge communes and large collective dining halls that characterized the Great Leap Forward did not last much more than three years before they practically disintegrated through neglect, though lip service often continued to be paid to them. The communes continued to function as administrative structures overseeing rudimentary welfare programs and small rural industries. In the end, as the state had to acknowledge the limits of the extraction from agriculture, it lowered procurement and introduced what was essentially a mixed economy in the countryside.

Local governments also reasserted their authority by tightening social control through registration, filing, and labeling systems. By strictly enforcing the *hukou* system, the government reestablished control over internal migration, especially rural-to-urban migration. It sent millions of people back to rural areas. By 1962, the urban population had been reduced by ten million. Another ten to fifteen million were relocated to the countryside in 1962–1963 to lower the workloads for the peasants and reduce the number of people receiving food from the government supply system.[3] Between these policies and better weather, China's economic recovery was undeniable. By 1965, agricultural production was back to what it had been in 1957 and total industrial production was double what it had been that year.

At the same time, the success of readjustment policies deepened Mao Zedong's political isolation as he was largely removed from economic decision-making and had resisted these policies. During the Seven Thousand Cadres Conference in January 1962, which was an enlarged Central Work Conference held in Beijing, Mao had been openly blamed for the failure of the Great Leap Forward and was even compelled to perform self-criticism in front of the seven thousand attendees. In the party, he was on the defensive.[4] Mao was of course frustrated by a situation he considered unfair. He was angered that he alone was blamed for the disastrous outcome of the Great Leap, and he felt betrayed by his comrades. He suspected that they wanted to uproot and replace him. Mao's assessment of the current political situation in China became critical and pessimistic. He no longer proclaimed visions of an imminent era of economic and political greatness. Instead, he came to conclude that it would take at least fifty years, or maybe even a century, for China to reach the economic levels of western capitalist countries.[5] Just as the promise of economic flourishing was indefinitely postponed, the attainment of a communist society seemed far more challenging and even uncertain. Mao was again often plagued by fears that the Chinese revolution would fail and be defeated by "bourgeois restoration." He worried openly that "the party of Marxism and Leninism will become the party of revisionism and fascism. China will then change its color. Think, comrades, what a dangerous and critical situation this will be."[6] Five years later, in 1967, Mao remarked to a delegation from Albania: "At the Seven Thousand Cadres Conference, I made a speech. I said that revisionism wanted to overthrow us. If we paid no attention and conducted no struggle, China would become a fascist dictatorship in either a few or a dozen years at the earliest or in several decades at the latest. This address was not published openly. It was circulated internally. We wanted to watch subsequent developments to see whether any words in the speech required revision. But at that time we already detected the problem."[7] Mao also was increasingly convinced: "the influence of foreign imperialism and domestic bourgeoisie are the social roots of revisionist thinking within the party. While carrying out struggle against class enemies at home and abroad, we must be at all times on guard and resolute in our opposition to all types of opportunistic ideological tendencies within the party."[8] Mao believed he had to weed out the forces of the "right" and undo the inequalities that had crept back in, not only by purging officials at the top, but by changing the values and orientations of the whole of society. Patriarchal hierarchy, family clans, technocracy, and corruption needed to be resolutely struggled against and eliminated, so that they could make a place for a pure reign of communism, a condition in which people shared public goods and services and worked altruistically for the good of all.

Since the Seven Thousand Cadres Conference, Mao was sidelined and had hardly any influence on economic policy and central decision making. Forced to focus his energies on other political fields, he picked education. Following the Tenth Plenum of the Eighth CCP Central Committee in September 1962, Mao launched a nationwide Socialist Education Campaign (Shehuizhuyi jiaoyu yundong) to renew class struggle in the urban and rural areas, as a means of "combating revisionism" and preventing "peaceful evolution."[9] This was the prelude for the Cultural Revolution, although the term was not yet in use. In Mao's analysis, the problems the Great Leap had run into were caused by inadequate attitudes and backward thinking in rural society that kept people from implementing policy correctly—not by the policies themselves, which were correct. To him, the Great Leap had failed because it was not only sluggishly carried out, but also sabotaged and resisted by other leaders and powerful cliques within the party. There was only one way to change the general political outlook and that was with a thorough education campaign. This campaign aimed to undo the resistance in the rural areas and in the party against collectivization. The Socialist Education Campaign framed complaints about the agricultural collectives and state purchasing policies as undermining socialism and an issue of class struggle. The campaign in the countryside was officially devoted to "the cleaning up of accounts, warehouses, workplaces and finances" and was therefore also referred to as the "four clean-ups" (siqing) movement. Inspectors and instructors

9.1. People in Qufu, Shangdong province, receiving instructions during the "four clean-ups" movement, 1964.
API / Getty Images / 840862260

scouted the countryside trying to identify corrupt, incapable, and politically unreliable cadres, and to uncover misappropriation of public funds and sloppy accounting. Those cadres were then subjected to public criticism and reeducation. After two years, the campaign was greatly scaled back, against Mao's wishes, since other leaders thought it was interfering with the readjustment policy.

The Socialist Education Campaign faded away in 1964 and 1965, never fulfilling Mao's hopes to reestablish class struggle and revolutionary purity. Instead, inner-party rivals twisted the campaign so that in the end it came to resemble an anti-corruption drive in the countryside. By 1964, Mao began to consider countermeasures. He refocused on the educational system, this time in the urban areas. He maintained that schools had become too elitist. He began to press hard for the establishment of "part-work, part-study" schools that would provide more vocational training. As Mao Zedong was pondering a campaign to deal with rising political challenges and to fight against the spread of revisionism, external pressures were again mounting.

Encirclement and Escalation

During the early 1960s, China went on the offensive in the international arena and escalated a number of conflicts along its borders. This development had tremendous repercussions for the situation inside China, as it led to a strengthening of the role of the PLA, which Mao and Lin Biao tried to make into a model organization.

Large-scale, armed uprisings of Tibetans in Qinghai and Tibet in 1958 and 1959 led to the flight of the Tibetan religious leader, the Dalai Lama, and also to conflict between India and China.[10] The unrest was originally caused by the implementation of the Great Leap Forward policy in the Tibetan areas of Amdo (which straddles the Qinghai, Gansu, and Sichuan provinces) and Kham (cutting across the Qinghai, Sichuan, and Yunnan provinces and part of the Tibet Autonomous Region). The ethnic minorities especially resented the establishment of communes and the forced settling of nomads during the early days of the Great Leap in June 1958, when a campaign to open up wastelands and to turn grasslands into agricultural land was vigorously enforced. Rumors that the PLA planned to kidnap the Dalai Lama triggered mass demonstrations in Lhasa in March 1959. When the PLA moved in to quell the uprising, the Dalai Lama fled to India. For China, it seemed clear that India had instigated unrest and that New Delhi sought to benefit from it. India allowed the Dalai Lama to set up a government in exile in the hill town of Dharamsala, just as it had already welcomed thousands of other Tibetan exiles. A second area of Sino-Indian conflict concerned three sparsely populated but strategically important stretches of land along the edge of the Tibetan plateau. This disputed territory was partly administered by China, partly by India, but in its entirety claimed by both countries. The areas were strategically important for both countries because they contained roads and mountain passes from Tibet into India. They were also important for China because a sizable population of ethnic Tibetans lived there. By the early 1960s, the relationship between the two countries was strained, culminating in the 1962 Sino-Indian War fought over the control of these territories. In this conflict, the PLA defeated the Indian Army in the border region, penetrating well beyond the Sino-Indian border. The conflict did not, however, produce any lasting change in control. The Chinese withdrew from most of the in-

9.2. The Dalai Lama (Tenzin Gyatso) escapes to India after the Chinese occupation of Tibet in 1959.
Tallandier / Bridgeman Images / TAD1752670

vaded areas and established a demilitarized zone on either side of the line of control.[11]

Most significantly, leadership seized on the army's victory and began to experiment with the possibility of creating a cult of "army heroes" to aid in popular mobilization. The party viewed the soldier-communist as the most suitable model for educating a future generation of leadership. Army uniformity and discipline, they believed, could transcend existing class differences, and troops could be trained to conform to rigorous political standards. These activities and movements in the PLA were initiated by Lin Biao, with the support of Mao Zedong, who found them simply "perfect." Starting in 1964, Mao insisted that political departments modeled on those in the PLA be established in all major government bureaucracies. In many cases, political commissars from the PLA itself staffed these new bodies, thus effectively penetrating the civilian government apparatus. Other efforts, such as a national propaganda campaign to learn from a purported army hero, Lei Feng, also contributed to enhancement of the PLA's prestige. Lei Feng was a soldier who had died in 1962 at the age of twenty-one and whose diary was alleged to have been found posthumously. The diary—perhaps concocted by party propaganda—is filled with praise of Mao Zedong as well as accounts of the soldier's efforts to help the common people and to inspire revolutionary zeal among his army colleagues.[12]

In the early 1960s, this effort was fused with the cult of Mao Zedong. In the aftermath of the Great Leap Forward, when the population was at its most disillusioned and politically apathetic, Mao's cult of personality was systematically developed to serve immediate political ends. Mao himself was the driving force behind it, but the entire leadership also felt it was useful for stabilizing party rule. Mao encouraged the mythology that grew up around him and was pleased when other leaders such as Lin Biao praised him and repeatedly used speeches, directives, and statements to spread it within Chinese society.

The General Political Department of the PLA under Lin Biao had the task of reviving and refashioning the cult. In this context, the General Political Department developed a simplified and dogmatized version of Mao's thought, eventually compiled in the form of the "little red book" of *Quotations from Chairman Mao* (*Mao zhuxi yulu*) and the somewhat longer *Selected Readings from the Works of Mao Zedong*. Both publications popularized Maoist thought so that it could be digested even by relatively uneducated military recruits and the broader masses. The hope was to make the army into "a great school for the study of Mao Zedong thought." As the military forces under Lin increasingly demonstrated that they could combine ideological purity with technical skill, Mao tried to expand the PLA's organizational authority and its political role. Beginning in 1963, Mao called on all Chinese to "learn from the PLA." Lin Biao orchestrated mass campaigns to study Mao's writings. In 1965, five million copies of *Quotations* were published and distributed, and over a million volumes of *Selected Readings*. By 1964–1965, the Mao cult was ubiquitous. In his instructions to a PLA political working meeting in 1967, Lin Biao said: "Chairman Mao's works are the supreme instructions for all the work of the PLA. Chairman Mao's words display the highest level, the greatest authority, and the strongest force. Every one of his words is truth, and carries greater weight than ten thousand empty words."[13]

The militancy of subsequent campaigns to learn from army heroes, or from the PLA as a whole, was echoed in international politics. As it moved to the world stage, the PRC demonstrated a fondness for military language and appearance. In a tour of Africa in late 1963 and early 1964, Zhou Enlai alarmed his hosts by calling for revolution in newly independent post-colonial states, and openly challenged the Soviet Union over the direction of the communist movement in the developing world.[14] The Soviet-US crisis in Cuba, in October 1962, had coincided with the Sino-Indian struggle, and in both cases China believed the Soviet Union had become untrustworthy and turned into a "capitulator." When the Soviet Union signed the Limited Nuclear Test Ban Treaty with the United States and Great Britain in August 1963, the Chinese press attacked the Soviet Union and reproached it for building an anti-Chinese conspiracy.

Internationally, China became ever more isolated. Substantial Soviet deployments along the Sino-Soviet border, including of nuclear weapons, threatened the country. In a drive to increase its own international influence, Moscow expanded its military aid to North Korea to gain that nation's loyalty. It pursued the same strategy to the south, using military assistance to keep North Vietnam on board. Both countries remained aligned with the Soviet Union. To both the north and the south, then, China was faced with Soviet allies. In Indonesia, many Chinese were killed in the course of General Suharto's anti-communist mass killings, because they were suspected to be leftists working for the CCP. Meanwhile, the US government repeatedly reconfirmed its policies of recognizing the Republic of China in Taiwan as the legitimate government of China. The United States also supported the exiled Dalai Lama. The incremental escalation of the US military presence in Vietnam in the early 1960s posed an additional threat to China. There was the possibility that US forces would start to bomb or invade North Vietnamese sanctuaries along the Chinese border, where North Vietnam had stockpiled ammunition and aircraft.

Confronted by this new strategic situation, the government boasted of the country's self-reliance. Mao's calls for revolution became more nationalistic and the PLA's influence on Chinese political and economic life grew stronger.[15] Against this backdrop, China also vigorously pursued the acquisition and development of nuclear weapons. Since the mid-1950s, the Soviet Union had hesitantly assisted China's nuclear program. The Sino-Soviet split in 1960 and the dramatic recall of Russian advisers was presumed to have delivered a major setback to it. China's own capable nuclear physicists and engineers nonetheless continued progress toward nuclear capability—assisted by a determined leadership that made substantial cuts in other defense spending and reallocated funds to the nuclear program. China conducted its first atomic test explosion on October 16, 1964.[16] While China celebrated that success, the international response from points both east and west was negative, which only deepened China's isolation. The development seemed to reinforce Mao's claim that domestic revolution would fuel the country's long-term power aspirations and defense capabilities. Indeed, soon after this, Mao began to articulate his "three worlds theory," where the two main superpowers constituted the First World that enjoyed a hegemonic relationship with the industrialized Second World, while China led the poor (and nonwhite) countries of the Third World in revolution. In the mid-sixties, China stood alone and faced pressure from all sides.

The external crisis led to an internal escalation of tensions. Threatened from all sides abroad, Mao looked for ways to enforce greater internal unity and discipline. In late 1963, the party started to call on intellectuals, including those in the cultural sphere, to reorient their academic and artistic work toward supporting China in its precarious situation. In December 1963 and June 1964, Mao criticized the communities producing art, literature, and scholarship for deviating from socialist principles and promoting feudalist and bourgeois ideas. The initial assignment for leading a movement to rectify the situation fell to Zhou Yang (1908–1989). A party intellectual and deputy director of the Central Committee's Propaganda Department, Zhou tried to enlist China's intellectuals in the ideological war against Soviet revisionism and in the struggle for rigidly pure political standards. In July 1964 he was appointed to the "five-man group" formed by the Central Committee, based on Mao's proposal, which was tasked with leading a rectification movement in literature and arts circles. The other members were long-serving party leaders Peng Zhen (mayor of Beijing), Lu Dingyi (head of the propaganda ministry), and Kang Sheng ([1898–1975] security tsar), and the editor of the *People's Daily*, Wu Lengxi (1919–2002). A similar drive was undertaken to target the "newborn forces" of the Communist Youth League, mainly in urban areas where Youth League membership tended to be highest. Meanwhile, "work teams" (*gongzuozu*) made up of party officials and government workers tried to reinvigorate the Socialist Education Campaign in rural areas. These efforts constituted the immediate prelude to the Cultural Revolution.

In 1963–1964, Mao Zedong also spent much of his time criticizing Khrushchev. By this point, Mao was adamant that Khrushchev was a "revisionist" and a danger to the communist movement. He warned against the rise of a Chinese Khrushchev. His year-long critique culminated in a long article entitled "On Khrushchev's Phony Communism and Its Historical Lessons for the World," published jointly in *People's Daily* (*Renmin Ribao*) and *Red Flag* (*Hongqi*) in July 1964, which summarized most of Mao's ideas on the continued need for class struggle in socialist societies and the danger of a restoration of capitalism. Mao claimed that a privileged bourgeois class had captured Soviet institutions and that China faced a similar danger. He wrote: "We must especially watch careerists and schemers such as Khrushchev and prevent such bad elements from seizing power from leaders at all levels of the CCP and the state."[17]

In early August 1964, US air strikes on North Vietnam raised the specter of war on China's southern border. The relationship with Soviet Union deteriorated, too. A debate ensued as to whether China should prepare rapidly for conventional war against the United States, or continue to struggle against the potential of revisionism in Chinese society, which in Mao's view had more fundamental, long-term importance for China's security. Liu Shaoqi and Deng Xiaoping argued for a delay of the internal political struggle. They also advocated responding to Soviet calls for "united action" in Vietnam and the reestablishment of closer Sino-Soviet ties. This, however, made them all the more suspicious in the eyes of Mao.[18] Meanwhile, Liu Shaoqi and Deng Xiaoping also asserted the need for further consolidation of the readjustment policy for economic development. Regulations issued in June 1964 for the organization of associations for poor and lower-middle peasants had reined in the cadres' authority, allowed experiments with a free-market system, and permitted the return to private ownership of rural plots. To Mao, these were efforts to downplay the importance of revolution in the rural areas. In his January 1965 directive on problems arising in the course of the Socialist Education Campaign, known as the "Twenty-three Articles," Mao stated, for the first time, that the principal enemies were revisionists and those within the

CCP who wanted to take the capitalist road. He also once more proclaimed the urgency of class struggle.

The dismissal of Nikita Khrushchev in October 1964 only increased Mao's worries, who knew the CCP did not wholeheartedly share his visions. While Mao had derided Khrushchev's policies, the coup in the Soviet Union made him fear a similar occurrence in China. Mao started to talk more about cultivating successors and became even more insistent in his demands for loyalty. This coincided with yet another secret working conference of the Central Committee, in which the Maoist group issued a call for a Cultural Revolution, convinced that the effort of 1964 had been deliberately sabotaged by senior party and military officials. Mao Zedong and Lin Biao decided to start a new campaign. As China turned its back on the war in Vietnam and the conflict with the Soviet Union, Mao's final struggle for China's future began.

Great Disorder under Heaven

In February 1965, Mao reportedly sent his wife of thirty years, Jiang Qing (1914–1991), a former actress, on a secret mission to Shanghai. Jiang had not played a public role before that moment, but her mission was to start a campaign criticizing party officials for not fully supporting Mao's revolutionary views. In these critical months, Shanghai became her base of operations. Newspapers published in that city reported the attacks on important figures in the Beijing party world who Mao believed were undoing his achievements and were out to unravel his policies. The first target was the historian Wu Han (1909–1969), who was also acting deputy mayor of Beijing. Wu had supposedly couched a criticism of Mao in his writing of a 1961 play about a ruthless emperor of the Ming dynasty. It was assumed that the play's hero, an honest minister named Huai Rui who was a true historical figure, was an allusion to Peng Dehuai, the minister of defense purged by Mao. That hero was portrayed as an upright official worried about the welfare of the peasants. The denunciation of Wu Han and the play "Huai Rui Dismissed from Office" as poisonous weeds in an article in the Shanghai *Wenhui bao* on November 10, 1965, was the first of many attacks unleashed on a range of important political figures. In quick succession, several high-ranking party members were dismissed, culminating in the fall of Peng Zhen, the mayor of Beijing, in April 1966. Peng Zhen was accused of shielding bad elements such as Wu Han, suppressing leftists, and running an "independent kingdom."[19] While some hoped this would be the end of the campaign, it was merely the beginning. Removal of Lu Dingyi, and subsequently Zhou Yang, indicated that this was to be a purge at the highest echelons of the party state. Further attacks resulted in many more dismissals and persecutions of officials, secretaries, and editors in Beijing, because they were denounced as "sworn followers" of those already purged. Increasingly, Mao and his supporters hinted at the existence of an anti-party "black gang" *(heibang),* especially in the fields of education and propaganda.

The conclusion of this opening phase of Mao's assault on his own party came with a series of notifications he wrote for presentation to the Politburo Standing Committee on May 16, 1966. The May 16 Notification (*Wuyiliu tongzhi,* sometimes also called May 16 Circular), which accompanied the material documenting Peng Zhen's transgressions, hinted at a larger, upcoming purge. It also announced the coming of a "cultural revolution." Mao described the depth of the problems confronting the nation. "Far from being a minor issue," the notification declared, "the struggle against this revisionist line is an issue of prime importance having a vital bearing on the destiny and future of our party and state, on the future complexion of our party and state, and on the world revolution." The May 16 Notification indicated that Mao was determined to widen the scope of his assault on the counterrevolutionary forces he seemed to believe had made their way deep into the party and its leadership—and through those organs to society as a whole. The text continued: "We should carry out the Great Proletarian Cultural Revolution to unmask academic authorities, who have revolted against socialism and who have supported the bourgeoisie.... While we have unmasked some of them, we also mistakenly trusted others or trained them to be our successors. Party committees at all levels should be alert to the Chinese Khrushchev within our party."[20]

In May 1966, Mao's most reliable group of allies, with his obvious encouragement, organized themselves in the form of the "Central Cultural Revolution Group" (it replaced the five-man group), also simply called the Small Group. Led by Chen Boda (1904–1989), Mao's political secretary, this informal body was to be the center of power. It became a top decision-making office of the party, directly answering to Mao. It overruled all the regular institutions and organs of the party, the state, and to some extent, even the military. The Small Group allowed Mao Zedong to mobilize the masses, to steer the Cultural Revolution, and to wield power independent of the structures of government. The Small Group ceased to work in April 1969 when, during the Ninth National Congress of the CCP, the regular apparatus was reshuffled.

With the May 16 Notification, Mao Zedong publicly launched the Cultural Revolution attack on "those in authority pursuing the capitalist road." Mao's concern, however, was no longer the economy, as it had been during the Great Leap Forward. In the mid-1960s, Mao's goal was broader and more ambitious: it was to transform Chinese society by changing its values to "all public and no private" *(dagong wusi)*. His tool: rebellion *(zaofan)*. In his July 8, 1966, "Letter to Comrade Jiang Qing" (his wife), Mao expressed his view that "great disorder under heaven" was good, because it would expose enemies, mobilize the masses, and ultimately lead to order.[21] The chaos of student demonstrations, mutual denunciations among party cadres, and orchestrated purges and public trials was intended to unravel the technocratic reforms of the readjustment period and remove the institutions built by Mao's opponents.

Following the May Notification, the focus shifted to the educational system, especially the universities. "Big-character posters" *(dazi bao)* spread from the principal campuses in Beijing throughout China. The first of the Cultural Revolution posters, posted on May 25, 1966, attacked the Peking University leadership for being a "bunch of Khrushchev-type revisionist elements."[22] University officials and professors were singled out for criticism while their students, encouraged by the party authorities, held mass meetings and began to organize themselves. Mao, who was in Hangzhou at that time, was in full support, declaring that this first poster was the "1960s equivalent of the Paris Commune Proclamation."[23] The movement spread quickly: sixty-five thousand posters were displayed at Tsinghua University in June. According to records in Shanghai, in the first three weeks of June, 2.7 million people joined the protest movements inside the city and some 88,000 posters appeared, attacking 1,390 people (by name) for various crimes.

On June 13, the government, acting on Mao's instructions, suspended classes at all schools and canceled the national examinations for university admissions nationwide. These standardized entrance examinations for high schools and universities had been used to recruit students since 1952.[24] Based on examination scores, first-year university students were usually allocated in accordance with unified enrollment plans—coordinated and carefully balanced between the national and regional levels—which stipulated the number of students to be enrolled from each region into each institution and specialty. All students were required to take these exams, but for university enrollment, family background and records of individual political activity were also taken into consideration. A red class background (signifying peasants, workers, soldiers) entitled a person to preferential treatment, while a black class background meant that a candidate needed higher test scores for admission.

The suspension of the entrance exams, the cancellation of classes, and the delay in reopening campuses in the fall freed up, for political action, around thirteen million students in middle and high schools and just over half a million at colleges and universities, plus more than one hundred million in primary schools.[25] When senior party leaders, especially Liu Shaoqi and Deng Xiaoping, ordered investigative work teams to go to campuses and schools and double-check the nature of the accusations being made and to restore some sort of order, Mao charged them with trying to suppress the revolutionary movement and censured them for "revisionist" behavior. At the end of July the investigative work teams had to be withdrawn from schools and workplaces. Once they were gone, the movement spread out and violence increased dramatically.

To show his support for the rising student upheaval, Mao issued his own first big-character poster with the provocative title "Bombard the Headquarters" *(paoda silingbu)*. Posted on August 5, it was later published in all newspapers, and was nothing less than a call for the denunciation and removal of the senior leadership. It declared that some leading comrades, from the central down to the local levels, had "enforced a bourgeois dictatorship and struck down the noisy and spectacular movement of the Great Proletarian Cultural Revolution":

They have stood facts on their head and juggled black and white, encircled and suppressed revolutionaries, stifled opinions differing from their own, imposed a white terror, and felt very pleased with themselves. They have puffed up the arrogance of the bourgeoisie and deflated the morale of the proletariat. How vicious they are! Viewed in connection with the right deviation in 1962 and the erroneous tendency of 1964, which was left in form but right in essence, shouldn't this prompt one to deep thought?[26]

misinterpret political motives

The poster—above all, with its references to 1962 (referring to the readjustment policy that Mao had resented) and 1964 (the winding down of the Socialist Education Campaign against Mao's will)—made unmistakably clear to other leaders in the CCP what the ultimate goal was. The person Mao Zedong was out to destroy was none other than his second in command and designated successor Liu Shaoqi. Evidently fearing that China would develop along the lines of the Soviet model and concerned about his own place in history, Mao was not only willing to throw China's cities into turmoil in a daring effort to rectify the revolution, but also wanted to topple the entire leadership of the state he had established and run for almost twenty years.

On August 8, 1966, the Eleventh Plenum of the CCP's Eighth Central Committee, where for the first time in CCP history, radical students and teachers were also in attendance (as non-voting members), adopted the first official public document regarding the Cultural Revolution. The decision became known as the "Sixteen Points" *(shiliu tiao)* and was on the front pages of all major Chinese newspapers. In part, it stated:

> At present our objective is to struggle against and crush those persons in authority who are taking the capitalist road, to criticize and repudiate the reactionary bourgeois academic "authorities" and the ideology of the bourgeoisie and all other exploiting classes, and transform education, literature, and art and all other parts of the superstructure that do not correspond to the socialist economic base, so as to facilitate the consolidation and development of the socialist system.... In the great proletarian cultural revolution, the only method is for the masses to liberate themselves.... Don't be afraid of disturbances.... Let the masses educate themselves in this great revolutionary movement and learn to distinguish between right and wrong.[27]

It was an unprecedented public call to seize power from "bourgeois" authorities. The locus of the struggle would be the urban caches of revisionists.

Despite the broad-ranging, grandiose, and lofty language in the key documents, in hindsight it is clear that Mao pursued very specific goals with the Cultural Revolution. First, he intended to replace the senior group of leaders in key positions with younger leaders more faithful to his current thinking. Since the Great Leap Forward's failure, he had been alienated from most of the senior party leaders and no longer had trust in their capabilities and their political convictions. Mao did not draw the same conclusions from the tragedy of the Great Leap that other leaders did. He saw traitors, saboteurs, and the return of capitalist oppression of the working people as the root causes of these unfavorable outcomes, and advocated a return to active, violent revolution. The Cultural Revolution was as much or even more about the elimination of leading cadres Mao suspected of opposing him and his policies as it was about changing China's culture. He viewed most of them as selfish opportunists who were politically unreliable and unpredictable. Moreover, he wanted to rectify the CCP because he felt that the party as a whole had deviated from the correct political line. He also sought to provide China's youth with a revolutionary experience, since he believed that without the chance to carry out a revolution, this generation would have no revolutionary vigor and passion. Finally, he wanted to shake up the new institutional order to make the institutions of the PRC more egalitarian and inclusive, especially in the educational, health care, and cultural sectors. He was convinced that newly formed hierarchies and special interests had distorted the institutions and made them accessible only to a few at the top of the party state, at the expense of the masses.

He pursued those goals through a massive mobilization of the country's urban youth, while instructing the CCP and the PLA to refrain from stopping the movement. As the Cultural Revolution gained momentum, Mao turned directly to students, young soldiers, and younger cadres to do what intellectuals and peasants in his opinion had failed to do: to rebel. In 1966, Mao famously declared "It is right to rebel!" Seeking to create a new system of education that would eliminate differences between town and country, workers and peasants, and mental and manual labor, Mao powerfully recognized the concerns of China's younger generation and tapped into their anxieties and grievances. It was their response that provided him with his most reliable support base. In 1966, the students officially formed the Red Guards (*hong weibing*) of the Cultural Revolution, the troops of Mao's uprising against his own party. A series of mass rallies were held. Mao attended the first rally in Tiananmen Square on August 18, 1966. Students had been entering the huge square since one o'clock in the morning. When Mao arrived at dawn, dressed in a green military uniform, he was met by roughly one million students and Red Guards. A participant recalled a frenetic scene:

Everybody was shouting "Long live Chairman Mao!" Around me girls were crying; boys were crying too. With hot tears streaming down my face, I could not see Chairman Mao clearly. . . . Earnestly we chanted: "We—want—to—see—Chairman—Mao!" He heard us! He walked over to the corner of Tian'anmen and waved at us. . . . My blood was boiling inside me. I jumped and shouted and cried in unison with a million people in the square. At that moment, I forgot myself; all barriers that existed between me and others broke down. . . . I would never be lonely again.[28]

Between August and November 1966, seven more large rallies were held, with millions of students in attendance. During these rallies, Mao and Lin Biao told the Red Guards to take to the streets of China's cities and towns to "crush the four olds" (that is, old ideas, customs, culture, and habits of mind), to root out capitalist roaders, and to "struggle against revisionists." Starting in October, a mass campaign was started against Liu Shaoqi and Deng Xiaoping, condemning their policy toward the work groups as bourgeois reactionary line.

The movement quickly escalated. Public criticism meetings began to take on new levels of violence as cadres, intellectuals, and leaders accused of political offenses were beaten up and humiliated, often in front of huge crowds or even in sports stadiums. The Red Guards forced people to march through scornful crowds, their heads crowned with dunce caps and their "crimes" outlined in heavy signboards hung from their necks.[29] With the Little Red Book in hand, the Red Guards rode roughshod over the ruined careers and in extreme cases even the dead bodies of Mao's alleged enemies and opponents. They also attacked their own parents in an effort to draw a "clear line of demarcation." The writer Ma Bo describes in his memoir how he turned himself into a Red Guard in 1966, when he was still a middle school (or junior high) student. He fervently reacted to the call of Mao "to rebel" by attacking his own mother, Yang Mo, author of the novel *The Song of Youth*. He even denounced her in public posters, inviting Red Guards to search his own home. He also stole money from his family to finance a trip to "make revolution in Vietnam."[30] The social chaos, particularly in 1966 and 1967, shattered China's cities and towns. Uncounted cultural sites were destroyed. Religious sites were a popular target. Red Guards smashed statues, burned scripts, and demolished temples. Such practices became more widespread after Mao and

9.3. Red Guards in Wuhan preparing big-character posters (*dazibao*) criticizing "revisionists," 1967.
VCG / Getty Images / 179599253

his allies began to speak of the need for, and value of, a "red terror" that would lead the "black gangs" of the present era to "tremble with fear and shake with fright."

The movement soon spun out of control. In late 1966, older students formed competing Red Guard units and a "rebel faction" *(zaofan pai),* often heavily armed, who clashed with earlier Red Guard groups, called the Old Red Guards, over the correct interpretations of the current political line. In many cities, civil war–like conditions erupted. The different factions barricaded themselves in streets and buildings, engaging in urban warfare and shelling each other's positions. Some also obtained support from worker militias. By early 1967, workers' organizations were formed, also along ideological lines, sometimes allied with student rebels and sometimes acting on their own. Workers also began making demands of their own and staged their own large-scale clashes with the "power holders" and the "center."[31]

With many factories closed and production often disrupted, industrial output fell and China's economy contracted by almost 5 percent for two years in a row (it needs to be noted, however, that in economic terms the Cultural Revolution did far less damage than the Great Leap Forward).[32] Attempts to rein in the PLA and prevent it from curbing major opposition with massive force and firepower led to a serious military mutiny in Wuhan and the arrest of two members of the Cultural Revolution Central Group in mid-1967 and to countless other outbreaks across China. China plunged into chaos. Death and injury from street battles were ubiquitous. Over the entire ten years of the Cultural Revolution, some 240,000 people may have been killed in such armed local clashes.[33] The conflicts revealed the tension and frictions that had built up in socialist society. Many groups also used the turmoil to secure gains, settle open disputes, and retaliate against past slights and humiliations. Here was a society that had intended to unify the people, yet the Cultural Revolution demonstrated that just the opposite had occurred. Simmering resentments beneath the surface, disgruntled groups, feelings of injustice, and obvious inequalities drove the violence of the Cultural Revolution.

The first phase of the Cultural Revolution ended in 1968, when a new system of "revolutionary committees" was instituted, consisting of three roughly equal parts, the PLA, the revolutionary masses, and the revolutionary cadres. The Revolutionary Committee replaced the traditional organs of the state on the provincial and local levels. All these groups should work together to establish a more stable yet truly revolutionary society. At the same the government brought urban warfare to an end by calling in the PLA to move into the cities and campuses to restore order. China's regular schools began to reopen, although the number of students in higher institutions represented only a small fraction of those three years before. In October 1968, the Twelfth Plenum of the Central Committee met to prepare the convening of a party congress in 1969 and to discuss the rebuilding of the CCP apparatus. But above all, the plenum sealed the fate of Liu Shaoqi. After his fall from power in autumn 1966, he was forced to write a self-criticism, a confession, and a self-examination laying out his mistakes and past transgressions. He was paraded through countless criticisms and struggle sessions. At the plenum, the party officially expelled Liu Shaoqi and dismissed him from his posts once and for all. At that time, he was already hospitalized. He died in November 1969. Deng Xiaoping, who had also written a lengthy self-criticism, was dismissed from all positions, too, but notably not expelled from the party. From 1969 to 1973, Deng Xiaoping was sent to the countryside and worked at a tractor repair shop in southern Jiangxi.

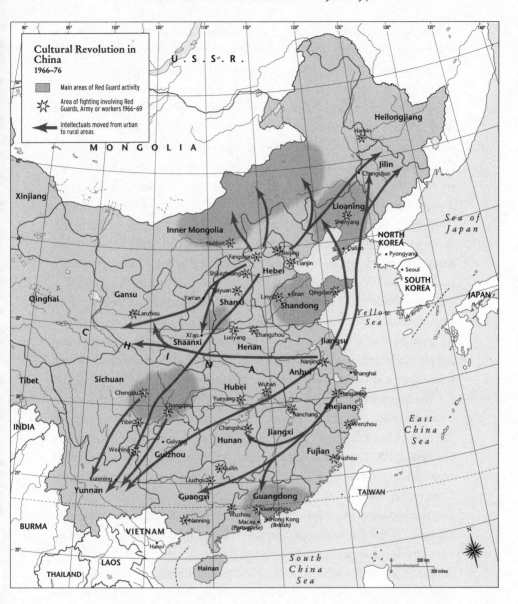

To further stabilize the situation, the Red Guards needed to be removed from the cities. In July 1968, Mao's "latest instructions" to the students called on them—now that they had had their taste of revolution—to become "ordinary peasants and ordinary workers."[34] Initially, these were primarily Red Guard activists, but the program soon took on a more general character, and it became expected that most graduates of middle school would head to the countryside. With this, the Red Guards were effectively dispersed as members were sent "up to the mountains and down to the villages" *(shang shan xia xiang)*. Altogether, around eighteen million "educated urban youth" *(zhishi qingnian* or abbreviated *zhiqing)* were sent out to the countryside to work and to "learn from the peasants." The response by the students was mixed. Some were enthusiastic about going to the countryside, but many felt frustrated, disappointed, and betrayed. Most were rusticated close to their hometowns, but some of the larger cities, such as Shanghai, Beijing, and Tianjin, sent large numbers of students to faraway places in Inner Mongolia, Xinjiang, Yunnan, and Heilongjiang. On average, they spent six years in factories or in the countryside. Sometimes, however, this could extend to ten years. The experience, too, could be very diverse. For most students, it was a time of hardship and great privations, but also of reflection and reckoning. Many were for the first time confronted with the extent of rural poverty. They encountered the existence of rural traditions that refused to be destroyed and a peasantry that was not nearly as enthusiastic about collectivization and people's communes as they had expected. The vast majority of these people found their way back to the cities after Mao's death.

The dispersion of the Red Guards by no means represented the end of violence. Violence continued between 1968 and 1970 with the campaign to "cleanse class ranks" used by the army to assault local power structures. "Cleansing the class ranks" was a campaign that was carried out by the new revolutionary committees. It aimed at eliminating all real or imagined resistance or opposition to the goals of the Cultural Revolution. These struggles also reached the countryside that, until 1968, had scarcely been involved in the fight. When the campaign arrived in villages and rural towns, it triggered uncontrolled violence against suspected local class enemies, including their families. There were the "four types" of enemies: landlords, rich peasants, counterrevolutionaries, and bad elements. Some villages became the sites of mass crimes intended to eliminate the class enemies, mobilizing local peasants as onlookers or rally participants.[35] In fact, this was the most violent phase of the Cultural Revolution, during which many more people were tortured, maimed, or killed, or committed suicide. From that point on, the issue of who would claim political power as the Cultural Revolution wound down became central to the clashes.

An especially harrowing case had been meticulously documented by Tan Hecheng, a Chinese witness of one instance of such a mass killing.[36] Across several weeks in August and September 1967, more than nine thousand people were murdered in Dao County (Daoxian), Hunan province. The killings were not random; they systematically aimed at eliminating the four types of class enemies. The brutal events were far from being the deeds of radicalized local peasants. Instead, the killings were organized by local party committees, which ordered the slaughters to be carried out in remote areas. Entire families, including infants, were murdered. Nationwide, probably one and a half million people were killed during this phase.

Government and party officials who were dismissed from their party posts were sent down to "May 7 Cadre schools"—usually farms run by a major urban unit. People from the urban unit had to live on the farm, typically in quite primitive conditions, for varying periods of time (for some, this amounted to a number of years, although by about 1973 the time periods were generally held to under a year). While on the farm, the urban cadres would both engage in rigorous manual labor and undertake intensive, supervised study of ideology. The object was to reduce their bureaucratic "airs."

The third stage of the Cultural Revolution decade started in 1970, which saw a moderation of the Cultural Revolution. Class struggle drew to a close, as campaigns and mass movements ceased. Junior cadres that had been purged were rehabilitated and returned to work in their former jobs. The party recognized that it had to refocus its policies on the economy, which was in bad shape. The exhausted country longed to leave the "great disorder under heaven" behind and go back to normal. Cultural Revolution ideas, however, continued to be visible and influential. Initiatives were carried out to reduce what were termed the "three major differences"—those separating intellectual from manual labor, worker from peasant, and urban from rural. Many measures were taken to make the educational system less elitist. The number of years at each level of schooling was decreased. Admission to a university was no longer based on a competitive examination. The criteria for selection would be a candidate's class status, their level of political activism, and positive recommendation letters from local leaders of work units or of Cultural Revolution committees.[37] Students were required to engage in at least several years of manual labor before attending a university and would be recruited directly from factories, people's communes, and military units, instead of from high schools. Within schools, education yielded in large measure to the study of political theory and to vocational training. Traditional learning formats were abolished, and emphasis was placed on collective and group study. The authority of teachers in the classroom was consistently questioned and rethought.

One widely reported incident reflected the unsettled public climate of this stage of the Cultural Revolution. The college examination system had been abolished in 1966, yet in 1973, there were still high schools that held their own informal, and possibly illegal, entrance examinations for those who had been recommended by local *danweis* or committees. A young student named Zhang Tiesheng from the province of Liaoning could not master the exam and handed in an empty sheet *(baijuan)*. On the back of it, he wrote a note to the leaders: "To speak frankly, I'm not won over by those bookworms who haven't done honest work for years, taking it easy and being carefree"[38] He also attacked the exams as "capitalist revenge." When Jiang Qing, Mao's wife, read about this in the newspapers, she noted: "The author of the empty sheet *(baijuan)* is a hero." Subsequently, cover stories in all newspapers praised the "hero of the empty sheet" *(baijuan yingxiong)*.

The system of medical care was also revamped. Serious efforts were made to force urban-based medical staffs to devote more effort to serving the needs of the peasants. This involved both the reassignment of medical personnel to rural areas and, more importantly, a major attempt to provide short-term training to rural medical personnel. These "barefoot doctors" *(chijiao yisheng)*. provided at least a minimal level of health care to many Chinese villages. Greater stress was also placed on the use of Chinese traditional medicine, which relied more heavily on locally available herbs and on more affordable methods such as acupuncture. Western medicine was simply too expensive and specialized to be used effectively throughout China's vast hinterlands. A new proletarian culture war was also vigorously promoted. Operas, posters, and literary texts portrayed and popularized the major ideas of the Cultural Revolution.[39]

In the absence of campaigns, people were able to place more focus on simply earning a living. The political relaxation was used in the countryside to revive individual farming and to expand private plots. Makeshift markets emerged in many places. Private workshops were established as side businesses. In low-key ways, village enterprises and factories were started. Supplies of many services and goods were scarce, and now that class enemies were re-moved and a more pragmatic attitude seemed permissible, local cadres hesi-tated to intervene. Beneath the planned economy, a lively economy of secondary markets emerged that allowed the rural population to trade and exchange important goods and products. This rapid emergence of markets and enterprises suggests that rural populations were reviving structures and insti-tutions that had existed in the past, although this contradicted official state policies.[40]

Despite the reappearance of social normalcy, human scars were not so easily erased. Scholars conclude that, in the period between 1966 and 1971, up to 27.2 million Chinese suffered from some form of persecution, harass-ment, or harm—often repeatedly. Of that total, at least 1.73 million people were killed and seven million were severely injured. Some 4.2 million were detained. The vast majority of casualties were not the result of rampaging Red Guards or even of armed combat between mass organizations competing for power. Instead, these people were the victims of organized action by the Cul-tural Revolution's organs of political and military power.[41]

The Succession Crisis Erupts

The succession crisis following the Twelfth Plenum of October 1968, which passed a draft of the new constitution mentioning Lin Biao as future leader, was deeply influenced by China's anxieties about a potential Soviet invasion. China's concern stemmed from the Soviet leadership's articulation of the Brezhnev Doctrine after its invasion of Czechoslovakia in August 1968. That doctrine justified the invasion in terms of an obligation that the Soviet Union and other socialist countries had to intervene if "socialist principles" became threatened in any country in which a communist party had held power. Even North Vietnam offered full support of this policy. The Soviet Union had long claimed that a "military-bureaucratic dictatorship" had seized power in China and distorted socialism. To add to China's concern, since 1966, the Soviet Union had been building up a sizable military force, including nuclear war-heads, along the formerly demilitarized Sino-Soviet border. While the forces stationed there were not sufficient for an invasion of China, they were cer-tainly menacing, especially given the political division and social chaos that prevailed in much of the country.

Almost immediately after the plenary meeting in October 1968, China tried to react to the threat, and called on the United States to resume ambassadorial-level talks in Warsaw. Beijing also renewed its conventional diplomacy; it had reduced its level of ambassadorial representation abroad to a single ambassador in Egypt, and now quickly sought to expand the range of countries with which it enjoyed diplomatic relations.[42]

When the National Party Congress convened in April 1969, it did so recoiling at violent Sino-Soviet border clashes that had arisen in early and mid-March. A series of combat operations at the border in Heilongjiang province along the Ussuri River, and a limited but bloody Soviet invasion several kilometers into the Uighur Autonomous Region of Xinjiang, escalated the tensions between the Soviet Union and China. The specter of war with the Soviet Union, perhaps even nuclear war, deeply unsettled the political leadership.

The rest of the year 1969 was consequently dominated by fears of impending war with the Soviet Union. Several measures were taken immediately. Defense spending was ratcheted up. Throughout the country, the population was told to be prepared for war and to build underground shelters. As a result of the spreading panic, the party even undertook the unusual step of writing into the new party constitution that Defense Minister Lin Biao was Mao's successor. The military tightened its grip on the party and the entire society. Both the Central Committee and the new revolutionary committees being established throughout the country were dominated by military men. Indeed, less than 30 percent of the Eighth Central Committee members elected in 1956 were reelected in 1969, and more than 40 percent of the members of the Ninth Central Committee chosen in 1969 held military posts.

In October, Lin Biao issued a directive, apparently without consulting Mao Zedong first, entitled "On Strengthening Defenses and Guarding against an Enemy Surprise Attack."[43] The directive was wide-ranging, putting the armed forces on high alert, speeding up defense industry production, and moving commanders into combat positions. Mao was infuriated. It seemed to him that Lin Biao had asserted his rising power by practically declaring something close to war, without having contacted him. This was most likely the beginning of the falling-out between the two men and the beginning of the next act of the succession crisis.

The continuous ascent of the military and of Lin Biao made Mao Zedong, Zhou Enlai, and Jiang Qing uneasy. It is doubtful that Mao Zedong had ever really wanted Lin Biao to take on important responsibilities beyond the military. To remove Liu Shaoqi, the old guard of political leaders, and much of the party apparatus and the state at the beginning of the Cultural Revolution, Mao had simply needed Lin Biao and the military. While Lin Biao had praised Mao at every possible opportunity, he showed little involvement during the Cultural Revolution. In fact, he was lukewarm at best on the policies favored by Mao. After 1969, Lin Biao's rapid rise to power must have started to feel threatening. Mao, Zhou, and the former members of the Cultural Revolution Small Group around Jiang Qing started to look for ways to cut back Lin Biao's power.

One way was to mitigate some of the external pressure by engaging the Soviets in direct negotiations on the border dispute. Zhou Enlai briefly met with Soviet Premier Aleksey Kosygin at the Beijing airport in mid-September 1969 and the two agreed to hold formal border talks. The door to the West was also opened. During this period, Zhou Enlai engaged in delicate and secret diplomatic exchanges with the United States. He managed to get the visibly aging Mao to agree to a secret visit to Beijing by the US national security adviser Henry Kissinger in July 1971. That visit was one of the most far-reaching events in the postwar international arena. At a time when the fighting in Vietnam continued to escalate, China and the United States took major steps to reduce their tensions in the face of the Soviet threat. Lin Biao strongly opposed this opening to the United States—probably in part because he knew that this development would strengthen the political stand of his opponents. Kissinger's visit was tantamount to a major defeat for Lin.

As the fear of war with the Soviet Union faded, Mao became ever warier of a successor who seemed to offer little specific support but wanted to assume power quickly. He began to maneuver against Lin. Mao's secretary, Chen Boda, decided to support Lin's cause, however. Therefore, while many measures were undertaken in 1970–1971 to bring order and normalcy back to society, increasingly severe strains split the top leadership. Tensions first surfaced at a meeting of the Central Committee in the summer of 1970, where Chen Boda, Lin Biao, and their supporters made a series of remarks that enraged Mao Zedong. Mao then reprimanded Chen Boda as a warning to Lin. At the end of 1970, Mao also censured Lin's top supporters in the military forces, accusing them of disregarding and undermining civilian authority. The tensions intensified during the spring of 1971 until Lin Biao's son, Lin Liguo, together with supporters in the military, evidently began to put together plans for a possible coup against Mao, should this prove the only way to save his father's position and life. The scheme had the code name "571" (*wuqiyi* is a homophone of the word for armed uprising). It contained a scathing condemnation of Mao Zedong, calling him "the biggest tyrant in Chinese history."[44] It also sketched out three possible ways to respond to Mao's tyranny: assassinate him, set up a rebel government in Guangzhou and start a civil war, or escape to a foreign country. No serious attempts seem to have been made to realize either of the first scenarios. But the third one was tried. In a confusing and unclear chain of events, Lin Biao's daughter secretly informed Zhou Enlai about her father's plotting and set events in motion leading to Lin Biao's immediate attempt to escape. In September 1971, Lin Biao, together with his closest family members, died in a plane crash over Mongolia. Apparently they had been on their way to the Soviet Union.

Details of the defection and death of Lin Biao are shrouded in mystery. This much is certain: Mao Zedong and the remaining leadership were deeply shocked by the narrow avoidance of a military coup. They drew one conclusion: the military's power in the party, and also in society at large, had to be curtailed. Following the Lin Biao incident, virtually every member of the Chinese high military command was purged or arrested. The PLA disappeared from politics and from the public.

China's people drew their own, very different conclusion: for many who had enthusiastically supported Mao during the Cultural Revolution, Lin's flight and death had a profoundly disillusioning effect. Lin had been the most public and most loyal supporter of the Mao cult, and millions had gone through tortuous struggles to back Lin and Mao in the fight against "revisionist" enemies. They had gone as far as to attack and torture respected teachers, mistreat elderly citizens, humiliate old revolutionaries, and even accuse former friends in bitter, often violent confrontations. The repugnant details of Lin's purported coup d'état and subsequent escape cast all this in the light of personal power struggles. Millions of people had cause to believe they had simply been used as pawns in a petty game.

Initially, it was Zhou Enlai who benefited most from Lin's death. From late 1971 through mid-1973, he tried to prod the system back toward stability. He encouraged an economic recovery and introduction of educational standards. He also rehabilitated former officials and brought them back into office. China began again to rebuild its trade and other links with the outside world, while the domestic economy continued the moderate growth that had been under way since 1969. Mao apparently approved of these developments but remained on the sidelines. He sensed that the falling-out with Lin Biao had cost him political capital and credibility.

In 1972, Mao suffered a serious stroke, and Zhou meanwhile learned that he was dying of cancer. These health crises heightened concerns over the still uncertain lines of succession. In early 1973, Zhou and Mao called Deng Xiaoping back from the tractor repair shop in Jiangxi. Deng had been the second most important victim purged by the radicals during the Cultural Revolution and his reemergence was opposed by Jiang Qing and her followers. From mid-1973, Chinese politics shifted back and forth between Jiang and her supporters—later dubbed the Gang of Four *(siren bang)*—and the faction around Zhou and Deng. The former group favored the continuation of the Maoist line, including political mobilization, class struggle, anti-intellectualism, and egalitarianism. The latter, however, advocated the primacy of economic growth, stability, educational progress, and a pragmatic opening to the West. Mao tried to maintain a balance among these different groups while continuing to search for the right successor.

The balance tipped back and forth between the two groups.[45] The leftists gained the upper hand from mid-1973 until the spring of 1974, during which time they initiated a campaign that used criticism of Lin Biao and of Confucius as an allegorical vehicle for attacking Zhou and Deng. By that spring, however, economic stagnation and mounting economic problems made Mao turn back toward Zhou and Deng, emphasizing the need for stability and unity. When Zhou Enlai was hospitalized in June, Deng assumed a vice-presidential post and gradually accrued power through the late fall of 1975. In April 1974, Deng was chosen by Mao to make the presentation for China at the Sixth Special Session of the UN General Assembly in New York, where he also met with Kissinger for the first time. Deng worked to revive the four modernizations (of agriculture, industry, science and technology, and defense). He also commissioned the drafting of an important group of documents in 1975 that laid out basic policies for work in the party, and the modernization realms of industry and science and technology. These policies, with their focus on consolidation in education, economy, and the military, were anathema to the leftists, who used their power in the mass media and the propaganda apparatus to attack Deng's efforts.

Jiang Qing and her radical supporters, however, finally succeeded in persuading Mao that Deng's policies would inevitably lead to a refutation of the Cultural Revolution—and even of Mao himself. Mao therefore sanctioned denunciations of these policies using the wall posters and public meetings that still were a powerful propaganda tool of the leftists. Zhou died in January 1976 and Deng delivered his eulogy. Mao's dissatisfaction with Deng had been accumulating, and after the funeral, Deng disappeared from public view and was once more formally stripped of all responsibilities (with Mao's backing) on April 8, 1976. The immediate cause of Deng's downfall was that a number of massive demonstrations were held in Beijing and other cities, taking advantage of the traditional Qingming Festival to remember Zhou Enlai and to decry radical leftist policies. Many of Deng's supporters were also removed from their posts and a political campaign was launched to "criticize Deng Xiaoping and his right deviationist attempt to reverse correct verdicts" on people during the Cultural Revolution.

On July 28, Tangshan, a town several hundred kilometers from Beijing in Hebei province, was hit by a catastrophic earthquake that, according to official figures, resulted in 242,000 deaths. The tremors jolted Beijing and damaged perhaps a third of Beijing's buildings. Some regarded the disaster as an ominous sign. Indeed, the catastrophe contributed to a general nervousness and uneasiness tangible in the public at that time. As the demonstrations had indicated, China was impatient for change. Mao's death on September 9, 1976, and the arrest of the Gang of Four less than one month later (on October 6, 1976) by a broad coalition of political leaders, police, and the military finally created the chance for a reset. It also brought the efforts to vilify Deng to a close. The Cultural Revolution was officially concluded by the Eleventh Party Congress in August 1977. In practical reality, it had ended with Mao's death, the purge of the Gang of Four, and the mixed feelings of grief and relief that had hit the public almost a year earlier. In 1981, the Gang of Four—among them, Mao's widow, Jiang Qing—were sentenced to lifelong prison terms for the excesses of the Cultural Revolution. The public trial, broadcast live on television, drew a huge audience.[46]

Although it was less damaging to property and human lives than the Great Leap Forward, the Cultural Revolution had very serious implications for Chinese society as a whole. In the short run, of course, the political instability and zigzags in economic policy produced no (or even negative) economic growth and caused a decline in the capacity of the government institutions to effectively deliver goods and services. Officials at all levels of the political system had learned that future unpredictable shifts in policy could easily jeopardize those who had enthusiastically worked for previous policy. The result was bureaucratic timidity. In addition, with the death of Mao and the end of the Cultural Revolution, nearly three million CCP members and other citizens awaited rehabilitation after having been purged, very often on the basis of wrongful accusations and fabricated cases. The Cultural Revolution violently disrupted the lives of tens of millions of Chinese people. Anyone with ties to foreigners was persecuted. Teachers and scholars, traditionally an object of great respect in Chinese society, were publicly criticized and humiliated by their students, driven from their jobs, and sent off to the countryside to do manual labor. The students themselves were then dispatched in large numbers to spend years in the countryside they normally would have spent in school. Factory managers and chief engineers were locked in factory rooms for months, and sometimes longer than a year. Most important, probably, was that a majority of the leadership of the Chinese government and of the Chinese Communist Party was persecuted, stripped of their positions, and relegated to the countryside to labor with the masses, as well. The institutions that party and state had expended so much energy to build, such as the planned economy, the education system, national security, and foreign relations, were suspended, disrupted, or outright abolished. The party-state bureaucracy was left weakened and divided by the campaigns. The result was a deepening of China's backwardness, widespread poverty, international isolation, and a growing gap between China and the industrialized world.[47]

The Cultural Revolution also left longer-term legacies. First, a generation gap had been created. Young adults had been denied an education and had learned to redress grievances by taking to the streets. Second, corruption had spread within the CCP and the government as the terror and accompanying scarcities of goods during the Cultural Revolution caused people to fall back on black markets and personal relationships. The black markets constituted a shadow economy in which many peasants sold whatever surplus they had produced in excess of state quotas. Third, the CCP leadership and the system itself suffered a further loss of faith in the system when millions of urban Chinese became disillusioned by the obvious power struggles that took place in the name of political purity in the early and mid-1970s. Fourth, the legacy of bitter factional strife continued to haunt Chinese society. Factional struggles were rampant as members of rival Cultural Revolution factions shared the same work units, each looking for ways to undermine the other's power.

Perhaps never before in human history had a political leader unleashed such forces against the very institutional system he had created. The resulting damage to that system was profound, and the goals Mao Zedong sought to achieve ultimately remained elusive. The agenda he left behind for his successors was extraordinarily challenging. This is the contradictory legacy of Mao: while he wrote the norms and rules of CCP leadership and represented its successes, he also became the voice of rebellion and the mirror of the party's flaws and failures. The reverberations of this ambiguity, and the impact of Mao's campaigns in the 1950s and 1960s, were profoundly influential for the time after Mao. The most famous slogan of the tumultuous Cultural Revolution, "it's right to rebel" *(zaofan youli)*, affected a whole generation. When former Red Guards and rusticated students returned to urban China from their stint in the countryside after two, three, and sometimes ten years, they had indeed learned from Mao, though not perhaps what Mao and the party wanted them to learn. They learned of the profound corruptibility of the party and the prevalence of archaic power struggles. They above all had absorbed that the biggest problem facing China was not the lack of revolution, but the lack of prosperity and progress.

❖ ❖ ❖

In March 1949, shortly after Beijing was captured by the PLA, Mao Zedong and Zhou Enlai were on their way to the future capital when Mao reminded Zhou of the fate of Li Zicheng, the leader of a huge popular uprising at the end of the Ming dynasty.[48] In 1644, Li Zicheng had marched into Beijing with great fanfare and proudly declared the establishment of a new dynasty with himself as emperor. Yet, shortly after the celebrations, Beijing was attacked by Manchu troops. The city was swiftly taken by conquerors from the north. Li Zicheng didn't stand a chance of defending the city and was killed as he attempted to escape. Thus, in the moment of his greatest triumph, Mao invoked the possibility of failure. The anecdote reflects the deep-seated anxieties that plagued the PRC leadership from the very beginning. The party leaders were aware that the CCP had won victory on the battlefield aided by a rapid disintegration of the GMD forces and by assistance from the Soviet Union. The CCP had won by military triumph, but it did not have a popular mandate to rule China. Leaders were deeply unsure that they could build such a consensus for their political program of radical transformation among the population and gain sustained popular support. It was the single most important problem they confronted. The possibility of failure and defeat was a threat that continued to haunt leadership, especially Mao Zedong.

In the first years of the PRC, both CCP leaders and their foreign supporters had concerns regarding regime stability. Stalin and the Soviet advisers frequently urged the CCP to enter a coalition government with the "democratic parties" in China and to work within existing political structures and institutions.[49] The CCP had come to power, after all, not by invoking socialism, communism, or Stalinism, but by dangling the concept of New Democracy. This implied that the CCP, while claiming leadership, would cooperate with the main political and social forces in China. More precisely, the new People's Republic was intended to rest on a broad social base, with its workers and peasants all part of a "national united front" that included the petty bourgeoisie and the national bourgeoisie. This policy had been pursued because the CCP was well aware of the challenges it faced in governing China and its lack of legitimacy given its violent assumption of power. When the party decided that it should gradually discard the slogan of New Democracy and, in the 1950s, began to stress the need for transformation and class struggle (a shift that by 1962 would find Mao proclaiming "never forget class struggle"), it created political ambiguity and uncertainty and exacerbated the lack of legitimacy. This, then, was a state and government that claimed to serve the people yet lacked any mandate. The profound transformation it was pursuing had not been sought by those for whom it was governing. With the push toward socialist transformation in 1953, the CCP departed from earlier assurances and faced growing mistrust. Cold War conflict, and later the conflict between China and the Soviet Union, created additional outside pressures that further increased feelings of vulnerability and a pervasive nervousness.

Given its profound lack of legitimacy, the institutions of the state were weak and vulnerable. The new government therefore felt it needed to exercise strict control of society and to constantly mobilize the people in support of the new system.

There were real reasons for insecurity. The CCP faced numerous challenges to its rule and was harried by constant internal and external threats to its viability. Well into the 1950s, the effects of the Second World War and subsequent civil war were evident everywhere: tens of millions of refugees uprooted by the strife migrated across the country and flooded into the cities. The conflicts had destroyed China's great cities, devastated its countryside, and ravaged its economies. Years of fighting and frequent changes of ruling powers and administrative structures had resulted in the collapse of social and political institutions. Many villages and towns were run by criminals, armed gangs, demobilized soldiers, and local strongmen. The rural economy had been ruined, food supply was insufficient, and urban economies were crippled by inflation.

The combination of vulnerability, distress, and security concerns permeated the body politic and shaped China's historical trajectory. A sense of crisis was very much on the minds of CCP leaders. When Mao spoke of the enemies of the people, he was quite aware of the tension between the supremacy of sovereign power and the institutions. On the one hand, leaders acknowledged that to be effective, the institutions of the state must be grounded in regulations and rules, especially constitutional law, rather than in arbitrary orders from powers above. On the other hand, they knew that the need for the use of "extraordinary power" made mass mobilization and violent struggle necessary. The state needed to be able to resort to unregulated violence against enemies and traitors. Since the new state saw itself as under siege or still at war, and was anxious about popular acceptance, security issues became of overwhelming importance. This caused the state to reimagine society and individuals in a way that constantly pushed security concerns to the foreground and, at the same time, devalued notions of institutional procedure and legality. It established powerful new contexts to construct threats to the social body of the Chinese nation and, as a result, to produce new forms of political subjects.

When social and cultural history focuses on legitimacy and the popularity of the regime, it amplifies rather than denies the centrality of politics in the

PRC. Show trials, mass rallies, public demonstrations, and spectacles were powerful and efficient vehicles for educating the masses and instilling discipline. The CCP introduced a new, highly politicized public culture into the young PRC that transformed the nation into a propaganda state, with the aim of consolidating the party's power. The CCP accomplished this by constructing monumental public buildings with patriotic and political themes, by mounting spectacular celebratory parades, and by disseminating propaganda through new art, literature, and a revised history of the CCP's accomplishments. These efforts were part of a larger policy of shaping, or generating, a shared rhetoric and set of ideas. This policy was supposed to form consensus by providing a common, meaningful framework. But it also produced jittery, restless states of emotion as the imagined utopian world of communism collided with the harshness of everyday life in Mao's China. The pervasive rumors about policy, campaigns, spies, scarcities, and other social dangers were a symptom of how fraught the atmosphere in this period was.

In the course of the 1950s and 1960s, the party also tried to shape new social norms and models in its lasting project to govern China, thus inscribing party and state itself into society. It was often the objective that the state or the party would be personified by a familiar neighbor, a model worker, or an exemplary soldier like Lei Feng. Such embodiments redefined the boundary between what is conventionally called the state and what constitutes society. The goal was to create a more diffuse state presence, an awareness of the state in society, and habits of self-fashioning with state norms in mind. One can, for instance, point to the capacity of social classification to generate social realities rather than simply reflect them. By "ascribing class" with class labels and other descriptors, and by generating a new sense of being Chinese by ascribing national, ethnic, or racial labels, the regime left deep and lasting imprints on the social construction of China and on the construction of the social and individual, because ascription was transmuted into self-definition and identification through thought reform and reeducation.

The periodic turn to crushing force and brutal violence in the course of endless campaigns and mass movements has to be understood, then, not as evidence of strength. Rather, as Hannah Arendt suggests in writing about totalitarian political systems, it reflects the weakness of the party state.[50] The relative weakness of the state was above all grounded in the comparatively low degree of institutional structures and weak institutional capacity. The

CCP had created a powerful centralized state that was able to subdue resistance by violence, but it was a "structureless" state, in Arendt's sense of that term, as it had no stable, legitimate institutions and lacked established procedures. Existing institutions from the time before 1949, such as villages, local communities, markets, private businesses, and the public sphere, were destroyed. Yet, the new institutions, such as people's communes, state-owned enterprises, and government planning agencies, remained weak, coercive, and inefficient. The personnel that the party could bring in to run the new institutions were limited in numbers, but were also largely made up of inexperienced and in many cases ruthless individuals, suffering from their own political ambiguities and insufficient skill sets. They were expected to govern a diverse population that was more consumed by the travails of everyday life than by political aspirations.

In the economy, heavy industry was to be developed by government command and elaborate planning. The necessary resources for this had to be obtained by collectivization of agriculture. This process entailed the abolition of private property rights to land, and the roundup of all peasants into people's communes. This made it possible for the government to seize agricultural output and use it to feed, clothe, and shelter workers deployed to building and operating the new factories. An extractive institutional system was created to allocate resources toward the heavy industries expected to generate growth. The extractive institutions were unable to generate sustained technological and economic development, however. A nationwide campaign such as the Great Leap Forward could try to compensate for the absence of impulses and innovations in the planned system, but the reality was that such a policy would fail disastrously. Reinvigorated central government command could solve some basic economic problems, but the extractive institutions were unable to motivate individuals and to launch technological progress. There was not only a lack of economic incentives, but also, once all the very inefficiently used resources had been reallocated to industry, there were few economic advances possible. The system hit a ceiling, with lack of innovation and poor economic incentives causing economic stagnation in the 1960s. Growth first slowed down and then collapsed—and stayed in that collapsed state for some time.

The centralized state was also based on an exclusive political institution: the party state. The party state secured the power of the CCP to impose control and permitted it to benefit from extraction. State centralization under one-party rule enabled certain achievements, especially in infrastructure, education, and welfare, but development under extractive political institutions was feeble and unstable because it encouraged infighting from rival factions within the CCP wishing to take control of the state and the extraction it generated.

Confronting these predicaments, Mao sought continuously to revolutionize the state, to "put politics in command," and to achieve a genuine social revolution capable of overriding economic calculations and social hierarchies. At the same time, Mao Zedong used war and revolution as a means of projecting a highly personalized, ambivalent, and amorphous regime of authority on the state. The most important issue, though, emerges from the observation that, during its first three decades, the CCP was unable to create and stabilize new social institutions with an overwhelmingly new elite.[51] Instead, for a long time, it had to rely on various unstable coalitions competing for power and resources. Maoism intended a revolution of the state and of the political system that it failed to achieve.

The turmoil in Chinese society caused by the Cultural Revolution was, above all, a dragged-out succession crisis at the top which saw intense jockeying in the leadership. Any one-party system that is hierarchically geared toward a central figure at the top faces the great challenge of political succession. A number of factors made succession in the Cultural Revolution decade volatile and unpredictable: weak institutions, the overwhelming authority of an incumbent who wanted to make his own pick, and ambitious contenders coveting the top job. Together these created an unstable situation. The Cultural Revolution was as much about the question of who would hold the greatest political power after Mao as it was about the creation of a new socialist culture. While Liu Shaoqi and many of the older leaders were removed from the equation, the succession issue was settled only with Mao's death.

The PRC had inherited indisputably difficult circumstances: bombed cities, broken dikes, land-hungry peasants, refugee movements across the country, and foreign interference. China in the mid-twentieth century was an enormously varied, profoundly shaken, and rough social terrain to be governed. The new authorities believed that monumental, even violent, efforts were required to eradicate, reeducate, or reconstruct, by means of coercion and persuasion, a preexisting world of capital and maritime connections. They made these efforts with varying degrees of success. There was an immense and resilient repository of cultural memory, traditional practices, and transnational links all captured in story and song, festival and ritual, street news and film. There were capitalists, Christians, Buddhists, liberal intellectuals, and other followers of value and faith, whose successful cooptation appeared to have long eluded the party and the state. There were also black markets, smuggling and gambling rings, and various forms of dissent and outright opposition.

To build a new China with varying degrees of fervor and success, the party felt compelled to invest enormous amounts in the forms of cultural capital, political energy, grassroots mobilization, and social engineering. Setting lofty goals such as social transformation had powerful effects and allowed the government to carry out a profound centralization in the 1950s, as society was regimented and absorbed into a hierarchical structure dominated by the state. The early PRC had, starting with "unified purchase and sale" *(tonggou tongxiao),* planned its economy *(jihua jingji)* and reduced the functions of the marketplace. Some of the policies did yield benefits, but many of the initiatives failed. To their dismay, cadres had to discover how ragged, uncompromising, and unruly Chinese society could be. Beyond campaigns and productions there were stubborn memories and aspirations, institutionalized or diffused, open or underground, informing subject positions and eluding party directives. The "old world" held on in bits and pieces. The "new world" struggled to be born. In retrospect, the PRC, from its founding to the end of the Cultural Revolution, was an era marked by the invasive use of governing technologies such as thought reform, rectification campaigns, and sheer violence, yet implementation of its policies remained uneven and its final victory proved elusive. The CCP had to contend with a China persistently in existence despite growing party power and the expanding reach of the state. All this suggests that the resilient powers of Chinese society should never have been underestimated.

PART FOUR

China Rising

In early August 1977, at a time of year when party leaders usually preferred to cool off at the seaside resort in Beihai, unanticipated activities kept the capital busy. Only two months after Deng Xiaoping, like others, had been allowed to return to power and had just assumed his former post as vice chairman of the Central Committee, he plunged himself into work on science and education as one of the four modernizations (along with industry, agriculture, and national defense). Deng realized that without the foundation of science and education, the other three modernizations would not occur. He proclaimed that "China must catch up with the most advanced countries in the world."[1] As one of his first actions, he set up and chaired a multiday forum on science and education in Beijing, which was attended by thirty-three leading Chinese scientists and educators—all of them from outside the party bureaucracy. The discussions quickly came to focus on the backwardness of China's education system. The participants agreed on the causes. After graduation, high school students were sent to work in the countryside, instead of attending universities. Enrollment in tertiary education depended on class background and not on individual performance. During the Cultural Revolution, education and scientific expertise had been looked down upon and treated as suspicious if not treasonous. It was still perceived to be better to be red than to be an expert. By contrast, Deng was convinced that the successful implementation of the four modernizations required a thorough revamping of the education system.

Based on proposals made by participants at his forum, Deng Xiaoping announced the reintroduction of the national entrance examination (*gaokao*) to all universities. The exams would be open to all students, regardless of their class status and level of political activism. Just four months after the meeting, in early December 1977, nationwide exams were held—something that had not happened since 1962. The level of participation was unexpected and overwhelming. Some 5.7 million high school graduates showed up to compete for 270,000 places at the universities. For the first time in the history of the People's Republic of China, enrollment in the universities was based exclusively on exam results. The reintroduction of the entrance examination system, which Deng Xiaoping pushed through against heavy odds and with much personal commitment and energy, had enormous impact. Competence and performance were made the criteria for university enrollment and therefore also the criteria for access to higher positions in state and society.

This reintroduction has to be seen as one of the most dramatic and important decisions made at the outset of China's era of reform and opening. From that time onward, the *gaokao* was held annually. By a few decades later, the number of candidates had climbed to about ten million—the year 2009 marked a historic high. In the context of a focus on institutions, it is also important to note that this was not based on transfers from the West. Rather, it revived a century-old Chinese institution. Public and open examinations for selecting the best talent to serve the state had been a hallmark of imperial China. In the reform era, the need was to implement a competitive system that promoted skills and qualifications instead of party loyalty and ideological submission. The imperial examination system provided the blueprint of a solution which also, thanks to its historical legacy, could enjoy a high degree of acceptance in society.

In 1977, under Deng Xiaoping's leadership, China entered a new era that saw it initiate bold domestic institutional reforms and opening to the outside world, especially with regard to education and the economy. The 1980s turned into a period of daring, hectic, and probing liberalization and experimentation in almost every sector of society and the economy. All this was abruptly checked in 1989, however, when a student-led democracy movement tested the limits of change and challenged the authority of the party. The movement was violently suppressed by the government, and hundreds of protesters were killed. Across the ensuing decades, under the leadership of Deng's successors, Jiang Zemin and Hu Jintao, the policies of reform and opening in the economy would continue to be vigorously and consistently debated. In the period from 1990 to 2012, aggressive economic reforms created an economic miracle that was the envy of the world. At the same time, political reform was not pursued by the party state.

China's resulting transformation was profound. A whole range of new institutions was established that laid the foundations for growth and prosperity. A successful market transition with impressively high GDP growth rates was achieved. As average incomes rose dramatically, hundreds of millions of Chinese people were lifted out of poverty. The progress marked an entirely new phase in the long evolution of modern China. As the country's wealth swelled and its needs for resources evolved, the PRC also pushed to extend its reach across the globe. While China had long been a global-scale contributor to the world economy, the country started to wield its economic weight with the confidence and purpose of a global superpower. As the global economy's center of gravity shifted, China began asserting its economic influence to win diplomatic allies, invest its vast wealth, expand its reach and secure much-needed natural resources. China's growing economic clout overlapped with an increasingly ambitious foreign and military policy. It built aircraft carriers, nuclear submarines, and stealth jets to secure trade routes. In the contested South China Sea, China turned reefs and atolls into artificial islands to mark its territorial claims.[2]

Institutional innovation and rapid economic growth also brought about a profound and unprecedented social transformation of Chinese society, reconfiguring its social structure and redistributing power between state and society. The state relaxed its control over society and public discourse. As a consequence, Chinese society became more complex, diverse, fluid, and dynamic. Massive migration and dramatic changes in working and living patterns fundamentally redefined the social structures of towns and villages. The open economy laid down a solid foundation for an increasingly mobile society, and saw the rise of middle classes and various forms of civil organizations that demanded more political participation. At the same time, China's economic miracle exacerbated income inequalities, environmental degradation, corruption, ethnic conflict, and social fragmentation. As China evolved rapidly from a society with a high degree of income equality under Mao to a relatively unequal one, marked increasingly by evidence of social injustice, popular protests arose of different magnitudes and natures. The rise of the internet in China enabled Chinese citizens to take part in active political discussions and to organize effective protests against perceived injustices. Cultural practices were also fundamentally transformed by market forces, as China was increasingly integrated into the global economy. Driven by technology and the marketplace, the formerly unified and relatively homogeneous public culture changed into a pluralized culture reflecting the diversity of individual experiences in the reform era. New, individualistic forms of cultural expression and lifestyles arose, including avant-garde art, commercial literature, independent films, and new styles of entertainment cinema.

China certainly no longer resembles Mao's China, much less a traditional, Soviet-style communist state. But neither is it anything approaching a liberal democratic system with a completely free-market economy. This is what has been called the "China puzzle."[3] The economy booms without clear protection of property rights, and state-owned enterprises continue to dominate the key sectors of the national economy. Increasing freedoms and relaxation of state control in some areas collide with the fact that the CCP remains firmly in control of state and society. New social spaces have opened up, but the party state has continued to retain a considerable degree of organizational power and has moved to extend its control to the new spaces. The results are new hybrid institutional settings that combine public and private actors in ways that defy Western patterns and models, and that are difficult to analyze with any precision.

The administration of Xi Jinping, who assumed office in 2012, coincided with the rise of new challenges. China's development had created wealth, national pride, and new forms of diversity, but also unmediated tensions and conflicts, creating profound uneasiness and restlessness. Those building pressures erupted repeatedly in scandals, disputes, and public protests. Nervous, anxious, and critical debates called into question the direction that Chinese society was taking in the midst of comprehensive and rapid change. Inside and outside of China, observers worried about the sustainability of those developments and the accruing strains of unresolved issues.

TEN

Reform and Opening

1977–1989

As in periods before, China's development from 1977 to 1989 was closely linked to changes in the international environment. China's active participation in these transnational developments changed global currents and had an enormous impact around the world, more so than ever before. In many ways, during the 1970s, tectonic shifts were underway—economically, politically, but also culturally. Societies in the East and West alike were faced with unprecedented global challenges, such the oil crisis in 1973 and growing economic interdependence, and had to confront them head-on. Very diverse events and processes—from the liberalization of capital markets, to the Soviet structural decline, to America's failure in Vietnam—combined to shatter the Cold War world. With a new, post–Cold War era dawning, this crumbling of existing global structures provided China with a unique chance to regain initiative, both on the global stage and at home.

Under Deng Xiaoping, Chinese society consistently capitalized on the opportunities generated by a changing world. Deng Xiaoping encouraged new, unideological thinking and called upon his countrymen to pursue opportunities and improve their lives, relying on their own talents and ideas. The removal of ideological blinders also prompted daring explorations into Chinese history and culture; the 1980s became one of the most liberal and intellectually interesting periods in China's modern history. Deng Xiaoping also created institutional conditions that allowed and incentivized individual initiative, performance, and risk-taking, while maintaining the overall planning system and state-owned enterprises. Of perhaps most consequence was China's opening to western markets, especially attracting foreign direct investment into what were designated special economic zones. By changing the rules of how the state managed economic transactions and by reducing the burden of extraction, China put its economy successfully on a growth path. Living standards in the rural areas rose, as well.

Toward the end of the 1980s, the limits of the model of combining market liberalization and state planning, often called "socialism with Chinese characteristics," became obvious. The economy was overheating, and rampant inflation evaded government control. Social tensions fueled political protest. Students, urban professionals, and workers took to the streets, demanding greater say and political participation. When tanks rolled into Tiananmen Square to suppress the revolt, the first phase of reform and opening came to an end in a blood-soaked incident that still haunts China today.

The Global 1970s

In the 1970s, the world in general made a major turn away from formal inequality, colonialism, and empire. The process of decolonization, which had begun after World War I, was essentially completed by the end of this decade. This hopeful era was shaped by great strides of emancipation and liberation movements worldwide. The liberation of Angola and Mozambique brought an end to the last great overseas empire, Portugal. White minority rule was upended in Rhodesia, the last of the racist states, which became Zimbabwe. Even in the last stronghold of legal white supremacy, South Africa, the revolt began to build in the black township of Soweto that would ultimately succeed in undermining minority rule. Vietnam rid itself of American intervention, Panama negotiated to gain control of its canal. Nicaragua ousted the ruthless, pro-American dictatorship of the Somoza family, and an Islamist insurgency forced Shah Reza Pahlavi of Iran into exile. At the end of the 1970s, when Red Army troops crossed the Amu Darya River into Afghanistan and confronted stubborn resistance by the Mujahedin fighters, the Soviet Union became tied down in the costly war that would bring about its demise. During the 1970s, opposition movements in Russia and Eastern Europe gained traction; in Poland, the first labor union in a communist state, called Solidarity, was established in 1980. To see even the working class revolting, perceiving that its well-being was unattainable under the current system, was a powerful indictment of communism and all its broken promises. Across the globe, human rights organizations such as Amnesty International also became an important force in international affairs in the 1970s, promoting concepts of equal rights and individual liberties.[1] This decade was a time of economic and political crisis, but also of experimentation and the search for a new and better world. It prompted efforts to break free from Cold War constraints, to overcome entrenched orthodoxies, and to look for new ways out of economic and social stalemate.

Hierarchies and inequities based on race, gender, and class had been denounced at least since the French Revolution, and communism was one of the most powerful articulations of this criticism. In the 1970s, however, the prominent struggles around the world were no longer based on wishes for collective solidarity or dreams of communism, but on a new ideology considered by many to be more fitting to a world transformed by industrialization and global capitalism. This ideology was based on individual rights and freedoms and was skeptical of most forms of collective control and government intervention. The widespread acceptance of the dignity and equal worth of all people coincided not with a surge in communist ideas, but with a resurgence of free market ideas. The new commitment to legal and cultural equality was yoked to an equally strong drive toward free markets. To the extent that barriers based on gender or national or cultural identity had been eliminated from public life, free marketers or liberals could more strongly claim that absolute equality was a mistaken goal and societies should rather focus on ensuring equal opportunities. If people were presented with equal opportunities, the inequalities that remained would be the reasonable result of letting them rise and fall based on their efforts and abilities, and allowing the natural laws of supply and demand to sort out the results.

The turn toward free markets in the 1970s was a broad global movement, in the same way that the decade's shifts toward greater formal equality in the post-colonial world and greater inclusiveness as in ending apartheid were worldwide rather than national trends. Political constituencies around the globe demonstrated that they had lost faith in the welfare states and socialist ideas that had emerged from World War II. They did so in Latin America and in Western Europe—particularly in the United Kingdom by electing the conservative Margaret Thatcher prime minister in 1979. They did so, too, in Eastern Europe with the founding of early anti-communist associations. Everywhere, it seemed, people were setting their hopes on the mechanisms of the market to stimulate economic growth after the worldwide recession of the early 1970s.

Helping, too, to advance free market ideas was the visible stagnation of the Soviet Union. The Soviet model of central planning and social order by government design could no longer be seen as successful. Doubts accumulated even in the Eastern Bloc, and by the 1970s it was clear that communism lacked innovation and transformative power. While communists in some countries were still convinced that their system was superior to capitalism, even they no longer expected it to achieve a truly egalitarian system or to create economies sufficiently dynamic to compete with capitalism. Both radical equality and economic dynamism seemed simply too difficult to reconcile with party dictatorship and the command economy.[2]

In Eastern Europe, while ambitions were trimmed regarding economic growth, a system of economic welfare that was stagnating but stable may have seemed acceptable, at least for a while. In a country like China, however, which still needed to create modern industries, that prospect became less and less desirable. Searching for a model of dynamic development, China no longer looked toward Eastern Europe, but increasingly focused on its immediate neighbors, South Korea, Hong Kong, and Taiwan, all pursuing a very different strategy of a state-driven but market-oriented development. This alternative strategy had lifted these East Asian countries up from poverty to a level of prosperity that came as a surprise to most Chinese when they were finally able to learn it in the 1970s. Increasingly, China's attempts at reform moved in a direction that, while not an exact copy of the Taiwanese or South Korean model, borrowed its basic approach and adapted it to Chinese conditions.

Coinciding with these ideological trends, other significant changes were underway in the arena of international politics. China soon found itself at the center of those developments. Since the late sixties, several US administrations had been thinking about how to benefit from the Sino-Soviet split. Yet, harsh Cold War rhetoric and the unfolding war against communism in Vietnam had initially made it impossible to justify any rapprochement with China. In the 1970s, under President Richard M. Nixon, the United States was determined to extricate itself from Vietnam. Moreover, Washington evaluated the Soviet military threat as increasingly serious under Brezhnev. In China, Zhou Enlai and other more pragmatic leaders saw the chance to reestablish relations with the United States. After several years of informal contact and behind-the-scenes talks, including Secretary of State Henry Kissinger's secret visit in 1971 (noted in Chapter 9), China and the United States arranged Nixon's historic trip to China. When it took place in February 1972, both declared: "This was the week that changed the world." The two sides agreed in the Shanghai Communiqué of 1972 to normalize their relationship. The transformation of China in the mind of the American public from communist menace to quasi-ally made it politically possible for Nixon to negotiate a face-saving withdrawal from the war in Vietnam. Beijing assisted by pressing Hanoi to accept the terms of the 1973 Paris Peace Accords, which temporarily stopped the fighting. Regarding Taiwan, Nixon assured Mao that the United States would no longer promote its independence or consider using the island as a base to attack China.

Nixon's meetings with the ailing Mao Zedong and Zhou Enlai created a geopolitical dynamic that western strategists called the "strategic triangle."[3] The triangle was important and remarkable in two ways. First, it positioned China, despite its poverty, isolation, and relative weakness, as the third most important strategic actor in the world after the United States and the Soviet Union. Because only China had the strategic importance and diplomatic flexibility to act as a swing player, it could play a more influential role than such traditional powers as England, France, Germany, and Japan. Second, this strategic triangle made China, the weakest of the three countries, the greatest beneficiary of their relationship. Most important, China was safe for the first time from both US and Soviet attacks. The USSR declared it would no longer pose a military threat to China. The United States, in turn, was no longer seen by China as a threat and could plausibly be regarded as a protector against whatever Soviet threat still lingered. US assistance strengthened China's position vis-à-vis the Soviet Union. The main US military ally in Asia, Japan, also moved quickly to establish diplomatic relations with China. Diplomatic recognition was also achieved between China and the European Community in 1975, although a number of European states had pursued this earlier.

China was favored by the United States because its pragmatic approach to socialism was considered preferable to the Soviet Union's more orthodox and much more threatening stance. For the United States, China was both a strategic partner against the Soviet Union and, after Mao's death, the pioneer of a more flexible variant of socialism that had the potential to evolve into a liberal society over time. As a result, the United States was willing to extend favorable policies—for instance, lower tariffs—more to China than to other countries. From this time on, relations with the United States played an outsized role in Chinese foreign policy. No other relationship has been as important, or as fraught, as that between America and China. The United States, as the largest economy, opened its doors to China's products and made significant investments, facilitating China's economic development. It also trained China's finest scientists and students, giving critical support to Chinese efforts to catch up in technology and science. Building steadily on small, initial forms of cooperation, the two nations grew more and more codependent. As the United States imported a growing amount of goods, China acquired US securities in return.

China opened its doors in the 1970s, a time when economies in the West were battling severe recessions. Japan's economy was maturing. By contrast, China held the promise of a vast market for investors and entrepreneurs—and offered, via Hong Kong, an easy way for capital, advanced technology, and entrepreneurship to flow in from the West. The late 1970s were thus a very opportune time for China to open its economy to the outside world. The role of timing in the eventual success of China's reform policies should not be underestimated. China was able to capitalize on a unique global opportunity that arose at the critical historical juncture just after Mao's death.

China after Mao

Inside China, the years between the end of the Cultural Revolution and the start of reform and opening (gaige kaifang) were marked by uncertainty. The crisis of legitimacy that had been brewing as living standards failed to improve across two decades was heightened by Mao's death in 1976. With it, an entire era shaped by Mao's personality, ideological beliefs, and political clout came to an end. His departure produced a huge vacuum, but also an opportunity for readjustment and recalibration. In many ways, the situation in China resembled the situation that had existed in the Soviet Union between 1953 and 1956. During that time, Khrushchev had been determined both to sustain a reformed communist system—"Soviet power" and "socialism," in his terms—and to consolidate and advance his own power within that system. Like Khrushchev, any new leader in China needed to assert the clear supremacy of the party bureaucracy over the military and leftists by emphasizing the need to overhaul the system to strengthen it. The senior members of the CCP who had suffered greatly during the Cultural Revolution all had a common interest in ensuring that no one ever be given as much license to act against rivals as Mao Zedong had been granted. Political relaxation and a strengthening of inner-party democracy constituted a policy that answered this general wish.

Hua Guofeng (1921–2008) immediately succeeded Mao Zedong as chairman of China's Communist Party by claiming that Mao had given him a note written on his deathbed saying: "With you in charge, my heart is at ease." The extreme leftist supporters of the Gang of Four were also soon purged and many party and government leaders who had been sent off to the countryside were returned to office and power. It became clear that the support of most of the population and the leadership of movements such as the Cultural Revolution and the Great Leap Forward had virtually disappeared. To many in China, the Cultural Revolution had proved the risks of popular mobilization as means of social reform and economic development, and discredited leftist dogmatism as a political direction. The years of abuse suffered by the country's leadership and most intellectuals had created a large constituency keen to see a reset of the socialist experiment. Many were more than ready to move past the chaos and power struggles that had characterized social life in China for a decade or more.

The Maoist era had produced a large, if inefficient, industrial base. It had also increased the number of educated people, despite closing universities and disrupting the schools during much of the Cultural Revolution. Still, the economic situation in the seventies was challenging, as China was plagued by high urban unemployment, stagnating levels of food production, deteriorating urban housing conditions, falling wages, widespread rural poverty, and sluggish productivity growth. The destruction and damage of the Cultural Revolution had created a widespread longing for policy that would bring stability and prosperity to China, and in that sense, set the stage for the gradual abandonment of the centrally planned command economy.[4]

Many hoped for a return to a more systematic and effective approach to governance in general, and to governance of the economy in particular. But what kind of governance of the economy was required? The failure of the Cultural Revolution had discredited the Maoist approach to economic and social development, but did not itself present a clear alternative. Essentially, there were two possibilities. First, China could go back to central planning on the grounds that it had never given the command-economy system a proper try (with the exception of a few years in the mid-1950s, when it had performed reasonably well). Second, China could aim for an altogether different model, discarding the planned economy for a market economy. During the second half of the seventies, the former viewpoint prevailed within the leadership. Deng Xiaoping, who was back in office by the end of 1977, was not committed to any particular economic system, but he certainly started the reform period with a view that the challenge was to make the planned economy work better, rather than abandon it altogether. Chen Yun (1905–1995), the other political leader with a major role in economic policy, fully agreed with that approach. The end of the Cultural Revolution therefore did not lead to liberalizing reforms as much as it led to an attempt to rebuild the planned economy. Indeed, it was logical for post-Mao leaders to seek to revitalize the plan precisely because of the disruptions to planning sustained under Mao. Since the system of economic planning had been shattered by the Cultural Revolution, however, it was difficult to simply revive the old system. The need for institutional change, in other words, was obvious.

Given the lingering economic crisis, Hua Guofeng, in his brief period of power, recognized that the new government had to produce results fast. Therefore, he attempted to carry out an economic policy focused on jump-starting industrial production by purchasing equipment and factories from foreign countries. The plan was to invest as much in this short period as had been invested from 1949 to 1977, with heavy industry still receiving the bulk of the resources. The program, dubbed the Great Leap Outward, also featured a state-led development strategy within the planned economy that resulted in massive projects like the Baoshan steel complex in Shanghai.

After the program failed to produce the intended results, however, economic course corrections were made. The Great Leap Outward was seen as having little effect on the general population's economic well-being. In its place, the new economic leaders grouped around Chen Yun launched an economic stabilization program that sidestepped heavy industry. In the words of Chen Yun: "Thirty years after [our] revolutionary victory, there are still beggars. [We] must improve living conditions. Balanced growth promises the fastest growth rates. We made the mistake of overemphasizing steel production in the past. Such a growth path cannot be continued."[5] Resources were deployed instead to light industry. As it happened, economic stabilization, the reorientation of economic strategy to consumer goods, and unexpectedly good agricultural harvests combined to relieve the shortages that had plagued China's command economy during the Cultural Revolution. The slightly improved economic environment gave breathing space to local cadres and resulted in a diminished role and desire for state redistribution and investment. In 1977–1978, when a few counties in Anhui and Sichuan were facing food shortages, local authorities permitted peasants in these areas to divide communal land among private households for cultivation, reintroducing individual household farming (while keeping the land under collective ownership).[6] If the peasants fulfilled certain quotas of grain delivery, they could keep anything they produced beyond the quota. The successes of those rural reforms in a few locales unleashed desires for more reforms in other regions and other spheres of economic life. The era of economic reform thus began, without a blueprint or grand vision, as a by-product of local experimentation and partial economic readjustment.[7]

Creating the Reform Era

Meanwhile, Deng Xiaoping was already maneuvering to replace Hua Guofeng. To consolidate power, Deng had to weaken the position of his main rival Hua Guofeng and his supporters.[8] He did this by first launching an ideological campaign in opposition to the "two whatevers"—a reference to an article that Hua Guofeng had ordered to be published in *Red Flag Journal* in February 1977. That article stated: "We will resolutely defend whatever political decisions were taken by Chairman Mao; we will unwaveringly follow whatever directives were issued by Chairman Mao." This statement was obviously a clear rejection of any open and critical assessment of the Maoist period. More importantly, it repudiated any attempts at political moderation or social reform. In response, Deng Xiaoping made a great effort to restructure official doctrine and to transform the radical and revolutionary party into a reform-oriented and pragmatic one. His goal was to establish a non-Maoist reform program and build political legitimacy for his own reform agenda. In 1977, Hu Yaobang (1915–1989), then vice president of the Central Party School, started an internal publication, *Theoretical Trend (Lilun dongtai)*, which published articles calling for emancipation of thought. In May 1978, the article "Practice Is the Sole Criterion for Testing Truth" was printed in the journal, and reprinted in other major newspapers such as *Guangming Daily*, *People's Daily*, and *PLA Daily*. The idea that practice, not political ideology, was the sole criterion for testing truth met with overwhelming support and spread quickly from Beijing to the rest of the country—and from party insiders to intellectuals. This campaign enabled Deng to promote a pragmatic and critical understanding of Mao Zedong's thought.

Deng was well prepared. As early as 1975, he had overseen the drafting of three party documents outlining a new political direction. The documents presented plans for the revitalization of the higher education system, the return to economic incentives in industry and agriculture, and the removal of "leftists" from the party. At the same time, Deng adopted Zhou Enlai's earlier "four modernizations," drafted back in 1964 but mostly ignored since. This agenda called for a fifteen-year "construction phase" to modernize agriculture, industry, science and technology, and national defense. Putting Zhou's four modernizations at the top of China's policy agenda once again, Deng started emphasizing the need for *fazhan* or "development," a term that would later become the mantra of party rule. Development should lead to "wealth and power." Deng lent his support to whatever changes he thought would move China toward that goal. From that moment on, economic development became the overriding quest of the party to which all other objectives were subordinated. He also selected advisers and officials who shared his emphasis on economic development and who were willing to experiment with new ideas and approaches. When these changes worked, they were rolled out more broadly. Those that failed had to be abandoned. Deng Xiaoping officially favored pragmatism and realism over ideological correctness and revolutionary zeal.

After removing ideological obstacles to reform, Deng and his supporters began to search for specific solutions to the serious problems China faced in the 1970s. The most urgent task was to replace the current political leadership, which had committed itself under Hua Guofeng to the line of the "two whatevers," with reform-minded leadership ready to implement necessary policy changes. To this end, a Central Working Conference of the CCP was held over the course of thirty-six days in the fall of 1978, before the Third Plenum of the Eleventh Central Committee in December. At the conference, Hua was pressured into conceding the mistakes of his policies. On December 13, 1978, at the Third Plenum, Deng Xiaoping gave a powerful and widely acclaimed political speech with the title "Liberate Thought, Seek Truth from Facts, and Unite to Look Forward." He explained: "So long as we unite as one, work in concert, emancipate our minds, use our heads, and try to learn what we did not know before, there is no doubt that we will be able to quicken the pace of our new Long March. Under the leadership of the Central Committee and the State Council, let us advance courageously to change the backward condition of our country and turn it into a modern and powerful socialist state."[9] The conference also unanimously decided on the major personnel reshuffling Deng Xiaoping had engineered. Hua was effectively stripped of his powers, although his period as chairman formally ended only in 1981. Chen Yun, Deng Yingchao (1904–1992), Wang Zhen (1908–1993), and Hu Yaobang were appointed to the Political Bureau. Chen also entered the Standing Committee and became the first secretary of the newly established Central Committee of Discipline Inspection. One of Hua's main supporters and a clear opponent of reform, Wang Dongxing, former head of Mao's personal security force, was removed from this position.

The Third Plenum was a watershed event in China's political, economic, and social development. The leadership formally announced the epochal change of policy from Maoist class struggle to economic development. A new tone was set, one that encouraged new thinking and a focus on practice and concrete improvement of living standards. It marked a sharp departure from the Mao era's insistence on doctrinal purity. There was an atmosphere of a new beginning, a turning point that fueled optimism and enthusiasm in China and abroad. Deng became the de facto head of the party, and was now able to embark on the reform and opening that would lay the foundation for China's rapid economic development in the following three decades.

The reforms also brought changes to the political system. Deng Xiaoping believed only the most qualified people should be allowed to join the Communist Party. To reach the higher levels of the party, cadres had to prove their effectiveness at lower levels. He also thought that leaders should retire at a certain age, and a new mechanism—seemingly unique among authoritarian systems—was created to periodically and peacefully renew and upgrade the political leadership.[10] Under Mao Zedong or in the Soviet Union, and in similar systems elsewhere, leaders refused to give up power even when their regimes weakened and declined. Because of the experience during the Mao period, Deng Xiaoping and later his successors, installed formal rules and informal norms to facilitate a peaceful turnover of political elites. With rare exceptions, officials would spend no more than fifteen years at a given rank. Unless granted special dispensation, they would retire from government and party posts at a fixed age which, depending on their rank, would fall between fifty-five and seventy-two.[11] For the top leadership positions, time in office was limited to two five-year terms. An official was normally not permitted to assume a top-level position in the province from which he or she hailed. The principle of collective leadership dictated that the members of the powerful Politburo Standing Committee must make policies in different domains by chairing various "leading small groups" *(lingdao xiaozu)* dealing with different fields of policy—for example, foreign affairs, national security, and financial and economic affairs. The Standing Committee would meet once a week and the full Politburo once a month to pass on the major decisions taken by these leading groups.

In 1981, the Sixth Plenum of the Eleventh Central Committee officially issued a "resolution on certain questions in the history of our party since the founding of the People's Republic of China."[12] The party led a long discussion to reach an agreement on the resolution. It was a challenge to come to terms with the long and complex period of Mao's rule. The resolution fundamentally approved of Mao's historical rule but did assert that he made leftist errors after 1958. Among his errors, the resolution mentioned the Great Leap Forward, but especially pointed to the Cultural Revolution. On this it said: "Chief responsibility for the grave 'Left' error of the 'cultural revolution,' an error comprehensive in magnitude and protracted in duration, does indeed lie with Comrade Mao Zedong."

At the beginning of the reform period, Deng and the other new leaders had neither a clear blueprint for how to bring wealth to the people and power to the country, nor anything close to a theory that would explain how liberalization and market orientation reforms would fit with Marxist or Mao Zedong thought.[13] Even as late as the mid-1980s, it was difficult to discern any larger political vision behind Deng's decisions. In the summer of 1984, Deng began using the term "socialism with Chinese characteristics," a striking but ambiguous phrase. It permitted stretching the acceptable ideological agenda to pursue market-oriented economic policies that improved living standards. Deng used the term to promote his goal of expanding the role of markets and launching comprehensive reforms in the areas of industry, commerce, science, and education, while at the same time maintaining party rule and loyalty to socialist values.

A more systematic theoretical framework eventually began to emerge only at the Thirteenth Communist Party Congress in 1987. At this congress, Zhao Ziyang (1919–2005) introduced the theory of "the primary stage of socialism," in an attempt to provide a new theoretical basis for economic reform and development.[14] Zhao Ziyang asserted that the reforms still intended to uphold socialism, and that the goal of achieving a higher stage of socialism remained in place, but that it might take as long as a century to reach that state. The new concepts—namely, that "planning should no longer be primary" and that China was only in the primary stage of socialism—provided a theoretical basis for continued use of market mechanisms. Zhao declared that commodity exchange should be allowed to develop according to the "law of value," with prices increasingly determined by fluctuations in value. That is if goods were in short supply, their prices would go up. Private enterprises should be permitted to employ more than seven people, and shareholders should be allowed to receive cash dividends. The congress also decided on a policy of "one center and two basic points." The center was economic growth and the two points were "reform and opening" and the "four basic principles" put forward by Deng in 1978: the socialist road; the dictatorship of the proletariat; the leadership of the Communist Party; and Marxism–Leninism and Mao Zedong Thought. These basic principles were meant to define the limits of what could be done under the banners of "reform" and "opening."

Institutional Innovations

To pursue economic reforms, China had to go through the difficult transition from a centrally planned economy, which followed Soviet-style heavy industrialization for several decades, toward a market-based economy. This required a great deal of institutional change and innovation. Existing rules needed to be modified and new rules had to be drafted. A broad range of transactions in society had to be conducted based on a new set of regulations.

A basic starting point for the reform and opening period was to establish better relations with other major countries. Along with the "opening" policy came the new buzzword of *jiegui*—literally, "connecting tracks" with the outside world. Deng Xiaoping was convinced that China under Mao had made

10.1. Deng Xiaoping wearing a cowboy hat at a rodeo near Houston during his official visit to the United States in 1979.
Bettmann / Getty Images / 515581898

grave mistakes in antagonizing neighboring countries and isolating itself. China's economic development depended on easing tensions with the world's leading nations. Unless it connected to the world and opened itself to an influx of foreign trade, technology, and knowledge, China could not be modernized.

The United States, as the biggest and most advanced economy, played a central role in China's strategy. Deng Xiaoping pushed to complete the normalization of relations with the United States as soon as possible, but even then, China negotiated hard, especially over the issue of Taiwan.[15] After many months of secret negotiations and mutual recognition of the need for a "peaceful reunification" between the PRC and the Taiwanese Republic of China, the deadlock was broken. On December 15, 1978, President Jimmy Carter announced the establishment of diplomatic relations between the United States and the PRC as of January 1, 1979. From January 29 to February 4, Deng Xiaoping made a triumphant visit to America, where he donned a cowboy hat, demonstrating that it was fine for the Chinese to sample

American culture. The Chinese leader was impressed by the advances of technology and productivity and the breadth of consumer choices he found in the United States. After returning home, he told his colleagues he had been unable to sleep for several nights, thinking about how China might achieve such abundance. One thing was clear to Deng: working with the United States on foreign affairs could open vast and indispensable opportunities for US technology transfers to China, both military and civilian. There were other important nations, too, to smooth out relations with. Deng Xiaoping was the first leader in Chinese history to visit Japan, where he met the Japanese emperor. He negotiated and signed a treaty of peace and friendship with Japan, promoted people-to-people exchanges, and expanded imports of Japanese movies, TV programs, and novels. His government's outreach also extended to the Soviet Union. In 1989, China welcomed Mikhail Gorbachev to Beijing to show the world that Sino-Soviet relations, broken since 1963, were back on track.

Maintaining a favorable international environment for economic growth was the top priority and main thrust of Chinese foreign policy after 1979. Numerous economic agreements were struck between China, the United States, and European countries. Some tensions flared up over Taiwan and the continued US arms sales taking place there. On those occasions, PRC leaders protested, but there were no serious disruptions in fundamental relationships. Sometimes human rights issues arose, but mutual economic interests always prevailed. China went to great lengths to avoid escalating disagreements and becoming involved in military conflicts with other countries. China favored secure world markets, opposed trading blocs, and worked for open access to foreign markets and foreign sources of energy and other commodities. China also actively collaborated with international organizations and supported international agreements governing trade, finance, nonproliferation, public health, and environmental policy. China's diplomats used negotiations and "soft power" to generate cooperation with like-minded states and influence decisions of international bodies. In all of these areas, China's actions were above all guided by its own economic interests.

Another area for institutional reform was the domestic economy. In the beginning, while Chen Yun and others believed it was desirable to supplement central planning with reliance on markets, he and most economists and politicians in China probably could not imagine displacing the former with the latter entirely. The goal, in other words, was merely to make the planned economy work better, by supplementing it with the market economy that had developed after the Cultural Revolution. China adopted its reforms gradually and incrementally during this period, extending and expanding ongoing changes. By so doing, it slowly introduced market forces into a centrally controlled economy, but without a fundamental and complete transformation into a privately owned economy. In essence, the approach was one in which the state continued to administer a planned economy flexibly, while permitting a market economy to expand alongside it. Economic reform in China was therefore a "partial reform strategy."[16] It was characterized by gradual institutional innovations and frequent regional experimentation. Deng Xiaoping and the leadership thought it wise to try new ideas in areas where leaders supported reforms and conditions were favorable. When new programs worked, leaders were brought in to observe the successes and those who led the experiments were sent around the country to explain how they succeeded. The reforms of the Deng government in 1979–1980 may have at first seemed like a cautious return to the "readjustment" policies promoted by Liu Shaoqi in the early 1960s to recover from the disaster of the Great Leap. Soon, however, they set off a surge of profound social and institutional changes that would eventually undermine many of the collective institutions in social and economic life built during the Maoist period.

About 80 percent of the Chinese people, or 795 million people, lived and worked in the countryside in 1980. It was here, within the agricultural sector, that the reform had to prove itself first. Initially, many rural cadres were opposed to ending rural communes, even though the system had proved incapable of feeding the population. Instead of confronting the opponents of change head-on by abolishing communes, Deng Xiaoping told local leaders that, if peasants were starving, farmers should be allowed to adapt. Deng also pointed to the experiments in Sichuan and Anhui where, after shortages, farms now flourished and surplus food was sold on the market, and Deng invited journalists to report on the successes. Within a year, most of the country chose to phase out communes. By 1982–1983, decisions were made to enforce decollectivization in the whole country. The 1982 state constitution legally abolished the people's communes, leaving them only as administrative hulls and turning their administration over to townships and village committees. This quickly led to the reintroduction of household farming nationwide.

Beyond doing away with collectivized agriculture, the essential thrust of those reforms was to introduce incentives and to motivate peasants to substantially increase production. The reformers clearly recognized that one of the biggest problems of the planned economy was its removal of motivating incentives. As local authorities pointedly remarked in 1980, the collectivization of agriculture "has caused suppression of the peasants' socialist initiative as well as insufficient exertion of the superiority of collectivization. Because the collective economy has not been doing satisfactorily, people in a few backward and poverty-stricken localities have even less faith in agricultural collectivization."[17]

Resource extraction from China's huge agricultural economy had been a major objective of Chinese governments throughout the twentieth century, including Mao's. Unlike the policies of the 1950s, however, the new policy was based on the commercialization of the rural economy—although this process was always to be under a great degree of state guidance. While the goals remained similar, the design of the institutions created to achieve that goal differed greatly. Two policies were at the center of the reform of rural institutions: the policy to implement the rural responsibility system, and the policy to develop rural enterprises. In September 1980, the party's Central Committee recommended adoption of what generally came to be called the "household responsibility system." Under the responsibility system, the government began to introduce a system of rural contracts that came to control commercial transactions between the rural producers, the state, and collective agencies responsible for agricultural inputs and outputs.

Individual peasant households could sign contracts with the production team for the cultivation of given portions of the team's "collective" land. In return, the households handed over to the team a contractually agreed share of their output to meet state tax and grain quota obligations. The transition to a more commercialized rural economy untied the bonds of the command economy that had previously subordinated the rural people's communes and their members to the dictates of the state plan. Individual contractors gained considerable latitude to sell their agricultural surplus to other peasants in local markets or to units managed by the collective or the state. The farming households were free to work the land in whatever fashion they wished and to dispose of the surplus as they chose. By 1984, party policy also permitted private individuals to provide services in the rural areas. Agricultural production teams and brigades (an administrative structure left over from the communes) allowed individuals to operate small-scale enterprises, agricultural machinery, technical services, and irrigation works for the commune, brigade, or team in return for fees. In April 1985, the government abolished the system of unified purchase (mandatory sales quotas) established in the 1950s. With this decision, the command economy in the countryside was all but dismantled.

These rural reform policies were hugely successful. Farmers opted for the household responsibility system in large numbers. As rural commercial production took off, farming households could choose where and to whom to sell their surplus goods and even how much surplus to produce. Between 1978 and 1982, agricultural product sales grew by 99 percent, and the average commodity rate (output sold as a proportion of total output) increased from 41 to 59 percent. The number of rural markets also rose by nearly 25 percent, and the volume of trade in the rural market jumped by almost 130 percent.[18] From 1978 to 1984, the gross value of agricultural production grew at an average annual rate of 7.4 percent. The grain output in 1984 was 33 percent higher than in 1978. There were outstanding gains in labor productivity in the countryside, rural per-capita income nearly doubled over those six years, and there was a visibly substantial rise in living standards across most of the countryside. The economic upsurge in the countryside could certainly be attributed to the reforms. It also stemmed from the 1979 price increases on agricultural products. The increases of 25 percent were decided by the state and were meant to alleviate the economic situation in the rural areas. Up to this point, market liberalization of commodity prices remained limited. Price changes in the planned economy were centrally administered and not driven by market forces. Although a market with flexible prices was gradually taking shape, it was only after 1985 that price liberalization was pursued in earnest.

The second policy of rural reform, the development of rural enterprises, started in 1979 when the central government began to encourage—in deed if not in word—the creation of "commune and brigade enterprises." Later, when there were no longer any communes and brigades, these were called "township and village enterprises," or TVEs.[19] TVEs were originally conceived during the Great Leap Forward campaign as a means to promote broader social goals, especially to reduce the gap between city and countryside standards of living. By the mid-1970s, the small factories (most of them rather primitive technologically) being operated by communes and brigades employed only twenty-eight million workers. In the market reform period, however, rural industry became a dynamic force in the Chinese economy. The removal of government-imposed barriers to the establishment of TVEs was enthusiastically embraced by rural local governments, which were eager to take advantage of the high profitability of industry. Rural industrial enterprises multiplied and developed quickly once the Deng government encouraged them, and thanks to the influx of capital from local governments, private investors and later, foreign investors (mostly overseas Chinese) and various local credit cooperatives. These rural enterprises also grew in terms of their numbers of employees, ranges of products, and extent of technological development. Through much of the 1980s, total production by TVEs grew at the stunning rate of 30 to 35 percent per year. By the 1990s, more than 125 million workers were employed in the rural industries, which was the most rapidly expanding sector of the Chinese economy. This institutional change generated innovation and dynamic growth in the rural economy.

The TVEs were officially classified as part of the "collective" sector of the Chinese economy, and they made up the largest part, by far, of what fell under that rather ambiguous designation. Yet most of the industrial enterprises in the countryside were owned and managed by private entrepreneurs and local governments, and operated in the national and global market economy. Probably unforeseen by the government, the resultant rapid expansion of the nonstate sector became the most powerful force that propelled China's transition to a market economy.[20] The entry of new nonstate producers greatly expanded the range of products and services available on the market and created competition for existing state-owned firms.

Encouraged by the positive results in the countryside, China introduced further reform into urban areas in 1984. Managers in state-owned enterprises were given more autonomy and allowed to keep parts of the profits. The government also permitted the adoption of various forms of the contract responsibility system, experiments with shareholding, and the development of a significant individual and service economy in urban areas.

In July 1979, the coastal provinces of Guangdong and Fujian were designated as platforms to launch China's new open-door policy. A year later, the central government selected the cities of Shenzhen, Zhuhai, Shantou, and Xiamen as special economic zones.[21] The primary intention of the government was to channel foreign capital, advanced technologies, and foreign expertise into export-oriented production and processing centers. In turn, the special economic zones gave foreign investors a degree of legal protection that was not enjoyed by Chinese enterprises. This was obviously sufficient to induce significant amounts of inward foreign direct investment into China in spite of an otherwise feeble legal system. Overseas, Chinese businessmen from Hong Kong and other countries started to establish new enterprises and set new standards for efficient management in the special economic zones. Between 1979 and 1982, 949 agreements for the special economic zones with foreign investors were reached, with a volume of foreign direct investment exceeding US$6 billion.

When these innovations and experiments worked, lessons were extended elsewhere. In January 1984, Deng Xiaoping toured Guangdong and Fujian, where he announced that the policy permitting the creation of special economic zones had proved a clear success. Television cameras captured images of the high-rise buildings and new cars beginning to change the Shenzhen landscape. The news coverage laid the basis for public acceptance of the opening of other coastal areas later in the year.[22] In April 1984, fourteen coastal cities stretching from Dalian in the northeast to Beihai, a port city in the southwestern province of Guangxi, were declared open to foreign direct investment. This policy continued throughout the 1980s. In 1988, the island of Hainan was opened as a special economic zone to foreign investment. Two years later, in 1990, the Pudong area in Shanghai was also declared a special economic zone. By the end of 1990, the number of agreements reached for using foreign capital reached 29,693, totaling $68.1 billion—a substantial amount of investments for China in that period. Most important to note is that the foreign investment flowing into these centers and the additional economic activity around it occurred largely outside of the state's plan, contributing to the erosion of the planned economy and the growth of the market economy.

Reforms were also pushed in the industrial sector. In industry, reform followed a dual-track approach. During the planned-economy era prior to

1978, raw materials, equipment, and other production materials had been allotted according to central planning, and their prices were set by state planning guidelines. As part of the reform and opening policy, state-owned enterprises, after selling planned output to the state at low, fixed prices, were allowed to sell any output that exceeded their designated quotas at market-determined prices. The state could thus meet its high-priority objectives while also providing incentives for market-oriented production. Since the new non-state enterprises were required to buy their production materials from the market, a dual-pricing system emerged. This dual-pricing system had complex effects on the Chinese economy. A dynamic sector of the economy entirely based on the market was opened up by this novel initiative.[23] Market forces started to penetrate the economic lives of all Chinese households and businesses. Furthermore, this landmark change avoided the economic or political earthquakes associated with full-scale privatization (which may have threatened people's livelihood) or full liberalization of prices (which may have eliminated long-standing subsidies and undercut the authority of plan agencies).

These innovations were able to work so well in a short period of time because they were rooted in relatively familiar institutional arrangements. Family farming and the contracting system resonated with historical patterns. The contracting system, for instance, was similar to the arrangements of traditional land leases. TVEs also harked back to historical institutions in which rural producers jointly invested in domestic rural production or trade through credit associations at the village level. The reforms were also successful because they had no losers and demanded no sacrifices. They were not contingent on cuts in other sectors such as heavy industry or state-owned enterprises, nor did they require investments on a large scale. Moreover, the benefits of the new arrangements were easily discernible and widely shared.[24]

These reforms, however, also led to new challenges. Incremental institutional reforms focused exclusively on the local level, while the macroeconomic institutional order remained unchanged. This produced a unique situation where several institutional systems coexisted on various levels. Institutional reform on the local level created intense competition and innovation. The central level approved of these changes, but itself remained outside the purview of reform. The state-owned enterprises, for instance, were not reformed. A hybrid combination of political centralization and economic regional decentralization and reform developed.[25] The national government continued to exercise a highly centralized control through appointment and promotion of local government officials. The governance of the economy, however, was by and large delegated to local governments competing for resources. The emerging regional economies (provinces, municipalities, and counties) were relatively self-contained and competitive, with their local governments holding responsibility for initiating and coordinating reforms.

Economic reforms also contributed to social change in China. The main driver was the rise of an entrepreneurial class, including both private entrepreneurs and professional managers. The Communist Party actively reacted to those social changes by coopting the new elites into its power structure. This happened on all levels of government, with the local level being the most dynamic. Embracing the new business elites allowed the CCP to stabilize its hold on power, but also made it possible for special, profit-seeking interests to gain access to local governments. While the Chinese government was a major player in shaping the contours of the reforms, it did not systematically plan or regulate China's transition to the market—at least not until long after the reform process had started. The reforms were pragmatic, piecemeal, and cautious, not wholesale or systemic. The result was a decentralized, fragmented, hybrid state-corporatist system.

This complex situation gave rise to inherent problems.[26] As competitive pressures built up, profit margins for firms of all ownership types steadily declined. Central government finance felt the strain, given its reliance on the financial health of state enterprises. Budget shortfalls were exacerbated by increased spending for infrastructure and large-scale construction, wage increases, and the use of foreign exchange. The 1980s also saw galloping inflation which, in 1988, even reached a hyperinflationary point that threatened the continuation of the reforms. The emergence and intensification of market competition thus yielded not only the dynamism and international competitiveness of Chinese industry but also the increasing difficulties facing state enterprises and central government finance, which had not been adjusted and were still governed by older institutions. There were many dynamics and dilemmas in the political economy of China's market transition.

The existence of the dual-pricing system led to rent-seeking behaviors and the spread of corruption, making it difficult to create a level playing field for competition among enterprises. Those who were well connected to politically powerful people were able to make a fortune by using their networks and influence to resell supplies earmarked for allocation by the state. The abuses were obvious enough to produce public outcry and frequent protests. In the mid- and late 1980s, an important topic of debate was how to further guide the reform of the dual-pricing system. It was not until 1993 that the scope of direct allocation of commodities and goods declined precipitously and the role of the dual-price system waned.

The politico-economic structure also was a major impediment to the emergence of a clear separation between the regulatory state and the market system in the rural areas. Perhaps most significant in this respect were the advantages rural party cadres discovered in the newly commercialized economy. Most rural officials initially resisted the return to household farming, partly out of ideological belief, but mostly because they feared loss of power and income. Many soon found out, however, that their political positions were uniquely valuable resources in pursuing commercial interests. Managing the process of decollectivization, many party cadres were able to get hold of the best lands and most valuable farm tools and machinery for themselves, their relatives, and their friends. Their political connections helped them acquire goods and materials in short supply, which could be used in lucrative dealings on the rapidly expanding black market.

Another problem that surfaced first in the countryside was related to ownership. An essential prerequisite for the development of rural markets was the privatization of land use, even if the question of outright ownership had been left open. Land originally used by family farmers under the household responsibility system was formally leased for short periods from the collective production teams and legally remained collective property. A 1984 government regulation permitted fields to be leased for periods of up to fifteen years. In 1993, that was extended by another thirty years, making forty-five-year leases possible, and it was generally understood that land could be inherited by the next generations. This effectively established a free market in land, with leased lands being rented, bought, sold, and mortgaged as if they were fully tradable private property. That the families had no real claims to the land, however, often became clear when the state confiscated agricultural land for infrastructure or commercial development.

In the 1970s and 1980s, reform and opening set off profound changes in Chinese society. Poverty slowly disappeared from most regions, 400 million peasants saw their living standards improve markedly for the first time in decades. Even in remote areas of the countryside, modern appliances such as refrigerators and washing machines became commonplace. While new high-rise buildings remained scant, and cars were still mostly government-owned, subtle and subsurface changes began to transform Chinese society. Released from the collective control of the commune, individuals and families took over responsibility for themselves and regained autonomy, but also had to learn to handle more risk. The family reemerged as an important social unit. The influence of the market entered the daily lives of almost all Chinese and pervaded everyday calculations and practices. State socialist structures partially gave way to a market economy, in a process that was liberating but also unsettling to ordinary citizens. New opportunities were opening up, but inequality and insecurity were increasing. New forms of differentiation entered Chinese society that would form the basis for future conflicts. While the party securely held sway, egalitarianism and collectivism slowly unraveled and became concepts of the past.

Debating Chinese Culture

China also changed profoundly in the areas of intellectual life and culture. The commitment to opening China fully to the outside world brought not only new trade and investments, but also new knowledge and ideas. Restrictions had been partially lifted in the course of the reform and opening policy that emphasized the liberation of thought from dogma. Contact with the outside world was steadily increasing, leading to passionate debates among intellectuals about how Chinese culture should change and also how its social and political system should be reformed. Deng Xiaoping and other leaders knew that China would face huge challenges from changes wrought by outsiders and from returning students, but they still firmly believed that China could only grow by "connecting tracks"—that is, opening up to trade, technology, and knowledge from the outside world.

To participate in intellectual and scientific exchanges with the West, China first needed to revive and revamp its higher education system. The system had to be realigned to promote knowledge and expertise instead of ideology and doctrine. Building on the international exchanges that started under Mao, back in the 1970s, China in the 1980s continued to send officials and students abroad in growing numbers, to translate foreign books and articles, and to welcome foreign advisers and business executives to China.[27] There was, however, also criticism from those who feared that Chinese lifestyles, beliefs, and interests would be adversely affected by this foreign influx. The overall mood in the Deng era oscillated between opposition to "leftist" ideas and "bourgeois liberalization," as windows were inevitably opened wider to the world. Deng followed a "middle course" and attempted to build political consensus by rejecting the Cultural Revolution's emphasis on class struggle. This course enabled a gradual, though not uninterrupted, depoliticization of Chinese institutions in education, culture, and the arts. While that trend was challenged at several points—most notably in the campaigns to criticize the writer Bai Hua, in 1981, to fight "spiritual pollution" in 1983, and to overcome "bourgeois liberalization" in 1987—the center of gravity of Chinese politics continued to shift toward greater depoliticization of society, greater use of market forces, and more recognition of societal and intellectual diversity. In many respects, the 1980s became the most liberal, most creative, and most daring decade in China's modern history.

As was often the case in China's modern period, the arts and literature pressed ahead and became the arenas where ideological limits were tested first and new ideas surfaced.[28] As mentioned in Chapter 7, leading Chinese writers such as Zhou Zuoren, Shen Congwen, Shi Zhecun, and Zhang Ailing had been removed from the bookshelves since the 1950s. Their works were available only to those considered ideologically advanced enough to be impervious to the "corrupting" influences of these authors—mainly party cadres and some academics. These same readers were also allowed to own and consult limited editions of translated works of modern western literature, known as the "brown cover books" *(huang pi shu)*, such as J. D. Salinger's *Catcher in the Rye* and Samuel Beckett's *Waiting for Godot*.[29] During the Cultural Revolution, copies of the "brown cover books" were exchanged among rusticated youths, since many were the children of party cadres with access to these forbidden reading materials. Some of them, inspired by foreign works and prompted by disillusionment with officially published literature, created a lively underground literary scene during the 1970s. The best of their texts were published in the late 1970s and eventually found their way into official literary journals in the early 1980s, in some cases more than a decade after they were written. Especially eye-catching were the "obscure" *(menglong)* poems by young authors such as Bei Dao, Shu Ting, Mang Ke, Gu Cheng, and Yang Lian, many of whom have since received international recognition. "Obscure poetry" was, however, a shock to a Communist Party literary system that, since the 1940s, had demanded that literature serve the revolution and use realism to reach out to the masses. By contrast, "obscure poetry" featured relatively apolitical content and difficult imagery. This new literature struck a chord with millions of readers, especially intellectuals, who were agonized by the Cultural Revolution, and delivered an urgent plea for political, social, and cultural change.

During the second half of the 1980s, state policies had been loosened enough for experimental works of narrative fiction to appear in official literary magazines. Experimental techniques involving unreliable narration, fragmentation, and especially the use of different language registers and dialects were also characteristic of another type of avant garde writing commonly known as "searching for roots" *(xungen)*. The explicit agenda of the roots seekers, drafted by their main representative, the author Han Shaogong (1953–), was to discover the diversity of Chinese cultural traditions and of the popular religions and cultures of ethnic minorities. This was an attempt to unearth roots that were obscured by the mainstream, orthodox cultural traditions. This search for roots was inspired in part by the authors' experiences as rusticated youth, and the life, language, and subcultures of remote countryside communities.

As the 1980s wore on, China's intellectual establishment became diverse and pluralistic.[30] There were intellectuals who had only minimal attachment to the state and felt alienated from politics—a trend that would continue, albeit with different content, in the 1990s. At the same time, liberal intellectuals pursued enormously ambitious publication projects focusing on western politics, economy, society, technology, and culture. They initiated a movement they called the "New Enlightenment" whereby groups worked to carve out a public space independent of the state and free from interventions by the authorities. During the 1980s, numerous western classics by the likes of Nietzsche, Kant, Weber, and Kafka were translated into the Chinese language and introduced to Chinese readers. China was engulfed in a reading frenzy for almost ten years, with books being sold in numbers unimaginable today. The most important of these New Enlightenment groups were gathered around book series and journals. The *Toward the Future (Zouxiang weilai congshu)* book series, for example, with Jin Guantao as chief editor, saw seventy-four volumes published within a period of only five years (from 1984 to 1988). The *Academy of Chinese Culture*, a series overseen at Peking University by Tang Yijie, Li Zhonghua, Wang Shucang, and others, organized lectures and publications. The book series *Culture: China and the World (Wenhua: Zhongguo yu shijie congshu)* was started by Gan Yang and Liu Xiaofeng. The magazine *Reading (Dushu)* also played a major role in this enlightenment movement. The Shanghai-based *World Economy Herald (Shijie jingji daobao)*, which daringly discussed China's political and economic reforms, had a circulation of three hundred thousand copies in its heyday. These publications replaced the old standard communist media and became bestsellers, wielding great influence over public debates.

Together, these groups and publications fueled the "cultural fever" *(wenhua re)* of the late 1980s, epitomized by the 1988 television series *River Elegy (He Shang)*.[31] The series' content was a sweeping and dramatic critique of the deep structure of Chinese culture. It intended to diagnose a long-standing defect at the core of China's tradition. In answering the perennial question of how the once mighty empire of China had fallen so far behind the western world, the documentary compared the "yellow" of the Yellow River and the Loess Plain with the "blue" of the ocean, the sky, and the planet earth as viewed from outer space. The script made use of the popular Chinese associations of the blue sea with foreignness (the word *yang* for "ocean" is also used for "foreign" or "western"), and connected it with images of maritime trade, exploration, capitalist expansion, and cultural vitality. By contrast, "yellow" in the documentary was portrayed as being associated with feudalism, conservatism, and rural backwardness. In particular, the Yellow River—muddy, turbulent, violent—served as a symbol for ignorance and backwardness within traditional Chinese culture. The documentary suggested that rescue could come only from opening up to the world and fully embracing western institutions and values—including markets, enlightenment, and democracy. It is easy to see the makers of the program rejecting the legacy of Maoism by pointing to historical trajectories in favor of the new western-oriented policies of economic reform.

The documentary aired twice on television, receiving a great deal of public attention and triggering passionate debates among students, intellectuals, and the party. It won both praise and criticism. The mere fact that this provocative series was made and broadcast on Chinese Central Television points to the rise of liberal positions within the party in the 1980s. Liberalism became the mainstream intellectual discourse in the 1980s. With the end of the Cultural Revolution, Chinese political and intellectual elites marveled at western cultural, material, and technological achievements that were seen to originate in the spirit of the enlightenment. Their previous belief in the supremacy of socialism was shattered and replaced by admiration for the liberal aspects of western culture and society. Also driving this trend were the political dynamics of the time—namely, the split in party leadership. The genuinely reformist faction headed by Hu Yaobang and Zhao Ziyang was opposed by skeptical, conservative hard-liners, resulting in a partial paralysis at the top of the leadership that translated into this fleeting period of astonishing openness.

June 4, 1989–A Point of No Return

Deng Xiaoping's call for openness, innovation, and undogmatic thinking in 1978 blazed the path to economic reform and artistic experimentation, but it also inevitably caused some Chinese—especially students and intellectuals—to anticipate more freedoms and increased political participation. Right at the outset of the new era, at the end of the 1970s, there were many students and intellectuals hoping for bold political reform alongside economic reform. In the debates and speeches at the Third Plenum in 1978 they saw hope for a political thaw. This became clear shortly after the plenum, during the Beijing Spring (1978–1981), when the "Democracy Wall" movement in Beijing caught worldwide attention. The surprised public in China could suddenly read astonishing posters pasted on a wall in Beijing's Xidan district, which described in great detail the abuses and suffering caused by the Cultural Revolution and which pointedly called upon the CCP to learn honestly from the mistakes of the past. Those mistakes, the posters and texts suggested, were above all related to the lack of democratic mechanisms. One poster written and signed by Wei Jingsheng (1950–) demanded "democracy" as the "fifth modernization!" (in addition to the four modernizations already articulated by Deng Xiaoping). The text explained:

> We want to be the masters of our own destiny. We need no gods or emperors, and we don't believe in saviors of any kind. We want to be masters of our universe, not the modernizing tools of dictators with personal am-

bitions. We want the modernization of people's lives. Democracy, freedom, and happiness for all are our sole objectives in carrying out modernization. Without this fifth modernization, all others are nothing more than a new promise. Comrades, I appeal to you: Let us rally under the banner of democracy. Do not be fooled again by dictators who talk of "stability and unity." Fascist totalitarianism can bring us nothing but disaster. Harbor no more illusions; democracy is our only hope.... Banish all self-proclaimed leaders and teachers, for they have already cheated the people of their most valuable rights for decades.[32]

The movement, although never coherent or united over most issues, thus offered a critique of Deng's policies of reform and opening, and called for a more comprehensive understanding of modernization. Its activists supported Deng Xiaoping's economic reforms and the four modernizations, but added their own vision of socialist democracy as an integral, and indeed necessary, part of a more complete and sustainable modernization of Chinese society. In the spring of 1979, the authorities ordered the relocation of the Democracy Wall to a small park in western Beijing, and declared that any who wished to put up posters must register their names and addresses with the authorities. When Deng Xiaoping reaffirmed the "four principles" in March 1979, emphasizing party rule and the socialist path, the leaders of the Democracy Wall (most notably, Wei Jingsheng) were arrested, tried, and jailed. Public advocacy of political democracy became taboo, as the reformers sternly insisted on the political limits of reform and opening. They argued that reform in China would not include tolerance of political free speech or any talk of individual rights. The party also demonstrated that it was ready to shut down public criticism or demonstrations by force, if necessary. In this respect, it explicitly did not break with the Mao era. The issue of democracy thus became one of the first and most fundamental challenges to the leadership, unavoidably originating from the consequences of reform.

Despite the strong-armed intervention of the government, the 1980s saw an unrelenting, steady rise of political dissent and discontent, with intellectuals increasingly willing to test the limits drawn by the party leadership.[33] Some called into question the ideological base of the regime. Parts of the intellectual elite even started to view communism as a central problem—and a market economy and western democracy as the only solution. Liu Binyan

(1925–2005), for instance, was an intellectual originally supportive of the party for whom the experience of living in the Maoist period suggested that more than just the economy must be reformed. He contributed to the "reportage" literature *(baogao wenxue)*, a genre that combined investigative reporting and literary narration, with one of his main themes being local corruption. He argued that it was necessary for writers to expose social problems and to criticize the party state so that it could amend its policies and better serve the people. He emphasized that, without freedom, this mission could not be accomplished. Asserting the indispensable role of intellectual and journalistic freedom to reveal social and political tribulations soon brought him into conflict with the authorities and the censors.[34] Another example of a thinker pressing for intellectual freedom was the scientist Fang Lizhi (1936–2012). Coming from a very different angle, Fang denied in his speeches and letters that Marxism was a science, as it was still considered to be in China. Instead, he painted Marxism as an outdated ideology from the nineteenth century. He also advocated freedom of opinion and speech as prerequisites to science and modernization in China.[35] To Fang Lizhi, the party needed to preserve intellectual freedom from both government meddling and big business pressures. Only if it was shielded from political intervention and able to pursue research without ideological restrictions could science hope to flourish in China and deliver its important contributions to the modernization of China. But the CCP under Deng had no tolerance for such aspirations, and Fang soon was labeled a dissident. At the end of the 1980s, Liu Binyan and Fang Lizhi both fled to the United States, where they lived out the rest of their lives in exile.

Not everybody in the party, and not even in the leadership, agreed with Deng's hard-line policies. In January 1987 Deng Xiaoping had Hu Yaobang fired from his post as the CCP general secretary, claiming he harbored sympathy for calls for democracy and had not dealt firmly enough with dissent in Chinese society. His successor was Zhao Ziyang, the premier, who was, however, also sympathetic to political reform. He worked with a number of academics and think tanks in Beijing, whom he had asked to conduct studies on the possibilities to gradually reform the political system. Inside and outside of the CCP, a growing number of people considered political liberalization and reform to be important topics.

Demands for freedom and democracy put universities and students in China in an uproar. But the expectations for change, for new freedoms, and for exciting opportunities to engage with liberal theories and knowledge collided time and again with the realities of party rule and the efforts to curtail the growing aspirations. Much of the energy of the Anti–Spiritual Pollution Campaign in 1983 and the Anti–Bourgeois Liberalization Campaign in 1987 was aimed at attacking writings and ideas connected to political liberalism, which orthodox Marxists in the party considered to be bourgeois and dangerous. Such campaigns riled up many students and intellectuals and pushed them toward radicalism.

In the late 1980s, economic uncertainties further exacerbated the situation and created the breeding ground for a larger protest movement. In 1988, the reforms in the monetary sector led to a serious loss of macroeconomic control, triggering an inflationary crisis that affected the entire society and that could not be brought under control. As inflation peaked in the last quarter of 1988, and austerity policies designed to reduce inflation caused dislocation and the erosion of real incomes, dissatisfaction spread in urban areas. Inflation and widespread corruption aroused a great deal of public dissatisfaction and contributed to the protests that were about to erupt in 1989.

The 1989 Beijing student movement was the largest spontaneous protest movement for political change and democracy since the founding of the People's Republic. The students demanded freedom and democracy, yet their protests were also a direct reaction to emerging social problems such as high inflation, rampant official corruption, and the worsening economic prospects for academics. Students from universities located in the Beijing area started the movement on April 15, 1989, upon learning of Hu Yaobang's sudden death. Cognizant of Hu's tolerance of dissent and calls for democracy, students gathered in Tiananmen Square with flowers and letters of condolences. Gradually, this commemoration of Hu Yaobang's life turned into a spontaneous, fragile political movement with a set of demands that also started to attract sympathy and support from the urban population. After a period of hesitation, *People's Daily* published an editorial inspired by Deng Xiaoping's denunciation of the movement as a "turmoil" manipulated by "a small handful of people with ulterior motives." When a hundred thousand students took to the streets on April 27 to protest the editorial, and gained the support of tens of thousands of additional citizens, it represented an unprecedented challenge to Deng and other leaders. The movement grew quickly as the students demanded that the editorial be officially disavowed.

10.2. Student protesters watching soldiers and tanks at Tiananmen Square in 1989.
Dario Mitidieri / Getty Images / SB100694370

In Beijing, the students also asked for a face-to-face meeting on equal terms with party leaders.[36] The unique demands of the protesters for a public political dialogue and official recognition shocked the leadership. After lengthy deliberations, the party signaled that it was willing to make a limited concession and offered a meeting behind closed doors. Meanwhile, a few students started a hunger strike on May 13 to make more radical demands for political freedom and above all for democracy. In a declaration of May 13, 1989, they explained their goals:

> Our honest feelings of patriotism and loyalty to the nation were distorted as "turmoil," and we were accused of being the tools of a "handful" who have "ulterior motives." . . . Our words were not heard in good faith. We were beaten by police when we marched, though we were only hungry for the truth. Our representatives knelt for hours, presenting our petition, only to be ignored by the government. Our request for dialogue has been put off again and again. The safety of our student leaders is now uncertain. . . . Democracy is supposed to be the highest of human aspirations

and freedom a sacred human right, granted at birth. Today these must be bought with our lives.[37]

These powerful words and the hunger strike rallied hundreds of thousands of sympathizers throughout the country. Once the condition of the hunger strikers deteriorated visibly, ordinary citizens, often organized by their *danweis,* took to the streets to show their support for the students. Protests now spread to hundreds of cities. Millions of urban citizens took part in demonstrations all over China. Support came from within the party, as well. As Zhao Ziyang recalled in his memoirs, many prominent public figures and senior party members mailed or phoned the Central Committee, urging the leadership to "treat the students properly, to acknowledge that the students' actions had been patriotic and to change the wrongful stance toward students."[38] The party was apparently deeply split on how to understand and handle the protests.

The hunger strike was an impressive success in mass mobilization by the students. With millions of citizens out on the street supporting the students against the government, the CCP faced determined resistance to its rule. The protests also interrupted the Sino-Soviet summit in 1989. With most of China's top state leaders now deeply antagonized, on May 20, the government announced martial law—which, however, it had difficulties enforcing. On the night of that same day, believing that the party had sent soldiers to harm the students in Tiananmen Square, Beijing residents went out by the hundreds of thousands. With major roadways and crossings all blocked by citizens, and old women and children camping in the streets, the army was stopped in the suburbs, unable to enter Beijing. The troops, who were mostly unarmed, were forced to withdraw and the occupation of Tiananmen Square was continued. The students and their supporters had scored their biggest victory.

Deng Xiaoping and Premier Li Peng (1928–) were horrified by the broad public revolt against state and party power. They were convinced that the defiance could not be accepted or else the situation in Beijing and other cities would spiral out of control. Qiao Shi (1924–2015), a member of the Politburo, characterized the situation as "riding the tiger, unable to get off." In a conversation with Zhao Ziyang on the evening of May 21, he observed: "the troops have been blocked from entering, martial law is ineffective, and millions of students, residents, workers, cadres from government organizations are out on the streets or gathered on Tiananmen Square. If this continues, the capital is in danger of becoming paralyzed."[39] On the basis of the rationale, the Politburo decided to clear the square using military force. On June 3, the army entered Beijing once more.[40] The troops were met with resistance again—but this time, with clear orders from the government, they opened fire on protesting residents and students. In the early morning hours of June 4, the soldiers forced their way through Beijing toward the square, leaving several hundred dead and thousands wounded.

With this massacre on the world stage, the government eventually stifled the democracy movement, calling it a counterrevolutionary political turmoil. But the party's order to open fire on unarmed young students caused widespread outrage inside and outside China. Despite censorship since, the movement is widely remembered. While the precise impact of this movement on China's top-level politics has yet to be fully explored, its effects reverberate through every field of social and political activity. Officially, China has sought to erase this event, but any thoughtful observer can feel its influence on present-day life. Chinese politics have in large part been infused with the spirit of the movement and its aftermath.[41]

Four immediate consequences are palpable. First, this unprecedented movement temporarily deepened the rift within the party. Zhao Ziyang, then the party's general secretary, opted for negotiation with the students, whom he declared to be "patriotic." He tried desperately to convince Deng of the necessity of adopting an accommodating line, but Deng could not accept compromise. After deciding to send in the army to crush the movement, he required Zhao Ziyang to support the party's decision. Zhao's refusal to back down was considered a deliberate attempt to split the CCP, and seen as a very serious transgression of one-party rule. He was investigated, dismissed from all posts, and put under house arrest. With this, not only was Zhao Ziyang silenced, but the considerable liberal and pro-democratic forces within the party lost ground. When the more liberal leaders were ousted, they were replaced by Jiang Zemin (1926–), and later Zhu Rongji (1928–). The new generation of leaders shared two qualities: they had been major leaders of the reform in big cities during the 1980s, and they prioritized stability when facing popular protest. With that, the inner-party split was resolved, and political reform was no longer discussed or advocated within the party. It became taboo. Moreover, the party tightened its control over universities, student organizations, the press and publishers, and arts and literature. In sharp contrast to the repeated political upheavals of the 1980s, China experienced a prolonged period of political stability—a counterintuitive outcome that has surprised many observers.

Second, after the economic disturbances in 1988 and the political disturbances in 1989, China's economic reforms came to a temporary halt. The economic debates over a planned economy versus a commodity economy implicitly became political debates about socialism versus capitalism. Therefore, concrete policy measures to curtail the privately run economy were implemented, including the development of TVEs and the strengthening of the dominant position of the state-owned enterprises. These policy measures had inevitable consequences, the most prominent of which was that the GDP growth fell sharply and unemployment began to swell. In 1989 and 1990, GDP growth was only 4.1 percent and 3.8 percent, respectively. On the other hand, the overheated economy cooled down and a more stable economic situation ensued.

Third, the 1989 social movement was an urban social movement. It exposed the contradictions in urban economic development and the social disruptions created in the course of market expansion. To prevent similar unrest in the future, urban reforms were deepened with the intention to improve living standards. As a result of the crisis in 1989, the rural versus urban divide had started to grow; by 1989–1991, peasant incomes had basically stagnated and the income gap between urban and rural areas had reached pre-1978 levels. Larger percentages of peasants therefore migrated out of rural areas, making a huge and inexpensive labor pool available to urban industries. After 1989, urban development was the clear priority. Often, this development was carried out at the expense of rural areas.

Fourth, the events in Tiananmen Square must be seen in the context of global developments. The year 1989 was, of course, also a year of momentous changes in Eastern Europe and the world. Ironically, the events in China, preceding the demonstrations elsewhere, helped to stimulate protest movements in Eastern Europe. The Chinese leaders' violent reaction to the demonstrations in 1989 discredited communism in the eyes of demonstrators in Eastern Europe, since it clearly revealed the violent downside of one-party rule. China's brutal suppression stood in dramatic contrast to the responses of its Soviet bloc counterparts who confronted similar circumstances but refrained from violence. In contrast to the shootings in Tiananmen Square, the greatest surprise of the smooth regime transitions in post-socialist Europe, the Baltic states, and Russia was precisely the relative peacefulness of the process, featuring rather sudden surrenders by the challenged regimes in most places.

Although the main events and effects of 1989 centered on the fall of communist systems in Europe, the case of China is a reminder that, in many regions and areas in the world, different conclusions were drawn from that tumultuous year. Frequent failures of markets, political institutions, and cultural norms in Eastern Europe after 1989 caused new forms of opposition to western order to mushroom. For example, political Islam was freed from its focus on the communist enemy and turned its fight against the liberal West. Latin American populism took on an increasing anti-western touch, and renewed forms of authoritarian rule emerged in many parts of the world, from Turkey to Russia. The renewal of authoritarianism in China was thus, to a large extent, an effort to avert the post-1989 crisis and malaise in Eastern Europe. In this sense, although the end of the Cold War has been felt most strongly in Europe, trends in China, and in fact in most parts of the world, have been divergent and unanticipated.

Those consequences of the suppression of the 1989 student movement more broadly related to two general characteristics of the post-1989 core political strategy, encapsulated in the phrase "strong on two fronts" *(liangshou yin).*[42] The two fronts referred to are economic reform and political stability, and the resolve was to remain firm with regard to both. Instead of simply representing a setback for reform, Tiananmen and 1989 permanently altered China's reform trajectory. From then on, economic reform accelerated and expanded, based on centralization and the availability of inexpensive migrant labor. At the same time, stability and security became overruling prerogatives in political, cultural, and social life. The basic issues and concerns raised by the 1989 social movement, such as democracy, liberty, and equal opportunities, were shunted aside. A new, authoritarian, yet self-confident China emerged. Amid the bloody chaos in Tiananmen Square and the transformations in the world of 1989, the China Model was born.

ELEVEN

Overall Advance

1990–2012

After the political and economic upheavals of 1989, China ceased all reform efforts for about three years. Conservative voices in the party proposed a return to the planned economy and spoke out against further liberalization of society. For a short time it looked as if China might in fact turn back the clock. In 1992, Deng Xiaoping intervened, proposing a new strategy that was called "overall advance with key breakthroughs."[1] Market-oriented reforms would be extended to the entire economy (making this an overall advance), and would emphasize changes to the state sector, taxation, banking, enterprises system, and foreign exchange (constituting the key breakthroughs). This strategy laid the foundation for a breathtaking achievement that catapulted China into the ranks of the economic superpowers. China's rise brought profound transformation of the country itself, but also sent change reverberating through the rest of the world. The economic development of China was an unparalleled global phenomenon of sufficient force to remake the world, step by step.

In marked contrast to its daring economic reforms, the CCP held back from any similarly bold reforms in the realm of politics. In the eyes of Chinese leadership, the rising popular discontent that had toppled communist parties in Russia and Eastern Europe in 1989 had been fueled mainly by poverty, backwardness, and all the economic problems that went with those. The collapse of the Soviet Union and the satellite states in Eastern Europe resonated deeply within the ranks of the CCP and had an enormous impact on its policies in the aftermath of the crisis.[2] To retain its control of state and society, the party cast its lot with rapid economic development. It also championed a spirit of nationalism as an active response aimed at strengthening its hold on society by emphasizing the need for unity against outside threats. The pursuit of national greatness and the rejuvenation of China became dominant themes of government propaganda. China also extended its global reach, building political and economic links with all regions in the world.

Closing Ranks within the Party

The negative, if not hostile, international reaction to the Tiananmen massacre had domestic repercussions, as well. Above all, it prompted the leadership to close ranks. This ironically provided the administration with a new level of clout and energy, permitting a consolidation of authority and resources at the top of the system and a deliberate choice of policies that were at once more state-oriented and stability-focused. The post-Tiananmen leaders Jiang Zemin, as general secretary from 1989 to 2002 and president from 1993 to 2003, and Zhu Rongji, as first vice premier from 1993 to 1998 (and later, premier from 1998 to 2003), developed a very good working relationship, especially regarding economic policy. There was an understanding that economic development was now the clear priority and that, without fast economic growth, political stability would be elusive. Meanwhile, the old generation of revolutionary leaders had begun to pass away. By 1997, all of the important elders, Deng Xiaoping among them, were deceased. As a result, Jiang and Zhu were able to end the fragmentation of ideology and of power within the top leadership. This strong internal accord allowed for a prolonged period relatively free of publicly noticeable inner-party strife. It also made for transitions between the different administrations that were remarkably smooth and peaceful.

An enhanced "priority to state interests" appeared after 1990 and led to a greater capacity for economic and societal management.[3] In this climate, a lively private sector was allowed to subsist and even to grow, but it did so only within the confines of a state sector that was much more rigorously supported than before. Under the dynamic and farsighted leadership of Zhu Rongji, who played an important role even before becoming premier in 1998, the reforms of the 1990s had three major thrusts: they focused on recentralizing and rebuilding the fiscal and monetary basis for macroeconomic stability; they stressed market unification; and they promoted reforms of ownership and improved regulation. At the same time, this heightened central authority also featured somewhat greater tolerance of small-scale and apolitical civil groups and nongovernmental organizations (NGOs), as long as they were

11.1. Jiang Zemin (right) and Zhu Rongji, April 2001.
Stephen Shaver / Getty Images / 51343359

not perceived as threats to party rule. NGOs were established in many realms, from labor activism to environmental protection.

Since the beginning of the reform period there had been an attempt to broaden the base of the party. In the 1990s, Jiang Zemin took active measures to recruit men and women from the world of business and markets into the party. This move obviously required a change in CCP doctrine, which had traditionally defined itself as a party of workers and peasants. Jiang Zemin justified this new policy of embracing capitalists by outlining a need for "three represents" *(san ge daibiao)*. He offered his longest and most important exposition of this concept in a speech on July 1, 2001, on the eightieth anniversary of the CCP's founding.[4] Jiang's policy signaled a turn toward elitism. In the age of economic reform, the party had to represent three forces: China's "advanced productive forces," its "advanced culture," and the "fundamental interests of the overwhelming majority" of the Chinese people. With this, Jiang called for the new elites in the economy (the first represented group), and the science and education community (the second represented group) that had emerged over the reform period, including private entrepreneurs, highly skilled specialists, scientists, innovators, and so on, to be admitted to the party. It was apparent that CCP leadership believed it needed to coopt the diverse groups in China that technological change, economic growth, and globalization had brought into influential positions. Jiang pushed the party to incorporate those forces into the CCP and allow them to have a voice within the party. The new ideological doctrine of the "three represents" recognized entrepreneurs, technical personnel, and managers of nonpublic and foreign enterprises as "builders of socialism with Chinese characteristics." By 2006, party membership had become much more diverse and larger; there were slightly more than seventy million party members.

While the party rejected a wholesale reform of the political system, it permitted gradual and limited changes at the local level. Limited institutional reforms were initiated in public administration, law, and local government. One effect of those reforms was to change the old cadre system into a modern civil service system, partly based on the historical precedent of the imperial examinations system. In this context, China also established standardized exams for civil servants in its central government—an important milestone for the move toward a transparent and meritocratic recruiting procedure based solely on clearly defined performance criteria. Open and equal exams were strictly implemented on all levels to ensure that advancement was competition- and qualification-based. Initially, implementation was difficult. It was discovered, for example, that some units had ignored test results in favor of their own selection criteria. From the very start, exams also included political questions on party ideology and history. In 2003, personal interviews were added to the process. The exams attracted many candidates. In 2008, about 775,000 people attended the exams, competing for about 13,500 positions in the civil service sector. The ministries receiving the highest numbers of applicants were the Ministry of Commerce, the Ministry of Foreign Affairs, and the National Development and Reform Commission.[5] Party membership was no longer formally required for a career in the civil service (although to this day it remains the case that 80 percent of all civil servants are party members). Some sensitive positions, such as positions in personnel management, were reserved for party members. Yet, even the highest government positions, including the positions of premier and prime minister, officially belonged to the civil service system. Ambitious civil servants and future top cadres had to pass exams, and for any single entry position in the central administration, applicants had to compete with hundreds if not thousands of other potential candidates. Even those striving for top state and government positions had to have achieved good results in positions at lower government levels first, and performance criteria grew more demanding at each rung. Every level of promotion required a new set of evaluations and tests to verify leadership skills. China built one of the most competitive systems in the world to recruit and promote government and state personnel.

Already in 1978, the government had introduced elections on the local level in selected rural localities. These reforms were subsequently conducted on a trial basis nationwide from 1988 onward. In 1998, the Chinese National People's Congress formally passed and promulgated the New Organic Law of the Village Committee, which instructed that all villages hold competitive elections for their village committee and that all candidates be nominated by villagers. Multiple candidates were allowed to run for three-year terms in the village committees. Voter turnout was usually high. By 2008, some 900 million people in more than 734,000 villages had voted in the elections of approximately 3.2 million village leaders. These elections represented a significant institutional development. By institutionalizing village-level elections, party leaders intended to make local administrations more accountable and improve the functionality of the existing administrative system.[6] The village elections were not, however, meant to lead to a democratization of the political system.

The CCP undertook a variety of steps to reform political institutions, open the policy process, and increase accountability, but these steps were limited and fell short of the broader political reforms some critics called for. While the CCP became a more pragmatic and patriotic governing party, it would be premature to assume the obsolescence or disappearance of ideology in China: government documents and official media were regularly couched in Marxist terminology.

The Deepening of Economic Reform

After three years of retrenchment and international isolation, China's reforms took on new life in 1992, when Deng Xiaoping expressed his strong support for the extension of economic reform and experimentation. He publicly toured South China to demonstrate his unwavering support for the continuation of the reforms. During this inspection tour, he said: "If we do not adhere to socialism, do not implement the policies of reform and opening up to the outside world, do not develop the economy and raise the people's living standards, we will find ourselves in a blind alley."[7] A year later, the Third Plenum of the Eighteenth Central Committee adopted the "Decision of the CCP Central Committee on Certain Issues in Establishing a Socialist Market Economy System," which clearly signaled not simply the continuation but the deepening of the reforms.[8] As a result of this shift, China would experience a remarkable economic boost and perhaps the fastest economic growth rate of any society in history. Its emerging market economy became deeply integrated into the global market, and the effects of globalization became visible everywhere.

It is useful to begin the discussion of this period by pointing to the substantial differences in reforms enacted before and after that watershed year, 1989.[9] In the 1990s, reform measures came to feature a systematic coherence that marked a clear contrast with those of the 1980s. The most crucial step was the adoption of a set of ambitious institutional reforms between 1993 and 1999, when China reached an agreement with the United States on its accession to the World Trade Organization (WTO).[10] In this phase, the government under the leadership of Premier Zhu Rongji implemented a flurry of measures that were all critically important steps in China's economic strategy of "overall advance."

The institutional innovations can be grouped into six categories. First and foremost was the strengthening of competition within public administration among counties and provinces.[11] Since 1949, China had already developed a system in which local cadres competed for attention and resource allocations from the central administration. Before the reforms, political and ideological criteria were mainly used to measure local cadres' performance. After the reforms, those criteria were replaced by development and growth indicators, such as GDP growth, exports, and inflows of foreign investment. Career opportunities for provincial leaders and local officials thus became contingent on the economic performance of their province or locale.[12] Officials had strong incentives to promote local growth, because their career prospects relied on the economic trajectory of the areas under their administration. Rapid local growth delivered prospects for local leaders to advance to national positions in the central administration, where they received recognition, promotion, and bonuses. Growth also, of course, meant that officials had expanded public revenue and enterprise profits over which they could exercise

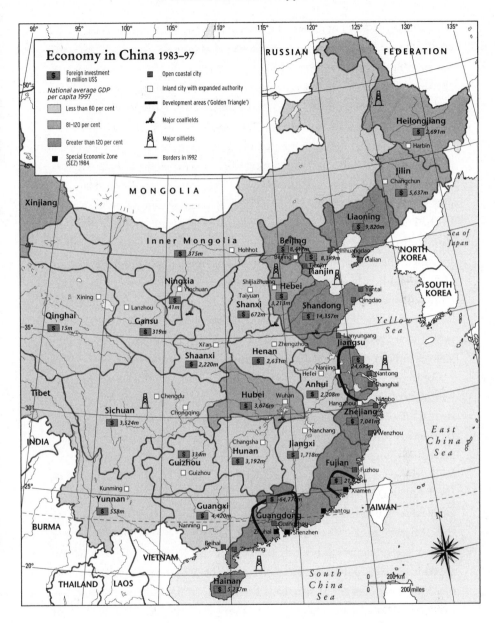

Economy in China 1983–97

$ Foreign investment in million US$

National average GDP per capita 1997

Less than 80 per cent

81–120 per cent

Greater than 120 per cent

■ Special Economic Zone (SEZ) 1984

■ Open coastal city

□ Inland city with expanded authority

━ Development areas ('Golden Triangle')

⚒ Major coalfields

⛏ Major oilfields

━ Borders in 1992

RUSSIAN FEDERATION

MONGOLIA

Xinjiang

Inner Mongolia
$ 375m

Hohhot □

Ningxia
Yinchuan □

$ 41m

Xining □

Qinghai
$ 15m

Gansu
$ 319m

Lanzhou □

Heilongjiang
$ 2,691m

Harbin □

Jilin
Changchun □
$ 5,637m

Liaoning
$ 9,820m

Beijing
$ 8,417m
Beijing □

Qinhuangdao □
Dalian □

NORTH KOREA

Sea of Japan

Tianjin
$ 8,349m

Shijiazhuang □
Taiyuan □

Hebei
$ 3,213m

Shanxi
$ 672m

Shandong
$ 14,357m

Yantai □
Qingdao □

SOUTH KOREA

Yellow Sea

Xi'an □

Shaanxi
$ 2,220m

Henan
$ 2,631m

Zhengzhou □

Lianyungang □

Jiangsu
$ 24,695m

Tibet

Chengdu □

Sichuan
$ 3,524m

Chongqing □

Hubei
$ 3,676m

Wuhan □

Nanjing □
Hefei □

Anhui
$ 2,208m

Hangzhou □

Nantong □
Shanghai □

Ningbo □

Zhejiang
$ 7,041m

East China Sea

INDIA

Changsha □

Hunan
$ 3,192m

Nanchang □

Jiangxi
$ 1,718m

Wenzhou □

Guizhou
$ 334m

Guizhou □

Fujian
$ 21,930m

Fuzhou □

Xiamen ■

Kunming □

Yunnan
$ 558m

Guangxi
$ 4,420m

Nanning □

Guangdong
$ 64,776m

Guangzhou □

Zhuhai ■ Shenzhen ■

Shantou ■

TAIWAN

N

BURMA

Beihai □

Zhanjiang □

VIETNAM

THAILAND LAOS

Hainan
$ 5,237m

South China Sea

0   200 km

0   200 miles

(533)

their varying degrees of control. They could enlarge business opportunities for families and friends and increase the rents (whether legal or illicit) directed toward official agencies and their managers. These policies therefore increased corruption and graft, but at the same time, they transformed China's local and provincial governments into keen promoters of growth and economic development. Counties in China began to compete with their neighbors in building airports, highways, science parks, telecommunications, and local industries. To be sure, central planning endured, but some latitude was created for local decisions and initiative. The resulting competition drove the persistent "investment hunger" visible in China's economy since the 1990s. In their intention to outdo other counties, local administrations often resisted central calls for restraint in building and expanding facilities and infrastructure. This competition for economic development is a unique feature of Chinese public administration, and stands in dramatic contrast to local government conduct in developing countries where local officials are indebted to local elites. Many such officials focus their energies on extracting resources rather than promoting growth. Local Chinese officials could extract resources only by promoting economic growth.

If strengthening of competition within public administration was the biggest institutional innovation of the 1990s, the second greatest impact came from China's effective devaluation of its currency, the renminbi, by 33 percent. Before this overhaul happened, at the start of 1994, China had two official foreign-exchange systems with confusingly different rates: an unfavorable one for foreigners and a better one for qualified Chinese enterprises. Because of the difference between the rates, profits could be made by illegally exchanging currencies, which led to a thriving black market and corruption. As part of the changes, China unified the two official foreign-exchange systems, setting the rate for foreigners at roughly the same level used internally by Chinese enterprises on swap markets. The devaluation opened the path for an increase of Chinese exports, and it also made foreign direct investments more attractive. Since China's share of the global economy was relatively small, the United States and other countries did not oppose the devaluation.

A third institutional innovation was that barriers to rural-to-urban migration were steadily lowered.[13] Barriers to mobility had restricted the transfer of not only labor, but also capital, commodities, and ideas across administrative boundaries under the planned economic system, perpetuating the gap in living standards between the cities and the countryside. The *hukou* system of residential permits functioned as a powerful tool of social control during the Maoist era, but in the reform period it also became a huge impediment to the transfer of workers out of agriculture into industry and urban service occupations. As such prior restrictions were relaxed, labor migrants from rural areas were now permitted to come to urban areas for work. Even though they were not permitted to relocate permanently, this easing of the *hukou* restriction allowed a steady increase in labor migration from the countryside to the city. This made a large pool of labor available to expanding urban industries, while keeping labor costs low.

With regional competition encouraged and barriers to domestic migration removed, a fourth institutional innovation followed: tax reform. Given the priority placed by the government on state interests, the tax reforms carried out in 1994 were designed to put China's finances on better footing. Budgetary revenues as a share of GDP hit a low point of 10.8 percent in 1995, but as the reforms took effect, they turned around abruptly to reach 16 percent in 2001 and 20.5 percent in 2008—a remarkable accomplishment. The success of the 1994 tax reforms expanded the tax base, raised revenues, and bolstered the government's central budget.

A fifth institutional factor that improved the budget situation of the central state was the massive trimming of the state-owned enterprise sector.[14] Specifically, publicly owned enterprises were exposed to much more open competition and stricter budget constraints on the financing side. Regulations on the operation of state enterprises issued in 1992 also gave managers of state-owned enterprises the authority to hire and dismiss workers, set wages, and conduct transactions involving enterprise assets. The dual-track pricing system, which had provided state-owned enterprises with a lifeline, was phased out and replaced by a unified market. Thousands of unprofitable state-owned firms closed down permanently. Privatization of small state-owned enterprises began on a large scale in 1995. Two years later, over half of these were privatized. Many small and medium state-owned enterprises, and even more township and village enterprises, were sold or given to domestic or foreign private owners. In the course of just over a decade, employment at traditional state-owned enterprises fell, through early retirements and buyouts, from forty-five million workers in 1992 to 17.5 million by the end of 2007. The total state enterprise workforce shrank by twenty-seven million workers—an almost

40 percent reduction.[15] Only the largest and most profitable firms, mostly in natural resources or strategic sectors, were maintained under central government control. About one thousand state-owned enterprises fell under that category. Where monopolies were still justified, state ownership was retained, but monopolies in energy and telecom were broken up into two or three competing state-owned firms, and better institutions of corporate governance were put in place. Many large-scale state enterprises were pushed onto stock markets or transformed into partnerships using a stock sharing model. The state was determined to keep China's "national champions" in state hands, but in general, the push toward ownership diversification was so aggressive that the wholly state-owned, nonfinancial enterprise became rare. State-owned enterprises were also permitted to undergo restructuring in the form of bankruptcies, liquidations, listings, sales to private firms, and auctioning of assets and liabilities. These institutional innovations increased the efficiency and profitability of the state sector, and while they did not eliminate dependence on state subsidies, they reduced it.

Finally, there was the very important question of how and to what extent China's economy should be linked to the international economy. Since China had first opened its doors in the late 1970s, its trade with the outside world had expanded rapidly. In the mid-1990s, in an effort to increase foreign investment, China relaxed its rules on foreign ownership. This brought a great increase in the amount of foreign direct investments and raised the question of whether rules on foreign investment should be relaxed. Such questions were, of course, linked to China's intention to join the World Trade Organization. An agreement on accession was reached in 1999 and formal membership started in 2001. Membership formalized not only a much greater openness to imports, but also a set of ground rules for foreign-invested enterprises to operate and sell freely in the Chinese domestic market. It obligated China to comply with the organization's rules and regulations concerning international copyright laws, trademarks, visas, business licenses, and protection of domestic industries. There were important modifications, however. China normally required international companies to transfer advanced key technologies and intellectual property when they established local operations in China. In many strategic sectors, China permitted foreign firms to do business only through joint ventures in which Chinese partners had majority ownership. These rules led to long complaints by international companies that China had strong-armed them to surrender business secrets and that they were treated unfairly.

The period of the 1990s was crucial for the success of the reforms, much more so than the 1970s or 1980s. Rather than retreat on reform and use administrative measures to rebalance the economy, Premier Zhu Rongji relied primarily on a stringent monetary policy and tighter budgets to drive a painful but necessary restructuring of the public sector—an effort that put him at odds with many vested interests in the central government and at the local level. Two aspects characterize the 1990s reforms. The first was a willingness to expose economic actors to increased competition on all levels, which quickly began to impose costs on individuals and social groups. The second was a determination to protect government resources and give priority to state interests. The central government succeeded in recentralizing fiscal resources to some degree and, as unemployment began to mushroom because of the reforms, constructed a safety net for the urban population, including unemployment insurance and antipoverty programs guaranteeing minimum livelihood, and a restructured pension system. The attention of reformers turned also to establishing effective corporate governance for newly reformed and newly privatized state enterprises; reforming and revitalizing the banking and financial system; and establishing a suitable regulatory regime for a market economy. As a result, the dramatic expansion of incentives, mobility, and markets created unprecedented opportunities for the establishment of new enterprises and the growth of existing firms, including foreign companies into new markets. The scale of market entry was astonishing; the number of manufacturing companies rose from 377,300 in 1980 to nearly eight million in 1996.[16]

China's Turn to Multilateralism

After 1989, China faced international isolation, putting the government under a great deal of pressure. The Tiananmen crackdown was a major turning point in China's foreign policy that forced leadership to readjust its perspective on the world. While the world had viewed Chinese reforms before 1989 with sympathy, this changed fundamentally. The change in views, particularly among liberal and neoconservative elites in the United States and Europe, was vehement, and influenced policymaking for years to come. In response to China's use of violence against its own people, the United States and other countries imposed sanctions on the country, complicating relations with China. Influencing the response of many was not just what had happened in China but also the timing of it. In the span of just a few years, as the Cold War came to an end, Eastern Europe and Russia seemed to back away from authoritarianism and embrace democratic freedoms. China's demonstration that any form of political liberalization was out of the question and would be met with repression put it seriously out of step with the times.

"China threat" theories began to proliferate in western academic and official circles during the 1990s. Seeing China as authoritarian and conflict-prone, these theorists based their warnings on the assumption that an eventual geopolitical showdown was unavoidable. In 1993, Harvard political scientist Samuel Huntington put forward his "clash of civilizations" thesis, portraying Confucian China as a threat to western civilization. Others warned that a "Greater China" superpower was in the making, as a result of the growing economic integration of coastal China, Hong Kong, Taiwan, and the overseas Chinese communities scattered across Asia. From a geopolitical perspective, China's coercive diplomacy against Taiwan, its increasing regional rivalry with Japan and India, and its challenge to America's global hegemony were all hints of greater dangers lurking behind a rising China.[17]

In the aftermath of Tiananmen, China made some efforts to engage with American and western criticisms of its human rights record. For example, it produced a white paper on the subject in October 1991, and received human rights delegations from foreign countries. At the same time, Beijing emphasized rights to subsistence and development, and attacked America's own human rights record regarding police brutality and racial discrimination, implying that the superpower was in no position to criticize others.[18]

Knowing that greater international acceptance would diminish the lingering effects of post-Tiananmen isolation, China initially concentrated its efforts on Asia. In 1990, it managed to gain diplomatic recognition from Indonesia and Singapore, from which it had long been estranged. It was also able to establish diplomatic relations with Saudi Arabia, followed by South Africa. Such diplomatic successes put Taiwan under greater pressure, but in the beginning did little to normalize China's relations with the United States.

The sanctions imposed on China were short-lived, however. By the autumn of 1991, the US administration was willing to lift them. After the end of the first Gulf War and the defeat of Iraq, the United States deepened its involvement in the Middle East. At the same time, the deteriorating situation in Eastern Europe and the Soviet Union, with the rise of nationalism and ethnic strife, also demanded western attention. To be able to focus on these two strategic areas, there was a sense in the United States that it should ease tensions with China and find a way back to normalized relations. Jiang Zemin, for his part, recognized that the continuation of economic reforms would be easier if relations with the United States were on firmer ground. The improvement of China's relations with the United States in the late 1990s culminated in Jiang's visit to America in 1997 and President Bill Clinton's visit to China in 1998.[19]

Maintaining a favorable international environment for economic growth was still the dominant priority of Chinese foreign policy. A second objective was to restore and defend territorial integrity. On this point, the overarching concerns were to work toward reunification with Taiwan, Hong Kong, and Macau and to maintain domestic political stability. Specifically, China blocked outside support for separatist movements in Tibet, Xinjiang, and the Inner Mongolian Autonomous Region and tried to impede or limit support for independence in Taiwan. It also signaled its readiness to uphold maritime claims in the East China and South China seas. As it worked to build support and sympathy among its neighbors, China was determined to prevent the domination of the Asian region by others. For the most part, it followed a pragmatic strategy designed to maintain territorial integrity, regional stability, and, above all else, high levels of undistracted economic growth. Regarding its concrete political and diplomatic policies, China stressed mutually beneficial outcomes, the maintenance of amicable ties with virtually all nations and institutions, and the expansion of those relationships that were most useful to its economic development.[20]

China's diplomacy turned toward multilateralism.[21] It invested in building "constructive strategic partnerships" with America and other powers and sought cooperation with multilateral security and economic institutions in Asia, such as the Asia-Pacific Economic Cooperation Forum and the Association of Southeast Asian Nations Regional Forum. China took the lead in developing strategic partnerships with Russia and other states of the former Soviet Union. A landmark strategic partnership between the PRC and the Russian Federation was signed in 1996 during a visit to Beijing by Russian president Boris Yeltsin. Moscow and Beijing also resolved a long-standing border conflict along the Amur River that had once threatened to engulf the Soviet Union and China in outright war. In the same year, the leaders of China, Russia, Kazakhstan, Kyrgyzstan, and Tajikistan met in Shanghai and agreed to finalize border settlements and to initiate confidence-building measures in Central Asia. The "Shanghai Five" security regime, as it became known, would evolve into a formal organization in 2001. China improved long-strained relations with India, which had been frozen since 1959 when India granted political asylum to the fourteenth Dalai Lama, then engaged in the brief border war in the Himalayas in the autumn of 1962.[22] In December 1991, Li Peng became the first Chinese premier in thirty-one years to visit India. Jiang Zemin visited India five years later, in November 1996. China also received Indian prime ministers and presidents on several occasions. After this diplomatic normalization, trade relations between the two countries developed very quickly. Jiang Zemin also initiated China's reengagement with Africa in 1996. In 1990, Yang Shangkun (1907–1998), then president, visited five countries in Latin America. His trip was the first of an increasing number of high-level missions. In 2001, Jiang Zemin completed a twelve-day mission to cement economic ties with Latin America. Key countries on his itinerary included Brazil, Argentina, and Venezuela.

China embraced multilateralism partly for very practical reasons. It wanted to end its post-Tiananmen international isolation and increase its influence in the world. It was also concerned about its international status, however, as it wanted to be recognized as a "responsible great power" by the international community. In the 2000s, China launched its global "charm offensive," attempting to improve its international image and build its soft power. A new government policy also encouraged Chinese commercial firms to "go out" (to invest abroad) and urged Chinese localities and organizations to more generally "go global." By the mid-2000s, considerable international moves were being initiated by a wide variety of Chinese organizations, localities, and individuals.

In 2004, Hu Jintao listed a number of objectives that highlighted the continued mission of securing stability along the borders, the growing importance of territorial disputes, the need to provide secure access to resources for China's economic growth, and the imperative of maintaining a military capability that would prevent other powers from launching a major war against China. He also sought to alleviate fears of China's rise by putting forward two basic concepts to describe the Chinese approach to foreign relations: pursuing peaceful development *(heping fazhan),* and the creation of a harmonious world *(hexie shijie).* "Peaceful development" was emphasized to allay widespread concerns in the West that China's rise would disrupt Asian and global stability. China stressed that both its current and future success depended on commercial and technological globalization, so that the only way to pursue its interests was through peaceful means. It also rejected any form of hegemonic and expansionist behavior. "Harmonious world" was a phrase intended to signal many things: China's continued support for multilateralism, international institutions, forums, and initiatives; its increasing contribution to global humanitarian and developmental assistance programs; its respect for the global diversity of political cultures, traditions, and values; and its defense of the principle of national sovereignty. It also reflected a general hope for the development of friendly relations based on the 1950s Chinese notion of the "five principles of peaceful coexistence," which were mutual respect for each other's territorial integrity and sovereignty; mutual nonaggression; mutual noninterference in each other's internal affairs; equality and cooperation for mutual benefit; and peaceful coexistence.

In Pursuit of National Greatness

As noted in earlier chapters, nationalism had already been a powerful driving force in China before the founding of the PRC. From Mao Zedong to Deng Xiaoping, early leaders adopted nationalist thought and rhetoric and within that frame portrayed the CCP as the only political party capable of leading China into an era of national unity and greatness. As the vestiges of socialism slowly disappeared from Chinese society in the 1990s, and some of the central promises of socialism—such as equality, social welfare, and social safety—became elusive for many Chinese, the nationalist element of political thinking became ever more virulent and important to the party. The party and government needed a reinvigorated vision that would give legitimacy to the emerging order. The simple recourse to Marxism as the dogmatic guideline for policy and development was no longer sufficient or persuasive. When it came to economic development, the party had already left behind most concepts and solutions in line with Marxist theory or Mao's beliefs. In general, starting in the late 1990s, the party highlighted narratives of national greatness.

In this context, as well, 1989 marked an important turning point. The party's violent suppression of student-led demonstrations in Tiananmen Square prompted a crisis of faith among the educated elite. The government first turned to drumming up patriotic feelings among the population as a way to regain control after the crisis. In 1991, Chinese leaders introduced the Patriotic Education Campaign that urged the students to unite behind its leadership. If they failed to do so, China would descend into chaos. The campaign also recalled Japanese wartime atrocities during WWII and more generally the indignities wrought by a century of foreign invasions after 1840. In September 1994, the Patriotic Education Campaign was expanded to include the entire population, including the military. This was followed by the publication of *Selected Works for Instruction in Patriotic Education* in November 1995, which compiled texts by Mao Zedong, Deng Xiaoping, and Jiang Zemin on patriotism. Jiang Zemin used the campaign to urge the party to rebuild itself "under the new banner of nationalism" and to urge the masses, especially students, to be "deeply inculcated" with the values of patriotism.[23] At the same time, the authorities generally discouraged writing about the "historical errors" committed by the party, such as the Great Leap Forward and the Cultural Revolution. The Patriotic Education Campaign in the 1990s was effective in that it engendered a nationalistic and conservative mood within Chinese society. The rise of nationalism intended to benefit the government and to restore some of the popular support lost in June 1989.

Beyond the need to maintain control, the party increasingly faced a more fundamental and systematic problem. In official statements, governments no longer focused on the attainment of communism as the clear goal, but rather advocated for the maintenance of order and stability and the achievement of high levels of growth and prosperity to create a "moderately well-off society" and thus facilitate the "revival" of the nation. Although the party still officially claimed legitimacy on the basis of Marxism–Leninism, which had important consequences for the political system, the government realized that it actually derived most of its legitimacy to rule China from its delivery of economic growth and national greatness. Most Chinese were becoming aware that *output legitimacy* in the form of economic growth and prosperity had become far more important than political ideology in justifying the government's continued claim to power. Consequently, the CCP had to transform itself from a "revolutionary party" *(gemingdang)* to a "ruling party" *(zhizheng-dang)* with the main task of promoting China's national welfare and strength. On the eightieth anniversary of the founding of the CCP in 2001, Jiang Zemin stated that making China strong and prosperous was the core mission of the CCP as a ruling party:

> Since the founding of New China, the economy and society have developed rapidly; the country has become increasingly prosperous; the people's social status, living standards and cultural and educational level have risen markedly. . . . The Chinese people and all the patriotic forces in China have come to realize that it is precisely the leadership of the Communist Party of China that has enabled the country to materialize the great historical transformation. China has thus come out of the most miserable plight and is now heading for a bright future. Without the Communist Party, there would have been no New China. . . . Every struggle that the Chinese people fought during the one hundred years from the mid-nineteenth to the mid-twentieth century was for the sake of achieving independence of our country and liberation of our nation and putting an end to the history of national humiliation once and for all. This great historic cause has already been accomplished. All endeavors by the Chinese people for the one hundred years from the mid-twentieth to the mid-twenty-first century are for the purpose of making our motherland strong, the people prosperous, and the nation immensely rejuvenated.[24]

Jiang Zemin's successor, Hu Jintao, also frequently used similar language evoking the "great rejuvenation of the Chinese nation."[25] The vision of a renewed, flourishing China made rich and strong by party stewardship was meant to galvanize the population behind the leadership.

In a sharp departure from Maoist positions and policies, the party under Jiang Zemin and Hu Jintao also started to redefine the relationship between China's Confucian tradition and "socialism with Chinese characteristics." It drew an analogy to a tree, arguing that China's traditional culture could be understood as the roots, Marxism–Leninism as the trunk, and the outstanding parts of various cultures from around the world as the branches.[26] Whereas the CCP traditionally rooted itself in the May Fourth tradition of discarding China's Confucian heritage, the tree analogy depicted contemporary China as growing out of the achievements of classical Chinese culture. Although this argument was criticized by the party's left wing, it can be understood as a continuation of efforts that had been made since the beginning of the reform period. The need had long been perceived to reconcile China's traditional heritage with its revolutionary legacy, so that the latter could be viewed as a continuation, rather than a dismissal, of the former.

Nationalism was not only an ideological replacement for an obsolete theory. It also worked as a uniting force to hold together a society experiencing the disruptive and divisive forces caused by rapid economic development. As social conflicts continued to sharpen, the party needed to divert attention. Nationalism provided social and political coherence for China by overcoming and combating the unpredictable political effects of economic development, including "ideological indifference," "a decline in patriotism," and the lamentable and increasing tendency to "worship money."[27]

The patriotic campaigns largely succeeded in forging a national identity based on an eclectic narrative that merged historical myths with historical traumas. Cultivated by the party to advance its agenda, Chinese nationalism after the 1990s was shaped by the contradictory feelings of historical humiliation and national pride. Chinese textbooks characteristically described a century of national humiliation *(guochi)* to define modern Chinese history.[28] The Opium Wars, when the British navy forced the opening of the Chinese empire to western trade, were seen as the beginning of that century. The discourse recounted how, at the hands of foreign invaders and corrupt Chinese regimes, sovereignty was mauled, territory was carved up, the Chinese people suffered tremendously, and China was thoroughly humiliated. This tale went on to list the various invasions, wars, occupations, lootings, and unequal treaties heaped on China by foreign aggressors and imperialists. Conveniently, the losses and destructions caused by China's self-inflicted disasters were left out in this narrative.

To overcome this bitter legacy of humiliation, the narrative continued, China had to become strong and modern. The party's vision of a "rejuvenated" China included a rising military power that would stand up to both domestic and international rivals—most notably Japan and its main ally, the United States. It would be a power capable of vigorously defending the nation's borders and strategic interests and asserting national sovereignty. The narrative of "national humiliation" and the earlier, weaker Chinese governments that allowed it became a strong element in official rhetoric. It formed Chinese perceptions of strategic realities, and therefore had an impact on China's actions in the international arena. China's perceived vulnerability as suggested by the national humiliation narrative engendered an urge not only to be safe and defensible in the world, but to be a power great enough to contend with any competitor in Asia or beyond. To be a great power would in part make up for the humiliation and shame of the past.

Beginning in the 1990s, the government invested considerable resources in actively promoting and sponsoring patriotic nationalism. These efforts did not, however, take place in a vacuum; the same period saw a partially independent, popular nationalism emerge from below and from within the society at large. As is well known from other countries' histories, nationalism always involves dynamics between government and population, and therefore has to be viewed as a powerful force that is not static but negotiated and contested. Neither the state nor the populace has full control over it. With regime legitimacy at stake, it is important to look at how the party and the Chinese people interacted with each other in the arena of Chinese nationalism. Popular nationalists supported but also challenged the state's claims to legitimacy, and issued their own competing nationalist visions. The party both suppressed and responded to challenges to its nationalist credentials. The suppression of legitimate nationalist claims, however, threatened to undermine regime stability. Successful responses to popular nationalist demands, by contrast, allowed the party to gain the approval of nationalist audiences, solidifying regime legitimacy.

The 1990s saw a surge of nationalism among Chinese intellectuals, and their readers and general audience, which occurred outside the domain of the government. Many well-educated Chinese social scientists, humanities scholars, writers, professionals, and above all, students added their voices to and even became activists for the nationalist agenda to create a flourishing China.[29] This was facilitated in large part by the rise of an urban commercial culture and thriving consumer culture. Sensationalist books and journals were published, often earning huge profits. Countless consumer-oriented TV series were aired, with Beijing TV, Central TV, and other local television stations leading the way. With the surge in economic and commercial activity, intellectuals and scholars turned to the market, a move called "jumping into the sea" *(xia hai)*. Among the topics that easily attracted large audiences were the nationalist themes of discrimination, humiliation, or mistreatment of China or Chinese at the hands of foreigners. The growing commercial publishing industry allowed previously unknown writers to capture the attention of the wider public. The most sensational and bestselling work to be published at the time was the essay collection *China Can Say No (Zhongguo keyi shuo bu)*. In it, young Chinese authors demanded that China stand up to the United States. The West was portrayed as a declining civilization, whereas a rejuvenated China was shown to be, based on its Confucian heritage, on the rise. Another book, *Behind the Demonization of China*, also caught public attention. It was written by eight graduates of top Chinese universities who had earned their graduate degrees or were still attending graduate school in the United States. Written to correct idealistic images of the United States, it made the case that America's government, media sector, and academic institutions worked together to construct a thoroughly evil and negative portrait of China.

These works, with their new and open defiance toward the West, took on strong significance in the narrative describing "popular nationalism" in the 1990s. They were viewed with alarm outside China because of the hostility they showed toward the western world and its values. Domestically, though, the more significant part of their message was the authors' implication that China was being held back as much by weak attitudes inside China as by any power that foreign forces could muster.

Popular nationalism burst into the open in several demonstrations and public protests.[30] In 1996, China confronted Japan over the ownership of eight tiny islands in the East China Sea, which the Chinese call *Diaoyutai* and the Japanese call *Senkaku*. Much to the surprise of the government, the dispute ignited a grassroots movement that mobilized Chinese communities not only in mainland China, but also in Hong Kong, Macau, Taiwan, and even in the United States and Canada, where demonstrations on September 22, 1996, drew some four thousand ethnic Chinese in San Francisco and twenty thousand in Vancouver. Even dissidents and outspoken critics of the PRC such as Wang Xizhe and Liu Xiaobo sent "open letters" to the authorities in Beijing and Taipei urging the deployment of military forces to recover the islands. This potential for popular nationalism to turn virulent alarmed the government in China. The CCP suddenly saw itself confronted with ever more radical demands from the street and as a result, decided to put an end to the protests and stop the demonstrations even at the risk of alienating the nationalist forces in the media.

Three years later, the NATO bombing of the Chinese embassy in Yugoslavia prompted large protests, too. Given the rise of popular nationalism, it was perhaps not surprising when many Chinese people reacted with rage to NATO's ostensibly mistaken bombing of the PRC embassy in Belgrade in June 1999 that killed three Chinese embassy staff. For three days, thousands of Chinese besieged the US embassy in Beijing and its consulates in ten cities across China, showering the buildings with rocks and bottles. In the city of Chengdu, rioters set fire to the consulate building. The Belgrade bombing protests were not manufactured by the party; to the contrary, as popular nationalists became outraged, party elites were barely able to control the situation. Again, suppressing the protests was risky, especially since Chinese lives had been lost and emotions were running high. To maintain nationalist legitimacy, and with regime stability at stake, the CCP needed to appease the protesters. Similar instances in the 2000s also suggest the emergence of a popular nationalism that increasingly challenged the CCP's claims to nationalist legitimacy. Although there were many common elements between popular nationalism and state nationalism in China, the independent existence of popular nationalism undermined the Communist Party's monopoly over nationalist discourse. It also pushed the party to a greater embrace of nationalism.

What is striking is that many of the intellectual elites who promoted nationalism had spent time in the West and, in the 1980s, even been advocates of liberal western ideas. The rise of nationalism was not simply a product of government propaganda, even though the party state found its uniting effects useful and certainly became a promoter of it. On the surface, specific events such as the NATO bombing played important roles as triggers in the rise of nationalistic sentiment in China. At a deeper level, however, at least among many intellectuals, nationalism was influenced by other, more persistent factors. During the 1980s, in the waning years of the USSR, most of them had been excited about Mikhail Gorbachev's policies of *perestroika* and *glasnost*—translated as "reform" and "openness"—which touched off the democratization of the Soviet Union. Chinese intellectuals admired glasnost's encouragement of the open discussion of political and social issues. They were also critical of Deng Xiaoping's focus on the authority of the CCP and the economy. The breakup of the Soviet Union and the chaotic internal politics and poor economic performance that ensued disappointed many Chinese, but also alarmed them. The possibility of a similar development in China became a fear that would haunt many intellectuals. They noted, moreover, that western countries failed to provide effective assistance to Russia in its painful democratic transition. Instead, the West seemed more interested in taking advantage of the weakening of Russia's international position. Meanwhile, although the intellectuals were aware of many problems in China, they personally started to benefit from all the positive economic development that had occurred since 1992. Finally, they were also very disappointed by the US media's generally negative coverage of China. Many students and intellectuals in China found a bias in the US media when it came to China that, to them, revealed the hegemonic political and cultural attitudes of the West. Many perceived a mentality of rivalry spreading among US politicians who looked at China's rise with growing distrust and hostility. To the extent that this was true, ironically it served to stimulate nationalistic passions in China.

Some Chinese intellectuals remained ambivalent, however, about the surge of nationalistic feelings. Wang Shuo (1958–) became China's most popular yet rebellious writer. His mocking books portrayed protagonists trying to cheat and play the system for their own benefit. The "Wang Shuo phenomenon," as it came to be known in the 1990s, reflected the development of an ironic antiestablishment popular culture that became a powerful force in its own right. Wang Shuo also wrote a scathing satire of China's wounded pride called *Please Don't Call Me Human*.[31] The book, with its parodies of the varying kinds of nationalist rhetoric and propaganda, amounted to a profound criticism of everything Chinese nationalism held sacred. Its plot is set in motion when the organizing committee of a freestyle elimination wrestling competition watches a video of a western wrestler trouncing his Chinese competitor. What can the Chinese nation do, asks the committee, to save face and not be humiliated by the West? First, it decides, it must change its own name, to MobCom (for mobilization committee). Then it starts looking for a national wrestling hero capable of winning the international respect China so richly deserves. That hero is found in the person of a pedicab driver named Tang, who is not only a martial arts master, but also said to be a Great Dream Boxer, a reincarnation of the nineteenth-century fighters of the Boxer uprising. Only by beating up someone else, realizes a member of MobCom, "can we overcome the frustrations of the past century." One pointed bit of dialogue starts with a comment by a citizen forced to celebrate publicly when the hero is found:

> "I seem to recall lining up like this once before, a long time ago, waving little flags and mumbling things to someone passing by."
>
> "It must have been 1949."
>
> "No, earlier than that."
>
> "Then it must have been 1937" [the start of the Sino-Japanese War, which began the spread of nationalist passions].

As the plot unfolds, and the Great Dream Boxer sadly proves unable to win any form of wrestling match, he is sent to participate in a new form of martial arts competition where athletes compete for a championship in "the art of endurance." It is a contest in which the advantage is held by the competitor who comes from the nation that can tolerate the most humiliation and pain. Indeed, China's champion perseveres through a barrage of hardships and tortures, including a self-humiliation trial consisting of hitting one's own face. Tang beats himself until he is "as purple as an eggplant," and the swelling under his thick skin has made it "as thin and translucent as paper." Yet, while the other competitors give up and fail, he revels in the pain. The athlete from China ends up prevailing literally by losing his face. Declared the undisputed world champion, he receives his award in an Olympic-style ceremony. The story ends with the raising of the Chinese flag and the playing of the national anthem, as all of China, tuned into a live broadcast of the ceremony, erupts in wild celebration.

At the risk of belaboring the point, Wang Shuo published his sharply satirical novel at a time when nationalistic sentiments were running high, and reminded readers both that Chinese nationalism had a long history, linked to the nation's suffering dating back to at least 1937, and that it stemmed from a need to save face that was deeply ingrained in Chinese thinking. His story was also designed to warn them that, by succumbing to its worst nationalist impulses, China could only lose face.

The Era of Super-High Growth

After its World Trade Organization accession in 2001, China went on to engineer an economic miracle that won worldwide admiration and envy. A booming market economy emerged that made China the "workshop of the world" and generated wealth and prosperity that benefited a large segment of Chinese society. Growth in the "productive forces"—that is, GDP and its underlying inputs—was the primary goal of the government, as reflected in a policy agenda that deliberately and successfully promoted rapid growth. To achieve and secure high growth rates, the Chinese government worked with every aspect of the economic system and experimented with many economic and social institutional modifications.[32]

When Chinese policymakers faced choices between different priorities, they consistently preferred the achievement of rapid growth over other targets. Evidence for this prerogative can be seen in many areas. At the very beginning of the reform process, China cut the investment rate—that is, fixed investment as a share of GDP—to give the economy space to breathe and allow consumption to increase. After that, it became a steady promoter of producer-friendly and growth-friendly policies favoring investments, which pushed the investment rate back up. Local governments became tireless developers of new investment opportunities by selling land for industrial zones or commercial projects. The result was an enormous, sustained mobilization of capital for investment, mostly in the export sector. These policies favored capital-intensive industries, which benefited most from the cheap loans from state-owned banks, an undervalued exchange rate, and low prices of key inputs such as land and energy. In addition, tax policies favored investments, low interest rates set by government monetary policy made credit inexpensive, and non-collectable debt was often forgiven.

China's investment rate grew higher than any other large country had ever achieved.[33] Between 1992 and 2002, the investment rate was already around 38–39 percent, comparable to the highest levels achieved in Japan, Korea, and Taiwan during their high investment and growth phases. From 2003 onward, the investment rate shot up more than 40 percent, an unprecedented level.[34] China financed some 60 percent of its gross capital formation through domestic savings, and the remaining 40 percent through foreign direct investment (FDI). This amounted to a massive influx of western capital.

China began its reform era at the end of the 1970s with less than $2 billion of FDI annually. Twenty years later, in the mid-1990s, FDI in China exceeded a cumulative total of $40 billion annually. With that number, China became the world's top recipient of FDI among the developing economies. From 1979 to 2011, on a cumulative basis, China absorbed a total of US$1,177 billion in FDI.[35] Most of the investment began flowing in 1992. China's record of attracting foreign investment is also impressive when put in a global context. Between 1992 and 1999, flows into China accounted for 8.2 percent of worldwide FDI and 26.3 percent of investments going to developing countries. During much of the 1990s, China was the world's second-largest recipient of FDI, trailing only the United States. By 2002, China passed the United States as the most favored destination for FDI. In 2010, the foreign investment into China stood at US$116 billion, about half of what came into the United States in the same year.

It is important to note, however, that investments by large western and Japanese multinational corporations constituted only a small portion of total foreign direct investment flows into China during much of the 1990s. Almost 60 percent of this came from "Greater China" sources, primarily in Hong Kong, Macau, and Taiwan. Most of the investors were small and medium enterprises, operating simple and labor-intensive production and assembly processes. Foreign enterprises made huge investments in a number of Chinese industries and acquired substantial control over China's export marketing channels to the world.[36] A major effect of foreign investment was not only the provision of capital, but also the acquisition of modern technology and the business expertise that permitted China to operate on global markets and increase its exports. Some four hundred of the world's five hundred largest companies invested in over two thousand projects in China. They included the world's leading computer, electronics, telecommunications equipment, pharmaceutical, and petrochemical companies. Transnational corporations such as Microsoft, Motorola, GM, GE, Samsung, Intel, Nokia, and Siemens, to name a few, established R&D ventures in China. Microsoft, for example, invested US$80 million in a Chinese research institute and announced its intention to make additional investments to create a Microsoft Asian Technology Center.[37]

The effect of FDI and the upgrade of its technological base could be seen in China's increasing ability to export high-tech products. In 2000, China exported US$37 billion worth of high-tech products, 81 percent of which were produced by foreign companies or joint ventures in China. But the effects of high foreign direct investment went further. These investments also created a highly competitive environment and encouraged the development of new institutions, at the firm level and through the legal system, by placing owner-ship and production in a more global and competitive context.

Growth in the export sector was mostly accomplished by private busi-nesses, not by the state-owned sector. The Chinese state sector was com-posed of two components, one central and one local. Most of the local state sector, which consisted of many medium-sized firms, was no longer in exis-tence, however, due to privatization of the township and village enterprises (TVEs). Yet the central segment made up of large and mostly unprofitable enterprises had so far weathered all reforms. The state realized that the state-owned sector urgently needed change to make it more competitive in the do-mestic and global markets. In 2003, China announced the creation of an ownership agency to exercise the central government's ownership oversight in a new institutional way.[38] The State Asset Supervision and Administration Commission (SASAC) assumed ownership of 196 of the largest nonfinan-cial state-owned enterprises, giving it nominal control over enormous wealth. Forty-five corporations on the global Fortune 500 list for 2012 were owned by SASAC, with combined assets totaling US$4.5 trillion. It became one of the most important and powerful organizations in the world, although few people ever heard its name. After the substantial downsizing of the state sector in the mid-1990s, the purpose of SASAC was to retain large state-owned cor-porations in select strategic sectors of the Chinese economy. While agricul-ture, industry, and commerce in China were already dominated by private businesses, large and powerful central government enterprises were to be maintained in areas such as natural resources, energy, communication, infra-structure, and defense. These sectors remained shielded from privatization and foreign investment, and thus were reserved for state ownership. Management buyouts of large state firms ceased, and the central government consolidated its ownership portfolio, even while privatization continued at the local level, albeit slowly and gradually. The establishment of SASAC therefore marked the virtual end of privatization of the larger state-owned enterprises through the central government and the beginning of the consolidation of the state-owned sector. This step was very successful, given that the state-owned sector thrived in the following years. The SASAC pushed through fundamental reforms of corporate management. More efficiency was encouraged through a process called corporatization *(gongsihua)*. The executive boards were given broader authorities and responsibilities (including restructuring, spin-offs, mergers, raising capital, and payments and salaries), and state interference in day-to-day business was restricted. The SASAC generally followed an agenda of professionalization, specialization, and the creation of internationally competitive firms that could eventually become leading world-class businesses.

As for the state-owned sector, the Chinese government engaged in an active effort to restructure large central government firms and shape their market environments. Generally, at least two large firms competed in each market segment. For instance, China National Petroleum Corporation (CNPC), the conglomerate that owned Sinopec and others, China Petrochemical Corporation (PetroChina), and China National Offshore Oil Corporation (CNOOC) divided the oil market, while China Mobile, China Unicom, and China Telecom partitioned the telecom market.[39] All these firms were centrally owned by SASAC. In the airline industry, there were three large central airlines, Air China, China Eastern, and China Southern, plus several smaller public and private airlines. On the one hand, market monopolies, seen as inefficient and easily corrupted, were avoided. On the other hand, the state kept control of strategic and sensitive sectors. The result was a system of structured competition among state-owned businesses. Due to this significant institutional innovation, the powerful state sector stabilized and became healthier. After hitting rock bottom in 1996–1998, the state sector saw a strong rise in profits during the 2000s.

A peculiar and hybrid economic system emerged, based on a few large centrally state-owned enterprises in strategic sectors, and on private entrepreneurs who maintained tight links with local government officials. Some scholars call this system "state capitalism," because the state continues to view state enterprises and state involvement as tools of not only government policy but, arguably, of regime identity and legitimacy.[40] State firms remained at the core of what Beijing officially called "market socialism with Chinese characteristics." The system enabled a period of rapid growth, generating the resources needed to support the state and its political class, and spreading benefits—both private and relating to social welfare—to a broader swath of the population. It also succeeded in smoothing over some of the system's inefficiencies. During this period of rapid structural change and peak economic growth, Chinese state capitalism was reasonably successful, benefiting the party state.

Despite pockets of state monopolies and local trade barriers, intense competition came to pervade everyday economic life. The automotive sector provides a perfect illustration. When China started to open its economy in the late 1970s, Beijing had to court companies and investors from abroad. One of the first multinationals to enter was American Motors Corporation, which built a factory in Beijing. The project was initially aimed at producing Jeeps for export to Australia, rather than building cars for Chinese consumers. Four decades later, Chinese car manufacturers produced twenty-four million cars per year, far more than any other country. Decades of intense competition transformed a lethargic, state-run oligopoly into a whirlwind of rivalries in which automaker upstarts like Chery and Geely wrestled for market share with state-sector heavyweights and global car producers. The results of rapid expansion of production, quality, variety, and productivity—along with galloping price reductions—created a dynamic new sector, bringing not just the manufacturing of vehicles, components, and materials, but also introducing auto dealers, service stations, parking facilities, car racing, publications, motels, and tourism into China's economy.[41] Price wars and advertising, two clear indicators of market competition, became everyday appearances. The decline of former industry leaders like Panda (televisions) and Kelon (home appliances) and the rise of new industry leaders like Alibaba (online trade), Wanxiang (auto parts), Haier (home appliances), or Tencent (internet) from obscure beginnings showed that competition had added new fluidity to Chinese market structures. China quickly grew into one of the largest and most dynamic economies in the world.

China's astounding development was only possible because the world markets made it the point of final assembly for a broad array of goods for export. Its seemingly limitless and comparatively inexpensive labor pool gave China an important comparative advantage in the labor-intensive final stages of global production processes. Labor market competition increased dramatically, too, although discrimination of migrant workers and segmented labor markets still provided some protection for urban workers.

The Chinese high growth model displayed downsides, too. The one-sided "pro-growth" policies led to distortions and imbalances by preferring high-return sectors of the economy. Allocation of capital to large and national champions also crowded out investment to higher-return, smaller, private companies. China's capital stock, for instance, climbed to 295 percent of

GDP in 2008, up from 248 percent in 2000, underscoring just how much China's double-digit growth in this period had been driven by capital spending and investment. But the overreliance of China's development on growth and investment created major macroeconomic imbalances. It limited job growth, holding down the share of labor in the economic system and depressing household consumption. The share of labor contributed only 0.9 percent to the economic growth. Making the economy even more lopsided, households in China did not benefit very much from the profits that state-owned firms made from their subsidized investments. There was, in fact, a plunge in the share of wages in national income to 39.7 percent in 2007, down from 52.8 percent a decade earlier. With income and job growth arrested, it was little wonder that Chinese household consumption accounted for only 37.1 percent of GDP in 2008, less than many other countries (especially the United States, at 61.1 percent).[42]

After China joined the World Trade Organization, therefore, questions arose concerning the long-term sustainability of its economic development. China tried to gradually adopt a new development strategy to reorient growth. Under the leadership of Hu Jintao and Wen Jiabao, policy sought to make China's growth more sustainable and to spread the benefits of growth more broadly among society.[43] After Hu Jintao rose to become general secretary of the CCP in the fall of 2002, social justice issues began to receive greater attention from the new administration.

In 2006, at the Sixth Plenum of the Sixteenth Central Committee, the party officially decided to shift the focus of reform from the uninhibited growth of Jiang's era to more balanced development. Thereafter, the second term of the Hu Jintao–Wen Jiabao administration (2007–2012) saw a flurry of government regulations and initiatives intended to redress many of the problems and grievances that had accrued during the previous thirty years of very high, yet highly unequal, growth. The new development strategy, sometimes referred to as the "Hu–Wen new policies" *(Hu–Wen xinzheng)* or the "scientific outlook on development" *(kexue fazhanguan)*, emphasized sustainable and equitable growth. Reflecting the direction of the new policies were key terms in policy documents and Hu's and Wen's speeches, such as "scientific outlook on development," "harmonious society" *(hexie shehui)*, "people's welfare" *(minsheng)*, "integrated and balanced urban-rural development" *(tongchou chengxiang)*, and "agricultural, rural, and peasant problems" (*nongye, nongcun, nongmin wenti,* or *sannong wenti*). The new strategy aimed to reduce inequalities and to protect the most economically vulnerable groups of the population. Specific measures included financial subsidies for agriculture, social welfare programs, tax reductions, minimum wage increases, and increased spending on poverty alleviation.[44] This program also included labor laws, medical insurance schemes, and pensions. Chinese reform was recalibrated to pursue the twin goals of advancing "humanity" (putting people first) and achieving a "harmonious society" (seeking balanced growth) with scientific development as the process to do so.

The policy also aimed at addressing the increasing disparity between the urban and rural economies.[45] A program called "New Socialist Countryside" (*shehui zhuyi xin nongcun*) promised to connect all villages to the outside by tar roads; to provide medical insurance for all farmers by 2020; to extend the minimum living allowance *(dibao)* policy from the cities to the rural areas; and to improve agricultural mechanization. One of the key issues at the subsequent Seventeenth National Congress of the Communist Party of China in October 2007 was whether to include in the party constitution a commitment to "balance" urban and rural development. Urban–rural integration was also at the heart of the Third Plenum of the Seventeenth Central Committee in October 2008, where the party's pledge to "rural reform and development" was renewed with a promise to double peasant income by 2020 and to further improve rural infrastructure. High-level leaders also indicated that they aimed to remove the urban–rural bias. In 2006, agricultural taxes were finally abolished in an effort to improve the economic situation in the countryside. This led to a modest improvement, but living standards still lagged far behind those in urban areas. Reforms to China's residence registration *(hukou)* system that would make it easier for peasants to take up residence in the cities were also promised.

Under the umbrella of this new development strategy, China's economy continued to grow. Imbalances persisted, however. Between 2002 and 2012, the benefits of growth were still not shared equally. Individual households benefited far less than companies and investors and urban areas were expanding their lead. By all accounts, the efforts under Hu Jintao to change the development model fell short. For example, the government introduced a national health care system. China managed to extend medical insurance to 95 percent of its citizens, but in practice, many workers fell through the cracks.

The quality and accessibility of medical care in contemporary China reflected the spatial divide between city and countryside. The disparity in access to quality health care between rural and urban areas, in essence, created a two-tiered system. Although the top level was similar to health care available in developed countries, the lower tier of the Chinese health care system was more typical of those found in developing countries.[46]

At the core of the problems in rural China were issues related to land ownership. All farmland was, by law, owned by the village collectively, and contracted out to individual peasants for cultivation (*chengbao*). That meant that land ownership was ultimately controlled by the state, giving officials the power to decide on what terms and when to develop land. In 1998, Jiang Zemin, trying to assure farmers, announced that land contracts would remain in effect for at least thirty years. After the late 1990s, local governments grew dependent on taking peasants' land or urban land for no or relatively little compensation, and selling it to developers for a huge uptick.[47] Lacking ownership of the land, peasants had little choice but to give up their plots and move to the cities in search of work. The central government transferred revenues to local governments, but kept the bulk of fiscal revenues. Many town and county officials complained that the amount from the central government was not enough to meet goals set by central leaders. The central government assigned many tasks to local governments that required substantial expenditures. Officials in county and city governments, eager to secure jobs for their constituents and to advance their careers, also went into perilous debt to pay for building and business projects that often used that land as collateral for loans, or to lure investors.

Although the peasants did not own the land, they started to trade contracted land use rights. The 2007 Property Law allowed transfer of the right to contracted use of land (called *chengbao tian*), and required local governments at the county level or above to issue rights certificates to *chengbao* holders. It also stated that rural land could not be used for non-agricultural purposes without governmental approval. Term of contract was specified as thirty years and, upon expiration of the contract term, the holder could "continue to fulfill the contract according to the relevant provisions of the state."[48] Some observers hoped that giving transfers of land use rights a legal basis would be an important step toward land concentration, which would be needed to create a more profitable agricultural economy. In 2009, a new law spelled out guidelines for land dispute resolutions that reaffirmed the land management rights and tried to strengthen the position of peasants in an area that had spawned some of the most contentious rural conflicts. Unless China's leadership found a way, however, to untie this knot of land and finance problems, many farmers would remain too poorly compensated for land redesigned by the state for development to make safe passages to life in cities.

In the 2000s, China started to increase investment in human capital, particularly by strengthening the education sector, which aimed to propel the nation to the next stage of economic development.[49] The country began an extraordinary expansion of its higher education system. China's universities also moved toward internationalization, a move linked to a campaign to improve research quality. In terms of the number of students educated, the recent changes in China's postsecondary education system were more dramatic than even the great postwar expansion of higher education in the United States or the growth of mass-enrollment universities in Europe in the 1970s and 1980s. After a decade in which most were shuttered, Chinese universities had opened their doors to fewer than a million students in 1978. By 1998, enrollment had reached 3.4 million, far short of the 14.5 million attending in the United States at the time. In 2017, 27.5 million students attended institutions of higher learning in China—some seven million more than the enrollment at US colleges and universities.[50] Private colleges and universities at this point accounted for more than a quarter of all higher education institutions in China, and were growing at a faster rate than public ones. Large companies were also getting involved. Alibaba's Taobao unit, for instance, established Taobao University, with the initial goal of training e-business owners, managers, and salespeople. In time, it said, it would offer online business education to more than a million students.

China began to turn out more PhDs each year than any other country in the world, as Chinese universities aimed to be cradles of high-level creative research with the capacity to transform research and innovation into higher productivity. The Chinese government and many other sources were pumping large amounts of funding into the leading institutions. Within ten years, the research budgets of China's elite universities were expected to approach those of their US and European peers. In engineering and science, Chinese universities were on the way to being among the world's leaders soon. But while there was need to further reform, as discussed in China's universities, the CCP remained deeply, and rather intriguingly, embedded in the fabric of the sector of higher education, possibly presenting a stumbling block to incite kick-off innovation.

To conclude, during the first decade of the twenty-first century, it became clear that the rapid development could not be sustained due to rising costs and burdens. The necessary readjustment of economic structure that was built around the presumption of very rapid growth was intensively discussed in the 2000s, but little was achieved. This rapid growth from a low income base was accomplished through a pro-growth development strategy that was based on industrialization, urbanization, and a vast migration of underemployed, low-skilled labor from the countryside to coastal cities. Enterprises, many of them state-owned, stockpiled their earnings rather than returning them to the public, which stunted families' incomes. At the same time, individual savings were high, in part because the social safety net was weak and families accumulated cash as a safeguard. As a result, Chinese spending was skewed, with very high rates of investment but a very low share of consumer demand in gross domestic product. This structure was workable as long as high economic growth offered sufficient investment opportunities. But doubts mounted toward the end of the Hu Jintao presidency. Investment seemed to have run into decreasing returns. Surging labor and energy costs in China were eroding its competitiveness in manufacturing. The reserve of surplus labor was dwindling, which meant that growth had to slow. According to the strategic consultancy Boston Consulting Group, manufacturing wages adjusted for productivity had almost tripled in China over the last decade, to an estimated $12.47 an hour in 2015, up from $4.35 an hour in 2004.[51] Textile production in China, for instance, was becoming increasingly unprofitable after years of rising wages, higher energy bills, mounting logistical costs, environmental requirements, and new government quotas on the import of cotton. The result was a transitional problem. China needed to wean itself from dependence on export-driven high growth and find a more sustainable model based on domestic demand and technological innovation. Many started to worry: What will happen if investment shrinks but consumption and innovation don't step up fast enough to fill the gap?

TWELVE

Ambitions and Anxieties

Contemporary China

In the second decade of the twenty-first century, China had to come to terms with the consequences of its rapid rise. In 2012, a new administration under Xi Jinping took office, which still seemed driven by anxiety that communist rule could founder in China as it had in the Soviet Union, unless the party maintained economic growth, projected political strength, and exercised strict control over an increasingly wealthy and diverse society. The government continued to promote and intensified with vigor a vision of national rejuvenation and of restoring China to its rightful place in the world. The Xi Jinping administration tightened oversight over potentially competing hubs of authority and power, including the business sector, the internet, the publishing industry, academia, the military, and other arms of state power—and for that matter, the more than eighty-nine million members of the CCP. Globally, China started to wield its considerable economic clout and to protect its interests with a more assertive and ambitious foreign policy. Many neighbors in the region and beyond started to worry about China's aggressive defense of its territorial claims. The government also renewed its efforts to make the military a first-class fighting outfit with global reach as it substantially raised military spending. With the "One Belt One Road" initiative, China invested in infrastructure-building overseas to acquire new allies and link their economies with its own. In search of resources, China built a global presence that started to shift the balance of power in the world.

Domestically, China had to grapple with a profoundly changed and diverse society and unresolved issues that had accumulated over time. The party recognized that development had been, in the words of President Xi Jinping, "unbalanced" *(bu pingheng)* and "inadequate."[1] The high-speed growth of the past decades had undoubtedly benefited many, but also created new tensions and conflicts. Inequalities were on the rise, and environmental pollution threatened quality of life. Some social groups, such as women, the elderly, and minorities, faced new forms of hardship and discrimination. Scandals revealed problems of governance and public responsibility. Various forms of public protest and internet activism calling for those problems to be addressed and demanding accountability elicited only the scorn of officials. Overall, there was growing concern and sometimes even outrage that the direction China took was not well advised and could not be sustained without modifications and substantial policy shifts. The most pressing concern that put many at unease in China was how the CCP would react if its claim to power was threatened. Would it embrace more democratic institutions or return to "strongman" rule? Deepening fissures emerged between the party's ideological and political conservatism and the pragmatic reality of a far more complex, concerned, restless, and dynamic society.

The Presidency of Xi Jinping

In late 2012, a new government with Xi Jinping as president assumed power in China.[2] The following year, in 2013, Li Keqiang was appointed prime minister. The new government realized that China needed to continue economic reforms to share the benefits of economic growth with a larger segment of the population and to deal with economic imbalances. Xi championed himself as the chief architect of economic policy—usually the prime minister's job—and vowed to reshape the economy. Based on his proposals, the Third Plenum of the Eighteenth Central Committee in 2013 adopted a bold reform program called "the sixty points."[3] Twenty-two of the sixty points outlined a new economic policy that called for "letting the market play the decisive role in allocating resources." The specific economic goals were to expand the role of the market in the energy and natural resources sectors, increase household investments and consumption, and relax controls over currency and financial markets. The remainder of the sixty points dealt with the continuation of legal reforms (with eleven points focusing on this goal), social policy (nine points), environment (four points), and the military (three points). Other points also announced the stepping up of social control and the enforcement of the party's political ideology.

Two years after Xi and Li came into office, the government faced a slowing of the Chinese economy. Government officials were alarmed by the fact that the economy had grown at its slowest pace in a quarter-century, and seemed to be decelerating further. In a sign of its apprehension, leadership in August 2015 implemented the biggest devaluation of the Chinese currency in more than two decades, sending stock prices down globally. China's leaders appeared to be frightened, for obvious political reasons, by the prospect of a recession, however brief. They tried to support domestic demand by, in effect, flooding the system with cheap credit and engineering a stock market boom. The government also propped up stock prices. Large shareholders were blocked from selling stocks; state-owned institutions and enterprises were instructed to buy shares; and many companies with falling prices were allowed to suspend trading. Worries about China's economic health were not ended by these policies. Instead, they were now fueled by growing debt and the existence of a "shadow banking" sector that had been essentially unregulated and could easily experience a wave of bank runs. Since the administration was busy dealing with immediate economic problems on many fronts, few of the bold reforms announced in 2013 were implemented.

The Xi Jinping administration also announced an official fight against the corruption that was threatening to undermine governance and party legitimacy. The spread of corruption was related to deeper and more systemic problems. The phenomenon could be interpreted as an indicator that internal interest groups—rather than the public interest—had been driving specific economic outcomes. A network of entrenched interest groups made up of businesses and officials had started to capture many institutions, such as state enterprises and government agencies. Revenues from lucrative land deals and profits of state-owned enterprises, for instance, were often not flowing into the state treasury, but rather being partially or even fully channeled to interest groups. One way to deal with these severe problems, which not only siphoned off important resources but also threatened regime legitimacy, could have been to improve transparency, competition, and public oversight (and even privatization). Xi Jinping's solution, however, was to crack down on "tigers and flies."[4] He began to carry out a vigorous anticorruption drive that took down some of the most powerful men (or tigers) in the country and sidelined more than a hundred thousand lower-ranking officials (the flies). The campaign against official corruption continued longer, reached higher, and achieved more than most had expected. Among those indicted were former president Hu Jintao's chief of staff, Ling Jihua (1956–), and the member of the Politburo who once controlled the internal security forces, Zhou Yongkang (1942–). Ling Jihua had been a protégé of Hu Jintao, while Zhou Yongkang owed his rise to Jiang Zemin. Xi Jinping also removed Bo Xilai (1949–), the former CCP secretary of Chongqing and member of the Politburo. All were sentenced to long prison terms for graft. Many believed that the campaign was used by Xi Jinping to remove some of his most powerful political rivals and enemies. The corruption investigations even reached into the top ranks of the military. General Guo Boxiong (1942–), who for a decade until his retirement in 2012 was the military's most senior serving officer, was officially placed under investigation in April 2015 and sentenced to life imprisonment in July 2016. General Xu Caihou (1943–2015) was indicted as well, but died while awaiting court-martial on bribery charges. Other powerful Chinese military leaders were placed under investigation, too. In 2015, fourteen generals were reported to have been convicted of or investigated for graft.

That campaign and other moves allowed Xi Jinping to exert greater control over the Chinese military than his predecessors had, and allowed him to appoint new commanders. After becoming head of the Communist Party and chairman of the Central Military Commission in November 2012, Xi Jinping closely associated himself with the People's Liberation Army. Unlike Jiang Zemin or Hu Jintao, Xi had some experience in the military before his elevation to the leadership. He started his rise through the party by spending several years as an aide to the minister of defense, starting in 1979, when China was briefly but disastrously at war with Vietnam. He often had visited military units to talk with soldiers and to push the military to embrace change, while praising it as a stronghold of party power.

Xi Jinping took the nationalist narrative even further by promoting "the China Dream" *(Zhongguo meng)*—an emotional appeal for national rejuvenation and military greatness. In his first public speech after becoming China's new general secretary of the CCP in November 2012, Xi Jinping explained that the "China Dream" was to "achieve the great rejuvenation of the Chinese nation" which he regarded as "the shared hope and expectation of every Chinese." "Rejuvenation" *(fuxing)*, the term used by Xi's predecessors Jiang Zemin and Hu Jintao before, meant that China needed to regain national strength and social stability to return to a leading central position in the world. His vision of the "China Dream" involved every individual, he stressed, because the country could only be rejuvenated with the "joint hard work of every generation of Chinese."[5] Only by following the common national goals devised by the Chinese Communist Party could the Chinese citizens hope to realize their collective dreams.[6] With this agenda, Xi Jinping continued to push a nationalist agenda, just as the Chinese public began to lose confidence in the party's main source of legitimacy: its ability to deliver economic growth.

Under Xi Jinping, the party also started to strengthen political ideology. Xi Jinping seemed self-consciously to resuscitate and reassemble prominent pieces of Maoist symbolism and propaganda. Over the New Year's holiday in 2016, Xi made a televised trip to Jinggangshan, where Mao had set up the first Chinese Soviet Republic as a self-governing region under CCP control in 1927. Footage showed Xi paternalistically "united with the masses," sharing a meal with peasants in front of a poster of Chairman Mao. In general, the party stressed the continued relevance of the revolutionary legacy and rhetoric to contemporary politics. There would be an ongoing rediscovery and redeployment of the power of "red culture."

Through campaigns and movements such as the anticorruption movement and the "China Dream," Xi Jinping acquired a greater degree of power and influence than his predecessors. He also took control of many of the central leading groups *(lingdao xiaozu)* in the CCP that dated from the 1950s and coordinated specific policies between the party and the government. They covered everything from Taiwan and Hong Kong to internet security, the legal system, and "preserving stability." The most important small groups formulated policy, such as the one focused on foreign affairs. They gathered data and carried out research before important decisions were made. There were also small groups dealing with more specific tasks or temporary initiatives such as the Three Gorges Dam or poverty alleviation. Finally, some short-term groups were set up to deal with emergencies or relief after disasters. By accumulating power, Xi Jinping's ascendance at least threatened to unhinge the principle of collective leadership that had been supported by a broad inner-party consensus since the death of Mao Zedong. More than *primus inter pares*, Xi became what party propaganda organs grandly touted as the "core" *(hexin)* of the party.

12.1. People in Beijing walking past a large billboard featuring the image of Xi Jinping and promotion of his hallmark slogan, "Chinese Dream," October 2017. Kyodo News / Getty Images / 862299474

In 2012, Xi Jinping visited Tsinghua University and Peking University. He made two points clear: that a central role for educational institutions was to train future party leaders, and that the party should have more, not less, influence on higher education. Faculty in Chinese universities faced stricter limitations on what they could talk about. The party touted "Seven No's"—a list of topics to avoid discussing with students. This meant that faculty should not talk about any past failures of the Communist Party. Other forbidden topics were separation between the judicial and executive arms of government, human rights, freedom of press, and freedom of civil society. Faculty were even prohibited from discussing whether or not the CCP was subject to the "constitutional rule" of China's constitution. It is hard to overstate the impact these strictures had on academic discourse and the intellectual environment. Censorship of critical publications in print or online was also increased. In 2015, China enacted a sweeping national security law intended to safeguard the country's "core interests" *(hexin liyi)*. The term referred to what Chinese leaders saw as three sacrosanct pillars of the nation: maintaining the political system and the unquestioned rule by the Communist Party; defending sovereignty claims and territorial integrity; and economic development. This represented a considerable expansion over previous administrations of what China considered to be nonnegotiable.

In the Xi Jinping era, then, the coming down of high growth rates and the need to continue social and political reforms coincided with a more repressive and conservative domestic policy. Even to raise the issue of political reform was anathema. This pointed out a fundamental but unresolved issue that loomed large and that threatened to derail the economic and social development. The question was: What kind of political system is suited for a transformed China and what could be the future of the CCP?[7] As long as these fundamental questions were not addressed, the danger of a "trapped transition" appeared real and China seemed at risk of slipping into a slow process of regime decay. The term "trapped transition" suggests a situation where necessary institutional reforms cannot be pursued and will inevitably be neglected because the party fears that those reforms will threaten its hold on power, its entrenched interests, and its access to national wealth. While China might manage to avert this development and maintain the status quo, risks like this spoke to the greater uncertainties that started to cloud China's future.

Global Ambitions

Most of China's global activities and foreign policy in the Xi Jinping era were closely related to China's economic development and its needs. Those needs also pushed China onto the global stage, where it occupied a prominent place.[8] China's global impact was increasingly felt on every continent, in most international institutions, and on many global issues. Its rapid growth reshaped the world economy, as a powerful driver of corporate strategies, financial markets, and geopolitical decisions. By many measures, China became the world's second leading power, after the United States, and its aggregate economy was predicted to surpass that of the United States around 2025.

While economic development brought wealth and power to China, it also created new demands—for instance, for energy and other commodities to power its economy, compelling China to look beyond its borders to make investments and to satisfy its needs for resources. Oil was on the leading edge of this investment push. China became the world's largest buyer of oil, which gave it substantial sway in oil-producing regions. Energy projects and stakes accounted for two-fifths of China's overseas investments in the period between 2005 and 2015.[9] With an increased dependence on foreign oil, China's leaders followed the United States and other large economies by seeking to own more overseas oil fields to ensure a stable supply. State-controlled Chinese oil companies acquired big stakes in oil operations in Africa, Central Asia, the Middle East, Latin America, and the United States.

China also became the biggest trading partner for many countries. For more than a decade, global prices for iron ore, a main ingredient in making steel, climbed as new skyscrapers, railway tracks, and other infrastructure were constructed across China. China's FDI—the money it spent overseas on land acquisitions, factory construction, and other business operations—was second only to that of the United States. In 2016, for the first time, the country sent more investments abroad than it received.[10] Chinese companies were at the center of a worldwide construction boom, building airports, highways, ports, and railways mostly financed by Chinese banks. Engineering became more important as Chinese companies built power plants in Eastern Europe, and glass and cement factories in Africa.

In Africa, for instance, China surpassed the United States as a trading partner and left its mark on the entire continent.[11] China followed a two-pronged approach by offering development loans (secured by collateral such as natural resource extraction rights) to oil- and mineral-rich nations like Angola, and developing special trade and economic cooperation zones in several countries, including Nigeria, Ethiopia, and Zambia. Special economic zones allowed African countries to improve poor infrastructure and inefficient institutions in those zones. By 2013, Africa had become China's second-largest source of crude oil imports.[12] China's largest suppliers of crude oil became Angola, Equatorial Guinea, Nigeria, the Republic of Congo, and Sudan. All of these countries were criticized for their lack of democratic procedures and transparent governance. China also often provided low-interest loans to governments with poor credit ratings allegedly in exchange for oil and mining rights.

China also established a substantial presence in Latin America.[13] Again, it was mainly China's demand for commodities that drove the growth of economic ties. Trade with China created economic booms in resource-rich countries like Brazil. Latin America's largest economy became the world's biggest exporter of some foodstuffs like sugar cane, orange juice, and soy-beans, largely owing to sales to China. China also bought oil from South America. To meet rising industrial needs and consumer demand, China pursued investments and agreements with a variety of Latin American oil producers in Brazil, Venezuela, and Ecuador.

Relations with Russia deepened.[14] Russia and China held joint naval exercises in the Mediterranean and the Sea of Japan in 2014. They joined forces at the United Nations in opposing American initiatives in Libya and Syria, and pursued a similar policy on Iran. In May 2014, China and Russia signed a US$400 billion gas deal, giving Moscow access to the profitable Chinese market for its leading export product, and further connecting the economies of the two major powers. Despite a rocky history of alliances and rivalries, Russia and China continued to draw closer. Both were motivated to balance the economic, political, and military dominance of the United States, and to a lesser extent of Europe, in global affairs, and worked to limit US influence in Central Asia, the Middle East, and the northern Pacific.

China built a highly visible global presence. Its economic development and growing trade smoothed relations on the periphery and opened access to the world strategically. Around 2010, China's state-owned Development Bank outdid the World Bank in issuing international loans. The effort to create an internationally funded institution to finance transportation and other infrastructure in the Asia-Pacific region led to the establishment of the Asian Infrastructure Investment Bank in 2014—which drew the support of fifty-seven countries, including several of the United States' closest allies, despite opposition from the United States. In late 2015, China's currency, the renminbi, was anointed as a global reserve currency, putting it on par with the dollar, the euro, the pound, and the yen. In 2016, China had nearly $4 trillion in foreign currency reserves, which it was determined to invest overseas, both to earn a profit and to exert its influence.

Under Xi Jinping, China set out on a new ambitious program known as "One Belt, One Road" (OBOR). The wording was confusing: "belt" meant the land-bound trading route through Central Asia and Europe, while "road" referred to the maritime route stretching from Southeast Asia across the Indian Ocean to the Middle East, Africa, and Europe. Through loans, infrastructure programs, and acquisitions, the program sought to revive the ancient silk roads by building ports, roads, rail, and telecommunications links in sixty-eight countries (to begin with), all connecting with China. OBOR was designed to build vital infrastructure, spread prosperity, and drive global development, but China also pushed its projects to secure access to key resources, to export its idle industrial capacity, and even to shape the world order in its favor.

Less positively for China, the deep immersion in global flows created a whole new category of security challenges. It caused new pressures and new levels of mutual vulnerability. Some pressures, such as the outbreak of global financial crises, currency shocks, and the fluctuations of global commodity markets, could not be contained by China alone. But specific geostrategic challenges, such as safeguarding China's global presence and securing global infrastructure, were met with a continued strengthening of the military.[15]

After the Communist Revolution in 1949, the People's Liberation Army had emerged as both a bulwark against external threats and a domestic guardian of the party's power. Its numbers were always tilted toward the land armies stationed across China to maintain domestic control. China's leaders tried to invest more in air and naval forces to project influence abroad and assert the country's claims to disputed islands and waters. To achieve its goals, China started to spend heavily on its navy, including on nuclear-powered submarines. After launching its first aircraft carrier in 2012, China began the construction of a second aircraft carrier to be commissioned in 2019. Its Coast Guard grew rapidly and acquired the world's largest cutter, a 10,000-metric-ton vessel built at the Jiangnan shipyard, where workers nicknamed it "the monster." The buildup of maritime power signified that China, traditionally a continental power, was transforming its capabilities. It would secure its interests along the vital sea lanes passing from the South China Sea through the Strait of Malacca and across the Indian Ocean to Africa and the Middle East into Europe—a route across which much of China's commercial trade and energy supplies traveled.

China's official defense spending nearly quintupled in terms of nominal renminbi since 2002. China's defense spending was roughly 1.3 percent of its (rapidly growing) GDP in 2017. It remained largely constant. The 2017 military budget was probably around $150 billion, making China the world's second-largest military spender after the United States, which paid more for its armed forces than the next eight highest-spending countries combined. China's actual military budget was almost certainly higher than the official number, but still far less than that of the United States. Widespread concerns about the objective reality of China's rapidly increasing military capabilities were complicated by low transparency of the government. The Chinese government did not issue regular statistics on its military forces, leaving experts to rely on estimates. It was widely assumed that the army had about 1.6 million personnel, the navy, 240,000, and the air force, 400,000. Many of its recruits were youths from the countryside, or just out of high school, who lacked the skills that are needed to work well in a modern military equipped with high technology. In 2015 Xi Jinping announced a cut that would shrink China's military personnel to two million. This was the biggest reduction since 1997, when half a million were demobilized, according to the state-run agencies. The Chinese military would remain the world's largest, compared with the United States' active-duty force of 1.4 million.[16]

China's military expansion was generally seen to be consistent with its economic size and growth. Nevertheless, China's increasingly powerful military and its modernization alarmed other Asian nations, many of which had come into diplomatic conflict with China in recent years. In territorial disputes with Japan, Vietnam, and other neighbors over rival maritime claims, China also signaled that its government would back its claims with force. China's policies toward territorial and resource disputes therefore constituted a contentious and critical issue in its relations with many Asian countries along its periphery. Japan, Vietnam, and the Philippines were among those most concerned, as was the United States, the preeminent military power in Asia. The United States stressed that it generally took no sides in territorial disputes but maintained stability and freedom of navigation in the region. Besides mapping out possible conflicts over territorial disputes in the East and South China seas, the military in China was focused on potential war scenarios over Taiwan, which China considered part of its territory. As part of its 1979 agreement with Taiwan, the US government had approved arms sales to Taiwan, to which China strongly objected. The United States had also pledged to defend Taiwan in case of attack.

China became a very large presence in international politics and in economic markets around the globe—however, it was often observed that, in many ways, China's presence on the world stage was "partial" or incomplete.[17]

There was a mismatch between its appearance and its real footprint. China became part of many international institutions, but often it was only loosely integrated. China often stood alone and didn't fully succeed in winning over close allies. Even its closest relations with Russia or North Korea remained beset with distrust and rivalry beneath the surface. Its diplomacy also seemed hesitant and narrowly self-interested. China often made known what it opposed, but rarely what it actively supported. Concepts such as a "peaceful rise" or "harmonious world" were not very persuasive, and Beijing was unable to credibly explain or convey its global ambitions. China's growing power and regional relationships were often marked by widespread uncertainties and insecurities about the future. Its behavior sometimes elicited backlash. Surging military spending and military modernization created a more volatile climate in East Asia. Long-standing disputes over maritime boundaries and territorial claims still simmered. In 2012, aggregate military spending in Asia surpassed that of Europe for the first time in modern history. Yet most important to note is that, regardless of China's actual intentions, the objective reality of Beijing's growing military power was threatening to other states and appeared assertive—particularly in light of its rapidly expanding military capabilities and policies regarding disputed territories and other features on its periphery.

China's economic global presence reflected similar uncertainties. The economic developments, as successful as they might have been, appeared fragile and vulnerable. Long an engine of global growth, China took on new risks by exposing itself to unstable political regimes, volatile emerging markets, and other economic forces beyond its control. While China's substantial assets allowed it to withstand serious economic setbacks, the overall health of the economy mattered. When China slowed down, the effects were felt worldwide by the companies, industries, and economies that depended on its growth. On the one hand, China had become a large and pervasive presence in the global economy, but on the other hand it exported uncertainty around the world. Industries and entire regions had predicated their strategies and plans on China's continued growth. Companies and whole countries stood to suffer setbacks should China's growth engine sputter.

To conclude, China's global record was mixed. It continued to dream about reviving historical greatness and becoming a rich, powerful, and modern country. Great strides were made, but the direction of the future remained opaque. Despite many achievements, much about China's international affairs left the impression that a long-term durable direction or blueprint was missing and that the government was instead preoccupied with coordinating a series of effective but short-term and ad hoc adjustments.

Rising Social Tensions

As China made the transition from a command economy to a market economy, the country enjoyed sustained double-digit growth and rising living standards. The social repercussions of the transition to a market economy that rippled through the economy, society, politics, and culture in China were far-reaching, perhaps even cataclysmic. As China's place in the world economy was redefined, changes also radiated through society, touching upon every citizen and inflicting costs on individuals and communities. The parameters of society and citizenship were fundamentally altered.

The development of the southern city of Shenzhen reflected both the successes and challenges of the nation's path. Shenzhen, in the Pearl River Delta near Hong Kong, had long been a poor village. When China opened to capitalism and foreign investment in 1979, Deng Xiaoping chose to start the reforms in Shenzhen as China's first Special Economic Zone. Development was faster here than anywhere else. Three decades later, the city had some of China's biggest skyscrapers and shopping malls, and a new subway. The majority of all consumer appliances sold worldwide were assembled in Shenzhen and the surrounding Guangdong province. The area was also recognized as a magnet for technology entrepreneurs. But Shenzhen's torrid and uncontrolled growth also mirrored many of China's most acute problems, such as overcrowding, corruption, pollution, and the absence of accountability. Shenzhen also became known for poor working conditions and questionable labor practices at its vast complex of electronics factories. The problems were highlighted by a spate of suicides and accidents at facilities owned by Foxconn, a Taiwanese company employing hundreds of thousands of Chinese workers and known for assembling Apple products like iPhones and iPads.[18] Suicides and accidents were said to be caused by long working hours and unsafe working conditions.

Beyond Shenzhen, new opportunities in a reformed China allowed society a greater degree of autonomy and the ability to engage in a broad range of productive and profitable activities. Social differentiation continued to play out and accelerate: many different social groups, including successful young urbanites, laid-off workers, peasants, migrant laborers, and even beggars, emerged to replace the few larger social classes of the past. But new risks and threats brought increased insecurity and material and cultural losses, especially to members of weaker groups in society, such as the elderly, migrant workers from rural areas, the young, women, and minorities. A society emerged that was characterized by deepening social rifts and dislocations, whether measured in terms of gender, generations, social classes, ethnic relations, or urban-versus-rural divisions. Different reactions could be observed to the widening inequalities that came with the new globalizing market economy.

The one-child policy, as it came to be known, became one of the most troubling, most contested, and most sensitive social issues of modern times. Announced by the government in September 1980, this decision to limit couples to having just one child generated major conflict and controversy within the country and outside of it. It bred intense resentment over the intrusions involved, including forced abortions and crippling fines, especially in the countryside. Of all the countries in the world that faced the fear of population explosion in the latter half of the twentieth century, only China resorted to such radical policies.

The policy dated back to the late 1970s, when Chinese scientists and officials started to discuss problems of population growth.[19] The immediate concern was to slow down the speed of population growth in China, which was seen as a major obstacle to successful modernization. China had accomplished great gains in average lifespans in the 1950s by establishing order and a health care system. The birth rate, meanwhile, rose, with the result that, according to census data, the population grew from 583 million in 1953 to just over one billion by 1982. Based on calculations by Chinese demographers and statisticians at the time, there were widespread fears that population growth would spin out of control, eating up economic gains and preventing China's escape from poverty. To the CCP, population control seemed a prerequisite for successful development. At first, in the 1970s, the party began a campaign urging late marriage, long birth intervals, and fewer

12.2. Pedestrians in front of a huge billboard extolling the virtues of China's one-child policy, 1985.

Peter Charlesworth / Getty Images / 158661292

children *(wan xi shao)*. That campaign succeeded in reducing the birth rate significantly, from 4.2 births per woman in 1974 to 3.5 in 1976, and further to 2.6 in 1980.[20]

Yet this reduction in the birth rate was not fast enough for the government, which looked for a quicker solution to the population problem. In 1980 it decided to enact a policy permitting no more than one child to each couple, which aimed to accelerate China's transformation into a wealthy, modern, global power. Systematic measures to make sure that couples had only one child were subsequently enforced. Some categories of people, however, were exempt from it. These included ethnic minorities, people living in the border areas, Chinese returned from overseas, and couples whose first child was disabled and would not be able to work. In rural areas, where sons especially were supposed to support their parents in old age, the policy often encountered resistance. The most important exception, which was introduced for rural areas after 1986, was that peasant couples whose first child was a girl could have a second child. Later, another exception was added: couples who were both single children themselves could have a second child. In 2002, a population and family planning law was passed to provide a legal basis for the state's control over family planning. China eased some restrictions on the one-child policy in 2013, allowing couples to have two children if even just one of the spouses was an only child. However, many eligible couples declined to have a second child, citing the expense and pressures of raising children in a highly competitive society. Driven by fears that an aging population could jeopardize China's economic ascent, Communist Party leadership relaxed its decades-old policy in October 2015, announcing that all married couples would be allowed to have two children.[21] In 2018, it was rumored that the government would soon lift the policy altogether. Due to the falling birth rates, it was even considering measures to persuade women to have more children.

In general, the one-child policy was implemented using both incentives and penalties. The Chinese government created various penalties through the work-unit system to enforce the one-child policy in urban areas, particularly in the 1980s. Those who had an extra child, according to the law, had to pay for the extra burden they imposed on society. They would necessarily use more public resources. Hence, couples violating the one-child policy were subject to high taxes, loss of jobs, decrease in wages, loss of benefits from the work units, and in some cases, loss of bonuses for their entire work group. In rural areas, the household incentive system was set up to offer a premium for those families who complied with this policy. In addition to a regular propaganda campaign, the State Planning Commission oversaw coercive measures such as forced abortions in makeshift facilities, compulsory intrauterine device insertion, and in some cases, compulsory sterilization. In all, an estimated 16.4 million women and 4.2 million men were sterilized. There were also many forced adoptions.

Based on the countrywide census in 2010, the government concluded that China's population had reached 1.34 billion (1.38 billion in 2016), an increase of 73.9 million, or 5.8 percent, from the last tally in 2000.[22] That was below the 1.4 billion that United Nations demographers had predicted, and the slowest rate of growth in nearly half a century. The Chinese government claimed that birth planning had helped prevent 400 million births and aided the nation's rapid economic development. This remained a subject of considerable controversy, however, in academic and population policy circles. There was reason to believe that without a coercive and costly policy, China's birthrate would have declined anyway. Meanwhile, there could be little doubt that the enforcement of the one-child policy in the reform era brought about a series of social problems and unforeseen consequences. The most severe consequences were the long-term demographic prospects. Fertility levels in China fell below the level of replacement, which is 2.1 children per couple. Across a decade of data, however, the level never exceeded 1.5 in many places. In Shanghai, where many young couples were allowed to have two children because both husband and wife were themselves only children, the 2010 census found a fertility level of 0.7, one-third of the replacement level. In 2013, for every elderly person receiving benefits, there were five taxpaying workers. Projections showed that this would soon drop to only two taxpaying workers. Rapidly, the state in China had to deal with the problems arising from an aging population. The consequences were particularly pronounced in the countryside, where massive out-migration had left elderly villagers with no adult children nearby to support them. With the gradual withdrawal of state support for the elderly, their care grew to depend more on the family system, thereby exacerbating this demographic problem. Aging societies presented a challenge that even advanced economies, like Germany and Japan, found difficult to address. The dilemma was intensified by the fact that wealth in China was so unevenly distributed. While the problem of an aging population was nothing new for many countries in the developed world, the grim observation was that "China will become old before it becomes rich."[23] Some demographers noted that, in the decades to come, China would find itself with an insufficient labor force.

Family size decreased, especially in urban areas. Among the social implications was a generation of only children who were nurtured by their parents and four grandparents. Their ability to monopolize so much loving attention led to a phenomenon that some called the "little emperor syndrome."[24] On the one hand, these only children were spoiled, but on the other hand, all their families' hopes were invested in them, creating great pressure to succeed.

The efforts to limit family size also led to a skewed sex ratio of males to females.[25] Historically and culturally, sons in Chinese families were responsible for taking care of the elderly, along with carrying the family name and inheriting the family property. As a result, male offspring were preferred in Chinese families, especially in rural areas. Under the one-child policy, female infanticide, while difficult to quantify, occurred on large scale. It has been estimated that, beginning in 1980, two hundred thousand female babies were killed each year. Female children were also frequently abandoned, though no estimates on the numbers are available. Many girls' births went unregistered, causing them to lose access to legal benefits, including educational opportunities and other forms of social welfare. Finally, the use of advanced technologies such as ultrasound increased the number of abortions of female fetuses. All of this left China with a significant gender gap. According to Chinese statistics, boys increasingly outnumbered girls among registered newborns in both rural and urban areas. Chinese census figures indicate that there were 107 infant boys for every 100 infant girls in 1982, 110 in 1990, and 117 in 2007. The ratio declined after the policy was reversed.[26]

Whatever its intentions, the one-child policy arose from a belief that social engineering was a legitimate activity for the state. It violated one of the most basic human rights and was most likely also largely unnecessary, for the previous policy based on voluntary measures was already diminishing fertility rates. The one-child policy might go down in history as China's worst policy mistake in the post-Mao era.

The reform and opening policy also had other consequences that were no less transformative. The reform policy relaxed the grip of the state in many realms. It opened the way for hundreds of millions of people to change their places of work and residence and seek new employment opportunities. There were massive rural labor outflows of workers in search of employment. The root cause for migration was the lack of sufficient employment in the countryside in many inland provinces. The economic impact of the reforms heavily favored coastal over inland areas with state investment, giving them privileged access to international capital and markets. State and private funds poured into rapidly industrializing coastal areas that spearheaded China's export boom. Rural migrant workers could choose between a low-paying farm job (or no job) at home and a better-paying, low-end job in a city. Most rural migrants decided to seek their luck in the cities to be able to send money back to families remaining in rural areas. Many went to nearby towns outside their villages, but some crossed thousands of kilometers to big cities on the coast.

The term "rural migrant labor" refers to the working population from the countryside that moved to a destination without a local *hukou* registration.[27] Most of this work was seasonal, operating in synchronization with farm work schedules (the outflow was larger in winter when there was not much work

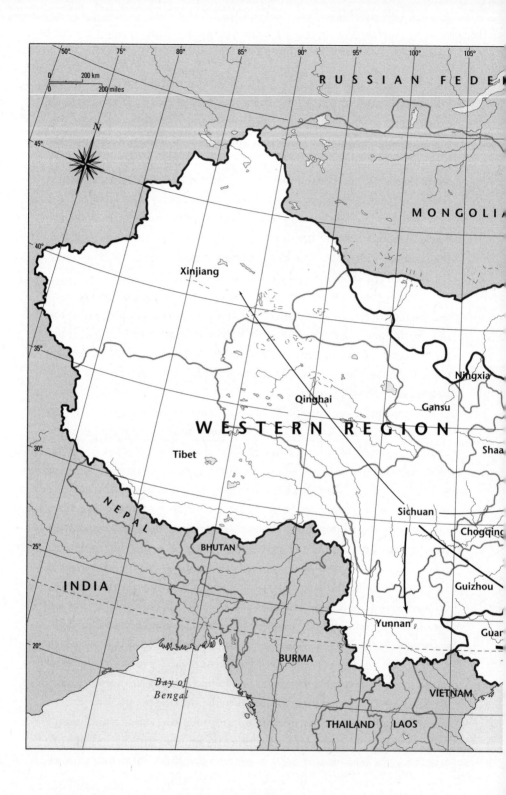

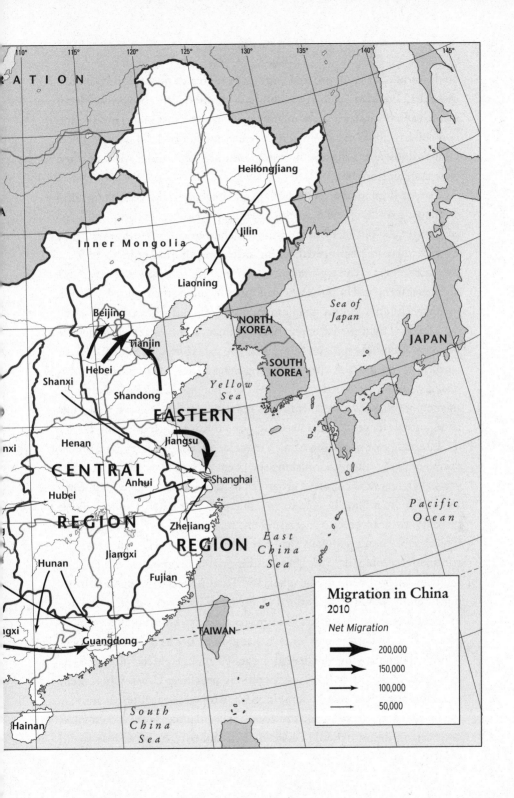

110° 115° 120° 125° 130° 135° 140° 145°

R A T I O N

Heilongjiang

Inner Mongolia

Jilin

Liaoning

Beijing

Tianjin

Hebei

Shanxi

Shandong

NORTH
KOREA

Sea of
Japan

JAPAN

SOUTH
KOREA

Yellow
Sea

EASTERN

nxi

Henan

Jiangsu

CENTRAL

Anhui

Shanghai

Hubei

REGION

Zhejiang

Hunan

Jiangxi

REGION

East
China
Sea

Pacific
Ocean

Fujian

ngxi

Guangdong

TAIWAN

Migration in China
2010

Net Migration

→ 200,000

→ 150,000

→ 100,000

— 50,000

Hainan

South
China
Sea

on the farm). Between 1992 and 2006, the number of rural migrant laborers more than doubled, from 53 million to 115 million. The 2010 census documented an even vaster internal migration, concluding that more than 261 million citizens (in 2017: 292 million)—nearly one in five—did not live where China's household registration system indicated they did.[28] Most of those were migrant laborers.

Despite the important contributions that migrant workers made to China's economic growth, migrant laborers faced numerous discriminations and disadvantages. As "outsiders" in the cities or richer agricultural areas where they worked, migrants confronted daunting formal and informal restrictions. Since they lacked valid urban registrations, they remained ineligible for many rights and benefits enjoyed by those who had them, including the right to education for their children in local public schools, health and welfare benefits, and even the legal right to rent or purchase apartments. They were also vulnerable to exploitation and expulsion from cities. The state continued to view migrant workers as second-class citizens, calling them a "floating population" (liudong renkou). It remained wary of them as a potential source of conflict. As their numbers soared, permanent urban residents also came to see the migrants as responsible for crime and, increasingly, as a threat to their own jobs.[29]

Internal labor migration of such magnitude resulted in regional imbalances and rapid urbanization along the coast. As a result, within thirty-five years after 1980, the country's urban population increased more than four-fold (from 190 million in 1980 to 792 million in 2015). It was projected that it would, by 2030, reach a staggering one billion people. This would make China's cities more populous than the entire North and South American continents combined.[30] The three fastest-growing regions were the urban municipalities of Beijing, Shanghai, and Tianjin. Between 2000 and 2010, both Beijing and Shanghai added about six million people, at an average annual growth rate of more than 3 percent. The two next highest-growth provinces were Guangdong and Zhejiang, both of them powerhouses of China's economic growth. Guangdong added about eighteen million to its population, making it the most populous province. Urban China went through a great real estate boom. In China's top cities, real prices grew by 13.1 percent annually from 2003 to 2013. Real land prices in the largest cities skyrocketed almost five-fold between 2004 and 2015. As prices rose, so did construction.

12.3. Headquarters of China Central Television amid the Beijing skyline of the central business district, August 2013.

Feng Li / Getty Images / 175373577

The reforms also dramatically changed the parameters that determined income and social status. In the 1990s, tens of millions of workers in state-owned enterprises lost their guarantees of lifetime employment and accompanying benefits. Moreover, when enterprises were privatized, the dismissed workers also lost welfare benefits such as pensions they had worked long and hard to secure. Those who retained their jobs were required to sign contracts with their employers, initially for a maximum of five years, and later often for just one year. The "iron rice bowl" of lifetime employment was smashed to the disadvantage of workers. Many more workers were hired on short-term contracts with neither security nor benefits of any kind, and had to compete with rural migrants ready to work for lower wages than formerly paid to state workers.[31] Low-skilled and older urban workers were also confronted with increasing competition from rural migrants and often found themselves locked out of the labor market. At the same time, rapid urban growth raised incomes for highly skilled, younger workers and those with special access to opportunities in the new economy. Income inequality grew considerably. The

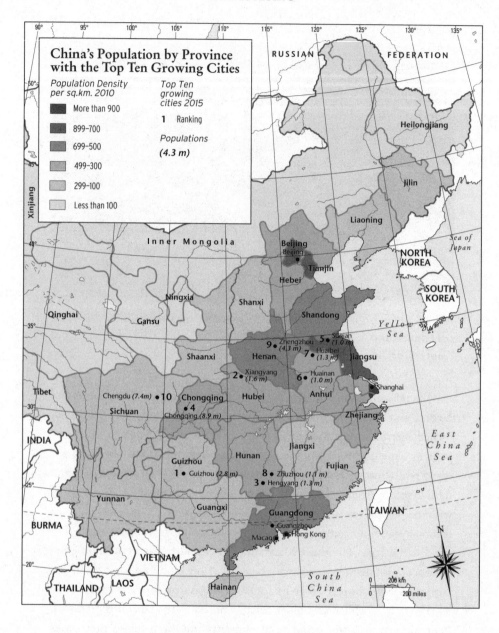

China's Population by Province with the Top Ten Growing Cities

Population Density per sq.km. 2010

More than 900
899–700
699–500
499–300
299–100
Less than 100

Top Ten growing cities 2015

1 Ranking

Populations

(4.3 m)

gap separating rich and poor, and the gap across social groups and ethnic lines, grew immensely. In contrast to the earlier emphasis on equality under Mao, reformers were ready to accept inequalities under Deng's reassuring slogan: "Let some get rich first." The substantial rise in social and economic inequality was documented in a wide range of studies by individual researchers, international organizations, and government agencies.[32] Naturally, estimates of the level of inequality vary, but all observers agree that after the 1990s, China, once a relatively egalitarian country, became, in terms of income, wealth, and opportunities, one of the world's most unequal societies.

Social institutions were altered as well. The *danwei* and even the *hukou*, for instance, lost much of their original function of providing welfare and social safety they originally had under Mao. But it would be a mistake to believe that they became completely obsolete; instead, in the transition to a market economy, they acquired different meaning. Institutions such as *danwei* moderated the effects of the market economy.[33] Preserving certain social entitlements embedded in the rural economy and in the urban work unit system, they often mitigated the worst exploitation workers were exposed to on the assembly lines. The work units, for instance, also allowed state workers to purchase former welfare housing at subsidized prices. This housing reform made them private property owners, providing an economic safety net even in the event of enterprise bankruptcy. The much-criticized household registration system that subjected migrant workers to second-class citizenship status, making them a cheap labor pool to be tapped by global capital, also conferred land-use rights to those with rural household registrations. These institutions generated a new degree of allegiance to the state—an effect that is often overlooked.

Gaps between regions and classes, as well as economic and social inequalities, were frequently widened by distinctions of ethnicity. The post-Mao leadership of China called upon ethnic minorities to unite forces behind China's drive to become a strong and wealthy country. Ethnic minorities made up roughly 8.5 percent of the country's population, or 110 million people. The areas in which they lived covered more than half of China's land, including 90 percent of its border area, and held much of its forests, animal husbandry, meat production, minerals, and medicinal plants.

The government maintained a policy of autonomy for minority regions. The 1984 (revised in 2001) Law of the People's Republic of China on Regional

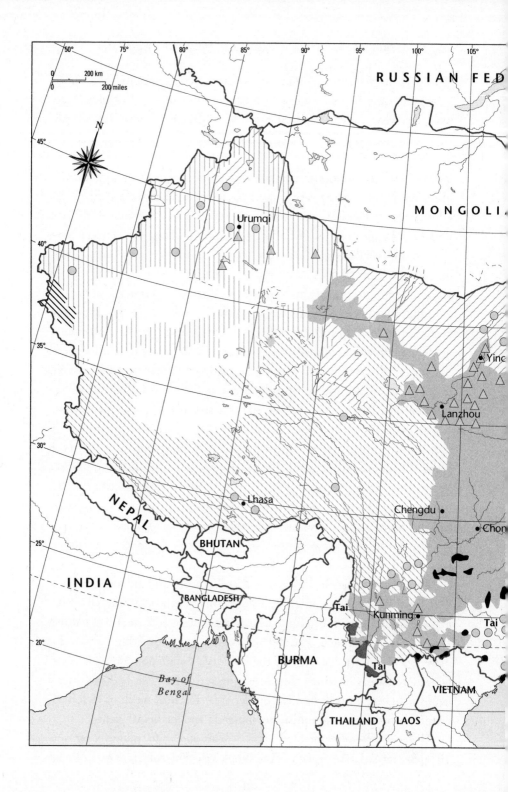

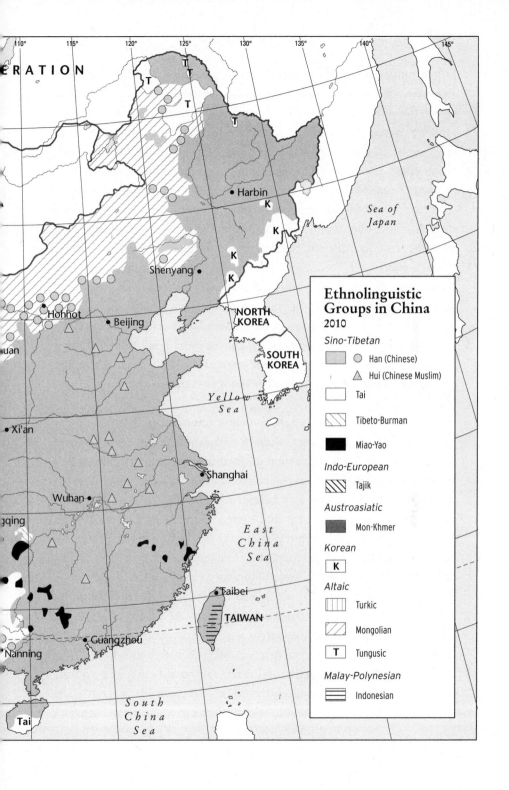

ΕRATION

Harbin
K

Sea of
Japan

Shenyang

NORTH
KOREA

Hohhot
Beijing

SOUTH
KOREA

uan

Yellow
Sea

Xi'an

Shanghai

Wuhan

East
China
Sea

jqing

Taibei

TAIWAN

Guangzhou

Nanning

South
China
Sea

Tai

**Ethnolinguistic
Groups in China**
2010

Sino-Tibetan

Han (Chinese)

Hui (Chinese Muslim)

Tai

Tibeto-Burman

Miao-Yao

Indo-European

Tajik

Austroasiatic

Mon-Khmer

Korean

K

Altaic

Turkic

Mongolian

T   Tungusic

Malay-Polynesian

Indonesian

Ethnic Autonomy stipulated that "regional autonomy shall be practiced in areas where minority nationalities live in concentrated communities." This included five province-level regions, thirty prefectures, 117 counties, and, after 1993, 1,173 autonomous or ethnic townships. Jiang Zemin gave a major speech on this issue during the First National Conference on Ethnic Affairs in 1992. He emphasized the need for national unity and refuted demands for independence from any minority area. However, he also announced that the government would continue the policies of ethnic autonomy. He highlighted the importance of economic development in the ethnic areas, which would allow them to keep pace with the rest of the country, and of social welfare for minority peoples.[34] Fifteen years later, reiterating many of the same points, Hu Jintao, in his speech to the Seventeenth National Congress in October 2007, stressed the need to "cement the great unity of the people of all ethnic groups, and enhance the great solidarity of all sons and daughters of the Chinese nation at home and overseas and of the Chinese people and peoples of other countries, which will give us immense strength to overcome all difficulties and obstacles and achieve new, greater victories in the cause of the party and the people."[35]

Many minorities welcomed the economic reforms, especially since many had suffered greatly during the Cultural Revolution. They were relieved to see a renewed emphasis on the cultural distinctiveness of minority cultures and more respect for their heritage and religions. However, conflicts appeared as the central government announced plans to develop the rich natural resources of some of the autonomous regions. Beijing also appeared to encourage Han Chinese to move to the border regions, and as word spread of readily available land and other incentives, the numbers of Chinese heading west increased. As a result, the ethnic groups in many autonomous areas were no longer in the majority. Most areas changed over to majority Han populations. With the influx of Han Chinese came economic disadvantages. As more Han people migrated from inland to the frontier to seek economic opportunities, they formed separate, booming economic networks, often excluding locals.[36]

Ethnic conflicts flared up time and again—above all, between Han on one side and Tibetans and Uighurs on the other.[37] Of particular concern to the government were rising tensions in oil-rich Xinjiang, home to the Uighurs, a Muslim group numbering some eight million people in the 1980s. Xinjiang was the site of secessionist governments in 1933 and 1944 (as noted in previous chapters), both of which sought to overthrow Chinese provincial governments and establish an independent East Turkestan. Tibet likewise could recall a history of independence from China given that, from 1912 to 1950, it was autonomously ruled. Simmering tensions and resentments sometimes culminated in large-scale riots, such as those on March 14, 2008, in Tibet and July 5, 2009, in Xinjiang. Between February 2009 and June 2015, in a little over six years, 146 Tibetans self-immolated in Tibetan areas, and more than a hundred of those are known to have died. The government characterized the riots and self-immolations as results of separatist instigation, but the reasons were far more complex than that. The riots were tied to structures of the regional economy, where minorities were at a disadvantage. They had a hard time finding employment and were paid less. Some minorities, especially Uighurs and Tibetans, came to believe that the Han Chinese state did not respect or value minorities, especially their political and economic interests. The state's national education also intended to "civilize" or educate minorities, especially in the restive provinces of Xinjiang and Tibet. To "civilize" minorities meant to push them to learn the Chinese language, culture, and history at the expense of their own languages, cultures, and histories.

The Chinese Communist Party and its government's strategy to deal with nationalist and separatist movements was twofold. First, separatism had to be suppressed ruthlessly in the short term by use of military force. Second, economic development and investment designed to improve the living conditions of the population of Xinjiang and Tibet were promoted as the long-term answers. Officials believed that the rise of living standards among minorities would create social stability. Those expectations, however, proved elusive, and the results of development in those regions were mixed. The Chinese government seldom responded to what minorities themselves demanded, such as the protection of their culture, religion, and political autonomy. Behind the rising ethnic conflicts in China were more fundamental issues, whether these were about national identity and education, about inequalities as a result of economic development, or about the problems of the state's ethnic policies.

The repercussions of the social transformation affected the social position of women, as well. During the Mao era, women enjoyed high symbolic importance, as promoting the equality of men and women was high on the agenda. In the post-Mao era, that political importance dwindled. Rapid social changes in the reform era brought many new opportunities, especially for younger and highly educated women. Before long, about 20 percent of all companies were run by women. Of the fourteen women appearing on the global Forbes list of self-made billionaires, half hailed from China. Many women in China had jobs and contributed to the family income. But there was a darker side: less educated middle-aged and older women were often left to fend for themselves against the onslaught of the market economy. Many younger, rural women migrated to cities in search of work. Known as working sisters or working girls (*dagong mei*), they comprised 30 to 40 percent of the "floating population" in the late 1990s. Some of them found themselves subject to exploitation and suppression by various forms of power and capital. If they had children, their children were mostly raised by their parents back in their rural homes, in the often difficult conditions typical of "left-behind children."

Urban women, more vulnerable to layoffs, often found themselves without jobs when state-owned enterprises were privatized or went bankrupt.[38] Middle-aged and older women, especially those lacking special skills and training, were treated as the most superfluous of all workers. Women textile workers, who constituted a major part of redundant women workers, were the least remunerated of all workers, and the first to be hit by workforce reductions. With job loss also came loss of welfare entitlements and social safety. Well-educated women were also confronted with discrimination. Female college graduates encountered want ads specifying "women need not apply." Suddenly, Chinese women realized that the revolutionary ideal of equality was a dream that was nearly gone or had never come true.

It would, however, be misleading to portray the changes originating from the transition to market economy completely and exclusively in negative terms of exploitation and discrimination. Despite the government's focus on economic reform, the fact that the political, economic, and social systems were intertwined in the past meant that reforming the economy inevitably would lead to fundamental changes that extended to political and social aspects. Individuals, families, and associations, which had been under state dominance, were increasingly able to make their own economic decisions. With the re-emergence of the private sector, individuals gained the freedom to pursue their personal interests and plans in the newly emerging markets. The reliance of individuals on the state was undone as the party state acted no longer as the key economic decision maker and no longer exercised full control over individuals and their livelihoods. To be sure, state officials still had power—for instance, to exchange official privileges for favors (for example, housing arrangements), to pursue personal benefits, or to silence criticism—but they lost the absolute control over economic and social resources they had had in the Maoist period. In the marketplace, individuals could access nearly all their everyday necessities, if they could afford them. The organizational dependency of individuals on work units and party cadres largely disappeared and power relations based on the patron-client ties in the workplace broke down. This process of decentralization and depoliticization also created new spaces for civil engagement. Many individuals used this increased freedom to engage in social activism and community involvement.[39] The reform period saw an impressive rise in social activism by a wide range of social groups, including workers, peasants, environmentalists, journalists, homeowners, feminists, religious communities, ethnic minorities, AIDS activists, and human rights advocates, among others. Aggrieved social groups deployed local resources like "barefoot lawyers," neighborhood solidarity groups, domestic Chinese law, and the courts, while engaging in local activism to pressure local officials. Activists in religious, cultural, feminist, and environmentalist movements established networks that crossed localities, regions, and even nations. Partially to deal with the challenges presented by social activism, and also to alleviate the anxieties and conflicts that accompanied the tremendous changes in both the economic and social arenas, the state initiated an expansion of the legal system. Based on the concept of "a socialist country under the rule of law," introduced by Jiang Zemin at the Fifteenth National Congress in 1997, broad legal reforms were pursued. While stressing the role of law, the party made it clear that there would be no change to the primacy of the state. Legal codes were issued that provided guidelines on a broad range of issues, including labor relations, intellectual property rights, environment, commerce, land use, property, and associational rights for NGOs. Between 1979 and 2006, the National People's Congress, China's supreme legislative body, enacted and updated more than two hundred laws that are generally consistent with accepted principles of international law.[40] A massive educational campaign was launched to publicize the new regulations. Mediation and arbitration offices, as well as the courts, were beefed up to handle the growing number of disputes and protests, in an effort to defuse conflicts that might otherwise produce violent confrontation. A further step toward a comprehensive overhaul of the legal system was taken on March 14, 2004, when China's parliament approved thirteen amendments to its constitution. The amendments addressed private property and human rights in general terms but did not limit the government's power to crack down on protests. For example, one amendment stated that "the state respects and preserves human rights." Another proclaimed that "citizens' lawful private property is inviolable," and that the state would compensate property owners when it confiscated their property.

Above all, by building a solid legal system, the government tried to move the arena of conflict from the streets to the courts. The government gradually ceded a good deal of authority to the market, to the courts, and to other institutions that grappled on a daily basis with the complex decisions and policies required of a rapidly changing economy and society on a daily basis. This partial withdrawal by the party provided a degree of political space for the development of a "rule of law with Chinese characteristics," as it were. As a result, it is no exaggeration to state that, across the span of more than a century, Chinese citizens had not enjoyed such a degree of legal protection and security—although, of course, the party was always able to infringe on those rights if its core interests were at stake.

Law is not just a tool of governance, but also a resource that may be appropriated by social groups who use the law as a terrain to make their claims and to pressure the state to keep its legal, contractual, and ethical obligations to the working people. In China, the rapid increase in the number of laws and regulations served to activate new social formations, as people with shared economic interests began to use the law to protect themselves against encroachment on their legal rights. Citizen's efforts to protect their legitimate interests and rights in the courts, however, were often disappointed. This led to protests and so-called "mass incidents" in which aggrieved peasants, workers, city residents, and homeowners staged protests over food safety, environmental pollution, or industrial accidents that challenged or engaged the state.[41] Some of their more confrontational tactics included blocking traffic, obstructing demolition, and even rioting and ransacking government offices. The state responded to such popular resistance by periodically closing down vocal newspapers or punishing critical journalists and editors, publicly denouncing influential intellectuals, arresting leaders, and harassing and directing violence against protesters. In many instances, however, the state made significant concessions. The public's mobilization has forced various state agencies to respond with revised decisions, policy changes, and reforms down the line, such as rural taxation and medical reform, revisions to labor and property rights law, and expansion of social security into the countryside, to mention but a few. Somewhat paradoxically, then, China's lack of democratic processes and institutions seemed to increase the urgency to deal with public problems and political challenges.[42] Public mass protests alarmed the government, and for that very reason forced it into quick action to assign blame, arrest officials, and pay compensations. While the lack of democratic procedure for expressing and solving popular discontent was certainly a main cause for the depth of a number of these social and political unrests, that same democratic deficit compelled the government to quickly find effective solutions to scandals and social problems.

The profound social and political changes discussed in this section were ambiguous and defy easy categorization. The transition to a market economy generated tremendous inequality in terms of opportunities, income, and market outcomes. This resulted in differentiations along the lines of generation, locality, ethnicity, and gender, and also fragmented the interests of citizens, social groups, and ethnic minorities across localities and factories. At the same time, the decentralization of economic and political power made local state officials more responsible for enforcing legal regulations, but also made them targets of local discontent and resistance, if policies did not work out or were mistaken, thus opening up new spaces for activism and civil engagement.

Growing Uncertainties

The world admired the speed and success of China's "economic miracle," which occurred when the economy grew, opened up, urbanized, and industrialized at breakneck speed. Inside China, however, the mood was far less upbeat. Neither the Chinese people nor their government seemed at ease with the achievements and results of the rapid development. To be sure, there was enormous popular pride taken in China's ascent to the ranks of global superpowers, and general satisfaction with the material benefits that both the poor and the rich gained from an expanding economy. However, rampant grass-roots protests revealed intense popular indignation at everything from land grabs to environmental pollution, while top officials themselves complained about the corroding effects of materialism, cadre corruption, and income inequality. On the Chinese internet, people vented their concerns, frustrations, and anger regarding a wide range of issues and problems that affected their lives or, in their view, the state of society and future of the nation. In a society notable for mobility and greater media access, including online communication, citizens displayed a heightened awareness of income disparities, lavish conspicuous consumption, and corrupt official practices. Social disparities and tensions fueled popular anger and at times resistance. There was great restlessness, anger about structural injustices and bad governance, and a search for new forms of spirituality and ethics to replace a collapsing moral order.[43] All of this contributed to anxieties and uncertainties regarding the future that shaped the mood of the public in China during the second decade of the twenty-first century.

To a large extent, these feelings are related to one elementary question surrounding China's political institutions. While the economic system was completely overhauled, and became arguably one of the most dynamic in the world, the political institutional order remained largely unchanged. It still was fundamentally a one-party system, in which a Leninist party exercised authoritarian rule. The mobile and innovative economy of China, based on inclusive institutions, was in tension with a political system based on exclusive institutions. The unmediated contradiction between an increasingly complex and open economy and society and a still intact Leninist party state was a persistent problem that China seemed not to be able to resolve. There was widespread skepticism of the long-term compatibility between a flourishing market economy and an authoritarian communist polity, fueling a pervasive feeling of uncertainty. Few people in China were convinced that the political system was set up for the future or that the political institutions were stable or strong enough to weather a big social crisis. This was in contrast to more mature political systems where, problems and conflicts notwithstanding, citizens acted on the assumption that their institutions were enduring and resilient.

The restlessness manifested itself in a number of phenomena that churned the public sphere in China. There was frequent outrage and despair about China's worsening environmental situation. The era of super high growth, above all, took a heavy toll on the environment. There was little question that economic growth came at the expense of the country's air, land, and water resources, much of them already degraded by decades of Stalinist economic planning that emphasized the development of heavy industries in urban areas, and by centuries of deforestation before the modern period.[44] In 2012, less than 1 percent of China's five hundred largest cities met the World Health Organization's air quality standards. The heavy air pollution in China was mostly caused by the use of fossil energy, especially coal, which China relied on for 70 percent of its energy needs. China had abundant supplies of coal and had been burning more of it per year than the United States, Europe, and Japan combined since 2007, although consumption declined after 2014. Energy consumption grew 130 percent from 2000 to 2010. As Chinese citizens became wealthier and moved into cities, they used more energy and contributed more to the environmental problems. Heavy traffic caused by increasing car ownership became the leading source of air pollution in Chinese cities.

Water was an equally acute challenge. China had only one-fifth as much water per capita as the United States. But while southern China was relatively wet, the north—home to about half of China's population—was an extensive, dry region at risk to become the world's biggest desert. Ten northern provinces fell below the World Bank's water-poverty level, resulting in high rates of land degradation and desertification. Industry and agriculture used nearly all of the country's water resources, but household consumption was also on the rise. China's water was also highly polluted. In many parts of China, factories and farms discarded waste into surface water. China's environmental monitors estimated that one-third of all river water, and many of China's great lakes—the Tai, Chao, and Dianchi—had the most degraded quality, rendering their waters unfit for agricultural use and human consumption.[45] At the same time, soil pollution from factories had seriously contaminated some of China's arable land. The Chinese government released a report in 2014 that said nearly one-fifth of its arable land was contaminated—an indication of the toxic results of China's rapid development and its lack of regulations over commercial activities.[46] The soil pollution had severe consequences for the national food chain. There was increasing concern among Chinese citizens and some officials over soil contamination in the main agricultural centers, because of the potential effects on food safety throughout the country.

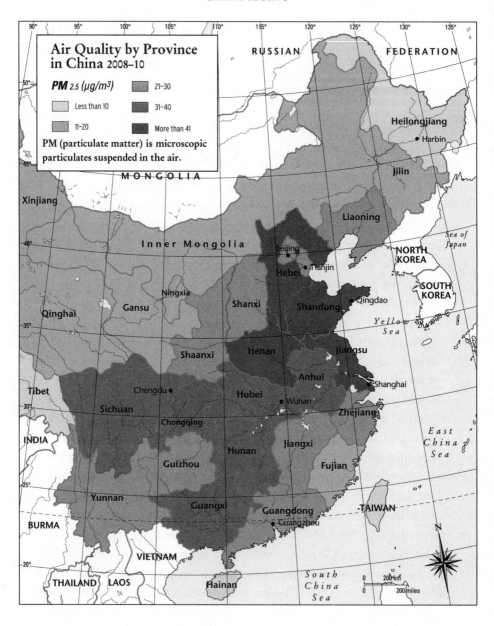

Air Quality by Province in China 2008–10

PM 2.5 *(µg/m³)*

Less than 10
11–20
21–30
31–40
More than 41

PM (particulate matter) is microscopic particulates suspended in the air.

Skyrocketing water and air pollution brought about a number of severe public health challenges. Rising toxic emissions from coal and fuel oil caused growing rates of respiratory and cardiovascular diseases, and so did acid rain. All along China's major rivers, Chinese citizens experienced rising rates of disease such as cancer, tumors, and other health problems related to pollution.

It seemed clear that China's significant environmental problems could only worsen with continued global warming. A 2015 report by the Chinese government provided a dire scientific assessment of the impact of climate change on China.[47] The report urged more spending on preparing to cope with the increasing likelihood of frequent natural calamities such as extreme droughts, floods, and heat waves. Rising sea levels were among the threats receiving most attention in the report. The concern was that, as polar ice melted and ocean temperatures rose, seas across the world would swell. Indeed, because the changes were uneven, the waters off China's coast had already been rising faster than the global average. According to the findings, the sea waters along the coast of eastern China will likely rise between forty and sixty centimeters by the end of the twenty-first century, exposing Shanghai and other cities to tidal floods and severe damage from storms and typhoons. The report also predicted that inland China would experience major shifts in rain and snowfall, which would reshape agriculture. Rising temperatures would also mean the air absorbed more moisture, which would then likely be dumped in increasingly erratic precipitation patterns, especially in northern China. The net effect, according to the report, was that China's water resources, already strained, could shrink 5 percent by midcentury. Irregular shifts in rainfall would not only result in major changes in farming, but could also put unanticipated heavy stress on infrastructure. In addition to environmental or economic risks to China, these changes implied national security issues. Alterations of current river flows and water volumes might then lead to struggles over cross-border water resources along China's southern borders and surges of transnational migration, triggering international disputes and conflict.

As the 2015 report demonstrated, awareness of the severity of the problems grew among the population and the authorities. The government started to address the problem. It set strict standards and ambitious targets, such as mandating the reduction of coal use for electricity generation and the installations of cleaner coal-burning generators in an effort to improve the abysmal

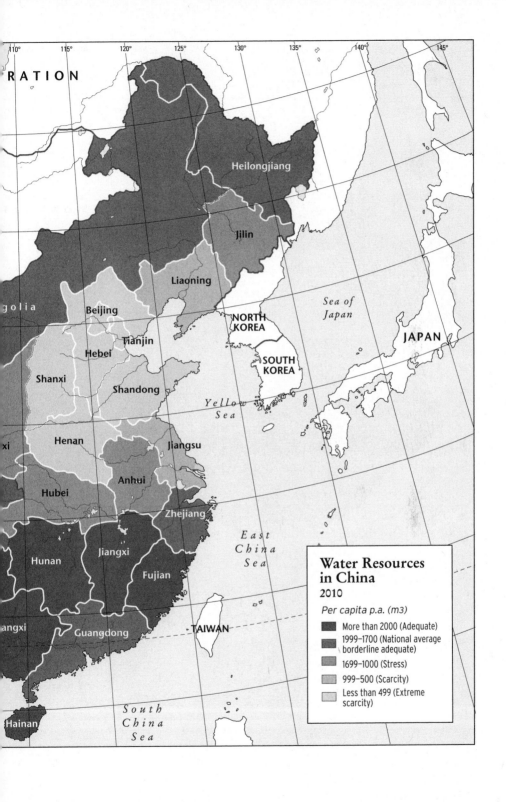

Water Resources in China
2010

Per capita p.a. (m3)

- More than 2000 (Adequate)
- 1999–1700 (National average borderline adequate)
- 1699–1000 (Stress)
- 999–500 (Scarcity)
- Less than 499 (Extreme scarcity)

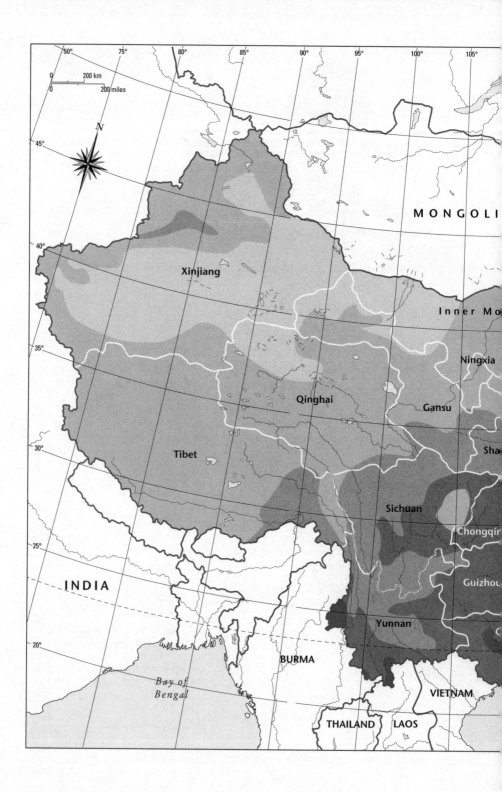

RUSSIAN FEDERATION

Heilongjiang

Jilin

Liaoning

Beijing

Tianjin

Hebei

Shanxi

Shandong

Henan

Jiangsu

Anhui

Hubei

Zhejiang

Hunan

Jiangxi

Fujian

Guangdong

Hainan

NORTH KOREA

SOUTH KOREA

JAPAN

Sea of Japan

Yellow Sea

East China Sea

South China Sea

TAIWAN

golia

xi

ngxi

Rainfall in China
2010

Millimeters	Inches
More than 1500	59.1
1000–1499	39.4–59.0
500–999	19.7–39.3
100–499	3.9–19.8
0–99	0–3.8

air quality in the big cities. In 2015, China claimed to have lowered its coal use by 8 percent compared to the year before. It upgraded vehicle emission standards and energy efficiency. Drones were used to detect factories that violated emissions laws. In 2014, the Environmental Protection Law was revised for the first time since 1989. The modified law strengthened environmental protection by fining polluters, and by even permitting NGOs to bring public-interest lawsuits against those who violated the law. It also held local officials accountable for the environmental standard in their regions. However, many of the requirements and targets were regularly unmet, owing to insufficient implementation or oversight. Local Chinese authorities failed to strictly enforce regulations for protecting the environment, because they sometimes were invested in local companies and profited from unrestricted economic development in their areas.[48] The decentralized nature of China's political system, which so many times in the past had worked to China's advantage in the economy, had a serious downside—namely, that Beijing often failed to get policy buy-ins from local officials.

Government inaction and inertia prompted the emergence of a vibrant environmental protest movement China.[49] When citizens' concerns were not addressed satisfactorily, they turned to protest to make their voices heard, either via the internet or on the street. In 2015, a former China Central Television journalist, Chai Jing, caused a video sensation with a self-made and self-financed documentary. Called *Under the Dome (qiongding zhi xia)*, it was posted on the internet.[50] The footage, consisting of commentary, interviews, and factory visits, documented the extent and dangers of air pollution in China. The film exposed the pollution caused by state-owned energy companies, steel producers, and coal factories. It also pointed to the inability of the Ministry of Environmental Protection to penalize the big polluters. The video was viewed over 150 million times within three days of its release. Chinese citizens also staged public demonstrations against the building of coal-fired power plants, chemical plants, oil refineries, waste incinerators, and the like. According to Chen Japing, a former leading member of the Communist Party's political and legislative affairs committee, the environment surpassed illegal land expropriation as the leading source of social unrest in China.[51] In August 2011, an estimated twelve thousand mainly middle-class protesters faced down riot police to demand the closing of a petrochemical plant in Dalian, in northeastern China. The local authorities were forced to back down in the face of environmental protests. The demonstrations in Dalian were largely peaceful. A year later, however, images posted on the internet from Shifang in southwestern China's Sichuan province showed scenes of bloodied protesters and police officers firing tear gas. The demonstrators voiced their protest against the planned construction of a $1.6 billion copper smelting complex, which would have been one of the largest smelting complexes on earth. The furious protests prompted local officials not just to suspend but to permanently cancel the project.

Other incidents that fueled anxiety and public protest included a host of scandals and manmade disasters in the recent decade which laid bare the perils of rapid growth and the failures of governance, such as lack of regulatory oversight, insufficient implementation of laws, corruption, bribery, graft, and general government mishandling and incompetence. Such public crises shattered the confidence of Chinese citizens and reflected poorly on the political institutions. They included a tainted milk scandal in 2008, a high-speed train crash in 2011, and explosions in residential areas in Tianjin in 2015.

In 2008, sixteen infants in China's Gansu province were diagnosed with kidney stones.[52] All of them had been given milk powder that was later found to have been polluted with the toxic industrial compound melamine. Four months later, an estimated three hundred thousand babies in China were reported sick from the contaminated milk. The kidney damage led to six fatalities. The Sanlu Group, one of the largest dairy producers in China, was identified as the polluter. But as the scandal unfolded, more Chinese dairy firms were implicated. The 2008 incident was one of the most severe food safety scandals in PRC history. In response, the government promulgated the food safety law in June 2009, which prohibited any use of unauthorized food additives. The law also led to the establishment of a central commission to facilitate interprovincial coordination and enforcement of food safety regulations at the national level. In March 2013, the China Food and Drug Administration was set up as a ministry-level agency to concentrate responsibilities regarding food and drug safety. China's efforts to strengthen food safety were complicated by the rampant pollution of water and soil. Rice and garden vegetables contaminated by heavy metals posed major health risks. The cleanup was expected to be highly costly and to take decades. Despite resolute government action following the milk scandal, however, consumer confidence in Chinese dairy products remained extremely weak.

Similar problems emerged from investigations into the railway accident in 2011 in the eastern coastal city of Wenzhou.[53] A train that stopped near Wenzhou was struck by another train, derailing six cars, two of which plunged from a viaduct. The disaster killed 40 people and injured 191. It was a serious setback to China's hopes to turn high-speed rail into a symbol of the nation's technological and industrial progress. The wave of public outrage online died down only after government authorities censored the domestic media. Later, Chinese investigators blamed the crash on a string of blunders, including design flaws, bidding irregularities, and lapses by safety inspectors who were supposed to ensure its quality. The failures of control and oversight were related to graft and corruption. The railway industry, which is mostly state-owned, was believed to be one of the most tarnished sectors in China, nurturing a "culture of corruption." The "Father of China's High-Speed Rail" and former vice chief engineer, Zhang Shuguang, was fired and arrested, prompting the Chinese government to launch an anticorruption campaign within the railway industry. In the years after 2009, a total of thirteen senior officials and senior managers from the state-owned railway companies were investigated for corruption and abuse of power for personal financial gain in scandals involving astonishing amounts of money. This form of collective corruption was able to unfold due to the lack of transparency and the absence of strong external checks and balances in this state monopoly.

Finally, in 2015 huge explosions in warehouses in the northern Chinese city of Tianjin killed 173 people and damaged more than 17,000 homes.[54] Evidence suggested that political malfeasance and rampant safety violations played significant roles in the accident. Facing growing public anger about the accident, the government began releasing information about the owners of the warehouse company, Rui Hai International Logistics. The two top executives, who deliberately had concealed their ownership stakes behind a shadowy corporate structure, apparently admitted to leveraging their personal relationships with government officials to obtain licenses for the site, despite clear violations of rules prohibiting the storage of hazardous chemicals within one kilometer of residential areas. The executives established Rui Hai in 2012 but had other people list their shares to avoid exposing the conflict of interest.

Throughout the reform period, the CCP struggled to strike a balance between cutting red tape and enforcing rules to protect the environment, workers, and public health. With little public scrutiny of their work, party officials were only occasionally punished for neglecting the regulations, and usually only after an accident. But they could count on being rewarded for economic growth with promotions and opportunities. Oversight was therefore often sloppy and safety regulations were often disregarded or bypassed. Companies exploited weak governance and used political connections to shield their operations from scrutiny with regard to labor or environmental standards. This also led to the spread of harsh working conditions. Workers had to work long hours. Some factories reportedly kept their doors locked to prevent the workers from leaving the production facilities. According to official statistics, over 263,500 people died in industrial accidents in two years (2004 and 2005). In the coal mining sector alone, nearly six thousand miners died in 2005. By the government's own count, nearly ten years later, in 2014, more than sixty-eight thousand people per year—two hundred every day— were killed in industrial accidents—most of them poor, powerless, and far from China's boomtowns.[55]

Frequent protests by workers, villagers, and victims of disasters showed the level of social discontent and public outrage.[56] In a large-scale study that surveyed a national sample of twenty thousand Chinese people, corruption of public officials and unfair distribution of wealth were found to be the two most significant social problems facing contemporary China.[57] In each of the scandals and accidents, top government officials placed the blame on others and refused to be held accountable. There was a more systemic problem at work, however: the scandals revealed China's failure to build effective regulatory institutions in its transition to a market economy. In addressing the scandals, the government resorted to a top-down, state-centric, regulatory, and legal approach. However, this approach did not sufficiently address China's regulatory problems. Without a vigorous civil society, free and socially responsible media, and independent judiciary to serve as sources of information and discipline in enforcing safety laws and regulations, it may not be possible to achieve a robust and sustainable regulatory capacity.

Despite the party's ban of the term, debates over democratization and public participation never waned. Although the Democracy Wall movement was silenced in China by 1981, some of its activists moved overseas and established a Democracy Wall movement there. In 1989, the question of democratization nearly caused the collapse of the regime. That the debate endured was again demonstrated in December 2008, for example, when a number of people (starting with a group of 303, which reportedly added up to over seven thousand) published a co-signed petition labeled *Charter 08*. The petition mapped out a road to democracy for the CCP. Liu Xiaobo, who wrote *Charter 08* and, in 2010 received the Nobel Peace Prize, died in prison in July 2017. His work had attempted to answer the question of how to create a more just, more transparent, and better-governed society, after thirty years of growing social inequality and corruption associated with China's economic miracle. The charter's signatories' answer was grounded in liberal democratic institutions of competitive elections, rule of law, and respecting human rights, but also in fairer distribution of wealth, environmental protection, and care for the weak.

There was also a notable change, however, in the demographics of activists. The Democracy Wall movement of 1979 and the Tiananmen protests were predominantly movements of youth and students. A distinctly high number of the signatories of the original *Charter 08*, however, were of middle class and well-educated professional origins. This was presumably a development that the CCP had feared. Its legitimacy had been based on economic growth, the promotion of nationalism, and rhetorical devices such as telling the Chinese people that there were no better alternatives to the party. One of its methods of staying in power had been to fraternize the emerging middle class by offering access, perks, and stability to allay its fears of chaos. For some members of the middle class, this was not working. Members of the middle class increasingly demanded good governance and a say in the decision-making that affected them and their neighborhoods.

The breakdown of socialist ideals, which began in the late Mao years, led to what scholars both inside China and outside sometimes refer to as a "values vacuum." The writer Yu Hua (1960–) sarcastically remarked: "China moved from Mao Zedong's monochrome era of politics in command to Deng Xiaoping's polychrome era of economics above all. 'Better a socialist weed than a capitalist seedling,' we used to say in the Cultural Revolution. Today we can't tell the difference between what is capitalist and what is socialist—weeds and seedling come from one and the same plant."[58] To him, this led to a "breakdown of social morality and a confusion in the value system of China today; it is an aftereffect of our uneven development.... We live in a frivolous society, one that doesn't set much store by matters of principle."[59] Chinese society was accustomed, for better or worse, to a powerful overwhelming public ideology. But when it evaporated, people longed for some kind of ethical belief system, as both a guide to their own decision-making in daily life and as a basis for assuming what is right and wrong.[60] In China's booming economy of recent years, moneymaking and materialism filled the space, becoming the most conspicuous public values. The widening sphere of private consumption and recreation was visible in pastimes ranging from interior decorating to basketball fandom.[61]

Consumption and material abundance were certainly satisfying after the scarcities under Mao, but only up to a point. As the pursuit of materialism gave rise to patterns of unscrupulous behavior and social injustice and as these patterns occasionally rested on special access to power, people looked for something better. Fundamental notions of right and wrong were deeply ingrained in the Chinese tradition. Many expressed online their uneasiness with a social world where only money counted, no matter how it was attained. In several ways, Chinese people struggled with big questions: What norms can we agree on? How can we put them into action? What do we want it to mean in the early twenty-first century, to be a good person (*zuo ren*)? What does it mean to be Chinese?

The economic reforms and the moral vacuum provided fertile ground for the revitalization of a wide array of religious practices, including divination, ancestor worship, temple festivals, going to church or mosque, funeral rites, pilgrimages, sectarianism, sutra chanting, and printing and distributing morality books. The surge of religion was impressive. China found itself in possession of the world's largest Buddhist population, as well as fast-growing Catholic and Protestant congregations, expanding Muslim communities, and active Daoist temples.[62] After having disappeared for nearly forty years after 1949, religious practices reemerged as an important part of everyday life in China.

Throughout Chinese history, "heterodox" religions were responsible for numerous uprisings, such as the White Lotus Uprising or the Taiping Rebellion. Heretic religious sects were traditionally considered a severe threat by authorities. This historical legacy contributed to the party state's suspicion toward all manner of spiritual beliefs and practices. The remarkable religious upsurge that swept China at the outset of the twenty-first century thus triggered special political concerns in the CCP.

The state was, unsurprisingly, slow to bestow official recognition on the myriad of new religious groups that emerged. In general, the state tolerated religions as long as no political lines were crossed. When those lines were crossed, however, the state suppressed the religious communities. The Falun Gong was a good example.[63] It emerged in 1992 as part of a general *qigong* boom, and combined *qigong*—that is, breathing and meditation techniques— with moral philosophy. Falun Gong practitioners believed this could lead them to better health and, ultimately, spiritual enlightenment. The Falun Gong quickly became one of the largest *qigong* organizations in China, consisting at its height in the mid-1990s of 28,263 base-level practice centers, 1,900 mid-level training stations, and thirty-nine main stations. The state tolerated the movement until a massive, peaceful Falun Gong demonstration took place outside of Communist Party headquarters in Beijing in late April 1999. The demonstrators protested against negative reports they had seen about their faith in the Chinese media. In the wake of this event, the authorities started to suppress the group rigorously.

The transition from socialism entailed a widespread commodification: labor, land, nature, and bodies were subjected to the forces of sprawling markets. It also triggered profound shifts in society's normative infrastructure. Standards of justice, dignity, entitlements, rights, and the value of labor were fundamentally changed. These moral consequences of commodification and commercialization—often ignored in western debates that privilege the role of economic interests and institutions—caused a bifurcation of institutional norms and an uneasy synchronicity of older Marxist, and newer market-liberal, discourses and ideologies. The philosopher Ci Jiwei described this unresolved and lamentable state of affairs with strong words:

> everyday norms of coexistence and cooperation—be they moral, legal, or regulatory—are breached on a massive scale. The sheer scale in question is astonishing. . . . Violations of such elementary norms have resulted in all too many instances of unsafe food (infant formula and so-called gutter oil among the most prominent examples), medicine, water, and traffic, not to mention coal mines. . . . By moral crisis I refer to a state of affairs in which large numbers of people fail to comply with more or less acceptable rules of social coexistence and cooperation. . . . Given this notion of a moral crisis, it is not surprising that the moral crisis in post-Mao China is at the same time a crisis of social order.[64]

Because it was a time of weak institutional norms and restless intellectual fluidity, it was also a politically poignant moment for Chinese citizens to get involved and partake of a wide range of social activism.[65] Never before had there been so many passionate debates in online media or elsewhere, that allowed for popular interests to play a greater role in shaping the outcomes of social and political conflicts. The debates furnished Chinese citizens with a rich repertoire of moral and cognitive resources to say their opinion and to make claims against the state. At the same time, the void of political reforms and the bewildering complexity of the post-utopian situation left many contemporary Chinese unsettled. Despite economic achievements and national pride, they saw themselves as a beleaguered and vulnerable nation with an uncertain future.

❖ ❖ ❖

In the late 1970s, the government led by Deng Xiaoping launched a series of reforms to help develop the country and invigorate its economy. China abandoned the planned economic system and autarkic policies that had been pursued under Mao Zedong to become the world's largest trading economy and the second-largest recipient of foreign direct investment. China's growth since the start of economic reforms was unprecedented in global economic history. No other country had grown as rapidly and for as long. By 2013, China's economy was twenty-five times larger in real terms than in 1978. As a result, China's share of global GDP more than quadrupled, shooting from under 3 percent up to 12 percent, and then to 14.8 percent in 2015. Its nominal GDP increased seventy-five times over. Along the way, it overtook a half-dozen advanced industrial countries to become the world's second-largest economy. Of course, its huge population meant that its rankings in per-capita terms were often much lower, but China nonetheless moved up in terms of per-capita income. In 1980, China, as a low-income economy, was among the world's poorest countries. By 2016, it was in the upper-middle-income category with a per-capita income of $12,400 and was ranked 106 in the world.[66]

China's reform era coincided with a new stage of globalization powered by rapid reductions in the cost of transport, communication, and information management. As a result, international markets provided China with opportunities that far exceeded those available at other times and to other countries after World War II. The development in China was critically dependent on open access to global markets and the unrestricted, transnational flow of capital and goods. The open-door policy tilted China's whole economy

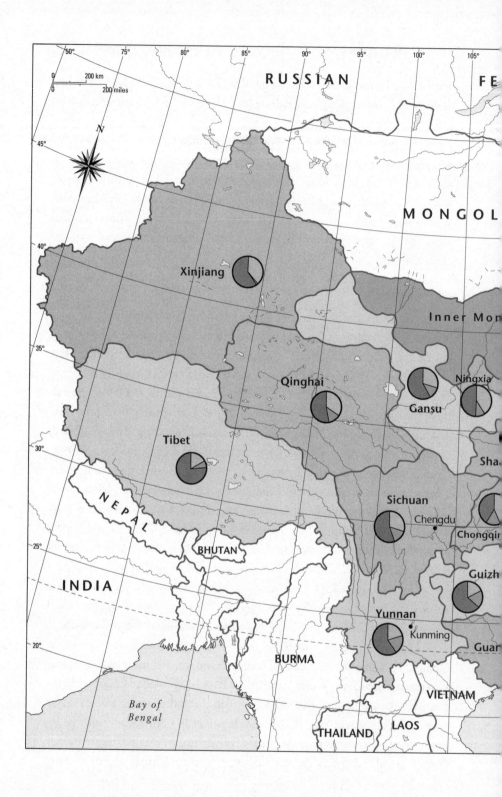

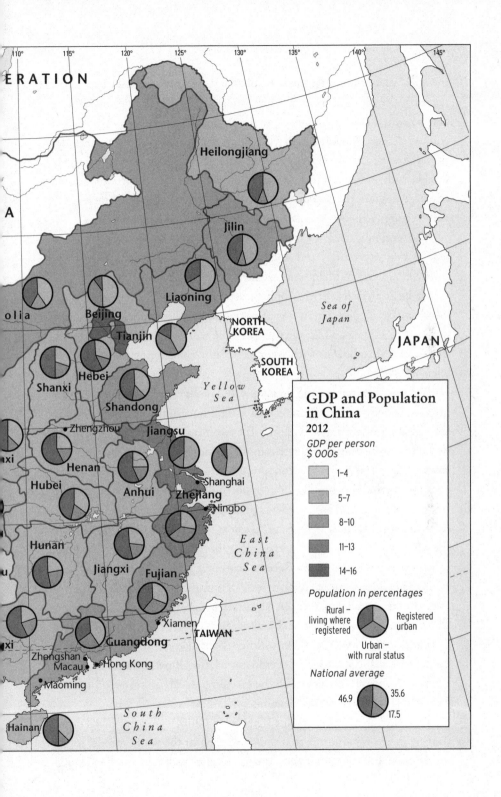

ERATION

A

olia

Heilongjiang

Jilin

Beijing

Liaoning

Tianjin

NORTH
KOREA

Sea of
Japan

JAPAN

Shanxi

Hebei

SOUTH
KOREA

Shandong

Yellow
Sea

Zhengzhou

Jiangsu

xi

Henan

Hubei

Anhui

Shanghai

Zhejiang

Ningbo

Hunan

Jiangxi

Fujian

East
China
Sea

u

Xiamen

xi

Guangdong

TAIWAN

Zhongshan

Macau

Hong Kong

Maoming

South
China
Sea

Hainan

**GDP and Population
in China**
2012

*GDP per person
$ 000s*

	1–4
	5–7
	8–10
	11–13
	14–16

Population in percentages

Rural –
living where
registered

Registered
urban

Urban –
with rural status

National average

46.9   35.6

17.5

toward the labor-intensive final assembly of parts produced elsewhere in the region or the world. Chinese workers, whose labor was their chief asset, were able to benefit, and China became the top trading partner of every other country in Asia. This resulted in rising wages and growing domestic consumption. By rewarding firms that raised quality standards toward global levels, foreign trade and investment pushed Chinese companies to start broad-based efforts to upgrade product quality, enabling a growing array of Chinese products to compete in overseas and domestic markets.

The economic rise since 1978 allowed China to gradually exert an increasingly pervasive economic influence in the world, backed by a more and more powerful military. With its wealth, China vastly strengthened its naval power. China built aircraft carriers, sophisticated missiles, and advanced submarines, and developed cyberwar capabilities that challenged western military dominance in Asia and in other parts of the world. The country started to pursue global ambitions with vigor, inevitably challenging the global balance of power,

The policy of reform and opening was based on injecting a growing degree of flexibility and openness into a rigid and statist economic system through gradual institutional reform. The reforms allowed China to break out of inefficient institutional patterns in the economy that caused poverty and to embark on a path to rapid economic growth. A greater degree of inclusiveness and openness afforded new opportunities to innovative and hardworking peasants and entrepreneurs to create and expand businesses, which over time would eclipse China's inefficient and wasteful state sector. Overall, the Chinese economic reform was driven by bottom-up initiatives rather than by grand visions from the top. Specific economic policies and, above all, cautious, gradual institutional reforms were of utmost importance. Institutional innovations included market liberalization; opening up the country step by step to foreign direct investment and overseas export markets; the creation of central banking and tax institutions essential to a functioning market economy; enhanced business-government relationships; and a gradual emergence of inclusive institutions in the economy which, if not yet fully rule-based, were at least more rule-leaning.

Profound challenges remained, however. China's growth slowed down starting in 2014, indicating that the "workshop of the world" model might not be economically sustainable. The model also caused environmental pollution on a huge scale, exacting a heavy price that seemed no longer acceptable to society. The central challenge became the need to wean China off heavy industry and low-end, low-wage manufacturing. The stakes were high for the government: making sure that while switching gears, the CCP itself continued to enjoy support from the people by producing growth and the creation of wealth. In other words, China's social stability—not just its economy—drove Chinese policy-making.

A fundamental institutional pillar of a capitalist market economy was still missing in China: a commitment to private property, considered to be the most efficient and fair way to organize the production of goods, provision of services, and allocation of economic and financial resources. Private ownership existed and spread in the Chinese economy, but in heavy industries and in certain service sectors, such as banking, insurance, and wholesaling, it remained relatively small. Operations of private firms were often burdened with higher regulatory, legal, and financial requirements than state-owned firms were. Although the privatization of state-owned enterprises accelerated after 1997, the government hesitated to privatize large state-owned enterprises. During the reform era as a whole, compared with the pace of market liberalization and opening to the outside world, changes in the ownership structure of the state sector, as both a policy goal and an economic reality, were limited. The size of the state sector, while it declined relative to nonstate firms, barely declined in absolute terms. The government remained committed to maintaining the state-owned sector, which also benefited from connections to the international financial markets and the private export sector. China's continued support of state-owned enterprises clearly defied Western theories and concepts of how a free-market economy should work.

Another persistent feature of China's market transition was the lack of political liberalization, although this is not to say that the Chinese political system stood still. China remained an authoritarian, one-party state, but after 1978, the party distanced itself from radical transformation and utopian goals. It became, perhaps, no longer communist except in name. Reforms of the civil service phased out the old cadre system and made administration more professional and accountable. Elections on the local level and intraparty democracy increased accountability throughout the political system. With the death of Deng Xiaoping, "strongman" politics were brought to a close. Yet, 2012 brought the bewildering attempt to reinstall president Xi Jinping as "core leader." The political climate teetered on the verge of becoming more rigid and perhaps more brittle than before.

The back and forth showed that the Chinese government had obviously not come to terms with de facto political and social change on the ground and had refused or at least delayed institution-building efforts to reform the political system. The combination of rapid economic liberalization and seemingly unchanged politics led many to characterize China's development as state-led, authoritarian capitalism—a form of government believed to be fragile and unsustainable. The unresolved question of popular participation in political decisions was the root cause of a series of political crises. The Democracy Wall in 1979, the student-led democracy movement of 1989, the *Charter 08* petition in 2008, and some smaller conflicts represented severe challenges to party rule.

When and how China will embrace a more participatory and legitimate system, and whether the party will survive that process, are the main questions that need to be asked about China's political future. China has developed a robust market for goods, but still lacks a free market for ideas. As the modern economy becomes more and more knowledge-driven and dependent on innovation, the gains from free exchange of ideas become too great and the costs of suppressing it become potentially very high.[67] China may well embrace political liberalization in the decades to come, just as it embraced market liberalization after 1978. This may or may not lead to a liberal democracy or multi-party system. But one conclusion can be safely drawn from history since 1978: without more pluralism and a greater degree of popular participation in political life, a more sustainable and stable development seems difficult to imagine and future political crises seem likely.

There are other factors and arguments that point to China's need to continue institutional reforms. Chinese society became diverse and pluralistic. At the same time, social tensions and conflicts increased, as well. China's level of economic inequality exceeds even that of the United States. Marxist ideology has almost completely collapsed and is being replaced by a combination of materialism and assertive nationalism. The vast migration of labor from countryside to city has continued apace. The pressures of a hypercompetitive market economy are ripping apart the traditional family. Political corruption has reached new heights. Environmental degradation has reached a level that poses increasing health risks. All those factors contributed to the

12.4. A pro-democracy protester draws on her tent at a campsite in the Admiralty district of Hong Kong, October 2014.
Nicolas Asfouri / Getty Images / 458093386

rise of critical and intense discussions, feelings of uncertainty, and outright social discontent. The increase in citizen protests, demonstrations, and petitions is driven in part by China's massive social and economic transformations. The internet has increasingly empowered the Chinese people to voice their political views and engage in political discussion. However, governance flaws at the heart of the Chinese state also fuel increasing social unrest. Entrenched interests of private and state firms have managed to capture many institutions and to manipulate policy outcomes in their favor, but at the expense of the public good. The anticorruption campaigns tried to address this critical development, but it is doubtful that they will work in the long term. Chinese citizens, however, lack independent political institutions to participate in the decisions that affect their lives. They also lack fully independent legal institutions to resolve their grievances against local officials. Thus, citizen discontent is channeled into the streets rather than into formal legal and political institutions.

The economic success story portrayed in this chapter is not the result of a grand "China model," or a systematic challenge to the existing world order, or an alternative development path.[68] Rather, it is the outcome of specific factors, incremental and opportunistic policies, historical legacies, and global opportunities. The key challenge in China's rise was to find a formula that would unlock historical potential. The country's historical advantages consisted of the comparative sophistication of premodern Chinese institutions, the country's emphasis on meritocracy and education, and its experience of running a complex administrative and economic system. Contemporary Chinese institutions such as nationwide entrance examinations draw on deep historical roots. This perspective, highlighting the central role of China's historical legacy in its current development, recognizes that the past influenced the future—not because Chinese agents were passive and under the spell of tradition, but because they found it necessary, useful, and desirable to draw on the past. They did so to determine how to behave in new situations when intentionally pursuing institutional change, and when contemplating the development or adoption of institutional and organizational innovations. The historical legacy of its social institutions and the creative adaptation of a broad spectrum of novel institutional reforms eventually allowed China to find adequate institutional solutions for some of the long-term problems facing the country (especially in the economy, but also other areas such as welfare and infrastructure).

China's reforms have made it an important, foundational part of the global economic and social order, and many of the problems China is currently grappling with are therefore global in compass and consequence. China brings both unique historical strengths and weaknesses to the global order. Yet, given the enmeshed nature of the world's markets and economies, imbalances in one large country cannot be contained there; they eventually radiate to other places. China, while a large and pervasive presence in the global arena, is also exporting risk around the world. The tectonic social and economic shifts in China in the present are an indication that the rapid and unprecedented, yet uneven, development that produced huge payoffs for China and global markets may sooner or later have to end. China, and the world, will ultimately have to learn to live within a more modest and sustainable reality.

Abbreviations

AB	Anti-Bolshevik
AIDS	Acquired Immune Deficiency Syndrome
CBI	China-Burma-India
CCP	Communist Party of China
CEC	Committee for Eliminating Counter-Revolutionaries
CMSC	China Merchant Steamship Company
CNOOC	China National Offshore Oil Corporation
CNPC	China National Petroleum Corporation
CPPCC	Chinese People's Political Consultative Conference
CPVA	Chinese People's Volunteer Army
FDI	Foreign Direct Investment
GDP	Gross Domestic Product
GE	General Electric
GM	General Motors
GMD	Guomindang, Nationalist Party of China
HSBC	Hong Kong and Shanghai Banking Cooperation
IBC	Imperial Bank of China
ID	Identification
NATO	North Atlantic Treaty Organization
NEP	New Economic Policy
NGO	Nongovernmental organization
NPC	National People's Congress
OBOR	One Belt, One Road
PLA	People's Liberation Army
PLA Daily	*People's Liberation Army Daily*
PPC	People's Republic Council
PRC	People's Republic of China
R&D	Research and Development
ROC	Republic of China
SACO	Sino-American Cooperation Organization
SASAC	State Asset Supervision and Administration Commission

SEZ	Special Economic Zone
SMC	Shanghai Municipal Council
SME	Small and Medium Enterprises
SOE	State-Owned Enterprise
SPC	State Planning Commission of China
TVEs	Township and Village Enterprises
UN	United Nations
US	United States
USSR	Union of Soviet Socialist Republics
WTO	World Trade Organization

Notes

Readers should be advised that a website has been created to house the maps herein, and to provide additional materials relevant to *Making China Modern*. These include a frequently updated list of further reading, a full bibliography, a glossary, and other elements, such as information on key people. The address is http://www.makingchinamodern.com/.

INTRODUCTION

1. Benjamin Carlson, "The World According to Xi Jinping," *The Atlantic,* September 21, 2015, http://www.theatlantic.com/international/archive/2015/09/xi-jinping-china-book-chinese-dream/406387/.

2. See chapters by Evelyn S. Rawski, Jack A. Goldstone, Jonathan Hay, and Lynn A. Struve in *The Qing Formation in World-Historical Time,* ed. Lynn A. Struve (Cambridge, MA: Harvard University Asia Center, 2004), 207–241, 242–302, 303–334, 335–482.

3. Daron Acemoglu and James A. Robinson, *Why Nations Fail: The Origins of Power, Prosperity and Poverty* (New York: Random House, 2012).

4. Douglass C. North explains institutions as "the rules of the game in a society or, more formally, the humanly devised constraints that shape human interaction." North, *Institutions, Institutional Change, and Economic Performance* (Cambridge: Cambridge University Press, 1990), 3.

5. According to Richard Scott, "Institutions are comprised of regulative, normative and cultural cognitive elements that, together with associated activities and resources, provide stability and meaning to social life." Scott, *Institutions and Organizations: Ideas and Interests,* 3rd ed. (Los Angeles: Sage Publications, 2008), 48.

6. Thus an institution "consists of an embodied (occupied by human persons) structure of differentiated roles. These roles are defined in terms of tasks, and rules regulating the performance of those tasks." Miller, "Social Institutions," The Stanford Encyclopedia of Philosophy Archive, last modified February 8, 2011, http://plato.stanford.edu/archives/win2014/entries/social-institutions/. See also Masahiko Aoki, "Endogenizing Institutions and Their Changes," *Journal of Institutional Economics* 3.1 (2007): 1–31; Stephan Haggard, "Institutions and Growth in East Asia," *Studies in Comparative International Development* 38.4 (2004): 53–81.

7. Avner Greif, *Institutions and the Path to the Modern Economy: Lessons from Medieval Trade* (Cambridge: Cambridge University Press, 2006), 188–190.

8. North, *Institutions,* 3.

9. Adrian Leftwich and Kunal Sen, *Beyond Institutions: Institutions and Organizations in the Politics and Economics of Poverty Reduction—Thematic Synthesis of Research Evidence* (Manchester: University of Manchester, 2010).

10. Daron Acemoglu and James A. Robinson, "Paths of Economic and Political Development," in *Handbook of Political Economy,* ed. Barry R. Weingast and Donald A. Wittman (Oxford: Oxford University Press, 2006), 673–692.

11. Susan H. Whiting, *Power and Wealth in Rural China: The Political Economy of Institutional Change* (New York: Cambridge University Press, 2001), 19–20.

12. Sabine Dabringhaus, *Geschichte Chinas, 1279–1949* (Munich: R. Oldenbourg, 2006), 118–120.

13. Victor H. Mair, "Kinesis versus Stasis, Interaction versus Independent Invention," in *Contact and Exchange in the Ancient World* (Honolulu: University of Hawai'i Press, 2006), 1–16.

14. Charles S. Maier, *Once Within Borders: Territories of Power, Wealth, and Belonging since 1500* (Cambridge, MA: Harvard University Press, 2016).

15. Alfred W. Crosby, "The Past and Present of Environmental History," *American Historical Review* 100 (1995): 1177–1189.

16. Mark Elvin and Liu Ts'ui-jung, *Sediments of Time: Environment and Society in Chinese History* (Cambridge: Cambridge University Press, 1998).

17. Pierre Bourdieu, *In Other Words: Essays towards a Reflexive Sociology* (Stanford, CA: Stanford University Press, 1990).

18. See Yeh Wen-hsin, "Introduction: Interpreting Chinese Modernity, 1900–1950," in *Becoming Chinese: Passages to Modernity and Beyond* (Berkeley: University of California Press, 2000), 1–30.

19. This is based on recent work by economic historians Loren Brandt, Debin Ma, and Thomas G. Rawski, "From Divergence to Convergence: Re-evaluating the History behind China's Economic Boom" (working paper, CAGE Online Working Paper Series, Department of Economics, University of Warwick, Coventry, UK, 2013), http://wrap.warwick.ac.uk/57944; Dwight H. Perkins, "China's Prereform Economy in World Perspective," in *The Rise of China in Historical Perspective,* ed. Brantley Womack (Lanham, MD: Rowman and Littlefield, 2010), 105–128.

20. Eleanor Albert and Xu Beina, "China's Environmental Crisis," Backgrounder, Council on Foreign Relations, January 18, 2016, http://www.cfr.org/china/chinas -environmental-crisis/p12608.

PART I. THE RISE AND FALL OF QING CHINA

1. Pamela K. Crossley, *The Wobbling Pivot: China since 1800, An Interpretive History* (Malden, MA: Wiley-Blackwell, 2010), xii.

1. AGE OF GLORY: 1644–1800

1. Much of the postwar liberal critique of China's political system was fixated on the alleged rigidity of ritual, social hierarchy, xenophobic nationalism, authoritarianism, and a lack of development and thus portrayed Qing society as stagnant and closed off. Recent research has by and large dismissed this picture.

2. Useful geographic data and maps are available at Harvard University, Center for Geographic Analysis, China GIS Data, http://www.gis.harvard.edu/resources/data/china-gis-data. See also Sun Jingzhi, ed., *Economic Geography of China* (Hong Kong: Oxford University Press, 1988); Arthur Waldron, *The Great Wall of China* (Cambridge: Cambridge University Press, 1990); Piper R. Gaubatz, *Beyond the Great Wall: Urban Form and Transformation on the Chinese Frontiers* (Stanford, CA: Stanford University Press, 1996).

3. Robert B. Marks, *China: Its Environment and History* (Lanham, MD: Rowman and Littlefield, 2012); Mark Elvin, *The Retreat of the Elephants: An Environmental History of China* (New Haven, CT: Yale University Press, 2004), 19–85; David A. Pietz, *The Yellow River: The Problem of Water in Modern China* (Cambridge, MA: Harvard University Press, 2015); Mark Elvin and Liu Cuirong, *Sediments of Time: Environment and Society in Chinese History* (Cambridge: Cambridge University Press, 1998); Robert Marks, *Tigers, Rice, Silk, and Silt: Environment and Economy in Late Imperial South China* (Cambridge: Cambridge University Press, 1998).

4. Jonathan Schlesinger, *A World Trimmed with Fur: Wild Things, Pristine Places, and the Natural Fringes of Qing* (Stanford, CA: Stanford University Press, 2017). On the global circulation of products during this time, see also Timothy Brook, *Vermeer's Hat: The Seventeenth Century and the Dawn of the Global World* (New York: Penguin, 2013).

5. Randall A. Dodgen, *Controlling the Dragon: Confucian Engineers and the Yellow River in the Late Imperial China* (Honolulu: University of Hawai'i Press, 2001); Richards L. Edmonds, ed., *Managing the Chinese Environment* (Oxford: Oxford University Press, 1998).

6. The best and most comprehensive study by historical demographers based on meticulously researched regional or county figures is Ge Jianxiong et al., *Zhongguo renkoushi* [History of China's Population], 6 vols. (Shanghai: Fudan, 2001). The best sources in English still are Ho Ping-ti, *Studies on the*

Population of China, 1368–1953 (Cambridge, MA: Harvard University Press, 1959) and James Z. Lee and Feng Wang, eds., *One Quarter of Humanity: Malthusian Mythology and Chinese Realities, 1700–2000* (Cambridge, MA: Harvard University Press, 1999).

7. Francesca Bray, *The Rice Economies: Technology and Development in Asian Societies* (Berkeley: University of California Press, 1994); Dwight H. Perkins, *Agricultural Development in China, 1368–1968* (Chicago: Aldine, 1969).

8. Pierre-Etienne Will and R. Bin Wong, with James Lee, *Nourish the People: The State Civilian Granary System in China, 1650–1850* (Ann Arbor: Center for Chinese Studies, University of Michigan, 1991).

9. Edward H. Schafer, "The Yeh Chung Chi," *T'oung Pao* (1990): 148.

10. This, despite the fact that Zhongguo is today probably the closest Chinese-language equivalent to our English word "China," and Zhonghua is the term officially used for China in the names of both the modern People's Republic and the Republic of China; see Lydia Liu, *Tokens of Exchange* (Durham, NC: Duke University Press, 1999).

11. James C. Y. Watt, "Art and History in China from the 3rd through the 8th Century," in *China: Dawn of a Golden Age, 200–750 AD,* ed. James C. Y. Watt and Prudence Oliver Harper (New York: Metropolitan Museum of Art, 2004), 2–46; Charles Holcombe, "Rethinking Early East Asian History," *Education about Asia* 11.2 (2006): 9–13.

12. Samuel Adrian M. Adshead, *T'ang China: The Rise of the East in World History* (Houndmills, Basingstoke, UK: Palgrave Macmillan, 2004), 30.

13. Samuel Adrian M. Adshead, *China in World History* (New York: St. Martin's Press, 1988).

14. Peter K. Bol, *"This Culture of Ours": Intellectual Transitions in T'ang and Sung China* (Stanford, CA: Stanford University Press, 1992); Dieter Kuhn, *The Age of Confucian Rule: The Song Transformation of China* (Cambridge, MA: Belknap Press of Harvard University Press, 2009).

15. The longest such dynasties were the Liao, Jin (1115–1234), Yuan (1271–1368), and Qing (1644–1911).

16. Evelyn S. Rawski, "Presidential Address: Reenvisioning the Qing: The Significance of the Qing Period in Chinese History," in *Journal of Asian Studies* 55.4 (1996): 829–850; Cho-yun Hsu, *China: A New Cultural History* (New York: Columbia University Press, 2012), 334.

17. The concept of *Tianming* first emerged to serve the political needs of Zhou dynasty (1045–256 BCE) rulers, who ended by conquest the Shang dynasty in the eleventh century BCE.

18. Scholars such as Prasenjit Duara, Michael Szonyi, and David Faure have demonstrated that religion played a central role in relating the Chinese imperial state

to local society: Prasenjit Duara, *Culture, Power, and the State: Rural North China, 1900–1942* (New York: ACLS History E-Book Project, 2005); Michael Szonyi, *Practicing Kinship: Lineage and Descent in Late Imperial China* (Stanford CA: Stanford University Press, 2002); David Faure, *Emperor and Ancestor: State and Lineage in South China* (Stanford CA: Stanford University Press 2007). On rainmaking rituals; see Jeffrey Snyder-Reinke, *Dry Spells: State Rainmaking and Local Governance in Late Imperial China* (Cambridge, MA: Harvard University Asia Center, 2009).

19. Benjamin A. Elman, *Civil Service Examinations and Meritocracy in Late Imperial China* (Cambridge MA: Harvard University Press 2013); Alexander Woodside, *Lost Modernities: China, Vietnam, Korea and the Hazards of World History* (Cambridge, MA: Harvard University Press, 2006); Ichisada Miyazaki, *China's Examination Hell: The Civil Examinations of Imperial China* (New York: Weatherhill, 1976); and Benjamin A. Elman, *A Cultural History of Civil Examinations in Late Imperial China* (Berkeley: University of California Press, 2000).

20. Officials in Qing China serving as examiners were expected to be familiar with those manuals spelling out in detail all applicable regulations. See Libu, comp., *Qinding kechang tiaoli*, 12 vols. (Taipei: Wenhai chubanshe, 1989).

21. Benjamin A. Elman, "Political, Social, and Cultural Reproduction via Civil Service Examinations in Late Imperial China," *Journal of Asian Studies* 50.1 (1991): 7–28.

22. Chang Chung-li, *The Chinese Gentry: Studies on their Role in Nineteenth-Century Chinese Society* (Seattle: University of Washington Press, 1955).

23. Numbers are extracted from Miyazaki, *China's Examination Hell;* Iona Man-Cheong, *The Class of 1761: Examinations, State, and Elites in Eighteenth-Century China* (Stanford, CA: Stanford University Press, 2004). The exams are described in Elman, *Civil Service Examinations and Meritocracy*, 213. Elman dates the exams on 1756, but there were no exams in that year; the source he cites refers to the 1766 exams.

24. Woodside, *Lost Modernities*.

25. Elman, *Civil Service Examinations and Meritocracy*, 229–230.

26. Benjamin A. Elman, "Changes in Confucian Civil Service Examinations from the Ming to the Ch'ing Dynasty," in *Education and Society in Late Imperial China, 1600–1900*, ed. Benjamin Elman and Alexander Woodside (Berkeley: University of California Press, 1994), 111–149.

27. John Dardess, Preface to *Governing China, 150–1850* (Indianapolis: Hackett, 2010), xii.

28. G. William Skinner, "Introduction: Urban Development in Imperial China," in *The City in Late Imperial China,* ed. G. William Skinner (Stanford, CA: Stanford University Press 1977), 1–32, here 19.

29. T'ung-tsu Ch'ü, *Local Government in China under the Ch'ing* (Cambridge, MA: Harvard University Press, 1962).

30. Joerg Baten, Debin Ma, Stephen Morgan, and Qing Wang, "Evolution of Living Standards and Human Capital in China in the 18–20th Centuries: Evidences from Real Wages, Age-Heaping, and Anthropometrics," *Explorations in Economic History* 47.3 (2010): 347–359.

31. Robert Gardella, "Squaring Accounts: Commercial Bookkeeping Methods and Capitalist Rationalism in Late Qing and Republican China," *Journal of Asian Studies* 51.2 (1992): 317–339; Evelyn S. Rawski, *Education and Popular Literacy in Ch'ing China* (Ann Arbor: University of Michigan Press, 1979).

32. William T. Rowe, *Crimson Rain: Seven Centuries of Violence in a Chinese County* (Stanford, CA: Stanford University Press, 2007), 17–42; David Robinson, *Bandits, Eunuchs and the Son of Heaven: Rebellion and the Economy of Violence in Mid-Ming China* (Honolulu: University of Hawai'i Press, 2001).

33. Lillian M. Li, *Fighting Famine in North China: State, Market, and Environmental Decline, 1690s–1990s* (Stanford, CA: Stanford University Press, 2007), 247. Perdue shows how Qing officials worked with local gentry to expand irrigation and flood control in Hunan province; see Peter C. Perdue, *Exhausting the Earth: State and Peasant in Hunan, 1500–1850* (Cambridge, MA: Harvard University Press, 1987). See also Will, Wong, and Lee, *Nourish the People.*

34. Jane K. Leonard, *Controlling from Afar: The Daoguang Emperor's Management of the Grand Canal Crisis, 1824–1826* (Ann Arbor: Center for Chinese Studies, University of Michigan, 1996).

35. Julia C. Strauss, *Strong Institutions in Weak Polities: State Building in Republican China, 1927–1940* (Oxford: Clarendon Press, 1998), 14.

36. William T. Rowe, *China's Last Empire: The Great Qing* (Cambridge, MA: Belknap Press of Harvard University Press, 2009), 11–30; Mark C. Elliott, *The Manchu Way: The Eight Banners and Ethnic Identity in Late Imperial China* (Stanford, CA: Stanford University Press, 2001); Pamela K. Crossley, *A Translucent Mirror: History and Identity in Qing Imperial Ideology* (Berkeley: University of California Press, 1999); Franz H. Michael, *The Origin of Manchu Rule in China: Frontier and Bureaucracy as Interacting Forces in the Chinese Empire* (New York: Octagon Books, 1972).

37. The "Account of Ten days at Yangzhou" by Wang Xiuchu provides a first-person eyewitness report of the massacre. It is translated in Lynn A. Struve, *Voices from the Ming-Qing Cataclysm: China in Tigers' Jaws* (New Haven, CT: Yale University Press, 1998), 28–48.

38. The following paragraphs are based on Hsu, *China: A New Cultural History,* 421–424.

39. Pamela K. Crossley, *Orphan Warriors: Three Manchu Generations and the End of the Qing World* (Princeton, NJ: Princeton University Press, 1991), 11.

40. Evelyn S. Rawski, *The Last Emperors: A Social History of Qing Imperial Institutions* (Berkeley: University of California Press, 1998); Crossley, *Translucent Mirror;* Nicola Di Cosmo, "Qing Colonial Administration in Inner Asia," *International History Review* 20.2 (1998): 287–309; Laura Hostetler, *Qing Colonial Enterprise: Ethnography and Cartography in Early Modern China* (Chicago: University of Chicago Press, 2001); Peter C. Purdue, *China Marches West: The Qing Conquest of Central Eurasia* (Cambridge, MA: Belknap Press of Harvard University Press, 2005); Evelyn S. Rawski, "The Qing Formation and the Early-Modern Period," in *The Qing Formation in World-Historical Time,* ed. Lynn Struve (Cambridge, MA: Harvard University Asia Center, 2004), 207–241; Frederic Wakeman, *The Great Enterprise: The Manchu Reconstruction of Imperial Order in Seventeenth-Century China* (Berkeley: University of California Press, 1985).

41. Richard J. Smith, *The Qing Dynasty and Traditional Chinese Culture* (Lanham, MD: Rowman and Littlefield, 2015), 85–123; Frederic Wakeman, Jr., "High Qing, 1683–1839," in *Modern East Asia: Essays in Interpretation,* ed. James B. Crowley (New York: Harcourt, Brace and World, 1970); Mark C. Elliott, *Emperor Qianlong: Son of Heaven, Man of the World* (New York: Pearson Longman, 2009); Evelyn S. Rawski and Jessica Rawson, *China: The Three Emperors, 1662–1795* (London: Royal Academy of Arts, 2005); Jonathan D. Spence, *Emperor of China; Self Portrait of K'ang Hsi* (New York: Knopf, 1974); Michael G. Chang, *A Court on Horseback: Imperial Touring and the Construction of Qing Rule, 1680–1785* (Cambridge, MA: Harvard University Asia Center, 2007), 428.

42. Smith, *The Qing Dynasty,* 118–119.

43. William T. Rowe, *Saving the World: Chen Hongmou and Elite Consciousness in Eighteenth-Century China* (Stanford, CA: Stanford University Press, 2001); Lin Manhong, *China Upside Down: Currency, Society, and Ideologies, 1808–1856* (Cambridge, MA: Harvard University Asia Center, 2006).

44. Anne Gerritsen and Stephen McDowall, "Material Culture and the Other: European Encounters with Chinese Porcelain, ca. 1650–1800," *Journal of World History* 23.1 (2012): 87–113, here 88; Peter Wilhelm Meister and Horst Reber, *European Porcelain of the Eighteenth Century,* trans. Ewald Osers (Ithaca, NY: Cornell University Press, 1983), 18; Benjamin A. Elman, *A Cultural History of Modern Science in China* (Cambridge, MA: Harvard University Press, 2008), 75–80.

45. The first work is available in English as Song Yingxing, *Chinese Technology in the Seventeenth Century = T'ien-kung k'ai-wu* (New York: Dover Publications,

1997). See also Benjamin A. Elman, *On Their Own Terms: Science in China, 1550–1900* (Cambridge, MA: Harvard University Press, 2005).

46. Rowe, *China's Last Empire,* 123.

47. Madeleine Zelin, "The Grandeur of the Qing Economy," Asia for Educators, Columbia University, 2005, http://afe.easia.columbia.edu/qing/downloads/economy.pdf.

48. See Richard von Glahn, *Economic History of China: From Antiquity to the Nineteenth Century* (Cambridge: Cambridge University Press, 2016), 295–347. The role of silver is discussed in Richard von Glahn, *Fountain of Fortune: Money and Monetary Policy in China, 1000–1700* (Berkeley: University of California Press, 1996), 113–141. Articles on silver and the Asian trade can be found in Dennis O. Flynn and Arturo Giraldez, eds., *Metals and Monies in an Emerging Global Economy* (Aldershot, UK: Variorum, 1997).

49. Loren Brandt, Debin Ma, and Thomas G. Rawski, "From Divergence to Convergence: Re-Evaluating the History behind China's Economic Boom" (Working Paper no. 117, CAGE Online Working Paper Series, Department of Economics, University of Warwick, 2013), http://wrap.warwick.ac.uk/57944.

50. Rowe, *China's Last Empire,* 43.

51. Madeleine Zelin, *The Merchants of Zigong: Industrial Entrepreneurship in Early Modern China* (New York: Columbia University Press, 2005); Kenneth Pomeranz, "'Traditional' Chinese Business Forms Revisited: Family, Firm, and Financing in the History of the Yutang Company of Jining, 1779–1956," *Late Imperial China* 18.1 (1997): 1–38.

52. The word "lineage" is used in Chinese social history to refer to groups of people of the same surname that can trace ancestry to a common ancestor.

53. Klaus Mühlhahn, *Criminal Justice in China: A History* (Cambridge, MA: Harvard University Press, 2009); Chen Fu-mei and Ramon Myers, "Customary Law and the Economic Growth of China during the Ch'ing Period," *Ch'ing shih wen t'i* 3.10 (1978): 4–27; Chen Fu-mei and Ramon Myers, "Coping with Transaction Costs: The Case of Merchant Associations in the Ch'ing Period," in *Chinese Business Enterprise in Asia,* ed. Rajeswary Ampalavanar Brown (London: Routledge, 1996), 252–274.

54. "Confucius" is the name used in the West for Kong Qiu, born in 551 BCE.

55. The Analects of Confucius is an anthology of brief passages that present the words of Confucius and his disciples, describe Confucius as a man, and recount some of the events of his life. The quoted passage is from Analects 2 / 3.

56. David L. Hall and Roger T. Ames, "Chinese Philosophy," in Routledge Encyclopedia of Philosophy, 1998, https://www.rep.routledge.com/articles/chinese-philosophy/v-1/.

57. Wm. Theodore de Bary and Irene Bloom, comp., *Sources of Chinese Tradition*, vol. 1 (New York: Columbia University Press, 1999), 849–850.

58. Benjamin A. Elman, "Ch'ing Dynasty Schools of Scholarship," in *Ch'ing-shih wen-t'i* 4.6 (1981): 1–44; Kang-i Sun Chang and Stephen Owen, eds., *The Cambridge History of Chinese Literature* (Cambridge: Cambridge University Press, 2010), 2: 157–162, 220–229; On Cho Ng, *Cheng-Zhu Confucianism in the Early Qing: Li Guangdi (1642–1718) and Qing Learning* (Albany: State University of New York Press, 2001); Elman, *Cultural History of Civil Examinations*.

59. Huang Zongxi and Wm. Theodore de Bary, *Waiting for the Dawn: A Plan for the Prince* (New York: Columbia University Press, 1993).

60. Wm. Theodore de Bary and Richard Lufrano, *Sources of Chinese Tradition: From 1600 through the Twentieth Century*, 2nd ed. (New York: Columbia University Press, 2010), 1:35–41. See also Gu Yanwu, *Record of Daily Knowledge and Collected Poems and Essays: Selections*, trans. and ed. Ian Johnston (New York: Columbia University Press, 2017).

61. R. Kent Guy, *The Emperor's Four Treasuries: Scholars and the State in the Late Ch'ien-Lung Era* (Cambridge, MA: Council on East Asian Studies, Harvard University, 1987).

62. Sebastian Conrad, "Enlightenment in Global History: A Historiographical Critique," *American Historical Review* 117.4 (2012): 999–1027.

63. Evelyn S. Rawski, "Chinese Strategy and Security Issues in Historical Perspective," in *China's Rise in Historical Perspective*, ed. Brantly Womack (Lanham, MD: Rowman and Littlefield, 2010).

64. I am drawing on the work of Takeshi Hamashita, Linda Grove, and Mark Selden, eds., *China, East Asia and the Global Economy* (Abingdon, UK: Routledge, 2008); Jean-Laurent Rosenthal and R. Bin Wong, *Before and Beyond Divergence: The Politics of Economic Change in China and Europe* (Cambridge, MA: Harvard University Press, 2011); R. Bin Wong, *China Transformed: Historical Change and the Limits of European Experience* (Ithaca, NY: Cornell University Press, 1997); Kenneth Pomeranz, *The Great Divergence: China, Europe, and the Making of the Modern World Economy* (Princeton, NJ: Princeton University Press, 2000); Andre G. Frank, *Reorient: Global Economy in the Asian Age* (Berkeley: University of California Press, 1998); Kaoru Sugihara, *Japan, China, and the Growth of the Asian International Economy, 1850–1949* (Oxford: Oxford University Press, 2005); Anthony Reid, *Southeast Asia in the Age of Commerce, 1450–1680* (New Haven, CT: Yale University Press, 1988).

65. The origins of the tribute system and its underlying ideas, values, and beliefs can be traced back to the Han dynasty (206 BCE–220 CE), when the tribute system was used to regulate China's trade and diplomacy with its neighbors.

General studies include: David C. Kang, *East Asia before the West: Five Centuries of Trade and Tribute* (New York: Columbia University Press, 2010); John King Fairbank, ed., *The Chinese World Order: Traditional China's Foreign Relations* (Cambridge, MA: Harvard University Press, 1968); Zhang Yongjin, "The Tribute System," in *Oxford Bibliographies in Chinese Studies*.

66. Kang, *East Asia before the West*, 56.

67. Alan Wood, *Russia's Frozen Frontier: A History of Siberia and the Russian Far East 1581–1991* (London: Bloomsbury Academic, 2011), 51–52; Jan Burbank and Frederick Cooper, *Empires in World History: Power and the Politics of Difference* (Princeton, NJ: Princeton University Press, 2011), 213–218.

68. Perdue, *China Marches West*, 211.

2. REORDERING THE CHINESE WORLD: 1800–1870

1. Pedro Machado, *Ocean of Trade: South Asian Merchants, Africa and the Indian Ocean, c. 1750–1850* (Cambridge: Cambridge University Press, 2014); Kirti Narayan Chaudhuri, *Trade and Civilisation in the Indian Ocean: An Economic History from the Rise of Islam to 1750* (Cambridge: Cambridge University Press, 1985); Donald F. Lach and Edwin J. Van Kley, *Asia in the Making of Europe* (Chicago: University of Chicago Press, 1965).

2. Emily Erikson, *Between Monopoly and Free Trade: The English East India Company, 1600–1757* (Princeton, NJ: Princeton University Press, 2014); Angela Schottenhammer ed. [see ch 3 n4], *The East Asian Maritime World 1400–1800: Its Fabrics of Power and Dynamics of Exchanges* (Wiesbaden: Harrassowitz, 2007); H. V. Bowen, *The Business of Empire: The East India Company and Imperial Britain, 1756–1833* (Cambridge: Cambridge University Press, 2006); Kirti Narayan Chaudhuri, *The Trading World of Asia and the English East India Company, 1660–1760* (Cambridge: Cambridge University Press, 1978).

3. Philip Thai, *China's War on Smuggling: Law, Economic Life, and the Making of the Modern State, 1842–1965* (New York: Columbia University Press, 2018) chapter 1.

4. William T. Rowe, *China's Last Empire: The Great Qing* (Cambridge, MA: Harvard University Press, 2009), 141–148.

5. Quoted in Frederick Wakeman, Jr., *The Fall of Imperial China* (New York: Free Press, 1975), 101. On the Macartney mission, see James Louis Hevia, *Cherishing Men from Afar: Qing Guest Ritual and the Macartney Embassy of 1793* (Durham, NC: Duke University Press, 2005).

6. J. Mason Gentzler, *Changing China: Readings in the History of China from the Opium War to the Present* (New York: Praeger, 1977), 25.

7. Historical research on the Chinese opium question has moved beyond the

narrow confines of the Sino-British war (1840–1842) to broader historiographical and theoretical issues. Recent contributors to the new scholarship include Timothy Brook and Bob Tadashi Wakabayashi, eds., *Opium Regimes: China, Britain, and Japan, 1839–1952* (Berkeley: University of California Press, 2000); Edward Slack, *Opium, State, and Society: China's Narco-Economy and the Guomindang, 1934–1937* (Honolulu: University of Hawai'i Press, 2001); Joyce Madancy, *The Troublesome Legacy of Commissioner Lin: The Opium Trade and Opium Suppression in Fujian Province, 1820s to 1920s* (Cambridge, MA: Harvard University Asia Center, 2003); Frank Dikötter, Lars Laamann, and Zhou Xun, *Narcotic Culture: A History of Drugs in China* (Chicago: University of Chicago Press, 2004); and David Anthony Bello, *Opium and the Limits of Empire: Drug Prohibition in the Chinese Interior, 1729–1850* (Cambridge, MA: Harvard University Asia Center, 2005).

8. On the Opium War, see Stephen R. Platt, *Imperial Twilight: The Opium War and the End of China's Last Golden Age* (New York: Alfred A. Knopf, 2018); Julia Lovell, *The Opium War: Drugs, Dreams and the Making of China* (London: Picador, 2011); Robert A. Bickers, *The Scramble for China: Foreign Devils in the Qing Empire, 1832–1914* (London: Allen Lane, 2011); Madancy, *The Troublesome Legacy of Commissioner Lin;* James Polachek, *The Inner Opium War* (Cambridge, MA: Council on East Asian Studies, Harvard University, 1992). The English versions of key articles of the treaty may be found in Gentzler, *Changing China,* 29–32.

9. The following paragraphs are based on Stephen R. Platt, *Autumn in the Heavenly Kingdom: China, the West, and the Epic Story of the Taiping Civil War* (New York: Alfred A. Knopf, 2012), 25–50; and John Yue-wo Wong, *Deadly Dreams: Opium, Imperialism, and the Arrow War (1856–1860) in China* (Cambridge: Cambridge University Press, 1998).

10. Harry Gelber, *Battle for Beijing, 1858–1860: Franco-British Conflict in China* (Switzerland: Palgrave Macmillan, 2016), 105–130; Michael Mann, *China, 1860* (Salisbury, Wiltshire: Russell, 1989).

11. See James L. Hevia, "Looting Beijing: 1860, 1900," in *Tokens of Exchange,* ed. Lydia Liu (Durham, NC: Duke University Press, 1999), 193–194.

12. Quoted in Arne O. Westad, *Restless Empire: China and the World since 1750* (New York: Basic Books, 2012), 51.

13. Mark Bassin, *Imperial Visions: Nationalist Imagination and Geographical Expansion in the Russian Far East, 1840–1865* (Cambridge: Cambridge University Press, 1999).

14. Sebastian Conrad and Klaus Mühlhahn, "Global Mobility and Nationalism: Chinese Migration and the Reterritorialization of Belonging, 1880–1910," in *Competing Visions of World Order: Global Moments and Movements,*

1880s–1930, ed. Sebastian Conrad and Dominic Sachsenmaier (New York: Palgrave Macmillan, 2007), 181–211; Walton Look Lai, *Indentured Labor, Caribbean Sugar: Chinese and Indian Migrants to the British West Indies, 1838–1918* (Baltimore, MD: Johns Hopkins University Press, 2003); Yen Ching-Hwang, *Coolies and Mandarins: China's Protection of Overseas Chinese during the Late Ch'ing Period (1851–1911)* (Singapore: Singapore University Press, 1985).

15. Rowe, *China's Last Empire,* 172–173.

16. Hans van de Ven, *Breaking with the Past: The Maritime Customs Service and the Global Origins of Modernity in China* (New York: Columbia University Press, 2014).

17. Teemu Ruskola, *Legal Orientalism: China, the United States, and Modern Law* (Cambridge, MA: Harvard University Press, 2013), 108–151; Pär Kristoffer Cassel, *Grounds of Judgment: Extraterritoriality and Imperial Power in Nineteenth-Century China and Japan* (Oxford: Oxford University Press, 2012).

18. Ann Laura Stoler and Carole McGranahan, "Refiguring Imperial Terrains," in *Imperial Formations,* ed. Ann Laura Stoler, Carole McGranahan, and Peter C. Perdue (Santa Fe, NM: School for Advanced Research Press 2007), 3–44.

19. Jürgen Osterhammel, *Colonialism: A Theoretical Overview* (Princeton, NJ: M. Wiener, 1997), 19; and Jürgen Osterhammel, "Semi-colonialism and Informal Empire in 20th-Century China," in *Imperialism and After: Continuities and Discontinuities,* ed. Wolfgang J. Mommsen and Jürgen Osterhammel (London: Allen and Unwin, 1986), 290–341.

20. Rebecca E. Karl, "On Comparability and Continuity: China, circa 1930's and 1990's," *boundary 2* (2005): 169–200.

21. There is a wealth of literature on the subject. Important titles include Robert A. Bickers and Isabella Jackson, *Treaty Ports in Modern China* (New York: Routledge, 2015); Bryna Goodman and David S. G. Goodman, *Twentieth-Century Colonialism and China: Localities, the Everyday and the World* (Milton Park, Abingdon, UK: Routledge, 2012); Robert Bickers and Christian Henriot, eds., *New Frontiers: Imperialism's New Communities in East Asia, 1842–1953* (Manchester, UK: Manchester University Press, 2000); Nicholas R. Clifford, *Spoilt Children of Empire: Westerners in Shanghai and the Chinese Revolution of the 1920s* (Hanover, NH: University Press of New England, 1991); John K. Fairbank, *Trade and Diplomacy on the China Coast: The Opening of the Treaty Ports, 1842–1854* (Cambridge, MA: Harvard University Press, 1953); Albert Feuerwerker, "The Foreign Presence in China," in *The Cambridge History of China* (Cambridge: Cambridge University Press, 1983), 12:129–208; Jürgen Osterhammel, "Britain and China, 1842–1914," in *The Oxford History of the British Empire,* ed. Andrew Porter (New York: Oxford University Press, 1999), 3:146–

169; Mark Peattie, "Japanese Treaty Port Settlements in China, 1895–1937," in *Japanese Informal Empire in China, 1895–1937*, ed. Peter Duus, Ramon Myers, and Mark Peattie (Stanford, CA: Stanford University Press, 1989), 166–209; Rudolf G. Wagner, "The Role of the Foreign Community in the Chinese Public Sphere," *China Quarterly* 142 (1995): 423–443.

22. Marie-Claire Bergère, *Shanghai: China's Gateway to Modernity* (Stanford, CA: Stanford University Press, 2009); Xiong Yuezhi, ed., *Shanghai tongshi* (Shanghai: Shanghai renmin chubanshe, 1999); Fairbank, *Trade and Diplomacy on the China Coast.*

23. Robert Bickers and Jeffrey N. Wasserstrom, "Shanghai's 'Dogs and Chinese Not Admitted' Sign: Legend, History, and Contemporary Symbol," *China Quarterly* 142 (1995): 444–466.

24. Klaus Mühlhahn, Wen-hsin Yeh, and Hajo Frölich, eds., "Introduction," in "Rethinking Business History in Modern China" special issue, *Cross-Currents* 4.2 (2015): 1–12; Wen-hsin Yeh, *Shanghai Splendor: Economic Sentiments and the Making of Modern China, 1843–1949* (Berkeley: University of California Press, 2007); David Faure, *China and Capitalism: A History of Business Enterprise in Modern China* (Hong Kong: Hong Kong University Press, 2006); Madeline Zelin and Andrea McElderry, "Guest Editors' Introduction" in "Business History in Modern China" special issue, *Enterprise & Society* 6.3 (2005): 357–363; Sherman Cochran, *Big Business in China: Sino-Foreign Rivalry in the Cigarette Industry, 1890–1930* (Cambridge, MA: Harvard University Press, 1980).

25. Bert Becker, "Coastal Shipping in East Asia in the Late Nineteenth Century," *Journal of the Royal Asiatic Society Hong Kong Branch* 50 (2010): 245–302; Howard Cox, Biao Huang, and Stuart Metcalfe, "Compradors, Firm Architecture, and the 'Reinvention' of British Trading Companies: John Swire & Sons' Operations in Early Twentieth-Century China," *Business History* 45.2 (2003): 15–34; Sherman Cochran, *Encountering Chinese Networks: Western, Japanese, and Chinese Corporations in China, 1880–1937* (Berkeley: University of California Press, 2000); William D. Wray, *Mitsubishi and the N.Y.K., 1870–1914: Business Strategy in the Japanese Shipping Industry* (Cambridge, MA: Harvard University Press, 1984); Hou Chi-ming, *Foreign Investment and Economic Development in China, 1840–1937* (Cambridge, MA: Harvard University Press, 1980); Liu Kwang Ching, *Anglo-American Steamship Rivalry in China, 1862–1874* (Cambridge, MA: Harvard University Press, 1956); Liu Kwang Ching, "British-Chinese Steamship Rivalry in China, 1873–85," in *The Economic Development of China and Japan,* ed. C. D. Cowan (New York: Praeger, 1964), 49–77.

26. Lillian Li, *China's Silk Trade: Traditional Industry in the Modern World* (Cambridge, MA: Harvard University Press, 1981); Wellington K. K. Chan, *Mer-*

chants, Mandarins, and Modern Enterprise in Late Ch'ing China (Cambridge, MA: East Asian Research Center, Harvard University, 1977).

27. Cheng Linsun, *Banking in Modern China: Entrepreneurs, Professional Managers and the Development of Chinese Banks, 1897–1937* (New York: Cambridge University Press, 2003); Niv Horesh, *Shanghai's Bund and Beyond: British Banks, Banknote Issuance, and Monetary Policy in China, 1842–1937* (New Haven, CT: Yale University Press, 2009); Frank H. H. King, *Eastern Banking: Essays in the History of the Hongkong and Shanghai Banking Corporation* (London: Athlone Press, 1983).

28. Sherman Cochran, *Chinese Medicine Men: Consumer Culture in China and Southeast Asia* (Cambridge, MA: Harvard University Press, 2006).

29. Rudolf G. Wagner, *Joining the Global Public: Word, Image, and City in Early Chinese Newspapers, 1870–1910* (Albany: State University of New York Press, 2007); Natascha Vittinghoff, "Readers, Publishers and Officials in the Contest for a Public Voice and the Rise of a Modern Press in Late Qing China (1860–1880)," *T'oung Pao* 87 (2001): 393–455; Natascha Vittinghoff, *Die Anfänge des Journalismus in China (1860–1911)* (Wiesbaden: Harassowitz, 2002); Barbara Mittler, *A Newspaper for China? Power, Identity and Change in Shanghai's News Media (1872–1912)* (Cambridge, MA: Harvard University Press, 2004); Henrietta Harrison, "Newspapers and Nationalism in Rural China, 1890–1929," *Past and Present* 106 (2000): 181–204; Joan Judge, *Print and Politics: "Shibao" and the Culture of Reform in Late Qing China 1996* (Stanford, CA: Stanford University Press, 1996).

30. Zhang Xiantao, *The Origins of the Modern Chinese Press: The Influence of the Protestant Missionary Press in Late Qing China* (London: Routledge, 2010); Wang Dong, *Managing God's Higher Learning: U.S.-China Cultural Encounter and Canton Christian College (Lingnan University), 1888–1952* (Lanham, MD: Lexington Books, 2007); Alvyn Austin, *China's Millions: The China Inland Mission and Late Qing Society, 1832–1905* (Grand Rapids, MI: W. B. Eerdmans, 2007); Edward J. M. Rhoads, *Stepping Forth into the World: The Chinese Educational Mission to the United States, 1872–81* (Hong Kong: Hong Kong University Press, 2011).

31. Christoph Kaderas, "The Founding of China's First Polytechnic Institution," *Asiatische Studien* 4 (1999): 893–903.

32. Laurence J. C. Ma, "The State of the Field of Urban China: A Critical Multidisciplinary Overview of the Literature," in "Urban China" special issue, *China Information* 20.3 (2006): 363–389; Joseph W. Esherick, "Modernity and Nation in the Chinese City," in *Remaking the Chinese City: Modernity and National Identity, 1900–1950,* ed. Joseph W. Esherick (Honolulu: University of Hawai'i Press, 2000); David Strand, "'A High Place Is No Better than a Low Place': The

City in the Making of Modern China," in *Becoming Chinese: Passages to Modernity and Beyond*, ed. Wen-hsin Yeh (Berkeley: University of California Press, 2000); Elizabeth J. Perry, "From Paris to the Paris of the East—and Back: Workers as Citizens in Modern Shanghai," in *Changing Meanings of Citizenship in Modern China*, ed. Merle Goldman and Elizabeth J. Perry (Cambridge, MA: Harvard University Press, 2002); Elizabeth J. Perry, *Shanghai on Strike: The Politics of Chinese Labor* (Stanford, CA: Stanford University Press, 1993); G. William Skinner, "Regional Urbanization in Nineteenth-Century China," in *The City in Late Imperial China*, ed. G. William Skinner (Stanford, CA: Stanford University Press, 1977).

33. Brian G. Martin, *The Shanghai Green Gang: Politics and Organized Crime, 1919–1937* (Berkeley: University of California Press, 1996).

34. Bryna Goodman, *Native Place, City and Nation: Regional Networks and Identities in Shanghai, 1853–1937* (Berkeley: University of California Press, 1995), 14–32.

35. Leo Ou-fan Lee, *Shanghai Modern: The Flowering of a New Urban Culture in China, 1930–1945* (Cambridge, MA: Harvard University Press, 1999), 203.

36. Tsai Weipin, *Reading Shenbao: Nationalism, Consumerism and Individuality in China, 1919–37* (Basingstoke, UK: Palgrave Macmillan, 2010); Rudolf G. Wagner, "The Role of the Foreign Community in the Chinese Public Sphere," *China Quarterly* 142 (1995): 423–443.

37. The estimate for the budget of the Board of Revenue is from Helen Dunstan, *State or Merchant: Political Economy and Political Process in 1740s China* (Cambridge, MA: Harvard University Asia Center, 2006), 446. On the reform policy, see Wang Wensheng, *White Lotus Rebels and South China Pirates: Crisis and Reform in the Qing Empire* (Cambridge, MA: Harvard University Press, 2014), 28. See also William T. Rowe, "Introduction: The Significance of the Qianlong-Jiaqing Transition in Chinese History," *Late Imperial China* 32.2 (2011): 74–88.

38. Richard von Glahn, *Economic History of China: From Antiquity to the Nineteenth Century* (Cambridge: Cambridge University Press, 2016), 553–564.

39. Lin Manhong, *China Upside Down: Currency, Society, and Ideologies, 1808–1856* (Cambridge, MA: Harvard University Asia Center, 2006); Lin Manhong, "Two Social Theories Revealed: Statecraft Controversies over China's Monetary Crisis, 1808–1854," *Late Imperial China* 2 (1991): 1–35.

40. Pierre-Etienne Will and R. Bin Wong, with James Lee, *Nourish the People: The State Civilian Granary System in China, 1650–1850* (Ann Arbor: Center for Chinese Studies, University of Michigan, 1991), 75–92; Pierre-Etienne Will, *Bureaucracy and Famine in Eighteenth-Century China* (Stanford, CA: Stanford University Press, 1990), 289–301; Susan Mann Jones and Philip Kuhn, "Dy-

nastic Decline and the Roots of Rebellion," in *The Cambridge History of China,* ed. John K. Fairbank (Cambridge: Cambridge University Press, 1978), 10:107–162; Peter C. Perdue, *Exhausting the Earth: State and Peasant in Hunan, 1500–1850* (Cambridge, MA: Harvard University Press, 1987).

41. Pei Huang, *Autocracy at Work: A Study of the Yung-cheng Period, 1723–1735* (Bloomington: Indiana University Press, 1974), 16; Hung Ho-fung, *Protest with Chinese Characteristics: Demonstrations, Riots, and Petitions in the Mid-Qing Dynasty* (New York: Columbia University Press, 2011), 131–133; Madeleine Zelin, *The Magistrate's Tael: Rationalizing Fiscal Reform in Eighteenth-Century Ch'ing China* (Berkeley: University of California Press, 1984); Jones and Kuhn, "Dynastic Decline and the Roots of Rebellion," 119–130.

42. Wang Yeh-chien, "Secular Trends of Rice Prices in the Yangzi Delta, 1638–1935," in *Chinese History in Economic Perspective,* ed. Thomas G. Rawski and Lillian M. Li (Berkeley: University of California Press, 1992), 35–68; Frederic Wakeman, *Strangers at the Gate: Social Disorder in South China, 1839–1861* (Berkeley: University of California Press, 1966), 133; Wang Yeh-chien, "Evolution of the Chinese Monetary System, 1644–1850," in *Modern Chinese Economic History: Proceedings of the Conference on Modern Chinese Economic History, August 26–29, 1977,* ed. Chi-ming Hou and Yu Tzong-shian (Taipei: Academia Sinica, 1979), 425–452.

43. Ralph W. Huenemann, *The Dragon and the Iron Horse: The Economics of Railroads in China, 1876–1937* (Cambridge, MA: Harvard University Press, 1984).

44. David Ownby and Mary F. Somers Heidhues, eds., *"Secret Societies" Reconsidered: Perspectives on the Social History of Early Modern South China and Southeast Asia* (Abingdon, Oxon, UK: Routledge, 2015); Dian Murray, in collaboration with Qin Baoqi, *The Origins of the Tiandihui: The Chinese Triads in Legend and History* (Stanford, CA: Stanford University Press, 1994); David Ownby, *Brotherhoods and Secret Societies in Early and Mid-Qing China: The Formation of a Tradition* (Stanford, CA: Stanford University Press, 1996); Jean Chesneaux, ed., *Popular Movements and Secret Societies in China, 1840–1950* (Stanford, CA: Stanford University Press, 1977).

45. Hakka or, in Mandarin, *kejia* (guest people) were originally from North China, but migrated to South China (especially Guangdong, Fujian, Jiangxi, and Guangxi provinces) during the fall of the Nan (Southern) Song dynasty in the 1270s. Having settled in South China in their own communities, the Hakka never became fully assimilated into the native population. During the eighteenth and nineteenth centuries, when conditions in South China deteriorated and land scarcity became prevalent, the Hakka were often involved in land feuds with the local population *(bendi).* Nicole Constable, *Guest People: Hakka Identity in China and Abroad* (Seattle: University of Washington Press, 2006); Sow-Theng Leong, Tim Wright, and G. W. Skinner, *Migration and Ethnicity in Chi-*

nese History: Hakkas, Pengmin, and Their Neighbors (Stanford, CA: Stanford University Press, 1997).

46. For the best summary of the debate, see Paul A. Cohen, *Discovering History in China: American Historical Writing on the Recent Chinese Past* (1984; New York: Columbia University Press, 2010); see also Hou Jiming, *Foreign Investment and Economic Development in China, 1840–1937* (Cambridge, MA: Harvard University Press, 1965); Andrew Nathan, "Imperialism's Effect on China," *Bulletin of Concerned Asian Scholars* [*Critical Asian Studies*] 4.4 (1972): 3–8; Joseph W. Esherick, "Harvard on China: The Apologetics of Imperialism," *Bulletin of Concerned Asian Scholars* [*Critical Asian Studies*] 4.4 (1972): 9–16.

47. Kenneth Pomeranz, *The Making of a Hinterland: State, Society, and Economy in Inland North China, 1853–1937* (Berkeley: University of California Press, 1993), 24.

48. Robert Y. Eng, *Economic Imperialism in China: Silk Production and Exports, 1861–1932* (Berkeley: Center for Chinese Studies, University of California, 1986), 11.

49. Cochran, *Encountering Chinese Networks;* Elisabeth Köll, *From Cotton Mill to Business Empire: The Emergence of Regional Enterprise in Modern China* (Cambridge, MA: Harvard University Asia Center, 2004); Aihwa Ong and Donald Macon Nonini, eds., *Ungrounded Empires: The Cultural Politics of Modern Chinese Transnationalism* (New York: Routledge, 1997); Daniel J. Meissner, *Chinese Capitalists versus the American Flour Industry, 1890–1910: Profit and Patriotism in International Trade* (Lewiston, NY: Edwin Mellen Press, 2005); Chan, *Merchants, Mandarins, and Modern Enterprise,* 79.

50. Mike Davis, *Late Victorian Holocausts: El Niño Famines and the Making of the Third World* (London: Verso, 2001); evidence of low temperatures and declining rainfall is cited by David D. Zhang, Jane Zhang, Harry F. Lee, and He Yuanqing, "Climate Change and War Frequency in Eastern China over the Last Millennium," *Human Ecology* 35.4 (2007): 403–414; Lillian M. Li, *Fighting Famine in North China: State, Market, and Environmental Decline, 1690s–1990s* (Stanford, CA: Stanford University Press, 2007), 27–30; Qing Pei and David D. Zhang, "Long-Term Relationship between Climate Change and Nomadic Migration in Historical China," *Ecology and Society* 19.2 (2014): 68.

51. Kathryn Edgerton-Tarpley, *Tears from Iron: Cultural Responses to Famine in Nineteenth-Century China* (Berkeley: University of California Press, 2008); Paul Richard Bohr, *Famine in China and the Missionary: Timothy Richard as Relief Administrator and Advocate of National Reform, 1876–1884* (Cambridge, MA: Harvard University Press, 1972).

52. Robert H. G. Lee, *The Manchurian Frontier in Ch'ing History* (Cambridge, MA: Harvard University Press, 1970); Thomas R. Gottschang and Diana Lary, *Swal-*

lows and Settlers: The Great Migration from North China to Manchuria (Ann Arbor: Center for Chinese Studies, University of Michigan, 2000); Philip A. Kuhn, *Chinese among Others: Emigration in Modern Times* (Lanham, MD: Rowman and Littlefield, 2008).

53. Joanna Handlin Smith, *The Art of Doing Good: Charity in Late Ming China* (Berkeley: University of California Press, 2009); Vivienne Shue, "The Quality of Mercy: Confucian Charity and the Mixed Metaphors of Modernity in Tianjin," *Modern China* 32.4 (2006): 411–452; William T. Rowe, *Hankow: Conflict and Community in a Chinese City, 1796–1895* (Stanford, CA: Stanford University Press, 1989), 100–103; Mary B. Rankin, *Elite Activism and Political Transformation in China* (Stanford, CA: Stanford University Press, 1986).

54. Elizabeth J. Perry, *Rebels and Revolutionaries in North China, 1845–1945* (Stanford, CA: Stanford University Press, 1980), 1–9. See also Roxann Prazniak, *Of Camel Kings and Other Things: Rural Rebels against Modernity in Late Imperial China* (Lanham, MD: Rowman and Littlefield, 1999).

55. Wang, *White Lotus Rebels,* 41–48; Richard Shek, "Ethics and Polity: The Heterodoxy of Buddhism, Maitreyanism, and the Early White Lotus," in *Heterodoxy in Late Imperial China,* ed. Kwang-Ching Liu and Richard H.-C. Shek (Honolulu: University of Hawai'i Press, 2004); Bernard J. ter Haar, *The White Lotus Teachings in Chinese Religious History* (Leiden: E. J. Brill, 1992); Susan Naquin, "Transmission of White Lotus Sectarianism in Late Imperial China," in *Popular Culture in Late Imperial China,* ed. David G. Johnson, Andrew J. Nathan, Evelyn S. Rawski, and Judith A. Berling (Berkeley: University of California Press, 1985); Hok-lam Chan, "The White Lotus—Maitreya Doctrine and Popular Uprisings in Ming and Ch'ing China," *Sinologica* 10 (1969): 211–233.

56. Manicheanism refers to a religion founded by the Persian prophet Mani in the 3rd century CE. It was introduced to China in the 6th century during the Tang dynasty. Manicheanism is considered a form of Gnosticism, a system of belief based on the importance of grasping religious mysteries with the mind. Sammuel L. C. Lieu, "Manicheism in China," *Encyclopædia Iranica,* online edition, 2002, http://www.iranicaonline.org/articles/manicheism-v-in-china-1.

57. Rowe, *China's Last Empire,* 157. On the Eight Trigram Rebellion, see Susan Naquin, *Millenarian Rebellion in China: The Eight Trigrams Uprising of 1813* (New Haven, CT: Yale University Press, 1976); Susan Naquin, *Shantung Rebellion: The Wang Lun Uprising of 1774* (New Haven, CT: Yale University Press, 1981); Pamela K. Crossley, *The Wobbling Pivot, China since 1800: An Interpretive History* (Malden, MA: Wiley-Blackwell, 2010), 59.

58. Perry, *Rebels and Revolutionaries,* 96–151.

59. The best available histories of the Taiping are Platt, *Autumn in the Heavenly Kingdom;* and Jonathan D. Spence, *God's Chinese Son: The Taiping Heavenly*

Kingdom of Hong Xiuquan (New York: W. W. Norton: 1996). The quotes are from Spence, pp. 116, 160. A reconstruction of the war through memories and personal texts is Tobie S. Meyer-Fong, *What Remains: Coming to Terms with Civil War in 19th Century China* (Stanford, CA: Stanford University Press, 2013).

60. The Taiping belief system and ideology is discussed in Rudolf G. Wagner, *Re-enacting the Heavenly Vision: The Role of Religion in the Taiping Rebellion* (Berkeley: Institute of East Asian Studies, Center for Chinese Studies, University of California, 1984); Philip Kuhn, "Origins of the Taiping Vision: Cross-Cultural Dimensions of a Chinese Rebellion," *Comparative Studies in Society and History* 19.3 (1977): 350–366.

61. Spence, *God's Chinese Son*, 171.

62. Taiping Imperial Declaration, cited in Kuhn, "Origins of the Taiping Vision," 360.

63. The following section is based on Platt, *Autumn in the Heavenly Kingdom*, chapter 3, and Spence, *God's Chinese Son*, 173–191; see also the important original document by Hong Rengan, Zizheng xinbian [A new work for the aid of government], trans. in Franz Michael, *The Taiping Rebellion: History and Documents* (Seattle: University of Washington Press, 1966–1971), 3:751–776.

64. "The Land System of the Heavenly Kingdom" (*Tianchao tianmu zhidu*), trans. in Theodore de Bary and Richard Lufrano, *Sources of Chinese Tradition: From 1600 through the Twentieth Century* (New York: Columbia University Press, 2000), 2:224–226.

65. See Document Nr. 208 in Michael, *The Taiping Rebellion*, 869–897.

66. Theda Skocpol, *States and Social Revolutions: A Comparative Analysis of France, Russia, and China* (Cambridge: Cambridge University Press, 1979).

67. The following section is based on Morris Rossabi, *A History of China* (Malden, MA: John Wiley and Sons, 2014), 307–311; David G. Atwill, *The Chinese Sultanate: Islam, Ethnicity, and the Panthay Rebellion in Southwest China, 1856–1873* (Stanford, CA: Stanford University Press, 2006), S. Frederick Starr, *Xinjiang: China's Muslim Borderland* (Armonk, NY: M.E. Sharpe, 2004); Kim Hodong, *Holy War in China: The Muslim Rebellion and State in Chinese Central Asia, 1864–1877* (Stanford, CA: Stanford University Press, 2004); Jonathan N. Lipman, *Familiar Strangers: A History of Muslims in Northwest China* (Seattle: University of Washington Press, 1998); Robert D. Jenks, *Insurgency and Social Disorder in Guizhou: The "Miao" Rebellion, 1854–1873* (Honolulu: University of Hawai'i Press, 1994).

68. Peter Lavalle, "Cultivating Empire: Zuo Zontang's Agriculture, Environment, and Reconstruction in the Kate Qing," in *China on the Margins*, ed. Sherman Cochran and Paul Pickowicz (Ithaca, NY: Cornell East Asia Program, 2010).

69. David Gillard, *The Struggle for Asia, 1828–1914: A Study in British and Russian Imperialism* (NY: Holmes and Meier, 1980).

70. Christopher I. Beckwith, *Empires of the Silk Road: A History of Central Eurasia from the Bronze Age to the Present* (Princeton, NJ: Princeton University Press, 2009), 241–242; Peter Frankopan, *The Silk Roads: A New History of the World* (New York: Alfred A. Knopf, 2016).

71. James A. Millward, *Eurasian Crossroads: A History of Xinjiang* (New York: Columbia University Press, 2007), 124–177.

72. Bruce Elleman and Stephen Kotkin, eds., *Manchurian Railways and the Opening of China: An International History* (Armonk, NY: M.E. Sharpe, 2010).

73. Philip A. Kuhn, *Rebellion and Its Enemies in Late Imperial China: Militarization and Social Structure, 1796–1864* (Cambridge, MA: Harvard University Press, 1970), 211–233.

3. LATE QING PREDICAMENTS: 1870–1900

1. Benjamin A. Elman, "Early Modern or Late Imperial? The Crisis of Classical Philology in Eighteenth-Century China," *Frontiers of History in China* 6.1 (2011): 3–25; Benjamin A. Elman, *From Philosophy to Philology: Intellectual and Social Aspects of Change in Late Imperial China* (Cambridge, MA: Council on East Asian Studies, Harvard University, 1984).

2. Elman, *From Philosophy to Philology*, 28. See also Elman, *On Their Own Terms: Science in China, 1550–1900* (Cambridge, MA: Harvard University Press, 2005).

3. Anne Cheng, "Nationalism, Citizenship and the Old Text / New Text Controversy in Late Nineteenth Century China," in *Imagining the People: Chinese Intellectuals and the Concept of Citizenship,* ed. Joshua A. Fogel and Peter G. Zarrow (Armonk, NY: M.E. Sharpe, 1997), 61–81; Benjamin A. Elman, *Classicism, Politics, and Kinship: The Ch'angchou School of New Text Confucianism in Late Imperial China* (Berkeley: University of California Press, 1990).

4. Jane Kate Leonard, *Wei Yuan and China's Rediscovery of the Maritime World* (Cambridge, MA: Council on East Asian Studies, Harvard University, 1984); Jane Kate Leonard, "Timeliness and Innovation: The 1845 Revision of The Complete Book on Grain Transport *(Caoyun quanshu),*" in *Chinese Handicraft Regulations of the Qing Dynasty: Theory and Application,* ed. Christine Moll-Murata, Song Jianze, and Hans Ulrich Vogel (Munich: Iudicum, 2005), 449–464; Jane Kate Leonard, "The Qing Strategic Highway on the Northeast Coast," in *The Perception of Maritime Space in Traditional Chinese Sources,* ed. Angela Schottenhammer and Roderich Ptak (Wiesbaden: Harrassowitz, 2006), 27–39.

5. Today's Jiangsu and Anhui were the combined province of Jiangnan (south of the Yangzi) in Qing China. Together with Jiangxi (west of the Yangzi) the

provinces were known as the two *jiangs*, hence the name *"Liangjiang."* There were nine governors-general *(zongdu)* who supervised provincial governments.

6. Wei quoted in Ssu-yü Teng and John K. Fairbank, eds., *Research Guide for China's Response to the West: A Documentary Survey, 1839–1923* (Cambridge, MA: Harvard University Press, 1979).

7. Orville Schell and John Delury, Introduction to *Wealth and Power: China's Long March to the Twenty-First Century* (New York: Random House, 2013); Helen Dunstan, *Conflicting Counsels to Confuse the Age: A Documentary Study of Political Economy in Qing China, 1644–1840* (Ann Arbor: Center for Chinese Studies, University of Michigan, 1996).

8. Philip A. Kuhn, "Reform on Trial," in *Origins of the Modern Chinese State* (Stanford, CA: Stanford University Press, 2002), 54–79.

9. Schell and Delury, *Wealth and Power,* 11–36.

10. J. Mason Gentzler, *Changing China: Readings in the History of China from the Opium War to the Present* (New York: Praeger, 1977), 70–71.

11. Wm. T. de Bary and Richard Lufrano, comp., *Sources of Chinese Tradition* (New York: Columbia University Press, 1960), 2:47.

12. On the Qing restoration and its industrial policies in general, see Shellen X. Wu, *Empires of Coal: Fueling China's Entry into the Modern World Order, 1860–1920* (Stanford, CA: Stanford University Press, 2015); Elisabeth Köll, *From Cotton Mill to Business Empire: The Emergence of Regional Enterprises in Modern China* (Cambridge, MA: Harvard University Asia Center, 2004); Samuel C. Chu and Liu Kwang-Ching, *Li Hung-Chang and China's Early Modernization* (Armonk, NY: M.E. Sharpe, 1994); Mary C. Wright, *The Last Stand of Chinese Conservatism: The T'ung-chih Restoration, 1862–1874,* rev. ed. (New York: Atheneum, 1965). On Zeng Guofan, see Jonathan Porter, *Tseng Kuo-fan's Private Bureaucracy* (Berkeley: Center for Chinese Studies, University of California, 1972); Hellmut Wilhelm, "The Background of Tseng Kuofan's Ideology," *Asiatische Studien* 3–4 (1949): 90–100; William J. Hail, *Tseng Kuo-fan and the Taiping Rebellion: With a Short Sketch of His Later Career* (New Haven, CT: Yale University Press, 1927).

13. On Zeng's song, see Stephen R. Platt, *Autumn in the Heavenly Kingdom: China, the West, and the Epic Story of the Taiping Civil War* (New York: Alfred A. Knopf, 2013), 175.

14. On Zeng's writings as one of modern China's most popular books, see Guo Yingjie and He Baogang, "Reimagining the Chinese Nation: The 'Zeng Guofan Phenomenon,'" *Modern China* 25.2 (1999): 142–170.

15. See Richard von Glahn, *Economic History of China: From Antiquity to the Nineteenth Century* (Cambridge: Cambridge University Press, 2016), 570, Table 9.7.

16. See David Faure, *China and Capitalism: A History of Business Enterprise in*

Modern China (Hong Kong: Hong Kong University Press, 2006), 50–56. On this model, see Wellington K. K. Chan, *Merchants, Mandarins, and Modern Enterprise in Late Ch'ing China* (Cambridge, MA: Harvard University Press, 1977).

17. Kuo Ting-Yee and Liu Kwang-Ching, "Self-Strengthening: The Pursuit of Western Technology," in *The Cambridge History of China,* volume 10: Late Ch'ing, 1800–1911, Part 1, ed. John K. Fairbank (Cambridge: Cambridge University Press, 1978), 491–542.

18. Liu Yun, "Revisiting Hanyeping Company (1889–1908): A Case Study of China's Early Industrialisation and Corporate History," *Business History* 52:1 (2010): 62–73; Elman, *On Their Own Terms,* 411.

19. David Pong, "Keeping the Foochow Navy Yard Afloat: Government Finance and China's Early Modern Defense Industry, 1866–75," *Modern Asian Studies* 21.1 (1987): 121–152.

20. William T. Rowe, *China's Last Empire: The Great Qing* (Cambridge, MA: Harvard University Press, 2009), 214.

21. Bert Becker, "Coastal Shipping in East Asia in the Late Nineteenth Century," *Journal of the Royal Asiatic Society Hong Kong Branch* 50 (2010): 245–302; Lai Chi-kong, "Li Hung-chang and Modern Enterprise: The China Merchants' Company, 1872–1885," *Chinese Studies in History* 25.1 (1991): 19–51; Albert Feuerwerker, *China's Early Industrialization: Sheng Hsuanhuai (1844–1916) and Mandarin Enterprise* (Cambridge, MA: Harvard University Press, 1958).

22. Faure, *China and Capitalism,* 53.

23. Daniel McMahon, *Rethinking the Decline of China's Qing Dynasty: Imperial Activism and Borderland Management at the Turn of the Nineteenth Century* (London: Routledge, 2015).

24. Dorothy Ko, "Footbinding and Anti-Footbinding in China: The Subject of Pain in the Nineteenth and Early Twentieth Centuries," in *Discipline and the Other Body: Correction, Corporeality, Colonialism,* ed. Steven Pierce and Anupama Rao (Durham, NC: Duke University Press, 2006), 215–242; Dorothy Ko, *Cinderella's Sisters: A Revisionist History of Footbinding* (Berkeley: University of California Press, 2005); Thoralf Klein, "Christian Mission and the Internationalization of China, 1830–1950," in *Trans-Pacific Interactions: The United States and China, 1880–1950,* ed. Vanessa Künnemann and Ruth Mayer (New York: Palgrave Macmillan, 2009), 141–160; Hong Fan, *Footbinding, Feminism, and Freedom: The Liberation of Women's Bodies in Modern China* (London: F. Cass, 1997).

25. There is a wealth of literature on the missionaries. Important titles include Daniel H. Bays, *A New History of Christianity in China: Blackwell Guides to Global Christianity* (Malden, MA: Wiley-Blackwell, 2012); Albert Monshan Wu, *From Christ to Confucius: German Missionaries, Chinese Christians, and*

the Globalization of Christianity, 1860–1950 (New Haven, CT: Yale University Press, 2016); Alvyn Austin, *China's Millions: The China Inland Mission and Late Qing Society, 1832–1905* (Grand Rapids, MI: Eerdmans, 2007); Michael G. Murdock, "Whose Modernity? Anti-Christianity and Educational Policy in Revolutionary China, 1924–1926," *Twentieth-Century China* 31.1 (2005): 33–75; Daniel H. Bays, ed., *Christianity in China: From the Eighteenth Century to the Present* (Stanford, CA: Stanford University Press, 1996); Kathleen L. Lodwick, *Crusaders against Opium: Protestant Missionaries in China, 1874–1917* (Lexington: University Press of Kentucky, 1996); John K. Fairbank, ed., *The Missionary Enterprise in China and America* (Cambridge, MA: Harvard University Press, 1974); Paul A. Cohen, *China and Christianity: The Missionary Movement and the Growth of Chinese Antiforeignism, 1860–1870* (Cambridge, MA: Harvard University Press, 1963); Jessie G. Lutz, *China and the Christian Colleges, 1850–1950* (Ithaca, NY: Cornell University Press, 1971).

26. Robert Lee, *France and the Exploitation of China, 1885–1901: A Study of Economic Imperialism* (Hong Kong: Oxford University Press, 1989).

27. Kirk W. Larsen, *Tradition, Treaties, and Trade: Qing Imperialism and Chosŏn Korea, 1850–1910* (Cambridge, MA: Harvard University Asia Center, 2008); S. C. M. Paine, *The Sino-Japanese War of 1894–1895: Perceptions, Power, and Primacy* (New York: Cambridge University Press, 2005); Michael R. Auslin, *Negotiating with Imperialism: The Unequal Treaties and the Culture of Japanese Diplomacy* (Cambridge, MA: Harvard University Press, 2004).

28. Pamela K. Crossley, *The Wobbling Pivot, China since 1800: An Interpretive History* (Malden, MA: Wiley-Blackwell, 2010), 96.

29. Klaus Mühlhahn, "A New Imperial Vision? The Limits of German Colonialism in China," in *German Colonialism in a Global Age,* ed. Bradley Naranch and Geoff Eley (Durham, NC: Duke University Press, 2015), 129–146; Klaus Mühlhahn, "Negotiating the Nation: German Colonialism and Chinese Nationalism in Qingdao, 1897–1914," in *Twentieth-century Colonialism and China: Localities, the Everyday and the World,* ed. Bryna Goodman and David S. G. Goodman (Milton Park, Abingdon, UK: Routledge, 2012), 37–56; George Steinmetz, *The Devil's Handwriting: Precoloniality and the German Colonial State in Qingdao, Samoa and Southwest Africa* (Chicago: University of Chicago Press, 2007), 433–508; John E. Schrecker, *Imperialism and Chinese Nationalism* (Cambridge, MA: Harvard University Press, 1971); Mechthild Leutner and Klaus Mühlhahn, *Musterkolonie Kiautschou: Die Expansion des Deutschen Reiches in China: Deutsch-chinesische Beziehungen 1897 bis 1914: Eine Quellensammlung* (Berlin: Akademie Verlag, 1997); Klaus Mühlhahn, *Herrschaft und Widerstand in der "Musterkolonie" Kiautschou: Interaktionen zwischen China und Deutschland 1897–1914* (Munich: Oldenbourg, 2000).

30. Leutner and Mühlhahn, *Musterkolonie Kiautschou,* 248.

31. Sixty percent of the degree holders of Shandong came from Gaomi or Jiaozhou; see Joseph Esherick, *The Origins of the Boxer Uprising* (Berkeley: University of California Press, 1987), 30.

32. Mühlhahn, "A New Imperial Vision," 138.

33. The fears of the Chinese population proved to be justified. In 1902, the whole region was flooded, destroying the year's harvest and washing away entire villages. The German governor sent a specialist to the Haoli district to investigate the cause. See report of engineer Born to Governor Truppel, September 4, 1902, in Leutner and Mühlhahn, *Musterkolonie Kiautschou,* 300–302.

34. See Paul Cohen, *History in Three Keys: The Boxers as Event, Experience, and Myth* (New York: Columbia University Press, 1997), 84–85. Other important studies include Robert Bickers and R. G. Tiedemann, eds., *The Boxers, China, and the World* (Lanham, MD: Rowman and Littlefield, 2007); Esherick, *The Origins of the Boxer Uprising;* David D. Buck, *Recent Chinese Studies of the Boxer Movement* (Armonk, NY: Sharpe, 1987).

35. Cohen, *History in Three Keys,* 14–56.

36. Wilhelm II: "Hun Speech" (1900), http://germanhistorydocs.ghi-dc.org/sub _document.cfm?document_id=755; see also Susanne Kuss, *German Colonial Wars and the Context of Military Violence,* translated by Andrew Smith (Cambridge, MA: Harvard University Press 2017), 146–147.

37. Mechthild Leutner and Klaus Mühlhahn, eds., *Kolonialkrieg in China: Die Niederschlagung der Boxerbewegung, 1900–1901* (Berlin: Links, 2007); James Hevia, *English Lessons: The Pedagogy of Imperialism in Nineteenth Century China* (Durham, NC: Duke University Press, 2003), 195–240; Xiang Lanxian, *The Origins of the Boxer War: A Multinational Study* (London: Routledge Curzon, 2003); Victor Purcell, *The Boxer Uprising: A Background Study* (Cambridge: Cambridge University Press, 1963).

38. See Leutner and Mühlhahn, *Musterkolonie Kiautschou,* 250.

39. Alfred Graf von Waldersee, *Denkwürdigkeiten des General-Feldmarschalls Alfred Graf von Waldersee,* ed. Heinrich Otto Meisner, vol. 3, *1900–1904* (Stuttgart: Deutsche Verlags-Anstalt, 1923), 36, 48, reprinted in Leutner and Mühlhahn, *Musterkolonie Kiautschou,* 501–502. On looting, see James Hevia, "Looting and Its Discontents: Moral Discourse and the Plunder of Beijing, 1900–1901," in Bickers and Tiedemann, *The Boxers, China, and the World,* 93–114.

40. Lewis Bernstein, "After the Fall: Tianjin under Foreign Occupation," in Bickers and Tiedemann, *The Boxers, China, and the World,* 133–146; Ruth Rogaski, *Hygienic Modernity: Meanings of Health and Disease in Treaty-Port China* (Berkeley: University of California Press, 2004), 165–192.

41. On the negotiations, see Chester Tan, *The Boxer Catastrophe* (New York: Norton, 1971); and Xiang, *The Origins of the Boxer War.*

42. Jung Chang, *Empress Dowager Ci Xi: The Concubine Who Launched Modern China* (London: Jonathan Cape, 2013), 298.

43. Charlotte Furth, "Intellectual Change: From the Reform Movement to the May Fourth Movement, 1895–1920," in *An Intellectual History of Modern China,* ed. Merle Goldman and Leo Ou-Fan Lee (New York: Cambridge University Press, 2002), 13–96; Chang Hao, *Chinese Intellectuals in Crisis: Search for Order and Meaning, 1890–1911* (Berkeley: University of California Press, 1987).

44. Rune Svarverud, "The Early Introduction of International Law: Translations and Language," in *International Law as World Order in Late Imperial China: Translation, Reception and Discourse, 1847–1911,* ed. Rune Svarverud (Leiden: Brill, 2007), 69–132; Richard S. Horowitz, "International Law and State Transformation in China, Siam, and the Ottoman Empire during the Nineteenth Century," *Journal of World History* 15.4 (2004): 445–486; Lydia H. Liu, *The Clash of Empires: The Invention of China in Modern World Making* (Cambridge, MA: Harvard University Press, 2004).

45. Paul A. Cohen, *Between Tradition and Modernity: Wang T'ao and Reform in Late Ch'ing China* (Cambridge, MA: Harvard University Press, 1974).

46. Ng Wai-ming, "The Formation of Huang Tsun-hsien's Political Thought in Japan (1877–1882)," *Sino-Japanese Studies* 8.1 (1995): 4–21; Noriko Kamachi, *Reform in China: Huang Tsun-Hsien and the Japanese Model* (Cambridge, MA: Council on East Asian Studies, Harvard University, 1981).

47. Huang Kewu, *The Meaning of Freedom: Yan Fu and the Origins of Chinese Liberalism* (Hong Kong: Chinese University Press, 2008); Benjamin I. Schwartz, *In Search of Wealth and Power: Yen Fu and the West* (Cambridge, MA: Belknap Press of Harvard University Press, 1964); James R. Pusey, *China and Charles Darwin* (Cambridge, MA: Council on East Asian Studies, Harvard University, 1983).

48. Yan Fu, "Learning from the West," in Teng and Fairbank, *Research Guide for China's Response to the West,* 151.

49. Wong Young-tsu, "Revisionism Reconsidered: Kang Youwei and the Reform Movement of 1898," *Journal of Asian Studies* 51.3 (1992): 513–544; Chang Hao, "Intellectual Change and the Reform Movement, 1890–1898," in *The Cambridge History of China,* ed. John K. Fairbank and Liu Kwang Ching (Cambridge: Cambridge University Press, 1980), 11:274–338.

50. Recent research has debated the extent to which Kang Youwei's radical ideas, including his Buddhist and Christian-inspired vision of *datong* (great harmony), played a role in these reforms. No consensus, however, has emerged: Shiping

Hua, *Chinese Utopianism: A Comparative Study of Reformist Thought with Japan and Russia, 1898–1997* (Washington, DC: Woodrow Wilson Center Press, 2009). See also Theodore Huters, *Bringing the World Home: Appropriating the West in Late Qing and Early Republican China* (Honolulu: University of Hawai'i Press, 2005); Luke S. K. Kwong, "Chinese Politics at the Crossroads: Reflections on the Hundred Days Reform of 1898," *Modern Asian Studies* 34.3 (2000): 663–695; Luke S. K. Kwong, *A Mosaic of the Hundred Days: Personalities, Politics, and Ideas of 1898* (Cambridge, MA: Council on East Asian Studies, Harvard University, 1984).

51. Joseph Richmond Levenson, *Liang Ch'i-ch'ao and the Mind of Modern China* (Cambridge, MA: Harvard University Press, 1953); Philip C. Huang, *Liang Ch'i-ch'ao and Modern Chinese Liberalism* (Seattle: University of Washington Press, 1972); Hao Chang, *Liang Ch'i-ch'ao and Intellectual Transition in China* (Cambridge, MA: Harvard University Press, 1971); Tang Xiaobing, *Global Space and the Nationalist Discourse of Modernity* (Stanford, CA: Stanford University Press, 1996); Andrew J. Nathan, *Chinese Democracy* (New York: Knopf, 1985); Pankaj Mishra, *From the Ruins of Empire: The Intellectuals Who Remade Asia* (New York: Farrar, Straus and Giroux, 2012).

52. Liang Qichao, "Observations on a Trip to America," quoted from *Chinese Civilization: A Sourcebook,* ed. Patricia Buckley Ebrey, 2nd ed. (New York: Free Press, 1993), 335–340.

53. Elman, *On Their Own Terms,* 379–382, 392–393.

54. Joanna Waley-Cohen, *The Culture of War in China: Empire and the Military under the Qing Dynasty* (London: I. B. Tauris, 2006); Nicolas Schillinger, *The Body and Military Masculinity in Late Qing and Early Republican China: The Art of Governing Soldiers* (Lanham, MD: Lexington Books, 2016).

55. Peter M. Worthing, *A Military History of Modern China: From the Manchu Conquest to Tian'anmen Square* (Westport, CT: Praeger Security International, 2007); Richard S. Horowitz, "Beyond the Marble Boat: The Transformation of the Chinese Military, 1850–1911," in *A Military History of China,* ed. David A. Graff and Robin Higham (Boulder, CO: Westview, 2002); Ralph L. Powell, *The Rise of Chinese Military Power, 1895–1912* (Princeton, NJ: Princeton University Press, 1955).

56. A classic author is Levenson, who wrote: "When traditionalists lost the will to develop tradition, and sought instead to repeat it, they changed its content. They saw it as an antithesis to the West, and development could only weaken it in that capacity. The strength which tradition would have brought them was lost." Joseph R. Levenson, *Confucian China and Its Modern Fate: The Problem of Intellectual Continuity* (Berkeley: University of California Press, 1958), 133. Levenson's analysis leads him to the conclusion that change occurred in China as

a direct result of western pressure. Much of this leads back to Max Weber's *Die Wirtschaftsethik der Weltreligionen: Konfuzianismus und Taoismus*—a work that had an enormous impact on western studies on China. For Weber, modern economic development was impossible in China, since China lacked the necessary *"Weltanschauung,"* informed by rationality and science.

57. Kenneth Pomeranz, *The Great Divergence: China, Europe, and the Making of the Modern World Economy* (Princeton, NJ: Princeton University Press, 2000); Jack A. Goldstone, "Efflorescences and Economic Growth in World History: Rethinking the 'Rise of the West' and the Industrial Revolution," *Journal of World History* 13.2 (2002): 323–389.

58. See Jürgen Osterhammel, *The Transformation of the World: A Global History of the Nineteenth Century,* trans. Patrick Camiller (Princeton, NJ: Princeton University Press, 2015), 392–468; Pamela K. Crossley, "The Late Qing Empire in Global History," *Education about Asia* 13.2 (2008): 4–7.

59. See Loren Brandt, Debin Ma, and Thomas G. Rawski, "From Divergence to Convergence: Re-Evaluating the History behind China's Economic Boom" (Working Paper no. 117, CAGE Online Working Paper Series, Department of Economics, University of Warwick, Coventry, UK, 2013), http://wrap.warwick.ac.uk/57944; Debin Ma, "Political Institution and Long-Run Economic Trajectory: Some Lessons from Two Millennia of Chinese Civilization," in *Institutions and Comparative Economic Development,* ed. Masahiko Aoki, Timur Kuran, and Gérard Roland (Basingstoke, UK: Palgrave Macmillan, 2012), 78–98.

60. Faure, *China and Capitalism,* 52.

61. Peter Zarrow, *After Empire: The Conceptual Transformation of the Chinese State, 1885–1924* (Stanford, CA: Stanford University Press, 2012).

62. Zheng Wang, *Never Forget National Humiliation: Historical Memory in Chinese Politics and Foreign Relations* (New York: Columbia University Press, 2012). On the cultural background, see Paul A. Cohen, *Speaking to History: The Story of King Goujian in Twentieth-Century China* (Berkeley: University of California Press, 2009).

PART 2. CHINESE REVOLUTIONS

1. Quoted in Orville Schell and John Delury, *Wealth and Power: China's Long March to the Twenty-First Century* (New York: Random House, 2013), loc. 2416–2419, Kindle.

2. Étienne Balibar and Immanuel M. Wallerstein, *Race, Nation, Class: Ambiguous Identities* (London: Verso, 1991), 86–106; Benedict Anderson, *Imagined Communities: Reflections on the Origin and Spread of Nationalism,* rev. ed. (London: Verso, 2016).

3. What is emphasized here is that the effort of state building was seen by almost all actors as not only a nationalist but also a revolutionary endeavor. The literature often treats these two themes separately or as unrelated parallel developments. This account, however, stresses that building a modern nation and a revolutionary state were overlapping projects that worked in tandem and augmented each other.

4. Jürgen Osterhammel, *The Transformation of the World: A Global History of the Nineteenth Century,* trans. by Patrick Camiller (Princeton: Princeton University Press, 2015), 514–522.

4. UPENDING THE EMPIRE, 1900–1919

1. Chang Jung, *Empress Dowager Cixi: The Concubine Who Launched Modern China* (New York: A. Knopf, 2013).

2. On various aspects of the New Policies, see Roger R. Thompson, "The Lessons of Defeat: Transforming the Qing State after the Boxer War," *Modern Asian Studies* 37.4 (2003): 769–773; Richard S. Horowitz, "Breaking the Bond of the Precedent: The 1905–6 Government Reform Commission and the Remaking of the Qing Central State," *Modern Asian Studies* 37.4 (2003): 775–797; Tong Lam, "Policing the Imperial Nation: Sovereignty, International Law, and the Civilizing Mission in Late Qing China," *Comparative Studies in Society and History* 52.4 (2010): 881–908; Douglas Reynolds, *China, 1898–1912: The Xinzheng Revolution and Japan* (Cambridge, MA: Council on East Asian Studies, Harvard University, 1993); Stephen R. MacKinnon, *Power and Politics in Late Imperial China: Yuan Shikai in Beijing and Tianjin* (Berkeley: University of California Press, 1980); Wolfgang Franke, *The Reform and Abolition of the Traditional Chinese Examination System* (Cambridge, MA: Harvard University Press, 1963); Hon Tze-Ki, "Educating the Citizens: Visions of China in Late Qing History Textbooks," in *The Politics of Historical Production in Late Qing and Republican China,* ed. Hon Tze-Ki and Robert J. Culp (Leiden: Brill, 2007), 791–805; Chuzo Ichiko, "Political and Institutional Reform, 1901–11," in *The Cambridge History of China,* ed. John K. Fairbank and Denis Crispin Twitchett (Cambridge: Cambridge University Press, 1980), 11:375–415.

3. Arthur Waldron, *From War to Nationalism: China's Turning Point, 1924–1925* (Cambridge: Cambridge University Press, 1995), 26; see also Andrew J. Nathan, *Chinese Democracy* (New York: Knopf, 1985), 247.

4. Quoted in Horowitz, "Breaking the Bond of the Precedent," 791.

5. Roger Thompson, *China's Local Councils in the Age of Constitutional Reform* (Cambridge, MA: Harvard University Press, 1995).

6. Klaus Mühlhahn, *Criminal Justice in China: A History* (Cambridge, MA: Harvard University Press, 2009), 60–62.

7. Dan Shao, "Chinese by Definition: Nationality Law, Jus Sanguinis, and State Succession, 1909–1980," *Twentieth-Century China* 35.1 (2009): 4–28.

8. William Kirby, "China, Unincorporated: Company Law and Business Enterprise in Twentieth Century China," *Journal of Asian Studies* 54.1 (1995): 43–63.

9. Chen Zhongping, *Modern China's Network Revolution: Chambers of Commerce and Sociopolitical Change in the Early Twentieth Century* (Stanford, CA: Stanford University Press, 2011).

10. Richard S. Horowitz, "Beyond the Marble Boat: The Transformation of the Chinese Military, 1850–1911," in *A Military History of China*, ed. David A. Graff and Robin Higham (Lexington: University of Kentucky Press 2012), 164–166; Nicolas Schillinger, *The Body and Military Masculinity in Late Qing and Early Republican China: The Art of Governing Soldiers* (Lanham, MD: Lexington Books, 2016), 29–30.

11. Elisabeth Kaske, "Fundraising Wars: Office Selling and Interprovincial Finance in Nineteenth Century China," *Harvard Journal of Asiatic Studies* 71.1 (2011): 69–141.

12. Benjamin A. Elman, *A Cultural History of Civil Service Examinations in Late Imperial China* (Berkeley: University of California Press, 2000), 569–626.

13. Stephen R. Halsey, *Quest for Power: European Imperialism and the Making of Chinese Statecraft* (Cambridge, MA: Harvard University Press, 2015), 93. See also Zhihong Shi, *Central Government Silver Treasury: Revenue, Expenditure and Inventory Statistics, ca. 1667–1899* (Leiden: Brill 2016), 59.

14. See Tong Lam, *A Passion for Facts: Social Surveys and the Construction of the Chinese Nation-State, 1900–1949* (Berkeley: University of California Press, 2011).

15. Rebecca Nedostup, *Superstitious Regimes: Religion and the Politics of Chinese Modernity* (Cambridge, MA: Harvard University Asia Center, 2009); Prasenjit Duara, "Knowledge and Power in the Discourse of Modernity: The Campaigns against Popular Religion in Early Twentieth-Century China," *Journal of Asian Studies* 50.1 (1991): 67–83.

16. Quoted from Chang, *Empress Dowager Cixi*, 325. See also Dorothy Ko, "Footbinding and Anti-Footbinding in China: The Subject of Pain in the Nineteenth and Early Twentieth Centuries," in *Discipline and the Other Body: Correction, Corporeality, Colonialism*, ed. Steven Pierce and Rao Anupama (Durham, NC: Duke University Press, 2006), 215–242; Fan Hong, *Footbinding, Feminism, and Freedom: The Liberation of Women's Bodies in Modern China* (London: F. Cass, 1997).

17. Frank Dikötter, Lars Laamann, and Zhou Xun, *Narcotic Culture: A History of Drugs in China* (Hong Kong: Hong Kong University Press, 2004); Zhou Yongming, *Anti-Drug Crusades in Twentieth-Century China: Nationalism, History, and State-building* (Lanham, MD: Rowman and Littlefield, 1999).

18. Zou Rong, *The Revolutionary Army: A Chinese Nationalist Tract of 1903,* trans. John Lust (The Hague: Mouton, 1968). See also Peter C. Perdue, "Erasing the Empire, Re-Racing the Nation: Racialism and Culturalism in the Imperial China," in *Imperial Formations,* ed. Ann Laura Stoler, Carole McGranahan, and Peter C. Perdue (Santa Fe, NM: School for Advanced Research Press, 2007), 141–169.

19. Elena Barabantseva, *Overseas Chinese, Ethnic Minorities and Nationalism: De-Centering China* (London: Routledge, 2011), 18–39; William C. Kirby, "When Did China Become China?" in *The Teleology of the Modern Nation-State: Japan and China,* ed. Joshua A. Fogel (Philadelphia: University of Pennsylvania Press, 2005), 105–116; Pamela K. Crossley, "Nationality and Difference in China: The Post-Imperial Dilemma," in Fogel, *The Teleology of the Modern Nation-State,* 138–160; Lowell Dittmer and Samuel S. Kim, eds., *China's Quest for National Identity* (Ithaca, NY: Cornell University Press, 1993).

20. David Strand, *An Unfinished Republic: Leading by Word and Deed in Modern China* (Berkeley: University of California Press, 2011), 236–382; Audrey Wells, *The Political Thought of Sun Yat-Sen: Development and Impact* (New York: Palgrave Macmillan, 2002); Marie-Claire Bergère, *Sun Yat-sen* (Stanford, CA: Stanford University Press, 2000).

21. Sun Yatsen, *San Min Chu I = The Three Principles of the People,* trans. Frank W. Price (Calcutta: Chinese Ministry of Information, 1942), 1.

22. Sun, *San Min Chu I,* 5.

23. Sun, *San Min Chu I,* 2.

24. Sun, *San Min Chu I,* 152 and 155.

25. Mary Clabaugh Wright, "Introduction: The Rising Tide of Change," in *China in Revolution: The First Phase 1900–1913,* ed. Mary Clabaugh Wright (New Haven, CT: Yale University Press, 1968), 1–66; Mary Backus Rankin, "Nationalistic Contestation and Mobilization Politics: Practice and Rhetoric of Railway-Rights Recovery at the End of the Qing," *Modern China* 28.3 (2002): 315–361, especially 316–318.

26. Peter Zarrow, *China in War and Revolution, 1895–1949* (London: Routledge, Taylor and Francis Group, 2007), 33.

27. Yong Ma, "From Constitutional Monarchy to Republic: The Trajectory of Yuan Shikai," *Journal of Modern Chinese History* 6.1 (2012): 15–32; Hirata Koji, "Britain's Men on the Spot in China: John Jordan, Yuan Shikai, and the Reorgani-

zation Loan, 1912–1914," *Modern Asian Studies* 47.3 (2013): 895–934; Jerome Ch'en, *Yuan Shih-k'ai*, 2nd ed. (Stanford, CA: Stanford University Press, 1972); Ernest Young, *The Presidency of Yuan Shih-k'ai: Liberalism and Dictatorship in Early Republican China* (Ann Arbor: University of Michigan Press, 1977).

28. Joshua Hill, "Seeking Talent at the Voting Booth: Elections and the Problem of Campaigning in the Late Qing and Early Republic," *Twentieth-Century China* 38.3 (2013): 213–229.

29. Julia C. Strauss, *Strong Institutions in Weak Polities: State Building in Republican China, 1927–1940* (Oxford: Clarendon Press, 1998), 31ff.

30. Lu Xun, *The Real Story of Ah-Q and Other Tales of China: The Complete Fiction of Lu Xun,* trans. Julia Lovell and Li Yiyun (New York: Penguin Classics, 2009).

31. Xu Guoqi, *China and the Great War: China's Pursuit of a New National Identity and Internationalization* (Cambridge: Cambridge University Press, 2005); Xu Guoqi, *Strangers on the Western Front: Chinese Workers in the Great War* (Cambridge, MA: Harvard University Press, 2011).

32. Xu Guoqi, *Asia and the Great War: A Shared History* (Oxford: Oxford University Press 2017), 32.

33. Xu Guoqi, *Strangers on the Western Front,* 48.

34. This and the following paragraphs are based on Klaus Mühlhahn, "China," in *1914–1918* online: *International Encyclopedia of the First World War,* last updated January 11, 2016, https://encyclopedia.1914-1918-online.net/article/china; doi: 10.15463/ie1418.10799. On the political discussions, see Strand, *An Unfinished Republic,* 1–12.

35. Zarrow, *China in War and Revolution,* 83.

36. Jörg Fisch, *The Right of Self-Determination of Peoples: The Domestication of an Illusion,* trans. Anita Mage (Cambridge: Cambridge University Press, 2015), 129–137.

37. Woodrow Wilson, "Address on the Fourteen Points for Peace," January 8, 1918, transcript available at Woodrow Wilson Presidential Library, http://www .woodrowwilson.org/digital-library/view.php?did=3863.

38. Vladimir I. Lenin, "Decree on Peace" (speech), October 26, 1917, in Izvestiia, *The First World War—A Multimedia History of World War One,* http://www .firstworldwar.com/source/decreeonpeace.htm.

39. Chow Tse-tsung, *The May Fourth Movement: Intellectual Revolution in Modern China* (Cambridge, MA: Harvard University Press, 1960), 93

40. Erez Manela, *The Wilsonian Moment: Self-Determination and the International Origins of Anticolonial Nationalism* (Oxford: Oxford University Press, 2007), 63–136.

41. Wen-hsin Yeh, "Progressive Journalism and Shanghai's Petty Urbanites: Zou Taofen and the Shenghuo Weekly (1926–45)," in *Shanghai Sojourners,* ed. Wen-hsin Yeh and Frederic E. Wakeman (Berkeley: Institute of East Asian Studies, University of California, 1992), 186–238; Parks Coble, "Chiang Kai-shek and the Anti-Japanese Movement in China: Zou Tao-fen and the National Salvation Association, 1931–1937," *Journal of Asian Studies* 44. 2 (1985): 293–310; the following quotes are from Rana Mitter, *A Bitter Revolution: China's Struggle with the Modern World* (Oxford: Oxford University Press, 2004), 129–130.

42. Mao Tse-tung, *Mao's Road to Power: Revolutionary Writings 1912–1949,* vol. 1: *The Pre-Marxist Period 1912–1920* (Armonk, NY: M.E. Sharpe, 1992), 335; Jonathan Spence, *Mao Zedong* (London: Weidenfeld and Nicolson, 1999), 57.

43. Manela, *Wilsonian Moment,* 175.

44. Simone M. Müller, *Wiring the World: The Social and Cultural Creation of Global Telegraph Networks* (New York: Columbia University Press, 2016).

45. Adam McKeown, "Global Migration, 1846–1970," *Journal of World History* 15.2 (2004): 155–189.

46. Philip A. Kuhn, *Chinese among Others: Emigration in Modern Times* (Lanham, MD: Rowman and Littlefield, 2008); Evelyn Hu-Dehart, "Chinese Coolie Labour in Cuba in the Nineteenth Century: Free Labour or Neo-Slavery?" *Slavery and Abolition* 14.1 (1993): 67–86.

47. Marilyn A. Levine, *The Found Generation: Chinese Communists in Europe during the Twenties* (Seattle: University of Washington Press, 1993), 24–26; Geneviève Barman and Nicole Dulioust, "The Communists in the Work and Study Movement in France," *Republican China* 13.2 (1988): 24–39; Xu Guoqi, *Strangers on the Western Front,* 218, 73; Chow, *The May Fourth Movement,* 37, 96.

48. Bruce A. Elleman, *Wilson and China: A Revised History of the Shandong Question* (Armonk, NY: M.E. Sharpe, 2002), 33–110.

49. Fabio Lanza, *Behind the Gate: Inventing Students in Beijing* (New York: Columbia University Press, 2010); Vera Schwarcz, *The Chinese Enlightenment: Intellectuals and the Legacy of the May Fourth Movement of 1919* (Berkeley: University of California Press, 1986); Yu Yingshi, "The Radicalization of China in the Twentieth Century," *Daedalus* 122.2 (1993): 125–150; Milena Doleželová-Velingerová and Oldřich Král, eds., *The Appropriation of Cultural Capital: China's May Fourth Project* (Cambridge, MA: Harvard University Asia Center, 2001); Kai-wing Chow, Tze-ki Hon, Hung-yok Ip, and Don C. Price, eds., *Beyond the May Fourth Paradigm: In Search of Chinese Modernity* (Lanham, MD: Lexington Books, 2008); Leo Ou-fan Lee, "Modernity and Its Discontents: The Cultural Agenda of the May Fourth Movement," in *Perspectives on Modern China: Four Anniversaries,* ed. Kenneth Lieberthal, Joyce Kallgren, Roderick

MacFarquhar, and Frederic Wakeman, Jr. (Armonk, NY: M.E. Sharpe, 1991), 158–177.

50. Lee, "Modernity and Its Discontents," 161–162.

5. REBUILDING DURING THE REPUBLICAN ERA: 1920–1937

1. Philip A. Kuhn, *Rebellion and Its Enemies in Late Imperial China: Militarization and Social Structure, 1796–1864* (Cambridge, MA: Harvard University Press, 1970).

2. Edward McCord, *The Power of the Gun: The Emergence of Modern Chinese Warlordism* (Berkeley: University of California Press, 1993); Jerome Ch'en, *The Military-Gentry Coalition: China under the Warlords* (Toronto: Joint Centre on Modern East Asia, 1979). Studies of single warlords include: Donald G. Gillin, *Warlord: Yen Hsi-shan in Shansi Province, 1911–1949* (Princeton, NJ: Princeton University Press, 1967); Diana Lary, *Region and Nation: The Kwangsi Clique in Chinese Politics, 1925–1937* (Cambridge: Cambridge University Press, 1975); James Sheridan, *Chinese Warlord: The Career of Feng Yü-hsiang* (Stanford, CA: Stanford University Press, 1966); Edward A. McCord, "Cries That Shake the Earth: Military Atrocities and Popular Protests in Warlord China," *Modern China* 31.1 (2005): 3–34; Ch'i Hsi-Sheng, *Warlord Politics in China, 1916–1928* (Princeton, NJ: Princeton University Press, 1976).

3. Christian socialism goes back to the French philosopher Henri de Saint-Simon, who proposed a "new Christianity" primarily concerned with the plight of the poor. The Saint-Simonians intended to effectively end the exploitation of the poor.

4. Zhang Yingjin, *Chinese National Cinema* (New York: Routledge, 2004), 13–57; Paul G. Pickowicz, "Melodramatic Representation and the 'May Fourth' Tradition of Chinese Cinema," in *From May Fourth to June Fourth: Fiction and Film in Twentieth Century China,* ed. Ellen Widmer and David Der-wei Wang (Cambridge, MA: Harvard University Press, 1993), 295–326.

5. Thomas Rawski, *Economic Growth in Prewar China* (Berkeley: University of California Press, 1989); Dwight H. Perkins, "China's Prereform Economy in World Perspective," in *China's Rise in Historical Perspective,* ed. Brantly Womack (Lanham, MD: Rowman and Littlefield, 2010), 118–119.

6. Bruce A. Elleman, *Wilson and China: A Revised History of the Shandong Question* (Armonk, NY: M.E. Sharpe, 2002), 138–140.

7. Arif Dirlik, *Anarchism in the Chinese Revolution* (Berkeley: University of California Press, 1991); Peter Zarrow, *Anarchism and Chinese Political Culture* (New York: Columbia University Press, 1990); Robert A. Scalapino and George T. Yu, *The Chinese Anarchist Movement* (Berkeley: Center for Chinese Studies,

Institute of International Studies, University of California, 1961). There was also an alternative version of anarchism that emphasized the rationality of science. This was popular among Chinese students in France: Gotelind Müller, *China, Kropotkin, und der Anarchismus* (Wiesbaden, Germany: Harrassowitz Verlag, 2001); and Edward S. Krebs, *Shifu: Soul of Chinese Anarchism* (Lanham, MD: Rowman and Littlefield, 1998).

8. Raoul David Findeisen, "Anarchist or Saint? On the Spread of 'Wisdom' (Sophia) in Modern Chinese Literature," *Asiatica Venetiana* 3 (1998): 91–104; Ding Ling, *Miss Sophia's Diary and Other Stories,* trans. William John Francis Jenner (Peking: Panda Books, 1985).

9. Ssu-Yü Teng and John King Fairbank, eds., *China's Response to the West: A Documentary Survey 1839–1923* (Cambridge, MA: Harvard University Press, 1954), 246–249. See also Maurice J. Meisner, *Li Ta-chao and the Origins of Chinese Marxism* (Cambridge, MA: Harvard University Press, 1967).

10. Karl Marx argued that a true "proletarian" (Marx's term to describe industrial workers) revolution could only happen in fully industrialized and capitalist countries. Vladimir Lenin insisted that underdeveloped and agricultural states such as the Russian empire could also become communist states. To that end Lenin modified the Marxist theory of a dictatorship of the urban workers to a dictatorship of the Communist Party.

11. Yoshihiro Ishikawa, *The Formation of the Chinese Communist Party,* trans. Joshua A. Fogel (New York: Columbia University Press, 2013); Alexander Pantsov, *The Bolsheviks and the Chinese Revolution, 1919–1927* (Honolulu: University of Hawai'i Press, 2000); Steven A. Smith, *A Road Is Made: Communism in Shanghai, 1920–1927* (Honolulu: University of Hawai'i Press, 2000); Hans J. van de Ven, *From Friend to Comrade: The Founding of the Chinese Communist Party, 1920–1927* (Berkeley: University of California Press, 1991); Lyman P. van Slyke, *Enemies and Friends: The United Front in Chinese Communist History* (Stanford, CA: Stanford University Press, 1967); Stephen Uhalley Jr., *A History of the Chinese Communist Party* (Stanford, CA: Hoover Institution Press, 1988).

12. Tony Saich, "The Chinese Communist Party during the Era of the Comintern (1919–1943)" (unpublished manuscript, no date, pdf), https://sites.hks.harvard.edu/m-rcbg/research/a.saich_iish_chinese.communist.party.pdf.

13. The following quotations from the Manifesto are from Tony Saich, ed., *The Rise to Power of the Chinese Communist Party: Documents and Analysis* (Armonk, NY: M.E. Sharpe, 1996), 11–13; On the background, see also Ishikawa, *Formation of the Chinese Communist Party,* 201–206.

14. The First Decision as to the Objects of the CCP (July–August 1921), quoted from Saich, *The Rise to Power of the Chinese Communist Party,* 18.

15. Quoted in Saich, *The Rise to Power of the Chinese Communist Party*, 16–18.

16. Tony Saich, *The Origins of the First United Front in China: The Role of Sneevliet (Alias Maring)* (Leiden: E. J. Brill, 1991).

17. Altogether, more than 30,000 cadets were trained at the academy between 1924 and 1949. Many of republican China's top military leaders were trained there. Chang Jui-te, "The National Army from Whampoa to 1949," in *A Military History of China*, ed. David A. Graff and Robin Higham (Boulder, CO: Westview Press, 2002), 193–209; Richard B. Landis, "Training and Indoctrination at the Whampoa Academy," in *China in the 1920s: Nationalism and Revolution*, ed. F. Gilbert Chan and Thomas H. Etzold (New York: New Viewpoints, 1976), 73–93; Lincoln Li, "The Whampoa Military Academy," in *Student Nationalism in China, 1924–1949* (Albany: State University of New York Press, 1994), 22–40; John Fitzgerald, *Awakening China: Politics, Culture and Class in the Nationalist Revolution* (Stanford, CA: Stanford University Press, 1998), 237–238.

18. Arthur Waldron, *From War to Nationalism: China's Turning Point, 1924–1925* (Cambridge: Cambridge University Press; 1995); Donald A. Jordan, *The Northern Expedition: China's National Revolution of 1926–1928* (Honolulu: University of Hawai'i Press, 1976); Hans J. van de Ven, *War and Nationalism in China, 1925–1945* (London: Routledge, 2003).

19. China's last war was the Sino-Vietnamese War, sometimes called the Third Indochina War, in early 1979. Chinese troops went over the border in retaliation for Vietnam's occupation of Cambodia in 1978, terminating the rule of the Chinese-backed Khmer Rouge. The wars between 1937 and 1952 are covered by Hans van de Ven, *China at War: Triumph and Tragedy in the Emergence of the New China* (London: Profile Books, 2017).

20. Peter Zarrow, *China in War and Revolution, 1895–1949* (London: Routledge, 2005), 249.

21. On the period in general, see Diana Lary, *China's Republic* (New York: Cambridge University Press, 2007); Van de Ven, *War and Nationalism in China*; Lloyd E. Eastman, "Nationalist China during the Nanking Decade 1927–1937," in *The Cambridge History of China*, vol. 13, pt. 2, eds. Denis Crispin Twitchett and John K. Fairbank (Cambridge: Cambridge University Press, 1986), 116–167; Robert E. Bedeski, *State Building in Modern China: The Kuomintang in the Prewar Period* (Berkeley: University of California Center for Chinese Studies, 1981); James E. Sheridan, *China in Disintegration: The Republican Era in Chinese History, 1912–1949* (New York: Free Press, 1975).

22. For a long time, T. V. Soong was described as privileged, corrupt, and money hungry. The release of his personal papers at the Hoover Institution at Stanford University, California, has allowed scholars to form a more nuanced assessment; see Wu Jingping, ed., *Song Ziwen yu zhanshi Zhongguo, 1937–1945*

[T. V. Soong and Wartime Nationalist China, 1937–1945] (Shanghai: Fudan Daxue Chubanshe, 2008).

23. Tien Hung-mao, *Government and Politics in Kuomintang China 1927–1937* (Stanford, CA: Stanford University Press, 1972), 45–46, 50.

24. Frederic Wakeman, *Spymaster: Dai Li and the Chinese Secret Service* (Berkeley: University of California Press, 2003); Chen Lifu, Sidney H. Chang, and Ramon H. Myers, *The Storm Clouds Clear over China: The Memoir of Ch'en Li-fu, 1900–1993* (Stanford, CA: Hoover Institution Press, 1994), 66–67.

25. Frederic Wakeman, "A Revisionist View of the Nanjing Decade: Confucian Fascism," *China Quarterly* 150 (1997): 395–432; Xu Youwei and Philip Billingsley, "Behind the Scenes of the Xi'an Incident: The Case of the Lixingshe," *China Quarterly* 154 (1998): 283–307; Maria Hsia Chang, *The Chinese Blue Shirt Society: Fascism and Developmental Nationalism* (Berkeley: Institute of East Asian Studies, Center for Chinese Studies, University of California, 1985); Maggie Clinton, "Ends of the Universal: The League of Nations and Chinese Fascism on the Eve of World War II," *Modern Asian Studies* 48.6 (2014): 283–307.

26. See Julia C. Strauss, "Symbol and Reflection of the Reconstituting State: The Examination Yuan in the 1930s," *Modern China* 20.2 (1994): 211–238.

27. See special issue of *Modern Asian Studies* 40.3 (2006) on Robert Hart and the Chinese Maritime Customs Service.

28. Andrew J. Nathan, "Political Rights in Chinese Constitutions," in *Human Rights in Contemporary China,* ed. R. Randle Edwards, Louis Henkin, and Andrew J. Nathan (New York: Columbia University Press, 1986), 77–124.

29. Klaus Mühlhahn, *Criminal Justice in China: A History* (Cambridge, MA: Harvard University Press, 2009), 63–67; Xu Xiaoqun, *Trial of Modernity: Judicial Reform in Early Twentieth Century China 1901–1937* (Stanford, CA: Stanford University Press, 2008); Kathryn Bernhardt and Philip C. C. Huang, eds., *Civil Law in Qing and Republican China* (Stanford, CA: Stanford University Press, 1994).

30. Allison W. Conner, "Training China's Early Modern Lawyers: Soochow University Law School," *Journal of Chinese Law* 8.1 (1994): 1–46.

31. There is an increasing amount of literature on education: Paul J. Bailey, *Reform the People: Changing Attitudes towards Popular Education in Early Twentieth Century China* (Edinburgh: Edinburgh University Press, 1990); Paul J. Bailey, *Gender and Education in China* (London: Routledge, 2007); Robert Culp, *Articulating Citizenship* (Cambridge, MA: Harvard University Asia Center, 2007); Suzanne Pepper, *Radicalism and Education Reform in Twentieth Century China* (Cambridge: Cambridge University Press, 1996); Stig Thøgersen, *A County of Culture: Twentieth Century China Seen from the Village Schools of*

Zouping, Shandong (Ann Arbor: University of Michigan Press, 2002); Timothy Weston, *The Power of Position: Beijing University, Intellectuals, and Chinese Political Culture, 1898–1929* (Berkeley: University of California Press, 2004); Ruth Hayhoe, *China's Universities, 1895–1995: A Century of Cultural Conflict* (New York: Garland, 1996); Xiaoqing Diana Lin, *Peking University: Chinese Scholarship and Intellectuals, 1898–1937* (Albany: State University of New York Press, 2005); Wen-hsin Ye, *The Alienated Academy: Culture and Politics in Republican China, 1919–1937* (Cambridge, MA: Harvard University Press, 1990); William C. Kirby, "The World of Universities in Modern China," in *Global Opportunities and Challenges for Higher Education Leaders: Global Perspectives on Higher Education,* ed. Laura E. Rumbley, Robin Matross Helms, Patti McGill Peterson, and Philip G. Altbach (Rotterdam: Sense Publishers, 2014).

32. Robert Culp, "Rethinking Governmentality: Training, Cultivation, and Cultural Citizenship in Nationalist China," *The Journal of Asian Studies* 65:3 (Aug. 2006), 529–554.

33. Janet Y. Chen, *Guilty of Indigence: The Urban Poor in China, 1900–1953* (Princeton, NJ: Princeton University Press, 2012); Zwia Lipkin, *Useless to the State: "Social Problems" and Social Engineering in Nationalist Nanjing, 1927–1937* (Cambridge, MA: Harvard University Press, 2006); Alan Baumler, "Opium Control versus Opium Suppression: The Origins of the 1935 Six-Year Plan to Eliminate Opium and Drugs," in *Opium Regimes: China, Britain and Japan, 1839–1952,* ed. Timothy Brook and Bob Tadashi Wakabayashi (Berkeley: University of California Press, 2000), 270–276; Gail Hershatter, *Dangerous Pleasures: Prostitution and Modernity in Twentieth Century Shanghai* (Berkeley: University of California Press, 1999).

34. Vincent Goossaert and David A. Palmer, *The Religious Question in Modern China* (Chicago: University of Chicago Press, 2011); David A. Palmer and Philip L. Wickeri, *Chinese Religious Life* (Oxford: Oxford University Press, 2011); Rebecca Nedostup, *Superstitious Regimes: Religion and the Politics of Chinese Modernity* (Cambridge, MA: Harvard University Asia Center, 2009); Mayfair Mei-hui Yang, *Chinese Religiosities: Afflictions of Modernity and State Formation* (Berkeley: University of California Press, 2008); Nara Dillon and Jean C. Oi, eds., *At the Crossroads of Empires: Middlemen, Social Networks, and State-Building in Republican Shanghai* (Stanford, CA: Stanford University Press, 2008).

35. Jay Taylor, *The Generalissimo: Chiang Kai-shek and the Struggle for Modern China* (Cambridge, MA: Harvard University Press, 2009), 77; Bernd Martin, ed., *Die Deutsche Beraterschaft in China 1927–1938: Militär-Wirtschaft—Außenpolitik* (Düsseldorf: Droste, 1981); William C. Kirby, *Germany and*

Republican China (Stanford, CA: Stanford University Press, 1984); Frederick Fu Liu, *A Military History of Modern China, 1924–1949* (Princeton, NJ: Princeton University Press, 1956), 61–64.

36. Wennan Liu, "Redefining the Moral and Legal Roles of the State in Everyday Life: The New Life Movement in China in the Mid-1930s," *Cross-Currents: East Asian History and Culture Review* 2.2 (2013): 335–365. https://cross-currents .berkeley.edu/sites/default/files/e-journal/articles/liu_0.pdf; Federica Ferlanti, "The New Life Movement in Jiangxi Province, 1934–1938," *Modern Asian Studies* 44.5 (September 2010): 961–1000.

37. Chiang Kaishek, *Outline of the New Life Movement* (Nanchang, China: Association for the Promotion of the New Life Movement, 1934), 6.

38. Timothy Cheek, *The Intellectual in Modern Chinese History* (Cambridge: Cambridge University Press, 2015), 8–9.

39. Taylor, *The Generalissimo,* 109–110.

40. Albert Feuerwerker, "Economic Trends 1912–1949," in *The Cambridge History of China,* vol. 12, pt. 1, ed. Denis Crispin Twitchett and John K. Fairbank (Cambridge: Cambridge University Press, 1983), 12:28–127. The "doomed to fail" thesis is especially pronounced in the work by Lloyd E. Eastman, *The Abortive Revolution: China under Nationalist Rule, 1927–1937* (Cambridge, MA: Harvard University Press, 1974); Lloyd E. Eastman, *Seeds of Destruction: Nationalist China in War and Revolution, 1937–1949* (Stanford, CA: Stanford University Press, 1984).

41. William C. Kirby, "Engineering China: Birth of the Developmental State, 1928–1937," in *Becoming Chinese: Passages to Modernity and Beyond,* ed. Wen-hsin Yeh (Berkeley: University of California Press, 2000), 137–160.

42. Margherita Zanasi, *Saving the Nation: Economic Modernity in Republican China* (Chicago: University of Chicago Press, 2006).

43. Charles D. Musgrove, "Building a Dream: Constructing a National Capital in Nanjing, 1927–1937," in *Remaking the Chinese City: Modernity and National Identity, 1900–1950,* ed. Joseph W. Esherick (Honolulu: University of Hawai'i Press, 2000), 139–157.

44. Musgrove, "Building a Dream," 144.

45. Morris L. Bian, "How Crisis Shapes Change: New Perspectives on China's Political Economy during the Sino-Japanese War, 1937–1945," *History Compass* 5 (2007): 1091–1110; Morris L. Bian, *The Making of the State Enterprise System in Modern China: The Dynamics of Institutional Change* (Cambridge, MA: Harvard University Press, 2005); Van de Ven, *War and Nationalism in China,* 151, 156–157; William C. Kirby, "The Chinese War Economy," in *China's Bitter Victory: The War with Japan, 1937–1945,* ed. James C. Hsiung and Steven I. Levine (Armonk, NY: M.E. Sharpe, 1992), 187–189.

46. Rana Mitter, *Forgotten Ally: China's World War II, 1937–1945* (New York: Houghton Mifflin Harcourt, 2013), 65.

47. Parks M. Coble, *The Shanghai Capitalists and the Nationalist Government in China 1923–1937* (Cambridge, MA: Harvard University Press, 1980), 36, 262.

48. Eastman, *Seeds of Destruction,* 136; Feuerwerker, "Economic Trends," 112–113.

49. The exact numbers for the economic indicators vary in the literature. I have relied on averages.

50. Wen-hsin Yeh, "Introduction: Interpreting Chinese Modernity, 1900–1950," in *Becoming Chinese: Passages to Modernity and Beyond,* ed. Wen-hsin Yeh (Berkeley, CA: University of California Press, 2000), 1–28.

51. Newer publications include Wen-hsin Yeh, *Shanghai Splendor: Economic Sentiments and the Making of Modern China* (Berkeley: University of California Press, 2007); Virgil K. Y. Ho, *Understanding Canton: Rethinking Popular Culture in the Republican Period* (Oxford: Oxford University Press, 2005); Madeleine Y. Dong, *Republican Beijing: The City and Its Histories* (Berkeley: University of California Press, 2003); Leo Ou-fan Lee, *Shanghai Modern: The Flowering of New Urban Culture in China, 1930–45* (Cambridge, MA: Harvard University Press, 1999); Lu Hanchao, *Beyond the Neon Lights: Everyday Shanghai in the Early Twentieth Century* (Berkeley: University of California Press, 1999); Sherman Cochran, ed., *Inventing Nanjing Road: Commercial Culture in Shanghai, 1900–1945* (Ithaca, NY: East Asia Program, Cornell University, 1999). For the literature before the mid-1990s, see Wen-hsin Yeh, "Shanghai Modernity: Commerce and Culture in a Republican City," *China Quarterly* 150 (1997): 375–394.

52. Hung-Yok Ip , Tze-Ki Hon, and Chiu-Chun Lee, "The Plurality of Chinese Modernity: A Review of Recent Scholarship on the May Fourth Movement," *Modern China* 29.4 (Oct. 2003): 490–509.

53. Frank Dikötter, *The Age of Openness: China Before Mao* (Berkeley, CA: University of California Press, 2008).

54. Christopher A. Reed, *Gutenberg in Shanghai: Chinese Print Capitalism, 1876–1937* (Honolulu: University of Hawai'i Press, 2004); Christopher A. Reed, "Advancing the (Gutenberg) Revolution: The Origins and Development of Chinese Print Communism, 1921–1947," in *From Woodblocks to the Internet: Chinese Publishing and Print Culture in Transition, circa 1800 to 2008,* ed. Cynthia Brokaw and Christopher A. Reed (Leiden: Brill, 2010), 275–311.

55. Cheek, *The Intellectual in Modern Chinese History,* 70–112; Wang Di, *The Teahouse: Small Business, Everyday Culture, and Public Politics in Chengdu, 1900–1950* (Stanford, CA: Stanford University Press, 2008); Lee Haiyan, *Revolution of the Heart: A Genealogy of Love in China, 1900–1950* (Stanford, CA: Stanford University Press, 2007); Eugenia Lean, *Public Passions: The Trial of Shi*

Jianqiao and the Rise of Popular Sympathy in Republican China (Berkeley: University of California Press, 2007); Madeleine Yue Dong and Joshua Lewis Goldstein, eds., *Everyday Modernity in China* (Seattle: University of Washington Press, 2006).

56. Edmund S. K. Fung, *The Intellectual Foundations of Chinese Modernity: Cultural and Political Thought in the Republican Era* (New York: Cambridge University Press, 2010); Elizabeth J. Perry, *Shanghai on Strike: The Politics of Chinese Labor* (Stanford, CA: Stanford University Press, 1993); Roger Jeans, *Democracy and Socialism in Republican China: The Politics of Zhang Junmai (Carson Chang)* (Lanham, MD: Rowman and Littlefield, 1997).

57. Robert Weatherly, *The Discourse of Human Rights in China: Historical and Ideological Perspectives* (Basingstoke, UK: Palgrave Macmillan, 1999); Edmund S. Fung, "The Human Rights Issue in China, 1929–1931," *Modern Asian Studies* 32.2 (1998): 431–457.

58. Fung, *The Intellectual Foundations of Chinese Modernity*, 22.

59. Liang Shuming, "Chinese Civilization vis-à-vis Eastern and Western Philosophies," in *Sources of Chinese Tradition: From 1600 through the Twentieth Century,* 2nd ed., comp. Wm. Theodore de Bary and Richard Lufrano (New York: Columbia University Press, 2000), 2:380–381.

60. Quoted from Sung Peng-Hsu, "Hu Shih," in *Chinese Thought: An Introduction,* ed. Donald H. Bishop (Delhi: Motilal Banarsidass Publishers, 1985), 364–392.

61. Mao Zedong, *Mao's Road to Power: Revolutionary Writings 1912–1949,* ed. Stuart R. Schram (Armonk, NY: M.E. Sharpe, 1992), 2:430.

62. Werner Meissner, *Das rote Haifeng: Peng Pai's Bericht über die Bauernbewegung in Südchina* (Munich: Minerva, 1987); Fernando Galbiati, *P'eng P'ai and the Hai-Lu-Feng Soviet* (Stanford, CA: Stanford University Press, 1985). A partial English translation of Peng Pai's report is in Patricia Ebrey, ed., *Chinese Civilization: A Sourcebook,* 2nd ed. (New York: Free Press, 1993), 364–372.

63. Kuo Heng-yü and Mechthild Leutner, *KPdSU(B), Komintern und die nationalrevolutionäre Bewegung in China: Dokumente: 1920–1925* (Münster: LIT, 2000), 1:198.

64. Mao, *Mao's Road to Power,* 3:30–31. See also Alexander V. Pantsov and Steven I. Levine, *Mao: The Real Story* (New York: Simon and Schuster, 2012), 190–206, 210.

65. Rebecca E. Karl, *Mao Zedong and China in the Twentieth Century World* (Durham, NC: Duke University Press, 2010), 36; Stephen C. Averill, *Revolution in the Highlands: China's Jinggangshan Base Area* (Lanham, MD: Rowman and Littlefield, 2005).

66. Stephen C. Averill, "The Origins of the Futian Incident," in *New Perspectives on the Chinese Communist Revolution,* ed. Tony Saich and Hans van de Ven (Armonk, NY: M.E. Sharpe), 109–110.

67. Guo Xuezhi, *China's Security State: Philosophy, Evolution, and Politics* (Cambridge: Cambridge University Press, 2012), 27–34; Michael Dutton, *Policing Chinese Politics* (Durham, NC: Duke University Press, 2005), 42–54.

68. Quoted from Mühlhahn, *Criminal Justice in China,* 162.

69. Sun Shuyun, *The Long March: The True History of Communist China's Founding Myth* (New York: Doubleday, 2007).

6. CHINA AT WAR: 1938–1948

1. Louise Young, *Japan's Total Empire: Manchuria and the Culture of Wartime Imperialism* (Berkeley: University of California Press, 1998), 89.

2. Andrew Gordon, *A Modern History of Japan: From Tokugawa Times to the Present* (Oxford: Oxford University Press, 2014), 188.

3. Quoted from Diana Lary, *China's Republic* (Cambridge: Cambridge University Press, 2007), 2:98.

4. Rana Mitter, *The Manchurian Myth: Nationalism, Resistance and Collaboration in Modern China* (Berkeley: University of California Press, 2000), 170–172.

5. Jay Taylor, *The Generalissimo: Chiang Kai-Shek and the Struggle for Modern China* (Cambridge, MA: Belknap Press of Harvard University Press, 2009), 95.

6. Donald Jordan, *China's Trial by Fire: The Shanghai War of 1932* (Ann Arbor: University of Michigan Press, 2001); Parks M. Coble, *Facing Japan: Chinese Politics and Japanese Imperialism, 1931–1937* (Cambridge, MA: Harvard University Press, 1991), 39–50.

7. Marjorie Dryburgh, *North China and Japanese Expansion 1933–1937: Regional Power and the National Interest* (Richmond, UK: Curzon, 2000), 84.

8. Mayumi Itoh, *Making of China's War with Japan: Zhou Enlai and Zhang Xueliang* (Singapore: Palgrave Macmillan, 2016), 115–116.

9. Rana Mitter, *Forgotten Ally: China's World War II, 1934–1945* (Boston: Houghton Mifflin Harcourt, 2013), loc. 1131–1188, Kindle; Hans J. van de Ven, *War and Nationalism in China, 1925–1945* (Abingdon, UK: Routledge, 2011), 183–188; Taylor, *The Generalissimo,* 117–137; Alexander Pantsov and Steven Levine, *Mao: The Real Story* (New York: Simon and Schuster, 2012), 295–303.

10. Quoted from Itoh, *Making of China's War,* 137.

11. Mitter, *Forgotten Ally,* loc. 1478, Kindle; Taylor, *The Generalissimo,* 149.

12. On August 2, 1937, Chiang Kai-shek legalized the Red Army; Mitter, *Forgotten Ally,* loc. 1478, Kindle.

13. Peter Zarrow, *China in War and Revolution, 1895–1949* (London: Routledge, 2005), 306.

14. Hans van de Ven, *China at War: Triumph and Tragedy in the Emergence of the New China* (London: Profile Books, 2017), 75–91; Peter Harmsen, *Shanghai 1937: Stalingrad on the Yangtze* (Philadelphia: Casemate Publishers, 2013).

15. John Faber, *Great News Photos and the Stories behind Them,* 2nd ed. (New York: Courier Dover Publications, 1978), 74–75.

16. Mark R. Peattie, Edward J. Drea, and Hans J. van de Ven, eds., *The Battle for China: Essays on the Military History of the Sino-Japanese War of 1937–1945* (Stanford, CA: Stanford University Press, 2011); R. Keith Schoppa, *In a Sea of Bitterness: Refugees during the Sino-Japanese War* (Cambridge, MA: Harvard University Press, 2001); Diana Lary, *Chinese People at War: Human Suffering and Social Transformation, 1937–1945* (Cambridge: Cambridge University Press, 2010); Diana Lary, "One Province's Experience of War: Guangxi, 1937–1945," in *China at War: Regions of China, 1937–1945,* ed. Stephen R. MacKinnon, Diana Lary, and Ezra F. Vogel (Stanford, CA: Stanford University Press, 2007), 314–334; Micah S. Muscolino, "Refugees, Land Reclamation, and Militarized Landscapes in Wartime China: Huanglongshan, Shaanxi, 1937–45," *Journal of Asian Studies* 69.2 (2010): 453–478.

17. On the Nanjing massacre, see Peter Harmsen, *Nanjing 1937: Battle for a Doomed City* (Philadelphia: Casemate Publishers, 2015); Mitter, *Forgotten Ally,* chap. 7; Iris Chang, *The Rape of Nanking: The Forgotten Holocaust of World War II* (New York: Penguin Books, 1998); Timothy Brook, *Documents on the Rape of Nanjing* (Ann Arbor: University of Michigan Press, 1999); Yang Daqing, "Convergence or Divergence? Recent Historical Writings on the Rape of Nanjing," *American Historical Review* 104 (1999): 842–865; Joshua A. Fogel, *The Nanjing Massacre in History and Historiography* (Berkeley: University of California Press, 2002); Zhang Kaiyuan, *Eyewitnesses to Massacre: American Missionaries Bear Witness to Japanese Atrocities in Nanjing* (Armonk, NY: M.E. Sharpe, 2001); John Latimer, *Burma: The Forgotten War* (London: John Murray, 2004); Bob Tadashi Wakabayashi, *The Nanking Atrocity, 1937–38: Complicating the Picture* (New York: Berghahn Books, 2007); MacKinnon, Lary, and Vogel, *China at War;* Erwin Wickert, ed., *The Good Man of Nanking: The Diaries of John Rabe* (New York: Knopf, 1998).

18. Wickert, *The Good Man,* 111–112.

19. Lary, *The Chinese People at War,* 61–62; Mitter, *Forgotten Ally,* loc. 2781, Kindle.

20. On Chongqing during the war, see Li Danke, *Echoes of Chongqing: Women in Wartime China* (Urbana: University of Illinois Press, 2010), 17; Lee McIsaac, "The City as Nation: Creating a Wartime Capital in Chongqing," in *Remaking*

the Chinese City: Modernity and National Identity, 1900–1950, ed. Joseph Esherick (Honolulu: University of Hawai'i Press, 2002), 174–191.

21. John Israel, *Lianda: A Chinese University in War and Revolution* (Stanford, CA: Stanford University Press, 1998).

22. Quoted from Li, *Echoes of Chongqing,* 112.

23. Ibid., 109.

24. Wu T'ien-wei, "Contending Political Forces during the War of Resistance," in *China's Bitter Victory: The War with Japan 1937–1945,* ed. James C. Hsiung and Steven I. Levine (Armonk, NY: M.E. Sharpe, 1992), 79–106; Li, *Echoes of Chongqing,* 20.

25. Mitter, *Forgotten Ally,* chap. 10; Felix Boecking, "Unmaking the Chinese Nationalist State: Administrative Reform among Fiscal Collapse, 1937–1945," *Modern Asian Studies* 45.2 (2011): 277–301; William C. Kirby, "The Chinese War Economy," in Hsiung and Levine, *China's Bitter Victory,* 185–212.

26. William C. Kirby, "Continuity and Change in Modern China: Chinese Economic Planning on the Mainland and on Taiwan, 1943–1958," *Australian Journal of Chinese Affairs* 24 (July 1990): 121–141.

27. Felix Boecking, *No Great Wall: Trade, Tariffs, and Nationalism in Republican China, 1927–1945* (Cambridge, MA: Harvard University East Asia Center, 2017).

28. There is substantial literature on the base areas, including David S. G. Goodman, *Social and Political Change in Revolutionary China: The Taihang Base Area in the War of Resistance to Japan, 1937–1945* (Lanham, MD: Rowman and Littlefield, 2000); Feng Chongyi and David S. G. Goodman, eds., *North China at War: The Social Ecology of Revolution, 1937–1945* (Lanham, MD: Rowman and Littlefield, 2000); Gregor Benton, *New Fourth Army: Communist Resistance along the Yangtze and the Huai, 1938–1941* (Berkeley: University of California Press, 1999); Tony Saich, "Introduction: The Chinese Communist Party and the Anti-Japanese Base Areas," *China Quarterly* 140 (1994): 1000–1006; Kathleen Hartford and Steven M. Goldstein, *Single Sparks: China's Rural Revolution* (Armonk, NY: Sharpe, 1990); Chen Yung-fa, *Making Revolution: The Communist Movement in Eastern and Central China* (Berkeley: University of California Press, 1986); Lyman P. Van Slyke, "The Chinese Communist Movement during the Sino-Japanese War, 1937–1945," in *The Cambridge History of China,* ed. John K. Fairbank and Albert Feuerwerker, vol. 13, *Republican China, 1912–1949: Part 2* (Cambridge: Cambridge University Press, 1986), 609–721; Mark Selden, *The Yenan Way in Revolutionary China* (Cambridge, MA: Harvard University Press, 1971).

29. Mao Zedong, "Reform Our Study," in *Selected Works of Mao Tse-tung,* vol. 3 (Beijing: Beijing Foreign Languages Press, 1971), 19.

30. Orville Schell and John Delury, *Wealth and Power: China's Long March to the Twenty-First Century* (New York: Random House, 2013), 444.

31. Stuart R. Schram, "Red Star over China?" in *Mao's Road to Power: Revolutionary Writings 1912–1949,* ed. Stuart R. Schram (Armonk, NY: M.E. Sharpe, 1992), 5:249.

32. Klaus Mühlhahn, *Criminal Justice in China: A History* (Cambridge, MA: Harvard University Press, 2009), 165; David E. Apter and Tony Saich, *Revolutionary Discourse in Mao's Republic* (Cambridge, MA: Harvard University Press, 1994), 163–192.

33. Michael Dutton, *Policing Chinese Politics: A History* (Durham, NC: Duke University Press, 2005), 90.

34. See the in-depth discussion in Dutton, *Policing Chinese Politics,* 71–132.

35. Pantsov and Levine, *Mao,* 296.

36. Norman Smith and Diana Lary, eds., *Empire and Environment in the Making of Manchuria* (Vancouver: UBC Press, 2017).

37. On Manchukuo, see Louise Young, *Japan's Total Empire: Manchuria and the Culture of Wartime* (Berkeley: University of California Press, 1998); Prasenjit Duara, *Sovereignty and Authenticity: Manchukuo and the East Asian Modern* (Lanham, MD: Rowman and Littlefield, 2003); Rana Mitter, *The Manchurian Myth: Nationalism, Resistance and Collaboration in Modern China* (Berkeley: University of California Press, 2000); Chao Kang, *The Economic Development of Manchuria: The Rise of a Frontier Economy* (Ann Arbor: Center for Chinese Studies, University of Michigan, 1982); Annika A. Culver, *Glorify the Empire: Japanese Avant-Garde Propaganda in Manchukuo* (Vancouver: UBC Press, 2014).

38. United States Government, *Report of the Lytton Commission of Inquiry* (Washington, DC: United States Government Printing Office, 1932), 30.

39. Pu Yi, *From Emperor to Citizen: The Autobiography of Pu Yi,* trans. William John Francis Jenner (Beijing: Foreign Language Press, 1965), 2:195. On the concentration camp system, see Klaus Mühlhahn, "The Concentration Camp in Global Historical Perspective," *History Compass* 8.6 (2010): 543–561, here 550–551; Sheldon H. Harris, *Factories of Death: Japanese Biological Warfare 1932–45 and the American Cover-Up* (London: Routledge, 1994), 26–33; on resistance in general, see Norman Smith, *Resisting Manchukuo: Chinese Women Writers and the Japanese Occupation* (Vancouver: UBC Press, 2014).

40. John Hunter Boyle, *China and Japan at War, 1937–1945: The Politics of Collaboration* (Stanford, CA: Stanford University Press, 1972), 83–134.

41. Kitamura Minoru and Lin Siyun, *The Reluctant Combatant: Japan and the Second Sino-Japanese War* (Lanham, MD: University Press of America, 2014), 70–73.

42. Timothy Brook, "The Creation of the Reformed Government in Central China, 1938," in *Chinese Collaboration with Japan, 1932–1945: The Limits of Accommodation,* ed. David Barrett and Larry Shyu (Stanford, CA: Stanford University Press, 2000), 79–101.

43. Ibid., 91.

44. Timothy Brook, *Collaboration: Japanese Agents and Local Elites in Wartime China* (Cambridge, MA: Harvard University Press, 2005); Poshek Fu, *Passivity, Resistance, and Collaboration: Intellectual Choices in Occupied Shanghai, 1937–1945* (Stanford, CA: Stanford University Press, 1996).

45. Sarah C. M. Paine, *The Wars for Asia, 1911–1949* (Cambridge: Cambridge University Press, 2012), 162.

46. Brian G. Martin, "Patriotic Collaboration? Zhou Fohai and the Wang Jingwei Government during the Second Sino-Japanese War," in *Japan as the Occupier and the Occupied,* ed. Christine de Matos and Mark Caprio (New York: Palgrave Macmillan, 2015), 152–171; Liu Jie, "Wang Jingwei and the 'Nanjing Nationalist Government': Between Collaboration and Resistance," in *Toward a History Beyond Borders: Contentious Issues in Sino-Japanese Relations,* ed. Yang Daqing et al. (Cambridge, MA: Harvard University Asia Center, 2012), 205–239.

47. The following paragraphs are based on Ronald Ian Heiferman, *The Cairo Conference of 1943: Roosevelt, Churchill, Chiang Kai-shek and Madame Chiang* (Jefferson, NC: McFarland, 2011); Mitter, *Forgotten Ally,* chaps. 10, 12, and 16; Odd Arne Westad, *Restless Empire: China and the World since 1750* (New York: Basic Books, 2015), chap. 7.

48. Lend Lease Bill of 1941, H.R. 1776, 77th Cong. (1941).

49. On SACO and the prison camps, see Mühlhahn, *Criminal Justice in China,* 133; Frederic Wakeman, *Spymaster: Dai Li and the Chinese Secret Service* (Berkeley: University of California Press, 2003), 217; Frederic Wakeman, "American Police Advisers and the Nationalist Chinese Secret Service, 1930–1937," *Modern China* 18.2 (1992): 107–137.

50. Robert Bickers, *Out of China: How the Chinese Ended the Era of Western Domination* (Cambridge MA: Harvard University Press, 2017).

51. Quoted from Mitter, *Forgotten Ally,* loc. 5432, Kindle.

52. Heiferman, *The Cairo Conference,* 127.

53. Ibid., 125.

54. Paine, *The Wars for Asia,* 199.

55. Paul Gordon Lauren, "First Principles of Racial Equality: History and the Politics and Diplomacy of Human Rights Provisions in the United Nations Charter," *Human Rights Quarterly* 5.1 (1983): 1–26.

56. Klaus Mühlhahn, "China, the West and the Question of Human Rights: A Historical Perspective," *Asien, Afrika, Lateinamerika* 24.3 (1996): 287–303, here 292.

57. Donald G. Gillin and Charles Etter, "Staying On: Japanese Soldiers and Civilians in China, 1945–1949," *Journal of Asian Studies* 42.3 (1983): 497–518.

58. Diana Lary, *China's Civil War: A Social History, 1945–1949* (Cambridge: Cambridge University Press, 2015); Odd Arne Westad, *Decisive Encounters: The Chinese Civil War, 1946–1950* (Stanford, CA: Stanford University Press, 2004); Paine, *The Wars for Asia,* 223–270; Kevin Peraino, *A Force So Swift: Mao, Truman and the Birth of Modern China, 1949* (New York: Crown, 2017); Richard Bernstein, *China 1945: Mao's Revolution and America's Fateful Choice* (New York: Alfred A. Knopf, 2015).

59. Quoted from Warren I. Cohen, "The Foreign Impact on East Asia," in *Historical Perspectives on Contemporary East Asia,* ed. Merle Goldman and Andrew Gordon (Cambridge, MA: Harvard University Press), 24.

60. Daniel Kurtz-Phelan, *The China Mission: George Marshall's Unfinished War, 1945–1947* (New York: Norton 2018), 11–16.

61. Daniel Kurtz-Phelan, *The China Mission,* 149–261.

62. National Security Council on United States Policy toward China, *Foreign Relations of the United States, 1949, The Far East: China* (Washington, DC: Government Printing Office, 1949), 9:492–495.

63. Cao Jianmin, *Zhongguo Minzhu Tongmeng Lishi Yanjiu* [The History of China's Democratic League] (Peking: Zhongguo renmin chubanshe, 1994), 48; Carson Chang, *The Third Force in China* (New York: Bookman Associates, 1952).

64. Roger B. Jeans, *Democracy and Socialism in Republican China: The Politics of Zhang Junmai, 1906–1941* (Lanham, MD: Rowman and Littlefield, 1997).

65. John Fitzgerald, "The Nationless State: The Search for a Nation in Modern Chinese Nationalism," *Australian Journal of Chinese Affairs* 33 (1995): 75–104; Arthur Waldron, "War and the Rise of Nationalism in Twentieth-Century China," *Journal of Military History* 57 (1993): 87–104.

66. William C. Kirby, "Engineering China: Birth of the Developmental State, 1928–1937," in *Becoming Chinese: Passages to Modernity and Beyond,* ed. Wenhsin Yeh (Berkeley: University of California Press, 2000), 137–160.

67. Julia Strauss, *Strong Institutions in Weak Polity, 1927–1949* (Oxford: Clarendon Press, 1998).

68. David Strand, *An Unfinished Republic: Leading by Word and Deed in Modern China* (Berkeley: University of California Press, 2011), 10–11.

69. Sebastian Veg, 1911: The Failed Institutional Revolution, October 10, 2011, http://www.thechinabeat.org/?tag=sebastian-veg.

PART 3. REMAKING CHINA

1. Li Zhisui and Anne F. Thurston, *The Private Life of Chairman Mao: The Memoirs of Mao's Personal Physician* (New York: Random House, 1996), 52.

7. SOCIALIST TRANSFORMATION: 1949–1955

1. Quoted from Alexander Pantsov and Steven I. Levine, *Mao: The Real Story* (New York: Simon and Schuster, 2012), 372.

2. Odd A. Westad, *Decisive Encounters: The Chinese Civil War, 1946–1950* (Stanford, CA: Stanford University Press, 2004), 121.

3. Andrew G. Walder, *China Under Mao: A Revolution Derailed* (Cambridge, MA: Harvard University Press, 2015), 100.

4. Legitimacy is "a generalized perception or assumption that the actions of an entity are desirable, proper, or appropriate within some socially constructed system of norms, values, beliefs, and definitions." Mark C. Suchman, "Managing Legitimacy: Strategic and Institutional Approaches," *Academy of Management Review* 20.3 (1995): 571–610, here 574. There are two main ways to build legitimacy— namely, either through approval and consent, which is called *input legitimacy*, or through the provision of crucial services such as security, food, and welfare, which is called *output legitimacy*. Without legitimacy, government institutions are necessarily unstable, unpredictable, and in a constant state of insecurity.

5. Frank Dikötter, *The Tragedy of Liberation: A History of the Chinese Revolution* (New York: Bloomsbury Press, 2013), 23; Pantsov and Levine, *Mao*, 356–358.

6. Nara Dillon, "New Democracy and the Demise of Private Charity in Shanghai," in *Dilemmas of Victory: The Early Years of the People's Republic of China*, ed. Jeremy Brown and Paul G. Pickowicz (Cambridge, MA: Harvard University Press, 2007), 80–102; Frederic Wakeman, "'Cleanup': The New Order in Shanghai," in Brown and Pickowicz, *Dilemmas of Victory*, 80–102.

7. Kenneth Lieberthal, *Revolution and Tradition in Tientsin, 1949–1952* (Stanford, CA: Stanford University Press, 1980), 40–41.

8. Lieberthal, *Revolution and Tradition*, 50–51; see also Elizabeth J. Perry, "Masters of the Country? Shanghai Workers in the Early People's Republic," in Brown and Pickowicz, *Dilemmas of Victory*, 59–79.

9. Elizabeth J. Perry and Sebastian Heilmann, *Mao's Invisible Hand: The Political Foundations of Adaptive Governance in China* (Cambridge, MA: Harvard University Asia Center, 2011).

10. Tianjin Shimin Zhengju [Tianjin Civil Affairs Bureau], "Guanyu shourong chuli qigai gongzuo de zongjie (1949.9.20) [Summary Report on the Work of Detaining and Processing Beggars (September 20, 1949)]," in *Tianjin jiefang*

[Liberation of Tianjin], ed. Tianjin Municipal Archives (Beijing: Zhongguo dangan chubanshe, 2009), 322–325. Quoted from Vanessa Bozzay, "Refugee Governance in Tianjin, 1945–1957" (master's thesis), Freie Universität Berlin, 2014, 37.

11. Bozzay, "Refugee Governance," 38.

12. Tianjin Shimin Zhengju [Tianjin Civil Affairs Bureau], "Guanyu Tianjinshi cishan tuanji de diaocha gongzuo zonghe baogao [Comprehensive Report on the Investigation of Charity Organizations in Tianjin]," April 8, 1949, Tianjin Municipal Archives, X0065-Y-000034-001, translated in Bozzay, "Refugee Governance," 31.

13. Lieberthal, *Revolution and Tradition,* 4.

14. Robert Bickers, *Out of China: How the Chinese Ended the Era of Western Domination* (London: Allan Lane, 2017), 270–282.

15. Du Ying, "Shanghaiing the Press Gang: The Maoist Regimentation of the Shanghai Popular Publishing Industry in the Early PRC (1949–1956)," *Modern Chinese Literature and Culture* 26.2 (2014): 89–141.

16. Perry, "Masters of the Country?" 59.

17. Christian Henriot, "'La Fermèture': The Abolishing of Prostitution in Shanghai, 1949–1958," *China Quarterly* 142 (1995): 467–486; Zhou Yongming, *Anti-Drug Crusades in Twentieth-Century China: Nationalism, History, and State Building* (Lanham, MD: Rowman and Littlefield, 1999); Lu Hong, Terance D. Miethe, and Liang Bin, *China's Drug Practices and Policies: Regulating Controlled Substances in a Global Context* (Farnham, Surrey, UK: Ashgate, 2009).

18. Mao Tse-tung, "On New Democracy," in *Selected Works of Mao Tse-tung* (Beijing: Foreign Languages Press, 1967), 2:339–384.

19. Mao, "On the People's Democratic Dictatorship," *Selected Works,* 4:411–424.

20. Mao, "On the People's Democratic Dictatorship," *Selected Works,* 4:417–418.

21. Walder, *China Under Mao,* 101–104; Kenneth Lieberthal, *Governing China: From Revolution through Reform* (New York: W.W. Norton, 2004), 173–179.

22. Zheng Shiping, *Party vs. State in Post-1949 China: The Institutional Dilemma* (Cambridge: Cambridge University Press, 1997).

23. Timothy Cheek, "Introduction: The Making and Breaking of the Party State in China," in *New Perspectives on State Socialism in China,* ed. Julian Chang, Timothy Cheek, and Tony Saich (Armonk, NY: M.E. Sharpe, 1997), 3–19.

24. Andrew J. Nathan and Andrew Scobell, *China's Search for Security* (New York: Columbia University Press, 2012), 192.

25. Shen Zhihua and Li Danhui, *After Leaning to One Side: China and Its Allies in the Cold War* (Washington, DC: Woodrow Wilson Center Press, 2011); Odd A. Westad, *Cold War and Revolution: Soviet-American Rivalry and the Origins of the Chinese Civil War, 1944–1946* (New York: Columbia University Press, 1993),

176; Chen Jian, *Mao's China and the Cold War* (Chapel Hill: University of North Carolina Press, 2001).

26. Mao, "On the People's Democratic Dictatorship," *Selected Works*, 4:415.

27. Thomas P. Bernstein and Hua-yu Li, eds., *China Learns from the Soviet Union, 1949–Present* (Lanham, MD: Lexington Books, 2010), 1–26.

28. Odd A. Westad, *Restless Empire: China and the World since 1750* (New York: Basic Books, 2012), 429; Odd A. Westad, *Brothers in Arms: The Rise and Fall of the Sino-Soviet Alliance, 1945–1963* (Washington, DC: Woodrow Wilson Center Press with Stanford University Press, 1998).

29. Deborah Kaple, "Agents of Change: Soviet Advisors and High Stalinist Management in China, 1949–1960," *Journal of Cold War Studies* 18:1 (Winter 2016): 1–26.

30. Hung Chang-Tai, *Mao's New World: Political Culture in the Early People's Republic of China* (Ithaca, NY: Cornell University Press, 2011), 25–50; Hung Wu, *Remaking Beijing: Tiananmen Square and the Creation of a Political Space* (Chicago: University of Chicago Press, 2005).

31. There is a large body of literature on the Korean War; important titles include Shen Zhihua, *Mao, Stalin and the Korean War: Trilateral Communist Relations in the 1950s* (New York: Routledge, 2012); Shen Zhihua and Xia Yafeng, *Mao and the Sino-Soviet Partnership, 1945–1959: A New History* (Lanham, MD: Lexington Books, 2015); Chen Jian, *China's Road to the Korean War* (New York: Columbia University Press, 1994); Chong Chae-ho, *Between Ally and Partner: Korea-China Relations and the United States* (New York: Columbia University Press, 2007); Bruce Cumings, *The Origins of the Korean War*, 2 vols. (Princeton, NJ: Princeton University Press, 1981); David Halberstam, *The Coldest Winter: America and the Korean War* (New York: Hyperion, 2007); Li Xiaobing, Yu Bin, and Allan Reed Millett, *Mao's Generals Remember Korea* (Lawrence: University Press of Kansas, 2001); Richard A. Peters and Li Xiaobing, *Voices from the Korean War: Personal Stories of American, Korean, and Chinese Soldiers* (Lexington: University Press of Kentucky, 2004); William Whitney Stueck, *The Korean War: An International History* (Princeton, NJ: Princeton University Press, 1995); Zhang Shu Guang, *Mao's Military Romanticism: China and the Korean War, 1950–1953* (Lawrence: University of Kansas Press, 1995); Allen S. Whiting, *China Crosses the Yalu: The Decision to Enter the Korean War* (New York: Macmillan, 1960); Max Hastings, *The Korean War* (New York: Simon and Schuster, 1987); Burton Ira Kaufman, *The Korean Conflict* (Westport, CT: Greenwood, 1999); Zhang Xiaoming, *Red Wings over the Yalu: China, the Soviet Union, and the Air War in Korea* (College Station: Texas A&M University Press, 2002); William Whitney Stueck, *The Korean War in World History* (Lexington: University Press of Kentucky, 2010).

32. Pantsov and Levine, *Mao,* 375.

33. Dikötter, *Tragedy of Liberation,* 142.

34. Shen, *Mao, Stalin and the Korean War,* 175–177.

35. Jay Taylor, *The Generalissimo: Chiang Kai-Shek and the Struggle for Modern China* (Cambridge, MA: Belknap Press of Harvard University Press, 2009), 420. See also Steven M. Goldstein, "The United States and the Republic of China, 1949–1978: Suspicious Allies" (working paper, Asia-Pacific Center, Institute for International Studies, Stanford University, February 2000), 5–26.

36. Chen Yun, "Kang Mei Yuan Chao kaishe hou caijing gongzuo de fangzhen" [The Direction of Financial Work after 'Resist America and Support Korea'], *Jianguo yilai zhongyao wenxian xuanbian* [Selection of Important Documents since the Founding of the Country], ed. Zhongguo gongchangdang and Zhongyang wenxian yanjiushi, vol. 1 (Beijing: Zhongyang wenxian chubanshe, 1992), 469.

37. Mao Zedong, "Guanyu jiasu jinxing tugai zhi Zhongnanju deng dian" [Cable to the Central South Bureau regarding accelerating land reform], *Gongheguo zou guo de lu: Jianguo yilai zhongyao wenxian zhuanti xuanji* [The Path of the Republic: Selection of Important Documents on Special Topics since the Founding of the Country], ed. Zhongguo zhongyang wenxianguan (Beijing: Zhonggong zhongyang wenxian chubanshe, 1991), 219.

38. Editorial, *Renmin Ribao,* March 17, 1949.

39. This and the following paragraphs are based on Klaus Mühlhahn, *Criminal Justice in China: A History* (Cambridge, MA: Harvard University Press, 2009), 178–185.

40. Albert P. Blaustein, *Fundamental Legal Documents of Communist China* (South Hackensack, NJ: F.B. Rothman, 1962), 215–221.

41. Mao Zedong, "On Ten Major Relationships," in *The Writings of Mao Zedong, 1949–1976,* ed. Michael Y. M. Kau and John K. Leung (Armonk, NY: M.E. Sharpe, 1992), 2:57.

42. Klaus Mühlhahn, "'Repaying Blood Debt': The Chinese Labor Camp System during the 1950s," in *The Soviet Gulag: Evidence, Interpretation, and Comparison,* ed. Michael David-Fox (Pittsburgh: University of Pittsburgh Press, 2016), 250–267. Numbers are mentioned in Yang Kuisong, "Reconsidering the Campaign to Suppress Counterrevolutionaries," *China Quarterly* 193 (2008): 102–121.

43. Quoted in Mühlhahn, *Criminal Justice in China,* 182.

44. Julia C. Strauss, "Paternalist Terror: The Campaign to Suppress Counterrevolutionaries and Regime Consolidation in the People's Republic of China, 1950–1953," *Comparative Studies in Society and History* 44 (2002): 80–105, here 97.

45. There were several types of campaigns, distinguished by their reach into society and their target groups; see Julia Strauss, "Morality, Coercion and State Building

by Campaign in the Early PRC: Regime Consolidation and After, 1949–1956," *China Quarterly* 188 (2006): 891–219. In the following, I focus mainly on two types of campaigns: the great mass campaigns, or *qunzhong yundong,* that took place in the years 1950 to 1953 and the frequent, more limited campaigns that were implemented through the bureaucracy and that targeted specific social or occupational groups. Both campaign types deployed tribunals.

46. See Shao Chuan Leng, *Justice in Communist China* (Dobbs Ferry, NY: Oceana Publications, 1967), 35–39.

47. Ibid., 36.

48. Sentences exceeding a five-year term of imprisonment needed to be ratified by the provincial government.

49. Dikötter, *Tragedy of Liberation,* 162; Michael M. Sheng, "Mao Zedong and the Three-Anti Campaign (November 1951 to April 1952): A Revisionist Interpretation," *Twentieth-Century China* 32.1 (2006): 56–80.

50. This and the following paragraph are based on Yang Kuisong, "Communism in China, 1919–1976," in *The Oxford Handbook of the History of Communism,* ed. Stephen A. Smith (Oxford: Oxford University Press, 2014), 220–229, here 226–227.

51. A total number of 800,000 executed counterrevolutionaries is often mentioned in official documents. In 1957, Mao Zedong himself explained that during the campaign to eliminate counterrevolutionaries in the years 1950 to 1953, 700,000 people had been killed. In the period from 1954 to 1957, an additional 70,000 people had been executed as counterrevolutionaries. He also admitted that mistakes had been made and innocent people had been killed; see Roderick MacFarquhar, Eugene Wu, and Timothy Cheek, eds., *The Secret Speeches of Chairman Mao: From the Hundred Flowers to the Great Leap Forward* (Cambridge, MA: Council on East Asian Studies, Harvard University, 1989), 142; See also Yang, *Reconsidering the Campaign;* Michael Dutton, *Policing Chinese Politics: A History* (Durham, NC: Duke University Press, 2005), 167.

52. Aminda M. Smith, "The Dilemma of Thought Reform," *Modern China* 39.2 (2013): 203–234.

53. Mühlhahn, *Criminal Justice in China,* 223–230.

54. Mühlhahn, *Criminal Justice in China,* 269.

55. A mass trial and a mass execution of around fifty landlords during the Land Reform movement is described in Gregory Ruf, *Cadres and Kin: Making a Socialist Village in West China, 1921–1991* (Stanford, CA: Stanford University Press, 1998), 86–87.

56. In 1950 and 1951, Mao Zedong wrote several comments on the "Movement to Suppress and Liquidate Counterrevolutionaries"; see Mao, *The Writings of Mao,* 1:189, 112. He expressed increasing uneasiness about the movement's getting out

of control. He saw two dangers: left deviation and right deviation. It seemed to him that in some places there was too much fervor against opponents and in others too much leniency. His comments therefore alternated between demanding a more orderly approach and calling for stricter and swifter punishments. In any case, Mao's frequent comments demonstrate how difficult it was to control the movement.

57. As Julia Strauss has argued with respect to the mass campaigns, an important audience was the "regional and local layers of the revolutionary state"; see Strauss, "Paternalist Terror," 85.

58. James Z. Gao, *The Communist Takeover of Hangzhou: The Transformation of City and Cadre, 1949–1954* (Honolulu: University of Hawai'i Press, 2004), 138–140.

59. Jerome Alan Cohen, *The Criminal Process in the People's Republic of China, 1949–1963: An Introduction* (Cambridge, MA: Harvard University Press, 1968), 20; Bing Ngeow Chow, "The Residents' Committee in China's Political System: Democracy, Stability, Mobilization," *Issues & Studies* 48 (2012): 71–126.

60. Gao, *The Communist Takeover,* 138–140.

61. See Tao Siju, *Xin zhongguo di yi ren gong'an buzhang—Luo Ruiqing* [Luo Ruiqing: New China's First Minister of Public Security] (Beijing: Qunzhong Chubanshe, 1996), 104.

62. David Bray, *Social Space and Governance in Urban China: The Danwei System from Origins to Reform* (Stanford, CA: Stanford University Press, 2005), 104; Morris L. Bian, *The Making of the State Enterprise System in Modern China: The Dynamics of Institutional Change* (Cambridge, MA: Harvard University Press, 2005); Tiejun Cheng and Mark Selden, "The Construction of Spatial Hierarchies: China's Hukou and Danwei Systems," in *New Perspectives on State Socialism in China,* ed. Timothy Cheek et al. (Armonk, NY: M.E. Sharpe, 1997), 23–50.

63. Andrew Walder, "Industrial Reform in China: The Human Dimension," in *The Limits of Reform in China,* ed. Ronald A. Morse (Boulder, CO: Westview Press, 1983), 59–60.

64. Yang Kuisong, "How a 'Bad Element' Was Made: The Discovery, Accusation, and Punishment of Zang Qiren," in *Maoism at the Grassroots: Everyday Life in China's Era of High Socialism,* ed. Jeremy Brown and Matthew D. Johnson (Cambridge, MA: Harvard University Press, 2015), 19–50; Jeremy Brown, "Moving Targets: Changing Class Labels in Rural Hebei and Henan, 1960–1979," in Brown and Johnson, *Maoism at the Grassroots,* 51–76; Elizabeth J. Perry, "Studying Chinese Politics: Farewell to Revolution?" *China Journal* 57 (January 2007): 1–22.

65. Timothy Cheek, *Propaganda and Culture in Mao's China: Deng Tuo and the Intelligentsia* (Oxford: Clarendon Press, 1997); Merle Goldman and Leo Ou-

Fan Lee, eds., *An Intellectual History of Modern China* (Cambridge: Cambridge University Press, 2002); Edward Gu and Merle Goldman, eds., *Chinese Intellectuals between State and Market* (London: Routledge, 2004); Matthew D. Johnson, "Beneath the Propaganda State: Official and Unofficial Cultural Landscapes in Shanghai, 1949–1965," in Brown and Johnson, *Maoism at the Grassroots,* 199–229.

66. The following paragraphs are based on Du, *Shanghaiing the Press Gang.*

67. Mi Zhao, "State Capitalism and Entertainment Markets: The Socialist Transformation of Quyi in Tianjin, 1949–1964," *Modern China* 44.5 (2018): 525–556.

68. Wang Ban, "Revolutionary Realism and Revolutionary Romanticism," in *The Columbia Companion to Modern Chinese Literature,* ed. Kirk A. Denton (New York: Columbia University Press, 2016), 237–244.

69. Chao Chin, "Introducing Hao Ran," *Chinese Literature* 4 (1974): 98–99. See also Richard King, *Milestones on a Golden Road: Writing for Chinese Socialism, 1945–80* (Vancouver: UBC Press, 2013); Bonnie S. McDougall and Paul Clark, *Popular Chinese Literature and Performing Arts in the People's Republic of China, 1949–1979* (Berkeley: University of California Press, 1984).

70. See Xu Jilin, *Dashidai zhong de zhishifenzi* [Intellectuals during the Great Age] (Beijing: Zhonghua shuju, 2012), 241–252.

71. Chen Yinghong, *Creating the "New Man": From Enlightenment Ideals to Socialist Realities* (Honolulu: University of Hawai'i Press, 2009); Theodore Hsien Chen, *Thought Reform of the Chinese Intellectuals* (Hong Kong: Hong Kong University Press, 1960), 54–56, 62–69; Timothy Cheek, *The Intellectual in Modern Chinese History* (Cambridge: Cambridge University Press, 2015).

72. Quoted in Eddy U, "The Making of Chinese Intellectuals: Representations and Organization in the Thought Reform Campaign," *China Quarterly* 192 (2007): 971–989.

73. Martin Whyte, *Small Groups and Political Rituals in China* (Berkeley: University of California Press, 1974).

74. Hsu Cho-yun, *China: A New Cultural History* (New York: Columbia University Press, 2012), 554–555.

75. There is little recent Western research on land reform: Louis G. Putterman, *Continuity and Change in China's Rural Development: Collective and Reform Eras in Perspective* (New York: Oxford University Press, 1993); John Wong, *Land Reform in the People's Republic of China: Institutional Transformation in Agriculture* (New York: Praeger, 1973); Anita Chan, Richard Madsen, and Jonathan Unger, *Chen Village: The Recent History of a Peasant Community in Mao's China* (Berkeley: University of California Press, 1992).

76. Strauss, "Paternalist Terror," 97.

77. Yunhui Lin, *Xiang Shehui Zhuyi guodu: Zhongguo Jingji yu Shehui de Zhuanxing, 1953–1955 [Transition to Socialism: The Transformation of Chinese Economy and Society, 1953–1955]* (Hong Kong: Xianggang Zhongwen Daxue Dangdai Zhongguo Wenhua Yanjiu Zhongxin, 2009), 32–44.

78. Zhang Xiaojun, "Land Reform in Yang Village: Symbolic Capital and the Determination of Class Status," *Modern China* 30 (2004): 3–45; Walder, *China Under Mao,* 51–53.

79. Luo Pinghan, "Tugai yu Zhonggong zhizheng diwei de queding" [Land Reform Movement and the Establishment of Chinese Communist Party's Rule], *Ershiyi Shiji* 111 (2009): 48–54; Gao Wang-ling and Liu Yang, "Tugai the Jiduanhua" [The Radicalization of the Land Reform Movement], *Ershiyi Shiji* 111 (2009): 36–47.

8. LEAPING AHEAD: 1955–1965

1. See Elizabeth J. Perry, *Anyuan: Mining China's Revolutionary Tradition* (Berkeley: University of California Press, 2012).

2. Wang Fei-Ling, *Organization through Division and Exclusion: China's Hukou System* (Stanford, CA: Stanford University Press, 2005); Cheng Tiejun and Mark Selden, "The Origins and Social Consequences of China's Hukou System," *China Quarterly* 139 (1994): 644–668.

3. Jeremy Brown, *City versus Countryside in Mao's China: Negotiating the Divide* (New York: Cambridge University Press, 2012), 32–33.

4. The quotes in this paragraph are from Tianjin Renmin Weiyuanhui [Tianjin Municipal People's Committee], "Tianjinshi dongyuan mangmu liujin renkou huixian gongzuo zongjie baogao" [Summary Report on Mobilizing Migrants for Repatriation], April 14, 1956, Tianjin Municipal Archives, X0053-C-001002-018, 70. Quoted from Vanessa Bozzay, "Refugee Governance in Tianjin, 1945–1957" (master's thesis, Freie Universität Berlin, 2014), 37. See also Greg Rohlf, *Building New China, Colonizing Kokonor: Resettlement to Qinghai in the 1950s* (Lanham, MD: Lexington Books, 2016).

5. The system was not abolished until 2014. See Zhang Zhanxin and Hou Huili, "Intensified Reform of the Labor Market and Abolishment of the Rural-Urban Divide," in *Chinese Research Perspectives on Population and Labor,* ed. Cai Fang (Boston: Brill, 2014), 1:185–207.

6. Sara L. Friedman, "Women, Marriage and the State in Contemporary China," in *Chinese Society: Change, Conflict and Resistance,* ed. Elizabeth J. Perry and Mark Selden (London: Routledge, 2010), 148–170, here 149; Sara L. Friedman, *Intimate Politics: Marriage, the Market, and State Power in Southeastern China* (Cambridge, MA: Harvard University Asia Center, 2006); Susan L. Glosser,

Chinese Visions of Family and State, 1915–53 (Berkeley: University of California Press, 2003); Yan Yunxiang, *Private Life under Socialism: Love, Intimacy, and Family Change in a Chinese Village, 1949–99* (Stanford, CA: Stanford University Press, 2003); Neil J. Diamant, *Revolutionizing the Family: Politics, Love, and Divorce in Urban and Rural China, 1949–68* (Berkeley: University of California Press, 2000).

7. Linda Benson, *China Since 1949* (London: Routledge 2002), 27–28.

8. Vincent Goossaert and David A. Palmer, *The Religious Question in Modern China* (Chicago: University of Chicago Press, 2011), 152–164; Rebecca A. Nedostup, *Superstitious Regimes: Religion and the Politics of Chinese Modernity* (Cambridge, MA: Harvard University Asia Center, 2009); Wang Xiaoxuan, "The Dilemma of Implementation: The State and Religion in the People's Republic of China," in *Maoism at the Grassroots: Everyday Life in China's Era of High Socialism,* ed. Jeremy Brown and Matthew D. Johnson (Cambridge, MA: Harvard University Press, 2015), 259–279.

9. S. A. Smith, "Redemptive Religious Societies and the Communist State, 1949 to the 1980s," in Brown and Johnson, *Maoism at the Grassroots,* 340–364.

10. Thomas S. Mullaney, *Coming to Terms with the Nation: Ethnic Classification in Modern China* (Berkeley: University of California Press, 2011).

11. Mullaney, *Coming to Terms,* 80, 90.

12. Mao Zedong, "On the People's Democratic Dictatorship," in *Selected Works of Mao Tse-tung* (Peking: Foreign Languages Press, 1967), vol. 4, 421, 411–421.

13. Case studies on the fate of entrepreneurs and firms after 1949 are in Sherman Cochran, ed., *The Capitalist Dilemma in China's Communist Revolution* (Ithaca, NY: East Asia Program, Cornell University, 2014).

14. Thomas Bernstein and Hua-Yu Li, "Introduction," in *China Learns from the Soviet Union, 1949–Present,* ed. Thomas Bernstein and Hua-Yu Li (Lanham, MD: Rowman and Littlefield, 2010), 1–24, here 9.

15. Li Hua-yu, *Mao and the Economic Stalinization of China, 1948–1953* (Lanham, MD: Rowman and Littlefield, 2006).

16. Quoted from Li, *Mao and the Economic Stalinization,* 135.

17. Robert K. Cliver, "Surviving Socialism: Private Industry and the Transition to Socialism in China, 1945–1958," in "Rethinking Business History in Modern China," ed. Wen-hsin Yeh, Klaus Mühlhahn, and Hajo Frölich, special issue, *Cross-Currents: East Asian History and Culture Review* 4.2 (2015): 694–722; Robert K. Cliver, "'Red Silk': Labor, Capital, and the State in the Yangzi Delta Silk Industry, 1945–1960" (PhD diss., Harvard University, 2007).

18. Dwight H. Perkins, "The Centrally Planned Command Economy (1949–84)," in *Routledge Handbook of the Chinese Economy,* ed. Gregory C. Chow and Dwight H. Perkins (Abingdon, Oxon, UK: Routledge, 2015), 41–54; Barry

Naughton, *The Chinese Economy: Transitions and Growth* (Cambridge, MA: MIT Press, 2007).

19. Preamble of the 1954 Constitution of the People's Republic of China, http://en .pkulaw.cn/display.aspx?cgid=52993&lib=law.

20. Suzanne Weigelin-Schwiedrzik, "The Distance between State and Rural Society in the PRC: Reading Document No. 1," *Journal of Environmental Management* 87.2 (2008): 216–225, here 217.

21. This paragraph draws on the discussion of the Soviet planned economy by Daron Acemoglu and James A. Robinson, *Why Nations Fail* (New York: Random House, 2012), chapter 5.

22. Mao Zedong, "Two Talks on Mutual Aid and Co-Operation in Agriculture, October and November 1953," *Selected Works,* 5:132.

23. Frederick C. Teiwes, *Politics at Mao's Court: Gao Gang and Party Factionalism in the Early 1950s* (Armonk, NY: M.E. Sharpe, 1990).

24. Mao Zedong, "The Question of Agricultural Cooperation," in *Sources of Chinese Tradition: From 1600 through the Twentieth Century,* 2nd ed., comp. Wm. Theodore de Bary and Richard Lufrano (New York: Columbia University Press, 2000), 2:458–459.

25. Liu Yu, "Why Did It Go So High? Political Mobilization and Agricultural Collectivisation in China," *China Quarterly* 187 (2006): 732–742.

26. Jean C. Oi, *State and Peasant in Contemporary China: The Political Economy of Village Government* (Berkeley: University of California Press, 1989), 15–16.

27. Frank Dikötter, *Tragedy of Revolution: A History of the Chinese Revolution, 1945–57* (London: Bloomsbury, 2017), 219.

28. Felix Wemheuer, "Collectivization and Famine," in *The Oxford Handbook of the History of Communism,* ed. Steven A. Smith (Oxford: Oxford University Press, 2014), 417–418.

29. Ezra Vogel, *Deng Xiaoping and the Transformation of China* (Cambridge, MA: Belknap Press of Harvard University Press, 2011), 111.

30. Zhu Dandan, *1956: Mao's China and the Hungarian Crisis* (Ithaca, NY: East Asia Program, Cornell University, 2013).

31. Y. Y. Kueh, *Agricultural Instability in China, 1931–1990: Weather, Technology, and Institutions* (Oxford: Clarendon Press 1995), 355. See also National Development and Reform Commission, People's Republic of China, China's National Climate Change Programme (June 2007), 4–5; http://en.ndrc.gov.cn /newsrelease/200706/P020070604561191006823.pdf.

32. Mao Zedong, "On Ten Major Relationships," *The Writings of Mao Zedong 1949–1976,* ed. Michael Y. M. Kau et al. (Armonk, NY: M.E. Sharpe, 1992), 2:56–57.

33. See Mao Zedong, "On Correctly Handling Contradictions among the People," in *The Writings of Mao*, 2:308–350.

34. Mao, "On Ten Major Relationships," *The Writings of Mao*, 2:45.

35. Roderick MacFarquhar, *The Hundred Flowers Campaign and the Chinese Intellectuals* (New York: Praeger, 1960).

36. Qu Anping, "Article in Guangming Daily," *Sources of Chinese Tradition*, 446–466.

37. Lin Xiling, "Speech at the Open-Air Forum of Beijing University, May 23," *Sources of Chinese Tradition*, 468.

38. Andrew J. Nathan and Andrew Scobell, *China's Search for Security* (New York: Columbia University Press, 2014), 75; Jeremy Scott Friedman, *Shadow Cold War: The Sino-Soviet Competition for the Third World* (Chapel Hill: University of North Carolina Press, 2015); Lorenz M. Lüthi, *The Sino-Soviet Split: Cold War in the Communist World* (Princeton, NJ: Princeton University Press, 2010); Odd A. Westad, *Brothers in Arms: The Rise and Fall of the Sino-Soviet Alliance, 1945–1963* (Washington, DC: Woodrow Wilson Center Press, 1998).

39. Yang Jisheng, "The Three Red Banners: Sources of the Famine," in *Tombstone: The Untold Story of Mao's Great Famine*, trans. Stacy Mosher and Guo Jian, ed. Edward Friedman, Guo Jian, and Stacy Mosher (New York: Straus and Giroux, 2012), 87–112; Felix Wemheuer, *Famine Politics in Maoist China and the Soviet Union* (New Haven, CT: Yale University Press, 2014); Felix Wemheuer and Kimberley E. Manning, *Eating Bitterness: New Perspectives on China's Great Leap Forward and Famine* (Vancouver: UBC Press, 2011); Frank Dikötter, *Mao's Great Famine: The History of China's Most Devastating Catastrophe, 1958–62* (New York: Walker and Co., 2010); Gail Hershatter, *The Gender of Memory: Rural Women and China's Collective Past* (Berkeley: University of California Press, 2011); Frederick Teiwes with Warren Sun, *China's Road to Disaster* (Armonk, NY: M. E. Sharpe, 1998).

40. An interesting report is Shahid Javed Burki, *A Study of Chinese Communes, 1965* (Cambridge, MA: East Asian Research Center, Harvard University, 1969). The author was able to visit a commune in 1965.

41. Mao Zedong, "Talks at Beidaihe Conference, 19 August 1958," in *The Secret Speeches of Chairman Mao: From the Hundred Flowers to the Great Leap Forward*, ed. Roderick MacFarquhar, Timothy Cheek, and Eugene Wu (Cambridge, MA: Council on East Asian Studies, Harvard University, 1989), 412.

42. Dwight H. Perkins, "China's Prereform Economy in World Perspective," in *China's Rise in Historical Perspective*, ed. Brantly Womack (Lanham MD: Rowman & Littlefield 2010), 122–123.

43. Andrew G. Walder, "Bending the Arc of Chinese History: The Cultural Revolution's Paradoxical Legacy," *China Quarterly* 12 (2016): 613–631, here 625.

44. Ralph Thaxton, *Catastrophe and Contention in Rural China* (Cambridge: Cambridge University Press, 2008); Hershatter, *The Gender of Memory;* Chen Yixin, "When Food Became Scarce," *Journal of Historical Studies* 10 (2010): 117–165; Anthony Garnaut, "The Geography of the Great Leap Famine," *Modern China* 40 (2014): 315–348.

45. Peng Xizhe has calculated twenty-three million deaths in fourteen provinces. Peng, "Demographic Consequences of the Great Leap Forward in China's Provinces," *Population and Development Review* 13.4 (1987): 639–670, here 649. Ansley Coale came to the conclusion that 16.5 million people died, and Basil Ashton counted thirty million deaths and thirty million missing births. Ashton and Kenneth Hill, "Famine in China, 1958–1961," *Population and Development Review* 10 (1984): 613–645, here 614. Jasper Becker estimated forty-three million to forty-six million casualties on the basis of an internal investigation by the Chinese government. Becker, *Hungry Ghosts: China's Secret Famine* (London: Murray, 1996), 272.

46. Gao Wenqian, *Zhou Enlai: The Last Perfect Revolutionary: A Biography* (New York: Public Affairs, 2007), 188.

47. Examples abound in Dikötter, *Mao's Great Famine.*

9. OVERTHROWING EVERYTHING: 1966–1976

1. The quotations are headlines from the *People's Daily: "niugui sheshen"* [Monsters and Demons], June 1, 1966, and *"jinxing daodi"* [Through the End], January 1, 1967. In retrospect and only a few months away from his death, Mao Zedong mentioned two flaws of the Cultural Revolution: "one, overthrowing everything; two, starting a full-scale domestic struggle." But, he continued, they were both in principle "appropriate" *(dui)* and "a valuable drill" *(duanlian),* although some measures and policies simply went too far. People should not have been killed. See Mao Zedong, "Mao Zedong zhongyao zhishi" [Important Instructions], in *Jianguo yilai Mao Zedong wengao,* vol. 13, *1969—1976* (Beijing: Zhong yang wen xian chubanshe, 1998), 488.

2. Zhou Enlai lays out this policy in his work report to the Third National People's Congress in December 1964. Frederick Teiwes ties the slogan of "four modernizations" back to Mao Zedong, who later abandoned the modernization program in favor of class struggle. See Frederick C. Teiwes, *Politics and Purges in China* (Armonk, NY: M. E. Sharpe, 1993), 438, 485.

3. The figure of twenty-six million less urban population from 1961 to 1963 is mentioned in Shang Changfeng, "Emergency Measures Taken during the Three-

Year-Period of Economic Difficulty," in *Selected Essays on the History of Contemporary China*, ed. Zhang Xingxing (Leiden: Brill, 2015), 71–92, here 80.

4. Frank Dikötter, *The Cultural Revolution: A People's History, 1962–1976* (New York: Bloomsbury Press, 2016), 10–26; Roderick MacFarquhar and Michael Schoenhals, *Mao's Last Revolution* (Cambridge, MA: Belknap Press of Harvard University Press, 2006), 8; Hu Angang, *Mao and the Cultural Revolution*, vol. 1, *Mao's Motivation and Strategy* (Honolulu: Silkroad Press, 2017), 58–59.

5. Stuart Schram, *Mao Tse-tung Unrehearsed* (Harmondsworth, UK: Penguin Books, 1974), 173–174.

6. Hu Angang, *Mao and the Cultural Revolution*, 65n120.

7. The quote, translated by Qiang Zhai, is from the memoirs of Bi Yibo, who was finance minister. See Qiang Zhai, "Mao Zedong and Dulles's 'Peaceful Evolution' Strategy: Revelations from Bo Yibo's Memoirs," *Cold War International History Project Bulletin* 6–7 (1995–1996): 230.

8. Quoted from Yang Jisheng, *Tombstone: The Untold Story of Mao's Great Famine*, trans. Stacy Mosher and Guo Jian, ed. Edward Friedman, Guo Jian, and Stacy Mosher (New York: Straus and Giroux, 2012), 502.

9. Hu Angang, *Mao and the Cultural Revolution*, 25.

10. Felix Wemheuer, *Famine Politics in Maoist China and the Soviet Union* (New Haven, CT: Yale University Press, 2014), 168–173.

11. John W. Garver, *Protracted Contest: Sino-Indian Rivalry in the Twentieth Century* (Seattle: University of Washington Press, 2001).

12. Xiaofei Tian, "The Making of a Hero: Lei Feng and Some Issues of Historiography," in *The People's Republic of China at 60: An International Assessment*, ed. William C. Kirby (Cambridge, MA: Harvard Asia Center 2011), 283–295.

13. Quoted from Hu Angang, *Mao and the Cultural Revolution*, 116; see also Daniel Leese, *Mao Cult: Rhetoric and Ritual during China's Cultural Revolution* (Cambridge: Cambridge University Press, 2011), and the articles in Alexander A. Cook (ed.), *Mao's Little Red Book: A Global History* (Cambridge: Cambridge University Press, 2014).

14. Sergey Radchenko, *Two Suns in the Heavens: The Sino-Soviet Struggle for Supremacy, 1962–1967* (Washington, DC: Woodrow Wilson Center Press, 2009).

15. Barry Naughton, "The Third Front: Defence Industrialization in the Chinese Interior," *China Quarterly* 115 (1988): 351–386.

16. Rosemary Foot, *The Practice of Power: US Relations with China since 1949* (Oxford: Clarendon Press, 1995), 183–184; Morton H. Halperin, *China and the Bomb* (New York: Praeger, 1965).

17. Mao Zedong, *On Khrushchev's Phony Communism and Its Historical Lessons for the World* (Beijing: Foreign Languages Press, 1964). Also in *The Cold War*

through Documents: A Global History, ed. Edward H. Judge, John W. Langdon (Lanham MD: Rowman and Littlefield, 2018), 200–201.

18. Yang Kuisong, "Changes in Mao Zedong's Attitude toward the Indochina War, 1949–1973" (Working Paper 34, Cold War International History Project, Woodrow Wilson International Center for Scholars, Washington, DC, 2002).

19. MacFarquhar and Schoenhals, *Mao's Last Revolution,* 32.

20. Quoted from Hu, *Mao and the Cultural Revolution,* 176.

21. MacFarquhar and Schoenhals, *Mao's Last Revolution,* 52

22. MacFarquhar and Schoenhals, *Mao's Last Revolution,* 57. The numbers for the posters are found on page 67.

23. Quoted from Hu, *Mao and the Cultural Revolution,* 195.

24. Jonathan Unger, *Education under Mao: Class and Competition in Canton Schools, 1960–1980* (New York: Columbia University Press, 1980).

25. MacFarquhar and Schoenhals, *Mao's Last Revolution,* 60.

26. MacFarquhar and Schoenhals, *Mao's Last Revolution,* 90.

27. Decision of the CCP Central Committee Concerning the Great Proletarian Cultural Revolution, in *Sources of Chinese Tradition: From 1600 through the Twentieth Century,* 2nd ed., comp. Wm. Theodore de Bary and Richard Lufrano (New York: Columbia University Press, 2000), 2:474–475.

28. Rae Yang, *Spider Eaters: A Memoir* (Berkeley: University of California Press, 1997), 123.

29. Various memoirs offer vivid descriptions of the turmoil engulfing Chinese society: Jung Chang, *Wild Swans: Three Generations of Chinese Women* (New York: Simon and Schuster, 1991); Nien Chen, *Life and Death in Shanghai* (London: Grafton, 1986); Anchee Min, *Red Azalea* (New York: Pantheon, 1994); Tingxing Ye, *A Leaf in the Bitter Wind: A Memoir* (Toronto: Doubleday Canada, 1997).

30. Ma Bo, *Blood Red Sunset: A Memoir of the Chinese Cultural Revolution* (New York: Viking, 1995).

31. Wu Yiching, *The Cultural Revolution at the Margins: Chinese Socialism in Crisis* (Cambridge, MA: Harvard University Press, 2014).

32. Liu Shucheng, *Chinese Economic Growth and Fluctuations* (Abingdon, Oxon, UK: Routledge, 2017), 91, figure 8.1.

33. Su Yang, *Collective Killings in Rural China during the Cultural Revolution* (Cambridge: Cambridge University Press, 2011), 37–38.

34. On the *zhiqing,* see Michel Bonin, *The Lost Generation: The Rustication of China's Educated Youth* (Hong Kong: Chinese University of Hong Kong Press, 2013); Thomas P. Bernstein, *Up to the Mountains and Down to the Villages: The Transfer of Youth from Urban to Rural China* (New Haven, CT: Yale University Press, 1977); Michel Bonin, "Restricted, Distorted but Alive: The

Memory of the Lost Generation of Chinese Educated Youth," in "Red Shadows: Memories and Legacies of the Chinese Cultural Revolution," ed. Patricia M. Thornton, Sun Peidong, and Chris Berry, special issue, *China Quarterly* 227 (2016): 154–174.

35. Su, *Collective Killings;* Yang Kuisong, "How a 'Bad Element' Was Made: The Discovery, Accusation, and Punishment of Zang Qiren," in *Maoism at the Grassroots: Everyday Life in China's Era of High Socialism,* ed. Jeremy Brown and Matthew D. Johnson (Cambridge, MA: Harvard University Press, 2015), 19–50.

36. Tan Hecheng, *The Killing Wind: A Chinese County's Descent into Madness during the Cultural Revolution* (New York: Oxford University Press, 2017).

37. Joel Andreas, *Rise of the Red Engineers: The Cultural Revolution and the Origins of China's New Class* (Stanford, CA: Stanford University Press, 2009), 188–210.

38. Chris Buckley, "Zhang Tiesheng: From Hero Under Mao to 'Hero of Wealth,'" August 18, 2014, https://sinosphere.blogs.nytimes.com/2014/08/18/zhang-tiesheng-from-hero-under-mao-to-hero-of-wealth/. See also the more complete and complex account in Jiaqi Yan and Gao Gao, *Turbulent Decade: A History of the Cultural Revolution* (Honolulu: University of Hawai'i Press, 1996), 418–419.

39. Barbara Mittler, *A Continuous Revolution: Making Sense of Cultural Revolution Culture* (Cambridge, MA: Harvard University Asia Center, 2012); Richard King et al., eds., *Art in Turmoil: The Chinese Cultural Revolution, 1966–76* (Vancouver: UBC Press, 2010).

40. Many more examples can be found in Dikötter, *The Cultural Revolution,* 270–300.

41. Andrew G. Walder and Yang Su, "The Cultural Revolution in the Countryside: Scope, Timing and Human Impact," *China Quarterly* 173 (March 2003): 82–107, here 95; Su, *Collective Killings,* 37.

42. Ma Jisen, *The Cultural Revolution in the Foreign Ministry of China* (Hong Kong: Chinese University Press, 2004).

43. MacFarquhar and Schoenhals, *Mao's Last Revolution,* 308–323.

44. Gao Wenqian, Peter Rand, and Lawrence R. Sullivan, *Zhou Enlai: The Last Perfect Revolutionary: A Biography* (New York: Public Affairs, 2007), 212.

45. A complete account of the complicated maneuverings of this period is found in Frederick C. Teiwes and Warren Sun, *The End of the Maoist Era: Chinese Politics During the Twilight of the Cultural Revolution, 1972–1976* (Armonk NY: M.E. Sharpe, 2007); see also Ezra F. Vogel, *Deng Xiaoping and the Transformation of China* (Cambridge, MA: Belknap Press of Harvard University Press, 2011), 91–183. The following paragraphs follow the briefer treatment

in Kenneth Pletcher (ed.), *The History of China* (Chicago: Britannica Educational Pub, 2011), 331–336.

46. See the full account of the trial in Alexander C. Cook, *The Cultural Revolution on Trial: Mao and the Gang of Four* (Cambridge: Cambridge University Press, 2017).

47. Andrew Walder, "Bending the Arc of Chinese History: The Cultural Revolution's Paradoxical Legacy," in Thornton, Sun, and Berry, *Red Shadows,* 15–33.

48. Alexander Pantsov and Steven I. Levine, *Mao: The Real Story* (New York: Simon and Schuster, 2012), 359.

49. Pantsov and Levine, *Mao,* 356–358.

50. Hannah Arendt, *The Origins of Totalitarianism* (New York: Harcourt, Brace and Co., 1951), 391, 419.

51. Frederick C. Teiwes, *Leadership, Legitimacy, and Conflict in China: From a Charismatic Mao to the Politics of Succession* (Armonk, NY: M.E. Sharpe, 1984).

PART 4. CHINA RISING

1. Ezra Vogel, *Deng Xiaoping and the Transformation of China* (Cambridge, MA, Harvard University Press, 2013), 201.

2. On China's island reclamation activities in maritime Southeast Asia, see Center for Strategic and International Studies, "Asia Maritime Transparency Initiative." Accessed March 29, 2016. http://amti.csis.org/island-tracker/.

3. Paul Gregory and Robert Stuart, "China, Party Dictatorship, Markets and Socialism," in *The Global Economy and Its Economic Systems* (Mason, OH: South-Western Cengage Learning, 2014), 427.

10. REFORM AND OPENING: 1977–1989

1. On the 1970s, see Akira Iriye, *Global Community: The Role of International Organizations in the Making of the Contemporary World* (Berkeley: University of California Press, 2002); Samuel Moyn, *The Last Utopia: Human Rights in History* (Cambridge, MA: Harvard University Press, 2010); Niall Ferguson et al., eds., *The Shock of the Global: The 1970s in Perspective* (Cambridge, MA: Belknap Press of Harvard University Press, 2010).

2. David Priestland, *The Red Flag: A History of Communism* (New York: Grove Press, 2009), 1107.

3. Andrew J. Nathan and Andrew Scobell, *China's Search for Security* (New York: Columbia University Press, 2012), 225.

4. Odd A. Westad, "The Great Transformation: China in the Long 1970s," in Ferguson et al., *The Shock of the Global;* Harry Harding, *China's Second Revolution: Reform after Mao* (Washington, DC: Brookings Institution Press, 1987);

Zheng Yongnian, *Contemporary China: A History since 1978* (Hoboken, NJ: John Wiley and Sons, 2014), 22–28.

5. Quoted from Victoria L. Mantzopoulos and Raphael Shen, *The Political Economy of China's Systemic Transformation: 1979 to the Present* (New York: Palgrave Macmillan, 2011), 37–38. Chen Yun, *Chen Yun Wenxuan* [Selected Writings of Chen Yun] (Beijing: People's Publishing House, 1995), 3:248–249.

6. David Zweig, *Freeing Chinese Farmers: Rural Restructuring in the Reform Era* (Armonk, NY: M.E. Sharpe, 1997), 12–15; Frederick C. Teiwes and Warren Sun, *Paradoxes of Post-Mao Rural Reform: Initial Steps toward a New Chinese Countryside, 1976–1981* (Basingstoke, UK: Taylor and Francis, 2016).

7. Cyril Lin, "Open-Ended Economic Reform in China," in *Remaking the Economic Institutions of Socialism: China and Eastern Europe,* ed. Victor Nee and David Stark (Stanford, CA: Stanford University Press, 1989), 95–136.

8. Alexander Pantsov and Steven I. Levine, *Deng Xiaoping: A Revolutionary Life* (Oxford: Oxford University Press, 2015), 328.

9. Deng Xiaoping, "Emancipate the Mind, Seek Truth from Facts and Unite as One in Looking to the Future," in *Selected Works of Deng Xiaoping (1975–1982),* ed. Editorial Committee for Party Literature, Central Committee of the Communist Party of China (Beijing: Foreign Languages Press, 1984), 2:151–165, here 165.

10. Li Cheng, *China's Leaders: The New Generation* (Lanham, MD: Rowman and Littlefield, 2001), 34–41.

11. Andrew Nathan, "China: The Struggle at the Top," *New York Review of Books,* February 9, 2017.

12. Alan Lawrence, *China since 1919: Revolution and Reform: A Sourcebook* (London: Routledge, 2004), 220–222.

13. Barry Naughton, *Growing Out of the Plan: Chinese Economic Reform, 1978–1993* (Cambridge: Cambridge University Press, 1995); Susan Shirk, *The Political Logic of Economic Reform in China* (Berkeley: University of California Press, 1993).

14. Zhao Ziyang, *Prisoner of the State: The Secret Journal of Zhao Ziyang,* trans. and ed. Bao Pu, Renee Chiang, and Adi Ignatius (New York: Simon and Schuster, 2009), 122–123.

15. Warren I. Cohen, *America's Response to China: A History of Sino-American Relations,* 5th ed. (New York: Columbia University Press, 2010), 215–231.

16. Linda Yueh, *The Economy of China* (Cheltenham, UK: Edward Elgar, 2010), 27; Wu Jinglian, *Understanding and Interpreting Chinese Economic Reform* (Mason, OH: Thomson / South-Western, 2005), 57.

17. Office of the CCP Dehong Dai Nationality and Qingbo Autonomous Zhou Committee, "Several Questions in Strengthening and Perfecting the Job

Responsibility Systems of Agricultural Production," November 7, 1980, in *Sources of Chinese Tradition: From 1600 through the Twentieth Century,* 2nd ed., comp. Wm. Theodore de Bary and Richard Lufrano (New York: Columbia University Press, 2000), 2:494–495.

18. Quoted from David Zweig, *Freeing Chinese Farmers: Rural Restructuring in the Reform Era* (Armonk, NY: M.E. Sharpe, 1997), 150–153. See *Zhongguo tongji nianjian* [Statistical Yearbook of China 1985] (Beijing: Chinese Statistical Publishing House, 1985), 477; and *Zhongguo tongji nianjian* [Statistical Yearbook of China 1983] (Beijing: Chinese Statistical Publishing House, 1983), 386.

19. Yuen Yuen Ang, *How China Escaped the Poverty Trap* (Ithaca, NY: Cornell University Press, 2016), 95.

20. Nicholas R. Lardy, *Markets over Mao: The Rise of Private Business in China* (Washington, DC: Peterson Institute for International Economics, 2014).

21. Mantzopoulos and Shen, *The Political Economy of China's Systemic Transformation,* 57–58.

22. Ezra F. Vogel, *Deng Xiaoping and the Transformation of China* (Cambridge, MA: Belknap Press of Harvard University Press, 2011), 418–419.

23. Loren Brandt and Thomas Rawski, introduction to *China's Great Economic Transformation* (Cambridge: Cambridge University Press, 2008), 10.

24. Wu, *Understanding and Interpreting,* 114.

25. Xu Chenggang, "The Fundamental Institutions of China's Reforms and Development," *Journal of Economic Literature* 49.4 (2011): 1076–1151; Jean C. Oi, *Rural China Takes Off: Institutional Foundations of Economic Reform* (Berkeley: University of California Press, 1999).

26. Maurice Meisner, *Mao's China and After: A History of the People's Republic of China* (New York: The Free Press), 463.

27. Julian B. Gewirtz, *Unlikely Partners: Chinese Reformers, Western Economists, and the Making of Global China* (Cambridge, MA: Harvard University Press, 2017).

28. Michael S. Duke, *Blooming and Contending: Chinese Literature in the Post-Mao Era* (Bloomington: Indiana University Press, 1985); David C. Lynch, *After the Propaganda State: Media, Politics, and "Thought Work" in Reformed China* (Stanford, CA: Stanford University Press, 1999). See also various chapters on the 1980s in David Der-wei Wang, ed., *A New Literary History of Modern China* (Cambridge, MA: Belknap Press of Harvard University Press, 2017).

29. Michel Hockx, "The Involutionary Tradition in Modern Chinese Literature," in Kam Louie, ed., *The Cambridge Companion to Modern Chinese Culture* (Cambridge: Cambridge University Press, 2008), 244–249.

30. Joseph Fewsmith, *China Since Tiananmen: The Politics of Transition* (Cambridge: Cambridge University Press, 2001), 12.

31. Su Xiaokang and Wang Luxiang, *Deathsong of the River: A Reader's Guide to the Chinese TV Series Heshang,* trans. Richard W. Bodman and Pin P. Wan (Ithaca, NY: East Asia Program, Cornell University, 1999).

32. Wei Jinsheng, "The Fifth Modernization—Democracy, 1978," *Sources of Chinese Tradition: From 1600 through the Twentieth Century,* 2nd ed., comp. Wm. Theodore de Bary and Richard Lufrano (New York: Columbia University Press, 2000), 2:499.

33. Timothy Cheek, *The Intellectual in Modern Chinese History* (Cambridge: Cambridge University Press, 2015), 262–315.

34. Liu Binyan and Perry Link, *People or Monsters? And Other Stories and Reportage from China after Mao* (Bloomington: Indiana University Press, 1983).

35. Fang Lizhi, "Democracy, Reform, and Modernization," in *Bringing Down the Great Wall: Writings on Science, Culture and Democracy in China,* ed. and trans. James H. Williams (New York: Knopf, 1991), 157–188.

36. Important studies include Philip J. Cunningham, *Tiananmen Moon: Inside the Chinese Student Uprising of 1989* (Lanham, MD: Rowman and Littlefield, 2014); Zhao Dingxin, *The Power of Tiananmen: State-Society Relations and the 1989 Beijing Student Movement* (Chicago: University of Chicago Press, 2004); Suzanne Ogden, *China's Search for Democracy: The Student and Mass Movement of 1989* (Armonk, NY: M.E. Sharpe, 1992); Tony Saich, ed., *The Chinese People's Movement: Perspectives on Spring 1989* (Armonk, NY: M.E. Sharpe, 1990); Jonathan Unger, ed., *The Pro-Democracy Protests in China: Reports from the Provinces* (Armonk, NY: M.E. Sharpe, 1991).

37. Eddie Cheng, based on Chai Ling, "Document of 1989: Hunger Strike Manifesto," Standoff at Tiananmen blog, posted May 12, 2009, http://www .standoffattiananmen.com/2009/05/document-of-1989-hunger-strike.html.

38. Zhao, *Prisoner of the State,* 30.

39. Zhao, *Prisoner of the State,* 32–33.

40. Zhang Liang, Andrew J. Nathan, and Perry Link, *The Tiananmen Papers* (New York: Public Affairs, 2001), 477.

41. Jean-Philippe Béja, *The Impact of China's 1989 Tiananmen Massacre* (London: Routledge, 2011).

42. Wang Hui, "The Year 1989 and the Historical Roots of Neoliberalism in China," in *The End of Revolution: China and the Limits of Modernity* (London: Verso, 2009), 37.

11. OVERALL ADVANCE: 1990–2012

1. Wu Jinglian, *China's Long March toward a Market Economy* (San Francisco: Long River Press, 2005), 40.

2. David L. Shambaugh, *China's Communist Party: Atrophy and Adaptation* (Washington, DC: Woodrow Wilson Center Press, 2008).

3. Joseph Fewsmith, "China Politics 20 Years Later," in *Socialism Vanquished, Socialism Challenged: Eastern Europe and China, 1989–2009,* ed. Nina Bandelj and Dorothy J. Solinger (Oxford: Oxford University Press, 2012), 44–60. The best overview is Joseph Fewsmith, *China since Tiananmen: From Deng Xiaoping to Hu Jintao* (New York: Cambridge University Press, 2008).

4. Bruce Dickson, *Red Capitalists in China: The Party, Private Entrepreneurs, and Prospects for Political Change* (Cambridge: Cambridge University Press, 2003), 103.

5. Wang Xiaoqi, *China's Civil Service Reform* (London: Routledge, 2012); John P. Burns, "Civil Service Reform in China," *OECD Journal on Budgeting* 7.1 (2007): 1–25.

6. Kevin J. O'Brien and Han Rongbin, "Path to Democracy? Assessing Village Elections in China," *Journal of Contemporary China* 18.60 (2009): 359–378; Gunter Schubert and Anna L. Ahlers, *Participation and Empowerment at the Grassroots: Chinese Village Elections in Perspective* (Lanham, MD: Lexington Books, 2012).

7. Deng Xiaoping, "Excerpts from Talks Given in Wuchang, Shenzhen, Zhuhai and Shanghai, January 18 to February 21, 1992," in *Selected Works of Deng Xiaoping,* vol. 3, *1982–1992* (Beijing: Foreign Languages Press, 1994), 358–370, here 358.

8. 18th Central Committee, "Decision of the CPC Central Committee on Certain Issues in Establishing a Socialist Market Economy System," *Beijing Review* 36, no. 47 (Nov. 22–28, 1993): 12–31.

9. Barry Naughton, "The 1989 Watershed in China: How the Dynamics of Economic Transition Changed," in Bandelj and Solinger, *Socialism Vanquished,* 125–146.

10. Qian Yingyi and Wu Jinglian, "China's Transition to a Market Economy: How Far across the River?" in *How Far across the River? Chinese Policy Reform at the Millennium,* ed. Nicholas C. Hope, Dennis T. Yang, and Li M. Yang (Stanford, CA: Stanford University Press, 2003), 31–64.

11. Loren Brandt and Thomas Rawski, *China's Great Economic Transformation* (Cambridge: Cambridge University Press, 2008), 17–18.

12. Susan H. Whiting, *Power and Wealth in Rural China: The Political Economy of Institutional Change* (Cambridge: Cambridge University Press, 2001); Li Hongbin and Zhou Li-An, "Political Turnover and Economic Performance: The Incentive Role of Personnel Control in China," *Journal of Public Economics* 89 (2005): 1743–1762.

13. Deliah Davin, *Internal Migration in Contemporary China* (Basingstoke, UK: Macmillan, 1999); Chan Kam Wing and Zhang Li, "The Hukou System and

Rural-Urban Migration in China: Processes and Changes," *China Quarterly* 160 (1999): 818–855.

14. Song Ligang, "State and Non-State Enterprises in China's Economic Transition," in *Routledge Handbook of the Chinese Economy,* ed. Gregory C. Chow and Dwight H. Perkins (London: Routledge, 2015), 188–193; Ross Garnaut et al., *China's Ownership Transformation: Process, Outcomes, Prospects* (Washington, DC: International Finance Corporation and the World Bank, 2005).

15. Data taken from China Labor Bulletin, Reform of State-owned Enterprises in China, 19/12/2007, http://www.clb.org.hk/en/content/reform-state-owned -enterprises-china#part1_3.

16. Brandt and Rawski, *China's Great Economic Transformation,* 13.

17. Robert F. Ash, David L. Shambaugh, and Seiichirō Takagi, *China Watching: Perspectives from Europe, Japan and the United States* (London: Routledge, 2007), 219.

18. Rosemary Foot, *Rights Beyond Borders: The Global Community and the Struggle over Human Rights in China* (Oxford: Oxford University Press, 2000); Ann Kent, *China, the United Nations, and Human Rights* (Philadelphia: University of Pennsylvania Press, 1999).

19. China had first applied to join the trade body, then known as the General Agreement on Tariffs and Trade (GATT), in 1986 but negotiations to complete China's entry were interrupted by Tiananmen. See Peter Nolan, *China and the Global Economy: National Champions, Industrial Policy, and the Big Business Revolution* (Houndmills, UK: Palgrave, 2001).

20. Andrew J. Nathan and Andrew Scobell, "What Drives Chinese Foreign Policy?" in *China's Search for Security* (New York: Columbia University Press, 2012), 3–36; Michael D. Swaine, *America's Challenge: Engaging a Rising China in the Twenty-First Century* (Washington, DC: Carnegie Endowment for International Peace, 2011), 32; Avery Goldstein, *Rising to the Challenge: China's Grand Strategy and International Security* (Stanford, CA: Stanford University Press, 2005), 118.

21. Wu Guoguang and Helen Lansdowne, introduction to *China Turns to Multilateralism: Foreign Policy and Regional Security* (London: Routledge, 2008), 1–18; Evan S. Medeiros, *China's International Behavior: Activism, Opportunism, and Diversification* (Santa Monica, CA: RAND, 2009); Chi-Kwan Mark, *China and the World since 1945: An International History* (London: Routledge, 2012), 118; Joshua Kurlantzick, *Charm Offensive: How China's Soft Power Is Transforming the World* (New Haven, CT: Yale University Press, 2007).

22. Amardeep Athwal, *China-India Relations: Contemporary Dynamics* (New York: Routledge, 2007); John W. Garver, *Protracted Contest: Sino-Indian Rivalry in the Twentieth Century* (New Delhi: Oxford University Press, 2001).

23. Maria Hsia Chang, *Return of the Dragon: China's Wounded Nationalism* (Boulder, CO: Westview Press, 2001), 177–179. On the campaign, see Zhao Suizheng, "A State-Led Nationalism: The Patriotic Education Campaign in Post-Tiananmen China," *Communist and Post-Communist Studies* 31 (1998): 287–302.

24. Jiang Zemin, "Speech at the Meeting Celebrating the 80th Anniversary of the Founding of the Communist Party of China," July 1, 2001, http://www.china.org.cn/e-speech/a.htm.

25. Hu Jintao, "Speech at a Meeting Commemorating the 90th Anniversary of the Communist Party of China," July 1, 2011, http://www.chinadaily.com.cn/china/19thcpcnationalcongress/2011-07/01/content_29714325.htm.

26. Fewsmith, *China since Tiananmen,* 186.

27. Chang, *Return of the Dragon,* 178.

28. William A. Callahan, *China: The Pessoptimist Nation* (Oxford: Oxford University Press, 2010), 31–90; Zhao Suisheng, *A Nation-State by Construction: Dynamics of Modern Chinese Nationalism* (Stanford, CA: Stanford University Press, 2004); Peter Hays Gries, *China's New Nationalism: Pride, Politics, and Diplomacy* (Berkeley: University of California Press, 2004).

29. Klaus Mühlhahn, "'Flourishing China': The Normative Dimension," *China Heritage Quarterly* 26 (June 2011), http://www.chinaheritagequarterly.org/features.php?searchterm=026_muhlhahn.inc&issue=026; Shen Yipeng, *Public Discourses of Contemporary China: The Narration of the Nation in Popular Literatures, Film, and Television* (New York: Palgrave Macmillan, 2015); Christopher R. Hughes, *Chinese Nationalism in the Global Era* (London: Routledge, 2006).

30. Peter Hays Gries, "Popular Nationalism and the State Legitimation in China," in *State and Society in 21st Century China: Crisis, Contention and Legitimation,* ed. Peter Hays Gries and Stanley Rosen (New York: Routledge Curzon, 2004), 180–194; Zhao Suisheng, "Chinese Intellectuals' Quest for National Greatness and Nationalistic Writing in the 1990s," *China Quarterly* 152 (1997): 725–745.

31. Geremie R. Barmé, *In the Red: On Contemporary Chinese Culture* (New York: Columbia University Press, 1999), 62–98.

32. Barry Naughton, "The Dynamics of China's Reform Era Economy," in *The Rise of China in Historical Perspective,* ed. Brantley Womack (Lanham, MD: Rowman and Littlefield), 129–148.

33. Naughton, "The Dynamics of China's Reform Era Economy", 132.

34. James Riedel, Jin Jing, and Gao Jian, *How China Grows: Investment, Finance, and Reform* (Princeton, NJ: Princeton University Press, 2007), 36–69; Mary Elizabeth Gallagher, *Contagious Capitalism: Globalization and the Politics of Labor in China* (Princeton, NJ: Princeton University Press, 2005), 30–32.

35. Huang Yasheng, "China's Inbound and Outbound Foreign Direct Investment," in Chow and Perkins, *Routledge Handbook,* 222–234.

36. Huang Yasheng, *Selling China: Foreign Direct Investment during the Reform Era* (Cambridge: Cambridge University Press, 2003), 2–6.

37. Paul Gregory and Robert C. Stuart, "China, Party Dictatorship, Markets and Socialism," in *The Global Economy and Its Economic Systems* (Mason, OH: South-Western Cengage Learning, 2014), 447.

38. Barry Naughton, "The Transformation of the State Sector: SASAC, the Market Economy, and the New National Champions," in *State Capitalism, Institutional Adaptation, and the Chinese Miracle,* ed. Barry Naughton and Kellee S. Tsai (Cambridge: Cambridge University Press, 2015), 46–72.

39. Jiang Binbin, "China National Petroleum Corporation (CNPC): A Balancing Act between Enterprise and Government," in *Oil and Governance,* ed. David G. Victor (Cambridge: Cambridge University Press, 2011), 379–417.

40. Sarah Eaton, *The Advance of the State in Contemporary China: State-Market Relations in the Reform Era* (Cambridge: Cambridge University Press, 2016); Barry Naughton, "China's Economic Policy Today: The New State Activism," *Eurasian Geography and Economics* 52 (2011): 313–329.

41. Loren Brandt and Eric Thun, "Competition and Upgrading in Chinese Industry," in Naughton and Tsai, *State Capitalism,* 154–199.

42. World Bank, World Development Indicators, 2015, "Household Final Consumption Expenditure (% of GDP)" [Data file], https://data.worldbank.org/indicator/NE.CON.PETC.ZS?locations=CN.

43. Naughton, "China's Economic Policy Today."

44. Shi Li, Hiroshi Sato, and Terry Sicular, "Rising Inequality in China: Key Issues and Findings," in *Rising Inequality in China: Challenges to a Harmonious Society*, ed. Shi Li, Hiroshi Sato, Terry Sicular (Cambridge: Cambridge University Press, 2013), 3.

45. Christian Göbel, *The Politics of Rural Reform in China: State Policy and Village Predicament in the Early 2000s* (London: Routledge, 2010).

46. William C. Hsiao, "Correcting Past Health Policy Mistakes," *Daedalus* 143 (2014): 53–68.

47. Qin Shao, *Shanghai Gone: Domicide and Defiance in a Chinese Megacity* (Rowman and Littlefield, 2013).

48. Property Law of the People's Republic of China, http://english.gov.cn/services/investment/2014/08/23/content_281474982978047.htm.

49. William C. Kirby, "The Chinese Century? The Challenges of Higher Education," *Daedalus* 143:2 (Spring 2014): 145–156.

50. Ministry of Education of the PRC, Number of Students of Formal Education by Type and Level, http://en.moe.gov.cn/Resources/Statistics/edu_stat2017

/national/201808/t20180808_344698.html; National Center for Education Statistics, Fast facts https://nces.ed.gov/fastfacts/display.asp?id=372.

51. Boston Consulting Group, "Made in America, Again: Why Manufacturing Will Return to the US," August 2011, https://www.bcg.com/documents /file84471.pdf.

12. AMBITIONS AND ANXIETIES: CONTEMPORARY CHINA

1. Xi Jinping, "Secure a Decisive Victory in Building a Moderately Prosperous Society in All Respects and Strive for the Great Success of Socialism with Chinese Characteristics for a New Era," speech at the 19th National Congress of the Communist Party of China, October 18, 2017, http://www.xinhuanet.com /english/download/Xi_Jinping%27s_report_at_19th_CPC_National _Congress.pdf.

2. Recent monographs dealing with the Xi Jinping government include Carl F. Minzner, *End of an Era: How China's Authoritarian Revival Is Undermining Its Rise* (New York, NY: Oxford University Press, 2018); Li Cheng, *Chinese Politics in the Xi Jinping Era: Reassessing Collective Leadership* (Washington, DC: Brookings Institution Press, 2016); Pei Minxin, *China's Crony Capitalism: The Dynamics of Regime Decay* (Cambridge, MA: Harvard University Press, 2016).

3. "Decision of the Central Committee of the Communist Party of China on Some Major Issues Concerning Comprehensively Deepening the Reform," adopted November 12, 2013, posted on China Internet Information Center, January 16, 2014, http://www.china.org.cn/china/third_plenary_session/2014 -01/16/content_31212602.htm.

4. Barry Naughton, "Is China Socialist?" *Journal of Economic Perspectives* 31.1 (2017): 3–24.

5. Lin Yunshi, "Xi Jinping: Kongtan Wuguo Shigan Xingbang" [Xi Jinping: Prattle Harms the Nation, Pragmatic Actions Help the State Flourish], *Caixin wang,* November 30, 2012, http://china.caixin.com/2012-11-30/100466950.html.

6. See Geremie R. Barmé, "Chinese Dreams (Zhongguo Meng)," in *Civilising China,* ed. Geremie R. Barmé and Jeremy Goldkorn, China Story Yearbook 2013 (Canberra: Australian Centre on China in the World, Australian National University, 2013), 6–8.

7. Susan L. Shirk, *China: Fragile Superpower: How China's Internal Politics Could Derail Its Peaceful Rise* (Oxford: Oxford University Press, 2007).

8. John Garver, *China's Quest: The History of the Foreign Relations of the People's Republic of China* (Oxford: Oxford University Press, 2016), 674–704.

9. See Clifford Kraus and Keith Bradsher, "China's Global Ambitions, Cash and Strings Attached," *The New York Times,* July 24, 2015.

10. Between 2005 and 2015, China has invested $640 billion US dollars abroad. See World Bank, World Development Indicators, 2016, "Foreign Direct Investment, Net Outflows (BoP, current $)" [Data file], https://data.worldbank .org/indicator/BM.KLT.DINV.CD.WD?end=2015&locations=CN&start =2005.

11. Howard W. French, *China's Second Continent: How a Million Migrants Are Building a New Empire in Africa* (New York: Vintage Books, 2014); David Hamilton Shinn and Joshua Eisenman, *China and Africa: A Century of Engagement* (Philadelphia: University of Pennsylvania Press, 2012); Deborah Brautigam, *The Dragon's Gift: The Real Story of China in Africa* (Oxford: Oxford University Press, 2009); Julia C. Strauss and Martha Saavedra, *China and Africa: Emerging Patterns in Globalization and Development* (Cambridge: Cambridge University Press, 2009); Larry Hanauer and Lyle J. Morris, *Chinese Engagement in Africa: Drivers, Reactions, and Implications for U.S. Policy* (Santa Monica, CA: RAND Corporation, 2014).

12. China shipped 1.3 million barrels a day, or 23 percent of what China was importing from abroad. Eleanor Albert, "China in Africa," Backgrounder, Council on Foreign Relations, last modified July 12, 2017, http://www.cfr.org/china /china-africa/p9557.

13. Gastón Fornés and Alan Butt Philip, *The China-Latin America Axis: Emerging Markets and the Future of Globalisation* (Basingstoke, UK: Palgrave Macmillan, 2012); Alex E. Fernández Jilberto and Barbara Hogenboom, *Latin America Facing China: South-South Relations beyond the Washington Consensus* (New York: Berghahn Books, 2010).

14. James Bellacqua, *The Future of China-Russia Relations* (Lexington: University Press of Kentucky, 2010).

15. Andrew J. Nathan and Andrew Scobell, "Military Modernization: From People's War to Power Projection," in *China's Search for Security* (New York: Columbia University Press, 2014), 278–317; Richard D. Fisher, *China's Military Modernization Building for Regional and Global Reach* (Westport, CT: Praeger Security International, 2008); David L. Shambaugh, *Modernizing China's Military: Progress, Problems, and Prospects* (Berkeley: University of California Press, 2002); Andrew Scobell, *China's Use of Military Force: Beyond the Great Wall and the Long March* (Cambridge: Cambridge University Press, 2003).

16. Jane Perlez, "China to Raise Military Spending, but Less than in Recent Years," *New York Times,* March 4, 2017.

17. David Shambaugh, *China Goes Global: The Partial Power* (Oxford: Oxford University Press, 2014), 1–13.

18. Rick Gladstone, "Shenzhen: The City Where China's Transformation Began," *New York Times,* December 21, 2015.

19. Fong Mei, *One Child: The Story of China's Most Radical Experiment* (Boston: Houghton Mifflin Harcourt, 2016); Kay Ann Johnson, *China's Hidden Children: Abandonment, Adoption and the Human Costs of the One-Child Policy* (Chicago: University of Chicago Press, 2016); Susan Greenhalgh, *Just One Child: Science and Policy in Deng's China* (Berkeley: University of California Press, 2008); Susan Greenhalgh and Edwin A. Winckler, *Governing China's Population: From Leninist to Neoliberal Biopolitics* (Stanford, CA: Stanford University Press, 2005).

20. Similar campaigns were carried out in the 1950s and 1960s; see Thomas Scharping, *Birth Control in China 1949–2000: Population Policy and Demographic Development* (London: Routledge, 2003). World Bank, World Development Indicators, 2016, "Fertility Rate, Total (births per woman)" [Data file], https://data.worldbank.org/indicator/SP.DYN.TFRT.IN?locations=CN.

21. Feng Wang, Gu Baochang, and Cai Yong, "The End of China's One-Child Policy," *Studies in Family Planning* 47.1 (2016): 83–86.

22. National Bureau of Statistics of China, "China Statistical Yearbook 2017," http://www.stats.gov.cn/tjsj/ndsj/2017/indexeh.htm.

23. Deborah S. Davis, "Demographic Challenges for a Rising China," *Daedalus* 143 (2014): 26–38.

24. Esther C. L. Goh, *China's One-Child Policy and Multiple Caregiving: Raising Little Suns in Xiamen* (London: Routledge Curzon, 2011).

25. Charis Loh and Elizabeth J. Remick, "China's Skewed Sex Ratio and the One-Child Policy," *China Quarterly* 222 (2015): 295–319.

26. World Bank, World Development Indicators, 2016, "Sex Ratio at Birth (male births per female births)" [Data file], https://data.worldbank.org/indicator/SP.POP.BRTH.MF?end=2015&locations=CN&start=1982.

27. Important work on this well-researched topic includes Beatriz Carrillo García, *Small Town China: Rural Labour and Social Inclusion* (Abingdon, UK: Routledge, 2011); Chan Kam Wing and Zhang Li, "The Hukou System and Rural-Urban Migration in China: Processes and Changes," *China Quarterly* 160 (1999): 818–855; Leslie T. Chang, *Factory Girls: From Village to City in a Changing China* (New York: Spiegel and Grau, 2008); Delia Davin, *Internal Migration in Contemporary China* (Basingstoke, UK: Macmillan, 1999); C. Cindy Fan, *China on the Move: Migration, the State, and the Household,* Routledge Studies in Human Geography 21 (New York: Routledge, 2008); Lee Ching Kwan, *Against the Law: Labor Protests in China's Rustbelt and Sunbelt* (Berkeley: University of California Press, 2007); Rachel Murphy, *How Migrant Labor Is Changing Rural China* (Cambridge: Cambridge University Press, 2002); Dorothy J. Solinger, *Contesting Citizenship in Urban China: Peasant Migrants, the State, and the Logic of the Market* (Berkeley: University of Cali-

fornia Press, 1999); Wang Fei-ling, "Reformed Migration Control and New Targeted People: China's Hukou System in the 2000s," *China Quarterly* 177 (2004): 115–132; Linda Wong, "Chinese Migrant Workers: Rights Attainment Deficits, Rights Consciousness, and Personal Strategies," *China Quarterly* 208 (2011): 870–892; Yan Hairong, *New Masters, New Servants: Migration, Development, and Women Workers in China* (Durham, NC: Duke University Press, 2008); Martin K. Whyte, ed., *One Country, Two Societies: Rural-Urban Inequality in Contemporary China* (Cambridge, MA: Harvard University Press, 2010).

28. Cai Yong, "China's New Demographic Reality: Learning from the 2010 Census," *Population and Development Review* 39 (2013): 371–396. 2017 data are from National Bureau of Statistics of China, "China Statistical Yearbook 2017," http://www.stats.gov.cn/tjsj/ndsj/2017/indexeh.htm.

29. Mark Selden and Elizabeth Perry, "Introduction: Reform, Conflict and Resistance in Contemporary China," in *Chinese Society: Change, Conflict and Resistance,* ed. Mark Selden and Elizabeth Perry, 3rd ed. (London: Routledge 2010), 6.

30. World Bank, World Development Indicators, 2016, "Urban Population" [Data file], https://data.worldbank.org/indicator/SP.URB.TOTL?locations=CN.

31. Mary Elizabeth Gallagher, "China's Workers Movement and the End of the Rapid-Growth Era," *Daedalus* 143.2 (2014): 81–95; Mary Elizabeth Gallagher, *Contagious Capitalism: Globalization and the Politics of Labor in China* (Princeton, NJ: Princeton University Press, 2011).

32. Martin King Whyte, "Soaring Income Gaps: China in Comparative Perspective," *Daedalus* 143.2 (2014): 39–52; Li Shi, Hiroshi Sato, and Terry Sicular, eds., *Rising Inequality in China: Challenges to a Harmonious Society* (Cambridge: Cambridge University Press, 2013); John Knight, *Inequality in China: An Overview* (Washington, DC: World Bank, 2013); Wang Feng, *Boundaries and Categories: Rising Inequality in Post-Socialist Urban China* (Stanford, CA: Stanford University Press, 2008); Azizur Rahman Khan and Carl Riskin, *Inequality and Poverty in China in the Age of Globalization* (Oxford: Oxford University Press, 2001); Carl Riskin, Zhao Renwei, and Li Shi, eds., *China's Retreat from Equality: Income Distribution and Economic Transition* (Armonk, NY: M.E. Sharpe, 2001).

33. Lee, *Against the Law,* xii. Ching Kwan Lee, "State and Social Protest," *Daedalus* 143.2 (2014): 124–134.

34. See Colin Macheras, *China's Ethnic Minorities and Globalisation* (London: Routledge Curzon, 2003), 38.

35. Hu Jintao, "Hold High the Banner of Socialism with Chinese Characteristics…," Report to the 17th Party Congress of the CPC, October 15, 2007, https://www.chinadaily.com.cn/china/2007-10/24/content_6204564.htm.

36. Grace Cheng, "Interpreting the Ethnicization of Social Conflict in China: Ethnonationalism, Identity, and Social Justice," in *Social Issues in China: Gender, Ethnicity, Labor, and the Environment,* ed. Hao Zhidong and Chen Sheying (New York: Springer, 2013), 127–144.

37. Gardner Bovingdon, *The Uyghurs: Strangers in Their Own Land* (New York: Columbia University Press, 2010); Michael Dillon, *Xinjiang—China's Muslim Far Northwest* (London: Routledge Curzon, 2004); S. Frederick Starr, *Xinjiang: China's Muslim Borderland* (Armonk, NY: M.E. Sharpe, 2004); Warren W. Smith, *Tibet's Last Stand? The Tibetan Uprising of 2008 and China's Response* (Lanham, MD: Rowman and Littlefield, 2010); Warren W. Smith, *China's Tibet? Autonomy or Assimilation* (Lanham, MD: Rowman and Littlefield, 2008); Melvyn C. Goldstein, *The Snow Lion and the Dragon: China, Tibet, and the Dalai Lama* (Berkeley: University of California Press, 1999).

38. Bian Yanjie, John R. Logan, and Shu Xiaoling, "Wage and Job Inequalities in the Working Careers of Men and Women in Tianjin," in *Redrawing Boundaries, Work, Households, and Gender in China,* ed. Barbara Entwisle and Gail Henderson (Berkeley: University of California Press, 2000), 111–133; Arianne M. Gaetano, *Out to Work: Migration, Gender, and the Changing Lives of Rural Women in Contemporary China* (Honolulu: University of Hawai'i Press, 2015); Liu Jieyu, *Gender and Work in Urban China: Women Workers of the Unlucky Generation* (London: Routledge, 2007); Tamara Jacka, *Rural Women in Urban China: Gender, Migration, and Social Change* (Armonk, NY: M.E. Sharpe, 2005); Rebecca Matthews and Victor Nee, "Gender Inequality and Economic Growth in Rural China," *Social Science Research* 29 (2000): 606–632.

39. Hsing You-tien and Lee Ching Kwan, *Reclaiming Chinese Society: The New Social Activism* (London: Routledge, 2010); Yang Guobin, *The Power of the Internet in China: Citizen Activism Online* (New York: Columbia University Press, 2009); Peter Ho and Richard L. Edmonds, *China's Embedded Activism: Opportunities and Constraints of a Social Movement* (London: Routledge, 2008).

40. On these developments, see Sarah Biddulph, *The Stability Imperative: Human Rights and Law in China* (Cambridge: Cambridge University Press, 2015); Wang Yuhua, *Tying the Autocrat's Hands: The Rise of the Rule of Law in China* (New York: Cambridge University Press, 2015); Stanley B. Lubman, *The Evolution of Law Reform in China: An Uncertain Path* (Cheltenham, UK: Edward Elgar, 2012); Randall P. Peerenboom, *Judicial Independence in China: Lessons for Global Rule of Law Promotion* (Cambridge: Cambridge University Press, 2010); Klaus Mühlhahn, *Criminal Justice in China: A History* (Cambridge, MA: Harvard University Press, 2009); Randall P. Peerenboom, *China's Long March towards the Rule of Law* (Cambridge: Cambridge University Press, 2002).

41. Chen Xi, *Social Protest and Contentious Authoritarianism in China* (New York: Cambridge University Press, 2012); Cai Yongshun, *Collective Resistance in China: Why Popular Protests Succeed or Fail* (Stanford, CA: Stanford University Press, 2010); Kevin J. O'Brien, *Popular Protest in China* (Cambridge, MA: Harvard University Press, 2008); Kevin O'Brien and Li Lianjiang, *Rightful Resistance in Rural China* (New York: Cambridge University Press, 2006).

42. Elizabeth J. Perry, "Growing Pains: Challenges for a Rising China," *Daedalus* 143:2 (April 2014): 5–13.

43. Perry Link, Richard Madsen, and Paul Pickowicz, *Restless China* (Lanham, MD: Rowman and Littlefield, 2013), 3–4.

44. Elizabeth Economy, "Environmental Governance in China: State Control to Crisis Management," *Daedalus* 143 (2014): 184–197; Robert Marks, *China: Its Environment and History* (Lanham, MD: Rowman and Littlefield, 2012), 312–318; Judith Shapiro, *China's Environmental Challenges* (Cambridge: Polity Press, 2012); Elizabeth Economy, *The River Runs Black: The Environmental Challenge to China's Future* (Ithaca, NY: Cornell University Press, 2004); Kristen A. Day, ed., *China's Environment and the Challenge of Sustainable Development* (Armonk, NY: M.E. Sharpe, 2005); Judith Shapiro, *Mao's War against Nature: Politics and the Environment in Revolutionary China,* Studies in Environment and History (Cambridge: Cambridge University Press, 2001); Anne Lora-Wainwright, *Fighting for Breath: Living Morally and Dying of Cancer in a Chinese Village* (Honolulu: University of Hawai'i Press, 2013).

45. Joseph Kahn and Jim Yardley, "As China Roars, Pollution Reaches Deadly Extremes," *New York Times*, August 26, 2017.

46. Xinhua, "China Alerted by Serious Soil Pollution, Vows Better Protection," Xinhua Insight, *China's Daily Online,* April 17, 2014, http://en.people.cn/90882/8602018.html.

47. Chris Buckley, "Chinese Report on Climate Change Depicts Somber Scenarios," *New York Times,* November 29, 2015.

48. Rachel E. Stern, *Environmental Litigation in China: A Study in Political Ambivalence* (Cambridge: Cambridge University Press, 2013).

49. Andrew C. Mertha, *China's Water Warriors: Citizen Action and Policy Change* (Ithaca, NY: Cornell University Press, 2008).

50. "Under the Dome: Air Pollution in China," documentary by Chai Jing, June 10, 2016, https://www.youtube.com/watch?v=pUY7nixXdNE.

51. Daniel K. Gardner, "China's Environmental Awakening," *New York Times,* September 14, 2014.

52. Huang Yanzhong, *Governing Health in Contemporary China* (New York: Routledge, 2013), 126–134.

53. Yu Hong, "Railway Sector Reform in China: Controversy and Problems," *Journal of Contemporary China* 96 (2015): 1070–1091.

54. Dan Levin, "Chinese Report Details Role of Political Connections in Tianjin Blasts," *New York Times,* August 19, 2015.

55. Chris Buckley, Andrew Jacobs, and Javier C. Hernández, "Behind Deadly Tianjin Blast, Shortcuts and Lax Rules," *New York Times,* August 31, 2015.

56. Lee, *Against the Law.*

57. Fan Hao et al., *Zhongguo dazhong yishixingtai baogao* [Public Report on the Chinese People's Ideology] (Beijing: Zhonghuo shehui kexue chubanshe, 2012).

58. Hua Yu, *China in Ten Words* (New York: Gerald Duckworth and Co., 2012), 153.

59. Ibid., 221.

60. Link, Madsen, and Pickowicz, *Restless China,* 3.

61. Elizabeth Croll, *China's New Consumers* (New York: Routledge, 2006); Deborah Davis, *The Consumer Revolution in China* (Berkeley: University of California Press, 2000).

62. Ian Johnson, *The Souls of China: The Return of Religion after Mao* (New York: Pantheon, 2017); Vincent Goossaert and David A. Palmer, *The Religious Question in Modern China* (Chicago: University of Chicago Press, 2012); Adam Y. Chau, *Religion in Contemporary China: Revitalization and Innovation* (Milton Park, UK: Routledge, 2011); Yoshiko Ashiwa and David L. Wank, *Making Religion, Making the State: The Politics of Religion in Modern China* (Stanford, CA: Stanford University Press, 2009).

63. James W. Tong, *Revenge of the Forbidden City: The Suppression of the Falungong in China, 1999–2005* (Oxford: Oxford University Press, 2009); David Ownby, *Falun Gong and the Future of China* (Oxford: Oxford University Press, 2008).

64. Ci Jiwei, *Moral China in the Age of Reform* (Cambridge: Cambridge University Press, 2014), 14–15. See also Gloria Davies, *Worrying about China: The Language of Chinese Critical Inquiry* (Cambridge, MA: Harvard University Press, 2007), 60–67.

65. Lee, *Against the Law,* xii.

66. Central Intelligence Agency, "The World Factbook," China: Economy, Overview, https://www.cia.gov/library/publications/the-world-factbook/geos/ch.html.

67. Ronald H. Coase and Ning Wang, *How China Became Capitalist* (New York: Palgrave Macmillan, 2012); Regina M. Abrami, William C. Kirby, and F. W. McFarlan, *Can China Lead? Reaching the Limits of Power and Growth* (Boston: Harvard Business Review Press, 2014).

68. A good discussion of common misconceptions about China's boom is Hung Ho-fung, *The China Boom: Why China Will Not Rule the World* (New York: Columbia University Press, 2016).

Acknowledgments

Why write a new history of China? It has become a widespread feeling that we live in a time of unsettling and violent global dislodgments, similar to the ones that accompanied Europe's transition to modernity in the eighteenth and nineteenth centuries. At the same time, the authority, attractiveness, and credibility of what used to be called the West has declined. The West is no longer the shining beacon of hope the rest of the world looks up to. It has also become less clear in which direction the world is moving. Contestations and conflicts spread as the world enters a phase marked by increasing volatility and uncertainty. The return of China to the center has been one of the main drivers of these profound shifts in the global landscape. China's ascent has tilted global conditions. Economically, but also politically and in terms of science and culture, China has built a tangible global presence that challenges the postwar dominance of the West. China offers the world new opportunities and initiatives, but it also poses new risks, as the country exports not only goods but also, inevitably, its imbalances and uncertainties.

China's astounding recent development has been based on a set of institutions that are unique and cannot be easily compared with institutions in other parts of the world. They are also not well understood. Understanding the particular institutional order in China requires, I believe, a deep historical approach. History plays a major role in China's evolution as its institutional drift contributes to institutional varieties and alternatives across the world. Small in the beginning, the variations were writ large when they interacted with critical historical junctures and turning points in Chinese history.

For a long time, however, historians and social scientists in the West assumed just the opposite. They believed that China would sooner or later adopt western models and institutions, in a process they called convergence. In our time, there is reason to seriously doubt that convergence is bringing China (or any other regions for that matter) much closer to the western world. The links and deals being made and remade across the globe increase by the day, but somehow the optimism that this will lead to one single world or a global village acting in unison has waned. Instead, resentments and bewilderments have taken hold on all sides.

These developments, like China's rapid evolution and the profound transformation of the world, call for current scholarship to reexamine conventional narratives and reconceptualize today's world from a historical perspective. This book has been a contribution to this endeavor.

There is a second reason that a new history of modern China has become necessary. The study of the Chinese past is now one of the most dynamic fields in the discipline of history. In the last two or three decades we have seen a tremendous outpouring of academic work from the United States, Europe, China and Taiwan. This onslaught of material dealing with modern China, both primary and secondary, presents a profound challenge because it increasingly calls into question assumptions and approaches that have dominated the field of Chinese history in the postwar period. The body of new scholarship on the development of Chinese society has placed projects on modern Chinese cultural, social, and intellectual history on completely new footing. The new insights generated by this massive new research effort mean that the histories of China written only three or four decades ago no longer reflect the current level of knowledge, and cannot adequately master even the most relevant aspects of modern Chinese history.

These considerations and concerns prompted me to start working on a new history of China. From its very beginning in 2011, the project has been very demanding. Combing through the constantly growing literature and synthesizing its seemingly disparate insights has been a staggering challenge. Given the countless books and articles, the crafting of a new narrative to tell the story of modern China was equally hard. While I am certain I was unable to do justice to many aspects of the burgeoning China field and subfields within it, I made a serious effort to integrate the most important results and explanations. It was nothing short of Sisyphean labor.

Going through this exciting new research has been rewarding and illuminating. It made clear to me how much the China field has matured in recent decades. I am convinced that, given the significance of China, we cannot hide behind narrow specializations. We need to continue to strive for a comprehensive, up-to-date representation of the country's complex history, even if this is an exceedingly hard and risky enterprise and even if there will inescapably be flaws and gaps. In researching this book, I mostly relied on the rich secondary literature produced by academics in Europe, the United States, China, and elsewhere, but occasionally added, where necessary, my own original research. I remain deeply intrigued by the subject and I feel very privileged and thankful that over the years I was able to invest my time and energy in work that mattered to me.

I was fortunate enough to receive a substantial amount of help in the course of my work. Without it, I could not have completed the book. A number of institutions provided me with generous support and inspiring opportunities. The East China Normal University in Shanghai hosted and funded me from December 2013 to May 2014, allowing me to write the first drafts of part 2 and part 3. My colleague Du Ying was kind enough to arrange my stay, for which I am very grateful to her. The Hoover Institution at Stanford University allowed me to work on its premises and also use its own and Stanford's rich and valuable academic resources several summers in a row, starting in 2012. In 2015, I received a generous summer grant from the Hoover Institution Library and Archives, which I gratefully acknowledge and which allowed me to write the draft for part 4. In 2016 and 2017, we also ran two joint Hoover-Freie Universität Berlin workshops on modern Chinese history. I particularly thank Eric Wakin and Lin Hsiao-ting for their cooperation. The German Research Foundation (DFG) supported three research projects, which made it possible to work with graduate students on specific topics such as the May Fourth movement (2011–2016) and governance in the early PRC (2012–2017). The latter project was part of the larger Collaborative Research Center (SFB) 700 on governance, headed by Thomas Risse. Risse and Tanja Börzel were consistently great inspirations, as were my collaborators in the projects, Yan He, Vanessa Bozzay, Hajo Frölich, Suy Lan Hopman, and Anja Blanke. The DFG funding also allowed me to undertake several trips to archives and libraries in the United States and China. A third DFG grant provided teaching release. The Volkswagen Foundation, the ACLS / Chiang Ch'ing-kuo Foundation, the Einstein Foundation in Berlin, and the Center for International Cooperation at Freie Universität Berlin provided funding for several workshops in Berlin (2011), Hong Kong (2013), Hanover (2014), and Berlin (2016) that allowed me to discuss specific historical issues with colleagues.

I was also lucky to have many colleagues who generously shared time and expertise with me. Essential insights were derived from my conversations with colleagues in China, among them especially a group of fantastic, erudite historians. These include Zhang Jishun, Yang Kiusong, Shen Zhihua, Feng Xiaocai, Xu Jilin, Wang Haiguang, Han Gang, Wang Hui, Mao Haijian, and Niu Dayong. I learned a great deal from all of them and thank them for their time and help. I also benefited considerably from advice and intellectual exchanges with many colleagues in the China field affiliated with European, American, and Hong Kong institutions. We met at workshops and meetings, and had long conversations over dinner or on other occasions. I owe great intellectual debts to all of them, including Debin Ma, Xu Guoqi, Frank Dikötter, Christian Henriot, Tom Gold, Andrew Nathan, David Der-wei Wang, Hsiung Ping-chen, Glen Tiffert, Matthew Johnson, Julia Strauss, William C. Kirby, Martin Dimitroff, Prasenjit Duara, Sabine Dabringhaus, Felix Wemheuer, Steve Smith, Susanne Weigelin-Schwierdzig, and Felix Boecking.

The exciting work of many global historians had a profound impact on my study. I want to particularly point out Fred Cooper, Sebastian Conrad, Stefan Rinke, and Andreas Eckert. A number of scholars of Russian history also helped me by asking provocative questions regarding the concept of Chinese characteristics. My thanks go to Paul Gregory, Stephen Kotkin, Amir Weiner, Mark Harrison, Deborah Kaple, Jörg Baberowski, Robert Service, and Jane Burbank. Here at FU Berlin, a number of colleagues were reliable and inspiring interlocutors. Colleagues at the Graduate School for East Asian Studies, which has a thematic focus on institutions, introduced me to theories of institutionalism. I owe special thanks to Verena Blechinger-Talcott, Eun-Jeung Lee, and Gregory Jackson. In 2015 and 2016, I used drafts of various chapters in my classes at FU Berlin and asked students for feedback. I was thrilled to receive so many helpful and insightful comments. Those responses helped me greatly as I revised the book.

Hajo Frölich, Nicolas Schillinger, Lena Weseman, Jessica Bathe-Peters, Lu Tian, Benjamin Wegener, Susanne Eberman, and Siyuan He have at various stages helped with specific tasks such as fact-checking, bibliographic references, and proofreading. I am very grateful for their dedication and superb work. Very big thanks need to go to the two reviewers of the manuscript. I was privileged to have two of the best China historians, Yeh Wen-hsin and Tim Cheek, go through it. I am deeply in awe that they completed this cumbersome task with so much knowledge, effort, and acuteness. I benefited immensely from their detailed comments and suggestions, and the book became much better as a result of their input. Over the years nobody has inspired me more than Yeh Wen-hsin, who often so generously shared her unparalleled knowledge and sharp intellect with me. All remaining errors and flaws are, of course, my sole responsibility.

Special thanks need to go to Kathleen McDermott, editor at Harvard University Press, for her long-term support and enthusiasm—and also her patience, as I was not able to meet the deadlines we first agreed upon. Julia Kirby's tireless, thorough, and creative copy editing was essential. It helped me make the book more readable and in many ways clearer. I am very grateful to her for her excellent work. Qiu Zhijie generously provided the art for the cover.

Last but not least, I gratefully acknowledge the unwavering support of my family and loved ones. My children, Sophia, Clara, and Julius, showed remarkable patience with me over the years and tolerated my absences with understanding, constantly rewarding me with their warmth and wit. My partner, Julia, not only gave constant, tender support, she also carefully read and commented on the entire manuscript and spent long hours with me discussing Chinese history. Her pointed questions and sharp eye for inconsistencies saved me from many mistakes. She also accompanied me on many trips and had my back on many occasions. I am deeply indebted to her for her help and confidence in me, and above all, for making my life meaningful and fulfilling.

Index

Page numbers in *italics* refer to maps and photographs.